CIMA Official
Learning System

CIMA

PUBLISHING

Revised edition relevant for
Computer-Based Assessments

C2 – Fundamentals of Financial Accounting

CIMA Certificate in Business Accounting

Henry Lunt

ELSEVIER

AMSTERDAM   BOSTON   HEIDELBERG   LONDON   NEW YORK   OXFORD
PARIS   SAN DIEGO   SAN FRANCISCO   SINGAPORE   SYDNEY   TOKYO

D1344859

CIMA Publishing is an imprint of Elsevier
Linacre House, Jordan Hill, Oxford OX2 8DP, UK
30 Corporate Drive, Suite 400, Burlington, MA 01803, USA

First edition 2008

British Library Cataloguing in Publication Data
A catalogue record for this book is available from the British Library

Library of Congress Cataloguing in Publication Data
A catalogue record for this book is available from the Library of Congress

978-1-85617-785-6

For information on all CIMA publications
visit our website at www.elsevierdirect.com

Typeset by Macmillan Publishing Solutions
(www.macmillansolutions.com)

Printed and bound in Italy

09 10 11   11 10 9 8 7 6 5 4 3 2 1

Contents

CONTENTS

10 The Regulatory Framework of Accounting

11 Incomplete Records; Income and Expenditure Statements

12 The Manufacturing Account

13 The Financial Statements of Limited Companies and the Statement of Cash Flows

14 The Interpretation of Financial Statements

The CIMA Learning System

How to use your CIMA *Learning System*

This *Financial Accounting Fundamentals Learning System* has been devised as a resource for students attempting to pass their CIMA computer-based assessments, and provides:

- a detailed explanation of all syllabus areas;
- extensive 'practical' materials;
- generous question practice, together with full solutions;
- a computer-based assessments preparation section, complete with computer-based assessments standard questions and solutions.

This Learning System has been designed with the needs of home-study and distance-learning candidates in mind. Such students require very full coverage of the syllabus topics, and also the facility to undertake extensive question practice. However, the Learning System is also ideal for fully taught courses.

The main body of the text is divided into a number of chapters, each of which is organised on the following pattern:

- *Detailed learning outcomes*. This is expected after your studies of the chapter are complete. You should assimilate these before beginning detailed work on the chapter, so that you can appreciate where your studies are leading.
- *Step-by-step topic coverage*. This is the heart of each chapter, containing detailed explanatory text supported where appropriate by worked examples and exercises. You should work carefully through this section, ensuring that you understand the material being explained and can tackle the examples and exercises successfully. Remember that in many cases knowledge is cumulative: if you fail to digest earlier material thoroughly, you may struggle to understand later chapters.
- *Activities*. Some chapters are illustrated by more practical elements, such as comments and questions designed to stimulate discussion.
- *Question practice*. The test of how well you have learned the material is your ability to tackle exam-standard questions. Make a serious attempt at producing your own answers, but at this stage do not be too concerned about attempting the questions in computer-based assessments conditions. In particular, it is more important to absorb the material thoroughly by completing a full solution than to observe the time limits that would apply in the actual computer-based assessments.

- *Solutions.* Avoid the temptation merely to 'audit' the solutions provided. It is an illusion to think that this provides the same benefits as you would gain from a serious attempt of your own. However, if you are struggling to get started on a question you should read the introductory guidance provided at the beginning of the solution, where provided, and then make your own attempt before referring back to the full solution.

Having worked through the chapters you are ready to begin your final preparations for the computer-based assessments. The final section of this CIMA *Learning System* provides you with the guidance you need. It includes the following features:

- A brief guide to revision technique.
- A note on the format of the computer-based assessments. You should know what to expect when you tackle the real computer-based assessments and in particular the number of questions to attempt.
- Guidance on how to tackle the computer-based assessments itself.
- A table mapping revision questions to the syllabus learning outcomes allowing you to quickly identify questions by subject area.
- Revision questions. These are of computer-based assessments standard and should be tackled in computer-based assessments conditions, especially as regards the time allocation.
- Solutions to the revision questions.

Two mock computer-based assessments. You should plan to attempt these just before the date of the real computer-based assessments. By this stage your revision should be complete and you should be able to attempt the mock computer-based assessments within the time constraints of the real computer-based assessments.

If you work conscientiously through this CIMA *Learning System* according to the guidelines above you will be giving yourself an excellent chance of success in your computer-based assessments. Good luck with your studies!

Guide to the Icons used within this Text

Key term or definition

Exam tip or topic likely to appear in the computer-based assessments

Exercise

Question

Solution

Comment or Note

Study technique

Passing exams is partly a matter of intellectual ability, but however accomplished you are in that respect you can improve your chances significantly by the use of appropriate study and revision techniques. In this section we briefly outline some tips for effective study during the earlier stages of your approach to the computer-based assessments. Later in the text we mention some techniques that you will find useful at the revision stage.

Planning

To begin with, formal planning is essential to get the best return from the time you spend studying. Estimate how much time in total you are going to need for each paper you are studying for the Certificate in Business Accounting. Remember that you need to allow time for revision as well as for initial study of the material. The amount of notional study time for any paper is the minimum estimated time that students will need to achieve the specified learning outcomes set out below. This time includes all appropriate learning activities, for example, face-to-face tuition, private study, directed home study, learning in the workplace, revision time, and so on. You may find it helpful to read *Better Exam Results: A Guide for Business and Accounting Students* by Sam Malone, Elsevier, ISBN: 075066357X. This book will provide you with proven study techniques. Chapter by chapter it covers the building blocks of successful learning and examination techniques.

The notional study time for the Certificate in Business Accounting paper *Fundamentals of Financial Accounting* **is 130 hours.** Note that the standard amount of notional learning hours attributed to one full-time academic year of approximately 30 weeks is 1,200 hours.

By way of example, the notional study time might be made up as follows:

	Hours
Face-to-face study: upto	40
Personal study: upto	65
'Other' study – e.g. learning in the workplace, revision, and so on: up to	25
	130

Note that all study and learning-time recommendations should be used only as a guideline and are intended as minimum amounts. The amount of time recommended for face-to-face tuition, personal study and/or additional learning will vary according to the type of course undertaken, prior learning of the student, and the pace at which different students learn.

Now split your total time requirement over the weeks between now and the exam. This will give you an idea of how much time you need to devote to study each week. Remember to allow for holidays or other periods during which you will not be able to study (e.g. because of seasonal workloads).

With your study material before you, decide which chapters you are going to study in each week, and which weeks you will devote to revision and final question practice.

Prepare a written schedule summarising the above – and stick to it!

The amount of space allocated to a topic in the Learning System is not a very good guide as to how long it will take you. For example, the material relating to the 'Conceptual and Regulatory Framework' and the 'Accounting Systems' both account for 20 per cent of the syllabus, but the latter has more pages because there are more numerical illustrations which take up more space. The syllabus weighting is the better guide as to how long you should spend on a syllabus topic. It is essential to know your syllabus. As your course progresses you will become more familiar with how long it takes to cover topics in sufficient depth. Your timetable may need to be adapted to allocate enough time for the whole syllabus.

Tips for effective studying

1. Aim to find a quiet and undisturbed location for your study, and plan as far as possible to use the same period of time each day. Getting into a routine helps to avoid wasting time. Make sure that you have all the materials you need before you begin so as to minimise interruptions.
2. Store all your materials in one place, so that you do not waste time searching for items around your accommodation. If you have to pack everything away after each study period, keep them in a box, or even a suitcase, which will not be disturbed until the next time.
3. Limit distractions. To make the most effective use of your study periods you should be able to apply total concentration, so turn off all entertainment equipment, set your phones to message mode, and put up your 'do not disturb' sign.
4. Your timetable will tell you which topic to study. However, before diving in and becoming engrossed in the finer points, make sure you have an overall picture of all the areas that need to be covered by the end of that session. After an hour, allow yourself a short break and move away from your Learning System. With experience, you will learn to assess the pace you need to work at.
5. Work carefully through a chapter, making notes as you go. When you have covered a suitable amount of material, vary the pattern by attempting a practice question. When you have finished your attempt, make notes of any mistakes you made, or any areas that you failed to cover or covered only skimpily.
6. Make notes as you study, and discover the techniques that work best for you. Your notes may be in the form of lists, bullet points, diagrams, summaries, 'mind maps' or the written word, but remember that you will need to refer back to them at a later date, so they must be intelligible. If you are on a taught course, make sure you highlight any issues you would like to follow up with your lecturer.
7. Organise your paperwork. Make sure that all your notes, calculations and articles can be effectively filed and easily retrieved later.

Computer-Based Assessments

CIMA uses objective test questions in the computer-based assessments. The most common types are:

- Multiple choice, where you have to choose the correct answer from a list of four possible answers. This could either be numbers or text.
- Multiple choice with more choices and answers, for example, choosing two correct answers from a list of eight possible answers. This could either be numbers or text.
- Single numeric entry, where you give your numeric answer, for example, profit is $10,000.
- Multiple entry, where you give several numeric answers, for example, the charge for electricity is $2,000 and the accrual is $200.
- True/false questions, where you state whether a statement is true or false, for example, external auditors report to the directors is FALSE.

- Matching pairs of text, for example, the convention 'prudence' would be matched with the statement 'inventories revalued at the lower of cost and net realisable value'.
- Other types could be matching text with graphs and labelling graphs/diagrams.

In every chapter of this Learning System we have introduced these types of questions. For convenience we have retained quite a lot of questions where an initial scenario leads to a number of sub-questions.

The Fundamentals of Financial Accounting Syllabus

The computer-based assessments for Financial Accounting Fundamentals is a 2-hour computer-based assessments comprising 50 compulsory questions, with one or more parts. There will be no choice and all questions should be attempted if time permits. CIMA are continuously developing the question styles within the CBA system and you are advised to try the online website demo at www.cimaglobal.com, to both gain familiarity with assessment software and examine the latest style of questions being used.

CIMA publishing have also developed eSuccess CD's specifically for Exam Practice. These can be bought from http://cimapublishing.com.

CIMA Certificate in Business Accounting

Syllabus Outline

The syllabus comprises:

Topic and Study Weighting

A	Conceptual and Regulatory Framework	20%
B	Accounting Systems	20%
C	Control of Accounting Systems	15%
D	Preparation of Accounts for Single Entities	45%

Learning Aims

This syllabus aims to test the student's ability to:

- explain the conceptual and regulatory framework of accounting;
- explain the nature of accounting systems and understand the control of such systems;
- prepare and interpret accounts for a single entity;
- calculate and interpret simple ratios.

Note:

This syllabus deals with the recording of accounting transactions and the preparation of accounting statements for *single entities*. Students will be required to be aware of the format and content of published accounts but are not required to prepare them. No knowledge of any specific accounting treatment contained in the International Financial Reporting Standards (IFRSs) – including the International Accounting Standards (IASs) – is necessary, except in terms of how they influence the presentation of financial statements. IAS 1 and IAS 7 formats will form the basis of those statements. The terminology used for all entities will be that seen in the IFRSs. This will enable students to use a consistent set of accounting terms throughout their studies.

Author's Note:

IAS 1 has been revised and the new terminology and presentation of financial statements will be assessable from May 2010. These changes mainly affect Chapter 13 'The Financial Statements of Limited Companies and Statement of Cash Flows'. A change, however, which does affect all of the Learning System is that a 'Balance Sheet' will be called a 'Statement of Financial Position' in the computer-based assessment from May 2010. The term 'statement of financial position' is used throughout the Learning System.

Students who are taking the computer based assessment before May 2010 may also use this book, but they should note the following differences between the old and revised versions of IAS 1.

		IAS 1	Revised IAS 1
		CBA Before May 2010	CBA from May 2010
1	Terminology	Balance sheet	The balance sheet is renamed 'Statement of financial position'
2	Terminology	Cash flow statement	The cash flow statement has been renamed 'Statement of cash flows'
3	Terminology	Income statement	In the accounts of limited companies, this has been renamed 'Statement of comprehensive income'
4	Gains on the revaluation of property.	The gain does NOT appear in the income statement. The gain is entered in the statement of changes in equity, and appears on its own separate line. The gain appears under the heading 'revaluation reserve'. See Chapter 13	The gain is included in the statement of comprehensive income, in the section 'other comprehensive income'. Total comprehensive income is transferred to the statement of changes in equity, and the gain on property revaluation is analysed under the heading 'revaluation reserve' See Chapter 13.

Assessment Strategy

There will be a computer-based assessments of 2 hours duration, comprising 50 compulsory questions, each with one or more parts.

A variety of objective test question types and styles will be used within the assessment.

A Conceptual and Regulatory Framework – 20%

Learning Outcomes

On completion of their studies students should be able to:

(i) identify the various user groups which need accounting information and the qualitative characteristics of financial statements;

(ii) explain the function of, and differences between, financial and management accounting systems;

(iii) identify the underlying assumptions, policies and changes in accounting estimates;

(iv) explain and distinguish capital and revenue, cash and profit, income and expenditure, assets and liabilities;

(v) distinguish between tangible and intangible assets;

(vi) explain the historical cost convention;

(vii) identify the basic methods of valuing assets on current cost, fair value and value in use bases, and their impact on profit measures and statement of financial position (previously known as a balance sheet) values;

(viii) explain the influence of legislation (e.g. Companies Acts, EC directives) and accounting standards on the production of published accounting information for organisations.

Indicative Syllabus Content

- Users of accounts and the qualitative characteristics of financial statements; functions of financial and management accounts; purpose of accounting statements; stewardship; the accounting equation.
- Underlying assumptions, policies and changes in accounting estimates, capital and revenue, cash and profit, income and expenditure, assets and liabilities.
- Tangible and intangible assets.
- Historical cost convention.
- Methods of asset valuation and their implications for profit measurement and the statement of financial position.
- The regulatory influence of company law and accounting standards; items in formats for published accounts.

B Accounting Systems – 20%

Learning Outcomes

On completion of their studies students should be able to:

  (i) explain the purpose of accounting records and their role in the accounting system;

  (ii) prepare cash and bank accounts, and bank reconciliation statements;

  (iii) prepare petty cash statements under an imprest system;

  (iv) prepare accounts for sales and purchases, including personal accounts and control accounts;

  (v) explain the necessity for financial accounting codes and construct a simple coding system;

  (vi) prepare nominal ledger accounts, journal entries and a trial balance;

  (vii) prepare accounts for indirect taxes;

  (viii) prepare accounts for payroll.

Indicative Syllabus Content

- The accounting system and accounting records.
- Ledger accounts; double-entry bookkeeping.
- Preparation of accounts for cash and bank, bank reconciliations, imprest system for petty cash.
- Accounting for sales and purchases, including personal accounts and control accounts.
- Financial accounting codes and their uses.
- Nominal ledger accounting, journal entries.
- Trial balance.
- Accounting for indirect taxes, for example value added tax (VAT).
- Accounting for payroll.

C Control of Accounting Systems – 15%

Learning Outcomes

On completion of their studies students should be able to:

  (i) identify the requirements for external audit and the basic processes undertaken;

  (ii) explain the purpose and basic procedures of internal audit;

  (iii) explain the meaning of fair presentation;

(iv) explain the need for financial controls;
(v) explain the purpose of audit checks and audit trails;
(vi) explain the nature of errors, and be able to make accounting entries for them;
(vii) explain the nature of fraud and basic methods of fraud prevention.

Indicative Syllabus Content

- External audit and the meaning of fair presentation.
- Internal audit.
- Financial controls, audit checks on financial controls, audit trails.
- Errors and fraud.

D Preparation of Accounts for Single Entities – 45%

Learning Outcomes

On completion of their studies students should be able to:

(i) prepare accounts using accruals and prepayments;
(ii) explain the difference between bad debts and allowances for receivables;
(iii) prepare accounts for bad debts and allowances for receivables;
(iv) calculate depreciation;
(v) prepare accounts using each method of depreciation and for impairment values;
(vi) prepare a non-current asset register;
(vii) prepare accounts for inventories;
(viii) prepare income statements, statement of changes in equity and statements of financial position from trial balance;
(ix) prepare manufacturing accounts;
(x) prepare income and expenditure accounts;
(xi) prepare accounts from incomplete records;
(xii) interpret basic ratios;
(xiii) prepare statements of cash flows (previously known as a cash flow statement).

Indicative Syllabus Content

- Adjustments to the trial balance; accruals and prepayments.
- Bad debts and allowance for receivables.
- Accounting treatment for depreciation (straight line, reducing balance and revaluation methods) and impairment.
- Non-current asset register.
- Accounting for inventories (excluding construction contracts); methods of inventory measurement (FIFO, LIFO and average cost).
- Income statements and statements of financial position from trial balance; statement of changes in equity.
- Manufacturing accounts.
- Income and expenditure accounts.
- Production of accounting statements from incomplete data.
- Ratios: return on capital employed; gross and net profit margins; asset turnover; trade receivables collection period and trade payables payment period; current and quick ratios; inventory turnover; gearing.
- Statement of cash flows.

1

The Accounting Scene

The Accounting Scene

1

1.1 Introduction

This chapter provides an introduction to the accounting framework and introduces the function of accounting systems. Much of the chapter relates to the first syllabus area 'conceptual and regulatory framework', which is also continued in Chapter 10. This chapter covers the objectives of accounting, an essential feature of which is a discussion of who uses accounts. This raises the question of how we can measure the usefulness of accounting information to those who use accounts.

1.2 What is accounting?

Accounting can be described as being concerned with *measurement* and *management*. Measurement is largely concerned with the recording of past data, and management with the use of that data in order to make decisions that will benefit the organisation.

The measurement process is not always easy. One of the most common problems is that of when to recognise a transaction. For example, if we are to obtain goods from a supplier with payment to be due 60 days after the goods are received, when should the transaction be recorded?

The following possibilities may be considered:

- when we place the order;
- when we take delivery of the goods;

- when we receive the invoice from the supplier; or
- when we pay the supplier for the goods.

Accounting, therefore, involves the exercising of judgement by the person responsible for converting data into meaningful information. It is this that distinguishes accounting from bookkeeping.

Accounting may be defined as:

- the classification and recording of monetary transactions;
- the presentation and interpretation of the results of those transactions in order to assess performance over a period and the financial position at a given date;
- the monetary projection of future activities arising from the alternative planned courses of action.

Note the three aspects considered in this definition: recording, reporting and forecasting:

1. Accounting is partly a matter of record-keeping. The monetary transactions entered into by a business need to be controlled and monitored, and for this a permanent record is essential. For an efficient system of record-keeping, the transactions must first be classified into categories appropriate to the enterprise concerned.
2. At appropriate intervals, the individual transactions must be summarised in order to give an overall picture.
3. Finally, accounting information can be the basis for planning and decision-making.

An alternative explanation is that accounting is part of the management information system (MIS) of an organisation. In this context, the accounting element is referred to as an accounting information system (AIS).

Accounting can thus be said to be a method of providing information to management (and other users) relating to the activities of an organisation. In order to do this it relies on the accurate collection of data from sources both internal and external to the organisation. The recording of this data is often referred to as bookkeeping.

1.2.1 The objectives of accounting

The objectives of accounting are to provide financial information to the managers, owners and other parties interested in an organisation. This is done by the production of financial statements. You will see in Chapter 10 that the International Accounting Standards Board (IASB) in their *Framework for the Preparation and Presentation of Financial Statements (Framework) state that*

 Providing useful information to investors is the main objective of financial reporting.

If these objectives are to be achieved, then the information provided by the accounting system must be reliable and easily understood, and prepared consistently not only from one accounting period to the next but also between similar organisations so that meaningful comparisons may be made. This need for consistency has led to a number of accounting rules being devised. Some of these rules are contained in legislation – these rules apply particularly to companies: some are included in accounting standards; some are included in documents such as the IASB's *Framework*; and others simply represent generally accepted accounting practice (GAAP). These rules are used by accountants to determine the treatment to be adopted in respect of certain financial transactions and the preparation of financial statements.

1.3 Who uses financial statements?

Accounting information is used by many people, both by individuals and in organisations. To get a feel for the purpose of accounts it is useful to classify these users into groups, and to look at the reasons why they use accounts and what they hope to get from them.

Any classification of this sort is somewhat arbitrary, and many users fall into more than one classification. However, the following groups are commonly recognised as having particular needs for accounting information:

(a) *The investor group.* This group includes both existing and potential owners of shares in companies. They require information concerning the performance of the company measured in terms of its profitability and the extent to which those profits are to be distributed to shareholders. They are also interested in the social/economic policies of the company so that they may decide if they wish to be associated with such an organisation.

(b) *The lender group.* This group includes both existing and potential providers of secured or unsecured, long- or short-term loan finance. They require information concerning the ability of the organisation to repay the interest on such loans as they fall due; and the longer-term growth and stability of the organisation to ensure that it is capable of repaying the loan at the agreed time. In addition, if the loan is secured, the value of the appropriate secured assets is important as a means of recovering the amount due.

(c) *The employee group.* This group includes existing, potential and past employees. They require information concerning the ability of the organisation to pay wages and pensions today. In addition, they are interested in the future of the organisation because this will affect their job security and future prospects within the organisation.

(d) *The analyst/adviser group.* This group includes a range of advisers to investors, employees and the general public. The needs of these users will be similar to those of their clients. The difference is, perhaps, that in some instances, the members of this group will be more technically qualified to understand accounting reports.

(e) *The business contact group.* This group includes customers and suppliers of the organisation. Customers will be concerned to ensure that the organisation has the ability to provide the goods/services requested and to continue to provide similar services in the future. Suppliers will wish to ensure that the organisation will be capable of paying for the goods/services supplied when payment becomes due.

(f) *The government.* This group includes taxation authorities, and other government agencies and departments. The taxation authorities will calculate the organisation's taxation liability based upon the accounting reports it submits to them. Other departments require statistical information to measure the state of the economy.

(g) *The public.* This group includes taxpayers, consumers and other community and special interest groups. They require information concerning the policies of the organisation and how those policies affect the community. The public is increasingly interested in environmental issues.

(h) *Internal users.* The management of the company require information to assist them in the performance of their duties. Three different levels of management can be identified:

- *Strategic.* This is the level of management found at the top of organisations. In a commercial organisation it is referred to as the board of directors. These people require information to assist them in decisions affecting the long-term future of the organisation.
- *Tactical.* This is often referred to as middle management. These people require information to assist them in monitoring performance and making decisions to enable the organisation to achieve its short- to medium-term targets.
- *Operational.* This is the level of management responsible for decisions concerning the day-to-day activities of the organisation. It is common for the information provided to them to be quantified in non-monetary units, such as hours worked, number of components produced, and so on.

1.4 The qualitative characteristics of financial statements

All of the above user groups, both internal and external to the organisation, require the information provided to be useful. In this context, information should:

(a) enable its recipient to make effective decisions;
(b) be adequate for taking effective action to control the organisation or provide valuable details relating to its environment;
(c) be compatible with the responsibilities and needs of its recipient;
(d) be produced at optimum cost;
(e) be easily understood by its recipient;
(f) be timely;
(g) be sufficiently accurate and precise for the purpose of its provision.

The IASB's *Framework* also suggests that financial statements should have certain qualitative characteristics, including relevance, reliability, completeness, comparability, understandability and timeliness.

For decisions to be made, the information must be relevant to the decision and be clearly presented, stating any assumptions upon which the information is based, so that the user may exercise judgement as appropriate.

Often, better information may be provided at additional cost or after an additional time delay. The adequacy of information is important, and factors such as the cost of the information and the speed with which it is available may be more important than it being 100 per cent accurate.

The information provided must be communicated to the person responsible for taking any action in respect of the information provided. In this regard it is better to distinguish information between that which relates to controllable aspects of the business and that which relates to non-controllable aspects. The controllable aspects may then be further divided into those that are significant and an exception reporting approach applied.

Exception reporting is the technique of reducing the size of management reports by including only those items that should be drawn to the manager's attention, rather than including all items.

Most organisations will set targets against which actual performance can be compared. You will learn more about the setting of such targets in your studies of management accounting. Their use enables exception reports to be produced to highlight the differences between the actual and target results. The use of exception reporting avoids wasting unnecessary management time reading reports that merely advise the management that no action is required and concentrates on those issues that do require management action.

In conclusion, therefore, internal information will be much more detailed than external information, and will be prepared on a more regular basis.

1.5 Terminology

1.5.1 Bookkeeping

Bookkeeping can be described as the recording of monetary transactions, appropriately classified, in the financial records of an entity, by either manual means or otherwise.

Bookkeeping involves maintaining a detailed 'history' of transactions as they occur. Every sale, purchase or other transaction will be classified according to its type and, depending on the information needs of the organisation, will be recorded in a logical manner in the 'books'. The 'books' will contain a record or *account* of each item showing the transactions that have occurred, thus enabling management to track the individual movements on each record, that is, the increases and decreases.

Periodically a list of the results of the transactions is produced. This is done by listing each account and its final position or *balance*. The list is known as a *trial balance* and is an important step prior to the next stage of providing financial statements.

1.5.2 Financial accounting

Financial accounting can be described as the classification and recording of monetary transactions of an entity in accordance with established concepts, principles, accounting standards and legal requirements, and their presentation, by means of various financial statements, during and at the end of an accounting period.

Two points in particular are worth noting about this description:

1. Financial statements must comply with accounting rules published by the various advisory and regulatory bodies. In other words, an organisation does not have a completely free hand. The reason for this is that the end product of the financial accounting process – a set of financial statements – is primarily intended for the use of people outside the organisation. Without access to the more detailed information available to insiders, these people may be misled unless financial statements are prepared on uniform principles.
2. Financial accounting is partly concerned with summarising the transactions of a period and presenting the summary in a coherent form. This again is because financial statements are intended for outside consumption. The outsiders who have a need for and a right to information are entitled to receive it at defined intervals, and not at the whim of management.

1.5.3 Management accounting

Management accounting can be described as the process of identification, measurement, accumulation, analysis, preparation, interpretation and communication of information used by management to plan, evaluate and control within an entity and to assure appropriate use of and accountability for its resources. Management accounting also comprises the preparation of financial reports for non-management groups such as shareholders, lenders, regulatory agencies and tax authorities.

Although the needs of external users of accounts are addressed in this definition, it can be seen that the emphasis of management accounting is on providing information to help managers in running the business. The kind of information produced, and the way in which it is presented, are at the discretion of the managers concerned; they will request whatever information, in whatever format, they believe to be appropriate to their needs.

1.6 The differences between external and internal information

External information is usually produced annually, though in organisations listed (or quoted) on a stock exchange, information may be produced more frequently, for example quarterly. External information is provided mainly by limited companies, in accordance with the relevant company legislation. These may prescribe the layouts to be used and the information that is to be disclosed either on the face of the financial statements or in the notes that accompany them. For other organisations that are not regulated by such legislation, accounts may have to be provided for other interested parties such as those dealing with taxation and lenders. For these organisations, the requirements of legislation are not mandatory and may not be appropriate. However, these requirements are often considered to be good accounting practice.

External information is often available publicly and is therefore available to the competitors of the organisation as well as its owners and employees. Of necessity, therefore, it is important that the information provided does not allow the organisation's competitors to obtain detailed information concerning the working of the organisation. Thus external information is summarised in order to protect the organisation from losing any competitive edge that it may possess.

Internal information is produced on a regular basis in order for management to compare the organisation's performance with its targets and to make decisions concerning the future. Accounting information is usually produced on a monthly basis, although other non-financial performance measures may be produced more regularly. Whereas external information is almost exclusively measured in monetary terms, internal information will most likely involve reporting financial and non-financial measures together. There is a very good reason for this: many managers, particularly those in control of operational matters, will not feel competent to understand accounting reports. They will understand differences in output levels and in usage of materials and labour much more readily than they will understand the implications of these same differences upon profit.

1.7 What is a business organisation?

A business is an organisation that regularly enters into transactions that are expected to provide a reward measurable in monetary terms. It is thus obvious from everyday life that many business organisations exist; what is less obvious is that their organisational (legal) structure and therefore their accounting requirements may differ.

There are two main reasons for the different organisational structures that exist – the *nature of their activities* and their *size*.

1.7.1 Profit-making organisations

Some organisations are formed with the intent of making profits from their activities for their owners:

(a) *Sole traders* (*sole proprietors*). These are organisations that are owned by one person. They tend to be small because they are constrained by the limited financial resources of their owner.

(b) *Partnerships.* These are organisations owned by two or more persons working in common with a view to making a profit. The greater number of owners compared with a sole trader increases the availability of finance and this is often the reason for forming such a structure.

(c) *Limited companies.* These are organisations recognised in law as 'persons' in their own right. Thus a company may own assets and incur liabilities in its own name.

The accounting of these organisations must meet certain minimum obligations imposed by legislation, for example, via company law and other regulations. Some of these requirements constitute recommended accounting practice for other types of organisation.

Two types of limited companies can be identified: *private* limited companies; and *public* limited companies.

Public limited companies can be further divided according to their size, and whether they are 'listed' on a stock exchange. These distinctions can be important when considering the accounting requirements. A common feature of private limited companies is that their owners are actively involved in running the business. In this way they are similar to sole traders and partnerships. This is rarely true of public companies, where the owners may not become involved in the day-to-day activities of the business. Listed companies may have many thousands of owners (shareholders) who are even further removed from the running of the business.

1.7.2 Non-profit-making organisations

Other organisations are formed with the intent of providing services, without intending to be profitable in the long term:

(a) *Clubs and societies.* These organisations exist to provide facilities and entertainments for their members. They are often sports and/or social clubs and most of their revenue is derived from the members who benefit from the club's facilities. They may carry out some activities that are regarded as 'trading' activities, in which profits are made, but these are not seen as the main purpose of the organisation.

(b) *Charities.* These exist to provide services to particular groups, for example people with special needs and to protect the environment. Although they are regarded as non-profit-making, they too often carry out trading activities, such as running shops.

(c) *Local and central government.* Government departments are financed by members of society (including limited companies). Their finances are used to provide the infrastructure in which we live, and to redistribute wealth to other members of society. You will not look at the accounts of government bodies in this Learning System.

1.8 Summary

In this chapter you have learnt:

- that 'accounting' involves recording, summarising and forecasting, to meet the information needs of different user groups;
- the qualitative characteristics of financial statements;
- the distinction between 'bookkeeping', 'financial accounting' and 'management accounting';
- the differences between internal and external information; the different types of business organisation.

Revision Questions

Question 1 Multiple choice

1.1 The main aim of accounting is to:

(A) maintain ledger accounts for every transaction.
(B) provide financial information to users of such information.
(C) produce a trial balance.
(D) record every financial transaction individually.

1.2 The main aim of financial accounting is to:

(A) record all transactions in the books of account.
(B) provide management with detailed analyses of costs.
(C) present the financial results of the organisation by means of recognised statements.
(D) calculate profit.

1.3 Financial statements differ from management accounts in that they:

(A) are prepared monthly for internal control purposes.
(B) contain details of costs incurred in manufacturing.
(C) are summarised and prepared mainly for external users of accounting information.
(D) provide information to enable the trial balance to be prepared.

1.4 Which *one* of the following does *not* apply to the preparation of financial statements?

(A) They are prepared annually.
(B) They provide a summary of the outcome of financial transactions.
(C) They are prepared mainly for external users of accounting information.
(D) They are prepared to show the detailed costs of manufacturing and trading.

1.5 Which of the following statements gives the best definition of the objective of accounting?

(A) To provide useful information to users.
(B) To record, categorise and summarise financial transactions.
(C) To calculate the taxation due to the government.
(D) To calculate the amount of dividend to pay to shareholders.

1.6 Which one of the following sentences does *not* explain the distinction between financial statements and management accounts?

(A) Financial statements are primarily for external users and management accounts are primarily for internal users.

(B) Financial statements are normally produced annually, and management accounts are normally produced monthly.

(C) Financial statements are more accurate than management accounts.

(D) Financial statements are audited by an external auditor and management accounts do not normally have an external audit.

Question 2

Match the following users with their information requirements.

1. Investors	A Firm's ability to provide goods now and in future and pay debts
2. Lenders	B Performance, profitability and dividends
3. Employees	C Profit levels, tax liability and statistics
4. Business contacts	D Firm's ability to pay interest and repay loans, the value of secured assets
5. Government departments	E Firm's ability to pay wages, cash resources, future prospects, pay pensions

Question 3

State six characteristics of useful accounting information?

(A) R ... ...

(B) R ... ...

(C) C ... ...

(D) C ... ...

(E) U ... ...

(F) T ... ...

Solutions to Revision Questions 1

 Solution 1

1.1   Answer: (B)

Maintaining ledger accounts, producing a trial balance and recording transactions are all part of the bookkeeping system.

1.2   Answer: (C)

Recording transactions is part of the bookkeeping function. This should be capable of providing management with internal information, but this is part of the management accounting function. The calculation of profit also results from the bookkeeping system and contributes towards the presentation of the financial results.

1.3   Answer: (C)

Management accounts are prepared monthly (or more frequently) for internal control purposes; they also contain detailed information such as costing figures. The trial balance is prepared from the bookkeeping system and is used as a basis for the preparation of financial statements.

1.4   Answer: (D)

Management accounts would provide detailed costs and other information regarding manufacturing and trading.

1.5   Answer: (A)

1.6   Answer: (C)

 Solution 2

1.   Answer: (B)
2.   Answer: (D)
3.   Answer: (E)
4.   Answer: (A)
5.   Answer: (C)

Solution 3

(A) Relevant
(B) Reliable
(C) Comparable
(D) Complete
(E) Understandable
(F) Timely.

The Framework of
Financial Statements

The Framework of Financial Statements

2

LEARNING OUTCOMES

When you have completed this chapter, you should be able to:

► explain and distinguish capital and revenue, cash and profit, income and expenditure, and assets and liabilities.

2.1 Introduction

In this chapter, we begin to look at what is contained in financial statements and how the information is compiled and presented. The chapter also introduces some of the basic conventions of accounting, although these are covered in more depth in Chapter 10. In particular, the chapter looks at the *accounting equation* as the basis on which accounting systems are built, and how the equation changes as financial transactions are undertaken. The chapter also considers the concept that an organisation must be regarded as an entity completely separate from the people who own it.

2.2 The separate entity convention

In discussing limited companies in Chapter 1, it was mentioned that the law recognises a company as a 'person' in its own right, distinct from the personalities of its owners (known as shareholders). In other words, if a company runs up debts in its own name and then has difficulty in paying them, its suppliers may be entitled to seize the assets owned by the company. But they have no claim against the personal assets owned by the shareholders: it is the company that owes money, *not* its owners. In law, this distinction does not exist with other forms of business entity, such as the sole proprietor. If Bill Smith is in business as a plumber, trading under the name of 'Smith & Co. Plumbing Services', the law recognises no distinction between the business and the individual. If there are large debts outstanding for plumbing supplies, and the business assets of Smith & Co. are insufficient to pay them, the suppliers can demand payment from Bill Smith the individual, who may be forced to sell his personal assets – home, car, and so on. But in this respect accounting conventions do not correspond with the strict legal form of the business. It is an absolutely crucial concept in accounting that, regardless of the legal form of a business – limited company, sole trader, partnership or whatever – the business is treated as a separate entity from its owner(s). For accounting purposes, Bill Smith the individual is not the same as Smith & Co. Plumbing Services. This reflects the fact that accounting information relates only to business transactions. What Bill Smith does as an individual is of no concern to the accountant, and his private activities must be kept quite separate from the business transactions of Smith & Co. Students often find this concept hard to grasp, particularly when they notice that, as a consequence of it, Bill Smith the individual can actually have business dealings with Smith & Co. For example, Bill may take some copper piping from the inventories held by Smith & Co. in order to repair the heating system in his own home. From the accounting point of view, a business transaction has occurred: Smith & Co. has supplied an individual called Bill Smith with some piping, and its value must be accounted for.

Despite its apparent artificiality, the importance of this convention will become apparent in the next section, where we look at an arithmetic relationship called the *accounting equation*.

2.3 The accounting equation

The accounting equation shows that

Assets = Liabilities + Capital

What do these terms mean?

Asset. A resource that may be used by a business or other organisation to derive revenue in the future.

Examples of assets are land, buildings, plant and machinery, motor vehicles, inventories of goods, receivables, bank balances and cash. Assets may be described as *tangible or intangible*. Tangible assets are those that can be physically seen or touched (e.g. land, buildings, equipment, inventories, etc.). Intangible assets cannot be physically seen or touched (e.g. goodwill, which represents the value of a business as a whole compared with the sum of the values of its individual assets and liabilities). As such, goodwill represents the value of the organisation's customer base, employee relationships, and so on. Other intangible assets might include patents and trademarks. You will learn more about intangible assets in Chapter 10.

Receivables. A person owing money to an entity.

These are assets to the business because they are eventually converted into cash, which is a resource that can be used by the business.

Liability. An entity's obligations to transfer economic benefits as a result of past transactions or events.

Thus a liability can be described as an amount owed by a business or organisation to an individual or other business organisation. Examples of liabilities are payables, loans received and bank overdrafts.

Payables. A person or an entity to whom money is owed as a consequence of the receipt of goods or services in advance of payment.

These are financial obligations or liabilities of a business until they are paid. These lists of assets and liabilities are not exhaustive, and you will encounter other examples as your studies progress.

Capital. In this context, capital is difficult to define, but it can be regarded as a special kind of liability that exists between a business and its owner(s).

To return to the accounting equation, you can perhaps see that the assets of an organisation have been provided, or 'financed', by liabilities either to outsiders or to the owner. This emphasises the importance of the separate entity concept described above. Because we regard the owner as being separate from the business, we can regard the amount owed by the business to its owner as a kind of liability. Effectively, we can restate the accounting equation in an even simpler form:

Assets of the business = Liabilities of the business

This statement is always true no matter what transactions the business undertakes. Any transaction that increases or decreases the assets of the business must increase or decrease its liabilities by an identical amount.

You may be wondering exactly what is meant by saying that capital is an amount 'owed' by the business to its owner. How can the business 'owe' anything in this way? How has it incurred a debt? The answer is that when a business commences, it is common for the owners to 'invest' some of their private resources in the business. As the business operates it generates its own resources in the form of profits, which technically belong to the owner. Some of the profits may remain in the business, while some may be withdrawn by the owner in the form of goods or cash. This withdrawal of profits in simple organisation structures such as sole traders is known as 'drawings'.

The equation that states that

Assets = Liabilities + Capital

can thus be seen to demonstrate the relationships that exist within any business. The equation is the basis of one of the most common accounting statements to be prepared – the *statement of financial position*. It is worth noting here that the presentation of a statement of financial position is based on the accounting equation.

2.3.1 The accounting equation in action

To see how this works, study the following example.

Example 2.A

On 31 March, Ahmed's employment with Gigantic Stores Ltd came to an end. On 1 April, Ahmed sets up in business by himself, trading as 'Ahmed's Matches', and selling boxes of matches from a tray on a street corner. Ahmed puts $100 into a bank account opened in the name of Ahmed's Matches. He persuades a supplier of matches to let him have an initial inventory of 400 boxes, costing 5p each, promising to pay for them next week. During his first day of trading he sells 150 boxes at 12¢ each – $18 in all. Feeling well pleased, he takes $5 from the cash tin and treats himself to supper at the local café. He also writes a cheque for $5 to his supplier in part payment for the initial inventory of boxes. Show what happens to the accounting equation as each of these transactions takes place.

Solution

To begin with, the only asset of the business is $100 in the business bank account. Capital invested by Ahmed also amounts to $100 and the accounting equation looks like this:

Assets		=	**Liabilities**		+	**Capital**	
Bank	$100	=	0		+	Capital	$100

The business then acquires matches worth $20 with a corresponding liability to the supplier. The accounting equation now looks like this:

Assets		=	**Liabilities**		+	**Capital**	
Bank	$100		Payables	$20		Capital	$100
Inventories	$20						
	$120	=		$20	+		$100

When Ahmed sells 150 boxes, he makes a profit of $(150 \times 7¢) = \$10.50$. His inventory falls to 250 boxes at 5¢ each ($12.50). He also acquires a further asset in the process: cash in hand of $18. The accounting equation now looks like this:

Assets		=	**Liabilities**		+	**Capital**	
Bank	$100		Payables	$20		Original capital	$100
Cash in hand	$18					Profit	$10.50
Inventories	$12.50						
	$130.50	=		$20	+		$110.50

Then Ahmed withdraws $5 from the business for his private use. This amount (referred to as *drawings*) reduces the sum owed to him by the business. The accounting equation now looks like this:

Assets		=	**Liabilities**		+	**Capital**	
Bank	$100		Payables	$20		Original capital	$100
Cash in hand	$13					Profit earned	$10.50
Inventories	$12.50					*Less*: drawings	($5)
	$125.50	=		$20	+		$105.50

Finally, Ahmed makes a payment to his supplier, reducing the funds in the business bank account, and also reducing the amount of his liability. The accounting equation now looks like this:

Assets		=	**Liabilities**		+	**Capital**	
Bank	$95		Payables	$15		Original capital	$100
Cash in hand	$13					Profit earned	$10.50
Inventories	$12.50					*Less*: drawings	($5)
	$120.50	=		$15	+		$105.50

 # Exercise 2.1

J Jones commenced business on 31 January 20X1, transferring $5,000 from her personal bank account into a business bank account.

During the first week of February 20X1 the following transactions occurred:

1 Feb.	Bought motor van costing $800 paying by cheque
2 Feb.	Bought goods on credit:
	P Smith $400
	E Holmes $250
3 Feb.	Sold goods for cash $600 (cost $400)
4 Feb.	Banked cash $600
	Paid P Smith $400 by cheque
5 Feb.	Bought goods on credit:
	P Smith $200
	A Turner $300

You are required to show the accounting equation at the end of each day's transactions.

✓ Solution

Assets	=	Liabilities	+	Capital	
31 Jan.					
Bank	5,000		Nil		5,000
1 Feb.					
Bank	4,200				
Van	800				
	5,000		Nil		5,000
2 Feb.					
Bank	4,200	P Smith	400		
Van	800	E Holmes	250		
Inventories	650				
	5,650		650		5,000
3 Feb.					
Bank	4,200	P Smith	400	Original capital	5,000
Van	800	E Holmes	250	Profit earned	200
Inventories	250				
Cash	600				
	5,850		650		5,200
4 Feb.					
Bank	4,400			Original capital	5,000
Van	800			Profit earned	200
Inventories	250	E Holmes	250		
	5,450		250		5,200
5 Feb.					
Bank	4,400	E Holmes	250	Original capital	5,000
Van	800	P Smith	200	Profit earned	200
Inventories	750	A Turner	300		
	5,950		750		5,200

2.4 The accounting equation and the statement of financial position

The statement of financial position is simply a statement of the assets, liabilities and capital of a business at a particular time. It is thus nothing more than a detailed representation of the accounting equation.

2.4.1 The contents of a statement of financial position

In its simplest form the statement of financial position is presented horizontally with assets being shown on the left and liabilities and capital being shown on the right. As a result the total of each side of the statement of financial position will be the same – hence *the statement of financial position balances*. When we prepare statements of financial position, assets are divided into two categories: non-current assets and current assets.

Non-current assets. Any asset acquired for retention by an entity for the purpose of providing a service to the business, and not held for resale in the normal course of trading.

In other words, a non-current asset is a resource acquired by an organisation with the intention of using it to earn income for a long period of time. Examples of non-current assets include land, buildings, motor vehicles, machinery and equipment.

Current assets. Cash or other assets – for example inventories, receivables and short-term investments – held for conversion into cash in the normal course of trading.

In other words, a current asset is one that is either already cash, or will be converted into cash within a short period of time. Liabilities are similarly divided into two categories, reflecting the time between the statement of financial position date and the date by which the liability should be settled. These categories are referred to as current liabilities and non-current liabilities.

Current liabilities. Liabilities that fall due for payment within 1 year. They include that part of non-current loans due for repayment within 1 year.

Non-current liabilities. Liabilities that are due for repayment more than 1 year after the statement of financial position date.

Example 2.B

Nadim had the following assets and liabilities on 1 January:

	$
Land	200,000
Buildings	60,000
Inventories	10,000
Receivables	15,000
Cash in hand	5,000
Bank balance	32,000
	322,000
Payables	17,000
Bank loan	240,000
	257,000

We can calculate the value of Nadim's capital using the accounting equation.

The total value of Nadim's assets on 1 January is $322,000; his liabilities totalled $257,000. Therefore his capital must be $65,000, that is:

Assets = Liabilities + Capital

$322,000 = 257,000 + 65,000$

We can now prepare Nadim's statement of financial position.

Statement of financial position of Nadim as at 1 January

Assets	$'000	$'000	Liabilites	$'000
Non-current asset			Capital	65
Land	200			
Buildings	60		Non-current liabilities	
		260	Bank loan	240
Current assets				
Inventories	10		Current liabilities	
Receivables	15		Payables	17
Bank balance	32			
Cash in hand	5			
		62		
		322		322

We can see from the above that the statement of financial position could be used to calculate the value of capital. If this method were used the capital value is the figure to make the statement of financial position balance. You should also note the order in which the current assets are listed. This is referred to as the order of liquidity. Liquidity is the measure of closeness of assets to being cash, and it is usual for current assets to be listed from the least liquid to the most liquid (as above). Returning to our example, let us assume that Nadim had the following transactions during the first week of January:

1. Bought office equipment costing $7,000, paying $2,000 deposit by cheque, the balance to be paid at the end of March.
2. Returned some office equipment to his supplier because it was faulty. Nadim had originally been charged $3,000 for it.
3. Received $8,000 from his receivables. They all paid him by cheque.

We can now see how these transactions affected his accounting equation.

1. Assets (office equipment) increase by $7,000
   Assets (bank balance) decrease by $2,000
   Liabilities (payables) increase by $5,000
   Nadim's accounting equation is amended to:

   Assets = Liabilities + Capital

   $327,000 = 262,000 + 65,000$

2. Assets (office equipment) decrease by $3,000
   Liabilities (payables) decrease by $3,000
   Nadim's accounting equation becomes:

   Assets = Liabilities + Capital

   $324,000 = 259,000 + 65,000$

3. Assets (receivables) decrease by $8,000
   Assets (bank balance) increase by $8,000
   This has no effect on Nadim's accounting equation.

Nadim's statement of financial position after these three transactions looks as follows:

Statement of financial position

Assets	$'000	$'000	Liabilities	$'000
Non-current assets			Capital	65
Land	200			
Buildings	60		Non-current liabilities	
Office equipment	4		Bank loan	240
		264		
Current assets			Current liabilities	
Inventories	10		Payables	19
Receivables	7			
Bank balance	38			
Cash in hand	5			
		60		
		324		324

2.4.2 Vertical presentation of a statement of financial position

The statement of financial position presentation used so far is known as the horizontal format. It may be thought of as representing a set of scales, whereby the amount on each side of the centre is equal. In this way it can be said to balance. In practice, a vertical presentation is used and an example is given below.

Statement of financial position: vertical format

Assets	$'000	$'000
Non-current assets		
Land	200	
Buildings	60	
Office equipment	4	
		264
Current assets		
Inventories	10	
Receivables	7	
Bank balance	38	
Cash in hand	5	60
		324
Capital and liabilities		
Capital		65
Non-current liabilities		
Bank loan		240
Current liabilities		
Payables		19
		324

The difference between the current assets and the current liabilities is known as the net current assets, if positive, or net current liabilities, if negative; it is also known as the working capital of the business. In later studies you will learn that this is an important measure of the short-term liquidity of an organisation. In Nadim's statement of financial position above, the net current assets (working capital) is $41 (60–19).

In order to prepare the above statement you should recognise that individual assets, capital and liabilities are grouped under five main headings as:

1. non-current assets
2. current assets
3. capital
4. non-current liabilities
5. current liabilities.

2.5　The income statement

In the course of his business, Nadim will attempt to earn money by selling his goods to customers. The money earned in this way is referred to as the *sales revenue* (or simply the *sales*) of the business. To sell goods, he first has to buy them (or manufacture them – but we shall assume that Nadim is a retailer rather than a manufacturer). Obviously, there is a cost involved in the buying of the goods. The difference between the cost of the goods he sells and the sales revenue earned from customers is called the *gross profit* of the business. Apart from having to purchase goods, Nadim incurs other costs in running his business. He must buy fuel for his delivery van. He probably pays rent for the warehouse or shop premises in which he stores his goods. If he employs anyone to help him he will have to pay wages. All of these costs have to be paid for from the gross profit earned by selling goods. The amount remaining after all of these expenses have been paid is called the *net profit* of the business.

What happens to this net profit once it has been earned?

- As a private individual, Nadim has living expenses like everyone else. He will need to withdraw some of the net profit from the business to pay for these; such a withdrawal is referred to as *drawings*.
- Any profit that Nadim does not need to withdraw simply remains in the business, increasing his capital.

In Example 2.A, you saw that Ahmed, trading as Ahmed's Matches, made a profit of $10.50, and withdrew $5 for himself, leaving the other $5.50 in the business to increase his capital.

Example 2.C

In the following month, Nadim sells goods on credit to his customers for $6,000. He already had some inventories, costing $10,000, so he used $1,000 worth of that existing inventory, and bought in another $3,000 worth of inventories that was all used to fulfil the order. He has not yet paid for this extra inventory. His rent bill for the month is $500 and his van running costs are $300. He withdraws $200 from the business for his private use.

Present an income statement for Nadim for this month, and a statement of financial position at the end of the month.

Solution

Income statement for the month

	$'000	$'000
Sales		6
Less: cost of goods sold		(4)
Gross profit		2
Less: Rent	0.5	
Van running costs	0.3	
		0.8
Net profit earned		1.2

Notes:

1. The cost of goods sold figure can be calculated as $1,000 from existing inventory, plus $3,000 bought specially. See Section 2.5.1 for another way to calculate the cost of goods sold.
2. Nadim's drawings are not business expenses, but are deducted from his capital on the statement of financial position below.

The part of the income statement which calculates gross profit is known as the trading account. This comprises sales less cost of goods sold equals gross profit. The trading account is thus a sub-section of the income statement although its name does not appear within the income statement. Nevertheless, it is a very important part of the income statement.

Statement of financial position at the end of the month

Assets	$'000	$'000
Non-current assets		
As before		264
Current assets		
Inventories (10–1)	9	
Receivables (7 + 6)	13	
Bank balance	38	
Cashinhand (5–0.5–0.3–0.2)	4	
		64
		328
Capital and liabilities		
Capital		66
Long-term liabilities		
Bank loan		240
Current liabilities		
Payables (19 + 3)		22
		328

Notice that the capital of the business has increased by $1,000 – the amount of net profit retained in the business. It is possible to prepare a statement of changes in capital, showing exactly how the figure of $65,000 has risen to $66,000.

Statement of changes in capital

	$'000	$'000
Capital at start of the month		65.0
Net profit earned in period	1.2	
Net profit withdrawn by Nadim	(0.2)	
Net profit retained in the business		1.0
Capital at end of month		66.0

You should see clearly from this statement how the income statement links up with the statement of financial position: the net profit earned, shown in the income statement, becomes an addition to capital in the statement of financial position, and Nadim's drawings are deducted from this.

In Chapter 13 we will learn more about the income statement and how it may be part of a statement of comprehensive income. However, until Chapter 13, we will just refer to the income statement.

2.5.1 The cost of goods sold

We shall be looking at the income statement in more detail later on, but at this stage it is worth noting one general point, which will be illustrated by the particular example of the cost of goods sold.

In computing the profit earned in a period the accountant's task is:

- first, to establish the sales revenue earned in the period;
- second, to establish the costs incurred by the business in earning this revenue.

This second point is not as simple as it might sound. For example, it would not be true to say that the costs incurred in an accounting period are equal to the sums of money expended in the period. This could be illustrated by many examples, some of which you will encounter later in the text. For now, we focus on one particular cost: The *cost of goods sold*.

A trader may be continually buying goods and selling them on to customers. At the moment he draws up his financial statements it is likely that he has inventories that have been purchased in the period but not yet sold. It would be wrong to include the cost of this closing inventory as part of the cost of goods sold, for the simple reason that these goods have not yet been sold.

Looking back to the beginning of the accounting period, it is likely that opening inventories were on hand. These have presumably been sold in this period and their cost must form part of the cost of goods sold, even though they were purchased in an earlier period.

What all this illustrates is that the cost of goods *sold* in an accounting period is not the same as the cost of goods *purchased* in the period. In fact, to calculate the cost of goods sold we need to do the following calculation (presented here using the figures from Nadim's business above):

	$
Cost of opening inventories at the start of the period	10,000
Cost of purchases during the period	3,000
	13,000
Less: cost of closing inventories at the end of the period	9,000
Cost of goods sold	4,000

It is this figure of $4,000 – not the purchases of $3,000 – that is matched with the sales revenue for the period in order to derive the figure of gross profit.

 ## Exercise 2.2

Explain briefly what is meant by the following terms:

- assets;
- liabilities;
- capital;
- revenue;
- expense.

 ## Solution

- *Assets.* Items possessed by an organisation, which may be used to provide income in the future. Includes non-current assets (land, buildings, machinery, etc.) and current assets (inventories, receivables, cash, etc.).
- *Liabilities.* Financial obligations or amounts owed by an organisation. Includes loans, overdrafts and payables.
- *Capital.* The amount of investment made by the owner(s) in the organisation, and not yet withdrawn. The amount includes initial and subsequent amounts introduced by the owner(s), plus any profits earned that have been retained in the organisation.
- *Revenue.* Amounts earned by the activities of the organisation, which eventually result in receiving money. Includes sales revenue, interest received and so on. Revenue increases profit.
- *Expense.* Costs used up in the activities of the organisation. Includes heat, light, local business tax, inventories consumed, wages and so on. Expenses reduce profit.

 ## Exercise 2.3

On 1 June 20X1, J Brown started business as a jobbing gardener with a capital of $2,000 in cash. A list of figures extracted from his records on 31 May 20X2 shows the following:

	$
Purchases of seeds, plants, etc.	700
New motor van	1,100
Mowing machine	70
Cultivator	250
Motor van expenses	300
Rent of garage	200
Paid to wife for clerical work	500
Insurance	200
Private expenses paid from bank	1,500
Cash in hand and bank	180
Cash received from customers	3,000
Capital at the start of the year	2,000
Inventories of seeds, plants, etc. at the end of the year	100

You are required to prepare:

(A) an account to show J Brown's profit or loss for the year ended 31 May 20X2,

(B) a statement of financial position as at 31 May 20X2.

 Solution

Income statement of J Brown for the year ended 31 May 20X2

	$	$
Sales		3,000
Purchases of seeds, plants	700	
Less: closing inventories of seeds, plants	(100)	
Cost of goods sold		600
Gross profit		2,400
Less: Motor van expenses	300	
Rent of garage	200	
Wife's wages	500	
Insurance	200	
		1,200
Net profit		1,200

Statement of financial position of J Brown as at 31 May 20X2

Assets	$	$
Non-current assets		
Motor van		1,100
Mowing machine		70
Cultivator		250
		1,420
Currents assets		
Inventories of seeds and plants	100	
Cash in hand and at bank	180	
		280
		1,700
Capital		
Capital introduced		2,000
Add: net profit for the year		1,200
		3,200
Less: drawings		(1,500)
Captital at the end of the period		1,700

2.6   Profit and cash

Note that in Example 2.C, Nadim's business made a profit of $1,200. But his bank balance remained unchanged and his cash holdings actually fell. This was because some of his transactions that affected profit did not affect cash at the same time. For example, his customers did not pay Nadim, nor did Nadim pay his suppliers, until after the end of the month. Also, there was a transaction that affected cash, but not profit – Nadim took $200 cash in drawings, which reduced his capital but not his profit. There are lots of other reasons why profit does not always result in an equal change in bank and cash balances. You will look at these in Chapter 13.

2.7 Capital and revenue

Note also that we do not include the cost of non-current assets in the profit calculation. We only include expenses that have been consumed, and have no future benefit for the organisation. Non-current assets have not been consumed, and do have a future benefit, as they will be used to earn profits in the following periods. This is why they are shown in the statement of financial position rather than in the income statement.

2.7.1 Capital transactions

The word 'capital' means different things in different contexts. You have already seen how the word is used to identify the investment by an owner in his business. Capital transactions are those that affect the organisation in the long term, as well as in the current period. Capital expenditure is expenditure on non-current assets, and capital receipts would result from the disposal of those assets. Other transactions that are regarded as capital transactions are the obtaining of, and repayment of, non-current finance. Capital transactions initially affect the figures in the statement of financial position. Of course, non-current assets are used up over a number of years, and so eventually they will be consumed. We account for this by including *depreciation* in the income statement. You will look at this in detail in Chapter 6.

2.7.2 Revenue transactions

Revenue transactions are those that affect the organisation in the current period. Revenue receipts come from sales, and sometimes in the form of income from investments. Revenue expenditure is expenditure on items that are consumed in the period, for example the running expenses of the organisation, cost of sales and so on. Revenue transactions affect the figures in the income statement.

2.8 Summary

In this chapter you have:

- seen how the separate entity convention works – for accounting purposes, a business is always regarded as an entity separate from its owners;
- seen how the accounting equation is defined as:

  Assets = Liabilities + Capital

  and how it changes as a result of financial transactions;

- learnt how to use the accounting equation to draw up a simple statement of financial position after certain transactions have occurred and how to prepare a statement of profit, including a calculation of cost of goods sold;
- learnt that profit does not always result in an equivalent change in bank and cash balances;
- that transactions can be classified as either 'capital' or 'revenue' according to whether they affect the statement of financial position or the income statement.

Revision Questions

 Question 1

1.1 Gross profit for 20X1 can be calculated from:

(A) purchases for 20X1, plus inventories at 31 December 20X1, less inventories at 1 January 20X1.
(B) purchases for 20X1, less inventories at 31 December 20X1, plus inventories at 1 January 20X1.
(C) cost of goods sold during 20X1, plus sales during 20X1.
(D) net profit for 20X1, plus expenses for 20X1.

1.2 The capital of a sole trader would change as a result of:

(A) a payable being paid his account by cheque.
(B) raw materials being purchased on credit.
(C) non-current assets being purchased on credit.
(D) wages being paid in cash.

1.3 The 'accounting equation' can be rewritten as:

(A) assets plus profit less drawings less liabilities equals closing capital.
(B) assets less liabilities less drawings equals opening capital plus profit.
(C) assets less liabilities less opening capital plus drawings equals profit.
(D) opening capital plus profit less drawings less liabilities equals assets.

1.4 An increase in inventories of $250, a decrease in the bank balance of $400 and an increase in payables of $1,200 results in:

(A) a decrease in working capital of $1,350.
(B) an increase in working capital of $1,350.
(C) a decrease in working capital of $1,050.
(D) an increase in working capital of $1,050.

1.5 A sole trader had opening capital of $10,000 and closing capital of $4,500. During the period, the owner introduced capital of $4,000 and withdrew $8,000 for her own use. Her profit or loss during the period was:

Profit or loss   Amount
$

1.6 The accounting equation at the start of the month was:

Assets $28,000 less liabilities $12,500
During the following month, the business purchased a non-current asset for $6,000, paying by cheque, a profit of $7,000 was made, and payables of $5,500 were paid by cheque.
  Capital at the end of the month would be:

$.......

1.7 The accounting equation can change as a result of certain transactions. Which *one* of the following transactions would *not* affect the accounting equation?

(A) Selling goods for more than their cost.
(B) Purchasing a non-current asset on credit.
(C) The owner withdrawing cash.
(D) Receivables paying their accounts in full, in cash.

1.8 The profit of a business may be calculated by using which one of the following formulae?

(A) Opening capital – drawings + capital introduced – closing capital.
(B) Closing capital + drawings – capital introduced – opening capital.
(C) Opening capital + drawings – capital introduced – closing capital.
(D) Closing capital – drawings + capital introduced – opening capital.

Question 2

The following table shows the cumulative effects of a series of separate transactions on the assets and liabilities of a sole trader's business. The transactions are labelled A to H, and the figures for each asset and liability in the column underneath represent values after the transaction has taken place.

		A	B	C	D	E	F	G	H
	($)	($)	($)	($)	($)	($)	($)	($)	($)
Non-current assets									
Land and buildings	45,000	65,000	65,000	65,000	65,000	65,000	65,000	65,000	65,000
Equipment	34,000	34,000	34,000	34,000	34,000	34,000	34,000	34,000	34,000
Motor vehicles	17,500	17,500	17,500	17,500	17,500	10,000	10,000	10,000	10,000
Current assets									
Inventories	20,800	20,800	20,800	27,000	27,000	27,000	27,000	27,000	23,000
Trade receivables	34,700	34,700	24,700	24,700	24,700	24,700	23,350	23,350	23,350
Prepaid expenses	1,300	1,300	1,300	1,300	1,300	1,300	1,300	1,300	1,300
Cash at bank	2,150	2,150	11,150	11,150	6,400	13,200	13,200	10,200	10,200
Cash on hand	320	320	320	320	320	320	320	320	320
	155,770	175,770	174,770	180,970	176,220	175,520	174,170	171,170	167,170
Capital	85,620	85,620	84,620	84,620	84,870	84,170	82,820	79,820	75,820
Loans	50,000	70,000	70,000	70,000	70,000	70,000	70,000	70,000	70,000
Current liabilities									
Trade payables	18,600	18,600	18,600	24,800	19,800	19,800	19,800	19,800	19,800
Accrued expenses	1,550	1,550	1,550	1,550	1,550	1,550	1,550	1,550	1,550
	155,770	175,770	174,770	180,970	176,220	175,520	174,170	171,170	167,170

Requirements

Identify, as clearly and as fully as the information permits, what transaction has taken place in each case by matching the transaction to the description below.

1. A supplier's invoice for $5,000 is paid by cheque; 5 per cent discount received.
2. An additional non-current loan of $20,000 is raised to finance the purchase of additions/improvements to buildings, costing $20,000.
3. $4,000 of inventories at cost is written off because they are obsolete.
4. A debt of $1,350 due from a customer is written off as bad.
5. $3,000 is withdrawn by the owner from the business bank account for personal use.
6. A customer pays off invoices totalling $10,000 by cheque, and receives 10 per cent discount.
7. Inventories costing $6,200 are purchased on credit.
8. A motor vehicle stated at $7,500 is sold for $6,800 – the amount being received by cheque. The resulting loss of $700 reduces capital.

 Question 3

You are given the following information relating to a business for the month of May 20XX.

	$
Sales of goods for cash	17,000
Sales of goods on credit	28,000
Purchases of inventories on credit	19,500
Wages paid in cash	2,000
Non-current assets bought on credit	12,000
Cash withdrawn by the owner	1,600
Inventories of goods at the start of the period	5,000
Inventories of goods at the end of the period	6,250

Requirement

Complete the following statement to determine the net profit for the period:

	$		$		$
Sales	....	+	....	=	....
Less: cost of sales					
Opening inventories			....		
Purchases			....		
			....		
Closing inventories			....		
Cost of goods sold					....
Gross profit					....
Less: expenses – wages					....
Net profit					....

Question 4

In addition to the information in Question 3, you are given the following information regarding assets and liabilities at the start of the period:

	$
Non-current assets	37,000
Receivables	7,000
Bank and cash	12,000
Payables	7,300

Requirement

Insert the missing figures below to prepare a statement of financial position at the start of the period.

	$
Capital at the start of the period:	
Non-current assets	....
Inventories	....
Receivables	....
Bank and cash	....
Total assets	....
Less: payables	....
Capital	....

Statement of financial position as at 31.5.XX

Assets	$	$
Non-current assets		....
Current assets		
Inventories	....	
Receivables	....	
Bank and cash	....	
Subtotal		....

Capital and liabilities	
Capital at the start of the period (as per above)	....
Net profit (as per Question 3)	....
Subtotal	....
Less: drawings	....
Capital at the end of the period	....
Current liabilities: payables	....

Solutions to Revision Questions

Solution 1

1.1 Answer: (D)

Working backwards often confuses candidates. Try drawing up a short example of an income statement using simple figures of your own, to prove or disprove the options given.

For example:

	$	$
Sales		20,000
Inventories at 31.12.20X0	2,000	
Purchases during 20X1	8,000	
	10,000	
Less: inventories at 31.21.20X1	(1,000)	
Cost of goods sold		9,000
Gross profit		11,000
Less: expenses		(4,000)
Net profit		7,000

Make all the figures different or you will make mistakes.

You can now see that options A, B and C will not give the correct answer.

1.2 Answer: (D)

Transactions that affect only assets and liabilities do not affect capital. Therefore, options A, B and C are irrelevant.

1.3 Answer: (C)

The 'standard' accounting equation is

$$\text{Assets} = \text{Liabilities} + \text{Capital}$$

and capital equals opening capital plus profits less drawings. The only rearrangement of this equation that maintains the integrity of the accounting equation is C.

1.4 Answer: (A)

The effect on working capital is calculated as:

	$
Increase in inventories = increase in working capital	250
Decrease in bank = decrease in working capital	(400)
Increase in payables = decrease in working capital	(1,200)
Overall decrease in working capital	(1,350)

1.5 Answer:

	$
Opening capital	10,000
Introduced	4,000
Drawings	(8,000)
Loss – balancing figure	(1,500)
Closing capital	4,500

1.6 Only the profit affects the capital at the end of the month. The capital at the start was $15,500 ($28,000 assets less $12,500 liabilities), so a profit of $7,000 increases this to $22,500. The purchase by cheque of a non-current asset affects only assets, and the payment of payables by cheque affects assets and liabilities, but neither affects capital.

1.7 Answer: (D)

The accounting equation changes when one or more of assets, liabilities or capital changes. Selling goods at a profit would change capital; purchasing a non-current asset on credit would change assets and liabilities; the owner withdrawing cash would change assets and capital; receivables paying their accounts in cash would not affect any of these.

1.8 Answer: (B)

☑ Solution 2

- This question requires you to ascertain the reason for changes in the assets and liabilities as a result of transactions that have occurred.
- Each column contains two changes that complement each other, because every transaction has two effects.

(A) Answer: 2
(B) Answer: 6
(C) Answer: 7
(D) Answer: 1
(E) Answer: 8
(F) Answer: 4
(G) Answer: 5
(H) Answer: 3

Solution 3

May 20XX	$	$
Sales ($17,000 + 28,000)		45,000
Less: cost of sales		
Opening inventories	5,000	
Purchases	19,500	
	24,500	
Less: closing inventories	(6,250)	
		18,250
Gross profit		26,750
Less: expenses – wages		(2,000)
Net profit		24,750

 ## Solution 4

First of all calculate the capital at the start of the period (not forgetting the inventories balance given in Question 3), then adjust the opening assets and liabilities for the changes given in Question 3. Finally, add the profit to the opening capital, and deduct drawings.

	$
Non-current assets	37,000
Inventories	5,000
Receivables	7,000
Bank and cash	12,000
	61,000
Less: payables	(7,300)
Capital	53,700

Statement of financial position as at 31.5.XX

Assets	$	$
Non-current assets (37,000 + 12,000)		49,000
Current assets		
Inventories	6,250	
Receivables (7,000 + 28,000)	35,000	
Bank and cash (12,000 + 17,000 – 2,000 – 1,600)	25,400	
		66,650
		115,650
Capital and liabilities		
Capital at the start of the period (as above)		53,700
Net profit (as in Question 3)		24,750
		78,450
Less: drawings		(1,600)
Capital at the end of the period		76,850
Current liabilities		
Payables (7,300 + 19,500 + 12,000)		38,800
		115,650

The Accounting System in Action

The Accounting System in Action

3

3.1 Introduction

In the last chapter, you were able to draw up a simple income statement and statement of financial position after considering a small number of transactions. Imagine an organisation with hundreds or thousands of transactions in a period, and how difficult (impossible, even) it would be to draw up the financial statements from just a list of transactions.

This chapter introduces you to the system of maintaining ledger accounts, to enable the income statement and statement of financial position to be prepared. It is known as the system of *bookkeeping*. Although nowadays most organisations maintain their accounts on computer, the basic principles of bookkeeping have remained unchanged for centuries, and are still important if you are to understand how such systems work, especially if adjustments need to be made to the system or its records.

Some of these topics will also be covered in more detail in subsequent chapters.

3.2 What is a ledger account?

An *account* is a record of the transactions involving a particular item. You may have a bank account yourself, which provides you with a record of the transactions you make; or you may have received an electricity account, which details how much electricity you have consumed and any payments you have made towards it. A ledger account may be thought of as a record kept as a page in a book. The book contains many pages – many accounts – and is referred to as a ledger. In this chapter we are concerned with the *nominal ledger*, which is the ledger containing all of the accounts necessary to summarise an organisation's transactions and prepare a statement of financial position and income statement. (Some organisations also maintain subsidiary ledgers in support of the nominal ledger: we shall look at this in Chapter 8.)

Each account comprises two sides: the left-hand side is referred to as the *debit* side, and the right-hand side is referred to as the *credit* side. The format is shown below:

Debit			*Credit*		
Date	Details	$	Date	Details	$

3.3 What is double-entry bookkeeping?

According to the CIMA *Official Terminology:*

Double-entry bookkeeping: The most commonly used system of bookkeeping based on the principle that every financial transaction involves the simultaneous receiving and giving of value, and is therefore recorded twice.

Earlier in this text we saw how some transactions affected the accounting equation and the statement of financial position. We saw that each transaction had two effects: this is referred to as the *dual aspect* or *duality* convention. For example, receiving payment from a receivable increases the asset 'cash', while reducing the asset 'receivables'; paying a supplier reduces the asset 'cash' while reducing the liability 'payables'; In both cases, the accounting equation remains intact. The fact that every transaction has two effects – equal and opposite – means that each transaction must be recorded in two ledger accounts. This is double-entry bookkeeping.

Bookkeeping is the technique of recording financial transactions as they occur so that summaries may be made of the transactions and presented as a report to the users of accounts. The double-entry bookkeeping technique applies to the recording of transactions in ledger accounts.

 Exercise 3.1

Explain what is meant by the term 'double-entry bookkeeping'.

 Solution

Double-entry bookkeeping is a system of keeping records of transactions in ledger accounts such that every transaction requires debit and credit entries of equal value. For example, there might be a debit entry of $100 equalled by two credit entries of $90 and $10, respectively. The result of this method is that the total of debit balances on ledger accounts equals the total of credit balances.

In the previous chapter, you learned the following terms:

- assets
- liabilities
- capital
- revenues
- expenses.

These five items can be grouped in pairs, according to whether they appear on the statement of financial position or in the income statement.

- Assets, liabilities and capital appear on the statement of financial position.
- Expenses and revenue appear in the income statement.

If you compare these pairs you will see that they are, in effect, two pairs of opposites.

Each type of asset, liability, capital, expense or income is recorded separately. This is achieved by using separate ledger accounts for each of them. We shall look first of all at recording assets, liabilities and capital.

Transactions are recorded on either the debit or the credit side of a ledger account according to the following table:

Debit	Credit
Increases in assets	Decreases in assets
Decreases in liabilities	Increases liabilities
Decreases in capital	Increases in capital

Entering transactions in ledger accounts is also called *posting* the transactions.

In the previous chapter, we saw how transactions would affect the accounting equation and the statement of financial position. Example 2.B is reproduced here so that the double-entry bookkeeping entries (or postings) may be compared with the solution given in Chapter 2.

Example 3.A

Nadim had the following assets and liabilities on 1 January:

	$
Land	200,000
Buildings	60,000
Inventories	10,000
Receivables	15,000
Cash in hand	5,000
Bank balance	32,000
	322,000
Payables	17,000
Bank loan	240,000
	257,000

First of all, we enter the opening balances into the ledger accounts. Assets have debit balances, and liabilities and capital have credit balances:

Assume that Nadim had the following transactions during the first week of January:

Land		
		$
1 Jan. Balance b/d		200,000

Buildings		
1 Jan. Balance b/d		60,000

Inventories		
		$
1 Jan. Balance b/d		10,000

Receivables		
		$
1 Jan. Balance b/d		15,000

Cash in hand		
		$
1 Jan. Balance b/d		5,000

Bank balance		
		$
1 Jan. Balance b/d		32,000

Payables		
		$
	1 Jan. Balance b/d	17,000

Bank loan		
		$
	1 Jan. Balance b/d	240,000

Capital		
		$
	1 Jan. Balance b/d	65,000

Notes:

1. The capital account balance is the difference between assets and liabilities.
2. 'Balance b/d' is short for 'balance brought down'. It is sometimes also called 'balance brought forward' or 'balance b/fwd'.

Assume that Nadim had the following transactions during the first week of January:

1. Bought office equipment costing $7,000, paying $2,000 deposit by cheque, the balance to be paid at the end of March.
2. Returned some office equipment to his supplier because it was faulty. Nadim had originally been charged $3,000 for it.
3. Received $8,000 from his receivables. They all paid him by cheque.

We now want to enter the January transactions into the ledger accounts. First, though, let us look at each transaction to determine how we are going to record it.

1. Office equipment is an asset, and is increasing. Therefore we want to debit the *office equipment* account.
   A cheque for $2,000 has been paid. The bank account, an asset, is decreasing, so we want to credit the *bank* account. $5,000 is still owing to the supplier (payable), so liabilities are increasing, leading us to credit *payables*.

2. Office equipment is being returned, so the asset of office equipment is decreasing. Therefore we want to credit the *office equipment* account.

     As Nadim has not yet paid for the goods, the amount will be included in the payables figure. If we return goods, the amount owed to payables decreases and, as payables are liabilities, we therefore want to debit the payables account.

3. Receivables are assets. If they pay their debts, the amount owed decreases, so we want to credit *receivables*. Bank is an asset. Paying money in increases the balance, so we want to debit *bank*.

     These transactions can now be entered into the ledger accounts, as follows:

Land

		$			
1 Jan.	Balance b/d	200,000			

Buildings

		$			
1 Jan.	Balance b/d	60,000			

Inventories

		$			
1 Jan.	Balance b/d	10,000			

Receivables

		$			$
1 Jan.	Balance b/d	15,000	Jan.	Bank	8,000

Cash in hand

		$			
1 Jan.	Balance b/d	5,000			

Bank balance

		$			$
1 Jan.	Balance b/d	32,000	Jan.	Office equipment	2,000
Jan.	Receivables	8,000			

Payables

		$			$
Jan.	Office equipment	3,000	1 Jan.	Balance b/d	17,000
			Jan.	Office equipment	5,000

Bank loan

					$
			1 Jan.	Balance b/d	240,000

Capital

					$
			1 Jan.	Balance b/d	65,000

Office equipment

		$			$
Jan.	Bank	2,000	Jan.	Payables	3,000
	Payables	5,000			

3.4 Bookkeeping entries for expenses and revenue

An expense is a cost connected with the activities of the organisation. Examples of expenses include rent, local business tax, light and heat, wages and salaries, postage, telephone and the cost of items bought for resale.

'Revenue' is the term used to describe the activities that will eventually lead to the organisation receiving money. The most common source of revenue is that derived from the sale of its goods or services, but others include the receipt of interest on bank deposits.

The dual aspect of transactions referred to earlier applies to expenses and revenue in the same way that it did to transactions simply involving the movement of assets and liabilities.

For example, the employment of workers will cause an expense (wages and salaries) and will also create a liability to pay them. Later, when workers are paid, the liability is ended but the balance at bank is reduced.

Similarly, the sale of goods on credit will represent revenue and will create a receivable (the customer) until the customer has paid for them. When payment occurs the asset of receivable is reduced and the balance at bank increases.

The same double-entry bookkeeping principle applies to recording the expenses and income of an organisation. The table shown earlier can now be extended to include expenses and income as follows:

Debit	*Credit*
Increases in assets	Decreases in assets
Decreases in liabilities	Increases in liabilities
Decreases in capital	Increases in capital
Increases in expenses	Decreases in expenses
Decreases in revenue	Increases in revenue

3.4.1 Bookkeeping entries for purchases and sales

We keep separate ledger accounts for the different types of inventory movement. Purchases and sales of inventories must always be kept in separate accounts, because one is at cost price and the other at selling price. You might have difficulty in determining how to classify purchases and sales. You could regard purchases as being assets, or you could regard them as being expenses. It all depends on whether they are consumed during the period, and that is unknown at the time they are bought. Similarly, sales could be regarded as decreases in inventory or as revenues. The fact is that *it does not matter* how you regard them. Both will result in the correct entry being made. For example, if you regard the purchase of inventories as an increase in an asset, you will make a debit entry; if you regard it as an increase in an expense, you will still make a debit entry. The same applies to sales – a decrease in inventories results in a credit entry, as does an increase in revenue. So, you will choose the right side for the entry, whichever way you classify these. The most important thing is to use the correct account – and *never* use the inventories account for purchases and/or sales as the inventories account is used only at the beginning and end of the accounting period.

Also note that you should *never* use either the purchases account or the sales account for anything other than the goods in which the business trades. Purchases of non-current assets, stationery and so on should all be recorded in their own ledger accounts.

 Exercise 3.2

Tick the correct box for each of the following:

		Debit	Credit
1.	Increases in assets	…	…
2.	Increases in liabilities	…	…
3.	Increases in income	…	…
4.	Decreases in liabilities	…	…
5.	Increases in expenses	…	…
6.	Decreases in assets	…	…
7.	Increases in capital	…	…
8.	Decreases in income	…	…

 Solution

The order of boxes should be debit; credit; credit; debit; debit; credit; credit; debit.

Example 3.B

The following example includes transactions involving all the above types of accounts. It might help you to determine the correct ledger entries by completing a table before you start, like this (the first item is done for you):

Date	Names of accounts involved	Type of accounts	Increase/decrease	Debit/credit
1 May	Capital	Capital	Increase	Credit
	Cash	Asset	Increase	Debit

Date	
1 May	BR starts business as a sole proprietor with $20,000 in cash
2 May	Pays $15,000 cash into a business bank account
4 May	Purchases goods on credit from JM for $2,000
6 May	Purchases goods from ERD on credit for $3,000
7 May	Pays wages in cash $60
10 May	Pays rent by cheque $80
12 May	Sells goods for cash $210
16 May	Buys furniture for $1,500 paying by cheque
19 May	Sells goods on credit to SP for $580
22 May	Buys goods for cash $3,900
24 May	Buys fittings for cash $600
25 May	Pays wages by cash $110
	Sells goods for cash $430
27 May	Receives part payment from SP of $330 by cheque
28 May	Pays advertising by cheque $25
	Sells goods for cash $890
29 May	Sells goods on credit to KM for $8,090
30 May	Withdraws $100 cash for his personal use

Solution

Capital

					$
			1 May	Cash	20,000

Cash

		$			$
1 May	Capital	20,000	2 May	Bank	15,000
12 May	Sales	210	7 May	Wages	60
25 May	Sales	430	19 May	Purchases	3,900
28 May	Sales	890	24 May	Fittings	600
			25 May	Wages	110
			30 May	Cash	100

Bank

		$			$
2 May	Cash	15,000	10 May	Rent	80
27 May	SP	330	16 May	Furniture	1,500
			28 May	Advertising	25

Purchases

		$
4 May	JM	2,000
6 May	ERD	3,000
22 May	Cash	3,900

JM

					$
			4 May	Purchases	2,000

ERD

					$
			6 May	Purchases	3,000

Wages

		$
7 May	Cash	60
25 May	Cash	110

Rent

		$
10 May	Bank	80

Sales

					$
			12 May	Cash	210
			19 May	SP	580
			25 May	Cash	430
			28 May	Cash	890
			29 May	KM	8,090

Furniture

		$
16 May	Bank	1,500

SP						
		$				$
19 May	Sales	580	27 May	Bank		330

Fittings		
		$
24 May	Cash	600

Advertising		
		$
28 May	Bank	25

KM		
		$
29 May	Sales	8,090

Drawings		
		$
30 May	Cash	100

 # Exercise 3.3

A Thompson commenced business on 1 February 20X1, paying $500 into a business bank account.

    During the next month the following transactions took place. All payments are made by cheque and all receipts are banked.

		$
1 Feb.	Bought goods for resale	150
5 Feb.	Paid rent	50
10 Feb.	Business takings to date	290
22 Feb.	Paid for advertising	25
26 Feb.	A Thompson's drawings	100
27 Feb.	Business takings	240

You are required to:

(i) write up the bank account;
(ii) write up all the other accounts.

Note: When you draw up your accounts, leave ten extra lines after the bank account, and four extra lines after all other ledger accounts – this exercise is continued in the next chapter.

THE ACCOUNTING SYSTEM IN ACTION

 # Solution

Bank

20X1		$	20X1		$
1 Feb.	Capital	500	1 Feb.	Purchases	150
10 Feb.	Sales	290	5 Feb.	Rent	50
27 Feb.	Sales	240	22 Feb.	Advertising	25
			26 Feb.	Drawings	100

Capital

			20X1		$
			1 Feb.	Bank	500

Purchases

20X1		$
1 Feb.	Bank	150

Rent

20X1		$
5 Feb.	Bank	50

Advertising

20X1		$
22 Feb.	Bank	25

Drawings

20X1		$
26 Feb.	Bank	100

Sales

			20X1		$
			10 Feb.	Bank	290
			27 Feb.	Bank	240

3.4.2 Nominal ledger accounts

At this stage in your studies, all your ledger accounts are kept in a single 'book'. In later chapters you will see how the ledger accounts can be divided into several books. The main book used is called the *nominal ledger*.

3.5 Balancing the accounts

From time to time it is necessary to determine the end result of the transactions recorded in each ledger account. For example, the cash account will contain a number of debit and credit entries, but no clear indication of how much cash is remaining. The same applies to other accounts. Receivables and payables accounts will have a number of debit and credit entries, but no indication of what is currently owed as a result of these entries.

3.5.1 Calculating the balance on the account

To determine the position on each account, each side is totalled: the difference between the two sides is called the *balance*. If the debit side is greater, the account has a 'debit balance', and *vice versa*.

As an example, look at the cash account that was produced in Example 3.B.

Cash

		$			$
1 May	Capital	20,000	2 May	Bank	15,000
12 May	Sales	210	7 May	Wages	60
25 May	Sales	430	19 May	Purchases	3,900
28 May	Sales	890	24 May	Fittings	600
			25 May	Wages	110
			30 May	Cash	100

The debit side totals $21,530 (meaning that that amount has been received) and the credit side totals $19,770 (meaning that that amount has been paid out). The balance, therefore, is $1,760 debit, which means there is still that amount held in cash.

The purpose of this section is to introduce you to what is meant by the balance on an account – it is simply the difference between the totals of the two sides of the account; a debit balance means that there is more on the debit side, a credit balance means that there is more on the credit side. In the next chapter you will see how these balances are shown in the ledger accounts.

 ## Exercise 3.4

Work out the balances on the other accounts in Example 3.B.

 ## Solution

Capital	$20,000	credit
Bank	$13,725	debit
Purchases	$8,900	debit
JM	$2,000	credit
ERD	$3,000	credit
Wages	$170	debit
Rent	$80	debit
Sales	$10,200	credit
Furniture	$1,500	debit
SP	$250	debit
Fittings	$600	debit
Advertising	$25	debit
KM	$8,090	debit
Drawings	$100	debit

THE ACCOUNTING SYSTEM IN ACTION

 ## Exercise 3.5

Work out the balances on the accounts from Exercise 3.3.

 ## Solution

Bank	$705	debit
Capital	$500	credit
Purchases	$150	debit
Rent	$50	debit
Advertising	$25	debit
Drawings	$100	debit
Sales	$530	credit

3.6 Summary

In this chapter you have:

* seen how financial transactions are recorded in ledger accounts, using double-entry principles;
* learned how to calculate the balance on an account at a point in time.

Double entry is the cornerstone of the entire accounting process. You will not get far in your studies of this subject unless you have a thorough grasp of its principles. Make sure you can follow the steps involved in the examples given in this chapter, and memorise the table:

Debit	Credit
Increases in assets	Decreases in assets
Decreases in liabilities	Increases in liabilities
Decreases in capital	Increases in capital
Increases in expenses	Decreases in expenses
Decreases in revenue	Increases in revenue

It is important that you fully understand the double-entry system, as it will enable you to understand how to record more complex transactions later on in your studies.

Try not to analyse the reason for the 'left and right' system for recording transactions. It is simply a rule that, if everyone abides by it, leads to a common system. It can be likened to the rule for driving a car. If the rule in a country is to drive on the left, then the system works as long as everyone abides by the rule.

Practise the examples in the chapter several times until you feel competent in them.

Revision Questions

Question 1 Multiple choice

1.1 A credit balance of $917 brought down on Y Ltd's account in the books of X Ltd means that

(A) X Ltd owes Y Ltd $917.
(B) Y Ltd owes X Ltd $917.
(C) X Ltd has paid Y Ltd $917.
(D) X Ltd is owed $917 by Y Ltd.

1.2 Which *one* of the following statements is correct?

(A) Assets and liabilities normally have credit balances.
(B) Liabilities and revenues normally have debit balances.
(C) Assets and revenues normally have credit balances.
(D) Assets and expenses normally have debit balances.

1.3 On 1 January, a business had a customer, J King, who owed $400. During January, J King bought goods for $700 and returned goods valued at $250. He also paid $320 in cash towards the outstanding balance. The balance on J King's account at 31 January is:

(A) $530 debit.
(B) $530 credit.
(C) $270 debit.
(D) $270 credit.

1.4 Alice had the following assets and liabilities at 1 January:

	$
Inventories	350
Payables	700
Receivables	400
Bank overdraft	125
Motor vehicles	880

Her capital at 1 January was: $...............

1.5   The correct entries needed to record the return of office equipment that had been bought on credit from P Young, and not yet paid for, are:

	Debit	*Credit*
A	Office equipment	Sales
B	Office equipment	P Young
C	P Young	Office equipment
D	Cash	Office equipment

1.6   Which *one* of the following statements regarding the balance on a ledger account is *not* correct?

(A)   A credit balance exists where the total of credit entries is more than the total of debit entries.

(B)   A debit balance exists where the total of debit entries is less than the total of credit entries.

(C)   A credit balance exists where the total of debit entries is less than the total of credit entries.

(D)   A debit balance exists where the total of debit entries is more than the total of credit entries.

1.7   Which of the following is the correct entry to record the purchase on credit of inventories intended for resale?

	Debit	*Credit*
A	Inventories	Receivable
B	Inventories	Payable
C	Purchases	Payable
D	Payable	Purchases

1.8   A receives goods from B on credit terms and A subsequently pays by cheque. A then discovers that the goods are faulty and cancels the cheque before it is cashed by B. How should A record the cancellation of the cheque in his books?

	Debit	*Credit*
A	Payables	Returns outwards
B	Payables	Bank
C	Bank	Payables
D	Returns outwards	Payables

? Question 2

The table below shows a selection of financial transactions. Complete the columns to identify the accounts and the debit/credit entries to be made in the ledger to record each of the transactions.

Transaction description	*Account to be debited*	*Account to be credited*
1. Sold goods on credit to Bashir		
2. Bought goods for sale on credit from P Walker		
3. Paid carriage on the goods purchased, in cash		
4. Returned goods to P Walker		
5. Bought office machinery on credit from W Print		
6. Returned office machinery to W Print		
7. Received a cheque from P Wright		
8. Received payment from T Wilkes by cheque		
9. Owner's private car brought into the business		
10. Cheque received from P Wright dishonoured		

Question 3

S Smart commenced in business as a decorator on 1 January.

1 Jan.	Commenced business by putting $1,000 of his own money into a business bank account.
3 Jan.	Bought a motor van on credit from AB Garages for $3,000.
4 Jan.	Bought decorating tools and equipment on credit from B & P Ltd for $650.
8 Jan.	Bought paint for $250, paying by cheque.
10 Jan.	Received $400 cash from a customer for work done.
12 Jan.	Bought paint for $150, paying in cash.
14 Jan.	Issued an invoice to a customer, K Orme, for $750 for work done.
18 Jan.	Returned some of the decorating tools, value $80, to B & P Ltd.
23 Jan.	Took $50 of the cash to buy a birthday present for his son.
28 Jan.	K Orme paid $250 by cheque towards his bill.

Requirement

Calculate the balance on each account at 31 January, by completing the ledger accounts provided below:

Date	Description	Amount ($)	Date	Description	Amount ($)

Capital

Date	Description	Amount ($)	Date	Description	Amount ($)

Bank

Date	Description	Amount ($)	Date	Description	Amount ($)

Motor van

Date	Description	Amount ($)	Date	Description	Amount ($)

AB Garages

Date	Description	Amount ($)	Date	Description	Amount ($)

Tools and Equipment

Date	Description	Amount ($)	Date	Description	Amount ($)

B and P Ltd

Date	Description	Amount ($)	Date	Description	Amount ($)

Purchases

Date	Description	Amount ($)	Date	Description	Amount ($)

Sales

Date	Description	Amount ($)	Date	Description	Amount ($)

Cash

Date	Description	Amount ($)	Date	Description	Amount ($)

K Orme

Date	Description	Amount ($)	Date	Description	Amount ($)

Drawings

Date	Description	Amount ($)	Date	Description	Amount ($)

The balances on the accounts are as follows:

	$	Debit/credit
Capital		
Bank		
Motor van		
AB Garages		
Tools and equipment		
B & P Ltd		
Purchases		
Sales		
Cash		
K Orme		
Drawings		

Question 4

B Baggins commenced in business as a market gardener on 1 March. Record the following transactions in the ledger accounts:

1 Mar.	Paid $70 rent for land for the month of March, from his own funds.
4 Mar.	Bought equipment on credit for $400 from JK Ltd.
8 Mar.	Bought plants for $2,000, paying from his own funds.
10 Mar.	Received $100 cash for a talk to the local horticultural society.
12 Mar.	Sold plants for $1,200, being paid by cheque. He opened a business bank account with this amount.
15 Mar.	Paid wages of $50 in cash.
18 Mar.	Bought plants for $800 on credit from BH Horticultural Ltd.
20 Mar.	Sold Plants for $500 on Credit to PB.
23 Mar.	Paid $100 local business tax by cheque.
28 Mar.	Paid wages of $20 in cash.
31 Mar.	Sold plants for $240, being paid in cash.

Calculate the balance on each account at 31 March by completing the ledger accounts provided below:

Rent payable

$ | $

Capital

$

JK Ltd

$

Equipment

$

Purchases

$

Sales

$

Cash

$ | $

The balances on the accounts are as follows:

	$	Debit/credit
Rent payable		
Capital		
Equipment		
JK Ltd		
Purchases		
Sales		
Cash		
Bank		
Wages		
BH Horticultural Ltd		
PB		
Local business tax		

Solutions to Revision Questions

 Solution 1

1.1   Answer: (A)

A credit balance in the books of X Ltd indicates that it owes money; none of the other distractors would result in a credit balance.

1.2   Answer: (D)

1.3   Answer: (A)

The ledger account would be as follows:

J King					
		$			$
1 Jan.	Balance b/f	400	Jan.	Returned goods	250
Jan.	Sales	700		Cash	320

The balance is the debit total ($1,100) less the credit total ($570): $530 debit.

1.4   Capital = Assets − Liabilities
           = ($350 + $400 + $880) − ($700 + $125)
           = $805

1.5   Answer: (C)

1.6   Answer: (B)

1.7   Answer: (C)

The inventories account is never used to record purchases.

1.8   Answer: (C)

Solution 2

- This question tests your ability to determine the debit and credit entries of a range of simple transactions.
- It is common for students to reverse the entries at this stage in their studies. Keep referring to the table until you are sure of your accuracy.

Debit	*Credit*
Increases in assets	Decreases in assets
Decreases in liabilities	Increases in liabilities
Decreases in capital	Increases in capital
Increases in expenses	Decreases in expenses
Decreases in revenue	Increases in revenue

	Account to be debited	*Account to be credited*
1.	Bashir	Sales
2.	Purchases	P Walker
3.	Carriage inwards	Cash
4.	P Walker	Purchase returns
5.	Office machinery	W Print
6.	W Print	Office machinery
7.	Bank	P Wright
8.	Bank	T Wilkes
9.	Car	Capital
10.	P Wright	Bank

 Solution 3

Capital					
					$
			1 Jan.	Bank	1,000

Bank					
		$			$
1 Jan.	Capital	1,000	8 Jan.	Puchases	250
28 Jan.	K Orme	250			

Motor van					
		$			
3 Jan.	AB Garages	3,000			

AB Garages					
					$
			3 Jan.	Motor van	3,000

Tools and equipment

		$			$
4 Jan.	B & P Ltd	650	18 Jan.	B & P Ltd	80

B & P Ltd

		$			$
18 Jan.	Tools	80	4 Jan.	Tools	650

Purchases

		$			$
8 Jan.	Bank	250			
12 Jan.	Cash	150			

Sales

					$
			10 Jan.	Cash	400
			14 Jan.	K Orme	750

Cash

		$			$
10 Jan.	Sales	400	12 Jan.	Purchases	150
			23 Jan.	Drawings	50

K Orme

		$			$
14 Jan.	Sales	750	28 Jan.	Bank	250

Drawings

		$			
23 Jan.	Cash	50	?	?	?

The balances on the accounts are as follows:

	$	
Capital	1,000	credit
Bank	1,000	debit
Motor van	3,000	debit
AB Garages	3,000	credit
Tools and equipment	570	debit
B & P Ltd	570	credit
Purchases	400	debit
Sales	1,150	credit
Cash	200	debit
K Orme	500	debit
Drawings	50	debit

Solution 4

Rent payable

		$
1 Mar.	Capital	70

Capital

			$
	1 Mar.	Rent	70
	8 Mar.	Purchases	2,000

JK Ltd

			$
	4 Mar.	Equipment	400

Equipment

		$
4 Mar.	JK Ltd	400

Purchases

		$
8 Mar.	Capital	2,000
18 Mar.	BH Horticultural Ltd	800

Sales

			$
	10 Mar.	Cash	100
	12 Mar.	Bank	1,200
	18 Mar.	PB	500
	31 Mar.	Cash	240

Cash

		$			$
10 Mar.	Sales	100	15 Mar.	Wages	50
31 Mar.	Sales	240	28 Mar.	Wages	20

Bank

		$			$
12 Mar.	Sales	1,200	23 Mar.	Local business tax	100

Wages

		$
15 Mar.	Cash	50
28 Mar.	Cash	20

BH Horticultural Ltd			
			$
	18 Mar.	Purchases	800

PB		
		$
20 Mar.	Sales	500

Local business tax		
		$
23 Mar.	Bank	100

The balances on the accounts are as follows:

	$	
Rent payable	70	debit
Capital	2,070	credit
Equipment	400	debit
JK Ltd	400	credit
Purchases	2,800	debit
Sales	2,040	credit
Cash	270	debit
Bank	1,100	debit
Wages	70	debit
BH Horticultural Ltd	800	credit
PB	500	debit
Local business tax	100	debit

4

Summarising the Ledger Accounts

Summarising the Ledger Accounts

4

4.1 Introduction

In this chapter, you will learn how the balances on the ledger accounts can be listed in a trial balance, where the total of the debits equals the total of the credits. This does not, however, prove that there are no errors as a trial balance can still balance and yet contain errors. A trial balance is a useful step before a trading account, income statement and statement of financial position are prepared. After these financial statements have been prepared the ledger accounts can be balanced off.

4.2 Preparing the trial balance

One way of checking the accuracy of the ledger entries is by listing the balances on each account, and totalling them. Because of the 'double-entry' rule that has been employed, the total of all the accounts with debit balances should equal the total of all the accounts with credit balances. This list is known as a trial balance.

Using Example 3.B, the trial balance at 31 May would appear as follows:

Trial balance

	Debit ($)	Credit ($)
Capital		20,000
Cash	1,760	
Bank	13,725	
Purchases	8,900	
JM		2,000
ERD		3,000
Wages	170	
Rent	80	
Sales		10,200
Furniture	1,500	
SP	250	
Fittings	600	
Advertising	25	
KM	8,090	
Drawings	100	
	35,200	35,200

Notice that the accounts with debit balances are either assets or expenses, while the accounts with credit balances are liabilities, capital or revenue accounts (except for drawings, which represents a reduction in capital).

The trial balance: A list of account balances in a double-entry accounting system. The sum of the debit balances will equal the sum of the credit balances, although certain errors such as the omission of a transaction or erroneous entries will not be disclosed by a trial balance.

The trial balance is thus a list of the balances on the ledger accounts. If the totals of the debit and credit balances entered on the trial balance are not equal, then an error or errors have been made either:

1. in the posting of the transactions to the ledger accounts; or
2. in the balancing of the accounts; or
3. in the transferring of the balances from the ledger accounts to the trial balance.

4.2.1 Does the trial balance prove the accuracy of the ledger accounts?

Just because the trial balance totals agree does not mean that there are no errors within the ledger accounts. There are a number of errors that might have been made that do not prevent the trial balance from agreeing. These are:

- Errors of *omission*, where a transaction has been completely omitted from the ledger accounts.
- Errors of *commission*, where one side of a transaction has been entered in the wrong account (but of a similar type to the correct account, for example, entered in the wrong receivable's

account, or in the wrong expense account). An error of commission would not affect the calculation of profit, or the position shown by the statement of financial position.

- Errors of *principle,* where the correct and incorrect accounts are of different types, for example, entered in the purchases account instead of a non-current asset account as for errors of commission. This type of error would affect the calculation of profit, and the position shown by the statement of financial position.
- Errors of *original entry,* where the wrong amount has been used for both the debit and the credit entries.
- *Reversal* of entries, where the debit has been made to the account that should have been credited and vice versa.
- *Duplication* of entries, where the transaction has been posted twice.
- *Compensating errors,* where two or more transactions have been entered incorrectly, but cancelling each other out, for example, electricity debited with $100 in excess, and sales credited with $100 in excess.

In all these cases, an account has been debited and an account has been credited with the same amount, so the trial balance will still be in agreement, even though it contains incorrect entries. You will learn more about errors, and how to correct them, in Chapter 9.

 ## Exercise 4.1
Explain the purpose of a trial balance.

 ## Solution
The purpose of a trial balance is to check the arithmetical accuracy of the entries made to the ledger accounts, that is, that the total of debit entries equals the total of credit entries.

 ## Exercise 4.2
Prepare a trial balance from the ledger accounts in Exercise 3.3.

 ## Solution

Bank	$705	debit
Capital	$500	credit
Purchases	$150	debit
Rent	$50	debit
Advertising	$25	debit
Drawings	$100	debit
Sales	$530	credit

Trial balance of A Thompson as at 28 February 20X1

	Debit ($)	Credit ($)
Bank	705	
Capital		500
Purchases	150	
Rent	50	
Advertising	25	
Drawings	100	
Sales		530
	1,030	1,030

4.3   Preparing a statement of profit

When the trial balance has been successfully completed, it is reasonably safe to assume that profit can now be accurately calculated. This is referred to as 'the income statement'. You should recall from Chapter 2 that the part of the income statement which calculates gross profit is known as the 'trading account'. This comprises sales, less cost of goods sold, equals gross profit. The trading account is thus a sub-section of the income statement although its name does not appear within the income statement. Nevertheless, it is a very important part of the income statement.

4.3.1   The trading account

The trading account is part of the double-entry bookkeeping system of an organisation that buys and sells goods with the intention of making a profit. It is part of the income statement and is regularly produced by such an organisation during the year, often on a monthly basis.

The trading account compares the revenue derived from selling the goods with the costs of obtaining the goods sold. A typical trading account is as follows:

Trading account for the year ending 31 December 20X1			
	$		$
Opening inventories	500	Sales	9,400
Purchases	6,400	Less: sales returns	(300)
	6,900		
Less: closing inventories	(430)		
Cost of goods sold	6,470		
Gross profit	2,630		
	9,100		9,100

This presentation, as a ledger account, is known as the *horizontal format*.

Transferring the balances to the trading account

The trading account is a ledger account in the normal sense, and must conform to the double-entry rule. Therefore, every entry in it must have an opposite entry elsewhere in the ledger accounts. For example, the credit in the trading account for 'sales' of $9,400 will also be debited in the sales account. In effect, the balance on the sales account is transferred into the trading account. In the example above, the sales account might have appeared as follows:

		Sales			
			20X1		$
			1 Jan.	B Nevitt	1,000
			10 Jan.	A Turner	5,400
			23 Jan.	G Fletcher	2,600
			30 Jan.	P Bajwa	400

Once the balance has been transferred to the trading account, the sales account will appear as follows:

		Sales			
20X1		$	20X1		$
31 Dec.	Trading account	9,400	10 Jan.	B Nevitt	1,000
			13 Mar.	A Turner	5,400
			6 Jun.	G Fletcher	2,600
			5 Dec.	P Bajwa	400
		9,400			9,400

Note that there is now no balance on the sales account, and so the two sides can be totalled to confirm that fact, and ruled off to prevent including them in the figures for the following year. The account is now said to be 'closed', although it can still be used to record the sales for the next period, below the totals.

This process is repeated with all the other figures that appear in the trading account, but there are some transfers that are worthy of special mention.

(a) *The inventories account.* In Chapter 3, you were told *never* to use the inventories account for the purchase, sale or return of inventories, but that it was used only at the beginning and the end of the period.

In a business that has been trading in the past, there will be a balance on the inventories account at the start of the period, which will be a debit balance (representing an asset). In the example above, the inventories account at the start of the period would appear as follows:

		Inventories		
20X1		$	20X1	$
1 Jan.	Balance	500		

As the trading account is being prepared, this balance is transferred into it, by crediting the inventories account and debiting the trading account. The inventories account then appears as follows:

Inventories

20X1		$	20X1		$
1 Jan.	Balance	500	31 Dec.	Trading account	500

The inventories account now has no balance, so it can be 'closed off' as with the sales account you saw earlier.

As the preparation of the trading account continues, it will be necessary to determine the value of the inventories at 31 December. This is often done by referring to a separate inventory control system, which is maintained outside the bookkeeping system (you will learn more about the valuation of inventories in Chapter 8). The figure is passed to the bookkeeper, who then debits the inventories account with the new value, and credits the trading account.

The inventories account now appears as follows:

Inventories

20X1		$	20X1		$
1 Jan.	Balance	500	31 Dec.	Trading account	500
31 Dec.	Trading account	430			

However, notice that in the trading account above, the closing inventories does not appear to have been credited to it, instead it has been *deducted* on the debit side of the account. This is not normal practice for most ledger accounts, but is commonplace when the trading account is being prepared, because it is then possible to show the cost of goods sold figure. An item deducted on the debit side of an account is equivalent to making a credit entry.

(b) *Sales and purchase returns*. The same type of entry is used with sales and purchase returns. In the trading account above, the sales returns have been deducted from the sales figure on the credit side of the account. This is the equivalent of making a debit entry. The opposite entry would be to credit the sales returns account.

The trading account thus brings together the revenue and costs of the trading function for a specified period of time, and by comparing them calculates the *gross profit*. It is common for the gross profit to be expressed as a percentage of the sales value, when it is known as the gross profit margin, or as a percentage of the cost of sales, when it is known as the gross profit mark-up.

The balance on the trading account

We have seen that the revenue from the sale of goods is compared with the cost of those goods in the trading account and the resulting difference is referred to as gross profit. This figure is the balance on the trading account.

This balance is then carried down within the income statement.

Vertical presentation of the trading account

An alternative presentation of the trading account is shown below. This is known as the *vertical format*, and is used when producing an income statement.

Trading account for the year ended 31 December 20X1

	$	$
Sales		9,400
Less: returns inwards		(300)
		9,100
Opening inventories	500	
Purchases	6,400	
	6,900	
Less: closing inventories	(430)	
		6,470
Gross profit		2,630

 ## Exercise 4.3

Prepare the trading account (in *horizontal* format) for Example 3.B, given that closing inventories were $1,200, and make the necessary entries in the ledger accounts.

 ## Solution

Trading account for the month ended 31 May

	$		$
		Sales	10,200
Opening inventories	Nil		
Purchases	8,900		
	8,900		
Less: closing inventories	1,200		
Cost of goods sold	7,700		
Gross profit	2,500		
	10,200		10,200

Note: There were no opening inventories in this case, as the company commenced trading only on 1 May.

Sales

		$			$
			12 May	Cash	210
			19 May	SP	580
			25 May	Cash	430
			28 May	Cash	890
31 May	Trading account	10,200	29 May	KM	8,090
		10,200			10,200

Purchases

		$			$
4 May	JM	2,000			
6 May	ERD	3,000			
22 May	Cash	3,900	31 May	Trading account	8,900
		8,900			8,900

Inventories

		$
31 May	Trading account	1,200

Exercise 4.4

Prepare the trading account for Exercise 3.3 (in *vertical* format), given that closing inventories were $50.

Solution

Trading account for the month ended 28 February 20X1

	$	$
Sales		530
Opening inventories	–	
Purchases	150	
	150	
Less: closing inventories	(50)	
		100
Gross profit		430

4.3.2 The income statement

The rest of the income statement performs a similar function to the trading account by comparing (in the case of trading organisations) the other costs of operating the business and any non-trading revenue (such as interest received) with the gross profit to identify whether the business has been profitable overall or not. In the case of organisations that provide a service rather than selling goods a trading account is not prepared. In this case, the word 'sales' is not normally used and some other word, such as 'services' or 'turnover', is used instead.

The income statement as a whole, just as the sub-section of the trading account, is part of the double-entry bookkeeping system. In the case of the trading account, the word 'account' appears and this makes it obvious that it is a ledger 'account' which can be debited and credited. The word 'account' does not appear in the name 'income statement' but it is nevertheless a ledger account which can be debited and credited.

A typical income statement, in *horizontal* format, is shown below:

Income statement for the year ended 31 December 20X1

	$		$
Rent	120	Gross profit b/d	2,630
Local business tax	80		
Light and heat	75		
Wages	1,120		
Printing and stationery	14		
Telephone	37		
Net profit	1,184		
	2,630		2,630

The income statement thus summarises all the costs and revenues of the business for a specified period of time. The various expenses (and sundry revenues, if there are any) are transferred out of the nominal ledger, and into the income statement. Those accounts are then closed off.

The resulting balance on the income statement is referred to as a *net profit* (if it is a credit balance), or *net loss* (if it is a debit balance).

It is common for the net profit (or loss) to be expressed as a percentage of the sales value shown in the trading account, and this is known as the *net profit percentage*.

The income statement is presented in a *vertical* format when it is presented as part of the financial statements. This is shown below:

Income statement for the year ended 31 December 20X1

	$	$
Gross profit		2,630
Less: Rent	120	
Local business tax	80	
Light and heat	75	
Wages	1,120	
Printing and stationery	14	
Telephone	37	
		(1,446)
Net profit		1,184

 Exercise 4.5

Prepare the income statement in horizontal format for Example 3.B, and make the necessary entries in the ledger accounts.

Solution

Income statement for the month ended 31 May

	$		$
Wages	170	Gross profit b/d	2,500
Rent	80		
Advertising	25		
Net profit	2,225		
	2,500		2,500

Wages

		$			$
7 May	Cash	60			
25 May	Cash	110	31 May	Income statement	170
		170			170

Rent

		$			$
10 May	Bank	80	31 May	Income statement	80

Advertising

		$			$
22 Feb.	Bank	25	31 Feb.	Income statement	25

 ## Exercise 4.6

Prepare the income statement in horizontal format for Exercise 3.3.

 ## Solution

Income statement of A Thompson for the month ended 28 February 20X1

Rent	50	Gross profit b/d	430
Advertising	25		
Net profit	355		
	430		430

4.3.3 The balance on the income statement

The balance on the income statement represents the owner's profit and has thus increased his investment in the business. At the end of the year this is transferred to the owner's capital account, by debiting the income statement and crediting the capital account. If the balance on the income statement is a debit balance, this represents a net loss, and the entries are reversed.

The capital account from Example 3.B would now appear as follows:

Capital

			$
1 May		Bank	20,000
31 May		Income statement	2,225

4.3.4 Dealing with drawings

The balance on the capital account is increased by the net profit (or decreased by a net loss). The balance is also affected by any drawings that have occurred, and that have been debited to a separate drawings account. The balance on this account now needs to be transferred to the capital account, by means of the following entries:

- credit the drawings account;
- debit the capital account.

Using Example 3.B again, the drawings and capital account would now look like this:

Capital

		$			$
31 May	Drawings account	100	1 May	Bank	20,000
			31 May	Income statement	2,225

Drawings

		$			$
30 May	Cash	100	31 May	Capital	100

4.4 Preparing the statement of financial position

The next stage is to prepare the balance sheet. The statement of financial position shows the assets, liabilities and capital that exist at the date at which it is drawn up. It will include *all* the ledger accounts that have balances on them.

It should be noted that the statement of financial position is not an 'account'. Its name is not the statement of financial position 'account' and it is not part of the double-entry book-keeping system. The statement of financial position, is a list of all the balances in the ledger accounts.

The ledger accounts for expenses and revenues will all have no balance remaining, as they have been transferred to the income statement (but see the next chapter for occasions when this is not the case). The inventories account will have a new balance, and the capital account will have had the net profit or net loss and drawings entered. The balances on the other assets and liabilities will be those used in order to prepare the trial balance. These, plus the inventories account and revised capital account balance, can be presented in the statement of financial position.

Refer Section 2.3 for the presentation of the balance sheet.

Exercise 4.7

Prepare the balance sheet for Example 3.B.

Solution

Balance sheet as at 31 May		
Assets	$	$
Non-current assets		
Furniture		1,500
Fittings		600
		2,100
Current assets		
Inventories	1,200	
Receivables	8,340	
Bank balance	13,725	
Cash in hand	1,760	
		25,025
		27,125
Capital and liabilities		
Capital		20,000
Net profit for the month		2,225
		22,225
Less: drawings		(100)
		22,125
Current liabilities		
Payables		5,000
		27,125

4.5 Balancing off the ledger accounts

The final task is to tidy up the remaining accounts in order to clearly show the final balance on each, in readiness for commencing posting the next period's transactions. This process is known as *balancing off* the accounts. In the previous chapter you saw how the balance is mathematically calculated in order to produce the trial balance, and to determine the amounts to be transferred to the income statement and included in the statement of financial position. Some accounts will now have no balance remaining, but those that appear on the statement of financial position will have, and this needs to be clearly identified.

The procedure can be shown in the following steps:

Step 1. Calculate the balance (or take the figure already used in the trial balance).

Step 2. Enter the balance on the *opposite* side of the account, for example, if there is a debit balance, enter it on the credit side. (Imagine the account as a pair of scales that was out of balance; entering the item on the opposite side brings the scales into balance.) Use the date at which the statement of financial position is prepared, and describe the balance as 'balance carried down', abbreviated to 'balance c/d'. This is, of course, making an entry in the ledger accounts, therefore an opposite entry needs to be made to conform to the double-entry rule – see step 4 for this.

Step 3. Total up each side, to confirm that the two sides now agree, and rule them off.

Step 4. Enter the balance on its *correct* side, beneath the totals. This completes the double entry from Step 2. Date the item as the first day of the next accounting period, for example, 1 January 20X2, and describe the balance as 'balance brought down', abbreviated to 'balance b/d'.

Step 5. Check that all accounts with debit balances are assets, and that all accounts with credit balances are either liabilities or capital, and compare them with the statement of financial position figures.

 Exercise 4.8

Balance off the asset, liability and capital accounts, from Example 3.B.

 Solution

Capital

		$			$
31 May	Drawings	100	1 May	Cash	20,000
	Balance c/d	22,125	31 May	Net profit	2,225
		22,225			22,225
			1 Jun.	Balance b/d	22,125

Cash

		$			$
1 May	Capital	20,000	2 May	Bank	15,000
12 May	Sales	210	7 May	Wages	60
25 May	Sales	430	19 May	Purchases	3,900
28 May	Sales	890	24 May	Fittings	600
			25 May	Wages	110
			30 May	Cash	100
			31 May	Balance c/d	1,760
		21,530			21,530
1 Jun.	Balance b/d	1,760			

Bank

		$			$
2 May	Cash	15,000	10 May	Rent	80
27 May	SP	330	16 May	Furniture	1,500
			28 May	Advertising	25
			31 May	Balance c/d	13,725
		15,330			15,330
1 Jun.	Balance b/d	13,725			

JM

					$
			4 May	Purchases	2,000

ERD

		$			$
10 May	Bank	80	6 May	Purchases	3,000
31 May	Balance c/d	2,920			
		3,000			3,000
			1 Jun.	Balance b/d	2,920

Furniture

		$			
16 May	Bank	1,500			

SP

		$			$
19 May	Sales	580	27 May	Bank	330
			31 May	Balance c/d	250
		580			580
1 Jun.	Balance b/d	250			

Fittings

		$			
24 May	Cash	600			

Advertising

		$			
28 May	Bank	25			

KM

		$			
29 May	Sales	8,090			

You should notice that the accounts that only have one entry have not been balanced off; this is because the balance on the account can easily be seen without balancing it. However, it is a good practice to balance off in the standard way at least once a year, to confirm that the account has been considered and included in the appropriate financial statement.

For example, the fittings account above would appear as follows:

Fittings

		$			$
24 May	Cash	600	31 May	Balance c/d	600
		600			600
1 Jun.	Balance b/d	600			

The balances brought down then become the first entries in each account for the following accounting period.

Exercise 4.9

Balance off the asset, liability and capital ledger accounts from Exercise 3.3, after transferring the net profit of $355 and the balance on the drawings account into the capital account. Remember that you also need to open an inventories account.

 ## Solution

Bank

20X1		$	20X1		$
1 Feb.	Capital	500	1 Feb.	Purchases	150
10 Feb.	Sales	290	5 Feb.	Rent	50
27 Feb.	Sales	240	22 Feb.	Advertising	25
			26 Feb.	Drawings	100
			28 Feb.	Balance c/d	705
		1,030			1,030
1 Mar.	Balance b/d	705			

Capital

20X1		$	20X1		$
28 Feb.	Drawings	100	1 Feb.	Bank	500
28 Feb.	Balance c/d	755	28 Feb.	Net profit	355
		855			855
			1 Mar.	Balance b/d	755

Inventories

20X1		$			
28 Feb.	Trading account	50			

 ## Exercise 4.10

Continue with the ledger accounts from Exercise 3.3 at 1 March, and enter the following transactions for March:

2 Mar.	Bought goods for resale, on credit from J Smith	100
5 Mar.	Paid rent	50
14 Mar.	Received a loan from L Lock	450
16 Mar.	Business sales	330
23 Mar.	A Thompson's drawings	75
24 Mar.	Paid J Smith by cheque	80
26 Mar.	Business sales, on credit to A Pitt	180
29 Mar.	Paid for advertising leaflets	30

Balance off the bank account at 31 March.

Solution

Bank

20X1		$	20X1		$
1 Mar.	Balance b/d	705	5 Mar.	Rent	50
14 Mar.	Loan	450	23 Mar.	Drawings	75
16 Mar.	Sales	330	24 Mar.	J Smith	80
			29 Mar.	Advertising	30
			31 Mar.	Balance c/d	1,250
		1,485			1,485
1 Apr.	Balance b/d	1,250			

Capital

			20X1		$
			1 Mar.	Balance b/d	755

Inventories

20X1		$
28 Feb.	Trading account	50

Purchases

20X1		$
2 Mar.	J Smith	100

J Smith

20X1		$	20X1		$
24 Mar.	Bank	80	2 Mar.	Purchases	100

Rent payable

20X1		$
5 Mar.	Bank	50

L Lock

			20X1		$
			14 Mar.	Bank	450

Sales

			20X1		$
			16 Mar.	Bank	330
			26 Mar.	A Pitt	180

Drawings

20X1		$
23 Mar.	Bank	75

A Pitt

20X1		$
26 Mar.	Sales	180

Advertising		
20X1		$
29 Mar.	Bank	30

4.6 Columnar ledger accounts

As an alternative to the traditional 'two-sided' ledger account seen above, ledger accounts can also be prepared in columnar format. This format was originally devised with the introduction of mechanised bookkeeping systems, and is often the format used by computerised systems. Instead of having two 'sides' to the account, with the date and details column repeated on each, there is a single date and details column, a debit column, a credit column, and, usually, a balance column. The balance is calculated after each transaction, or perhaps each day's transactions, so that it is always available at a glance.

To illustrate the layout and operation of columnar accounts (also called *three-column accounts*), the bank account for March in Exercise 4.10 would appear as follows:

					Bank	
Date	*Details*	*Ref.*	*Debit* ($)	*Credit* ($)	*Balance* ($)	
1 Mar.	Brought forward				705	debit
5 Mar.	Rent	123		50	655	debit
14 Mar.	Loan		450		1,105	debit
16 Mar.	Sales		330		1,435	debit
23 Mar.	Drawings	124		75	1,360	debit
24 Mar.	J Smith	125		80	1,280	debit
29 Mar.	Advertising	126		30	1,250	debit

With this layout, there is sufficient room to add other columns, for example, for cheque numbers, and the balance is readily visible every day.

4.7 Summary

In this chapter you have looked at:

- the preparation of the trial balance;
- the form and content of the trading account within the income statement;
- the form and content of the income statement;
- the ledger entries needed to prepare an income statement;
- the entries needed to record profit and drawings in the capital account;
- the preparation of the statement of financial position;
- the balancing off the ledger accounts at the end of the period.

This chapter is one of the most 'technical' chapters you will study. Do practise the techniques you have learned here to ensure that you have a thorough understanding of them.

Revision Questions

4

Question 1 Multiple choice

1.1 Where a transaction is credited to the correct ledger account, but debited incorrectly to the repairs and renewals account instead of to the plant and machinery account, the error is known as an error of:

(A) omission.
(B) commission.
(C) principle.
(D) original entry.

1.2 If a purchase return of $48 has been wrongly posted to the debit side of the sales returns account, but has been correctly entered in the supplier's account, the total of the trial balance would show:

(A) the credit side to be $48 more than the debit side.
(B) the debit side to be $48 more than the credit side.
(C) the credit side to be $96 more than the debit side.
(D) the debit side to be $96 more than the credit side.

1.3 The debit side of a trial balance totals $50 more than the credit side. This could be due to:

(A) a purchase of goods for $50 being omitted from the payables account.
(B) a sale of goods for $50 being omitted from the receivables account.
(C) an invoice of $25 for electricity being credited to the electricity account.
(D) a receipt for $50 from a debtor being omitted from the cash book.

1.4 An invoice from a supplier of office equipment has been debited to the stationery account. This error is known as:

(A) an error of commission.
(B) an error of original entry.
(C) a compensating error.
(D) an error of principle.

1.5   The double-entry system of bookkeeping normally results in which of the following balances on the ledger accounts?

	Debit balances	*Credit balances*
A	Assets and revenues	Liabilities, capital and expenses
B	Revenues, capital and liabilities	Assets and expenses
C	Assets and expenses	Liabilities, capital and revenues
D	Assets, expenses and capital	Liabilities and revenues

1.6   Which one of the following is an error of principle?

(A) A gas bill credited to the gas account and debited to the bank account.

(B) The purchase of a non-current asset credited to the asset at cost account and debited to the payables account.

(C) The purchase of a non-current asset debited to the purchases account and credited to the payables account.

(D) The payment of wages debited and credited to the correct accounts, but using the wrong amount.

1.7   Recording the purchase of computer stationery by debiting the computer equipment at cost account would result in:

(A) an overstatement of profit and an overstatement of non-current assets.

(B) an understatement of profit and an overstatement of non-current assets.

(C) an overstatement of profit and an understatement of non-current assets.

(D) an understatement of profit and an understatement of non-current assets.

? Question 2

On 1 January, P Roberts starts a business with $2,500 in the bank and $500 cash. The following transactions occur:

2 Jan.	He buys raw materials on credit for $700 from J Martin.
3 Jan.	He sells goods for $300 on credit to G Goddard.
7 Jan.	He sells goods for $1,100 to K Lemon on credit.
12 Jan.	He buys equipment for $3,000, paying by cheque.
18 Jan.	He pays wages of $50 by cheque.
20 Jan.	He buys raw materials for $350, paying by cheque.
	He takes $80 from the cash box for himself.
28 Jan.	He pays J Martin $250 by cheque.
30 Jan.	He transfers $200 cash into the bank from his cash box.

Requirements

(a)   Record the above transactions in the ledger accounts provided below.

Capital

		$				$
31 Jan.	Drawings	...	1 Jan.	Bank		...
	Balance c/d	...		Cash		...
			31 Jan.	Net profit		...
		...				...
			1 Feb.	Balance b/d		...

Bank

		$				$
1 Jan.	Capital	...	12 Jan.	Equipment		...
30 Jan.	Cash	...	18 Jan.	Wages		...
31 Jan.	Balance c/d	...	20 Jan.	Purchases		...
			28 Jan.	J Martin		...
		...				...
			1 Feb.	Balance b/d		...

Cash

		$				$
1 Jan.	Capital	...	20 Jan.	Drawings		...
			30 Jan.	Bank		...
			31 Jan.	Balance c/d		...
		...				...
1 Feb.	Balance b/d	...				

Purchases

		$				$
2 Jan.	J Martin	...	31 Jan.	Trading a/c		...
20 Jan.	Bank	...				
		...				...

J Martin

		$				$
28 Jan.	Bank	...	2 Jan.	Purchases		...
31 Jan.	Balance c/d	...				
		...				...
			1 Feb.	Balance b/d		...

Sales

		$				$
31 Jan.	Trading a/c	...	3 Jan.	G Goddard		...
			7 Jan.	K Lemon		...
		...				...

G Goddard

		$				$
3 Jan.	Sales	...				

K Lemon

		$				$
7 Jan.	Sales	…				

Equipment

		$				$
12 Jan.	Bank	…				

Wages

		$				$
18 Jan.	Bank	…	31 Jan.	Income statement		…
		…				…

Drawings

		$				$
20 Jan.	Cash	…	31 Jan.	Capital account		…
		…				…

(b) Insert the missing figures into the following trial balance.

Trial balance of P Roberts as at 31 January

	Debit ($)	Credit ($)
Capital		…
Bank		…
Cash	…	
Purchases	…	
Payables		…
Sales		…
Receivables	…	
Equipment	…	
Wages	…	
Drawings	…	—
	…	…

(c) Insert the missing figures into the income statement for January, given that closing inventories are $200.

Income statement of P Roberts for the month ended 31 January

	$	$
Sales		…
Less: cost of goods sold		
Purchases	…	
Closing inventories	…	
		…
Gross profit		…
Less: expenses – wages		…
Net profit		…

(d) Insert the missing figures into the statement of financial position at 31 January.

Statement of financial position of P Roberts as at 31 January

	$	$
Assets		
Non-current assets		
Equipment		...
Current assets		
Inventories	...	
Receivables	...	
Cash	...	
		...
		...
Capital and liabilities		
Opening capital		...
Add: net profit		...
		...
Less: drawings		...
Current liabilities		
Payables	...	
Bank overdraft	...	...
		...

Solutions to Revision Questions

4

✓ Solution 1

1.1   Answer: (C)

This is a straightforward test of your knowledge of the types of errors that can exist. If the wrong account is used, and this results in an incorrect statement of profit, then an error of principle has been made. Debiting the repairs and renewals account results in an extra charge for expenses in the income statement, when the item should be included as a non-current asset on the statement of financial position.

1.2   Answer: (D)

A purchase return should be credited to the purchase returns account. If it has been debited to an account (whether the correct account or not), and also debited to the supplier's account (which is correct), then two debit entries will have been made with no corresponding credit. $96 (2 × $48) will have been debited, and nothing credited. Thus, the debit side will exceed the credit side by $96.

1.3   Answer: (A)

(B) and (D) are incorrect as they would give a lower debit side. (C) is incorrect because it would give a higher credit side.

1.4   Answer: (D)

An error of principle occurs where an entry is made in the wrong account, and that account is of a different category from the correct account – thus affecting the view given by the financial statements. Office equipment is a non-current asset, while stationery is an expense, so both profit and non-current assets will be incorrect.

1.5   Answer: (C)

Assets and expenses have debit balances; liabilities, capital and revenue have credit balances.

1.6   Answer: (C)

An error of principle is where one side of an entry has been recorded in the wrong account, and where that account is classified differently to the correct account. In this case, debiting a non-current asset to the purchases account would result in the profit calculation being incorrect, and the value of assets shown on the statement of financial position being incorrect.

1.7 Answer: (A)

Stationery is an expense and should be used to reduce profits; therefore profits would be overstated. Computer equipment is shown in the statement of financial position, and therefore the figure for non-current assets would be overstated.

 Solution 2

(a)

Capital

		$				$
31 Jan.	Drawings	80	1 Jan.	Bank		2,500
	Balance c/d	3,420		Cash		500
			31 Jan.	Net profit		500
		3,500				3,500
			1 Feb.	Balance b/d		3,420

Bank

		$				$
1 Jan.	Capital	2,500	12 Jan.	Equipment		3,000
30 Jan.	Cash	200	18 Jan.	Wages		50
31 Jan.	Balance c/d	950	20 Jan.	Purchases		350
			28 Jan.	J Martin		250
		3,650				3,650
			1 Feb.	Balance b/d		950

Cash

		$				$
1 Jan.	Capital	500	20 Jan.	Drawings		80
			30 Jan.	Bank		200
			31 Jan.	Balance c/d		220
		500				500
1 Feb.	Balance b/d	220				

Purchases

		$				$
2 Jan.	J Martin	700	31 Jan.	Trading account		1,050
20 Jan.	Bank	350				
		1,050				1,050

J Martin

		$				$
28 Jan.	Bank	250	2 Jan.	Purchases		700
31 Jan.	Balance c/d	450				
		700				700
			1 Feb.	Balance b/d		450

Sales

		$				$
31 Jan.	Trading account	1,400	3 Jan.	G Goddard		300
			7 Jan.	K Lemon		1,100
		1,400				1,400

G Goddard

		$
3 Jan.	Sales	300

K Lemon

		$
7 Jan.	Sales	1,100

Equipment

		$
12 Jan.	Bank	3,000

Wages

		$			$
18 Jan.	Bank	50	31 Jan.	Income statement	50
		50			50

Drawings

		$			$
20 Jan.	Cash	80	31 Jan.	Capital account	80
		80			80

(b)   Trial balance of P Roberts as at 31 January

	Debit ($)	Credit ($)
Capital		3,000
Bank		950
Cash	220	
Purchases	1,050	
Payables		450
Sales		1,400
Receivables	1,400	
Equipment	3,000	
Wages	50	
Drawings	80	
	5,800	5,800

(c)   Income statement of P Roberts for the month ending 31 January

	$	$
Sales		1,400
Less: cost of goods sold		
Purchases	1,050	
Less: closing inventories	(200)	
		(850)
Gross profit		550
Less: expenses – wages		(50)
Net profit		500

(d)   Statement of financial position of P Roberts as at 31 January

Assets	$	$
Non-current assets		
Equipment		3,000
Current assets		
Inventories	200	
Receivables	1,400	
Cash	220	
		1,820
		4,820
Capital and liabilities		
Opening capital		3,000
Add: net profit		500
		3,500
Less: drawings		(80)
		3,420
Current liabilities		
Payables	450	
Bank overdraft	950	1,400
		4,820

Further Aspects of Ledger Accounting

Further Aspects of Ledger Accounting

5

LEARNING OUTCOMES

When you have completed this chapter, you should be able to:

▶ prepare accounts for indirect taxes, for example value added tax (VAT);

▶ prepare accounts for payroll;

▶ prepare accounts using accruals and prepayments;

▶ explain the difference between, and prepare accounts for, bad debts and allowances for receivables.

5.1 Introduction

In this chapter we continue looking at ledger accounts, and look at ones of special significance. These are

- carriage costs,
- sales tax (e.g. VAT in UK, TVA in France),
- wages and salaries,
- accruals and prepayments,
- bad debts,
- allowance for receivables,
- the exchange of goods and services.

5.2 Accounting for specialised transactions

5.2.1 Carriage costs

Organisations may pay for carriage and delivery charges on items that they buy and/or sell.

Carriage and delivery charges on non-current assets are included with the cost of the non-current asset, and are debited to that non-current asset's account, along with the cost of the item. But carriage charges on the purchase and sale of goods in which the organisation trades are recorded separately as follows.

(a) *Carriage outwards*. This is carriage paid by the organisation on goods that it sells. It is debited to a separate 'carriage outwards' ledger account, and treated as any other expense, that is, it is transferred to the income statement at the end of the period.

(b) *Carriage inwards*. This is carriage paid by the organisation on goods that it buys. It is debited to a separate 'carriage inwards' ledger account. However, some purchases may have the carriage costs paid for by the supplier, and these costs will be included in the purchase price. This creates a situation where the purchases account is debited with some items already containing an element of carriage costs, and some that do not. So that all purchases are treated in the same way, the carriage costs borne by the organisation itself are transferred into the trading account at the end of the period, and added to the cost of purchases.

This additional cost does make the calculation of cost of goods sold a little more complicated, especially when there are purchase returns to consider as well. The following illustration (using imaginary figures) shows how the cost of goods sold calculation might look.

	$	$
Opening inventories		2,600
Purchases	18,500	
Carriage inwards	500	
	19,000	
Less: purchase returns	(1,700)	
		17,300
		19,900
Less: closing inventories		(2,150)
Cost of goods sold		17,750

5.2.2 Discounts

A discount is a reduction in the amount paid for goods and services. Discounts may be received from suppliers or allowed to customers. There are two types of discount: trade discounts and cash discounts.

Trade discounts. A trade discount may be offered to customers who are also traders, which is where the term 'trade discount' originates. However, nowadays it might be offered for a variety of other reasons, such as to existing customers, new customers, customers buying in bulk and so on. Once the discount has been offered, it cannot be taken away for whatever reason, so it simply means that a lower price is being charged. Trade discount is deducted from the quoted price (sometimes referred to as a 'list' price, or a 'catalogue' price), and only the net amount is recorded in the ledger accounts.

Example 5.A

On 1 January, AB buys goods for resale on credit from XY, with a list price of $250, subject to trade discount of 20 per cent. The trade discount is $50, and therefore the net amount payable is $200. The purchases account is debited with $200, and the account of XY is credited with $200.
Note: Once this net figure has been agreed, any further calculations (see below for cash discounts and sales tax) are based on the *net* figure.

Cash discounts. A cash discount may be offered to encourage prompt payment. The term used to apply only to payments made in cash at the time of sale, but nowadays it applies to payments by many different methods, provided that payment is made within a certain time. If the payment is *not* made within that time, the discount is withdrawn.

The difficulty is that, at the time of sale, it will not be known whether the payment will be made in time (unless, of course, it is made at once), but the transaction still needs to be entered in the ledger accounts. Thus, at the time of sale, no account is taken of the cash discount.

Example 5.B

Continuing with Example 5.A, suppose that XY also offers cash discount of 5 per cent for payment within ten days. At the time of purchase, AB is not certain to pay within the 10 days, so the transaction is entered ignoring the cash discount (but after adjusting for the trade discount). The ledger accounts would appear as follows:

Purchases

20X1		$			
1 Jan.	XY	200			

XY

			20X1		$
			1 Jan.	Purchases	200

If the account is not settled in the 10 days, the full amount of $200 is payable.

Let us suppose, however, that AB pays on 7 January. Five per cent is deductible, so only $190 is paid (by cheque). The bank account will be credited with $190, and the account of XY will be debited, thus:

XY

20X1		$	20X1		$
7 Jan.	Bank	190	1 Jan.	Purchases	200

The account has been settled, and yet there is still a balance of $10 credit in the ledger account, which gives the impression that there is still $10 owing to XY. This is not the case. The account needs to be cleared, to give a true impression, by debiting it with a further $10, and a credit is made to 'discounts received' account. This account is a form of revenue, and will be transferred to the income statement at the end of the period, to increase profit.

The ledger accounts after recording the cash discount are as follows:

XY					
20X1		$	20X1		$
7 Jan.	Bank	190	1 Jan.	Purchases	200
	Discount received	10			

Discount received					
			20X1		$
			7 Jan.	XY	10

Cash discount allowed will arise where an organisation allows its customers to deduct an amount for prompt payment. The receivables account will be credited with the discount, and a 'discounts allowed' account will be debited. The balance on this is treated like any other expense and transferred to the income statement at the end of the period.

5.3   Accounting for sales tax

In many countries certain organisations are required to charge a sales tax. In the UK this is 'VAT', and in France 'TVA'. In this section we shall use the generic name 'sales tax'. As a consequence the amount that they charge their customers for goods and services supplied will increase by the addition of sales tax.

The rate of sales tax varies between countries and will also vary between the nature of the goods and services supplied. The sales tax collected does not belong to the organisation that charges and collects it and the tax must therefore be remitted to the tax authorities on a regular basis. It is a tax that ultimately must be paid to the tax authorities. Because it does not belong to the organisation collecting it, it does not affect the value of its sales. However, it does mean that customers will have to pay to the organisation the full amount, including sales tax.

The organisation may also have to pay sales tax itself on goods and services that it buys. This sales tax paid can normally be reclaimed. Even though the organisation has to pay the supplier the full amount, if the sales tax is reclaimable then it does not affect the value of the item purchased.

Such organisations will, as a consequence, be both receiving and paying sales tax. The organisation may offset sales tax paid against the sales tax received from customers, and only the difference is payable to/by the tax authority. The sales tax paid to suppliers is therefore an asset (receivable) and the amount received from customers is a liability (payable), until they are offset when a net asset or (more likely) a net liability arises.

Sales tax received can be referred to as 'output' sales tax, and sales tax paid can be referred to as 'input' sales tax.

The double-entry bookkeeping records need to show the goods and sales tax values separately so that the purchases, expenses and sales are posted net (i.e. without the addition of sales tax) and the sales tax amounts are posted to a separate sales tax account.

Example 5.C

During October, W had the following credit transactions:

1 Oct.	Purchased goods from H $360 subject to 20 per cent trade discount
3 Oct.	Sold goods to HG for $80
5 Oct.	Sold goods to PL for $15
8 Oct.	Bought goods from KJ for $4,000 subject to 10 per cent trade discount
12 Oct.	Received a credit note from KJ for goods returned valued at $1,200 list price
15 Oct.	Sold goods to RW for $2,000
18 Oct.	Issued credit note for $500 to RW for goods returned

All of these transactions are subject to sales tax at the rate of 17.5 per cent.

Before entering these items in the ledger accounts, first calculate the relevant figures and determine the entries to be made. The following table illustrates this:

Date	Calculations	Debit entries	$	Credit entries	$
1 Oct.	Trade discount $72 (deduct from list price)				
	Net goods value $360 − $72 = $288	Purchases	288		
	Sales tax 17.5% × $288 = $50.40	Sales tax	50.40	H	338.40
3 Oct.	Sales tax 17.5% × $80 = $14	HG	94	Sales	80
				Sales tax	14
5 Oct.	Sales tax 17.5% × $15 = 2.62	PL	17.62	Sales	15
				Sales tax	2.62
8 Oct.	Trade discount $400 (deduct from list price)				
	Net goods value $4000 − $400 = $3,600	Purchases	3600.00		
	Sales tax 17.5% × 3,600 = $630	Sales tax	630.00	KJ	4,230
12 Oct.	Trade discount $120 (deduct from list price)				
	Net goods value $1200 − $120 = $1,080			Purchase returns	1,080
	Sales tax 17.5% × $1,080 = $189	KJ	1,269	Sales tax	189
15 Oct.	Sales tax 17.5% × $2,000 = $350	PQ	2,350	Sales	2,000
				Sales tax	350
18 Oct.	Sales tax 17.5% × $500 = $87.50	Sales returns	500	RW	587.50
		Sales tax	87.50		

Notice that the amounts debited and credited to sales, purchases and returns accounts exclude the sales tax. The sales tax account would appear as follows:

Sales Tax

20X1		$	20X1		$
1 Oct.	H	50.40	3 Oct.	HG	14.00
8 Oct.	KJ	630.00	5 Oct.	PL	2.62
18 Oct.	RW	87.50	12 Oct.	KJ	189.00
			15 Oct.	PQ	350.00
			31 Oct.	Balance c/d	212.28
		767.90			767.90
1 Nov.	Balance b/d	212.28			

The balance on the account is now $212.28 debit, which signifies that a refund of this amount is due from the tax authorities. This amount will be shown as a current asset on the statement of financial position at 31 October.

 ## Exercise 5.1

Explain the meaning of the terms 'input sales tax' and 'output sales tax', and describe their treatment in the accounts.

 ## Solution

Input sales tax is the sales tax that an organisation suffers on the goods and services that it buys. It can normally be reclaimed from the tax authorities. It does not contribute towards the cost of the goods and services.

Output sales tax is the sales tax that an organisation must add to the goods and services that it sells. It must pay over this sales tax to the tax authorities. It does not contribute to the sales revenue earned by the organisation.

The treatment of sales tax in the accounts is as follows:

- Input sales tax is debited to the sales tax account (or to a separate sales tax input account, if required). The value of the goods purchased is debited to the relevant account, while the total of the invoice is credited to the payables account until paid.
- Output sales tax is credited to the sales tax account (or to a separate sales tax output account). The value of the goods sold is credited to the sales account, while the total of the invoice is debited to the receivables account, until paid.
- Sales tax on goods returned is debited or credited to the sales tax account as appropriate: for returns inwards the sales tax account is debited, for returns outwards it is credited.
- The balance on the sales tax account is shown as an asset (if a debit balance) or a liability (if a credit balance) on the statement of financial position. A credit balance must be paid over to the tax authorities while a debit balance can be reclaimed.
- Inventories are valued, excluding sales tax.

Exercise 5.2

The following transactions relate to Patel & Sons during December 20X1.

2 Dec.	Bought goods on credit from R Williams, list price $350, trade discount 20 per cent
8 Dec.	Bought goods on credit from Samuel Ltd, list price $750, trade discount 30 per cent
10 Dec.	Sold goods to Mary Smythe for $400, no discount, payment terms 30 days
18 Dec.	Bought goods on credit from Amir, list price $1,000, trade discount 25 per cent
26 Dec.	Sold goods on credit John Blair, $800, no discount

All transactions are subject to sales tax at 17.5 per cent.

Show the entries in the ledger accounts of Patel & Sons.

 Solution

Purchases

20X1		$
2 Dec.	R Williams	280.00
8 Dec.	Samuel Ltd	525.00
18 Dec.	Amir	750.00

Sales Tax

20X1		$	20X1		$
2 Dec.	R Williams	49.00	10 Dec.	Mary Smythe	70.00
8 Dec.	Samuel Ltd	91.87	26 Dec.	John Blair	140.00
18 Dec.	Amir	131.25			

R Williams

			20X1		$
			2 Dec.	Purchases	329.00

Samuel Ltd

			20X1		$
			8 Dec.	Purchases	616.87

Amir

			20X1		$
			18 Dec.	Purchases	881.25

	Sales		
	20X1		$
	10 Dec.	Mary Smythe	400.00
	26 Dec.	John Blair	800.00

	Mary Smythe		
20X1		$	
10 Dec.	Sales	470.00	

	John Blair		
20X1		$	
26 Dec.	Sales	940.00	

5.3.1 Sales tax on non-current assets and expenses

Input sales tax is also suffered on the purchase of non-current assets and expenses, and can be reclaimed in the normal way. There are, however, generally some items on which input sales tax cannot be reclaimed, although the detail will vary between countries. Examples in the UK are:

- Sales tax on passenger cars;
- Sales tax on entertainment expenses.

In both the above cases, the sales tax cannot be reclaimed, so it is included with the cost of the item. For example, the purchase of a passenger car, costing $10,000, plus sales tax of 17.5 per cent, in effect costs $11,750, and so the motor cars account would be debited with that amount.

5.3.2 Sales tax in separate ledger accounts

When completing the sales tax return to the tax authorities, it is necessary to provide separate totals of input and output sales tax. Therefore, some organisations may keep separate ledger accounts for these.

5.3.3 Non-registered businesses

Some businesses may not be required to account for sales tax; this may be because of their small size or because of the nature of the goods/services they provide. Such businesses are referred to as 'non-registered' businesses for sales tax purposes. In this case, they are not allowed to add sales tax to their sales, but on the other hand they cannot reclaim the sales tax on their purchases, either. Thus, where input sales tax is paid it is included with the cost of the item in the ledger accounts.

For example, if a non-registered business purchases goods costing $100, plus sales tax at 17.5 per cent, it will debit the purchases account with the full $117.50.

5.3.4 Zero-rated and exempt supplies

Supplies of some goods and services are *zero-rated*, which means that although they are taxable, the rate used is zero. Common examples in the UK include basic foodstuffs and children's clothing. Businesses that make such supplies add zero sales tax to their outputs, but are still able to reclaim the sales tax on inputs in full.

Yet other goods and services are *exempt* from sales tax. Businesses supplying such goods cannot reclaim the sales tax on their inputs.

Consider three businesses: A, B and C. All three make monthly cash sales of $10,000, before adding any applicable sales tax. Company A's supplies are all standard-rated, B's supplies are all zero-rated and C's supplies are all exempt. All three make monthly cash purchases of $4,000, plus sales tax at 17.5 per cent. Their results for a month will be as follows:

	A ($)	B ($)	C ($)
Sales	10,000	10,000	10,000
Sales tax	1,750	–	–
Cash received	11,750	10,000	10,000
Purchases	4,000	4,000	4,000
Sales tax	700	700	700
Cash paid	4,700	4,700	4,700
Sales tax payable	1,750	–	–
Sales tax reclaimable	(700)	(700)	–
Net payment/(refund)	1,050	(700)	–
Total cash in	6,000	6,000	5,300

You can see that C is at a disadvantage compared with A and B. This is because it has suffered sales tax that he cannot reclaim. This will affect its profit. A and B can both reclaim their sales tax, so their profit is not affected by the charging or suffering of sales tax.

A and B's profit can be calculated as sales (excluding sales tax), minus purchases (excluding sales tax), that is, $10,000 − $4,000 = $6,000, whereas C's profit is sales minus purchases (including sales tax), that is $10,000 − $4,700 = $5,300.

5.4 Accounting for wages and salaries

In this section we shall see how the wages cost is recorded in the ledger accounts of an organisation.

5.4.1 Gross pay and net pay

Example 5.E

George is paid $5.50 per hour for a basic 36-hour week. Any overtime is paid at basic rate plus 50 per cent. During a particular week, George worked for 42 hours.

The first step is to calculate the amount of George's gross earnings:

	$
36 hours @ $5.50 per hour=	198.00
6 hours @ $8.25 per hour=	49.50
	247.50

Unfortunately for George, he will have to pay income tax, and also in some countries a social security tax, which will be deducted from his gross earnings of $247.50. Let us assume that he will be liable to pay income tax at 25 per cent on all his weekly earnings in excess of $75, and in addition he will be liable to pay social security tax (SS) of 9 per cent of his total earnings. In addition to George's SS, assume his employer is also liable to a further 10.5 per cent SS contribution based on George's gross earnings. The revised position is therefore:

	$	$
George's gross earnings		247.50
Less: income tax (25% × $172.50)	43.13	
SS (9% × $247.50)	22.27	
		65.40
George's net earnings		182.10
Employer's SS contribution: 10.5% × $247.50		25.99

George's employer will deduct George's income tax and SS and pay George his net earnings. The employer will then pay George's income tax and all of the SS contributions over to the government. Thus it can be seen that the total cost of employing George during the week amounted to $273.49 (the total of George's gross earnings and the employer's SS contributions).

This wages cost will be recorded in the employer's ledger accounts as follows:

Gross wages expense

	$		
Wages payable	247.50		

SS and Income Tax payable

			$
		Wages payable	65.40
		Employer's SS	25.99

Employer's SS Expense

	$		
SS & Income tax payable	25.99		

Wages payable

	$		$
Income tax payable	65.40	Gross wages	247.50

The liability on the wages payable account will be eliminated when the wages are paid. The liability to pay the income tax and SS will be eliminated when the employer pays the government.

5.4.2 Other deductions

The deduction of income tax and SS from George's gross wages by his employer are *statutory* deductions. George is required to pay these by law. However, George may also authorise his employer to make other deductions from his wages – these *voluntary* deductions are made from George's net earnings, as they do not affect his liability to income tax and SS.

For example, George's employers may have a sports and social club with a weekly membership fee of $1.25. George may also ask his employer to pay $20.00 a week directly into a savings plan (SP) scheme. The deductions will have the following effect:

	$	$
George's net earnings		182.10
Less:		
Sports and social club	1.25	
SP scheme	20.00	
		(21.25)
Net pay to be received by George		160.85

The wages payable account would appear as follows:

Wages payable

	$		$
Income tax payable	65.40	Gross wages	247.50
Sports club payable	1.25		
SP scheme payable	20.00		

Two further payable accounts would be required:

Sports club payable

			$
		Wages payable	1.25

SP scheme payable

			$
		Wages payable	20.00

The liability to pay the sports club and SP scheme will be eliminated when the employer pays them, which may be weekly or monthly.

5.4.3 Pension contributions

Many employees contribute to pension schemes by allocating a percentage of their gross pay to the pension fund, for example 5 or 6 per cent. This amount is deducted from the employee's gross pay, and is payable to the pension-fund company.

Example 5.F

Lesley earns $200 gross in week 21. Pension contributions are 5 per cent. The ledger entries to record this are:

- debit wages payable with $10;
- credit pension company with $10.

 Exercise 5.3

List the ledger entries required to record the following pay details, and the subsequent payment to the employee by cheque:

Gross pay	$1,200
Social security tax – employee's	9% of gross pay
Pension	6% of gross pay
Income tax	$185
Social security tax – employer's	10% of gross pay
Trade union subscription	$5 per week

 Solution

Debit wages expense account	$1,200 (Gross wages)
Debit wages expense account	$120 (Employer's SS)
Credit income tax payable account	$108 (Employee's SS)
	$120 (Employer's SS)
	$185 (Income tax)
Credit pension payable account	$72
Credit trade union payable account	$5
Credit wages payable account	$830 (Net wages owing)
Debit wages payable account	$830 (Net wages paid)
Credit bank	$830

5.5 Accruals and prepayments

The most common application of accruals and prepayments is in accounting for expenses.

Accrued expenses. Charges that are brought into the financial statements at the end of a period because, although goods and services have been provided, they have not yet been charged for by the suppliers. For example, electricity, invoiced in arrears, generally requires an accrual at the end of each accounting period.

An accrued expense is a *liability* because it is owed to the relevant supplier of those goods and services, irrespective of the fact that an invoice has not yet been received. If the business were to close down at the end of the accounting period, the expense would still have to be paid.

The opposite of an accrual is a prepayment:

Prepayment. Expenditure on goods or services for future benefit, which is to be charged to future operations, for example, rentals paid in advance. These amounts are included in current assets.

A prepayment is an *asset* because the business has yet to enjoy or utilise the benefit from it. Depending on the type of expense, if the business were to close down at the end of the accounting period, the amount prepaid may well be refunded. As an example, local business tax is often levied annually, for example the year to 31 March. A business with a year end of 31 December may have already paid in full for its local business tax for the year to 31 March following. If it is closed down at 31 December, it would receive a refund of the 3 months' excess paid, for which it did not receive the services of the local government.

So far, you have dealt with entries in expense ledger accounts on the basis of payments made during the period. It does happen, however, that some expenses that have been incurred or consumed during a period do not require to be paid during that accounting period, but are paid some time later. Hence, at the time that the trial balance is drawn up, they have not been entered in the ledger accounts.

On the other hand, there are sometimes expenses that have been paid during the accounting period that cover a future period, instead or as well as the period in which they have been paid.

However, the income statement must be credited with all revenue earned during a period (we credit all sales to the sales account, irrespective of whether or not the bills have been paid), and it should be debited with all expenses incurred during the same period (irrespective of whether or not the bills have been paid – or even received).

This is known as the convention of *matching*, that is, comparing the revenue earned during a period with the expenditure incurred *in earning that revenue*. Thus, if a telephone has been used to make calls during a period, to help earn revenue, the cost of those calls should be included in the expenses of the period, even if the telephone bill has not yet been received.

In addition, the organisation must make sure that its statement of financial position reflects all assets and liabilities at that date, and thus prepaid expenses will be shown as current assets, while accrued expenses will be shown as current liabilities.

In order to account for accrued expenses the organisation must make an estimate of the cost incurred during the accounting period. This is usually based on past records or in some cases may be calculated based on the consumption of a resource by metering the resource concerned, for example, gas and electricity. The extent of any prepayment is usually calculated by reference to time. It is normally assumed that the expense is incurred equally during the passage of time, thus the amount prepaid is simply a proportion of the total invoiced amount.

While adjustment for accruals and prepayments is most common with regard to expenses, it is also possible to have situations where *revenue* has been prepaid or should be accrued. The principles are the same as those of expenses, the intention being to make the adjustments necessary to ensure that the accounting statements produced show the extent of the revenue and costs that have arisen during the period being reported.

5.5.1 Recording accruals and prepayments in the ledger accounts

So far you have learned how to record revenue and expenditure on the basis of invoices issued and received, or payments made. However, there are a number of occasions when this method does not fairly reflect the true revenue and expenditure that has arisen during the period, and adjustments therefore need to be made.

Example 5.G

Draw up the heat and light account from the following information:

Owing at 1 Jan. 20X1	$125
Bills received and paid during 20X1:	
28 Feb.	$460
31 May	$440
30 Aug.	$390
30 Nov.	$420
Bill received on 28 Feb. 20X2	$450 (for the period 1 Dec. 20X1 to 28 Feb. 20X2)

The year end is 31 December.

Solution

Heat and light

20X1		$	20X1		$
28 Feb.	Bank	460	1 Jan.	Balance b/d	125
31 May	Bank	440			
30 Aug.	Bank	390			
30 Nov.	Bank	420			
31 Dec.	Balance c/d	150	31 Dec.	Income statement	1,735
		1,860			1,860
			20X2		
			1 Jan.	Balance b/d	150

The credit balance of $150 represents one-third of the bill received on 28 February 20X2 (i.e. the amount applicable to the month of December 20X1). This amount will appear on the statement of financial position under current liabilities.

Example 5.H

Draw up the rent payable account from the following information.

Rent is payable quarterly in advance on 1 March, June, September and December. The current annual rental is $4,800.

	$
Rent prepaid at 1 Jan. 20X1	800 (for January and February 20X1)
Rent paid during 20X1:	
1 Mar.	1,200
1 Jun.	1,200
1 Sep.	1,200
1 Dec.	1,500

The annual rental is increased to $6,000 per annum with effect from 1 December 20X1, and the year end is 31 December.

Solution

Rent payable

20X1		$	20X1		$
1 Jan.	Balance b/fwd	800			
1 Mar.	Bank	1,200			
1 Jun.	Bank	1,200			
1 Sep.	Bank	1,200	31 Dec.	Income statement	4,900
1 Dec.	Bank	1,500	31 Dec.	Prepaid c/d	1,000
		5,900			5,900
20X2					
1 Jan.	Balance b/d	1,000			

The balance brought down represents the prepayment for January and February 20X2, which is at the new rate of $500 per month. The charge to the income statement can be confirmed as being 11 months at the old rate of $400 per month, and one month at the new rate of $500 per month, that is, $4,900.

5.6 Bad debts and allowance for receivables

When a business sells goods on credit, it assumes that the customer will pay up in full. However, it sometimes happens that a customer does not pay in full, or even at all, and thus it is incorrect to retain his balance as an asset, or to treat the sale as having created profit.

There may also be occasions when an organisation feels that a proportion of receivables may fail to pay their debts, but is not certain who they are, or the amount that may become unpaid.

Both of these situations need to be considered in preparing the financial statements.

5.6.1 Accounting for bad debts

When it becomes known that a customer is unlikely to pay, the receivable balance must be removed (since it is no longer an asset of the business) and transferred to the income statement as an expense of the period in which the bad debt arises. This is done by debiting a bad debts account and crediting the receivable's account.

Example 5.I

X sold goods to Y on credit on 1 January 20X1 valued at $350. On 30 November 20X1, X was advised that Y was unable to pay the debt.

Prior to X receiving this information Y's account was as follows:

		Y		
		$		
1 Jan.	Sales	350		

But now it is necessary to remove the asset and instead treat the outstanding balance as an expense. The entries are shown below:

		Y			
		$			$
1 Jan.	Sales	350	30 Nov.	Bad debts	350

		Bad debts	
		$	
30 Nov.	Y	350	

There may be circumstances where only part of the debt needs to be written off as an expense. For example, if Y had paid $200 on 30 June 20X1 and only the balance was to be written off, then the accounts would appear as follows:

		Y			
		$			$
1 Jan.	Sales	350	30 Jun.	Bank	200
			30 Nov.	Bad debts	150
		350			350

		Bad debts	
		$	
30 Nov.	Y	150	

One bad debts account is used to record all bad debts occurring during a year. At the end of the year the balance on the bad debts expense account is transferred to the income statement.

5.6.2   Bad debts recovered

It is possible that debts that have previously been written off may later be paid. If this happens, then the entries made to write off the debt as an expense must be reversed before recording the receipt of the payment from the customer.

Example 5.J

P sold goods to Q on credit valued at $500. Q did not pay and his debt was written off in 2X10. The original ledger account entries were as follows:

		Q	
	$		$
2X10		2X10	
Balance b/d	500	Bad debts	500

		Bad debts	
	$		$
2X10		2X10	
Q	500	Income statement	500

On 31 December 2X11, Q paid the debt in full. The entries required to record this in the ledger accounts are shown below:

		Q	
	$		$
2X10		2X10	
Balance b/d	500	Bad debts	500
2X11		2X11	
Bad debts	500	Bank	500

		Bad debts	
		2X11	$
		Q	500

The credit balance on the bad debts expense account will be credited to the income statement at the end of 2X11.

Sometimes a part payment of a debt previously written off is made. If Q had paid $200 as full and final settlement, then the entries made would have been:

		Q	
	$		$
Balance b/d	500	Bad debts	500
Bad debts	500	Bank	200
		Bad debts	300
	500		500

Bad debts			
2X11	$	2X11	$
Q	300	Q (bad debt brought back)	500

The reason for reinstating the full amount of the original debt and then writing off the resulting $300 is so that if P were to trade with Q again in the future it would be clear that a bad debt arose from their previous trading activities. If only the part of the debt settled were reinstated it may appear that no bad debt occurred.

5.6.3   Allowance for receivables

While some debts are definitely bad – it is known for *certain* that the customer will not pay – others may be only *doubtful*. In this case it would not be appropriate to eliminate the receivable balance because he/she may pay after all. But we have to recognise that the value of the asset 'receivables' is probably less than it appears to be. The technique used is to create an *allowance for receivables*.

Both writing off bad debts and allowances for receivables are in accordance with the convention of *prudence*, which you will learn more about in Chapter 10. Adopting a prudent approach is simply ensuring that profits and assets are not overstated, by estimating likely losses and decreases in assets as soon as they become apparent.

This estimate can be made using a number of different techniques. For example:

1. using experience and knowledge of customers and the economic climate;
2. listing all receivables and scrutinising them individually for their ability to pay;
3. calculating an overall percentage of the outstanding receivable balances;
4. preparing a schedule of receivables according to the length of time that their debt has been outstanding, and using different percentages depending on the age of the debt. This is known as an aged receivables schedule.

Example 5.K

Age of debt	Amount ($)	%	Allowance ($)
Less than 1 month	8,000	1	80
1–2 months	3,000	2	60
2–3 months	700	5	35
More than 3 months	140	20	28
	11,840		203

This technique is based on the belief that the older the debt the more likely it is to become a bad debt.

When the allowance for receivables is first created, the ledger account entries are as shown below:

Bad debts	
20X1	$
Allowance for receivables	203

Allowance for Receivables	
20X1	$
Bad debts	203

The balance on the bad debts account is transferred to the income statement at the end of the period. Thus the balance on this account will be reduced to nil.

The balance on the allowances account is used to decrease the value of receivables shown on the statement of financial position at the end of the period. This balance will remain in the ledger accounts.

Note that no entries are made in the receivables accounts for the allowance.

Once the allowance has been created it must be reviewed and increased or decreased depending on the circumstances of the business.

For example, if the above allowance were to be decreased to $130 in 20X2, then the entries would appear as follows:

Bad debts	
20X2	$
Allowance for receivables	73

Allowance for Receivables			
20X2	$	20X2	$
Bad debts	73	Balance b/d	203
Balance c/d	130		
	203		203
		20X3	
		Balance b/d	130

Note that it is possible to avoid the use of the bad debts account if the entry is only being made once a year, since the income statement can be debited directly, but most modern accounting systems provide monthly profit statements for internal management use, and in these circumstances it is common to use the ledger accounts shown.

Exercise 5.4

The following information is given regarding the allowance for receivables:

Receivables at 31 December 20X0	$30,000
Receivables at 31 December 20X1	$25,000
Receivables at 31 December 20X2	$35,000
Receivables at 31 December 20X3	$40,000

The allowance at each year end is to be 5 per cent of receivables, after writing off bad debts. Bad debts to be written off are as follows:

31 December 20X1	$3,000
31 December 20X2	$2,000

Write up the allowance for receivables account for the years 20X0 to 20X3.

 Solution

Allowance for Receivables account

20X0		$	20X0		$
31 Dec.	Balance c/d	1,500	31 Dec.	Increase in allowance	1,500
20X1			20X1		
31 Dec.	Decrease in allowance	400	1 Jan.	Balance b/d	1,500
	Balance c/d	1,100			
		1,500			1,500
20X2			20X2		
			1 Jan.	Balance b/d	1,100
31 Dec.	Balance c/d	1,650	31 Dec.	Increase in allowance	550
		1,650			1,650
20X3			20X3		
			1 Jan.	Balance b/d	1,650
31 Dec.	Balance c/d	2,000	31 Dec.	Increase in allowance	350
		2,000			2,000
			20X4		
			1 Jan.	Balance b/d	2,000

 Exercise 5.5

On 31 August 20X4, the sundry receivables of Henry Higgins stood at $10,000 and the balance on the allowance for receivables account at that date was $200. Of the receivables it was considered that $500 were irrecoverable and should be written off. It was decided that the allowance for receivables should be made equal to 5 per cent of the outstanding accounts.

At 31 August 20X5, the receivables balances had fallen to $8,000, of which $100 were considered to be irrecoverable and should be written off. The allowance for receivables was to be at the same rate as in 20X4. You are required to:

1. show the bad debts account at 31 August 20X4 and 20X5;
2. show the allowance for receivables account at 31 August 20X4 and 20X5;
3. show the relevant figures in the statements of financial position for the 2 years 20X4 and 20X5.

 ## Solution

Bad debts

20X4		$	20X4		$
31 Aug.	Receivables	500	31 Aug.	Income statement	775
	Allowance for receivables	275			
		775			775
20X5			20X5		
31 Aug.	Receivables	100	31 Aug.	Allowance for receivables	80
				Income statement	20
		100			100

Allowance for receivables

20X4		$	20X4		$
			31 Aug.	Balance b/f	200
31 Aug.	Balance c/f	475		Bad debts	275
		475			475
20X5			20X5		
31 Aug.	Bad debts	80	1 Sep.	Balance b/f	475
	Balance c/f	395			
		475			475
			20X6		
			1 Sep.	Balance b/f	395

Balance sheet extracts

		$	
20X4		$	
Receivables		9,500	
Less: allowance		475	
			9,025
20X5		$	
Receivables		7,900	
Less: allowance		395	
			7,505

In this and the previous examples, both the bad debts and the change in the allowance for receivables have been charged to a bad debts account in the income statement. In some organisations (and in some assessment questions) you may be asked to show these in separate ledger accounts. In this case, there would be a 'bad debts' account and a 'change in allowance for receivables' account. As the latter name implies, the expense in the income statement shows the change in the allowance; the statement of financial position shows the actual allowance. In the year that an organisation first creates an allowance for receivables, the full amount will be charged to the income statement. (This is logical as the change is from NIL to the first allowance, which must equal the first allowance.)

Thus in the example above, the bad debts account would show debits of $500 and $100 in 20X4 and 20X5, respectively.

The change in allowance for receivables account would show a debit $275 in 20X4 and a credit of $80 in 20X5.

The 'allowance for receivables' account would not be affected.

Payments received from 'doubtful' receivables

Because there is no adjustment made in the account of the receivable when an allowance is made there is no need to make any particular entries if that receivable eventually pays. The adjustment to the previous period's allowance will take place when the current year's receivables are assessed for the likelihood of being paid, and that debt will be ignored in the calculation of the allowance for the current year. It is accepted that, in making allowances, there is some doubt as to the absolute accuracy of the estimates made. An over allowance or an under allowance can occur, but provided that these do not make a significant (material) difference to the view portrayed by the financial statements, no action is taken.

Specific allowances

In some situations a 'specific allowance' is made. This is where the identity of the receivable is known, but the amount of the likely bad debt is unknown. It particularly arises where a receivable is known to be in difficulties, but is making efforts to repay his or her debt. He might have agreed to pay in instalments, and he has paid some, but missed others. It is prudent to write off any known bad receivables, but in this situation it is also prudent to consider the likelihood of only part of the debt being repaid. A specific allowance is treated in the same way as a general allowance, that is, it is debited to the bad debts account, and credited to the allowance for receivables account.

5.7　The exchange of goods

When a business sells goods or services it will normally receive cash/cheques in exchange. However, it will sometimes occur that two businesses will exchange goods or services with each other. For example, an electrician may do some work for a plumber, and the plumber may do some work for the electrician. If the agreed value of the work is, say, $100, then each will record in their books $100 sales and $100 purchases. It would be incorrect to just ignore this transaction and contra one against the other.

Sometimes the exchange may not be equal; for example, an accountant may have a client who is a printer, and the accountant may exchange his professional services for the supply of letterheads. If, for example, the accountant's fees are $500 and the letterheads are $200, then the printer will pay $300 to the accountant. The accountant will record fees of $500 in his books and the cost of stationery $200. The printer will record sales of $200 and accountancy fees $500. It would be incorrect for the accountant just to record fees of $300 and to ignore the stationery expense; it would be incorrect for the printer just to record accountancy fees of $300 and to ignore the sale of $200.

Thus these transactions are recorded in the books at the full amount. Where there is a barter for the exchange of goods, these must not be ignored; where there is a difference in the value of the goods exchanged, and some cash changes hands, then this transaction is recorded at the gross amounts and is not netted off. Although the inclusion of these transactions in the accounts at the gross, as opposed to the net amount, does not affect profit, the sales and the expenses would not be correctly stated if no adjustment was made for the barter.

It is not always easy to place a value on the goods exchanged if a business sells goods but is negotiable on the price it charges. This is particularly important if the exchange involves a non-current asset. For example, a car dealer (C) may buy a second-hand car for $15,000 and advertise the car at $20,000, but expect to receive only $19,000 and may be prepared to sell at $18,000, if it is a poor trading month (the customer will not know that C is prepared to do this). Suppose another business (G) has goods in inventories which cost $16,000 which it normally sells for $18,500, which it is prepared to exchange for the car.

What is the profit G has made on exchanging the goods and how should the car be valued in its books? The cost of the goods to G is $16,000; the value of the car could be regarded as $20,000, or $19,000, or $18,000 or even $15,000. In the first two cases, G would have made more profit than normal; in the third case, it would be less profit than normal; and in the last case it would be a loss. This is not, therefore, a very satisfactory approach to the problem.

The better solution to the problem is to look at what G gave up in exchange for the car. G gave up goods valued at $18,500 and this is therefore the value that he places on the car. The sale of the goods should, therefore, be recorded at $18,500 and the car should be included in non-current assets at a cost of $18,500.

However, suppose that G's normal selling price was $21,000, it does not follow that the car should be valued at $21,000. This would not be a sensible solution, as it would have been better for G to sell its inventories for $21,000 in the normal course of business, and then pay $20,000 for the car, as it would have been better off by $1,000. In these circumstances, it must be assumed that the maximum price that G could have obtained for its goods is $20,000 and the car should be valued at this price.

The bartering of goods and services illustrates the prudence convention (see Chapter 10) which means that G should not overstate the profit that it has made on selling its goods.

5.8 Summary

In this chapter you have looked at the bookkeeping and accounting treatment of a number of different transactions.

- carriage costs
- sales tax
- wages and salaries
- accruals and prepayments
- bad debts and allowances for receivables
- the exchange of goods and services.

All of these (especially accruals and prepayments, bad debts and allowances for receivables) are likely to appear in *every* computer-based assessment involving either the preparation of ledger accounts or, more commonly, the preparation of financial statements.

The topics in this chapter are very important. The principles involved are discussed in more detail in Chapter 10.

In particular, the adjustments made for accruals and prepayments, and allowances for receivables, involve the *accruals* and *matching* conventions. The idea is that the revenue earned during a period is 'matched' in the income statement with the expense incurred in earning that revenue. So, the mere fact that something has been paid for during a period does not necessarily mean that it has been consumed during that period in earning revenue, and therefore some adjustment is needed to the ledger accounts to fairly reflect what *has* been consumed.

Another important concept is the *realisation* convention, which states that we 'recognise' (i.e. account for) revenue when it is *earned*, not necessarily when it is *received*. An important convention that affects accounting is the *prudence* convention, which states that revenue and assets should not be recognised unless it is probable that they can be valued reliably. This is also the case for expenses and losses, but a degree of caution should be exercised in making any judgement, such that revenue/assets are not overstated and expenses/liabilities are not understated. Perhaps it is this philosophy that has earned accountants the reputation of being 'miserable'!

Some of the topics contained in this chapter involve a degree of 'judgement', rather than hard evidence and fact, and it is important that accountants have sufficient guidance as to how to exercise that judgement when drawing up the financial statements. In other words, some items dealt with in the financial statements are 'subjective', that is, subject to different measurement and interpretation: as accountants are human beings they may well differ in their degree of subjectivity. For this reason, Chapter 10 discusses various sources of guidance for accountants, and their importance. Some of these ideas will also be encountered in the next chapter.

Revision Questions

? Question 1 Multiple choice

1.1 Which of the following transactions would result in an increase in capital employed?

(A) Selling inventories at a profit.
(B) Writing off a bad debt.
(C) Paying a payable in cash.
(D) Increasing the bank overdraft to purchase a non-current asset.

1.2 Rent paid on 1 October 19X2 for the year to 30 September 19X3 was $1,200 and rent paid on 1 October 19X3 for the year to 30 September 19X4 was $1,600. Rent payable, as shown in the income statement for the year ended 31 December 19X3, would be:

(A) $1,200
(B) $1,600
(C) $1,300
(D) $1,500

1.3 A decrease in the allowance for receivables would result in:

(A) an increase in liabilities.
(B) a decrease in working capital.
(C) a decrease in net profit.
(D) an increase in net profit.

1.4 At the end of the month, an organisation needs to accrue for one week's wages. The gross wages amount to $500, tax amounts to $100, employer's social security tax is $50, employees' social security tax is $40, and employees' contributions to a pension scheme amount to $30. The ledger entries to record this accrual would be:

		$		$
(A)	Debit wages expense	500	Credit social security tax payable	90
			Credit income tax payable	100
			Credit pension scheme payable	30
			Credit wages accrued	280

123

		$		$
(B)	Debit wages expense	550	Credit social security tax payable	90
			Credit income tax payable	100
			Credit pension scheme payable	30
			Credit wages accrued	330
(C)	Debit wages expense	280	Credit wages accrued	500
	Debit social security tax expense	90		
	Debit income tax expense	100		
	Debit pension scheme expense	30		
(D)	Debit wages expense	330	Credit wages accrued	550
	Debit social security tax expense	90		
	Debit income tax expense	100		
	Debit pension scheme expense	30		

1.5 The sales account is:

(A) credited with the total of sales made, including sales tax.
(B) credited with the total of sales made, excluding sales tax.
(C) debited with the total of sales made, including sales tax.
(D) debited with the total of sales made, excluding sales tax.

1.6 Stationery paid for during 19X5 amounted to $1,350. At the beginning of 19X5 there were inventories of stationery on hand of $165 and an outstanding stationery invoice for $80. At the end of 19X5, there were inventories of stationery on hand of $140 and an outstanding stationery invoice for $70. The stationery figure to be shown in the income statement for 19X5 is:
$...................

1.7 A business had a balance at the bank of $2,500 at the start of the month. During the following month, it paid for materials invoiced at $1,000 less trade discount of 20 per cent and cash discount of 10 per cent. It received a cheque from a receivable in respect of an invoice for $200, subject to cash discount of 5 per cent. The balance at the bank at the end of the month was:
$...................

1.8 An error of commission is one where:

(A) a transaction has not been recorded.
(B) one side of a transaction has been recorded in the wrong account, and that account is of a different class from the correct account.
(C) one side of a transaction has been recorded in the wrong account, and that account is of the same class as the correct account.
(D) a transaction has been recorded using the wrong amount.

1.9 A business commenced with capital in cash of $1,000. Inventories costing $800 is purchased on credit, and half is sold for $1,000 plus sales tax, the customer paying in cash at once.

The accounting equation after these transactions would show:

(A) assets $1,775 less liabilities $175 equals capital $1,600.
(B) assets $2,175 less liabilities $975 equals capital $1,200.

(C) assets $2,575 less liabilities $800 equals capital $1,775.

(D) assets $2,575 less liabilities $975 equals capital $1,600.

1.10 A sole trader's business made a profit of $32,500 during the year ended 31 March 19X8. This figure was after deducting $100 per week wages for himself. In addition, he put his home telephone bill through the business books, amounting to $400 plus sales tax at 17.5 per cent. He is registered for sales tax, and therefore has charged only the net amount to his income statement.

His capital at 1 April 19X7 was $6,500. His capital at 31 March 19X8 was:

$...................

1.11 An employee is paid at the rate of $3.50 per hour. Earnings of more than $75 a week are taxed at 20 per cent. Employees' social security tax is 7 per cent, and employer's social security tax is 10 per cent. During week 24, the employee works for 36 hours.

The amounts to be charged to the income statement and paid to the employee are:

	Income statement	Paid to employee
A	$126.00	$94.38
B	$126.00	$106.98
C	$138.60	$94.38
D	$138.60	$106.98

1.12 An organisation's year end is 30 September. On 1 January 19X6, the organisation took out a loan of $100,000 with annual interest of 12 per cent. The interest is payable in equal instalments on the first day of April, July, October and January, in arrears. How much should be charged to the income statement for the year ended 30 September 19X6, and how much should be accrued on the statement of financial position?

Income statement	Statement of financial position
$........................	$.....................

1.13 The electricity account for the year ended 30 June 20X0 was as follows:

	$
Opening balance for electricity accrued at 1 July 19X9	300
Payments made during the year:	
1 August 19X9 for 3 months to 31 July 19X9	600
1 November 19X9 for 3 months to 31 October 19X9	720
1 February 20X0 for 3 months to 31 January 20X0	900
30 June 20X0 for 3 months to 30 April 20X0	840

What is the appropriate entry for electricity?

Accrued at 30 June 20X0	Charge to income statement year ended 30 June 20X0
$..................	$..

1.14 The year end of M plc is 30 November 20X0. The company pays for its gas by a standing order of $600 per month. On 1 December 19X9, the statement from the gas supplier showed that M plc had overpaid by $200. M plc received gas bills for the four quarters commencing on 1 December 19X9 and ending on 30 November 20X0 for $1,300, $1,400, $2,100 and $2,000, respectively.

What is the correct charge for gas in M plc's income statement for the year ended 30 November 20X0?

$...................

1.15 A company has been notified that a receivable has been declared bankrupt. The company had previously made an allowance for this receivable. Which of the following is the correct double entry?

	Debit	*Credit*
A	Bad debts	The receivable
B	The receivable	Bad debts
C	Allowance for receivables	The receivable
D	The receivable	Allowance for receivables

1.16 An employee has a gross monthly salary of $1,000. In September the tax deducted was $200, the employee's social security tax was $60, and the employer's social security tax was $100. What was the charge for salaries in the income statement?

$...................

1.17 The turnover in a company was $2 million and its receivables were 5 per cent of turnover. The company wishes to have an allowance of 4 per cent of receivables, which would make the allowance of 33 per cent higher than the current allowance. What figure would appear in the income statement for bad debts?

Debit or Credit	$
....	....

1.18 A business purchases a machine on credit terms for $15,000 plus sales tax at 15 per cent. The business is registered for sales tax. How should this transaction be recorded in the books?

		Debit ($)	*Credit($)*
A	Machinery	15,000	
	Payables		15,000
B	Machinery	17,250	
	Payables		17,250
C	Machinery	15,000	
	Sales tax	2,250	
	Payables		17,250
D	Machinery	17,250	
	Sales tax		2,250
	Payables		15,000

1.19 On 1 May 20X0, A Ltd pays a rent bill of $1,800 for the period to 30 April 20X1. What is the charge to the income statement and the entry in the statement of financial position for the year ended 30 November 20X0?

Income statement	Statement of financial position	Accrual or Prepayment
$	$	

1.20 S Ltd exchanged inventories for a delivery vehicle with T Ltd. The inventories had cost S Ltd $10,000 and the normal selling price was $12,000; the delivery vehicle had cost T Ltd $9,000 and the normal selling price was $13,000.

How should S Ltd value the vehicle in its statement of financial position?

$...................

1.21 B is a builder with a staff of ten employees. In April 20X1, he paid the following amounts:

	$
Net salaries after tax and social security tax	14,000
Tax and employee's social security tax for March 20X1	5,000
Employer's social security tax for March 20X1	1,400

He owes the following amounts in respect of tax and social security tax for April 20X1:

	$
Tax and employee's social security tax	6,000
Employer's social security tax	1,500

The correct expense for employee costs to be shown in the income statement for April 20X1 is

$...................

1.22 X exchanged inventories for a machine with Y. The inventories had cost X $15,000 and the normal selling price was $17,000; the machine had cost Y $14,000 and the normal selling price was $18,000.

How should X value the machine in its statement of financial position?

$...................

1.23 M Ltd exchanged inventories for equipment with Z Ltd. The inventories had cost M Ltd $10,000 and the normal selling price was $16,000; the equipment had cost Z Ltd $12,000 and the normal selling price was $14,000.

How should M Ltd value the machine in its statement of financial position?

$...................

Question 2

From the information given below *you are required* to show the rent, local business tax and insurance account in the ledger of CPF Ltd for the year ended 30 June 20X6, showing clearly the prepayments and accruals at that date and the transfer to income statement for the year. The balances on the account at 1 July 20X5 were

	$
Rent accrued	200
Local business tax prepaid	150
Insurance prepaid	180

Payments made were as follows:

20X5		$
10 Aug.	Rent, 3 months to 31 July 20X5	300
26 Oct.	Insurance, 1 year to 31 October 20X6	600
2 Nov.	Local business tax, 6 months to 31 March 20X6	350
12 Dec.	Rent, 4 months to 30 November 20X5	400
20X6		
17 Apr.	Rent, 4 months to 31 March 20X6	400
9 May	Local business tax, 6 months to 30 September 20X6	350

Use the following pro forma to enter your answer:

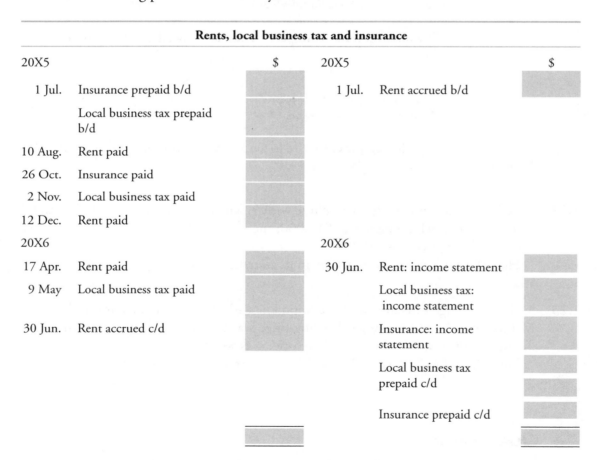

? **Question 3**

PQR Ltd has a year end of 31 December. At 30 November 20XX, the following balances exist in the ledger for the sales tax, bank and receivables accounts:

	$
Sales tax owing to the tax authorities	3,250
Bank overdraft	6,250
Receivables	127,000

During December 20XX, the following transactions take place:

(i) Sales of $85,000 plus sales tax are made on credit.

(ii) A motor car costing $8,000 plus sales tax is bought and paid for by cheque (assume that sales tax is not reclaimable on cars).

(iii) Materials are purchased on credit for $27,000 plus sales tax.

(iv) Materials costing $3,000 plus sales tax are returned to the supplier and a refund given by cheque.

(v) Administration expenses of $2,400 plus sales tax are incurred and paid for by cheque.

(vi) A sales tax refund of $1,567 for the quarter ended 31 October 20XX is received by cheque from the tax authorities.

(vii) Receivables pay the balance outstanding at 30 November 20XX by cheque, deducting $2,000 cash discount.

(viii) Payables are paid $42,000 by cheque.

Sales tax is 17.5 per cent in all cases.

Requirements

(a) Insert the missing figures into the sales tax account for December 20XX, showing the closing balance.

Sales tax

	$		$
Purchases		Balance b/f	
Administration expenses		Sales	
Balance c/f		Purchases returns	
		Sales tax repayment	

(b) Insert the missing figures into the bank ledger account given below in order to calculate the bank balance at 31 December 20XX.

Bank

	$		$
Materials refund		Balance b/f	
Sales tax repayment		Vehicle	
Receivables		Administration expenses	
		Payables	
		Balance c/f	

(c) Explain the purpose of a trial balance by completing the gaps in this sentence.
The main purpose is to check _____ accuracy of the _____ system, that is each transaction has matching _____ and _____ entries. Total _____ balances should equal total _____ balances.

(d) Match the four different types of error that could occur in the trial balance, which would prevent its agreement, with the examples in the table below.

Type of error

(A) Transposition
(B) Posting one entry only
(C) Posting both entries on the same side
(D) Bringing the opening balance down on the wrong side

Example

1. A sale of $432 to Wang debited correctly in Wang's account, but recorded in the sales account as $423. The trial balance would have $9 more on the debit total.
2. If a debit balance on Wang's account was brought down on the credit side, the trial balance would not agree.
3. Again using the same transaction as in 1 – if the $432 was debited in the sales account as well as in Wang's account, the trial balance would disagree.
4. Using the same transaction as in 1 – if the credit entry was not posted, but the debit was, then the debit trial balance total would be $432 higher than the credit total.

? Question 4

On 1 October 19X5, the following balances were brought forward in the ledger accounts of XY:

	$
Rent payable	$1,500 debit
Electricity account	$800 credit
Interest receivable	$300 debit
Allowance for receivables account	$4,800 credit

You are told the following:

- Rent is payable quarterly in advance on the last day of November, February, May and August, at the rate of $6,000 per annum.

Electricity is paid as follows:

	$
5 Nov. 19X5	$1,000 (for the period to 31 October 19X5)
10 Feb. 19X6	$1,300 (for the period to 31 January 19X6)
8 May 19X6	$1,500 (for the period to 30 April 19X6)
7 Aug. 19X6	$1,100 (for the period to 31 July 19X6)

On 30 September 19X6, the electricity meter shows that $900 has been consumed since the last bill was received.

Interest was received during the years as follows:

	$
2 Oct. 19X5	$250 (for the 6 months to 30 September 19X5)
3 Apr. 19X6	$600 (for the 6 months to 31 March 19X6)

- You estimate that interest of $300 is accrued at 30 September 19X6.

- On 30 September 19X6, the balance of receivables amounts to $125,000. The allowance for receivables is to be amended to 5 per cent of receivables.

Requirements

(a) Insert the missing information into the following ledger accounts:

    (i) rent payable;
    (ii) electricity;
    (iii) interest receivable;
    (iv) allowance for receivables;

and bring down the balances at 30 September 19X6.

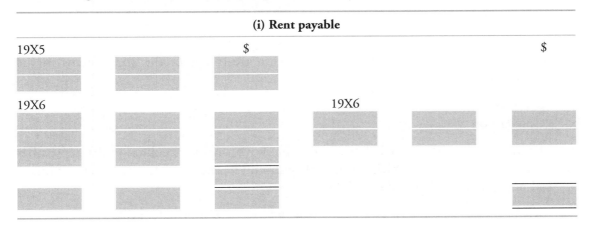

(i) Rent payable

19X5			$				$

| 19X6 | | | | 19X6 | | | |

(ii) Electricity

19X5		$	19X5		$
19X6			19X6		

(iii) Interest receivable

19X5		$	19X5		$
19X6			19X6		

(iv) Allowance for receivables

		$	19X5		$
19X6			19X6		

(b) State *two* accounting conventions that govern treatment of the above items in the accounts of XY.

   Convention 1 ....
   Convention 2 ....

(c) Describe *each* of the four balances brought down on the accounts at 30 September 19X6, *and* state under which heading they should be shown in the statement of financial position at 30 September 19X6.

	Description	Statement of financial position Heading
Rent payable		
Electricity		
Interest receivable		
Allowance for receivables		

Solutions to Revision Questions

5

✓ Solution 1

1.1   Answer: (A)

Capital employed is increased by making a profit, or by adding more capital. Writing off a bad debt is clearly the opposite of making a profit; transactions such as (B) and (C) merely adjust the split of assets and liabilities but do not add anything overall.

1.2   Answer: (C)

The year to 31 December 19X3 includes 3/4th of the rent for the year to 30 September 19X3 and 1/4th of the rent for the year to 30 September 1994, that is:

$$\frac{3}{4} \times £1,200 + \frac{1}{4} £1,600 = £1,300$$

1.3   Answer: (D)

The change in allowance for receivables is taken to the income statement – an increase is debited and therefore decreases net profit, while a decrease is credited and therefore increases net profit. The resultant balance on the allowance for receivables account is deducted from receivables (current assets), which in turn affects working capital. A decrease in the allowance would increase net profit, and would also increase current assets. The latter is not one of the options, therefore (D) is the answer.

1.4   Answer: (B)

A is incorrect as the employer's social security tax has been deducted from the net wages accrued. (C) is incorrect as there has been no deduction from wages accrued for tax, social security tax or pension contributions. Nor is there any record of liability for these items. (D) is similar, with the added error of employer's SS being included with wages accrued.

1.5   Answer: (B)

Sales tax is excluded from sales and purchases accounts, so (A) and (C) are incorrect. Sales is revenue, and therefore the sales account is credited.

1.6 The stationery ledger account would appear as:

	$		$
Opening inventories b/d	165	Outstanding invoice at 1.1.19X5	80
Paid during year	1,350	Closing inventories c/d	140
Outstanding invoice at 31.12.19X5	70	Income statement	1,365
	1,585		1,585

1.7 Reconstruction of the bank account:

	$		$
Balance b/d	2,500	Payment (1,000 − 20%) − 10%	720
Receipt (200 − 5%)	190	Balance c/f (diff)	1,970
	2,690		2,690

1.8 Answer: (C)

A is incorrect as this is an error of omission. (B) is incorrect as an error of principle occurs where the two accounts are of different classes. (D) is an example of an error of original entry.

1.9 Answer: (D)

Opening statement of financial position and adjustments required:

	$		$
Assets (cash)	1,000	Liabilities (capital)	1,000
Transaction 1 (inventories)	800	Payables	800
Transaction 2 (cash)	1,175	Sales tax owing	175
Inventories	(400)	Profit (add to capital)	600
Closing balance	2,575		2,575

Assets ($2,575) less liabilities ($975) = capital ($1,600)

1.10

	$
Capital at 1/4/ X7	6,500
Add: profit (after drawings)	32,500
Less: sales tax element	(70)
Capital at 31/5/ X8	38,930

1.11   Answer: (D)

Income statement		Paid to employee	
	$		$
36 × $3.50	126.00	Gross pay	126.00
Employer's SS (10%)	12.60	7% SS	(8.82)
Gross wages cost	138.60	Tax	(10.20)
		Net pay	106.98

1.12   The charge to the income statement is $9,000 for 9 months' interest, at an annual rate of $12,000 (12 per cent of $100,000). The payment for the third quarter ending 30 September 19X6 is not paid until 1 October 19X6, so 3 months' interest is accrued, that is, $3,000.

1.13

	Electricity			
		$		$
			Balance b/f	300
19X9				
1 Aug.	Paid bank	600		
1 Nov.	Paid bank	720		
20X0				
1 Feb.	Paid bank	900		
30 Jun.	Paid bank	840		
30 Jun.	Accrual c/d ($840 × 2/3)	560	Income statement	3,320
		3,620		3,620

1.14

	Gas supplier					
		$				$
	Balance b/f	200				
	Bank ($600 × 12)	7,200	28 Feb.	Invoice		1,300
			31 May	Invoice		1,400
			31 Aug.	Invoice		2,100
			30 Nov.	Invoice		2,000
			30 Nov.	Balance c/d		600
		7,400				7,400

	Gas				
		$			$
28 Feb.	Invoice	1,300			
31 May	Invoice	1,400			
31 Aug.	Invoice	2,100			
30 Nov.	Invoice	2,000	30 Nov.	Income Statement	6,800
		6,800			6,800

1.15   Answer: (C)

1.16   The charge for the salary in the income statement is the gross salary plus the employer's social security tax contribution. This is $1,000 plus $100, a total of $1,100.

1.17   Debit $1,000

1.18   Answer: (C)

1.19   Income statement $1,050; Statement of financial position $750; Prepayment

1.20 $12,000

1.21 $21,500

1.22 $17,000

1.23 $14,000

 Solution 2

- Start by entering the balances brought forward at 1 July 20X5.
- Enter the transactions in chronological (i.e. date) order.
- Calculate the amounts to be carried forward for accrued and/or prepaid expenses at 30 June 20X6.
- Calculate the amounts to be transferred to the income statement.
- Carry down the balances at 1 July 20X6.

		Rents, local business tax and insurance				
20X5			$	20X5		$
1 Jul.	Insurance prepaid b/d		180	1 Jul.	Rent accrued b/d	200
	Local business tax prepaid b/d		150			
10 Aug.	Rent paid		300			
26 Oct.	Insurance paid		600			
2 Nov.	Local business tax paid		350			
12 Dec.	Rent paid		400			
20X6				20X6		
17 Apr.	Rent paid		400	30 Jun.	Rent: income statement	1,200
9 May	Local business tax paid		350		Local business tax: income statement	675
30 Jun.	Rent accrued c/d		300		Insurance: income statement	580
					Local business tax prepaid c/d	175
					Insurance prepaid c/d	200
			3,030			3,030
20X5			$	20X5		$
1 Jul.	Local business tax prepaid b/d		175	1 Jul.	Rent accrued b/d	300
1 Jul.	Insurance prepaid b/d		200			

You should note how the account shows the extent of any balance to be carried forward and also the amount transferred to the income statement.

The three individual figures for the income statement could be combined in a single figure of $2,455.

The statement of financial position at 30 June would include the following figures:

	$
Current assets	
Local business tax prepaid	175
Insurance prepaid	200
Current liabilities	
Rent accrued	300

 # Solution 3

- Remember that sales tax on sales is owed to the tax authorities, while sales tax on purchases is refundable from the tax authorities.
- Remember that sales tax is not reclaimable on passenger cars.

(a)

Sales tax

	$		$
Purchases	4,725	Balance b/f	3,250
Administration expenses	420	Sales	14,875
Balance c/f	15,072	Purchases returns	525
		Sales tax repayment	1,567
	20,217		20,217

(b)

Bank

	$		$
Materials refund	3,525	Balance b/f	6,250
Sales tax repayment	1,567	Vehicle	9,400
Receivables	125,000	Admin expenses	2,820
		Payables	42,000
		Balance c/f	69,622
	130,092		130,092

(c) The main purpose is to check arithmetical accuracy of the double-entry system, that is each transaction has matching debit and credit entries. Total debit balances should equal total credit balances.

(d) (A) 1
   (B) 4
   (C) 3
   (D) 2

Solution 4

- Deal with each ledger account in turn.
- Enter the balances at 1 October 19X5, using the correct side, as given in the question.
- Record the payments or receipts in chronological (i.e. date) order.
- Calculate the balance to be carried forward at the end of the period.
- Calculate the amount to be transferred to the income statement.
- Bring down the balances at 1 October 19X6.
- For Part (b), accounting conventions are covered in more detail in Chapter 10.

(a)

(i) Rent payable

19X5		$				$
1 Oct.	Prepayment b/d	1,500				
30 Nov.	Bank	1,500				
19X6			19X6			
29 Feb.	Bank	1,500	30 Sep.	Income statement		6,000
31 May	Bank	1,500	30 Sep.	Prepayment c/d		1,500
31 Aug.	Bank	1,500				
		7,500				7,500
1 Oct.	Prepayment b/d	1,500				

(ii) Electricity

19X5		$	19X5			$
5 Nov.	Bank	1,000	1 Oct.	Accrual b/d		800
19X6			19X6			
10 Feb.	Bank	1,300	30 Sep.	Income statement		5,000
8 May	Bank	1,500				
7 Aug.	Bank	1,100				
30 Sep.	Accrual c/d	900				
		5,800				5,800
			1 Oct.	Accrual b/d		900

(iii) Interest receivable

19X5		$	19X5			$
1 Oct.	Accrual b/d	300	2 Oct.	Bank		250
19X6			19X6			
30 Sep.	Income statement	850	30 Apr.	Bank		600
			30 Sep.	Accrual c/d		300
		1,150				1,150
1 Oct.	Accrual b/d	300				

(iv) Allowance for receivables

		$	19X5		$
			1 Oct.	Balance b/f	4,800
19X6			19X6		
30 Sep.	Balance c/d	6,250	30 Sep.	Income statement	1,450
		6,250			6,250
			1 Oct.	Balance b/f	6,250

(b)   Convention 1 Accruals
      Convention 2 Prudence (conservatism)

Ledger Account	Description	Statement of financial position Heading
Rent payable	Prepayment	Current assets
Electricity	Accrual	Current liabilities
Interest receivable	Accrued income	Current assets
Allowance for receivables	Allowance	Current assets (netted off receivables)

Accounting for
Non-current Assets

Accounting for Non-current Assets

6

LEARNING OUTCOMES

When you have completed this chapter, you should be able to:

▸ explain and distinguish capital and revenue;

▸ identify the basic methods of valuing assets on current cost, fair value and value in use bases and their impact on profit measures and statement of financial position values;

▸ explain and calculate the methods of depreciation including straight line, reducing balance and revaluation methods, and prepare accounts using each method and impairment;

▸ prepare a non-current asset register.

6.1   Introduction

We have already learned that a non-current asset is a resource acquired by an organisation with the intention of using it to earn revenue for a long period of time. Examples of tangible non-current assets include land, buildings, motor vehicles, machinery and equipment. In this chapter we shall look at the important distinction between capital expenditure and revenue expenditure, where capital expenditure is defined as expenditure on non-current assets. We shall also learn about the concept of depreciation and how this is applied in practice. The chapter also looks at the sale of non-current assets and how non-current assets are controlled.

The chapter concludes with a brief discussion on another class of non-current assets known as 'intangible non-current assets'.

6.2   Capital and revenue expenditure

Capital expenditure is expenditure likely to increase the future earning capability of the organisation, whereas revenue expenditure is that associated with maintaining the organisation's present earning capability.

Thus, new items of plant and machinery that are bought from external manufacturers, vehicles, buildings and purchases of land are clearly capital expenditure to be included in a statement of financial position. However, when assets are internally manufactured or when existing assets are modified or repaired, it is sometimes difficult to determine whether the expenditure is of a capital or revenue nature. The general principle to be followed is that if the expenditure significantly improves earnings capability, then it is to be treated as capital expenditure. When making this comparison in the context of expenditure on repairs, it is necessary to consider the effects in relation to the position prior to the need for repair.

Example 6.A

Consider the situation where a computer is repaired by replacing a faulty floppy disk drive and a faulty hard drive. The replacement floppy disk drive is identical to that which it replaced. The faulty hard drive had a storage capacity of 500 megabytes, its replacement is a 5 gigabyte (i.e. 5,000 megabyte) unit. At the same time a CD-ROM drive is fitted. How should these 'repair' costs be classified?

Solution

The replacement of the faulty floppy disk drive with an identical unit is clearly a repair, and as such will be treated as an expense.

The fitting of the CD-ROM drive is clearly not a repair because the computer did not have a CD-ROM drive previously. This is an addition to the asset, which should be capitalised.

It is the cost of the hard disk drive that presents the classification problem. To the extent that it replaced the original hard drive it is a repair, but the new drive has ten times the capacity of the original. As it enhances the storage capacity of the computer it is capital expenditure. Thus this cost must be divided, part of it is treated as an expense and the remainder as capital expenditure.

The distinction between capital and revenue expenditure is important because of the implications for the financial statements. Revenue expenditure will be reflected in full in the measurement of profit in the period in which it is incurred. In contrast, capital expenditure will be reflected in an increase in asset values in the statement of financial position. This will diminish over the life of the asset as it is depreciated (see later), with a corresponding reduction in the profit reported.

 ## Exercise 6.1

Explain briefly the difference between capital and revenue transactions.

 ## Solution

Capital transactions are those affecting the long-term operations of the organisation. They might affect non-current assets, non-current borrowing and so on. Revenue transactions are those affecting the immediate future of the organisation. They might include the purchase or sale of inventories, the incurring of expenses such as wages, heat and light, and so on.

Revenue transactions would also include the repair and maintenance of non-current assets, even though the initial purchase of those assets was a capital transaction. Expenditure that does not provide any additional benefit is classed as revenue.

Capital transactions would also include the cost of acquisition of non-current assets, such as legal fees, carriage and delivery, and installation costs. If the equipment needs to be tested prior to use, these costs can also be included.

 ## Exercise 6.2

Classify each of the following transactions into capital or revenue transactions:

- Complete repaint of existing building.
- Installation of a new central heating system.
- Repainting of a delivery van.
- Providing drainage for a new piece of water-extraction equipment.
- Legal fees on the acquisition of land.
- Carriage costs on a replacement part for a piece of machinery.

 ## Solution

- Complete repaint: revenue.
- Installation of new heating system: capital.
- Repainting van: revenue.
- Drainage for new equipment: capital.
- Legal fees on acquisition of land: capital.
- Carriage costs on replacement part: revenue.

6.3 Depreciation

The cost of the non-current asset will contribute to the organisation's ability to earn revenue for a number of accounting periods. It would be unfair if the whole cost were treated as an expense in the income statement in the year of acquisition. Instead, the cost is spread over all of the accounting periods in which the asset is expected to be making a contribution to earnings (this is known as the asset's *useful life*). The process by which this is achieved is called *depreciation*.

We shall look at the calculation of depreciation in detail in the next section. For now, we shall just focus on the main principles.

- When we acquire a non-current asset, we credit cash (or creditors), and debit an account called 'non-current assets' or 'plant and machinery' or another suitable description.
- If we were to prepare a set of financial statements immediately afterwards we would display the balance on the asset account – the cost of the asset – on the statement of financial position. It would not appear as an expense in the income statement at all, because we have not yet begun to 'consume' it in earning revenue.
- During the periods that the asset is in use – its useful life – we must allocate its original cost on some fair basis. An appropriate proportion of the cost must be recorded as an expense – called depreciation charge – in the income statement of each period concerned.

- We achieve this by, in effect, changing the balance in the asset account. Each year we decide that some proportion of the original cost has now been 'consumed' in operating the business. This proportion is transferred to the income statement, where it is shown as an expense, and the amount remaining on the statement of financial position is correspondingly reduced. (This remaining balance is referred to as the *carrying amount* of the asset.)
- Eventually we reach a point where the whole of the original cost has been consumed and the carrying amount for the asset on the statement of financial position has declined to zero (or perhaps to some small residual value that it may realise on disposal).

It is extremely important to understand this basic notion of depreciation as a means of allocating the cost of a non-current asset over a number of accounting periods. It has nothing whatever to do with 'valuing' the asset, in the sense of estimating what its fair value might be at the end of each accounting period. (Fair value is the estimated amount for which an asset could be sold.) Indeed, it is not likely, in general, that the carrying amount of a non-current asset is anything like an approximation to its fair value. Nor does depreciation have anything to do with providing a fund for replacing the non-current asset when it is consumed. The process of transferring amounts from statement of financial position to income statement each year does not in any sense generate funds for the business. It may indeed be desirable to plan ahead for asset replacement by setting aside cash for the purpose, but this is an exercise quite separate from the process of charging depreciation.

 ## Exercise 6.3

Explain what you understand by the term 'depreciation'.

 ## Solution

Depreciation is the systematic allocation of the cost of an asset, less its residual value, over its useful life. In practice, it is usually taken as being the original cost of the asset spread over its estimated useful life. The cost is reduced by any expected residual value, which is the estimated amount that may be received if the asset is sold at the end of its useful life. The depreciation might be an equal amount every year (the straight-line basis) or might be a percentage of its opening value each year (the reducing-balance basis). There are other methods, including revaluation for small items.

The amount of depreciation each year is charged against the profits, and reduces the asset's carrying amount. Depreciation is not a method of providing for the replacement of the asset, and no cash movement is involved.

6.4 Calculating depreciation

There are a number of methods that accountants use to depreciate a non-current asset. The two most common methods that are used will each be examined in this section of the chapter using the same basic information about a single non-current asset:

Cost – 1 January 20X5	$50,000
Estimated useful life	10 years
Estimated residual value at the end of its life (residual value)	$1,280

6.4.1 The straight-line method

This method allows an equal amount to be charged as depreciation to each accounting period over the expected useful life of the asset. If the depreciation charge were to be shown on a graph it would be a straight line parallel to the horizontal axis (hence the name of the method). The amount to be charged to each accounting period is given by the formula:

$$\text{Depreciation per annum} = \frac{\text{Original cost} - \text{estimated residual value}}{\text{Estimated useful life}}$$

Using the data above, the annual depreciation charge would be

$$\frac{£50,000 - £1,280}{10} = £4,872$$

The effect of the above would be that the carrying amount of the asset shown in the organisation's statement of financial position would be reduced by $4,872 each year. The corresponding effect would be to reduce profits in the income statement by charging depreciation as an expense.

The ledger entries to record the depreciation are

- credit an accumulated depreciation account;
- debit the income statement with the annual depreciation.

As each year passes, the balance on the accumulated depreciation account will increase as follows:

Accumulated depreciation

		$
31 Dec. X5	Income statement	4,872
31 Dec. X6	Income statement balance	4,872
		9,744
31 Dec. X7	Income statement balance	4,872
		14,616

and the asset would be shown on the statement of financial position as follows:

	Cost ($)	Accumulated depreciation ($)	Carrying amount ($)
(31 Dec. 20X5) non-current assets	50,000	(4,872)	45,128
(31 Dec. 20X6) non-current assets	50,000	(9,744)	40,256
(31 Dec. 20X7) non-current assets	50,000	(14,616)	35,384

The example above shows the depreciation account in respect of the single asset used in the example; however, each asset would not normally have a separate ledger account. While it is necessary to calculate the depreciation of each asset separately, it is usual for the ledger accounts to summarise the depreciation charge and the accumulated depreciation in respect of different categories of assets such as buildings, motor vehicles, and plant and equipment.

6.4.2 The reducing-balance method

Some assets give a greater service – and therefore depreciate more – in their early years than they do in later years. For this reason, it is considered sensible to charge a higher amount of depreciation in the earlier years. This method of depreciation is known as the reducing-balance method. With this method a constant percentage is applied to the cost not yet treated as an expense at the end of the previous accounting period. This results in the depreciation charged as an expense being greater in the earlier years of an asset's life than in the later years.

This can be illustrated using the data from the previous example. In this case the annual depreciation rate works out as 30.7 per cent. For the purposes of illustration this will be rounded up to 31 per cent.

	$	
Original cost	50,000	
Year 1 depreciation	15,500	(31% of 50,000)
	34,500	
Year 2 depreciation	10,695	(31% of 34,500)
	23,805	
Year 3 depreciation	7,380	(31% of 23,805)
	16,425	

At the end of the asset's useful life the remaining amount should equal its estimated residual value of $1,280 subject to any difference caused by rounding the percentage to be used for the amounts of annual depreciation.

The double-entry bookkeeping will be the same in principle as that illustrated earlier for the straight-line method. Clearly, though, the amount charged as an expense and the corresponding reduction in the value of the asset will be different depending on the method of depreciation used, until the end of the asset's useful life.

 Exercise 6.4

A machine is purchased on 1 May 2000 for $1,000 cash. The financial year ends on 30 April each year.

Show the account or accounts in the ledger for the first 3 years assuming that the machine is depreciated by 20 per cent per annum on the reducing-balance method.

Income statement and statement of financial position entries are not required.

Solution

Machine at cost		
2000		$
1 May	Cash	1,000

Accumulated depreciation for machinery					
2001		$	2001		$
30 Apr.	Balance c/f	200	30 Apr.	Income statement	200
			1 May	Balance b/f	200
2002			2002		
30 Apr.	Balance c/f	360	30 Apr.	Income statement	160
		360			360
			1 May	Balance b/f	360
2003			2003		
30 Apr.	Balance c/f	488	30 Apr.	Income statement	128
		488			488

6.4.3 The machine-hour method/units of production method

Some non-current assets depreciate according to their usage. If the asset has a measurable 'life' in terms of the number of hours it is likely to be used, or the number of units of output it is likely to produce, it can be depreciated according to that rate.

For example, a computer printer might have an expected total output of 50,000 sheets. If it produces 10,000 sheets in a year, it can be said to have used up one-fifth of its cost in that year.

6.4.4 The revaluation method

This method of calculating depreciation differs from the straight-line and reducing-balance methods explained above by not being a calculation based on the original cost of an individual asset. Instead, the method relies on an estimated cost being made in respect of a group of similar small-value assets when preparing the financial statements. The following example illustrates the principles involved.

Example 6.B

On 1 January 20X1, X commenced trading as a mobile mechanic, introducing small tools with an estimated cost of $2,400 as part of the opening capital. During the year, small tools costing $980 were purchased. On 31 December 20X1, X estimated the cost of the small tools at $3,150.

Using the revaluation method, the depreciation charge for the year is:

	$
Opening estimated cost	2,400
Add: additional items costing	980
	3,380
Closing estimated cost	(3,150)
Depreciation	230

This depreciation charge of $230 represents the total loss in the estimated cost of 'non-current asset: small tools' in the period. If there had been any disposals during the year for which sale proceeds were received, the proceeds received would have been deducted in the above calculation.

6.4.5 Depreciation in the year of acquisition and disposal

Non-current assets are acquired at various dates throughout the year so, strictly speaking, if the asset has been owned for only part of a year, only that proportion of the annual depreciation should be accounted for. This is known as depreciation on an 'actual time basis'. Conversely, when the asset is sold, only a proportion of the final year's depreciation should be charged.

However, it is common for small organisations to charge a full year's depreciation in the year of acquisition, irrespective of the date of purchase, and to charge none in the year of disposal.

6.5 Accounting for the disposal of a non-current asset

At the end of the asset's life it will be either abandoned or sold. This is known as a 'disposal' in accounting terminology. At this time a comparison is made of the difference between the carrying amount of the asset at the date of its disposal and the proceeds received (if any). The difference is referred to as the *profit or loss arising on the disposal of the asset*. It effectively represents the extent to which the depreciation charged during the life of the asset was incorrect.

If the proceeds received on disposal are less than the carrying amount at that date the difference is a loss on disposal, which is treated as an expense when calculating the organisation's profitability.

The following example will be used to show the calculation of the profit or loss arising on the disposal of an asset.

Example 6.C

X purchased a van on 1 January 20X5 for $10,000. He estimated that its resale value on 31 December 20X0 after 6 years' use would be $400, and depreciated it on a straight-line basis. He sold it on 30 June 20X7 for $5,500.

The amount of depreciation to be charged each year was:

$$\frac{\text{Original cost} - \text{estimated residual value}}{\text{Estimated useful life}} = \frac{£10,000 - £400}{6} = £1,600$$

X owned the asset for 2 years and 6 months, thus the total depreciation charged since acquisition is $1,600 × 2.5 = $4,000. This means that the carrying amount at the date of the disposal was $10,000 − $4,000 = $6,000.

Since the sale proceeds only amounted to $5,500 there has been a 'loss on disposal' of $500.

When there has been a disposal of an asset, entries must be made in the ledger accounts of the organisation so as to remove the original cost and accumulated depreciation of the asset disposed of. This is so that the balance on these accounts only relates to the assets owned by the business at that date. The bookkeeping entries related to this example are as follows:

Van at cost

20X5		$	20X7		$
1 Jan.	Bank	10,000	30 Jun.	Disposal	10,000

Accumulated depreciation – van

		$	20X5		$
			31 Dec.	Depreciation	1,600
			20X6		
			31 Dec.	Depreciation	1,600
20X7			20X7		
30 Jun.	Disposal	4,000	30 Jun.	Depreciation	800
		4,000			4,000

Non-current asset disposal – van

20X7		$	20X7		$
30 Jun.	Van at cost	10,000	30 Jun.	Accumulated depreciation – van	4,000
				Bank	5,500
				Loss (to income statement)	500
		10,000			10,000

Exercise 6.5

Write up the relevant accounts for a non-current asset that was purchased on 23 March 20X1 for $3,500. Its residual value is expected to be $200, and its expected useful life is 4 years. The asset is sold on 18 January 20X4 for $1,300. A full year's depreciation is to be charged in the year of purchase. The organisation's year end is 31 December.

 Solution

Non-current assets at cost

20X1		$	20X4		$
23 Mar.	Cash	3,500	18 Jan.	Disposals	3,500

Accumulated depreciation

		$	20X1		$
			31 Dec.	Income statement	825
			20X2		
			31 Dec.	Income statement	825
20X4			20X3		
18 Jan.	Disposals a/c	2,475	31 Dec.	Income statement	825
		2,475			2,475

Non-current asset disposals

20X4		$	20X4		$
18 Jan.	Cost	3,500	18 Jan.	Accumulated depreciation	2,475
31 Dec.	Profit on disposal	275		Proceeds	1,300
		3,775			3,775

6.6 A Comprehensive example

A business bought the following machines:

- Machine A on 3 February 20X1, costing $1,000,
- Machine B on 18 March 20X2, costing $1,200,
- Machine C on 27 June 20X3, costing $2,000.

None of the machines has any expected residual value, and all are depreciated on the straight-line basis over 10 years, with a full year's depreciation in the year of purchase. Machine A is sold for $720 on 30 June 20X4. The business's year end is 31 December. Annual depreciation is:

- Machine A $100,
- Machine B $120,
- Machine C $200.

Because there are three machines bought at different times, it is a good idea to tabulate the depreciation as follows:

Year	Machine A	Machine B	Machine C	Total
	$	$	$	$
20X1	100	Nil	Nil	100
20X2	100	120	Nil	220
20X3	100	120	200	420
20X4	Nil	120	200	320

The total column gives the depreciation to be charged each year. Remember to dispose of Machine A in 20X4. The ledger accounts are as follows:

Machines at cost

		$			$
20X1			20X1		
3 Feb.	Cash	1,000	31 Dec.	Balance c/d	1,000
20X2			20X2		
1 Jan.	Balance b/d	1,000			
18 Mar.	Cash	1,200	31 Dec.	Balance c/d	2,200
		2,200			2,200
20X3			20X3		
1 Jan.	Balance b/d	2,200			
27 Jun.	Cash	2,000	31 Dec.	Balance c/d	4,200
		4,200			4,200
20X4			20X4		
1 Jan.	Balance b/d	4,200	30 Jun.	Disposals a/c	1,000
			31 Dec.	Balance c/d	3,200
		4,200			4,200
20X5					
1 Jan.	Balance b/d	3,200			

Accumulated depreciation on machines

		$			$
20X1			20X1		
31 Dec.	Balance c/d	100	31 Dec.	Income statement	100
20X2			20X2		
			1 Jan.	Balance b/d	100
31 Dec.	Balance c/d	320	31 Dec.	Income statement	220
		320			320
20X3			20X3		
			1 Jan.	Balance b/d	320
31 Dec.	Balance c/d	740	31 Dec.	Income statement	420
		740			740
20X4			20X4		
30 Jun.	Disposals a/c	300	1 Jan.	Balance b/d	740
31 Dec.	Balance c/d	760	31 Dec.	Income statement	320
		1,060			1,060
			20X5		
			1 Jan.	Balance b/d	760

Non-current asset disposals

		$			$
20X4			20X4		
30 Jun.	Machines at cost	1,000	30 Jun.	Accumulated depreciation	300
31 Dec.	Income statement	20	30 Jun.	Cash	720
		1,020			1,020

The profit on disposal is credited to the income statement.

6.7 Controlling tangible non-current assets

Most organisations will own a number of non-current assets and in large organisations their control is vital to the efficient running of the organisation. Management will need to be aware of:

1. the location of each asset;
2. the extent to which it is being used;
3. the repairs that have been carried out on the asset and the cost of those repairs;
4. the expiry dates of any licences permitting the organisation to use the asset.

In addition, for accounting purposes, the following information is required:

1. the date of purchase;
2. the name and address of the asset's supplier;
3. the cost of the asset;
4. the estimated useful life of the asset;
5. the estimated residual value of the asset at the end of its useful life;
6. a description of the asset;
7. a code number for the asset so that it can be found easily on a computerised system;
8. the method of depreciation to be used for the asset;
9. whether any government grants have been obtained to assist in the purchase of the asset;
10. the accumulated depreciation of the asset;
11. details of the disposal of the asset when it has occurred.

This information is normally recorded in a *non-current asset register*. The efficiency of the organisation can be greatly improved if the register is stored on a computer. Specialist computer packages exist for the recording of an organisation's non-current assets, but much the same effect can be obtained by using a spreadsheet or database program, particularly in smaller organisations or where the information is recorded within each department.

In the context of a non-current asset register, each asset would be given a code number. There would be a separate record on the computer file for each non-current asset, and within each record there would be a field for each data item to be recorded. The asset code would normally be used as the key field so that the record of any particular asset could be located easily.

The use of a computerised non-current asset register would allow the calculation of depreciation to be automated and various reports could be produced showing, for example:

- the depreciation charge for the accounting period analysed by asset and by department as required;
- a list of assets requiring servicing;
- a list of assets at a particular location;
- the extent of any repair expenditure on each asset;
- a list of assets continuing in use beyond their estimated useful life.

The use of a computerised system greatly improves the speed and accuracy of reporting and allows management to design different reports specific to their needs. These needs will vary for different managers and the use of a computerised system means that the basic data needs to be entered only once, and the computer can then sort it in different ways in order to produce the report required.

 Exercise 6.6

List the information that might be contained in a non-current asset register.

 Solution

The information that might be contained in a non-current asset register is

- description of asset;
- date of purchase;
- name of supplier;
- cost of asset;
- asset code number;
- location;
- estimated useful life;
- estimated residual value;
- method of depreciation;
- depreciation to date;
- carrying amount;
- insurance details;
- maintenance details, for example regular servicing;
- major amendments/refinements;
- disposal details (when disposed of).

6.8 Accounting for intangible non-current assets

An *intangible asset*. An asset that does not have a physical substance, for example trademarks and patents.

Assets of this type, although regarded as non-current assets for accounting purposes in the same way as are plant and equipment, are different because they cannot be touched. They do have a value, however. Another example of an intangible asset is a brand. A brand is a name given by an organisation to one of its products and which is used in the marketing of that product. For this reason, brand names are often more well known than the name of the organisation making the product. This familiarity may lead to customer brand loyalty, which will result in future sales. Clearly, this is valuable to the organisation and the brand should therefore be accounted for as an intangible fixed asset.

Intangible assets, just like tangible assets, may have useful lives. For example, a patent may have a life of 10 years before the patent expires. Thus intangible assets need to be 'amortised', which is the same as depreciation, but the word 'amortisation' is used when it applies to an intangible asset.

The straight-line method is used for amortisation and there will be no residual value.

6.8.1 What is goodwill?

Goodwill. The difference between the fair value of a business as a whole and the aggregate of the fair values of the separable and identifiable assets and liabilities.

This implies that it is not possible to identify goodwill separately from the business, and this is largely because it is an intangible asset.

The definition above explains that goodwill is the value placed upon a business in excess of the sum of its individual assets; thus goodwill represents the value of the business continuing as a going concern, as compared with its assets being sold individually. However, it could be said to be more than that. All established businesses have some goodwill. Goodwill comprises business contacts, good staff relations, the right to occupy certain pieces of land and so on. All of these have a value – the difficulty lies in placing a value on them.

Purchased and non-purchased goodwill

When a business first starts, it is either created by its owners or purchased from an existing business. In the latter case there will have been a certain amount of negotiation over the purchase price. The vendors will obviously seek to obtain the highest price possible, whereas the purchaser will seek to minimise the price. It is likely, however, that the final price will be greater than the purchaser's valuation of the tangible assets taken over. This is accepted because the price includes the rights to the existing business's customer base, possibly its name, its staff, and their experience and expertise, and so on. This difference is the goodwill and, more precisely, is said to be *purchased goodwill*.

However, whether the business is created as a new start-up business or is the result of the acquisition of another business, new goodwill is earned or created by the new owners over a period of time. This is known as *non-purchased goodwill*.

Accounting treatment

The accounting treatment of purchased goodwill is for the purchaser to place a fair value on the net tangible assets (i.e. assets–liabilities) of the business acquired and to consider the difference between the sum of these values and the total purchase price to be goodwill. This amount is debited to the goodwill ledger account. The purchaser will hope that the value of the goodwill will at least be maintained and that, if he were to sell the business, he would be paid for its goodwill.

However, it is important to note, when applying the concept of prudence, that assets should not be overstated. It could be that the factors which caused goodwill to exist in the past, for example location and customer base, no longer apply and that the value of the goodwill is now less than the price paid for it.

It is therefore necessary to estimate, on an annual basis, the value of the goodwill. If the current estimated value is less than the amount in the statement of financial position, then the goodwill is said to be 'impaired'. Impairment occurs when the value of a non-current asset is less than its carrying amount in the statement of financial position. In this situation, the goodwill is reduced to its new lower value and the difference (the 'impairment') is charged to the income statement as an expense.

It may be noted that impairment can also apply to tangible and other non-tangible non-current assets and will occur at any time that the carrying amount of an asset in a statement of financial position is overstated.

Example 6.D

X Ltd has recently acquired the assets and liabilities of A Ltd for $1,500,000. The assets and liabilities acquired were valued by X Ltd as follows:

	$
Land and buildings	750,000
Plant and equipment	240,000
Inventories	65,000
Receivables	38,000
Payables	(41,000)
	1,052,000

The difference between the sum of the individual net assets and the purchase price is goodwill. In this example the value of goodwill is $448,000. If in the future X Ltd values the goodwill at only $400,000, then the impairment of $48,000 will be charged to the income statement and the goodwill in the statement of financial position will be reduced to $400,000.

Non-purchased (or 'internal') goodwill is not recognised in the statement of financial position. The reason for this is that it is not possible to obtain a reliable measurement of its value. In the case of purchased goodwill, the fact that someone has paid for goodwill does mean that it has a value and that this can be measured by the price paid. In the case of internal goodwill, there has been no such external transaction and there is no basis on which the internal goodwill can be valued.

6.9 Summary

In this chapter, we have looked at the accounting issues associated with non-current assets. These issues can be summarised as:

- the classification of expenditure as capital or revenue;
- the allocation of non-current asset cost to accounting periods using depreciation;
- accounting entries to record the acquisition, depreciation and disposal of non-current assets;
- the control of tangible non-current assets;
- accounting for intangible non-current assets, such as purchased goodwill.

Revision Questions

Question 1 Multiple choice

1.1 A non-current asset register showed a carrying amount of $67,460. A non-current asset costing $15,000 had been sold for $4,000, making a loss on disposal of $1,250. No entries had been made in the non-current asset register for this disposal. The balance on the non-current asset register is:

(A) $42,710
(B) $51,210
(C) $53,710
(D) $62,210

1.2 Your firm bought a machine for $5,000 on 1 January 20X1, which had an expected useful life of 4 years and an expected residual value of $1,000; the asset was to be depreciated on the straight-line basis. On 31 December 20X3, the machine was sold for $1,600. The amount to be entered in the 20X3 income statement for profit or loss on disposal is:

$ . . . .

1.3 An organisation's non-current asset register shows a carrying amount of $135,600. The non-current asset account in the nominal ledger shows a carrying amount of $125,600. The difference could be due to a disposed asset not having been deducted from the non-current asset register:

(A) with disposal proceeds of $15,000 and a profit on disposal of $5,000.
(B) with disposal proceeds of $15,000 and a carrying amount of $5,000.
(C) with disposal proceeds of $15,000 and a loss on disposal of $5,000.
(D) with disposal proceeds of $5,000 and a carrying amount of $5,000.

1.4 A non-current asset costing $12,500 was sold at a loss of $4,500. Depreciation had been accounted for using the reducing balance, at 20 per cent per annum since its purchase. Which of the following correctly describes the sale proceeds and length of time for which the asset had been owned?

	Sale proceeds	*Length of ownership*
(A)	Cannot be calculated	Cannot be calculated
(B)	Cannot be calculated	2 years
(C)	$8,000	Cannot be calculated
(D)	$8,000	2years

1.5 A machine costs $9,000. It has an expected useful life of 6 years, and an expected residual value of $1,000. It is to be depreciated at 30 per cent per annum on the reducing-balance basis. A full year's depreciation is charged in the year of purchase, with none in the year of sale. During year 4, it is sold for $3,000. The profit or loss on disposal is:

$ . . . .

1.6 The most appropriate definition of depreciation is:

(A) a means of determining the decrease in fair value of an asset over time.
(B) a means of allocating the cost of an asset over a number of accounting periods.
(C) a means of setting funds aside for the replacement of the asset.
(D) a means of estimating the fair value of the asset.

1.7 A non-current asset was disposed of for $2,200 during the last accounting year. It had been purchased exactly 3 years earlier for $5,000, with an expected residual value of $500, and had been depreciated on the reducing-balance basis, at 20 per cent per annum. The profit or loss on disposal was:

$ . . . .

1.8 The purpose of charging depreciation on non-current assets is:

(A) to put money aside to replace the assets when required.
(B) to show the assets in the statement of financial position at their fair value.
(C) to ensure that the profit is not understated.
(D) to spread the net cost of the assets over their estimated useful life.

1.9 The phrase 'carrying amount' when applied to non-current assets means that

(A) the assets are shown in the statement of financial position at their original cost.
(B) the assets are valued at their likely selling price.
(C) the assets have been depreciated using the reducing-balance method.
(D) the assets are shown in the statement of financial position at their cost less accumulated depreciation.

1.10 Which of the following statements regarding goodwill is *not* correct?

(A) Goodwill is classed as an intangible non-current asset.
(B) Goodwill is the excess of the value of a business as a whole over the fair value of its separable net assets.
(C) Purchased goodwill may be shown on the statement of financial position and may be reduced by impairment.
(D) Non-purchased goodwill is a liability.

1.11 W Ltd bought a new printing machine from abroad. The cost of the machine was $80,000. The installation costs were $5,000 and the employees received specific training on how to use this particular machine, at a cost of $2,000. Before using the machine to print customers' orders, a test was undertaken and the paper and ink cost $1,000. What should be the cost of the machine in the company's statement of financial position.

$ . . . .

1.12 A car was purchased by a newsagent business in May 20X0 for:

	$
Cost	10,000
Annual vehicle licence tax	150
Total	10,150

The business adopts a date of 31 December as its year end.

The car was traded in for a replacement vehicle in August 20X3 at an agreed value of $5,000.

It has been depreciated at 25 per cent per annum on the reducing-balance method, charging a full year's depreciation in the year of purchase and none in the year of sale.

What was the profit or loss on disposal of the vehicle during the year ended December 20X3?

$ . . . .

1.13 The carrying amount of a company's non-current assets was $200,000 at 1 August 20X0. During the year ended 31 July 20X1, the company sold non-current assets for $25,000 on which it made a loss of $5,000. The depreciation charge for the year was $20,000. What was the carrying amount of non-current assets at 31 July 20X1?

$ . . . .

1.14 Which one of the following should be accounted for as capital expenditure?

(A) The cost of painting a building.
(B) The replacement of windows in a building.
(C) The purchase of a car by a garage for resale.
(D) Legal fees incurred on the purchase of a building.

1.15 A car was purchased for $12,000 on 1 April 20X0 and has been depreciated at 20 per cent each year, straight line, assuming no residual value. The company policy is to charge a full year's depreciation in the year of purchase and no depreciation in the year of sale. The car was traded in for a replacement vehicle on 1 August 20X3 for an agreed figure of $5,000. What was the profit or loss on the disposal of the vehicle for the year ended 31 December 20X3?

$ . . . .

1.16 Which of these two graphs illustrate the straight-line method of depreciation and the reducing-balance method?

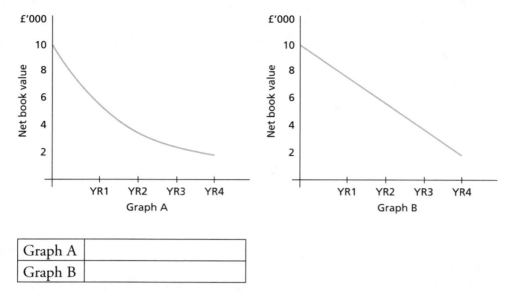

Graph A	
Graph B	

1.17 A non-current asset register is:

(A) an alternative name for the non-current asset ledger account.

(B) a list of the physical non-current assets rather than their financial cost.

(C) a schedule of planned maintenance of non-current assets for use by the plant engineer.

(D) a schedule of the cost and other information about each individual non-current asset.

? Question 2

ABC Ltd had the following balances on its motor vehicles accounts at 30 September 20X5:

	$
Motor vehicles at cost	10,000
Accumulated depreciation of motor vehicles	4,000

During the year to 30 September 20X6, the following transactions occurred:

31 Jan. 20X6	Bought a motor van (plant number M V11) costing $9,000
24 Apr. 20X6	Sold a motor van (plant number MV05) for $500, which had originally cost $4,000 in January 20X3

During the year to 30 September 20X7, the following transactions occurred:

20 Feb. 20X7	Bought a motor van (plant number M V12) costing $12,000
31 Aug. 20X7	Traded-in van bought on 31 January 20X6 (plant number M V11) for a new van (plant number M V13) costing $14,000. The trade-in allowance was $7,400.

ABC Ltd accounts for depreciation on its motor vehicles at a rate of 25 per cent per annum using the reducing-balance method. It is company policy to make a full year's charge against all assets held at the end of its financial year (30 September).

Requirements

Insert the missing figures into the ledger accounts below to record the above transactions, showing the values that will be transferred to the company's income statement and statement of financial position at the end of each of the financial years to 30 September 20X6 and 20X7.

Motor vehicles at cost

		$				$
1.10.X5	Balance b/d		24.04.X6	Disposal		
31.01.X6	Bank		30.09.X6	Balance c/d		
1.10.X6	Balance b/d		31.08.X7	Disposal		
20.02X7	Bank					
31.08.X7	Bank					
	Disposal		30.09.X7	Balance c/d		
1.10.X7	Balance b/d					

Motor vehicles – accumulated depreciation

		$				$
24.04.X6	Disposal [W1]		1.10.X5	Balance b/d		
30.09.X6	Balance c/d		30.09.X6	Income statement [W2]		
31.08.X7	Disposal [W3]		1.10.X6	Balance b/d		
30.09.X7	Balance c/d		30.09.X7	Income statement [W4]		
			1.10.X7	Balance b/d		

ACCOUNTING FOR NON-CURRENT ASSETS

Workings

		$		%		$
W1	Year ended 30 Sep. 20X3		×		=	
	Year ended 30 Sep. 20X4		×		=	
	Year ended 30 Sep. 20X5		×		=	
	Total					
W2	Depreciation y/e 30.09.X6		×		=	
W3	Depreciation (disposal) y/e 30.09.X7		×		=	
W4	Depreciation y/e 30.09.X7		×		=	

Motor vehicles – disposal

		$			$
24.04.X6	Motor vehicles cost		24.04.X6	Motor vehicles – accumulated depreciation Bank	
			30.09.X6	Income statement	
31.08.X7	Motor vehicle cost		31.08.X7	Motor vehicle – accumulated depreciation	
30.09.X7	Income statement			Motor vehicle cost	

⟨?⟩ Question 3

ABC Ltd prepares financial statements to 31 December each year. On 1 January 20X5, it had the following balances on its non-current assets accounts:

	Debit	Credit
	$	$
Motor vehicles at cost	15,000	
Plant and equipment at cost	24,000	
Motor vehicles – accumulated depreciation		9,000
Plant and equipment – accumulated depreciation		10,500

During the year to 31 December 20X5, the following transactions took place:

(i) purchased a new machine on 1 February at a cost of $7,500;

(ii) installed office equipment in its office building on 14 March at a cost of $11,500;

(iii) sold equipment on 1 April for $2,000. It had originally been purchased on 1 January 20X1 for $5,600;

(iv) sold a motor vehicle on 31 July for $3,400 that had been purchased on 1 August 20X2 for $9,400, including $100 annual vehicle licence tax and $300 warranty against mechanical defects for 2 years;

(v) purchased a motor vehicle on 1 August for $10,000, including $500 delivery, $100 annual vehicle licence tax and $400 extended warranty against mechanical defects for 3 years;

(vi) carried out major repairs to some equipment on 1 October costing $15,000. This included a new motor costing $5,000, which increased the efficiency of the equipment by 200 per cent.

The company accounts for a full year's depreciation on non-current assets held at the end of each year using the following methods and rates:

Motor vehicles	25% per annum, reducing balance
Plant and equipment	20% per annum, straight line

Requirements

(a) Insert the missing figures for the transactions numbered (i)–(vi) above in the ledger accounts of ABC Ltd and account for depreciation as appropriate for the year ended 31 December 20X5.

(b) Insert the missing figures in the extract from the income statement for the year ended 31 December 20X5 in respect of the above transactions.

(a)

Motor vehicles at cost

$

Motor vehicles expenses

$

Plant and equipment at cost

$

Repairs and maintenance

$

Motor vehicles – accumulated depreciation

$

Plant and equipment – accumulated depreciation

$

Plant and equipment – disposal

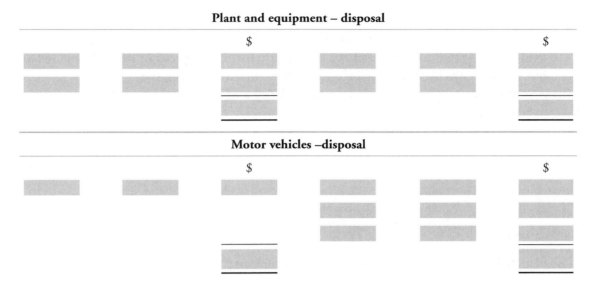

Motor vehicles –disposal

(b) Income statement extract – year ended December 20X5

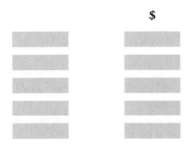

? Question 4

SBJ's non-current asset register gives the cost and accumulated depreciation to date for every non-current asset held by the company. Prior to charging depreciation for 20X4, the total carrying amount of all non-current assets on the register at 31 December 20X4 was $147,500. At the same date, the non-current asset accounts in the nominal ledger showed the following balances:

	Cost to date	Accumulated Depreciation
	($)	($)
Motor vehicles	48,000	12,000
Plant and machinery	120,000	30,000
Office equipment	27,500	7,500

You are told that

(i) An item of plant costing $30,000 has been sold for $23,500 during 20X4. The loss on disposal was $800. No entries have been made for this disposal in the nominal ledger, but the asset has been removed from the non-current asset register.

(ii) A motor car was purchased on 1 October 20X4 and correctly recorded in the nominal ledger. Its cost was as follows:

List price of vehicle	$24,000
Trade discount	20%
Sales tax added at 17.5%	
Insurance	$360
Annual vehicle licence tax	$130
Painting of company name	$100 (no sales tax)

The vehicle has not been entered in the non-current asset register.

(iii) Office equipment was purchased during 20X4, and entered on the non-current asset register but not in the nominal ledger. Until the omission can be investigated fully, its cost is deemed to be the difference between the balances on the non-current asset register and the nominal ledger at 31 December 20X4 (prior to charging depreciation for the year).

(iv) Depreciation for 20X4 is to be charged as follows:

Motor vehicles	25% per annum straight line on an actual time basis
Plant and machinery	10% per annum straight line, with a full year's depreciation in the year of purchase
Office equipment	10% per annum reducing balance, with a full year's depreciation in the year of purchase

Requirements

(a) Insert the balances at 31 December 20X4 for cost and depreciation to date on the three non-current asset accounts in the nominal ledger (prior to the charging of depreciation for 20X4).

Motor vehicles	$
List price	
Less: 20%	
Add: sales tax 17.5%	
Add: Cost of painting name	
Amount to add to non-current asset register	

Plant and machinery	Cost ($)	Accumulated depreciation ($)
Balance as per nominal ledger		
Less: Disposal		

Office equipment

Revised nominal ledger balances	Cost ($)	Accumulated depreciation ($)	Carrying amount ($)
Motor vehicles			
Plant and machinery			
Office equipment			
Revised non-current asset register			

(b) Insert the depreciation for each class of non-current asset for 20X4.

Depreciation for 20X4

Motor vehicles	$	
		(rounded)
Plant and machinery		
Office equipment		

Question 5

Your organisation maintains a non-current asset register that contained the following details at 1 April 20X7:

	Cost at 1 April 20X7 ($)	Accumulated depreciation at 1 April 20X7 ($)
Land	120,000	Nil
Buildings	80,000	18,000
Plant		
Machine A	60,000	27,000
Machine B	40,000	24,000
Machine C	26,000	11,700
Machine D	18,000	13,500
Office equipment		
Computer	20,000	7,200
Scanner	1,000	600
Printers (2)	600	250
Small tools	1,200	300

Buildings are depreciated at 2.5 per cent per annum on cost. The cost of small tools is estimated annually, the value at 31 March 20X8 being $800. Plant is depreciated at 7.5 per cent per annum on cost, and office equipment is depreciated at 7.5 per cent per annum on cost.

During the year ended 31 March 20X8, the following transactions occurred:

  (i) Machine E was purchased by cheque for $17,000.
 (ii) Machine C was sold for $13,000 to A Jones, on credit.
(iii) The computer memory was upgraded by the manufacturer at a cost of $2,000.
 (iv) The scanner was repaired at a cost of $300.
  (v) Machine F was purchased by cheque for $42,300 including sales tax at 17.5 per cent. The purchase price included delivery and installation of $1,200 plus sales tax, and a 1-year maintenance contract of $2,000 plus sales tax.
 (vi) The total on the non-current asset register at 1 April 20X7 was compared with the ledger accounts, and it was discovered that one of the printers had been passed to a supplier in part-payment of his debt during December 20X6, but had never been removed from the non-current asset register. The cost of the printer was $400 and depreciation of $200 had been charged up to 1 April 20X6.

Notes:

1. Ignore sales tax on all items except for those in transaction (v).
2. The organisation's policy is to charge a full year's depreciation in the year of purchase.

Requirements

(a) Insert the figures in the non-current asset accounts (at cost) and the accumulated depreciation accounts for each of the above categories of non-current asset, commencing with the totals in the non-current asset register on 1 April 20X7. Make entries for additions, disposals, adjustments and depreciation for the year ended 31 March 20X8.

Ledger Accounts

Land at cost

$

Buildings at cost

$

Plant at cost

$ $

Office equipment at cost

$ $

Small tools at cost

$

Buildings accumulated depreciation

$ $

Plant accumulated depreciation

$ $

Office equipment accumulated depreciation

$ $

Small tools accumulated depreciation

$ $

(b) Insert the figures in the non-current asset disposals account for the year ended 31 March 20X8.

Disposal of non-current assets

$ $

(c) Describe the information that could be held on a non-current asset register.

1. _____
2. _____
3. _____
4. _____
5. _____
6. _____
7. _____
8. _____
9. _____

10. _____
11. _____
12. _____

? Question 6

(a) Depreciation is the systematic _____ of the cost of an asset, less its _____, over its _____. The purpose of depreciation is to ___ the cost of a non-current asset over its _____ and thus match the ___ of an asset in a period with the _____. It is an example of the application of the ___ convention.

(b) A transport company started business on 1 January 20X7 and purchased truck A for $80,000. Truck A was destroyed in a road accident on 1 March 20X8 and the insurance company paid out $60,000 to the transport company.

On 1 April 20X8, truck B was purchased for $90,000.

On 1 July 20X8, car C was purchased for $20,000.

On 1 August 20X9, car C was traded in for car D, which cost $25,000, less a part-exchange allowance on car C of $15,000.

The depreciation policy of the company is:

- depreciate trucks at 40 per cent each year on a reducing-balance basis;
- depreciate cars at 25 per cent each year using a straight-line basis;
- assume a residual value for cars of 10 per cent of the original cost;
- if a vehicle is owned for part of a year, calculate depreciation according to the number of months for which the vehicle is owned.

The year end of the company is 31 December.

Including entries for each relevant year, and working to the nearest $, write up the following accounts using the ledger accounts provided.

Motor vehicles at cost						
20X7		$	20X7			$
20X8			20X8			
Jan.	Balance b/d					
			Dec.	Balance c/d		
20X9			20X9			
Jan.	Balance b/d					
			Dec.	Balance c/d		

Accumulated depreciation on motor vehicles

20X7		$	20X7		$
Dec.	Balance c/d		Dec.	Depreciation charge – Income statement	
20X8			20X8		
			Jan.	Balance b/d	
Dec.	Balance c/d		Dec.	Depreciation charge – Income statement	
20X9			20X9		
			Jan.	Balance b/d	
Dec.	Balance c/d		Dec.	Depreciation charge – Income statement	

Disposal of motor vehicles

20X8		$	20X8		$
20X9			20X9		

Workings: Depreciation

Year acquired	Truck A 20X7 ($) 80,000	Truck B 20X8 ($) 90,000	Car C 20X8 ($) 20,000	Car D 20X9 ($) 25,000	Total ($)
Depreciation charge 20X7					
Depreciation charge 20X8					
Written back on disposal					
Depreciation charge 20X9					
Written back on disposal					
Balances c/d					

Solutions to Revision Questions

 Solution 1

1.1   Answer: (D)

The carrying amount of the disposed asset needs to be deducted from the non-current asset register. The asset was sold for $1,250 less than its carrying amount, thus its carrying amount must have been $4,000 + $1,250 = $5,250.

The balance can be calculated as follows:

	$
Balance on the register	67,460
Less: carrying amount of the disposed asset	(5,250)
	62,210

1.2   The profit or loss on disposal is the difference between the carrying amount at the time of disposal and the disposal proceeds. An excess of disposal proceeds over carrying amount indicates a profit on disposal, while an excess of carrying amount over disposal proceeds indicates a loss on disposal.

The annual depreciation on the machine is calculated as:

$$\frac{\text{Cost} - \text{residual value}}{\text{Useful life}} = \frac{5,000 - 1,000}{4 \text{ years}} = 1,000 \text{ per year}$$

Depreciation by 31 December 20X3 would be 3 × $1,000 = $3,000, therefore the carrying amount of the machine at the date of disposal would be $2,000. Disposal proceeds were $1,600, therefore there was a loss on disposal of $400.

1.3   Answer: (A)

The difference between the two records is $10,000, therefore the disposed asset must have had a carrying amount of this amount. B and D are clearly wrong, and C would produce a carrying amount of $20,000.

1.4 Answer: (A)

There is insufficient information to calculate the proceeds or the length of ownership.

1.5

	$	
$9,000 \times 0.7 \times 0.7 \times 0.7 =$	3,087	(carrying amount)
Proceeds of sale	(3,000)	
Loss on disposal	87	

1.6 Answer: (B)

Depreciation never provides a fund for the replacement of the asset, nor does it aim to show assets at their fair values.

1.7

	$	
$5,000 \times 0.8 \times 0.8 \times 0.8 =$	2,560	(carrying amount)
Receipt	(2,200)	
Loss on disposal	360	

1.8 Answer: (D)

Depreciation is not connected with the putting aside of money for the replacement of the asset, nor does it aim to show assets at their fair values. The charging of depreciation ensures that profits are not overstated.

1.9 Answer: (D)

Non-current assets should, except in certain circumstances, be depreciated over their expected useful life. Answer A would almost never be appropriate. Assets are rarely valued at their expected selling price – if this is more than their cost, this would be imprudent, and if less than cost would contravene the 'going concern' convention, which is discussed in a later chapter. The method of depreciation is irrelevant.

1.10 Answer: (D)

(A), (B) and (C) are all correct, in most situations.

1.11

	$
Cost of machine	80,000
Installation	5,000
Training	2,000
Testing	1,000
	88,000

1.12

		$
Cost		10,000
20X0 Depreciation		(2,500)
		7,500
20X1 Depreciation		(1,875)
		5,625
20X2 Depreciation		(1,406)
		4,219
20X3 Part-exchange		(5,000)
Profit		781

1.13

	$	$
Carrying amount at 1 August 20X0		200,000
Less: depreciation		(20,000)
Proceeds	25,000	
Loss	5,000	
Therefore carrying amount		(30,000)
		150,000

1.14 Answer: (D)

1.15

	$
Cost	12,000
20X1 Depreciation	(2,400)
	9,600
20X2 Depreciation	(2,400)
	7,200
20X3 Depreciation	(2,400)
	4,800
Proceeds on disposal	(5,000)
Profit	200

1.16 Graph A Reducing-balance method of depreciation. Graph B Straight-line method of depreciation.

1.17 Answer: (D)

Solution 2

- This is a straight test of double-entry bookkeeping principles for non-current assets.
- It requires a calculation of the accumulated depreciation of the disposed asset up to the date of disposal in accordance with the method and policy stated in the question, and then to calculate the depreciation charge for each of the 2 years.
- The purchases and sales of vehicles do *not* involve purchases and sales accounts.
- The sale proceeds are part of the calculation of the profit or loss on disposal – do not use this figure in transferring the asset at cost out of its ledger account.

Motor vehicles at cost

		$			$
1.10.X5	Balance b/d	10,000	24.04.X6	Disposal	4,000
31.01.X6	Bank	9,000	30.09.X6	Balance c/d	15,000
		19,000			19,000
1.10.X6	Balance b/d	15,000	31.08.X7	Disposal	9,000
20.02.X7	Bank	12,000			
31.08.X7	Bank	6,600			
	Disposal	7,400	30.09.X7	Balance c/d	32,000
		41,000			41,000
1.10.X7	Balance b/d	32,000			

Motor vehicles – accumulated depreciation

		$			$
24.04.X6	Disposal [W1]	2,313	1.10.X5	Balance b/d	4,000
30.09.X6	Balance c/d	5,015	30.09.X6	Income statement [W2]	3,328
		7,328			7,328
31.08.X7	Disposal [W3]	2,250	1.10.X6	Balance b/d	5,015
30.09.X7	Balance c/d	10,074	30.09.X7	Income statement [W4]	7,309
		12,324			12,324
			1.10.X7	Balance b/d	10,074

Workings

		$
W1	Year ended 30 September 20X3 ($4,000 @ 25%)	1,000
	Year ended 30 September 20X4 ($3,000 @ 25%)	750
	Year ended 30 September 20X5 ($2,250 @ 25%)	563
		2,313
W2	($15,000–($4,000–2,313)) @ 25%	3,328
W3	Year ended 30 September 20X6 ($9,000 @ 25%)	2,250
W4	($32,000–($5015–2,250)) @ 25%	7,309

Motor vehicles – disposal

		$				$
24.04.X6	Motor vehicles cost	4,000	24.04.X6	Motor vehicles – acc. dep'n Bank		2,313
						500
			30.09.X6	Income statement		1,187
		4,000				4,000
31.08.X7	Motor vehicle cost	9,000	1.08.X7	Motor vehicle – acc. dep'n		2,250
30.09.X7	Income statement	650		Motor vehicle cost		7,400
		9,650				9,650

✅ Solution 3

- Identify the revenue items – for example tax and insurance – and exclude from the non-current asset accounts.
- A full year's depreciation is to be charged on all assets in possession at the end of the year.

(a)

Motor vehicles at cost

		$			$
1 Jan.	Balance b/d	15,000	31 Jul.	Disposal	9,000
1 Aug.	Bank	9,500	31 Dec.	Balance c/d	15,500
		24,500			24,500
1 Jan.	Balance b/d	15,500			

Motor vehicles expenses

		$			$
1 Aug.	Bank	500	31 Dec.	Income statement	156
				Balance c/f	344
		500			500

Plant and equipment at cost

		$			$
1 Jan.	Balance b/d	24,000	1 Apr.	Disposal	5,600
1 Feb.	Bank	7,500			
14 Mar.	Bank	11,500			
1 Oct.	Bank	5,000	31 Dec.	Balance c/d	42,000
		48,000			48,000
1 Jan.	Balance b/d	42,400			

Repairs and maintenance

		$			$
1 Oct.	Bank	10,000	31 Dec.	Income statement	10,000

Motor vehicles – accumulated depreciation

		$			$
31 Jul.	Disposal	5,203	1 Jan.	Balance b/d	9,000
31 Dec.	Balance c/d	6,723	31 Dec.	Income statement	2,926
		11,926			11,926
			1 Jan.	Balance b/d	6,723

Plant and equipment – accumulated depreciation

		$			$
1 Apr.	Disposal	4,480	1 Jan.	Balance b/d	10,500
31 Dec.	Balance c/d	14,500	31 Dec.	Income statement	8,480
		18,980			18,980
			1 Jan.	Balance b/d	14,500

Plant and equipment – disposal

		$			$
1 Apr.	Plant and equipment at cost	5,600	1 Apr.	Plant and equipment accumulated depreciation	4,480
31 Dec.	Income statement	880	1 Apr.	Bank	2,000
		6,480			6,480

Motor vehicles – disposal

		$			$
31 Jul.	Motor vehicles at cost	9,000	31 Jul.	Motor vehicles accumulated depreciation	5,203
			31 Jul.	Bank	3,400
			31 Dec.	Income statement	397
		9,000			9,000

(b)   Income statement extract – year ended December 20X5

	$
Depreciation charge for the year	11,406
Net profit on disposal of assets	(483)
Equipment repairs	10,000
Annual vehicle licence tax	100
Vehicle warranty (5/36×$400)	56

 Solution 4

- Set aside a separate page for workings, and label them clearly.
- Remember to deduct the discount on the motor vehicle before calculating the amount of sales tax to be added; remember also that the annual vehicle licence tax and insurance are revenue expenses, and should not be included with the cost of the vehicle. The resulting total needs to be added to the non-current asset register, *not* to the ledger accounts.
- Deduct the cost and depreciation of the disposed plant from the ledger.
- Calculate the value of office equipment purchased by comparing the ledger total with the non-current asset register total.
- In Part (b), note that the motor vehicle is depreciated on an actual time basis.

(a)

Motor vehicles

	$
List price	24,000
Less: 20%	(4,800)
	19,200
Add: sales tax 17.5%	3,360
	22,560
Add: Cost of painting name	100
Amount to add to non-current asset register	22,660

Plant and machinery	*Cost ($)*	*Acc. dep'n ($)*	
Balance as per nominal ledger	120,000	30,000	
Less: Disposal	(30,000)	(5,700)*	(*i.e. ($30,000–$24,300))
	90,000	24,300	

Office equipment

Revised nominal ledger balances	*Cost ($)*	*Acc. dep'n($)*	*Carrying amount ($)*
Motor vehicles	48,000	(12,000)	36,000
Plant and machinery	90,000	(24,300)	65,700
Office equipment	27,500	(7,500)	20,000
	165,500	(43,800)	121,700
Revised non-current asset register ($147,500 + $22,660)			170,160
Therefore purchase of office equipment was			48,460

(b) Depreciation for 20X4

Motor vehicles		
25% × $48,000	12,000	
25% × $22,660 × 3/12	1,416	(rounded)
	13,416	
Plant and machinery		
10% × $90,000	9,000	
Office equipment		
10% × $68,460	6,846	

☑ Solution 5

- Remember to deduct the sales tax that is included in the price of machine F, as well as the cost of the maintenance agreement (which is a revenue expense).

(a) Ledger Accounts

Land at cost

		$			
1/4/X7	Balance b/fwd	120,000			

Buildings at cost

		$			
1/4/X7	Balance b/fwd	80,000			

Plant at cost

		$				$
1/4/X7	Balance b/fwd	144,000		Disposal a/c	26,000
	Bank a/c	17,000	31/3/X8	Balance c/fwd	169,000
	Bank a/c	34,000			
		195,000			195,000

Office equipment at cost

		$				$
1/4/X7	Balance b/fwd	21,600	31/3/X8	Adjustment	400
	Bank	2,000		Balance c/fwd	23,200
		23,600			23,600

Small tools at cost

		$			
1/4/X7	Balance b/fwd	1,200			

Buildings – accumulated depreciation

		$				$
			1/4/X7	Balance c/fwd	18,000
31/3/X8	Balance c/fwd	20,000	31/3/X8	Income statement	2,000
		20,000			20,000

Plant – accumulated depreciation

		$				$
31/3/X8	Disposal a/c	11,700	1/4/X7	Balance b/fwd	76,200
	Balance c/fwd	77,175		Income statement	12,675
		88,875			88,875

Office equipment – accumulated depreciation

		$				$
31/3/X8	Adjustment	200	1/4/X7	Balance b/fwd	8,050
	Balance c/fwd	9,590	31/3/X8	Income statement	1,740
		9,790			9,790

Small tools – accumulated depreciation

		$				$
			1/4/X7	Balance b/fwd	300
31/3/98	Balance c/d	400	31/3/X8	Income statement	100
		400			400

Workings

Machine F	$
Total cost	42,300
Inc. sales tax	(6,300)
Exc. sales tax	36,000
Less: maintenance	(2,000)
Plant a/c	34,000

(b)

Disposal of non-current assets

		$			$
31/3/X7	Plant at cost a/c	26,000	31/3/X7	Plant accumulated depreciation a/c	11,700
				A Jones	13,000
				Loss on disposal	1,300
		26,000			26,000

The office equipment at cost and accumulated depreciation accounts could commence with the balances after adjusting for the disposed printer, that is, $21,200 (office equipment at cost) and $7,850 (office equipment accumulated depreciation).

(c) A non-current asset register should normally include:

1. a description of the asset;
2. the location of the asset;
3. the original cost of the asset;
4. the date of acquisition;
5. the purchase order reference;
6. the supplier's name and address;
7. the estimated life of the asset;
8. the estimated residual value of the asset;
9. the rate and method of depreciation to be used;
10. the accumulative depreciation charged to date;
11. maintenance agreements and history;
12. insurance details.

Solution 6

(a) Depreciation is the systematic allocation of the cost of an asset, less its residual value, over its useful life.

(b) The purpose of depreciation is to allocate the cost of a non-current asset over its useful life and thus match the cost of an asset in a period with the benefit from its use. It is an example of the application of the accruals concept.

Motor vehicles at cost

20X7		$	20X7		$
Jan.	Bank – Truck A	80,000	Dec.	Balance c/d	80,000
20X8			20X8		
Jan.	Balance b/d	80,000	Mar.	Disposal a/c – Truck A	80,000
Apr.	Bank – Truck B	90,000			
July	Bank – Car C	20,000	Dec.	Balance c/d	110,000
		110,000			110,000
20X9			20X9		
Jan.	Balance b/d	110,000	Aug.	Disposal a/c – Car C	20,000
Aug.	Disposal a/c – Car C part-exchange Car D	15,000			
	Bank – Car D	10,000	Dec.	Balance c/d	115,000
		135,000			135,000

Accumulated depreciation on motor vehicles

20X7		$	20X7		$
Dec.	Balance c/d	32,000	Dec.	Depreciation charge – Income statement	32,000
20X8			20X8		
Mar.	Disposal a/c – Truck A	35,200	Jan.	Balance b/d	32,000
			Mar.	Depreciation charge Truck A – Income statement	3,200
Dec.	Balance c/d	29,250	Dec.	Depreciation charge – Income statement	29,250
		64,450			64,450
20X9			20X9		
			Jan.	Balance b/d	29,250
Aug.	Disposal a/c – Car C	4,875	Aug.	Depreciation charge Car C – Income statement	2,625
Dec.	Balance c/d	54,544	Dec.	Depreciation charge – Income statement	27,544
		59,419			59,419

Disposal of motor vehicles

20X8		$	20X8		$
Mar.	Vehicle cost a/c – Truck A	80,000	Mar.	Accumulated depreciation on vehicle a/c – Truck A	35,200
Dec.	Income statement	15,200	Mar.	Bank – proceeds from Truck A	60,000
		95,200			95,200
20X9			20X9		
Aug.	Vehicle cost account – Car C	20,000	Aug.	Accumulated depreciation on vehicle a/c – Car C	4,875
			Aug.	Vehicle cost account – Car C part-exchange Car D	15,000
			Dec.	Income statement	125
		20,000			20,000

Workings: Depreciation

Year acquired	Truckz A 20X7 ($) 80,000	Truck B 20X8 ($) 90,000	Car C 20X8 ($) 20,000	Car D 20X9 ($) 25,000	Total ($)
Depreciation charge 20X7 $80,000 × 40%	(32,000)				(32,000)
Depreciation charge 20X8 ($80,000 − $32,000) × 40% × 2/12	(3,200)				(3,200)
$90,000 × 40% × 9/12		(27,000)			(27,000)
$20,000 × 90% 25% × 6/12			(2,250)		(2,250)
					(29,250)
Written back on disposal	35,200				
Depreciation charge 20X9 $20,000 × 90% × 25% × 7/12			(2,625)		(2,625)
($90,000 − $27,000) × 40%		(25,200)			(25,200)
$25,000 × 90% × 25% × 5/12				(2,344)	(2,344)
					(27,544)
Written back on disposal			4,875		
Balance c/d		(52,200)		(2,344)	(54,544)

7

Preparation of Financial Statements with Adjustments

Preparation of Financial Statements with Adjustments

7

Learning Outcome

When you have completed this chapter, you should be able to:

► prepare income statements and statements of financial position from trial balances and adjustments.

7.1 Introduction

This chapter looks at the preparation of financial statements (i.e. income statement and statement of financial position) from a trial balance, with various adjustments to be made.

These adjustments include:

- closing inventories at the end of the period,
- accruals,
- prepayments,
- bad debts and allowance for receivables,
- depreciation.

The trial balance is often extracted from the ledger accounts prior to the consideration of adjustments for accruals and prepayments, depreciation and allowance for receivables, and so on, and these are given as notes following the trial balance.

The chapter contains a complete worked example.

7.2 The trial balance

The following trial balance has been extracted from the nominal ledger of Yusuf on 30 November 20X3.

Trial balance of Yusuf as at 30 November 20X3

	$	$
Sales		125,658
Returns	6,341	1,902
Receivables and payables	11,257	7,983
Office equipment		
Cost	10,000	
Acc. Depreciation at 1 December 20X2		1,550
Vehicles		
Cost	3,500	
Acc. Depreciation at 1 December 20X2		700
Purchases	64,726	
Inventories at 1 December 20X2	5,000	
Carriage inwards	908	
Carriage outwards	272	
Vehicle expenses	1,349	
Electricity	1,803	
Wages and salaries	11,550	
Rent and local business tax	8,800	
Stationery and postages	2,681	
Bank deposit account	10,000	
Bank	4,797	
Discount allowed and received	5,652	3,765
Sales tax payable		1,325
Employee income tax payable		453
Capital at 1 December 20X2		4,300
Drawings	15,000	
Loan		16,000
	163,636	163,636

7.3 The adjustments

Following the extraction of the above trial balance from the ledgers and an examination of the accounting records, the following additional information was obtained:

1. The value of the inventories on hand at 30 November 20X3 was $5,700.
2. The bank deposit was made on 1 June 20X3. This account earns interest at 8 per cent per annum. The balance shown in the ledgers is the only deposit made into this account. Interest is credited on 31 December annually.
3. Bank charges accrued to 30 November 20X3 are estimated to be $60.
4. Vehicle expenses include annual vehicle licence tax of $125 per annum for a vehicle, which expires on 31 December 20X3, and vehicle insurance of $360 per annum which was paid on 1 July 20X3.
5. There is one employee whose gross wage is $1,050 per month. The wage for November 20X3 has not yet been entered in the ledgers.

6. The balance of the rent and local business tax account includes a payment of rent for the 3 months to 31 December 20X3 of $1,200 and a payment of local business tax for the 6 months to 31 March 20X4 of $4,000.
7. Following a review of receivables at the year end, it is decided that a bad debt of $1,207 should be written off, and an allowance for receivables made, of 2 per cent of receivables.
8. Office equipment is to be depreciated at 10 per cent per annum on cost, and motor vehicles are to be depreciated at 20 per cent per annum on cost.
9. Loan interest of 10 per cent per annum is to be accrued.

Requirement

Using the above information, prepare an income statement of Yusuf for the period ended 30 November 20X3 together with his statement of financial position at that date.

7.4 Step 1: Labelling the trial balance

The trial balance contains all of the account balances from the ledger of Yusuf. It, therefore, includes assets, liabilities, capital, expenses and revenue. You should remember that the assets, liabilities and capital are shown in the statement of financial position, and the expenses and revenue in the income statement where they are used to calculate net profit, which is then also transferred to the statement of financial position. If you are unsure about the correct category for any of the items in the trial balance it might help to remember the following:

Debit balances usually represent either assets or expenses and these are always shown in the left-hand column of a trial balance. Therefore, credit balances (shown in the right-hand column) are usually revenue, liabilities or capital.

You should also remember that values shown in the trial balance have, by definition, been posted to the ledger accounts and that, therefore, the double entry is complete. Other pieces of information given by way of a note have not been recorded in the ledger accounts and consequently will require both a debit and a credit entry (which is usually effected by entering them in both the income statement and the statement of financial position).

The first step, then, is to identify the items in the trial balance that are to be entered in the trading account part of the income statement; those to be entered in the rest of the income statement, and those to be entered in the statement of financial position. These are shown below marked with 'T', 'I' or 'B'. In addition, it is useful to mark those values that are to be affected by the additional information. This has been done with an asterisk (*) and the note number in the layout below.

			$	$
Sales	T			125,658
Returns	T		6,341	1,902
Receivables and payables	B		11,257	7,983
Office equipment				
Cost	B		10,000	
Accumulated depreciation at 1 December 20X2	B	*8		1,550
Vehicles				
Cost	B		3,500	
Accumulated depreciation at 1 December 20X2	B	*8		700
Purchases	T		64,726	
Inventories at 1 December 20X2	T		5,000	
Carriage inwards	T		908	
Carriage outwards	I		272	
Vehicle expenses	I	*4	1,349	
Electricity	I		1,803	
Wages and salaries	I	*5	11,550	
Rent and local business tax	I	*6	8,800	
Stationery and postages	I		2,681	
Bank deposit account	B	*5	10,000	
Bank	B		4,797	
Discount allowed and received	I		5,652	3,765
Sales tax payable	B			1,325
Employee income tax payable	B			453
Capital at 1 December 20X2	B			4,300
Drawings	B		15,000	
Loan	B	*9		16,000
			163,636	163,636

7.5 Step 2: Preparing workings

Each of the notes should be considered in turn, and you should head up a page entitled 'workings' on which any calculations and adjustments should be clearly shown and labelled.

1. Closing inventories of $5,700 is to be entered in the income statement (trading account part) and the statement of financial position.
2. There will be an entry in the income statement for accrued interest received and the outstanding amount will be shown on the statement of financial position as an asset. The deposit was made on 1 June 20X3, so that the interest earned to 30 November is:

$$£10,000 \times 8\% \times 6/12 = £400 \text{ Income statement/balance sheet assets}$$

3. These will be shown as an additional expense to the income statement and as a liability in the statement of financial position.
4. This account includes prepayment as follows:

Annual Vehicle licence tax: 1 month, therefore $£125 \times \frac{1}{12} \approx £10$

Insurance: 7 months, therefore $£360 \times \frac{7}{12} = £210$

	$	
Vehicle expenses as per trial balance	1,349	
Less: prepaid expenses	(220)	(Statement of financial position: assets)
Income statement	1,129	

5. The wages for November are a cost of the period, so the value shown in the trial balance should be increased by this amount.

	$	
Wages as per trial balance	11,550	
Accrued wages	1,050	(Statement of financial position: liabilities)
Income statement	12,600	

6. Rent and local business tax includes prepayments as follows:

Rent: 1 month, therefore £1,200 $\times \frac{1}{3}$ = £400

Local Business Tax: 4 months, therefore £4,000 $\times \frac{4}{6}$ = £2,667

	$	
Rent and local business tax as per trial balance	8,800	
Less: prepayments	(3,067)	(Statement of financial position: assets)
Income statement	5,733	

7. Bad debts to be written off: $1,207 (income statement)

New receivables figure: $11,257 − $1,207 written off = $10,050.
Allowance for receivables to be made: 2% $\times$ $10,050 = $201 (Income statement)
Deduct from receivables figure: $201 (balance sheet)

8. Depreciation on office equipment

	$	
10% $\times$ $10,000	1,000	(Income statement)
Accumulated depreciation as per the trial balance	1,550	
Accumulated depreciation	2,550	(Statement of financial position)

Depreciation on Vehicles

	$	
20% $\times$ 3,500	700	(Income statement)
Accumulated depreciation as per the trial balance	700	
Accumulated depreciation	1,400	(Statement of financial position)

9. Loan interest accrued

10% $\times$ $16,000	$1,600	(Income statement)
	$1,600	(Statement of financial position: current liabilities)

Total accruals for the statement of financial position comprise item 3 ($60), item 5 ($1,050) and item 9 ($1,600), totalling $2,710.

We can now prepare the financial statements.

7.6 Step 3: Preparing the financial statements

- *Hint*. Tick each item in the trial balance and/workings as it is entered.
- *Hint*. Enter the reference number of the 'workings' where relevant.

Income statement of Yusuf for the period ended 30 November 20X3

	$	$	$
Sales			125,658
Less: returns			(6,341)
Net sales			119,317
Opening inventories		5,000	
Purchases	64,726		
Carriage inwards	908		
	65,634		
Less: returns	(1,902)		
Net purchases		63,732	
		68,732	
Less: closing inventories (W1)		(5,700)	
Cost of goods sold			(63,032)
Gross profi			56,285
Bank deposit interest (W2)			400
Discount received			3,765
			60,450
Bank charges		60	
Carriage outwards		272	
Vehicle expenses (W4)		1,129	
Electricity		1,803	
Wages and salaries (W5)		12,600	
Rent and local business tax (W6)		5,733	
Bad debts (W7)		1,207	
Allowance for receivables (W7)		201	
Stationery and postages		2,681	
Discount allowed		5,652	
Depreciation			
Office equipment (W8)		1,000	
Vehicles (W8)		700	
Loan interest (W9)		1,600	
			(34,638)
Net profit			25,812

Statement of financial position of Yusuf as at 30 November 20X3

Assets	Cost ($)	Acc. Depreciation ($)	Carrying amount ($)
Non-current assets			
Office equipment	10,000	(2,550)	7,450
Vehicles	3,500	(1,400)	2,100
	13,500	(3,950)	9,550
Current assets			
Inventories		5,700	
Receivables	11,257		
Less: bad debts	(1,207)		
Less: allowance for receivables	(201)	9,849	
Prepayments		3,287	
Accrued interest receivable		400	
Bank deposit		10,000	
Bank		4,797	
			34,033
			43,583
Capital and liabilities			
Capital at the start of the year			4,300
Add: net profit			25,812
			30,112
Less: drawings			(15,000)
Capital at the end of the year			15,112
Non-current liabilities			
Loan			16,000
Current liabilities			
Payables		7,983	
Accruals ($60 + $1,050 + $1,600)		2,710	
Sales tax payable		1,325	
Employee income tax payable		453	
			12,471
			43,583

 # Exercise 7.1

From the following trial balance:

(a) distinguish between assets, liabilities, capital, revenue and expenditure;

(b) distinguish between items to be found in the income statement (including the trading account) or balance sheet; and

(c) prepare an income statement for the year ended 31 December 20X3 and a statement of financial position at that date.

Trial balance of XYZ as at 31 December 20X3

	Debit ($)	Credit ($)
Sales		126,500
Purchases	99,850	
Premises		
Cost	100,000	
Accumulated depreciation at 1 January 20X3		25,000
Plant		
Cost	18,000	
Accumulated depreciation at 1 January 20X3		2,300
Wages and salaries	8,900	
Rent and local business tax	7,500	
Inventories at 1 January 20X3	5,000	
Capital at 1 January 20X3		80,000
Drawings	25,000	
Carriage inwards	4,000	
Receivables	27,500	
Payables		16,000
Bad debts written off	5,000	
Rent		2,000
Bank balance		18,950
Bank loan		30,000
	300,750	300,750

1. Closing inventories is $12,500.
2. Wages and salaries accrued amount to $700.
3. Rent prepaid amounts to $300.
4. Bank loan interest of 10 per cent per annum is outstanding.
5. Allowance for receivables of 2 per cent is to be made.
6. Depreciation is to be charged at 2 per cent of cost on premises, and at 10 per cent of cost on plant.

Solution

If you have successfully completed Parts (a) and (b) of the exercise, you should be able to complete Part (c) as follows:

Income statement of XYZ for the year ended 31 December 20X3

	$	$	$
Sales			126,500
Less: cost of sales			
Opening inventories		5,000	
Purchases	99,850		
Carriage inwards	4,000		
		103,850	
		108,850	
Less: closing inventories		(12,500)	
			(96,350)
Gross profit			30,150
Rent receivable			2,000
			32,150
Wages and salaries		9,600	
Rent and local business tax		7,200	
Bad debts written off		5,000	
Bank loan interest		3,000	
Allowance for receivables		550	
Depreciation			
Premises		2,000	
Plant		1,800	
			(29,150)
Net profit			3,000

Statement of financial position of XYZ as at 31 December 20X3

Assets

Non-current assets	Cost ($)	Acc. Depreciation ($)	Carrying amount ($)
Premises at cost	100,000	(27,000)	73,000
Plant at cost	18,000	(4,100)	13,900
	118,000	(31,100)	86,900

Current assets			
Inventories		12,500	
Receivables	27,500		
Less: allowance	(550)		
		26,950	
Prepayments		300	
			39,750
			126,650

Capital and liabilities

Capital at start of year			80,000
Add: net profit			3,000
			83,000
Less: drawings			(25,000)
Capital at end of year			58,000
Non-current liabilities			
Bank loan			30,000
Current liabilities			
Payables		16,000	
Accruals		3,700	
Bank overdraft		18,950	
			38,650
			126,650

Exercise 7.2

JW Ltd had, among others, the following balances in the books at 30 June 20X9

	Debit ($)	Credit ($)
Motor vehicles at cost	200	
Motor vehicles acc. depreciation at 1 July 20X8		70
Fixtures at cost	60	
Fixtures acc. depreciation at 1 July 20X8		20
Office equipment at cost	125	
Office equipment – acc. depreciation at 1 July 20X8		45
Trade receivables	580	
Allowance for receivables at 1 July 20X8		10
Insurance	90	

The following adjustments have not yet been made in the books:

(i) Motor vehicles are depreciated over 4 years on the straight-line basis. On 31 March 20X9, a motor vehicle that had cost $20,000 on 1 July 20X6 was disposed of for $8,000. It is the company's policy to charge a full year's depreciation in the year of purchase, and hence none in the year of disposal. No entries have been made for the disposal.

(ii) Fixtures are depreciated on the straight-line basis over 10 years, on an actual time basis (i.e. from the date of acquisition). On 1 October 20X8, fixtures were purchased for $40,000, which have not been entered in the books.

(iii) Office equipment is depreciated at 20 per cent per annum on the reducing-balance basis.

(iv) On 30 June 20X9, it was decided to write off a bad debt of $80,000 and to make an allowance for receivables of 3 per cent of the remaining receivables.

(v) The insurance figure above covers the period 1 July 20X8 to 30 September 20X9.

(vi) Sales representatives are paid commission, which amounts to 5 per cent of the previous month's sales. The commission is due for payment on the 15th of the following month. During June 20X9, sales amounted to $120,000.

Requirements

(a) Prepare ledger accounts for all the above items, showing clearly all calculations, transfers to the income statement for the year ending 30 June 20X9, and balance to be carried down at 30 June 20X9.

(2 marks)

(b) Show the 'expenses' section of the income statement for the year ending 30 June 20X9, to include all the items above.

(2 marks)

(c) Show the extracts from the non-current assets, current assets and current liabilities sections of the balance sheet at 30 June 20X9, which includes balances for the above items.

(2 marks)

(d) Explain briefly why depreciation is charged in the income statement, but does not affect cash balances.

(4 marks)
(Total marks = 20)

Solution

This solution does not utilise a 'depreciation expense' account or a 'bad debts expense' account. Although many businesses do maintain such accounts, it is often considered unnecessary and time-consuming to produce them in the computer-based assessment. Instead of transferring the depreciation to such an expense account, the amount is transferred directly to the income statement.

(a)

Motor vehicles at cost

		$			$
1 Jul. X8	Balance b/fwd	200	31 Mar.X9	Disposals a/c	20
			30 Jun.	X9 Balance c/fwd	180
		200			200

Motor Vehicles – accumulated depreciation

		$			$
31 Mar. X9	Disposals (W1)	10	1 Jul.98	Balance bfwd	70
30 Jun. X9	Balance c/fwd	105	30 Jun. X9	Income statement (W2)	45
		115			115

Disposal of non-current assets

		$			$
31 Mar. X9	Motor vehicles at cost	20	31 Mar. X9	Motor vehicle accumulated depreciation	10
				Cash	8
				Loss on disposal (IS)	2
		20			20

Fixtures at cost

		$			$
1 Jul. X8	Balance b/fwd	60	30 Jun. X9	Balance c/fwd	100
1 Sep. X8	Purchase (bank)	40			
		100			100

Fixtures – accumulated depreciation

		$			$
30 Jun. X9	alance c/fwd	29	1 Jul. X8	Balance b/fwd	20
			30 Jun. X9	Income statement (W3)	9
		29			29

Office equipment at cost

		$			$
1 Jul. X8	Balance b/fwd	125	30 Jun. X9	Balance c/fwd	125
		125			125

Office equipment – accumulated depreciation

		$			$
30 Jun. X9	Balance c/d	61	1 Jul. X8	Balance b/fwd	45
			30 Jun. X9	Income statement (W4)	16
		61			61

Bad debts written off

		$			$
30 Jun. X9	Receivables	80	30 Jun. X9		80
		80			80

Trade receivables

		$			$
30 Jun. X9	Balance c/fwd	580	30 Jun. X9	Bad debts (IS)	80
				Balance c/fwd	500
		580			580

Allowance for receivables

		$			$
30 Jun. X9	Balance c/fwd	15	1 Jul. X8	Balance b/fwd	10
				Income statement (W5)	5
		15			15

Insurance

		$			$
1 Jul. X8	Bank	90	30 Jun. X9	Prepaid c/fwd (W6)	18
				Income statement	72
		90			90

Sales commission payable

		$			$
30 Jun. X9	Bank (during year)	40	30 Jun. X9	Income statement	46
	Accrued c/fwd (W7)	6			
		46			46

Workings

(W1) Motor Vehicles – depreciation on disposed vehicle

	$'000
Cost on 1 July 20X6	20
Depreciation y/e 30 June 20X7: 20 ÷ 4	5
Depreciation y/e 30 June 20X8: 20 ÷ 4	5
Total depreciation to be removed	10

(W2) Motor vehicles – depreciation

Motor vehicles – cost at 30 June 20X9	180
Depreciation = 180 ÷ 4 years =	45

Note: The depreciation rate could also be expressed as 25% on cost.

(W3) Fixtures – depreciation on existing items

	$'000	$'000
Cost at 1 July 20X8	60	
Depreciation = 60 ÷ 10		6
Depreciation on new items:		
Cost at 1 September 20X8	40	
Depreciation = 40 ÷ 10 × 9/12		3

(W4) Office equipment – depreciation

	$'000
Cost b/fwd	125
Depreciation b/fwd	(45)
Carrying amount b/fwd	80

(W5) Allowance for receivables

	$'000
Receivables (prior to bad debts)	580
Bad debts written off	(80)
Revised receivables	500
Allowance for receivables 3% × 500=	15
Less: existing allowance for receivables	(10)
	5

(W6) Insurance Prepaid

	$'000
Insurance paid for 15 months	90
Prepaid = 3/15 × 90	(18)
Income statement charge	72

(W7) Sales commission accrued

	$'000
Sales commission paid	40
Accrued = 5% × 120	6
Income statement charge	46

(b) Income statement for the year ended 30 June 20X9 (extract)

Expenses	$'000
Depreciation	
Motor vehicles	45
Fixtures	9
Office equipment	16
Loss on disposal of non-current assets	2
Bad debts written off	80
Allowance for receivables	5
Insurance	72
Sales commission	46

(c) Statement of financial position at 30 June 20X9 (extract)

	Cost ($'000)	Acc. Dep'n ($'000)	Carrying amount ($'000)
Non-current assets			
Motor vehicles	180	(105)	75
Fixtures	100	(29)	71
Office equipment	125	(61)	64
	405	(195)	210
Current assets			
Receivables		500	
Less: allowance for receivables		(15)	
			485
Prepaid insurance			18
Current liabilities			
Accrued commission			6

(d) Depreciation is a means of spreading the cost of non-current assets (less any expected sale proceeds) over their expected useful life, so as to charge the income statement with a portion of their cost to reflect the usage of assets in earning revenue.

If depreciation were not charged then the profits would be overstated. There is a danger that these profits would be paid out as dividends (or as drawings in the case of a sole trader), thereby depleting the cash balances and the capital employed in the business. When the asset was disposed of, the whole of the decrease in value since purchase would appear as a charge in that period's income statement, thereby distorting the profits.

Cash is paid out when a non-current asset is paid for, not when depreciated. Cash comes in when the asset is disposed of. Accounting for depreciation does not involve any movement of cash and does not provide a means of replacing non-current assets at the end of their lives, unless cash is set aside as a separate transaction.

7.7 Summary

This chapter has shown how:

- a transaction can be traced from a ledger account to a trial balance, and from there to the financial statements – income statement or statement of financial position;
- financial statements are prepared from a trial balance and a list of adjustments, which need to be made to finalise the financial statements.

The whole of this chapter should be regarded as a 'must know' topic you are to be successful in passing the examination. This chapter has brought together much of what has been learnt in Chapters 2–6 inclusive. It is a good point to consolidate your studies before moving on to Chapter 8 and the remaining chapters in this learning system.

Revision Questions

 Question 1 Multiple choice

1.1 The following is an extract from the trial balance of ABC Ltd at 31 December 20X4:

	Debit ($)	Credit ($)
Sales		73,716
Returns	5,863	3,492
Discounts	871	1,267

The figure to be shown in the trading account for net sales is:

(A) $66,586
(B) $66,982
(C) $67,853
(D) $70,224

1.2 A company's working capital was $43,200. Subsequently, the following transactions occurred:

- payables were paid; 3,000 by cheque;
- a bad debt of $250 was written off;
- inventories valued at $100 were sold for $230 on credit.

Working capital is now:
$................

1.3 Working capital will reduce by $500 if:

(A) goods costing $3,000 are sold for $3,500 on credit.
(B) goods costing $3,000 are sold for $3,500 cash.
(C) non-current assets costing $500 are purchased on credit.
(D) non-current assets with a carrying amount of $750 are sold for $250 cash.

1.4 A business has opening inventories of $12,000 and closing inventories of $18,000. Purchase returns were $5,000. The cost of goods sold was $111,000. Purchases were:
$...............

1.5 At the beginning of the year, the balance on the allowance for receivables account was $6,000, representing 4 per cent of receivables. At the end of the year, receivables amounted to $150,000, but it was decided that the allowance should be increased to 5 per cent of receivables. Which of the following is correct?

Account entry	Income statement	Net receivables on statement of financial position	Allowance for receivables account
A	$1,500 credit	$142,500	$7,500 credit
B	$1,500 debit	$148,500	$1,500 debit
C	$1,500 debit	$142,500	$7,500 credit
D	$7,500 debit	$142,500	$13,500 credit

1.6 The following is an extract from the trial balance of a business for its most recent year.

	Debit ($)	Credit ($)
Opening Inventories	28,000	
Sales		310,000
Purchases	225,000	
Returns	22,000	26,000
Carriage inwards	7,000	
Carriage outwards	8,000	

You are also told that closing inventories were $23,000.

Using some or all of the figures above, the correct gross profit is:
$...............

1.7 The following is an extract from the trial balance of a business for its most recent year:

	Debit ($)	Credit ($)
Heat and light	22,000	
Rent and local business tax	27,000	
Non-current assets	80,000	
Acc. depreciation on non-current assets		20,000

Gross profit has already been calculated as being $85,000. Depreciation is to be calculated at 25 per cent on the reducing balance. At the end of the year, heat and light accrued is $4,000, and rent and local business tax prepaid is $2,500.

The correct net profit is:
$...............

Question 2

GBA is a sole trader, supplying building materials to local builders. He prepares his financial statements to 30 June each year. At 30 June 20X5, his trial balance was as follows:

	Debit ($)	Credit ($)
Capital at July 20X4		55,550
Purchases & Sales	324,500	625,000
Returns	2,300	1,700
Discounts	1,500	2,500
Inventory of building materials at 1 July 20X4	98,200	
Packing materials purchased	12,900	
Distribution costs	17,000	
Rent and insurance	5,100	
Telephone	3,200	
Car expenses	2,400	
Wages	71,700	
Allowance for receivables at 1 July 20X4		1,000
Heat and light	1,850	
Sundry expenses	6,700	
Delivery vehicles cost	112,500	
Delivery vehicles acc. depreciation at July 20X4		35,000
Equipment cost	15,000	
Equipment acc. depreciation at July 20X4		5,000
Receivables and payables	95,000	82,000
Loan		10,000
Loan repayments	6,400	
Bank deposit account	15,000	
Bank current account	26,500	
	817,750	817,750

The following additional information at 30 June 20X5 is available:

1. Closing inventories:

	$
Building materials	75,300
Packing materials	700

There was also an unpaid invoice of $200 for packing materials received and consumed during the year.

2. Prepayments:

	$
Rent and insurance	450

3. Accrued expenses:

	$
Heat and light	400
Telephone	500

4. Wages includes $23,800 cash withdrawn by GBA.

5. Receivables have been analysed as follows:

	$
Current month	60,000
30 to 60 days	20,000
60 to 90 days	12,000
Over 90 days	3,000

Allowance to be made for receivables as follows:

30 to 60 days	1%
60 to 90 days	2.5%
Over 90 days	5% (after writing off $600)

6. Sundry expenses includes $3,500 for GBA's personal tax bill.

7. The loan was taken out some years ago, and is due for repayment on 31 March 20X6. The figure shown in the trial balance for loan repayments includes interest of $800 for the year.

8. The bank deposit account was opened on 1 January 20X5 as a short-term investment; interest is credited at 31 December annually; the average rate of interest since opening the account has been 6 per cent per annum.

9. At 1 July 20X4, GBA decided to bring one of his family cars, valued at $8,000, into the business. No entries have been made in the business books for its introduction.

10. Depreciation is to be provided as follows:

   - 20 per cent on cost for delivery vehicles;
   - at 25 per cent on the reducing balance for the car;
   - at 25 per cent on the reducing balance for equipment.

Requirements

(a) Insert the missing items into the income statement for the year ended 30 June 20X5, set out below.

Income statement of GBA for the year ended 30 June 20X5

	$	$	$
Sales			625,000
Less: Returns inwards			...
			...
Cost of sales			
Opening inventories		98,200	
Purchases	324,500		
Less: Returns outwards	...		
		...	
		...	
Less: Closing inventories		...	
			...
Gross profit			...
Add:			
Interestondeposit account			...
Discounts received			...
Decrease in allowance for receivables			...
Less:			
Discounts allowed		...	
Packing materials consumed		...	
Distribution costs		17,000	
Rent and insurance		...	
Telephone		...	
Car expenses		2,400	
Wages		...	
Heat and light		...	
Sundry expenses		...	
Interest on loan		...	
Bad debts written off in year		...	
Depreciation of delivery vehicles		...	
Depreciation of cars		...	
Depreciation of equipment		...	
			...
Profit			...

(b) Insert the missing figures into the statement of financial position set out below.

Statement of financial position of GBA as at 30 June 20X5

Assets	Cost ($)	Acc. Dep'n ($)	Carrying Amount ($)
Non-current assets			
Delivery assets	112,500	...	...
Cars	...	...	...
Equipment	15,000	...	...
	...	...	...
Current assets			
Inventories		...	
Receivables	...		
Less: allowance	...		
		...	
Prepayments		...	
Accrued revenue		...	
Bank Deposit account		15,000	
Bank current account		26,500	
			...
			...
Capital and liabilities			
Capital at July 20X4			55,500
Add: Capital introduced			...
Add: Profit for the year			...
Less: drawings			...
Current liabilities			
Payables		...	
Accruals		...	
Loan		...	
			...
			...

(c) With regard to the transaction in the business of GBA, which of the following transactions affect:

- profit
- cash at bank

	Affects Profit	Affects Cash at Bank
Payments to suppliers		
Depreciation		
Sales invoiced to customers		
Drawings in cash		
Loan repayment		
Bad debts written off		

Question 3

PLJ has been in business for some years and has kept her drawings slightly below the level of profits each year. She has never made a loss, and therefore feels that her business is growing steadily. You act as her accountant, and she has passed you the following list of balances at 30 April 20X7.

	$'000
Capital at 1 May 20X6	228
Drawings	14
Plant at cost	83
Plant – acc. Depreciation at May 20X6	13
Office equipment at cost	31
Office equipment – acc. depreciation at May 20X6	8
Receivables	198
Payables	52
Sales	813
Purchases	516
Returns inwards	47
Discount allowed	4
Allowance for receivables at 1 May 20X6	23
Administration costs	38
Salaries	44
Research costs	26
Loan to a friend, repayable in 6 months	25
Bank	50
Bad debits written off	77

You ascertain that inventories at 1 May 20X6 was $84,000 and inventories at 30 April 20X7 was $74,000. On 1 November 20X6, she brought her personal computer, valued at $2,000, from home into the office; no entries have been made for this.

You are also given the following information at 30 April 20X7:

(i) Depreciation on plant is charged at 10 per cent per annum on cost. Depreciation on office equipment is charged at 20 per cent per annum on the carrying amount at the year end.

(ii) Administration costs include insurance prepaid of $3,000.

(iii) Salaries accrued amount to $2,000.

(iv) The research costs are all in relation to pure research.

(v) It is agreed that the allowance for receivables figure is to remain at $23,000.

Requirements

(a) Insert the missing items into the trial balance at 30 April 20X7, set out below, after adjusting for the computer that PLJ has brought from home, but prior to making any other adjustments.

Trial balance of PLJ as at 30 April 20X7

	Debit ($)		*Credit* ($)
Capital at 1.5.X6	...	or	...
Capital introduced	...	or	...
Drawings	...	or	...
Plant at cost	...	or	...
Plant – Acc. plant depreciation at 1.5.X6	...	or	...
Office equipment at cost or value	...	or	...
Office equipment – acc. depreciation at 1.5.X6	...	or	...
Receivables	...	or	...
Payables	...	or	...
Sales	...	or	...
Purchases	...	or	...
Returns inwards	...	or	...
Discount allowed	...	or	...
Allowance for receivables at 1.5.X6	...	or	...
Administration costs	...	or	...
Salaries	...	or	...
Research costs	...	or	...
Loan to friend	...	or	...
Bank	...	or	...
Bad debts written off	...	or	...
Inventories at [insert date] ...	...	or	...

(b) Insert the missing figures into the income statement set out below.

Note: Expenditure on pure research is to be treated as a revenue expense.

	$'000	$'000
Sales		813
Less: returns inwards		...
		...
Less: cost of goods sold		
Opening inventories	...	
Purchases	516	
	...	
Closing inventories	...	
		...
Gross profit		...
Less: expenses		
Discount allowed	...	
Administration costs	...	
Salaries	...	
Research costs	26	
Bad debts written off	77	
Depreciation of plant	...	
Depreciation of office equipment	...	
		...
Net profit		...

(c) Insert the missing figures into the statement of financial position set out below.

Assets	Cost ($'000)	Acc. Depreciation ($'000)	Carrying amount ($'000)
Non-current assets			
Plant and machinery	83	...	...
Office equipment	...	...	...
	...	...	...
Current assets			
Inventories		...	
Receivables	198		
Less: allowance	...		
		...	
Loan		...	
Prepayments		...	...
			...
			...
Capital and liabilities			
Capital			...
Net profit			...
Less: drawings			(14.0)
			...
Current liabilities			
Payables		52	
Accruals		...	
Bank overdraft		...	
			...
			...

Question 4

The following trial balance was extracted from the ledger of Stella Parkinson at the end of her most recent year.

	$	$
Buildings at cost	240,000	
Plant at cost	160,000	
Accumulated depreciation at start of year		
On buildings		40,000
On plant		76,000
Purchases and sales	500,000	808,800
Inventories at start of year	100,000	
Discounts	36,000	9,600
Returns	4,400	30,000
Wages and salaries	117,600	
Bad debts written off	9,200	
Other expenses	45,600	
Receivables and payables	76,000	72,000
Bank and cash	3,200	
Drawings	48,000	
Allowance for receivables		1,000
Opening capital		302,600
	1,340,000	1,340,000

The following information is also given at the end of the year:

(a) Closing inventories are $84,000.
(b) Wages and salaries accrued amount to $1,600.
(c) Other expenses prepaid amount to $600.
(d) The allowance for receivables is to be adjusted to 2 per cent of receivables.
(e) Depreciation for the year is to be calculated as:
  • 1.5 per cent per annum straight line on buildings;
  • 25 per cent per annum reducing balance on plant.

Requirements

(a) Prepare the income statement for the year by inserting the missing figures below.

Income statement of Stella Parkinson for the year ended . . .

	$	$	$
Sales			▆
Less: returns			▆
Net sales			▆
Less: cost of sales			
Opening inventories		▆	
Purchases	▆		
Less: returns	▆		
		▆	
		▆	
		▆	
Less: closing inventories		▆	
			▆
Gross profit			▆
Add: discounts received			▆
			▆
Less: expenses		▆	
Discounts allowed		▆	
Wages and salaries		▆	
Bad debts written off		▆	
Other expenses		▆	
Allowance for receivables		▆	
Depreciation			
Buildings (1.5% × 240,000)		▆	
Plant (25% × 84,000)		▆	
			▆
Net profit			▆

(b) Prepare the statement of financial position at the end of the year by inserting the missing figures below.

Statement of financial position of Stella Parkinson as at . . .

Assets	Cost ($)	Acc. Depreciation ($)	Carrying amount ($)
Non-current assets			
Buildings			
Plant			
Current assets			
Inventories			
Receivables			
Less: allowance			
Prepayments			
Bank and cash			
Capital and liabilities			
Opening capital			
Net profit for the year			
Less: drawings			
Current liabilities			
Payables			
Accruals			

Solutions to Revision Questions

 Solution 1

1.1 Answer: (C)

Net sales is calculated as follows:

	$
Sales	73,716
Less: returns inwards	(5,863)
Net sales	67,853

Discounts are those arising from prompt payment (i.e. cash discounts) and do not appear in the trading account section of the income statement, but are brought into the income statement after the calculation of gross profit.

1.2 Working capital is not affected by movements between current assets and current liabilities, so the payment of payables by cheque would result in a lower bank balance and lower payables, but would have no effect on working capital. The writing off of a bad debt of $250 would reduce receivables, and hence working capital. The sale of inventories would increase receivables by $230, but only decrease inventories by $100, so working capital would be increased by $130. The net effect of these items on working capital would be to decrease working capital by $120, so the final result would be $43,200 − $120 = $43,080.

1.3 Answer: (C)

(A) and (B) both involved the exchange of an asset (inventories) with another asset of $500 more. This would result in an increase in working capital of $500. (D) would result in an increase in working capital of $250. Only (C) will result in a decrease in working capital, as a non-current asset is acquired by increasing payables.

1.4 Reconstruction of cost of goods sold to establish the purchases figure:

	$	$
Opening inventories		12,000
Add: purchases*	122,000	
Less: returns	(5,000)	
		117,000
Less: Closing inventories		(18,000)
Cost of goods sold		111,000

* Found by difference

1.5 Answer: (C)

The final allowance must be 5 per cent of receivables of $150,000, that is, $7,500. This will provide the balance for the allowance account, to be deducted from the receivables figure. Therefore, receivables are $142,500. Thus, only answers (A) or (C) can be considered. The change in the allowance from $6,000 to $7,500 is an additional charge to the income statement, thus (C) is the correct answer.

1.6 Draw up the following:

	$	$	$
Sales			310,000
Less: returns			(22,000)
Net sales			288,000
Less: cost of sales			
Opening inventories		28,000	
Purchases	225,000		
Carriage inwards	7,000		
	232,000		
Less: returns	(26,000)		
Net purchases		206,000	
		234,000	
Less: closing inventories		(23,000)	
			211,000
Gross profit			77,000

Common errors include:

- reversing returns;
- not adding carriage inwards to the cost of purchases (or deducting it);
- adding carriage outwards to the cost of purchases.

1.7 The income statement would be:

	$	$
Gross profit as calculated		85,000
Less: expenses		
Heat and light (22,000 + 4,000)	26,000	
Rent and local business tax (27,000 − 2,500)	24,500	
Depreciation (25% × 60,000)	15,000	
		(65,500)
Net Profit		19,500

 # Solution 2

- You will find it helpful to set out workings for most of the adjustments. They will help you to derive the correct figures to enter into the boxes provided.
- Remember there is already a balance on the allowance for receivables account.
- Notice that the deposit account has been open for only part of the year, and calculate interest accordingly.
- Make sure you deal correctly with returns and discounts.
- Remember to adjust for the cash taken by the proprietor.
- Divide the loan repayment figure between interest (for the income statement) and the repayment of capital (to be deducted from the opening loan figure), notice also the repayment date of the loan.

(a) Income statement of GBA for year ended 30 June 20X5

	$	$	$
Sales			625,000
Less: Returns inwards			(2,300)
			622,700
Cost of sales			
Opening inventories		98,200	
Purchases	324,500		
Less: Returns outwards	(1,700)		
		322,800	
		421,000	
Less: Closing inventories		(75,300)	
			(345,700)
Gross profit			277,000
Add:			
Interest on deposit account			450
($15,000 × 6% × 6/12)			
Discounts received			2,500
Decrease in allowance for receivables			
($1,000 − $620)			380
			280,330
Less:			
Discounts allowed		1,500	
Packing materials consumed		12,400	
Distribution costs		17,000	
Rent and insurance ($5,100 − $450)		4,650	
Telephone ($3,200 + $500)		3,700	
Car expenses		2,400	
Wages ($71,700 − $23,800)		47,900	
Heat and light ($1,850 + $400)		2,250	
Sundry expenses ($6,700 − $3,500)		3,200	
Interest on loan		800	
Bad debts written off in year		600	
Depreciation of delivery vehicles		22,500	
Depreciation of cars		2,000	
Depreciation of equipment		2,500	
			(123,400)
Profit			156,930

(b) Statement of financial position of GBA as at 30 June 20X5

Assets	Cost ($)	Acc. Depn. ($)	Carrying Amount ($)
Non-current assets			
Delivery vehicles	112,500	(57,500)	55,000
Cars	8,000	(2,000)	6,000
Office equipment	15,000	(7,500)	7,500
	135,500	(67,000)	68,500
Current assets			
Inventories ($75,300 + $700)		76,000	
Receivables	94,400		
Less: allowance	(620)		
		93,780	
Prepayments		450	
Accrued revenue		450	
Bank deposit account		15,000	
Bank current account		26,500	
			212,180
			280,680
Capital and liabilities			
Capital at 1 July 20X4			55,550
Add: capital introduced			8,000
Add: profit for the year			156,930
Less: drawings ($23,800 + $3,500)			(27,300)
			193,180
Current liabilities			
Payables		82,000	
Accruals ($400 + $500 + $200)		1,100	
Loan ($10,000 − $5,600)		4,400	
			87,500
			280,680

(c) With regard to the transactions in the business of GBA, which of the following transactions affect:

- profit
- cash at bank

	Affects profit	*Affects Cash at bank*
Payments to suppliers		√
Depreciation	√	
Sales invoiced to customers	√	
Drawings in cash		√
Loan repayment		√
Bad debts written off		

Solution 3

- Take care to choose the correct side for the items in the trial balance, in particular returns, discounts and allowance for receivables.
- Remember to add in the computer that the proprietor has introduced, and to depreciate it.
- Notice that there is no change in the allowance for receivables, so there is no charge to the income statement, but remember to deduct the balance from receivables on the statement of financial position.

(a) Trial balance of PLJ as at 30 April 20X7

	Debit $'000	*Credit* $'000
Capital at 1.5.X6		228
Capital introduced		2
Drawings	14	
Plant at cost	83	
Plant – acc. depreciation at 1.5.X6		13
Office equipment at cost	33	
Office equipment – acc. depreciation at 1.5.X6		8
Receivables	198	
Payables		52
Sales		813
Purchases	516	
Returns inwards	47	
Discount allowed	4	
Allowance for receivables at 1.5.X6		23
Administration costs	38	
Salaries	44	
Research costs	26	
Loan to friend, repayable in 6 months	25	
Bank		50
Bad debts written off	77	
Inventories at 1.5.X6	84	
	1,189	1,189

(b) Income statement of PLJ for the year ended 30 April 19X7

	$'000	$'000
Sales		813
Less: returns inwards		(47)
		766
Less: cost of goods sold		
Opening inventories	84	
Purchases	516	
	600	
Less: Closing inventories	(74)	
Cost of sales		(526)
Gross profit		240
Less: expenses		
Discount allowed	4	
Administration costs	35	
Salaries	46	
Research costs	26	
Bad debts written off	77	
Depreciation of plant	8.3	
Depreciation of office equipment	5	
		(201.3)
Net profit		38.7

(c) Statement of financial position of PLJ as at 30 April 20X7

Assets	Cost ($'000)	Acc. Depreciation ($'000)	Carrying amount ($'000)
Non-current assets			
Plant	83	(21.3)	61.7
Office equipment	33	(13.0)	20.0
	116	(34.3)	81.7
Current assets			
Inventories		74	
Receivables	198		
Less: allowance	(23)		
		175	
Loan		25	
Prepayment		3	
			277
			358.7
Capital and liabilities			
Capital			230.0
Net profit			38.7
Less: drawings			(14.0)
			254.7
Current liabilities			
Payables		52	
Accruals		2	
Bank overdraft		50	
			104
			358.7

Solution 4

- Tick off each item on the trial balance as you use it.
- Calculate adjustments from the additional information carefully.
- Take care with the allowance for receivables.

(a) Income statement of Stella Parkinson for the year ended . . .

	$	$	$
Sales			808,800
Less: returns			4,400
Net sales			804,400
Less: cost of sales			
Opening inventories		100,000	
Purchases	500,000		
Less: returns	(30,000)		
		470,000	
		570,000	
Less: closing inventories		(84,000)	
			(486,000)
Gross profit			318,400
Add: discounts received			9,600
			328,000
Less: expenses			
Discounts allowed		36,000	
Wages and salaries (117,600 + 1,600)		119,200	
Bad debts written off		9,200	
Other expenses (45,600 − 600)		45,000	
Allowance for receivables (2% × 76,000)-		520	
1,000 already provided			
Depreciation			
Buildings (1.5% × 240,000)		3,600	
Plant (25% × 84,000)		21,000	
			234,520
Net profit			93,480

(b) Statement of financial position of Stella Parkinson as at . . .

Assets	Cost ($)	Acc. Depreciation ($)	Carrying Amount ($)
Non-current assets			
Buildings	240,000	(43,600)	196,400
Plant	160,000	(97,000)	63,000
	400,000	(140,600)	259,400
Current assets			
Inventories		84,000	
Receivables	76,000		
Less: allowance	(1,520)		
		74,480	
Prepayments		600	
Bank and cash		3,200	
			162,280
			421,680
Capital and liabilities			
Opening capital			302,600
Net profit for the year			93,480
			396,080
Less: drawings			(48,000)
			348,080
Current liabilities			
Payables		72,000	
Accruals		1,600	
			73,600
			421,680

8

Organising the
Bookkeeping System

Organising the Bookkeeping System

8

LEARNING OUTCOMES

When you have completed this chapter, you should be able to:

- explain the purpose of accounting records and their role in the accounting system;
- prepare accounts for sales and purchases, including personal accounts;
- prepare cash and bank accounts;
- prepare petty cash statements under an imprest system;
- prepare nominal ledger accounts;
- prepare journal entries;
- prepare accounts for indirect taxes (e.g. sales tax);
- explain, calculate and prepare accounts for inventories.

8.1 Introduction

So far, the bookkeeping exercises you have seen and tried for yourself have involved only a small number of transactions, and you have therefore been able to keep all your ledger accounts in one place (even on one page!), with no difficulty in locating a particular ledger account or transaction if you wanted to check it again. Furthermore, producing a trial balance from a small number of ledger accounts is fairly quick, and any errors can easily be located by tracing through the entries again.

In this chapter we look at ways of organising the bookkeeping system for organisations with a larger number of transactions, where the ledger accounts may be too numerous to keep in one place, and where the number of transactions is too great for one person to handle. We also look at some of the supporting books and systems that help to maintain accuracy, security and control over the accounting records. A final section in this chapter deals with the inventories records and the cost of inventories.

8.2 Organising the ledger accounts

In larger organisations, a single ledger may not be sufficient to hold all the ledger accounts, there may be too many transactions for one person to maintain, and it might become difficult to trace individual accounts. It is common for the ledger accounts to be divided into sections, known as 'divisions of the ledger'. Double entry is still maintained as before, but ledger accounts of the same type are grouped together.

A common division of the ledger is as follows:

- all receivable accounts kept in the *sales ledger* (also known as the *receivables ledger*);
- all payable accounts kept in the *purchase ledger* (also known as the *payables ledger* or *bought ledger*);
- all bank and cash accounts kept in a *cash book* with perhaps a separate *petty cash book* as well;
- all others accounts kept in the *nominal ledger* (also known as the *general ledger*).

Other divisions are possible, if the organisation has additional requirements.

Do note that the sales and purchase ledgers are for personal accounts. They do not contain the sales and purchases accounts – these are found in the nominal ledger.

8.2.1 Advantages of dividing the ledger

The advantages of dividing the ledger are the following:

- individual ledger accounts can be located more easily;
- the workload can be shared among several members of the staff;
- by having one person entering one 'half' of a transaction (e.g. crediting the sales account), and another person entering the other 'half' of the transaction (e.g. debiting the receivables account), it is possible to reduce the chance of errors and fraud;
- staff who maintain one of the divisions, for example the sales ledger, can become experts in that area;
- additional controls can be built into the bookkeeping system to check accuracy.

We shall look at this last advantage in more detail in Chapter 9.

8.3 Supporting books and records

With a larger number of transactions, more errors are likely to occur, and with the ledger now divided into sections, with different people maintaining them, it is possible that there may be delays in keeping the accounts up to date, or that transactions may be omitted.

It is possible to maintain other books, records, lists and so on, that, although not part of the ledger, help in recording and controlling the transactions in the ledger. These books are known by various names:

- *daybooks* (because they are intended to be written up on a daily basis);
- *journals* (another word for 'diary' which also means 'a daily record');
- *books of prime entry* ('prime' means 'first') – and the transactions are 'captured' here first, before being entered in the ledger accounts.

These books are part of 'the classification of monetary transactions' that we mentioned in Chapter 1. We begin by classifying accounting transactions in a number of categories – sales to credit customers, purchases from suppliers, receipts of cash, payments of cash and so on. We keep a separate record for each of these categories, and we log each transaction as it arises in the appropriate record.

Most businesses of any size maintain records of their transactions in the following books of prime entry:

- *sales daybook* records goods sold to credit customers;
- *purchases daybook* records goods purchased on credit from suppliers (e.g. finished goods for resale in the case of a retail business; or raw materials for use in a manufacturing business). Traditionally, the purchases daybook was used only for such purchases, as businesses had few other types of purchase on credit – nowadays businesses have a much wider variety of expenses, and thus the purchases daybook is often used for all credit purchases and expenses. In practice, this usually means all purchases and expenses, as few businesses buy things for immediate payment;
- *returns inwards daybook* (or *sales returns daybook*) records goods returned by customers, perhaps because they were defective;
- *returns outwards daybook* (or *purchases returns daybook*) records goods returned to suppliers;
- *cash book* records payments made from the business bank account, and receipts of money into the business bank account;
- *petty cash book* records small payments made in cash (i.e. notes and coins);
- *journal* records 'unusual' items, not falling into any of the categories above. The journal is also used for rectifying errors in the accounting entries.

Notice that the cash book and petty cash book are also mentioned as 'divisions of the ledger' in Section 8.1. This is because these books fulfil a dual role. They are 'of prime entry' because it is important that cash and bank accounts are kept as up to date as possible, so we want no delays in capturing such transactions, and they are also ledger accounts because they record the movements in cash and bank.

8.3.1 Source documents

Every transaction should be evidenced by a document showing the details of the transaction. These are known as 'source documents'. There are different kinds for different types of transaction. Some originate outside the organisation (such as invoices received from suppliers), some originate inside the organisation but are sent to outsiders (such as invoices sent to customers), and others originate inside and remain inside the organisation (such as details of accruals at the end of the period).

We shall look at the cash books and the journal later in this chapter. First, we shall look at the first four daybooks described above – those that deal with credit sales and purchases.

8.4 Sales, purchases and returns daybooks

The source document for sales and purchases is known as an invoice; for returns, the source document is a credit note. A typical invoice (or credit note) will contain the following details:

- invoice (credit note) number and date;
- name and address of the supplier;

- name and address of the customer;
- quantity and description of the goods supplied;
- the price per unit for the goods, with details of any trade discount given;
- the total price charged for the goods, excluding sales tax;
- the amount of sales tax;
- the total payable, before any cash discounts;
- the amount and terms of cash discount available;
- the due date for payment.

You should note that the content of the invoice is the same for both purchases and sales. When the business sells goods to a customer, it prepares a sales invoice requesting payment; when the business purchases goods from a supplier it receives a purchase invoice from that supplier.

Credit notes should show the same information as an invoice.

8.4.1 Recording transactions in the daybooks

The four types of transaction identified earlier in this chapter are each recorded in their own specialist daybook.

Each of the books can be thought of as a listing device. They each contain columns to record the facts of the transaction. At regular intervals, they are totalled as part of the summarising process.

Such a daybook will have the following headings:

Date	Doc. No.	Personal details	Goods value ($)	Sales tax ($)	Total invoice/credit note value ($)

The personal details would be the name of the supplier or customer as appropriate.

The use of daybooks will enable the recording of such transactions to be delegated to junior staff who may not even be considered to be part of the accounts department. This will reduce the burden of work placed on the accounts department of the organisation.

Example 8.A

ABC Ltd had the following transactions during the first week of July 20X2:

1 Jul.	Bought goods on credit from JB cost $1000
	Sold goods on credit to JSA & Co. for $800
2 Jul.	Sold goods on credit to PB Ltd for $80
	Returned goods to JB because they were faulty $80
3 Jul.	Bought goods from AL Ltd cost $600
4 Jul.	JSA & Co. returned unwanted goods $200
5 Jul.	Returned goods to AL Ltd $120
6 Jul.	Sold goods to CAL for $400
7 Jul.	CAL returned goods as unsuitable $120
	Sold goods to BC for $240

All items are subject to sales tax at 17.5 per cent.

Purchases daybook

Date	Doc. no.	Personal details	Goods value ($)	Sales tax ($)	Total invoice/credit note value ($)
1 Jul.	001	JB	1,000	175	1,175
3 Jul.	002	AL Ltd	600	105	705
			1,600	280	1,880

Sales daybook

Date	Doc. no.	Personal details	Goods value ($)	Sales tax ($)	Total invoice/credit note value ($)
1 Jul.	101	JSA & Co.	800	140	940
2 Jul.	102	PB Ltd	80	14	94
6 Jul.	103	CAL	400	70	470
7 Jul.	104	BC	240	42	282
			1,520	266	1,786

Returns inwards daybook

Date	Doc. no.	Personal details	Goods value ($)	Sales tax ($)	Total invoice/credit note value ($)
4 Jul.	901	JSA & Co.	200	35	235
7 Jul.	902	CAL	120	21	141
			320	56	376

Returns outwards daybook

Date	Doc. no.	Personal details	Goods value ($)	Sales tax ($)	Total invoice/credit note value ($)
2 Jul.	9001	JB	80	14	94
5 Jul.	9002	AL Ltd	120	21	141
			200	35	235

Remember that if there was trade discount given on any of the above transactions, it would be deducted prior to calculating the sales tax, and the net amount would be recorded in the 'goods value' column.

8.4.2 Making the ledger entries

It is important that the ledger accounts of receivables and payables are kept up to date, otherwise the organisation could make incorrect decisions, such as allowing a customer to have further goods when he has not yet paid for the previous delivery, or not knowing that a payables account has been reduced by a credit note. Therefore, the ledger entries are made at once to the receivables and payables accounts, probably by passing over the invoices and credit notes to the relevant ledger clerk. Remember that it is the total of the invoice or credit note that is entered in the personal accounts.

The entries to the sales, purchases, returns and sales tax accounts are not so urgent. They will probably only be required to be up to date on a monthly basis. In addition, as the daybooks contain a complete list of all sales, purchases and returns (and the sales tax thereon), there is no need to repeat all this in those ledger accounts. Thus, the daybooks can be totalled (and cross-checked for accuracy), and the totals entered in the nominal ledger accounts periodically.

Cross-referencing the entries

To enable the source of the ledger entries to be traced, a system of cross-referencing can be used. Each page in the daybooks is given a reference – for example, sales daybook page 23 (abbreviated to SD23) – and each page in the ledger accounts is given a reference, for example, SLC3 might indicate the sales ledger, Section C, p. 3, where CAL's (a customer) ledger account can be found. Extra columns can be added to the daybooks and ledger accounts to show these cross-references. These columns are called 'folio columns'. Thus the ledger entries for all of the above items can be shown as follows:

Sales Ledger

BC (B22)

		$			
4 Jul.	104	282			

CAL (C14)

		$			$
6 Jul.	103	470	7 Jul.	902	141

JSA & Co. (J4)

		$			$
1 Jul.	101	940	4 Jul.	901	235

PB Ltd (P35)

		$			
2 Jul.	102	94			

Purchase Ledger

AL Ltd (A42)

		$			$
5 Jul.	9002	141	3 Jul.	002	705

		JB (J7)			
		$			$
2 Jul.	9001	94	1 Jul.	001	1,175

Nominal Ledger

Purchases (01)

		$			
7 Jul.	PDB97	1,600			

Sales (02)

					$
			7 Jul.	SDB118	1,520

Returns outwards (03)

		$			
7 Jul.	RIDB28	320			

Sales tax (99)

		$			$
7 Jul.	PDB97	280	7 Jul.	SDB118	266
	RIDB28	56		RODB25	35

The double entry is now complete.

 Exercise 8.1

Describe briefly the purpose, contents and use of the sales daybook.

 Solution

The purpose of the sales daybook is to list all the normal sales of the organisation made on credit prior to recording the transactions in the ledger accounts. The sales daybook is a book of original or prime entry. The book can be totalled periodically, say monthly, and the totals can be used to credit the sales and sales tax accounts instead of crediting them with each sale as it is made.

The book normally contains the invoice number and date, the total of the goods or services, the sales tax thereon and the total invoice value. Sometimes trade discount is also recorded. If the organisation uses a customer numbering system, this will be listed and/or the name of the customer. Some organisations also break down the invoice into the various goods and services sold.

The sales daybook can be used to credit the sales and sales tax accounts in total, to provide a complete list of sales on credit, and to provide a means of preventing and locating errors.

Exercise 8.2

List as many books of prime entry as you can.

Solution

Books of prime entry include:

- sales daybook;
- sales returns daybook;
- purchase daybook;
- purchase returns daybook;
- journal;
- cash book;
- petty cash book.

Exercise 8.3

Enter the following transactions for the month of March in the appropriate daybooks and ledgers of PQR, an office equipment retailer.

March

1	Sold four typewriters to Office Services, list price $80 each, allowing 10% trade discount
4	Bought six calculators from Abdul & Co. at $12 each net
12	Sold duplicating machine to J. Hoy for $350
16	Sold four calculators to Chow, list price $20 each, allowing 10% trade discount
17	Office Services returned one damaged typewriter
20	Bought six typewriters from Ace Co., list price $40 each. Allowed 15% trade discount
25	Sold two duplicating machines to Mills & Co., list price $350, allowing 10% trade discount

All items carry sales tax at 17.5 per cent.

Solution

Sales daybook

Date	Doc. no.	Personal details	Goods value ($)	Sales tax ($)	Total invoice/credit note value ($)
1 Mar.	001	Office Services	288.00	50.40	338.40
12 Mar.	002	J. Hoy	350.00	61.25	411.25
16 Mar.	003	Chow	72.00	12.60	84.60
25 Mar.	004	Mills & Co	630.00	110.25	740.25
			1,340.00	234.50	1,574.50

Purchases daybook

Date	Doc. no.	Personal details	Goods value ($)	Sales tax ($)	Total invoice/credit note value ($)
4 Mar.	101	Abdul & Co.	72.00	12.60	84.60
20 Mar.	102	Ace Co.	204.00	35.70	239.70
			276.00	48.30	324.30

Sales returns daybook

Date	Doc. no.	Personal details	Goods value ($)	Sales tax ($)	Total invoice/credit note value ($)
17 Mar.	999	Office Services	72.00	12.60	84.60
			72.00	12.60	84.60

Sales Ledger

Office Services

		$			$
1 Mar.	001	338.40	17 Mar.	999	84.60

J Hoy

		$
12 Mar.	002	411.25

Chow

		$
16 Mar.	003	84.60

Mills & Co.

		$
25 Mar.	004	740.25

Purchase Ledger

Abdul & Co.

			$
	4 Mar.	101	84.60

Ace Co.

			$
	20 Mar.	102	239.70

Nominal Ledger

Sales

			$
	31 Mar.	Sales daybook	1,340.00

Purchases

		$			
31 Mar.	Purchases daybook	276.00			

Sales returns

		$			
31 Mar.	Sales returns daybook	72.00			

Sales tax

		$			$
31 Mar.	Purchases daybook	48.30	31 Mar.	Sales daybook	234.50
	Sales returns daybook	12.60			

8.4.3 Extending the use of daybooks

The examples above assumed that only sales of the organisation's products, and purchases of its goods for sale or raw materials, were entered in the daybooks. This used to be the case when most of an organisation's transactions were in goods for sale. Nowadays, organisations have a wide range of expenses and services too, and the daybooks can be extended to cater for these also. As an example, consider a purchase daybook that is used to record all the organisation's purchases on credit as follows:

Date	Doc. no.	Details	Purchases ($)	Stationery ($)	Heat and light ($)	Motor expenses ($)	Sales tax ($)	Total ($)
1 Jan.	001	ABC Ltd	1,000				175	1,175
2 Jan.	002	XYZ		400			70	470
3 Jan.	003	PQ Ltd	2,000				350	2,350
4 Jan.	004	GL Motors				120	21	141
	005	ABC Ltd	4,000				700	4,700
5 Jan.	006	XYZ		200			35	235
	007	Genlec			600		105	705
6 Jan.	008	RS Motors				240	42	282
7 Jan.	009	Goodgas			400		70	470
		Totals	7,000	600	1,000	360	1,568	10,528

The credit entries to the payables accounts would be made immediately, but the nominal ledger entries to purchases, stationery, heat and light, motor expenses and sales tax would be made in total at the end of the period.

8.5   The cash books

Again, the term 'cash book' dates back to the days when organisations dealt only in actual cash transactions. Nowadays businesses rarely deal in cash, and so the term 'cash book' refers to any book that records monies received and paid.

It was stated earlier that the cash books have a dual purpose, both as books of prime entry and as part of the ledger. As part of the ledger, they are used to maintain the bank and cash ledger accounts, but because of the importance of keeping bank and cash records up to date they are the first place of entry for *all* bank and cash transactions.

8.5.1   The banking system

Today's banking system is highly automated, with large numbers of transactions being conducted electronically. However, many organisations still use cheques to make payments, and paying-in slips to make deposits to their accounts. Some common methods of transacting business through a bank account are as follows:

- *By cheque.* The *drawer* makes out a cheque to the person being paid (the *payee*). The cheque is entered in the drawer's ledger accounts at once, and sent to the payee. The payee pays it into his own bank account some days later, using a paying-in slip to record its details and that of other cheques paid in at the same time. The bank *clearing system* passes it to the drawer's bank for approval and payment, with the result that it is taken out of the drawer's bank account. This is known as *presenting a cheque* for payment.

Until the cheque is accepted by the drawer's bank, it is considered to be *uncleared* and the bank has the right to return it as *dishonoured* if there is something amiss with it, or there are insufficient funds in the drawer's account. The time delay between making out a cheque and it being cleared depends on various factors, such as postal delays, administrative delays, holiday periods and so on. Each cheque has a reference number by which it can be identified.

- *By bankers automated clearing system* (BACS). This avoids the use of the postal system and the writing of numerous cheques by creating a transfer between the bank accounts of different organisations. It is a faster means of payment and it is also more cost-effective when there are regular payments to the same people. The account holder produces a list of the payments to be made at any particular time. There are also specialised types of automated payments suitable for the immediate transfer of funds both within the country and outside the country.
- *By direct debit or standing order.* These work in a similar manner to each other, and are suitable for regular payments to a particular person. The bank makes the transfer automatically.
- *By bank-initiated transactions.* The transactions such as the charging of fees for maintaining the account (bank charges), interest paid on overdrawn balances, interest received, charges for dealing with dishonoured cheques and so on.

An organisation may both make and receive payments by any of these methods.

Tight control of cash and bank balances is vital, and it is important to take account of the fact that some methods of transaction involve delays, and organisations may not be aware of, or may forget, automated transactions.

8.5.2 The cash book

At its simplest, the cash book is no more than an ordinary ledger account, used to record the movements in the bank account. Some organisations use it to record cash movements as well as bank movements, by using two 'money' columns on each side as follows:

Date	Details	Ref.	Bank ($)	Cash ($)	Date	Details	Ref.	Bank ($)	Cash ($)
1 Jan.	Balance b/fwd		400	50	3 Jan.	ABC Ltd	000123	100	
4 Jan.	XYZ Ltd	101	200		5 Jan.	Wages			20
8 Jan.	Cash sales			120	7 Jan.	Office equipment	000124	300	
10 Jan.	PQR Ltd	102	150		8 Jan.	Advertising	000125	125	
	RST Ltd	102	170		12 Jan.	Wages			30
14 Jan.	Cash banked	103	50		14 Jan.	Cash banked			50
					14 Jan.	Balance c/d		445	70
			970	170				970	170
15 Jan.	Balance b/d		445	70					

Discount columns

The cash book can also be used to indicate cash discount that has been given or received. We looked at the recording of cash discount in Chapter 5. We saw how, when cash discount is received or given, the amount is credited/debited to discounts received/discounts allowed account. Cash discount often involves a large number of small-value transactions, so it is possible that the nominal ledger (which contains the discount accounts), would soon fill up with the detail of a large number of small-value transactions. By adding an extra column to each side of the cash book, the discount can be identified at the point of payment (which is when it becomes known), and the total of those columns used to make the entries in the discount accounts.

Example 8.B

Zadie Traders Ltd had a favourable balance of $216 in its business bank account as at the start of business on 2 May 20X8. The following is a list of bank transactions for the week ending 7 May 20X8:

2 May	Paid an insurance premium of $130 by cheque
3 May	Paid an invoice for $110 from Goodies Ltd in full after deducting 10% for prompt settlement
4 May	Received a cheque for $314 from Freda Dexter, a credit customer. Ms Dexter was settling an invoice for $320 and had been entitled to $6 discount
6 May	Paid employees their week's wages of $182 by cheque

You are required to record these transactions in the cash book of Zadie Traders Ltd below.

Solution

Date	Details	Bank ($)	Disc. all'd ($)	Total ($)	Date	Details	Bank ($)	Disc. all'd ($)	Total ($)
1 May	Balance b/f	216			2 May	Insurance	130		130
4 May	Dexter	314	6	320	3 May	Goodies	99	11	110
					6 May	Wages	182		182
						Balance c/f	119		
		530	6	320			530	11	422
7 May	Balance b/f	119							

For the transaction on 3 May, Goodies will be debited with $110, and for the transaction on 4 May, Dexter will be credited with $320, whereas the bank account has only been debited/credited with the amount received/paid. The discount accounts have yet to have their entries made, and this can be done at the end of the period by totalling the discount columns and debiting discount allowed with $6, and crediting discount received with $11.

Analysed cash books

It is common for cash books to have a number of columns, called *analysis columns*, in which receipts and payments of a similar nature may be collected together and eventually totalled. An example is given below.

ORGANISING THE BOOKKEEPING SYSTEM

Date	Details	Rec. from Receivables	Other income	Total rec'd	Date	Details	Paid to Payables	Petty cash	Wages	Sales tax	Sundry	Total

As well as entering the amount of each payment and receipt in the total columns, the amount would also be entered in one or other of the analysis columns. This means that when the book is totalled, at regular intervals, it will be immediately apparent how much cash has been received from receivables, how much paid to payables, how much paid in wages and so on. The totals can be used to make ledger entries, but can also be used in the control process covered in Chapter 9.

Exercise 8.4

N Ramrod keeps cash and bank records. At the close of business on 29 May 20X1 he reached the bottom of a page and carried forward the following:

	Discount ($)	Cash ($)	Bank ($)	
Total b/f	27.40	114.10	214.30	Debit side
Total b/f	40.10	74.50	210.00	Credit side

The following sums were received on 30 May 20X1:
Cheque from J Cuthbertson for $120 in settlement of an account for $125
Cash from N green $40
Cheque from Xu for $75 in settlement of an account for $76.50
The following payments were made on 30 May 20X1:
Cheque to Morris Brown for $140.40
Cheque to local council in payment of local business tax for the half-year $150.40
N Ramrod cashed a cheque for private drawings and took $50 from the office cash for the same purpose.
Write up N Ramrod's cash and bank records and balance them at close of business on 30 May 20X1.

Solution

Date	Details ($)	Disc. all'd ($)	Cash ($)	Bank ($)	Date	Details	Disc. all'd ($)	Cash ($)	Bank ($)
29 May	Balance b/f	27.40	114.10	214.30	29 May	Balance b/f	40.10	74.50	210.00
30 May	J Cuthbertson	5.00		120.00	30 May	Morris Brown			140.40
	N Green		40.00			Rates			150.40
	Xu	1.50		75.00		Drawings		50.00	50.00
	Balance c/f			141.50		Balance c/f		29.60	
		33.90	154.10	550.80			40.10	154.10	550.80

Authorising bank payments

All payments out of the bank account should be authorised by a senior member of staff. Two signatories may be required for amounts of more than a certain, fixed figure.

All items to be paid should be evidenced by source documents, for example, invoices, that have been approved for payment.

8.5.3   The petty cash book

The petty cash book is similar in many ways to the cash books described earlier in this chapter except that it is intended to be used for small payments made in cash.

It usually operates on an *imprest* system whereby an agreed balance of cash is held by an individual nominated as the petty cashier. This person can often be a junior member of staff due to the fact that he or she is responsible only for small sums of money that are tightly controlled. Small payments of cash and reimbursements of expenses to employees are then made via the petty cash system and at the end of each week (or other agreed period) the amount paid out of petty cash is reimbursed from the main cash book to restore the imprest (balance) to its agreed level. The amount to be reimbursed is evidenced by *petty cash vouchers* raised by the petty cashier, and signed by the person receiving the cash, as evidence of receipt. The cash itself can be counted and compared to the balance in the petty cash book.

The petty cash book would not normally receive income other than from the main cashier, although such a possibility does exist, and so its design concentrates on the analysis of expenditure by using a columnar approach as illustrated by the example below. At the end of each accounting period the columns are totalled. The balance on the petty cash account is carried forward to the next accounting period.

Example 8.C

Beechfield Ltd make use of a petty cash book as part of their bookkeeping system. The following is a summary of the petty cash transactions for the month of November 20X9.

		$
1 Nov.	Opening petty cash book float received from cashier	350
2 Nov.	Cleaning materials	5
3 Nov.	Postage stamps	10
6 Nov.	Envelopes	12
8 Nov.	Taxi fare	32
10 Nov.	Petrol for company car	17
14 Nov.	Typing paper	25
15 Nov.	Cleaning materials	4
16 Nov.	Bus fare	2
20 Nov.	Visitors' lunches	56
21 Nov.	Mops and brushes for cleaning	41
23 Nov.	Postage stamps	35
27 Nov.	Envelopes	12
29 Nov.	Visitors' lunches	30
30 Nov.	Photocopying paper	40

You are required to draw up a petty cash book for the month using analysis columns for stationery, cleaning, entertainment, travelling and postages. Show clearly the receipt of the amount necessary to restore the float and the balance brought forward for the start of the following month.

Solution

Debit ($)	Date	Details	Total ($)	Stat'y ($)	Cleaning ($)	Ent'ment ($)	Travel ($)	Post ($)
350	1 Nov.	Cashier						
	2 Nov.	Materials	5		5			
	3 Nov.	Stamps	10					10
	6 Nov.	Envelopes	12	12				
	8 Nov.	Taxi	32				32	
	10 Nov.	Petrol	17				17	
	14 Nov.	Paper	25	25				
	15 Nov.	Materials	4		4			
	16 Nov.	Bus fare	2				2	
	20 Nov.	Lunches	56			56		
	21 Nov.	Mops, etc.	41		41			
	23 Nov.	Stamps	35					35
	27 Nov.	Envelopes	12	12				
	29 Nov.	Lunches	30			30		
	30 Nov.	Paper	40	40				
321	30 Nov.	Cashier	321					
	30 Nov.	Balance c/d	350					
671			671	89	50	86	51	45

The totals of the various expense columns are then debited to those accounts in the nominal ledger.

 Exercise 8.5

Explain briefly the operation of the imprest system of controlling petty cash.

 Solution

The imprest system of controlling petty cash is based on a set 'float' of cash that the petty cashier commences with. This amount is used to pay for small items during the coming week or month, for which a petty cash voucher should be prepared. At the end of the period (or when the cash runs out), the vouchers can be totalled and the amount spent is reimbursed to the petty cashier so as to commence the next period with the same 'float'.

8.6   The journal

In a bookkeeping system involving the use of books of prime entry, it is inevitable that there will be transactions that do not correspond with the main books of prime entry used, that is, the daybooks and cash books. In order to complete the system, another book is needed in which to capture sundry items prior to entering them in the ledger. This book is called 'the journal' and is used for a wide variety of transactions, such as:

• the purchase and sale of non-current assets on credit;
• depreciation;

- the write-off of bad debts;
- allowances for receivables;
- accruals and prepayments;
- transfers between accounts, such as the transfers to income statement at year end;
- the correction of errors;
- opening entries when a new business is formed;
- entries when another business in acquired;

The correction of errors will be considered in the next chapter.

The journal is used to record any transaction that does not fit into any of the other books of prime entry, that is, transactions that are not sales or purchases on credit, and transactions not involving cash.

The journal has debit and credit columns. However, these are not part of the double-entry system. They are merely a memorandum of what is going to be recorded in the ledger accounts for a particular transaction or adjustment. It is also common for journal entries to be authorised by a senior accountant. In the narrative to a journal entry it is possible to add more information about the transaction, and to cross reference to other documentation.

It is common for a computer-based assessment question to ask for the journal entries for a transaction.

This is sometimes used as an alternative to asking for the ledger entries. You must, therefore, know how to layout a journal and record the debits and credits of a transaction.

8.6.1 The layout of the journal

The basic layout is as follows:

Date	Account name/details	Debit ($)	Credit ($)	Explanation

8.6.2 Using the journal for miscellaneous transactions

The following transactions are to be entered in the journal:

1 May Purchased plant on credit from J Smith for $1,000 plus sales tax at 17.5%

3 May Wrote off the following bad debts

P Taylor	$500
M Morris	$300
Y Bhatti	$100

4 May Sold office machinery for $800 to A Bell on credit. The machinery had cost $1,000 and had been depreciated by $400

✓ Solution

Date	Account name/details	Debit ($)	Credit ($)	Explanation
1 May	Plant	1,000		Purchase of plant on credit, see invoice No. X123
	Sales tax	175		
	J Smith		1,175	
3 May	Bad debts written off	900		Bad debts – see bad debt file reference May 003
	Taylor		500	
	Morris		300	
	Bhatti		100	
4 May	Office machinery at cost		1,000	Office machinery sold on credit, see invoice No. Y345
	Office machinery accum. depreciation	400		
	A Bell	800		
	Disposals account		200	Profit on disposal

8.6.3 Using the journal for end-of-year transactions

The following year end adjustments are to be made to the accounts:

		$	
1.	Depreciation of fixtures	500	
2.	Electricity accrued	150	
3.	Allowance for receivables	240	
4.	Transfer of balances		
	(a) sales	12,000	
	(b) opening inventories	1,500	
	(c) purchases	8,000	
	(d) closing inventories	1,200	
	(e) heat and light	700	(excluding the adjustment above)
	(f) wages	4,300	

The journal entries would be as follows:

Date	Account name/details	Debit ($)	Credit ($)	Explanation
(1)	Income statement	500		
	Accumulated Depreciation		500	
(2)	Income statement	150		
	Heat and light account		150	
(3)	Income statement	240		
	Allowance for Receivables		240	
(4)	Sales account	12,000		
	Trading account		12,000	
	Trading account	1,500		Balances transferred at year end.
	Inventories account		1,500	
	Trading account	8,000		
	Purchases account		8,000	
	Inventories account	1,200		
	Trading account		1,200	
	Income statement	700		
	Heat and light		700	
	Income statement	4,300		
	Wages account		4,300	

Authorisation of journal entries

Because journal entries involving adjustments and transfer have no source documents to support them, it is vital that all such entries are authorised by a senior member of staff. This can be done by signing the journal entries, or by referencing them to other forms of authorisation, for example, letters, minutes and so on.

8.7 Inventory records and methods of inventory measurement

The measurement of inventories is important because, as we have already learned, it is part of the overall value of an organisation shown in the statement of financial position. From your work in preparing an income statement it should already be clear that the value placed on inventories affects the amount of profit or loss made by an organisation during a period of time.

This ability to alter the profit of an organisation by changing its inventories measurement explains the need to regulate the methods to be used when valuing inventories.

Inventories should be valued at the lower of cost and net realisable value (NRV).

- Cost is the total cost incurred in bringing the product to its present location and condition. For bought-in items this will be the cost of the items themselves plus the costs of carriage associated with obtaining them.
- NRV is the selling price of the item less any costs to be incurred in making the item suitable for sale. These might include packaging and costs of delivering the items to customers.

For example, if some items have been bought at a cost of $5 each but, owing to market conditions, they can be sold for just $6 each and the cost of packaging and delivering them to customers is $1.50 each, it can be seen that

Cost	$5.00
Net realisable value	$4.50

In other words, when the items are eventually sold for $6 each there will be a loss of $0.50 per item.

	$	$
Selling price		6.00
Less: Purchase cost	5.00	
Packaging/delivery cost	1.50	
		(6.50)
Loss		(0.50)

By valuing the inventories at their net realisable value of $4.50 we are recognising the foreseeable loss of $0.50 per item.

The fall in value should be recognised as soon as it is known about. Suppose that we bought 100 of the above items, and sold 60 in the first month, with the remainder being carried forward to the next month. The calculation of the loss in the first month would be as follows:

	$	$
Sales (60 × $6.00)		360
Less: cost of sales		
Purchases (100 × $5.00)	500	
Packaging costs (60 × $1.50)	90	
	590	
Less: closing inventory (40 × $4.50)	(180)	(410)
Loss		(50)

The whole of the loss is accounted for in the first month, not just the loss on those sold. In the second month, assuming the remaining items were all sold, the calculation would be as follows:

	$	$
Sales (40 × $6.00)		240.00
Less: cost of sales		
Opening inventories (as above)	180.00	
Packaging costs (40 × $1.50)	(60.00)	
		(240.00)
Profit/(Loss)		–

This treatment is an example of applying the convention of 'prudence', which is explained more fully in Chapter 10.

8.7.1 The process of inventories measurement

The value of inventories are obtained at a particular point in time – there are two ways to achieve this: either physically measure the quantity of inventories held at that time and then value it, or record the movement of inventories on a regular basis and verify such records randomly over a period of time. These inventories records are then used as the basis of the measurement.

Physical inventories count

The physical measurement of the quantity of inventories held at a particular time is known as a physical inventories count. It is not always possible to count inventories at the time required and in these circumstances cut-off procedures are applied to adjust the quantity actually measured to that which would have been measured had the inventories been measured at the appropriate time.

Example 8.D

On 3 June, a physical inventories count was carried out that revealed that XYZ Ltd held 405 units of inventory. According to the company's records they had received a delivery of 250 units on 2 June and had sold 110 units since 31 May.

Solution

The inventories that existed on 31 May were therefore:

	Units
Quantity as per physical inventories count	405
Add: units sold/used before physical inventories count	110
	515
Less: units received before the physical inventories count	(250)
Theoretical inventories on 31 May	265

The cost measurement of these items is then obtained by multiplying the quantity by the cost price per unit.

This technique is most common in small organisations. Larger organisations keep records of the movement of inventories using *bin cards* or *stores ledger cards*, but even so they should physically check their inventories from time to time and compare it with the inventory recorded on the bin or stores ledger card, and make any necessary investigations and/or adjustments.

A bin card is a document, traditionally made of cardboard, on which is manually recorded the movement of inventory. It is called a bin card because in storekeeping terminology a 'bin' is the location of an item in the stores. This record is usually kept with the items in the stores so that any movement of the inventory is recorded as it occurs.

The stores ledger card is similar except that in addition to recording quantities, cost values are also recorded so that the value of inventories can be seen at any time.

Each item of inventory has its own inventory reference code and bin card/stores ledger card.

8.7.2 Application of methods of inventory measurement (also known as cost formulas)

Consider the following information regarding the movements of inventories during March:

1 Mar.	Opening inventories Nil
2 Mar.	Bought 10 units @ $3 each
4 Mar.	Sold 5 units @ $8 each
7 Mar.	Bought 20 units @ $4 each
10 Mar.	Sold 15 units @ $8 each
13 Mar.	Bought 20 units @ $5 each
17 Mar.	Sold 5 units @ $8 each

Using these figures we can calculate that the inventories remaining after these transactions had occurred was 25 units. The difficulty is in measuring those units. Are the remaining inventories made up of items bought recently, or is it made up of items bought earlier? Or is a mixture of the two? How do we know?

Well, in practice, we do not know. It is up to the storekeeper to exercise good management of inventories, but it is up to the accountant to determine the cost of those inventories.

Three cost formulas (or methods) are commonly used in financial accounting. Each of them gives different measurements of the closing inventories. Each of these methods will now be considered.

First in, first out (FIFO). This cost formula assumes that the items bought earliest are those used (or sold) first. This assumption is made only for cost purposes, it does not have any connection with the physical usage of the inventories.

Stores ledger card FIFO

Date	Units	Receipts $/unit	$	Units	Issues $/unit	$	Units	Balance $/unit	$
1 Mar.							Nil		Nil
2 Mar.	10	3	30				10	3	30
4 Mar.				5	3	15	5	3	15
7 Mar.	20	4	80				20	4	80
10 Mar.				5	3	15			
				10	4	40	10	4	40
13 Mar.	20	5	100				20	5	100
17 Mar.				5	4	20	5	4	20
							20	5	100
Totals	50		210	25		90	25		120

Note that the card is 'ruled off' each time there is an 'issue' of inventory.

This cost formula gives a closing inventory cost of $120 and the cost of sales (obtained by totalling the cost of each issue) amounted to $90. Using this cost formula, the trading account would be as follows:

	$	$
Sales (25 units @ $8)		200
Opening inventories	–	
Purchases	210	
	210	
Closing inventories	(120)	
Cost of sales		(90)
Gross profit		110

Last in, first out (LIFO). This cost formula assumes that the items bought most recently are those used first. Again, this assumption is made only for cost purposes, it does not have any connection with the physical usage of the inventories.

Stores ledger card – LIFO

Date	Receipts Units	Receipts $/unit	Receipts $	Issues Units	Issues $/unit	Issues $	Balance Units	Balance $/unit	Balance $
1 Mar.							Nil		Nil
2 Mar.	10	3	30				10	3	30
4 Mar.				5	3	15	5	3	15
7 Mar.	20	4	80				20	4	80
10 Mar.				15	4	60	5	3	15
							5	4	20
13 Mar.	20	5	100				20	5	100
17 Mar.				5	5	25	5	3	15
							5	4	20
							15	5	75
Totals	50		210	25		100	25		110

This cost formula gives a closing inventory cost of $110 and the cost of sales (obtained by totalling the cost of each issue) amounted to $100. Using this cost formula, the trading account would be as follows:

	$	$
Sales (25 units @ $8)		200
Opening inventories	Nil	
Purchases	210	
	210	
Closing inventories	(110)	
Cost of sales		(100)
Gross profit		100

ORGANISING THE BOOKKEEPING SYSTEM

You can see that this results in a higher cost of sales total than with the FIFO cost formula, and hence a lower gross profit, in times of inflation. It also results in a lower closing inventories figure, as the inventories are valued at earlier prices. The cost formula is not acceptable when preparing financial statements for external reporting although it may be useful for management accounts. It can be argued that the profit is more realistic than with the FIFO cost formula, as it values cost of sales at a value nearer to the current cost of replacing the inventories sold with new inventories.

Weighted average cost formula (AVCO). This cost formula recalculates a new weighted average cost each time a new delivery of units is received using the formula:

$$\frac{\text{Previous balance value} + \text{new reciepts value}}{\text{Previous units} + \text{new units}}$$

Issues are then valued at the new weighted average cost.

Stores ledger card – Weighted average

| | | Receipts | | | Issues | | | Balance | |
Date	Units	$/unit	$	Units	$/unit	$	Units	$/unit	$
1 Mar.							Nil	2	Nil
2 Mar.	10	3	30				10	3	30
4 Mar.				5	3	15	5	3	15
7 Mar.	20	4	80				25	3	95
10 Mar.				15	3.8	57	10	3.8	38
13 Mar.	20	5	100				30	4.6	138
17 Mar.				5	4.6	23	25	4.6	115
Totals	50		210	20		95			

This cost formula gives a closing inventories cost of $115 and the cost of sales (obtained by totalling the cost of each issue) amounted to $95.

Using this cost formula the trading account would be as follows:

	$	$
Sales (25 units @ $8)		200
Opening inventories	Nil	
Purchases	210	
Closing inventories	(115)	
Cost of sales		(95)
Gross profit		105

You can see from this example that, in times of rising prices, the weighted average cost formula gives a lower closing inventories cost than FIFO and, consequently, a lower profit, but a higher closing inventories cost than the LIFO cost formula, and consequently a higher profit. It is an acceptable cost formula for reporting in financial statements.

It might be useful for you to see the profit calculation of the three cost formulas together, to compare them:

	FIFO	LIFO	AVCO
	$	$	$
Sales	200	200	200
Less: cost of sales			
Opening inventories	Nil	Nil	Nil
Purchases	210	210	210
Less closing inventories	(120)	(110)	(115)
	(90)	(100)	(95)
Gross profit	110	100	105

8.7.3 Issues and receipts

The three examples above used the words 'receipts' to mean 'purchases' and 'issues' to mean 'sales', but note that 'receipts' could also include inventories returned by customers, and 'issues' could also include inventories returned to suppliers. 'Issues' could also mean inventories taken out of the general store and sent to another department, for example, a production department.

Take care when doing exercises that require you to calculate cost of sales and purchases, as well as the closing cost of inventories, if your receipts and issues columns contain items other than sales and purchases. Remember also that the sales column indicates the cost of sales, not the selling price.

Exercise 8.6

Explain what is meant by inventories cost using FIFO, LIFO and AVCO.

Solution

The FIFO cost formula is based on the assumption that those received first are used first. This results in those inventories remaining being valued at more recent prices. In times of rising prices, this cost formula gives lower cost of sales figures and hence a higher gross profit, and a higher closing inventories cost than might otherwise be the case. The LIFO cost formula is based on the assumption that those received most recently are used first, and hence those remaining are valued at earlier prices. The result is a lower profit figure and a lower inventories cost. The AVCO cost formula incorporates each new purchase with the existing inventories, weighted according to the quantity purchased. The result is a profit figure and an inventories cost of somewhere in between the other two cost formulas.

Exercise 8.7

M Lord had inventory on 1 January 20X1 consisting of 400 articles bought at $4 each. His purchases during the month of January consisted of 800 at $4.20 each purchased on 8 January, and 2,000 at $3.80 each on 18 January. He sold 2,400 at $5.00 each on 28 January. Forty of those sold were returned in perfect condition on 31 January.

You are required:

(a) to ascertain, by means of an inventory account:

- the number of articles held in inventory on 31 January 20X1;
- the unit price and total cost of the inventory.

(b) to show the trading account for the month ended 31 January 20X1;
(c) to calculate the gross profit as a percentage of cost of sales.

Note: Lord uses the FIFO cost formula.

 Solution

Date	Receipts Units	Receipts $/unit	Receipts $	Issues Units	Issues $/unit	Issues $	Balance Units	Balance $/unit	Balance $
1 Jan.							400	4.00	1,600
8 Jan.	800	4.20	3,360				800	4.20	3,360
18 Jan.	2,000	3.80	7,600				2,000	3.80	7,600
28 Jan.				400	4.00	1,600			
				800	4.20	3,360			
				1,200	3.80	4,560	800	3.80	3,040
31 Jan.	40	3.80	152				840	3.80	3,192

(a) Inventory at 31 January – 840 articles.
(b) Unit price $3.80, total cost $3,192.

(A) Trading account for January:

	$	$
Sales		12,000
Less: returns		(200)
		11,800
Opening inventory	1,600	
Purchases	10,960	
	12,560	
Less: closing inventory	(3,192)	
Cost of sales		(9,368)
Gross profit		2,432

Gross profit percentage 2,432/11,800 = 20.6%

8.8 Summary

This chapter introduced you to a variety of books, records and documents that can assist in the recording of financial transactions, especially applicable to larger organisations.

These include:

- daybooks (books of prime entry);
- the use of the journal;
- divisions of the ledger;
- cash books;
- inventories records.

Much of the chapter is concerned with the physical maintenance of these books and records, but you should also appreciate how they fit into the overall system of control of the bookkeeping system.

Revision Questions

? **Question 1** Multiple choice

1.1 An organisation's cash book has an opening balance in the bank column of $485 credit. The following transactions then took place:

- cash sales $1,450, including sales tax of $150;
- receipts from customers of $2,400;
- payments to payables of $1,800 less 5 per cent cash discount;
- dishonoured cheques from customers amounting to $250.

The resulting balance in the bank column of the cash book should be:

$............

1.2 An organisation restores its petty cash balance to $500 at the end of each month. During January, the total column in the petty cash book was recorded as being $420, and hence the imprest was restored by this amount. The analysis columns, which had been posted to the nominal ledger, totalled only $400.
This error would result in:

(A) no imbalance in the trial balance.
(B) the trial balance being $20 higher on the debit side.
(C) the trial balance being $20 higher on the credit side.
(D) the petty cash balance being $20 lower than it should be.

1.3 A book of prime entry is one in which:

(A) the rules of double-entry bookkeeping do not apply.
(B) ledger accounts are maintained.
(C) transactions are entered prior to being recorded in the ledger accounts.
(D) subsidiary accounts are kept.

1.4 The following totals appear in the daybooks for March 20X8:

	Goods exc. sales tax	sales tax
	$	$
Sales daybook	40,000	7,000
Purchases daybook	20,000	3,500
Returns inwards daybook	2,000	350
Returns outwards daybook	4,000	700

Both opening and closing inventories are $3,000. The gross profit for March 20X8 is:
$.............

1.5 The petty cash imprest is restored to $100 at the end of each week. The following amounts are paid out of petty cash during week 23:

Stationery	$14.10, including sales tax at 17.5%
Travelling costs	$25.50
Office refreshments	$12.90
Sundry payables	$24.00 plus sales tax at 17.5%

The amount required to restore the imprest to $100 is:
$.............

1.6 Inventories are stated using FIFO. Opening inventories were 10 units at $2 each. Purchases were 30 units at $3 each, then issues of 12 units were made, followed by issues of 8 units. Closing inventories were:
$.............

1.7 In times of rising prices, the FIFO cost formula for inventories cost, when compared with the average cost method, will usually produce:

(A) a higher profit and a lower closing inventories value.
(B) a higher profit and a higher closing inventories value.
(C) a lower profit and a lower closing inventories value.
(D) a lower profit and a higher closing inventories value.

1.8 Your firm uses the weighted average cost formula for inventories. On 1 October 20X8, there were 60 units in inventories valued at $12 each. On 8 October, 40 units were purchased for $15 each, and a further 50 units were purchased for $18 each on 14 October. On 21 October, 75 units were sold for $1,200. The value of closing inventories at 31 October 20X8 was:
$.............

1.9 Inventory movement for product X during the last quarter were as follows:

January	Purchases	10 items at $19.80 each
February	Sales	10 items at $30 each
March	Purchases	20 items at $24.50 each
	Sales	5 items at $30 each

Opening inventory at 1 January was six items valued at $15 each.

Gross profit for the quarter, using the weighted average cost formula, would be:

$............

1.10   A firm uses the LIFO cost formula. Information regarding inventories movements during a particular month are as follows:

1	Opening balance	200 units valued at $1,600
10	Purchases	800 units for $8,000
14	Sales	400 units for $4,800
21	Purchases	800 units for $10,000
23	Sales	600 units for $9,000

The cost of inventories at the end of the month would be:

$............

1.11   S & Co. sells three products – Basic, Super and Luxury. The following information was available at the year end:

	Basic $ per unit	Super $ per unit	Luxury $ per unit
Original cost	6	9	18
Estimated selling price	9	12	15
Selling and distribution costs	1	4	5

	Units	Units	Units
Units in inventories	200	200	150

The value of inventories at the year end should be:

$............

1.12   Inventories record card shows the following details:

1 Feb.	50 units in inventory at a cost of $40 per unit
7 Feb.	100 units purchased at a cost of $45 per unit
14 Feb.	80 units sold
21 Feb.	50 units purchased at a cost of $50 per unit
28 Feb.	60 units sold

What is the cost of inventories at 28 February using the FIFO cost formula?

$............

1.13   W Ltd is registered for sales tax. The managing director has asked four staff in the accounts department why the output tax for the last quarter does not equal 17.5 per cent of sales (17.5 per cent is the rate of sales tax). Which one of the following four replies she received was not correct?

(A)   The company had some exports that were not liable to sales tax.

(B)   The company made some sales of zero-rated products.

(C)   The company made some sales of exempt products.

(D)   The company sold some products to businesses not registered for sales tax.

1.14 When measuring inventories at cost, which of the following shows the correct method of arriving at cost?

	Include inward transport costs	*Include production overheads*
A	Yes	No
B	No	Yes
C	Yes	Yes
D	No	No

 # Question 2

Shown below is the sales and returns inwards daybook of XY, a sole trader, who employs a bookkeeper to maintain her personal account records but she maintains the nominal ledger herself.

Date 1992	Customer	Goods ($)	Sales tax ($)	Total ($)
7 Feb.	ANG Ltd	4,600	805	5,405
10 Feb.	John's Stores	2,800	490	3,290
14 Feb.	ML Ltd	1,000	175	1,175
17 Feb.	ML Ltd	(600)	(105)	(705)
25 Feb.	ANG Ltd	1,200	210	1,410
		9,000	1,575	10,575

Requirements

(a) Is the transaction on the 17 February:

(A) The payment for goods by ML Ltd
(B) The purchase of goods from ML Ltd by XY
(C) The return of goods by ML Ltd
(D) The writing off of the debt from ML Ltd

(b) Using the data in the sales and returns inwards daybook, insert the missing figures into the ledger accounts set out below:

ANG Ltd

		$
7 Feb.	SDB	
25 Feb.	SDB	

Sales

					$
			28 Feb.	SDB	

John's Stores

		$
10 Feb.	SDB	

Returns inward

		$
28 Feb.	SDB	

ML Ltd

		$			$
14 Feb.	SDB		16 Feb.	SDB	

Sales tax

					$
			28 Feb.	SDB	

? Question 3

Your organisation had the following transactions during the last month:

Transaction 1	Purchase of raw materials on credit from J Smith, list price $3,000, trade discount 25 per cent, rate of sales tax 17.5 per cent.
Transaction 2	Payment by cheque to a supplier, L Taylor, outstanding amount $2,400 less cash discount of 5 per cent.
Transaction 3	Contra entry between sales and purchase ledgers of $300, receivable K Green.
Transaction 4	Motor vehicle worth $2,000 received in part-payment of a debt due from a customer, S Long.
Transaction 5	Staff wages earned during the month of $3,000 gross, with income tax of $450, employee's social security contributions of $120 and employer's social security contributions of $130. All payments are to be made after the month end.

Requirements

Complete the table below for each transaction.

Item	Book of prime entry	Debit entries: Account name	$	Credit entries: Account name	$
1.					
2.					
3.					
4.					
5.					

? Question 4

The following information is to be recorded:

1. Opening balances are:
   Cash — $50
   Bank — $100
2. Cash sales — $500
3. Credit purchases from P — $400
4. Wages paid in cash — $100
5. Cash banked — $200
6. Credit sales to Q — $300
7. Paid P $250 less 10% discount, by cheque
8. Received cash from Q, $200 less 5% discount
9. Sent goods to R on approval (i.e. on sale or return) costing $60 with selling price $135
10. Wages paid by cheque — $100
11. R returns one-third of the goods sent on approval, accepts one-third and delays a decision on the remainder
12. Bank charges notified — $30
13. Receive balance due from Q, less discount of 4% in cash.

Requirement

Enter the missing figures in the three-column cash book.

Cash book

Item	Disc. ($)	Cash ($)	Bank ($)	Item	Disc. ($)	Cash ($)	Bank ($)
▨		▨	▨	▨		▨	
▨		▨		▨		▨	
▨			▨	▨	▨		▨
▨	▨	▨		▨			▨
▨	▨	▨		▨			▨
▨			▨	▨		▨	
	▨	▨	▨		▨	▨	▨

Trial balance

	Debit ($)	Credit ($)
▨		▨
▨	▨	
▨		▨
▨		▨
▨	▨	
▨		▨
▨		
▨		
▨	▨	
	▨	▨

Question 5

Your organisation has recently employed a new ledger accounts assistant who is unsure about the correct use of books of original entry and the need for adjustments to be made to the ledger accounts at the end of the year. You have been asked to give the new assistant some guidance.

You use the following examples of transactions to be recorded in the books of prime entry:

(i) Purchase of raw materials on credit from Pandya, list price $27,000 less trade discount of 33½ per cent, plus sales tax of 17.5 per cent.

(ii) Payment to a supplier, P Barton, by cheque in respect of a debt of $14,000, less cash discount of 2 per cent.

(iii) Receipt of a piece of office equipment in payment of a debt of $2,500 from a customer, Arif.

(iv) Write-off of a debt of $500 due from A Scholes.

(v) Returns of goods sold to J Lockley, total invoice value of $470, including sales tax of 17.5 per cent.

(vi) Purchase of a motor vehicle on credit from A Jackson, for $1,400, including annual vehicle licence tax of $75.

Requirements

(a) Complete the table below for each the above transactions:

Item	Book of prime entry	Debit entries: Account name	$	Credit entries: Account name	$
(i)					
(ii)					
(iii)					
(iv)					
(v)					
(vi)					

(b) Rates are paid annually on 1 April, to cover the following 12 months. The local business tax for 19X8/X9 is $1,800, and for 19X9/20X0 is increased by 20 per cent. Rent is paid quarterly on the first day of May, August, November and February, in arrears. The rent has been $1,200 per annum for some time, but increased to $1,600 per annum from 1 February 19X9. Complete the missing figures in the rent and local business tax account for the year ended 30 April 19X9, given below.

Rent and local business tax account

19X8		$	19X8		$
1 May	Balance b/f		1 May	Balance b/f	
1 May	Bank				
1 Aug.	Bank				
1 Nov.	Bank				
19X9			19X9		
1 Feb.	Bank		30 Apr.	Income statement	
1 Apr.	Bank		30 Apr.	Balance c/f	
30 Apr.	Balance c/f				
1 May	Balance b/f		1 May	Balance b/f	

Solutions to Revision Questions

 Solution 1

1.1 The calculation is as follows:

	$
Opening overdraft	(485)
Add: receipts, inc. sales tax	(3,850)
	3,365
Less: payments after discount	(1,710)
	1,655
Less: dishonoured cheques	(250)
	1,405

1.2 Answer: (C)

The petty cash book will have been credited with $420 to restore the imprest, whereas the expense accounts will have been debited with only $400. Therefore, the credit side of the trial balance will be $20 higher than the debit side.

1.3 Answer: (C)

(A) is incorrect as the journal is one of the books of prime entry in which double-entry rules do apply. (B) is incorrect – ledger accounts are not maintained in books of prime entry. (D) is incorrect as subsidiary accounts are ledger accounts that are maintained outside the main ledgers.

1.4 Reconstruction of the trading account

	$	$
Sales		40,000
Less: Returns inwards		(2,000)
		38,000
Less: Opening inventories	3,000	
Purchases	20,000	
Returns outwards	(4,000)	
Closing inventories	(3,000)	
		(16,000)
Gross Profit		22,000

1.5

	$
Stationery	14.10
Travel	25.50
Refreshments	12.90
Sundry payables ($24 × 1.175)	28.20
	80.70

1.6 The first issues (twelve units) would use up the opening inventory of ten units and two units of the purchases at $3 each, leaving 28 units at $3 each. The next issues would be of $3 units, leaving twenty units at $3 each, that is $60.

1.7 Answer: (B)

The closing inventories figure reduces the cost of goods sold figure, which in turn increases the gross profit.

Therefore, a higher closing inventories figure means a lower cost of goods sold figure, and hence a higher gross profit. In times of rising prices, the FIFO cost formula will produce higher closing inventories values, and therefore a higher gross profit figure.

1.8

	Qty	*Value ($)*	
1 October (60 × $12)	60	720	
8 October (40 × $15)	100	1,320	
14 October (50 × $18)	150	2,220	(i.e. average cost $14.80)
21 October (75 × $14.80)	75	1,110	

1.9 Summarised inventories card

	Qty	$	
6 × $15	6	90	
10 × $19.80	10	198	
	16	288	($18 each)
10 × $18	10	(180)	
	6	108	
20 × $24.50	20	490	
	26	598	($23 each)
5 × $23	(5)	(115)	
	21	483	

Note: Issues are shown in brackers.

Trading account

	$	$
Sales (15 × $30)		450
Less: Opening inventories	90	
Purchases	688	
	778	
Less: Closing inventories	(483)	
		(295)
Profit		155

1.10 The sale of 400 units on the 14th will take up 400 of those purchased on the 10th, leaving 400 of those (4,000) and the opening inventory of 200 (1,600). Value of inventory remaining at that point is 5,600. The sale of 600 units on the 23rd will take up 600 of those purchased on the 21st, leaving 200 of those (2,500), plus the previous balance of 5,600: total 8,100.

1.11

	Cost ( )	Net realisable value ( )	Lower of cost & NRV ( )	Units	Cost ( )
Basic	6	8	6	200	1,200
Super		8	8	250	2,000
Luxury	18	10	10	150	1,500
					4,700

1.12 There are 60 units in inventory at 28 February. These are deemed to comprise the 50 units purchased on 21 February at cost 50 per unit = 2,500, and ten units from the units purchased on 7 February at 45 per unit = 450, which is 2,950 in total.

1.13 Answer: (D)

1.14 Answer: (C)

Solution 2

- Part (b) is a straightforward double-entry question involving daybooks and ledger accounts.

(a) Answer: (C)

(b)

		ANG			
		$			
7 Feb.	SDB	5,405			
25 Feb.	SDB	1,410			

		Sales			
					$
			28 Feb.	SDB	9,600

		John's Stores			
		$			
10 Feb.	SDB	3,290			

		ML Ltd			
		$			$
14 Feb.	SDB	1,175	16 Feb.	SDB	705

		Sales tax			
					$
			28 Feb.	SDB	1,575

 # Solution 3

- This is another test of knowledge of books of prime entry and of the double-entry principles, but using a table rather than asking for the accounts to be drawn up.
- Remember to deduct trade discount before calculating sales tax.
- Remember that it is the total invoice price that is entered in the personal accounts, but the net amount in the purchases account.
- In Transaction 5, make clear that there are liabilities outstanding in respect of wages.

Item	Book of Prime entry	Debit entries Account name	$	Credit entries Account name	$
1.	Purchase day book	Purchases	2,250.00	J Smith	2,643.75
		Sales tax	393.75		
2.	Cash book	L Taylor	2,400.00	Bank	2,280.00
				Discount received	120.00
3.	Journal	K Green (receivable)	300.00	K Green (receivable)	300.00
4.	Journal	Motor vehicles	2,000.00	S Long	2,000.00
5.	Journal	Wages expense	3,000.00	Income tax payable	450.00
		SS expense	130.00	Wages payable	2,430.00
				SS payable	250.00

☑ Solution 4

- This question covers basic double-entry bookkeeping and at this stage in your studies should pose no particular problems.
- The only difficult area concerns the sales to R on approval, which requires you to consider the realisation convention – the sale should not be recognised in the financial statements until it is certain – and in this example only one-third is certain by the end of the period. Therefore, only one-third of the total sales ($45) should be included with sales, with the remainder in inventories, valued at $40.

Cash book

Item	Disc ($)	Cash ($)	Bank ($)	Item	Disc ($)	Cash ($)	Bank ($)
(1)		50	100	(4)		100	
(2)		500		(5)		200	
(5)			200	(7)	25		225
(8)	10	190		(10)			100
(13)	4	96		(12)			30
Balance			55	Balance		536	
	14	836	355		25	836	355

Note: The remaining 'sale or return' goods are taken out of sales (at selling price); their cost, $20, must be debited to 'inventories on sale or return' account when preparing the trading account, and accounted for as current assets in preparing the statement of financial position.

Trial balance

	Debit ($)	Credit ($)
Capital		150
Cash	536	
Bank		55
Discounts	14	25
Sales		890
Purchases	400	
Payables		150
Wages	200	
Receivables	45	
Bank charges	30	
Sales returns	45	
	1, 270	1, 270

✓ Solution 5

- Notice that it is the 'book of prime entry' that is asked for, not the ledger.
- For the debit and credit entries, be sure to state the name of the ledger accounts.
- In Part (b), a single rent and local business tax account is required.

(a)

Book of Prime entry	Debit entries Account name	$	Credit entries Account name	$
(i) Purchases daybook	Purchases	18,000	Pandya	21,150
	Sales tax	3,150		
(ii) Cash book	P Barton	14,000	Bank	13,720
			Discount received	280
(iii) Journal	Office equipment	2,500	Arif	2,500
(iv) Journal	Bad debts	500	A Scholes	500
(v) Returns inwards daybook	Returns inwards	400	J Lockley	470
	Salex tax	70		
(vi) Journal	Vehicle at cost	1,325	A Jackson	1,400
	Motor expenses	75		

(b)

Rent and local business tax

19X8		$	19X8		$
1 May	Balance b/f[1]	1,650	1 May	Balance b/f[2]	300
1 May	Bank	300			
1 Aug.	Bank	300			
1 Nov.	Bank	300			
19X9			19X9		
1 Feb.	Bank	300	30 Apr.	Income statement	3,130
1 Apr.	Bank	2,160	30 Apr.	Balance c/f	1,980
30 Apr.	Balance c/f	400			
		5,410			5,410
1 May	Balance b/f	1,980	1 May	Balance b/f	400

Notes:

1. Rates prepaid $= \frac{11}{12}$ of $1,800 = $1,650

2. Rent accrued $= \frac{1}{4}$ of $1,200 = $300

9

Controlling the
Bookkeeping System

Controlling the Bookkeeping System

9.1 Introduction

No bookkeeping system can be guaranteed to be entirely free of errors. Human beings are fallible, and even automated and computerised systems are less than perfect. For example, a computer cannot possibly know that a supplier has sent you an invoice that never arrived.

In this chapter we look at a number of ways in which the bookkeeping system can be checked for accuracy, and ways in which errors and omissions can be rectified.

Specific topics which are covered include:

• bank reconciliations
• control accounts
• suspense accounts.

9.2 Preventing errors

There are a number of ways in which errors can be prevented, or at least limited in their number and effect. Many of these also prevent deliberate fraud.

9.2.1 Authorisation procedures

Transactions should be authorised at an appropriate level. For example,

- the purchase of major non-current assets should be justified/agreed by senior management and recorded in the minutes of meetings;
- cheques for large amounts should require two signatures;
- new receivable and payable accounts should be authorised by a senior person;
- all purchase orders should be authorised by a responsible officer;
- all payments made should be approved. In particular,
  - payments to suppliers should be checked against goods received, invoices and credit notes;
  - refunds to customers should be authorised;
  - payrolls should be checked and authorised prior to making payment.

9.2.2 Documentation

Documentation should be used to give evidence of transactions, and should be properly filed and referenced. This helps to provide an 'audit trail' of transactions through the system. As an example, consider the ordering of goods for resale, and the documentation involved.

- *Raising of the order*. On official order forms, properly authorised, after obtaining several quotations.
- *Receipt of goods*. Checked on arrival, checked with order, shortages and breakages recorded.
- *Receipt of invoice*. Checked with order and receipt of goods; prices, discounts and calculations checked.
- *Payment of invoice*. Only after all credit notes have been received, and checked with purchase ledger account prior to payment.

9.2.3 Organisation of staff

Staff should be properly recruited, trained and supervised. No one person should have complete control over any section of the bookkeeping system. Duties should be shared out between different members of staff. This is known as *segregation of duties*.

This can be illustrated by considering the procedures arising from selling goods on credit. In summary the tasks involved are:

- issuing sales invoices;
- issuing credit notes;
- credit control;
- banking receipts from customers.

If one person were to be solely responsible for all (or even more than one) of these tasks, it would be easy for money to be diverted and the corresponding paperwork destroyed or falsified. Staff should also rotate their duties from time to time.

9.2.4 Safeguarding assets

Assets should be properly maintained, insured, utilised, valued and recorded.

9.3 Detecting errors

Some errors may come to light purely by chance, and some are never found at all. For example, if you receive a cheque from a customer who has no outstanding balance on his account, it is possible that an invoice has been omitted from the books. If you never receive the cheque, the error might never come to light.

It would be extremely unwise to trust to chance, and therefore there are several checks that can be incorporated to help detect errors.

9.3.1 Spot checks

These are particularly useful in detecting fraud. For example, spot checks on petty cash balances may uncover 'teeming and lading' activities, whereby an employee borrows money from the petty cash on a regular basis, but puts it back when the imprest is being checked, only to remove it again afterwards.

Spot checks are also commonly carried out on bank balances, ledger accounts and inventories.

9.3.2 Comparison with external evidence

External evidence is among the most useful in determining the reliability of records. Examples include:

- confirmation of balances with receivables and payables;
- confirmation of bank balances with the bank.

9.3.3 Reconciliations

A reconciliation is a comparison of records to identify differences and to effect agreement. There are several types of reconciliation that can be carried out.

- Producing a trial balance. If the debit and credit totals do not agree, it is obvious that an error has been made.
- Reconciling the accounts of the organisation with records received from other organisations. Two common reconciliations of this type are:
  - *bank reconciliations*, where the bank account maintained by the organisation is reconciled with the statement issued by the bank;
  - *supplier reconciliations*, where the ledger account maintained by the organisation is reconciled with a statement of the ledger account in the supplier's books.
  Both of these types of reconciliation are considered in more detail later in this chapter.
- Reconciling groups of ledger accounts with a *control account*. Control accounts are considered in more detail later in this chapter.

9.3.4 Carrying out an audit

An audit is a check on the accounting records and financial statements of the organisation. It does not entail a complete check on every bookkeeping entry, but rather examines the systems and procedures in place that should contribute to the reliability of the accounting records. The role of audit is discussed in more detail in Chapter 10.

9.4   Bank reconciliation statements

Bank reconciliations are an essential 'must know' topic.

The purpose of a bank reconciliation statement is to check the accuracy of an organisation's bank account record by comparing it with the record of the account held by the bank. In Chapter 8 we saw that there is often a timing delay between the transaction occurring (and therefore being recorded in the cash book) and it being processed by the bank. It is this timing difference that is usually the cause of any difference between the balances. However, there are some transactions of which the organisation will not be aware until they receive their bank statement. These include bank charges, commissions and dishonoured cheques (where the drawer's bank has refused to honour the cheque drawn upon it), and may also include direct debits and standing orders if the account holder has not been separately notified of their being paid.

In order to ensure that both the bank's and the organisation's records are correct, a comparison is made of the two sets of records and a reconciliation statement produced.

Example 9.A

The following extract from the cash book of ABX Limited for the month of June shows the company's bank transactions:

	$		$
Balance b/f	9,167	Purchase ledger	1,392
Sales ledger	4,023	Employees' income tax	2,613
Cash sales	2,194	Sales tax payable	981
Sales ledger	7,249	Cheques cashed	3,290
		Balance c/f	14,357
	22,633		22,633

The company's bank statement for the same period is as follows:

	Debit ($)	Credit ($)	Balance ($)
Opening balance			7,645
Lodgement 000212		2,491	10,136
Cheque 000148	969		9,167
Insurance D/D	2,413		6,754
Lodgement 000213		4,023	10,777
Cheque 000149	1,392		9,385
Cheque 000150	2,613		6,772
Cheque 000152	3,290		3,482
Lodgement 000214		2,194	5,676
Bank charges	563		5,113

You are required to reconcile the balances shown in the cash book and the bank statement.

Solution

The first step is to compare the entries shown in the cash book with those on the bank statement and match them. This is shown below where letters have been used to match the items together.

	$		$
Balance b/fwd	9,167	Purchase ledger (c)	1,392
Sales ledger (a)	4,023	Employees' income tax (d)	2,613
Cash sales (b)	2,194	Sales tax payable	981
Sales ledger	7,249	Cheques cashed (e)	3,290
		Balance c/f	14,357
	22,633		22,633

	Debit ($)	Credit ($)	Balance ($)
Opening balance			7,645
Lodgement 000212		2,491	10,136
Cheque 000148	969		9,167
Insurance D/D	2,413		6,754
Lodgement 000213		4,023 (a)	10,777
Cheque 000149	1,392 (c)		9,385
Cheque 000150	2,613 (d)		6,772
Cheque 000152	3,290 (e)		3,482
Lodgement 000214		2,194 (b)	5,676
Bank charges	563		5,113

When the matching is complete there will usually be items on the bank statement that are not shown in the cash book, and items entered in the cash book that are not shown on the bank statement.

Some of these may relate to the previous period – in this example the opening balances were not the same. There is a lodgement (reference 000212) and a cheque (number 000148) that are not in the cash book of the period. A simple calculation shows that these items represent the difference between the opening balances. These are, therefore, timing differences that do not affect the bank reconciliation at 30 June.

There are some items on the bank statement that have not been entered in the cash book. These are the direct debit for insurance and the bank charges. The cash book balance needs to be amended for these:

	$	$
Balance as shown in cash book		14,357
Less:		
Insurance	2,413	
Bank charges	563	
		(2,976)
Amended cash book balance		11,381

The remaining difference between the amended cash book balance and the bank statement balance is caused by timing differences on those items not matched above:

	$
Balance as per bank statement	5,113
Add: uncleared lodgement	7,249
	12,362
Less: unpresented cheque	(981)
Balance as per cash book	11,381

You should note that this statement commenced with the balance as per the bank statement and reconciled it to the balance shown in the cash book. A less common alternative is to commence with the balance as per the cash book and reconcile it to the bank statement. To do this, the mathematical additions and subtractions must be reversed. Try it.

Exercise 9.1

From the following information, prepare a statement that shows any necessary corrections to the cash book balance and a statement that reconciles the bank statement balance with the corrected cash book balance.

	$
Balance as per cash book	1,245
Unpresented cheques	890
Bank charges not entered in cash book	100
Receipts not yet credited by bank	465
Dishonoured cheque not entered in cash book	170
Balance as per bank statement	1,400

 Solution

	$
Original cash book balances	1,245
Less: amounts not yet entered	
Bank charges	(100)
Dishonoured cheque	(170)
Corrected cash book balance	975
Balance per bank statement	1,400
Add: outstanding lodgements	465
Less: unpresented cheques	(890)
Balance as per corrected cash book	975

 Exercise 9.2

Cash book (bank columns only)

		$			$
1 Jan.	Balance	600	18 Jan.	D Anderson	145
13 Jan.	Umberto	224	28 Jan.	R Patrick	72
13 Jan.	L Bond	186	30 Jan.	Parveen	109

Bank statement

		Debit ($)	Credit ($)	Balance ($)
1 Jan.	Balance			635
3 Jan.	H Turner	35		600
13 Jan.	Umberto		224	824
23 Jan.	D Anderson	145		679
31 Jan.	Standing order	30		649

Using the information given above:

(a) prepare a corrected cash book;
(b) draw up a bank reconciliation statement.

Solution

Cash book

		$			$
1 Jan.	Balance b/f	600	18 Jan.	D Anderson	145
13 Jan.	Umberto	224	28 Jan.	R Patrick	72
31 Jan.	L Bond	186	30 Jan.	Parveen	109
			31 Jan.	Standing order	30
			31 Jan.	Balance c/f	654
		1,010			1,010
1 Feb.	Balance b/f	654			

Bank reconciliation statement at 31 January

	$
Balance as per bank statement	649
Add: receipts not lodged	186
Less: unpresented cheques (109 + 72)	(181)
Balance as per cash book	654

9.5 Reconciliation of suppliers' statements

Many suppliers send monthly statements to their customers, showing the position of that customers, account in their own records, and this provides an ideal opportunity to check the accuracy of the organisation's records with those of another. A reconciliation of payable balances to supplier statements is no different from carrying out a bank reconciliation, as shown below.

Example 9.B

Included in the payables ledger of J Cross, a shopkeeper, is the following account that disclosed that the amount owing to one of his suppliers at 31 May 20X4 was $472.13.

Payables ledger

20X4		$	20X4		$
18 May	Purchase returns	36.67	1 May	Balance b/d	862.07
27 May	Purchase returns	18.15	16 May	Purchases	439.85
27 May	Adjustment (overcharge)	5.80	25 May	Purchases	464.45
31 May	Discount received	24.94	25 May	Adjustment (undercharge)	13.48
31 May	Bank	1,222.16			
31 May	Balance c/d	472.13			
		1,779.85			1,779.85

J Cross in account with Nala Merchandising Company – Statement of account

20X4		Debit ($)	Credit ($)	Balance ($)
1 May	BCE			1,538.70 Dr
3 May	DISC		13.40	1,525.30 Dr
	CHQ		634.11	891.19 Dr
5 May	ALLCE		29.12	862.07 Dr
7 May	GDS	256.72		1,118.79 Dr
10 May	GDS	108.33		1,227.12 Dr
11 May	GDS	74.80		1,301.92 Dr
14 May	ADJ	13.48		1,315.40 Dr
18 May	GDS	162.55		1,477.95 Dr
23 May	GDS	301.90		1,779.85 Dr
25 May	ALLCE		36.67	1,743.18 Dr
28 May	GDS	134.07		1,877.25 Dr
29 May	GDS	251.12		2,128.37 Dr
30 May	GDS	204.80		2,333.17 Dr
31 May	GDS	91.36		2,424.53 Dr
31 May	BCE			2,424.53 Dr

Abbreviations: BCE – balance; CHQ – cheque; GDS – goods; ALLCE – allowance; DISC – discount; ADJ – adjustment.

You are required to prepare a statement reconciling the closing balance on the supplier's account in the payables ledger with the closing balance shown on the statement of account submitted by the supplier.

Solution

As we saw with bank reconciliation statements the technique is to match the items first and then construct a reconciliation statement.

Payables ledger

20X4		$	20X4		$
18 May	Purchase returns (a)	36.67	1 May	Balance b/d	862.07
27 May	Purchase returns (r)	18.15	16 May	Purchases (b)	439.85
27 May	Adjustment (overcharge) (t)	5.80	25 May	Purchases (c)	464.45
31 May	Discount received (s)	24.94	25 May	Adjustment (undercharge) (d)	13.48
31 May	Bank (s)	1,222.16			
31 May	Balance c/d	472.13			
		1,779.85			1,779.85

J Cross in account with Nala Merchandising Company – Statement of Account

20X4		Debit ($)	Credit ($)	Balance ($)
1 May	BCE			1,538.70 Dr
3 May	DISC		13.40(p)	1,525.30 Dr
	CHQ		634.11(p)	891.19 Dr
5 May	ALLCE		29.12(p)	862.07 Dr
7 May	GDS	256.72(b)		118.79 Dr
10 May	GDS	108.33(b)		1,227.12 Dr
11 May	GDS	74.80(b)		1,301.92 Dr
14 May	ADJ	13.48(d)		1,315.40 Dr
18 May	GDS	162.55(c)		1,477.95 Dr
23 May	GDS	301.90(c)		1,779.85 Dr
25 May	ALLCE		36.67(a)	1,743.18 Dr
28 May	GDS	134.07(q)		1,877.25 Dr
29 May	GDS	251.12(q)		2,128.37 Dr
30 May	GDS	204.80(q)		2,333.17 Dr
31 May	GDS	91.36(q)		2,424.53 Dr
31 May	BCE			2,424.53 Dr

The items marked 'p' reconcile the opening balances.

Reconciliation statement

	$	$
Balance as per payables ledger		472.13
Add:		
Goods despatched by supplier not entered in ledger (q)	681.35	
Returns not yet recognised by supplier (r)	18.15	
Payments/discounts not yet recognized by supplier (s)	1,247.10	
Adjustment not yet recognised by supplier (t)	5.80	
		1,952.40
Balance as per supplier's statement		2,424.53

9.6 Control accounts

Control accounts are an essential 'must know' topic.

When the ledger accounts are divided into sections, it is possible to introduce an additional control on each section, known as a *control account*. Common control accounts include the *sales ledger control account* and the *purchase ledger control account*. A control account contains exactly the same information as in the individual accounts in the ledger that it controls, but using totals rather than individual transactions. In fact, they are sometimes referred to as *total accounts*.

As we saw in Chapter 8, transactions are first entered into the appropriate books of prime entry as follows:

- daybooks – sales, purchases and returns on credit;
- cash book – receipts, payments, discounts and dishonoured cheques;
- journal – bad debts written off.

Receivables and payables accounts are always kept up to date, with transactions being entered immediately as they arise. The daybooks and so on are totalled periodically, and the 'opposite' entries made in the nominal ledger accounts at the end of the period.

These totals in these books of prime entry can be use to create a 'copy' of the receivables and payables accounts, which can be used as a control mechanism.

Example 9.C

An organisation has four receivables, with the following balances at 1 January 20X1:

	$
Khan	437
P Binns	1,046
J Harris	93
C Bloggs	294
Total	1,870

The sales daybook for January is as follows:

Sales daybook

Date	Customer	Goods ($)	Sales tax ($)	Total ($)
20X1				
10 Jan.	J Harris	200	35	235
17 Jan.	P Binns	400	70	470
23 Jan.	Khan	600	105	705
		1,200	210	1,410

The sales returns daybook for January is as follows:

Sales returns daybook

Date	Customer	Goods ($)	Sales tax ($)	Total ($)
20X1				
12 Jan.	J Harris	80	14	94
20 Jan.	P Binns	120	21	141
		200	35	235

The cash book (debit side) for the same day includes the following entries:

Received from receivables

Date	Details	($)	Discount ($)
20X1			
14 Jan.	C Bloggs	125	5
16 Jan.	P Binns	570	30
		695	35

You are required to write up the personal accounts in the sales ledger and the control account, and to reconcile the control account to the total of the sales ledger balances.

Solution

Sales ledger accounts

Khan

20X1		$	20X1		$
1 Jan.	Balance b/f	437			
12 Jan.	Invoice	705	31 Jan.	Balance c/d	1,142
		1,142			1,142
1 Feb.	Balance b/d	1,142			

P Binns

20X1		$	20X1		$
1 Jan.	Balance b/f	1,046	16 Jan.	Cash	570
17 Jan.	Invoice	470	16 Jan.	Discount	30
			20 Jan.	Sales returns	141
			31 Jan.	Balance c/d	775
		1,516			1,516
1 Feb.	Balance b/d	775			

J Haris

20X1		$	20X1		$
1 Jan.	Balance b/f	93	12 Jan.	Sales returns	94
10 Jan.	Invoice	235	31 Jan.	Balance c/d	234
		328			328
1 Feb.	Balance b/d	234			

C Bloggs

20X1		$	20X1		$
1 Jan.	Balance b/f	294	1 Jan.	Cash	125
				Discount	5
			31 Jan.	Balance c/d	164
		294			294
1 Feb.	Balance b/d	164			

A list of receivables' balances extracted at 31 January 20X1 is as follows:

	$
Khan	1,142
P Binns	775
J Harris	234
C Bloggs	164
Total	2,315

The sales ledger control account can be compiled from the total of the entries made to the individual receivables accounts, using the totals in the various books of prime entry, as follows:

Sales ledger control account

20X1		$	20X1		$
1 Jan.	Balance b/f	1,870	31 Jan.	Sales returns daybook	235
31 Jan.	Sales daybook	1,410	31 Jan.	Cash book Received	695
				Discount allowed	35
			31 Jan.	Balance c/d	2,315
		3,280			3,280
1 Feb.	Balance b/d	2,315			

If all has gone well, the individual postings to the sales ledger should exactly equal the total postings made to the nominal ledger. It follows that if we add up the balances on all the personal accounts in the sales ledger we should reach a total that exactly equals the balance on the receivables control account in the nominal ledger. The same applies in the case of the purchase ledger. By performing this exercise at regular intervals we are, in effect, checking that postings to the ledgers are accurate. The exercise is sometimes seen as performing a 'trial balance' on the ledgers.

9.6.1 The status of the control account

The status of a control account is not an easy concept to grasp. Particular care should be made in ensuring that you understand this issue as it is the basis of many computer-based assessment questions.

So far we have considered that the double entry is completed by entering each transaction in the receivables personal accounts in the sales ledger, and entering the totals of sales, returns, sales tax, cash received and discounts allowed in the nominal ledger. Now that we have introduced a control account, it might appear that we are duplicating the entries in the sales ledger. Obviously, this cannot happen, as the ledger accounts will be out of balance. We cannot have *both* the receivables accounts *and* the control account as part of the double-entry system. Therefore, one or other of these must be treated as being outside the double-entry system. The records that are outside the double-entry system are known as *memorandum accounts*.

In computerised systems, it is common for the sales ledger to be a separate component of the bookkeeping system, and for the control account to exist in the nominal ledger. But it is also acceptable to regard the control account as a memorandum account.

 Exercise 9.3

Briefly explain the meaning of each of the entries in the following receivables account:

			P Richmond				
		$					$
1 Jan.	Balance b/f	465		13 Jan.	Cheque		450
6 Jan.	Sales	240			Discount		15
8 Jan.	Sales	360		17 Jan.	Returns		40
				31 Jan.	Balance c/d		560
		1,065					1,065
1 Feb.	Balance b/d	560					

 Solution

- 1 January: balance. P Richmond owes this amount at 1 January.
- 6/8 January: sales. P Richmond has been sold these amounts on credit.
- 13 January: cheque and discount. P Richmond has paid $450 by cheque to clear a debt of $465, having been allowed a cash discount of $15. It is likely that this was in payment of the opening balance on 1 January.
- 17 January: P Richmond has returned goods and been allocated a credit of $40 to be offset against the amount owing.
- 31 January: balance $560. P Richmond owes this amount at 31 January.

Example 9.D

You have been asked to prepare control accounts in order to produce end-of-year figures for receivables and payables for inclusion in the draft final accounts of Korrinna Company for the year ended 30 November 20X8.
   You obtain the following totals for the financial year from the books of original entry:

Cash book

	$
Discounts allowed	6,805
Cash and cheques from customers	287,601
Discounts received	3,415
Cash and cheques paid to suppliers	233,078
Customer's cheque dishonoured	251

The following totals have been extracted from the daybooks for the year:

	$
Purchases daybook	247,084
Sales daybook	306,580
Returns inwards daybook	6,508
Returns outwards daybook	4,720

According to the audited financial statements for the previous year, receivables and payables as at the close of business on 30 November 20X7 were $44,040 and $63,289, respectively.
   You are required to draw up the relevant control accounts for the year ending 30 November 20X8, entering the closing balances for receivables and payables.

Solution

Sales ledger control account

	$		$
Balance b/d	44,040	Discounts allowed	6,805
Sales	306,580	Cash and cheques	287,601
Cheque dishonoured	251	Returns inwards	6,508
		Balance c/d	49,957
	350,871		350,871

Purchase ledger control account

	$		$
Discounts received	3,415	Balance b/d	63,289
Cash and cheques	233,078	Purchases	247,084
Returns outwards	4,720		
	69,160		
	310,373		310,373

The entries in the control accounts reflect respectively the effect of the transactions on the value of Korrinna Company's receivables (sales ledger control account) and payables (purchase ledger control account).
   In the sales ledger control account the debit entries are those transactions that cause the asset of receivables to increase, whereas decreases are recorded on the credit side of the control account.
   In the purchase ledger control account the debit entries are those transactions that cause the liability of payables to decrease, whereas increases are recorded on the credit side of the control account.

Debit	*Credit*
Increases in assets	Decreases in assets
Decreases in liabilities	Increases in liabilities

Note that the transactions are entered individually in the personal accounts of the customers and also entered in total in the control account.

You should also note that every entry in the personal accounts should also be included in the control account and *vice versa* – if the control account balance agrees with the total of the individual account balances it is highly likely that the double entry has been posted correctly. Note, however, that if a transaction is posted to the wrong personal account this will not be found by the reconciliation of the control account balance.

 ## Exercise 9.4

Explain the purpose of control accounts. Describe the contents of a sales ledger control account and state the source of the main items of information contained therein.

 ## Solution

Control accounts are a means of controlling a complete ledger or group of ledger accounts, by containing duplicate information in total or summary form. The balance on the control account should equal the balances on the individual ledger accounts that it controls. It can be used as a means of checking the accuracy of the entries, and assists in the speedy production of financial statements.

A sales ledger control account would contain summary information regarding receivables ledger accounts. Debit entries would include opening balances, sales made on credit, dishonoured cheques; credit entries would include sales returns, monies received and cash discount allowed, bad debts written off, transfers to other ledgers, closing balances.

The sources of the main items would be the sales daybook, sales returns daybook and cash book.

 ## Exercise 9.5

Ascertain the value of sales from the following information:

	$
Opening receivables	23,750
Closing receivables	22,400
Cash sales	14,000
Receipts from receivables	215,000
Discounts allowed	4,500
Bad debts written off	2,250
Dishonoured cheques	2,500

 ## Solution

Sales ledger control account

	$		$
Opening receivables	23,750	Receipts	215,000
Sales	?	Discounts	4,500
Dishonoured cheques	2,500	Bad debts w/off	2,250
		Closing receivables	22,400
	244,150		244,150

The sales figure is the balancing figure required, that is $244,150 − $23,750 − $2,500 = $217,900.

9.6.2 Contra entries

When a business is both a supplier and a customer of your business it is common for an agreement to be made to set off the sums receivable and payable, and for a single cheque to be sent between the parties to settle the net balance. The entry to record the setting off of the balances is known as a *contra entry.*

Example 9.E

The following accounts are taken from the accounting records of Z Ltd:

Sales ledger

AP Ltd

	$		
Balance b/d	1,815		

Purchase ledger

AP Ltd

			$
		Balance b/d	792

Solution

The balance of $792 in the purchase ledger is set off against the sales ledger balance using a contra entry:

Sales ledger

AP Ltd

	$		$
Balance b/d	1,815	Purchase ledger (contra)	792

Purchase ledger

AP Ltd

	$		$
Sales ledger contra	792	Balance b/d	792

AP Ltd would send a cheque to Z Ltd for $1,023 to clear its sales ledger balance.

The same entries must be made in the control accounts, that is debit the purchase ledger control account with $792, and credit the sales ledger control account with $792. Note that it is always the *smaller* of the two balances that is transferred, but the entries of 'debit purchase ledger' and 'credit sales ledger' always occur.

The contra would also be entered in the journal (as its book of prime entry), but remember that the journal is not part of the double-entry system.

9.6.3 Credit balances in the sales ledger; debit balances in the purchase ledger

Normally, sales ledger accounts have debit balances, and purchase ledger accounts have credit balances. But it can happen that the reverse occurs. For example, a receivable may have paid his invoice, and then returns some goods that are faulty. The entries on the return would be to debit returns inwards and credit the receivable – which means that he acquires a credit balance. The same might occur with a supplier, whereby you have paid his invoice and later return goods. Strictly speaking, receivables with credit balances are payables, and vice versa, but it is not normal to move them from one ledger to the other.

Thus it is possible to have credit balances in the sales ledger and debit balances in the purchase ledger. Very often, these balances are wiped out when the customer orders more goods, or we order goods from the supplier. But sometimes it happens that there are no further orders, and a refund is required. With receivables, the entries are debit the receivable and credit bank, and with payables the entries are credit the payable and debit bank.

 Exercise 9.6

Compile a sales ledger control account from the following information:

	$
Opening balances	Debit 14,500, credit 125
Sales on credit	27,500
Sales return	850
Bad debts written off	500
Cash sales	420
Cheques received from receivables	19,800
Cash discount allowed	480
Dishonoured cheques	700
Contras to the purchases ledger	340
Refunds to credit customers	125

 Solution

Sales ledger control account

	$		$
Opening balances	14,500	Opening balances	125
Sales on credit	27,500	Sales returns	850
Dishonoured cheques	750	Bad debts w/off	500
Refunds	125	Cheques received	19,800
		Cash discount allowed	480
		Contras to purchase ledger	340
		Closing balances	20,780
	42,875		42,875

9.6.4 The control account and allowance for receivables

An allowance for receivables is made when it is felt that a proportion of receivables may not honour their debts in full, but the identity of the individual receivables is not known. Refer back to Chapter 5 to refresh your memory on the bookkeeping treatment of these provisions.

The important point to remember is that *no entries are made in the receivables ledger accounts* for allowances for receivables, and therefore no entry is made in the sales ledger control account either.

9.6.5 Advantages of control accounts

- They check the accuracy of the ledger accounts that they control.
- They enable 'segregation of duties' by allocating the job of maintaining the sales/ purchase ledger to one person, and the job of maintaining the control account to another person, thereby reducing the risk of fraud.
- They enable the trial balance to be prepared more speedily, as the receivables and payables total can be extracted from the control accounts rather than waiting for the individual accounts to be balanced and totalled.
- They enable speedier identification of reasons why the trial balance may not balance – if the control account disagrees with its ledger balances, it prompts investigation into the entries in that area.

9.6.6 Reconciling control accounts and ledger accounts

The control account must be checked against the total of balances in the relevant ledger, on a regular basis, and any difference between the two must be investigated. Assuming that the control account has been prepared using totals from the books of prime entry, it is usual to 'work backwards' through the tasks that have been carried out, before checking individual entries. The sequence for a sales ledger control account could be as follows:

  (i) Rework the balance on the control account; check that bad debts have been entered, contras have been properly recorded, and that the account does not contain the allowance for receivables.
 (ii) Check that all totals have been correctly transferred from the books of prime entry to the control account (look especially for discounts allowed, which may have been omitted).
(iii) Recalculate the list of receivable balances (look especially for credit balances listed as debits, check contras and bad debts written off).
(iv) Recalculate the columns in the books of prime entry (look at the sequence of invoice numbers to see if one is missing; look also in the cash book for refunds made to receivables).
 (v) If the balances are still incorrect, it will be necessary to start looking at entries in detail:
   – cross-check the net, sales tax and totals for each invoice/credit note in the daybooks;
   – cross-check the net, discount and total for each receipt in the cash book;
   – cross-check the calculation of the balances on the individual receivable accounts;
   – cross-check the entry of each invoice, credit note, receipt and so on in the receivable accounts.

In computerised systems there is much less chance of arithmetical error, but omissions and mispostings can still occur.

Once the errors have been identified, corrections must be made to the sales ledger accounts, the control account or both.

Example 9.F

Cathy maintains a sales ledger control account. At 31 March 20X1, the balance on the control account was calculated as being $128,545, while the total of individual balances extracted from the sales ledger was $128,106. An examination of the books and records revealed the following:

(i) The total of $29,450 for sales in the sales daybook had been posted as $29,540.
(ii) The credit balance of $128 on a receivable account had been listed as a debit balance.
(iii) A bad debt of $240 had been correctly written off in the receivable account, but no entry had been made in the control account.
(iv) Discounts allowed totalling $185 had been entered on the wrong side of the control account.
(v) A credit balance of $95 in the purchase ledger had been set off against the same person's balance in the sales ledger, but no entries had been made in the control account.
(vi) The total on the debit side of a receivable account had been overcast by $100.

You are required to reconcile the two totals.

Solution

Each adjustment is likely to affect either the control account or the individual balances; it is also possible that an error affects both.

Adjustments to receivables balance	$
Total per original list	128,106
(ii) credit balance listed as debit	(256)
(vi) debit side overcast	(100)
Revised total	127,750

Adjustments to control account (probably easiest to show this as a ledger account):

	$		$
Balance b/d	128,545	(i) error in sales daybook	90
		(iii) bad debts written off	240
		(iv) discounts allowed	370
		(v) contra	95
		Revised balance	127,750
	128,545		128,545

9.7 Suspense accounts and the correction of errors

The nature of a suspense account is not an easy concept to grasp. Particular care should be made in ensuring that you understand this issue as it is the basis of many computer-based assessment questions. To record transactions is difficult enough; to put right a transaction which has already been recorded incorrectly is more difficult. This ability to correct errors is a good test of bookkeeping competence and thus is a common computer-based assessment question.

We have already seen that since every transaction has debit and credit entries of equal value, then when the accounts are balanced and a trial balance extracted the sum of the debit and credit balances are equal. However, this is to assume that all of the transactions are correctly posted to the ledger accounts and that the ledger account balances are correctly calculated. If the trial balance does not balance, then an error or errors have been made.

There are many different reasons why a trial balance may not balance:

(a) incorrect additions in individual ledger accounts;
(b) only one side of the transaction has been posted;
(c) different values have been entered to the debit and credit sides of the respective ledger accounts.

When the trial balance does not balance, every effort should be made to find the errors and correct them, but occasionally they cannot be found quickly and in these circumstances a *suspense account* is opened and used to record the difference until the errors can be found. The use of the suspense account allows financial statements to be prepared subject to the correction of the errors. The prudent approach is to treat the suspense account balance as an expense (rather than an asset) if it is a debit balance and as a liability (rather than as revenue) if it is a credit balance. When the errors are found they should be corrected and an explanation given.

The corrections are made through the journal in the first instance, and then in the ledger accounts. If the error is one that has affected the agreement of the trial balance, then the suspense account will be involved in the correction of the error.

Example 9.G

On 31 December 20X1 a trial balance was extracted from the ledgers of Marconi and the total of the debit side was found to be $77 less than the total of the credit side. A suspense account was opened to record the difference. Later, the following errors were discovered:

(1) A cheque for $150 paid to Bond had been correctly entered in the cash book but not in Bond's account or the control account.
(2) The purchases account had been undercast by $20.
(3) A cheque received for $93 from Smith had been correctly entered in the cash book but had not been entered in Smith's account or the control account.

Solution

The journal entry and resulting entries in the suspense account are as follows:

Journal	Dr $	Cr $
Bond	150	
Suspense		150
(Being correction of an error whereby only one entry was posted)		
Purchases	20	
Suspense		20
(Being correction of an error of addition in the purchases account)		
Suspense	93	
Smith		93
(Being correction of an error whereby only one entry was posted)		

Suspense			
	$		$
From trial balance	77	Bond	150
Smith	93	Purchases	20
	170		170

Exercise 9.7

The following trial balance was extracted from the books of Jane Smith on 31 March 20X1:

	Dr $	Cr $
Premises	50,000	
Motor vans	7,400	
Sundry receivables	1,680	
Sundry payables		2,385
Purchases	160,260	
Sales		200,490
Wages	12,000	
Drawings	1,600	
Capital		30,000
	232,940	232,875

As the trial balance totals did not agree, the difference was posted to a suspense account. The following errors were discovered:

1. The purchase of a motor van had been entered in the motor van account as $3,860 instead of $3,680.
2. The total of the purchases book $32,543 had been posted to the purchases account as $32,453.
3. The proprietress had withdrawn $140 for private use during March that had been debited to the wages account.
4. A cash discount of $25 allowed by Diane Jones, a payable, had not been entered in Diane Jones's account.

You are required to take the above information into account and show:

(a) journal entries to correct the errors;
(b) the suspense account written up and balanced;
(c) the corrected trial balance.

 Solution

Journal entries		Dr ($)	Cr ($)
Item 1	Suspense account	180	
	Motor vans		180
Item 2	Purchases	90	
	Suspense account		90
Item 3	Drawings	140	
	Wages		140
Item 4	Diane Jones (trade payable)	25	
	Suspense account		25

Suspense account

	$		$
Motor van	180	Balance b/f	65
		Purchases	90
		Sundry payables	25
	180		180

Trial balance

	Dr ($)	Cr ($)
Premises	50,000	
Motor vans	7,220	
Sundry receivables	1,680	
Sundry payables		2,360
Purchases	160,350	
Sales		200,490
Wages	11,860	
Drawings	1,740	
Capital		30,000
	232,850	232,850

9.8   Computers in accounting

The use of computers to maintain bookkeeping records and produce financial statements is now widespread, even in small organisations. The use of computers is not specifically part of your syllabus, but no accounting textbook would be complete without mentioning some of the features and problems that such systems possess.

It is important, however, that you recognise that computers must perform the same bookkeeping tasks that have been described manually in this book. The double-entry system must still be maintained, and adequate controls must be in place to ensure its accuracy. In computer-based assessment questions, you will normally be required to answer questions on the assumption that the system is a manual one, so if you work in an organisation that has a sophisticated computerised accounting system, try to relate the principles of bookkeeping described here to those that take place in the computerised system.

Using computers provides a range of benefits such as:

- speed of input and processing of data;
- speed and flexibility of producing information;
- ability to manage large numbers of accounts and transactions;
- improved accuracy;
- automatic update of all related accounts in a transaction, with a single entry;
- less storage space required;
- additional checks on the input of data, for example, dates (31 November is not allowed), limits (no person can work more than 100 hours in a week), ranges (hourly wage rates are between $7.60 and $12.50) and so on.

However, the biggest single drawback of computerised systems is that the user cannot physically see what is happening to the bookkeeping system and errors and omissions cannot be readily identified.

Of course, many computerised accounting systems are 'self-balancing', in that a single transaction is input, and is used to update the ledger accounts, the daybooks, the control accounts, perhaps even the inventory records, and it is all too easy to assume that everything has been done correctly. Unfortunately, this is not always the case.

9.8.1 Aspects of computerised accounting systems

There are many different types of computerised system. Some lend themselves to large organisations, others to smaller organisations. Typical configurations are:

(i) a mainframe computer that has a very large capacity, supported by a minicomputer (slightly smaller) and perhaps several personal computers for individual users. Such a system might involve the users in entering data into the system, and accessing the results directly.

(ii) Networked computers, where the files are held centrally, but updated and accessed from remote locations by users.

(iii) Stand-alone computers, where files are held on individual computers, updated by those users.

All of these configurations have security implications. For example, some may allow individual users to update the ledger accounts. It is important that there is sufficient segregation of duties in this situation. Others may only allow access to the balances, but not the facility to amend those balances.

In all cases, the ledger accounts will have to balance and a trial balance will be produced. This may be part of the 'month-end routine', which typically produces totals of the transactions during, and balances at the end of, the month. The month-end routine would provide lists and totals of invoices issued and received, payments made, expenses incurred, as well as end-of-month balances of receivables, payables, inventories, bank and cash, and expenses.

The computer system will also be capable of making adjustments to the accounts for accruals, prepayments, allowance for receivables and so on. These will normally be input via a journal entry, as in a manual system.

9.9 Accounting coding systems

By now you will realise that a busy organisation will have a large number of ledger accounts and subsidiary records within and outside the accounting system. Using the titles of accounts to locate and cross-reference transactions could be difficult in such situations. Imagine the tax authorities maintaining all the records of taxpayers according to their names. There will be hundreds of thousands of taxpayers with the surnames Smith, or Khan or Jones – and thousands called John Smith or Helen Jones. Each needs a unique code to identify them from the others. The same applies to accounting systems. The ledger accounts require unique codes, as do inventory items, employees on the payroll and so on.

We could simply number them 1, 2, 3 and so on, but that would not be particularly helpful in locating an individual item. Some kind of coding system is needed. This is particularly important in computerised systems, which use codes to transfer data throughout the system.

Organisations could perhaps start with the five main categories of ledger accounts, for example:

- Assets Code 1
- Liabilities Code 2
- Capital Code 3
- Expenses Code 4
- Revenues Code 5

and then further subdivide them into more minor categories, for example:

- Non-current assets Code 12
- Current assets Code 13

Non-current assets could be further divided into types, for example, plant (1), motor vehicles (2), office equipment (3) and so on.

Codes could be included to identify the location of such items within the organisation, e.g. sales department, purchasing department, wages department, factory locations. This would enable depreciation to be charged to the department that utilises the item.

The following structure illustrates how a coding system may be used for a nominal ledger in a large organisation.

A six-digit code is used: the first digit represents the functional analysis; digits 2 and 3 represent the cost centre (i.e. the department); and digits 4–6 represent the type of expense involved.

Function	*Cost centre (within production)*	*Nominal ledger expense analysis*
1 Production	10 Machining	100 Raw material X
2 Sales	11 Assembly	101 Raw material Y
3 Administration	12 Finishing	201 Skilled-labour wages
		202 Unskilled-labour wages
		203 Salaries
		301 Rent
		601 Postage
		602 Stationery

An example code could be 110202, which represents unskilled-labour wage cost incurred in the machining cost centre of the production function.

It is generally accepted that codes should be:

(a) *Unique*. In order to avoid ambiguity, each item must have only one possible code.
(b) *Useful*. There is no point in using a code if there is to be no benefit from its use. The code will have to be learned by the users of the system so that it may be both applied and understood.
(c) *Compact*. It is generally accepted that the shorter the code the easier it is to learn and therefore the likelihood of mistakes and confusion is reduced. Thus, a code should be as short and compact as possible.
(d) *Meaningful*. If the code can be made meaningful by the characters of the code being connected in some way to the item that the code represents, the code will be more easily remembered and understood.

(e) *Self-checking*. The biggest problem with the use of codes is that users of the codes remember them incorrectly. To ensure that the information to be provided by the system is of value, each of the codes used must be validated. If a numeric code is used it can be designed in such a way as to be self-checking – this will help in identifying coding mistakes and avoid the production of incorrect information.

(f) *Expandable*. When designing a coding system it is important to consider the requirements of the organisation in the future. The design of accounting systems often involves a large amount of time and this is then followed by a period when the users are learning the system. If the code is not expandable, then it is likely that the system will have to be changed sooner rather than later. This will be costly in design time and will cause difficulties because the users of the system will have to learn the new system.

(g) *Standard size*. If codes are of varying size, then different users may write the same code differently. For example, if a part of a coding system comprises up to four characters, then the three-digit code AB1 could be written in a number of ways, with spaces and dashes in different places. Using AB01 would prevent this.

9.10 Summary

This chapter has outlined a variety of controls and checks that can be incorporated into or alongside the bookkeeping system to:

- help prevent errors and fraud;
- detect errors if they do occur;
- correct errors, often via the journal, once they have been discovered.

These controls and checks include:

- bank reconciliations,
- control accounts,
- suspense accounts.

The chapter concluded with an explanation of:

- computers in accounting,
- coding systems.

Revision Questions

? Question 1 Multiple choice

1.1 Following the preparation of the income statement, it is discovered that accrued expenses of $1,000 have been ignored and that closing inventories have been over-valued by 1,300. This will have resulted in:

$...............

1.2 The cash book shows a bank balance of $5,675 overdrawn at 31 August 20X5. It is subsequently discovered that a standing order for $125 has been entered twice, and that a dishonoured cheque for $450 has been debited in the cash book instead of credited. The correct bank balance should:

$...............

1.3 A supplier sends you a statement showing a balance outstanding of $14,350. Your own records show a balance outstanding of $14,500. The reason for this difference could be that:

(A) the supplier sent an invoice for $150 that you have not yet received.
(B) the supplier has allowed you $150 cash discount that you had omitted to enter in your ledgers.
(C) you have paid the supplier $150 that he has not yet accounted for.
(D) you have returned goods worth $150 that the supplier has not yet accounted for.

1.4 From the following information, calculate the value of purchases:

	$
Opening payables	142,600
Cash paid	542,300
Discounts received	13,200
Goods returned	27,500
Closing payables	137,800

$...............

1.5 A suspense account shows a credit balance of $130.
This could be due to:

(A) omitting a sale of $130 from the sales ledger.
(B) recording a purchase of $130 twice in the purchases account.
(C) failing to write off a bad debt of $130.
(D) recording an electricity bill paid of $65 by debiting the bank account and crediting the electricity account.

1.6 You are given the following information:

	$
Receivables at 1 January 20X3	10,000
Receivables at 31 December 20X3	9,000
Total receipts during 20X3	
(including cash sales of $5,000)	85,000

Sales on credit during 20X3 amount to:
$...............

1.7 Your cash book at 31 December 20X3 shows a bank balance of $565 overdrawn. On comparing this with your bank statement at the same date, you discover that

- a cheque for $57 drawn by you on 29 December 20X3 has not yet been presented for payment;
- a cheque for $92 from a customer, which was paid into the bank on 24 December 20X3, has been dishonoured on 31 December 20X3.

The correct bank balance to be shown in the statement of financial position at 31 December 20X3 is:
$...............

1.8 After calculating your company's profit for 20X3, you discover that

- a non-current asset costing $50,000 has been included in the purchases account;
- stationery costing $10,000 has been included as closing inventories of raw materials, instead of as inventories of stationery.

These two errors have had the effect of:

(A) understating gross profit by $40,000 and understating net profit by $50,000.
(B) understating both gross profit and net profit by $40,000.
(C) understating gross profit by $60,000 and understating net profit by $50,000.
(D) overstating both gross profit and net profit by $60,000.

1.9 The sales ledger control account at 1 May had balances of $32,750 debit and $1,275 credit. During May, sales of $125,000 were made on credit. Receipts from receivables amounted to $122,500 and cash discounts of $550 were allowed. Refunds of $1,300 were made to customers.
The closing balances at 31 May are:

Debit	Credit
$...............	$...............

1.10 Your firm's cash book at 30 April 20X8 shows a balance at the bank of $2,490. Comparison with the bank statement at the same date reveals the following differences:

	$
Unpresented cheques	840
Bank charges not in cash book	50
Receipts not yet credited by the bank	470
Dishonoured cheque not in cash book	140

The correct bank balance at 30 April 20X8 is:

$...............

1.11 The following information relates to a bank reconciliation.

(i) The bank balance in the cash book before taking the items below into account was $8,970 overdrawn.

(ii) Bank charges of $550 on the bank statement have not been entered in the cash book.

(iii) The bank has credited the account in error with $425, which belongs to another customer.

(iv) Cheque payments totalling $3,275 have been entered in the cash book but have not been presented for payment.

(v) Cheques totalling $5,380 have been correctly entered on the debit side of the cash book but have not been paid in at the bank.

What was the balance as shown by the bank statement *before* taking the items above into account?

$...............

1.12 Which of the following is *not* the purpose of a sales ledger control account?

(A) A sales ledger control account provides a check on the arithmetic accuracy of the personal ledger.

(B) A sales ledger control account helps to locate errors in the trial balance.

(C) A sales ledger control account ensures that there are no errors in the personal ledger.

(D) Control accounts deter fraud.

1.13 When reconciling the payables ledger control account with the list of payable ledger balances of M, the following errors were found:

- the purchase daybook had been overstated by $500;
- the personal ledger of a supplier had been understated by $400.

What adjustment must be made to correct these errors?

	Control account	*List of payable balances*
A	Cr $500	Decrease by $400
B	Dr $500	Increase by $400
C	Dr $400	Increase by $500
D	Cr $400	Decrease by $500

1.14 In a receivables report, which *one* of the following would you *not* expect to see?

   (A) Total receivable balances outstanding for current and previous months.
   (B) Receivable balances, excluding sales tax.
   (C) Credit limit.
   (D) Sales to date.

1.15 Z's bank statement shows a balance of $825 overdrawn. The bank statement includes bank charges of $50, which have not been entered in the cash book. There are unpresented cheques totalling $475 and deposits not yet credited of $600. The bank statement incorrectly shows a direct debit payment of $160, which belongs to another customer.

   The figure for the bank balance in the statement of financial position should be:

$.......... overdrawn

1.16 I Ltd operates the imprest system for petty cash. On 1 July there was a float of $150, but it was decided to increase this to $200 from 1 August onwards. During July, the petty cashier received $25 from staff for using the photocopier and a cheque for $90 was cashed for an employee. In July, cheques were drawn for $500 for petty cash.

   How much cash was paid out as cash expenses by the petty cashier in July?

$...............

? Question 2

A business had the following transactions from 1 March 20X1 to 31 May 20X1:

	Purchases				Sales		
Supplier	*Net $*	*Sales tax $*	*Gross $*	*Customer $*	*Net $*	*Sales tax $*	*Gross $*
A	300	52.50	352.50	V	700	122.50	822.50
B	200	35.00	235.00	W	400	70.00	470.00
C	800	140.00	940.00	X	1,200	210.00	1,410.00
D	1,000	175.00	1,175.00	Y	200	35.00	235.00
E	100	17.50	117.50	Z	500	87.50	587.50
	2,400	420.00	2,820.00		3,000	525.00	3,525.00

	Payments			Receipts	
Supplier	*$*		*Customer*	*$*	
A	300		V	600	
B	180		W	2	
C	920		X	1,000	
D	700		Y	115	
E	85		Z	475	
	2,185			2,190	

Brought forward balances at 1 March 20X1 were $470 for trade receivables and $600 for trade payables.

Requirements

Write up the following accounts

Receivables control

	$		$
Balance b/f		Cash	
Sales		Balance c/f	
Sales tax			

Payables control

	$		$
		Balance b/f	
Cash		Purchases	
Balance c/f		Sales tax	

Sales tax

	$		$
Payables		Receivables	
Balance c/f			

Sales

	$		$
Income statement		Receivables	

Purchases

	$		$
Payables		Income statement	

? Question 3

The assistant accountant of BC Ltd has prepared a sales ledger control account at 30 September 20X5 for you to reconcile with the list of sales ledger balances at that date. The control account balances are:

Debit balances	$226,415
Credit balances	$1,250

The list of balances extracted from the sales ledger totals $225,890. You discover the following:

  (i) The credit balances have been included on the list of receivables as debit balances.

 (ii) A sales invoice for $6,400 plus sales tax at 17.5 per cent has been recorded in the sales daybook as $4,600 plus sales tax at 17.5 per cent. It has been entered correctly in the sales ledger.

(iii) Cash discounts allowed amounted to $840 and cash discounts received amounted to $560; the only entry in the control account for discounts is a debit for cash discounts received.

(iv) A dishonoured cheque for $450 from a customer has been recorded correctly in the control account, but no entry has been made in the receivable's personal account.

 (v) A contra entry between the sales and purchase ledgers of $750 has been omitted from the control account.

(vi) The control account contains receipts from cash sales of $860 but does not contain the invoices to which these receipts refer; no entries have been made in the sales ledger for these invoices or receipts.

(vii) No entries have been made in the control account for bad debts written off ($2,150) and allowance for receivables ($2,400). Ignore sales tax for item (vii)

Requirements

(a) Complete the table below to show the entries needed in the sales ledger control account to correct the present balance; consider each of the seven items mentioned-if no entry is required in the control account, write N/E' in the 'Description' column and ignore the other columns.

Item	Description (max. 4 words each)	Debit or credit?	Amount ($)
(i)			
(ii)			
(iii)			
(iv)			
(v)			
(vi)			
(vii)			

(b) Complete the missing figures given below to calculate the revised sales ledger control account balance:

	$
Original balance	225,165
Add: debit entries required	
Less: credit entries required	
Revised balance	

(c) *Two* of the seven items noted above required adjustment to the list of sales ledger balances. Insert the missing entries into the statement given below:

	$
Original sales ledger balances	225,890

Items requiring adjustment

Item no.	Description (max. two words each)	Adjustment $

Total adjustment

Corrected total

(d) State four facilities that a computerised sales ledger system might offer to BC Ltd (*max. 3 words each*).

(i)

(ii)

(iii)

(iv)

Question 4

BH commenced in business some years ago, maintaining a single ledger for all accounts, plus a cash book. His business has now expanded to the extent that he now needs to consider improving his accounting system by dividing the ledger into sections and introducing a petty cash system.

Requirements

(a) Complete the missing word in this sentence.

A system for recording petty cash payment is the _____ system.

(b) State the names of 4 daybooks.

(i)

(ii)

(iii)

(iv)

(c) From the following information, draw up a sales ledger control account for the month of February 20X7 by entering the missing figures in the control account below.

	$
Owing by customers at 1 February 20X7	103,670
Owing to customers at 1 February 20X7	1,400
Sales, excluding sales tax	175,860
Sales tax on sales	10,350
Returns inwards, including sales tax	9,500
Sales tax on returns inwards	1,300
Refunds to customers	800
Cash sales, including sales tax	12,950
Cheques received from receivables	126,750
Discounts allowed to customers	1,150
Contra entries to purchase ledger	750
Bad debts written off	2,300
Dishonoured cheques from receivables	1,580

In addition, BH has been notified that he will receive a dividend of 10p in the pound from a previously written-off bad debt of $3,000. The amount has not yet been received.

On 28 February 20X7, an allowance for receivables is to be made of 2 per cent of the net balance that existed at 1 February 20X7.

Amounts owing to customers at 28 February 20X7 amounted to $840.

BH – Sales ledger control account

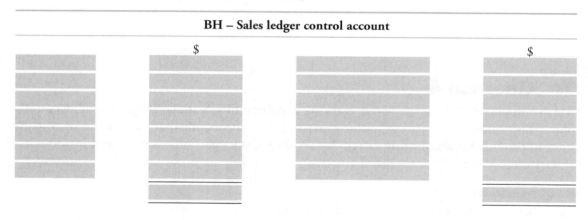

? Question 5

The following balances appeared in your company's sales ledger at 1 April 20X8:

		$
Receivable P	Debit	5,000
Receivable Q	Debit	1,200
Receivable R	Debit	1,045
Receivable S	Debit	8,750
Receivable T	Credit	140
Receivable U	Credit	900
Receivable V	Debit	400

During April 20X8, the following transactions occurred:

Receivable		$	
Sales	P	4,700	
	Q	1,175	
	R	3,520	
	U	9,400	
Returns	P	1,400	
	R	800	
	S	750	
Receipts	P	9,740	
	Q		Balance at 1 April 20X8 less 5 per cent cash discount (cheque dishonoured later in the month)
	R	1,520	
	S	7,500	
Refunds	T		Balance at 1 April 20X8

The balance on V's account is written off as bad. The remaining balance on S's account is offset against his balance in the purchase ledger. An allowance for receivables of 5 per cent of closing balances is to be made.

Requirements
(a) Complete the missing figures in the following table in order to calculate the total of receivable balances at 30 April 20X8. Where a figure is to be deducted from the balance, show it in brackets. If no figure is required in a particular box, leave it blank.

	P ($)	Q ($)	R ($)	S ($)	T ($)	U ($)	V ($)	Total ($)
Balance 1/4/X8								
Credit sales								
Returns								
Receipts								
Discount allowed								
Dishonoured cheque								
Refund								
Bad debt w/off								
Set off								
Balance 30/4/X8								

(b) Complete the missing figures in the sales ledger control account given below.

Sales ledger control account

	$		$
Balance b/f		Balance b/f	
Sales		Receipts	
Dishonoured cheque		Returns	
Refund		Discounts allowed	
Balance c/f		Bad debts written off	
		Set off/contra	
		Balance c/f	
Balance b/f		Balance b/f	

(c) Insert the missing word in this sentence:

(i) The principle purpose of a control account is to check on the accuracy of the _____ _____ accounts in the relevant ledger that it controls.

(ii) It is called a 'total account' because it contains the total of all transactions posted to the _____ accounts, taken from summary daybooks, cash books and so on.

? Question 6

After calculating net profit for the year ended 31 March 20X8, WL has the following trial balance:

	Debit ($)	Credit ($)
Land and buildings – cost	10,000	
Land and buildings – acc. depreciation at 31 March 20X8		2,000
Plant – cost	12,000	
Plant – acc. depreciation at 31 March 20X8		3,000
Inventories	2,500	
Receivables	1,500	
Bank	8,250	
Payables		1,700
Rent prepaid	400	
Wages accrued		300
Capital account		19,400
Profit for the year ended 31 March 20X8		9,750
	34,650	36,150

A suspense account was opened for the difference in the trial balance.

Immediately after production of the above, the following errors were discovered:

(i) A payable account had been debited with a $300 sales invoice (which had been correctly recorded in the sales account).

(ii) The heat and light account had been credited with gas paid $150.

(iii) G Gordon had been credited with a cheque received from G Goldman for $800. Both are receivables.

(iv) The insurance account contained a credit entry for insurance prepaid of $500, but the balance had not been carried down and hence had been omitted from the above trial balance.

(v) Purchase returns had been overcast by $700.

Requirements

(a) Complete the table below to indicate the journal entries necessary to correct each of the above errors.

Item	Name of account	Debit amount ($)	Credit amount ($)
(i)			
(ii)			
(iii)			
(iv)			
(v)			

(b) Insert the missing items into the suspense account given below, in respect of any errors that you have identified in (a), and total the account:

Suspense account

	$	Description	Item no.	$
Balance as per trial balance				

(c) Name the type of error that has occurred in each of items (i)__(iii) (*max. five words each*).

(i)

(ii)

(iii)

(d) Insert the missing items into the boxes below to show the recalculated net profit for the year to 31 March 20X8:

		$
First draft profit		9,750
Adjustment re:		
Adjustment re:		
Revised net profit		

(e) Insert the missing figures into the statement of financial position of WL at 31 March 20X8, given below:

Assets	Cost ($)	Acc. Depreciation ($)	Carrying Amount ($)
Non-current assets			
Land and buildings	10,000	2,000	
Plant	12,000	3,000	
	22,000	5,000	
Current assets			
Inventories			
Receivables			
Prepayments			
Bank			
Capital and liabilities			
Capital			
Profit for the year			
Current liabilities			
Payables			
Accrual			

? Question 7

You are the payroll administrator in your organisation, and your responsibilities include the preparation of the monthly payroll for 100 employees.

Each employee is paid a basic monthly wage, with overtime at time and a third. Employees complete an overtime report form that they submit direct to you each month. You input the necessary data to a computerised payroll system, in batches, which are processed as a single run at the end of each month.

The system produces a monthly summary of payroll data. You then journalise the totals to provide input to the nominal ledger.

You make out cheques in the following month for employees' net wages.

The highest-paid employee earns $2,000 basic pay per month gross.

An extract from the payroll printout for the month ended 31 October 20X8 was as follows:

Employee number	Gross wages ($)	Tax ($)	Employees' SS ($)	Pension payments	Employer's SS ($)
1	6,000	1,000	200	360	520
2	2,222	360	200	132	160
3	2,160	340	180	125	150
4	1,760	300	160	105	120
etc					
100	600	2	48	40	60
Totals	78,000	12,800	5,600	4,600	5,250

Requirements

(a) Insert the missing items into the boxes given below in respect of the ledger entries to be made for wages:

(i)

	DR or CR?	Amount ($)
Total wages expense account		

This is made up of the figures from the following columns in the question:

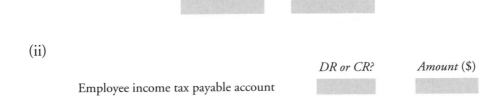

Column heading	Amount ($)

(ii)

	DR or CR?	Amount ($)
Employee income tax payable account		

This is made up of the figures from the following columns in the question:

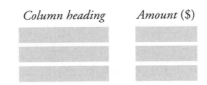

Column heading	Amount ($)

(iii)

	DR or CR?	Amount ($)
Pension scheme payable account		

(iv)

	DR or CR?	Amount ($)
Wages payable account (i.e. net wages payable)		

(b) Insert into the box the amount to be debited to the income statement for the month of October, in respect of wages costs:

$....................

? Question 8

The trial balance of E Ltd did not balance and the following errors have been discovered:

 (i) A cheque for $1,000 received from a receivable had been credited to the sales account and debited to the bank account.
 (ii) The cash book had been undercast by $250.
(iii) A machine costing $5,000 had been debited to the machinery repairs account. Machinery is depreciated at 10 per cent on cost and no residual value is assumed.

Requirements

(a) Insert the missing items into the table below to show the correction of the above errors.

Item	Account	Debit ($)	Credit ($)
(i)			
(ii)			
(iii)			
(iv)			

(b) (i) Insert the missing words in this sentence.
        Financial control is important to prevent _____ and _____ .
    (ii) Insert the missing words:

   - An example of financial control is the _____ ledger _____ account.
   - An example of financial control is the bank _____.

Solutions to Revision Questions

 Solution 1

1.1 Ignoring accrued expenses means that insufficient expense has been charged against profits, thus making profits too high (i.e. overstated); overvaluing closing inventories will have resulted in cost of goods sold that is too low, hence gross profit will be too high (i.e. overstated). Both errors result in an overstatement of profit, so the correct answer is an overstatement of $1,000 + $1,300 = $2,300.

1.2 The correct bank balance can be found as follows:

	$	
Cash book balance	5,675	overdrawn (credit)
Correct standing order error	125	debit
Reverse error of dishonoured cheque	450	credit
Enter dishonoured cheque correctly	450	credit
Correct balance	6,450	overdrawn

1.3 Answer: (B)

The supplier's records show a smaller amount owing than your own records. This could not be due to an invoice not received as this would further increase the amount owing according to your records. If you have paid the supplier, this would further reduce the balance in his records. If you have returned goods, this would also reduce the balance in his records. If you are to account for cash discount in your records, this would reduce the balance in your records to agree to the supplier's.

1.4 Purchases can be found by constructing a control account:

	$		$
Cash paid	542,300	Opening payables	142,600
Discount received	13,200	Purchases	?
Goods returned	27,500		
Closing payables	137,800		
	720,800		720,800

Purchases = $720, 800 − $142, 600 = $578, 200

1.5 Answer: (B)

A credit balance on the suspense account indicates that the debit total of the trial balance was higher than the credit total. An error that could cause this would involve either too great a value having been debited, too little a value having been credited, or a combination of these where an item has been recorded as a debit when it ought to have been a credit.

(A) would result in too little having been debited to the customer's account.
(B) would result in an additional debit entry, therefore this is the correct answer.
(C) would not cause any imbalance in the trial balance as both the debit and credit entries will have been omitted.
(D) would not cause any imbalance in the trial balance as both a debit and a credit entry have been made even though they were the wrong way round.

1.6 Sales can be found by constructing a mini sales control account:

	$		$
Receivables at 1.1.X3	10,000	Receipts, less cash sales	80,000
Sales	?	Receivables at 31.12.X3	9,000
	89,000		89,000

Sales = $79,000

1.7 The cash book balance needs adjusting for the dishonoured cheque, and the bank balance needs adjusting for the unpresented cheque. The correct balance for the statement of financial position is therefore:

$565 overdrawn + dishonoured cheque $92 = $657 overdrawn

1.8 Answer: (A)

Including a non-current asset in the purchases account has overstated purchases, and hence has overstated cost of goods sold; this has the effect of understating gross profit. Including stationery inventories with closing inventories of raw materials has the effect of increasing closing inventories of raw materials, which then understates the cost of goods sold, and hence overstates gross profit. So, gross profit has been understated by $50,000 and overstated by $10,000 – a net understatement of $40,000.

Inventory of stationery should reduce the total of stationery expenses in the income statement. Omitting to consider the closing inventories will have overstated the expenses. An overstatement of gross profit and an overstatement of expenses by the same amount (because of the stationery error) will have no effect on net profit. Therefore, the only effect on net profit will be the understatement due to the non-current asset error.

The result, therefore, is that gross profit has been understated by $40,000 and the net profit understated by $50,000.

1.9   The closing balance is calculated as:

	$	
Opening balance (32,750 – 1,275)	31,475	Debit
Sales	125,000	Debit
Receipts	(122,500)	Credit
Cash discounts	(550)	Credit
Refunds	1,300	Debit
Closing balance	34,725	Debit

1.10

	$
Original cash book figure	2,490
Adjustment re: charges	(50)
Adjustment re: dishonoured cheque	(140)
	2,300

1.11

Cash book	$	Bank statement	$
Balance	(8,970)	Balance	(11,200)
Bank charges	(550)	Credit in error	(425)
		Unpresented cheques	(3,275)
		Outstanding deposits	5,380
	(9,520)		(9,520)

1.12   Answer: (C)

1.13   Answer: (B)

1.14   Answer: (B)

1.15

	$
Bank statement – overdrawn	(825)
Unpresented cheques	(475)
Deposits outstanding	600
Direct debit error	160
Bank balance – overdrawn	(540)

1.16

	$
Petty cash balance at 1 July	150
Photocopies receipts	25
Cheque cashed	(90)
	85
Cheques drawn for cash	500
	585
Petty cash balance at 1 August	(200)
Cash paid out for expenses	385

Solution 2

This question involves the ledger entries to be made from sales and purchase daybooks (journals). The total invoice values are debited/credited to the receivable/payable accounts (and hence to the control accounts), while the sales and purchases accounts contain only the net amounts. Input sales tax is debited to the sales tax control, and output sales tax is credited.

Receivables control				
	$			$
Balance b/f	470	Cash		2,190
Sales	3,000	Balance c/f		1,805
Sales tax	525			
	3,995			3,995

Payables control				
	$			$
		Balance c/f		600
Cash	2,185	Purchases		2,400
Balance c/f	1,235	Sales tax		420
	3,420			3,420

Sales tax				
	$			$
Payables	420	Receivables		525
Balance c/f	105			
	525			525

Sales				
	$			$
Income statement	3,000	Receivables		3,000
	3,000			3,000

Purchase				
	$			$
Payables	2,400	Income statement		2,400
	2,400			2,400

Solution 3

- Remember to include the sales tax element in the incorrect sales invoice.
- Allowance for receivables never appears in the control account, nor is it adjusted for in the individual's account.

(a)

	Description	Debit/Credit?	Amount $
(i)	N/E		
(ii)	Error in daybook	Debit	2,115
(iii)	Discount allowed	Credit	560
	Discount received	Credit	840
(iv)	N/E		
(v)	Contra	Credit	750
(vi)	Cash sales	Debit	860
(vii)	Bad debts written off	Credit	2,150

(b)

	$
Original balance	225,165
Add: debit entries required	2,975
Less: credit entries required	(4,300)
Revised balance	223,840

(c)

	Description (max. two words each)	Adjustment $	
	Sales ledger balances	225,890	
(i)	Credit balances	(2,500)	(This is a reversal)
(iv)	Dishonoured cheque	450	
		223,840	

(d) (i) Speed.
(ii) Accuracy.
(iii) Control accounts.
(iv) Aged receivable analysis.

 Solution 4

- In Part (c), take care with the opening and closing balances, and the inclusion of sales tax on credit sales.
- Cash sales should be ignored, as they are not entered into any sales ledger account.
- Refunds and contras to the purchase ledger often cause difficulties.
- Dishonoured cheques and bad debts recovered also need careful attention.
- The allowance for receivables can be ignored, as no entries are made in the sales ledger for this allowance.

(a) A system for recording petty cash payments is the imprest system.

(b)   (i) Sales daybook.
     (ii) Purchase daybook.
   (iii) Sales returns daybook.
   (iv) Purchase returns daybook.

(c)

BH – Sales ledger control account

	$		$
Opening receivables b/d	103,670	Credit balances b/d	1,400
Sales	175,860	Returns inwards	9,500
Sales tax on sales	10,350	Payments received	126,750
Refunds	800	Discounts allowed	1,150
Dishonoured cheques	1,580	Contra to purchase ledger	750
Bad debts written back	300	Bad debts written off	2,300
Credit balances c/d	840	Closing receivables c/d	151,550
	293,400		293,400

✅ Solution 5

- Take your time with Part (a) – accuracy will improve your chances of answering Part (b).
- If you also add a 'total' column at the end of your table, this will assist in answering Part (b).

(a) Receivable balances

	Receivables							
	P	Q	R	S	T	U	V	Total
	$	$	$	$	$	$	$	$
Balance 1/4/X8	5,000	1,200	1,045	8,750	(140)	(900)	400	15,355
Credit sales	4,700	1,175	3,520	–	–	9,400	–	18,795
Returns	(1,400)	–	(800)	(750)	–	–	–	(2,950)
Receipts	(9,740)	(1,140)	(1,520)	(7,500)	–	–	–	(19,900)
Discount allowed	–	(60)	–	–	–	–	–	(60)
Dishonoured cheque	–	–	1,520	–	–	–	–	1,520
Refund	–	–	–	–	140	–	–	140
Bad debt w/off	–	–	–	–	–	–	(400)	(400)
Set off	–	–	–	(500)	–	–	–	(500)
Balance 30/4/X8	(1,440)	1,175	3,765	–	–	8,500	–	12,000

List of balances

	$
P	1,440 Cr
Q	1,175 Dr
R	3,765 Dr
S	–
T	–
U	8,500 Dr
V	–
	12,000 Dr

(b)

Sales ledger control account

	$		$
Balance b/f	16,395	Balance b/d	1,040
Sales	18,795	Receipts	19,900
Dishonoured cheque	1,520	Returns	2,950
Refund	140	Discounts allowed	60
Balance c/d	1,440	Bad debts written off	400
		Set off/contra	500
		Balance c/d	13,440
	38,290		38,290
Balance b/d	13,440	Balance b/d	1,440

(c) (i) The main purpose of a control account is to check on the accuracy of the personal accounts in the relevant ledger that it controls.

(ii) It is called a 'total account' because it contains the total of all transactions posted to the individual accounts, taken from summary daybooks, cash books and so on.

☑ Solution 6

- Part (a) is straightforward, but take care to identify those corrections that involve the suspense **account**.
- To assist with Part (d), examine the journal entries; identify those that affect profit (i.e. revenue or expense accounts); if they are being debited, this will reduce profit; if they are being credited this will increase profit.

(a) Journal entries

		Debit	Credit
		$	$
(i)	Receivable	300	
	Payable		300
(ii)	Heat and light	300	
	Suspense account		300
(iii)	G Gordon	800	
	G Goldman		800
(iv)	Insurance	500	
	Suspense account		500
(v)	Purchase returns	700	
	Suspense account		700

(b)

Suspense account			
	$		$
Balance as per trial balance	1,500	Heat and light (ii)	300
		Insurance (iv)	500
		Purchase return (v)	700
	1,500		1,500

(c) (i) Error of principle
(ii) Reversal of entries
(iii) Error of commission

(d)

	$
First draft profit	9,750
Adjustment re: heat and light	(300)
Adjustment re: purchase returns	(700)
Revised net profit	8,750

(e) Statement of financial position of WL as at 31 March 20X8

	Cost $	Acc. Depn. $	Carrying Amount $
Assets			
Non-current assets			
Land and buildings	10,000	(2,000)	8,000
Plant	12,000	(3,000)	9,000
	22,000	(5,000)	17,000
Current assets			
Inventories		2,500	
Receivables (1,500 + 300)		1,800	
Prepayments (400 + 500)		900	
Bank		8,250	
			13,450
			30,450
Capital and liabilities			
Capital			19,400
Add: Profit for the year			8,750
			28,150
Current liabilities			
Payables (1,700 + 300)		2,000	
Accrual		300	
			2,300
			30,450

 Solution 7

- In Part (a), there are several alternative ways of journalising wages entries, but all should end up with the same final balance on each account.
- Remember that employees' income tax, employees' social security and employee contributions to a pension scheme are all deducted from their gross wages, and therefore reduce the balance on the wages payable account.
- Remember that employer's social security is an additional charge to the wages expense account.
- The question states that employees are paid in the following month; therefore do not include any payments in your journal entries.

(a) Journal entries

		$
(i) Total wages expense account	DR	83,250
This comprises:		
Gross wages		78,000
Employers' SS		5,250
(ii) Employee income tax payable account	CR	23,650
This comprises:		
Tax		12,800
Employees' SS		5,600
Employers' SS		5,250
(iii) Pension scheme payable account	CR	4,600
(iv) Wages payable account	CR	55,000

(b) The amount to be debited to the income statement for October is $83,250, made up as follows:

	$
Gross wages	78,000
Employer's SS	5,250
	83,250

 Solution 8

(a)

	Debit $	Credit $
(i) Sales	1,000	
Receivables		1,000
(ii) Bank	250	
Suspense account		250
(iii) Machinery	5,000	
Machinery repairs		5,000
(iv) Charge for depreciation of machinery	500	
Accumulated depreciation on machinery		500

(b) (i) Financial control is important to prevent error and fraud.

 (ii) • An example of financial control is the sales ledger control account.

  • An example of financial control is the bank reconciliation.

10

The Regulatory Framework of Accounting

The Regulatory Framework of Accounting

10

LEARNING OUTCOMES

When you have completed this chapter, you should be able to:

▸ identify the underlying assumptions, policies and changes in accounting estimates;

▸ identify the basic methods of valuing assets on current cost, fair value and value to the business bases and their impact on profit measures and statement of financial position values;

▸ explain the influence of legislation (e.g. Companies Acts) and accounting standards on the production of published accounting information for organisations;

▸ identify the requirements for external audit and the basic processes undertaken;

▸ explain the purpose and basic procedures of internal audit;

▸ explain the meaning of fair presentation (or 'true and fair view');

▸ explain the purpose of audit checks and audit trails.

10.1 Introduction

The objective of accounting is to present financial information to users, as we saw in Chapter 1. Users need to be able to rely on the information provided in those financial statements to enable them to make appropriate decisions.

You have perhaps realised by now that there are often several alternative ways of valuing items entered in the bookkeeping system, and different methods of determining how much of an item should be shown in the income statement and how much in the statement of financial position. You will probably also realise that some of these depend entirely on judgement and opinion.

For example, you have seen how depreciation is an estimate of the cost of a non-current asset consumed during a period. It depends on judgement as to how long it is likely to be in use, what its residual value may be, and whether it should be depreciated on a straight line, reducing balance or some other basis. You have looked at three different ways of measuring inventories. You have seen how estimates of accruals and prepayments are entered into the financial statements. All of these 'estimates' affect the profit and the position shown by the statement of financial position.

Accountants need some guidance in the way in which they prepare the financial statements. This chapter looks at some of the ways in which accountants take decisions on methods of accounting and valuation for certain items. This chapter also looks at the role of auditors, who check that the rules on accounting have been followed.

10.2 Accounting conventions

There is no agreed list of accounting conventions. Authors differ in the relative importance they attribute to each of the possible conventions that can be identified. But there is a fair degree of consensus that the conventions discussed below are of particular importance.

In this section we have referred to 'conventions' but they could also be described as 'concepts', 'rules', 'practices', assumptions and so on. The important point is for you to understand what the terms mean and not worry about how they should be described.

They are presented in a list, which is not in order of importance. Later in your studies you will learn that some are regarded as more importance than others, but at this stage you should concentrate on knowing what each convention means.

The conventions can be related to each other, and they can also be related to the qualitative characteristics discussed in Chapter 1, Section 1.4. However, at this stage they are presented as stand-alone individual conventions.

The list of conventions below are all key terms.

10.2.1 The business entity convention

This convention separates the individual(s) behind a business from the business itself, and only records transactions in the accounts that affect the business. This convention can be interpreted in two ways:

- In the case of a sole trader or partnership, the entity is viewed as a vehicle through which the owner(s) engage in economic activity with a view to profit.
- In the case of a company, the entity is viewed as having a separate identity with its own objectives, the owners merely being other interested parties having claims against the entity.

10.2.2 The money measurement convention

This limits the recognition of accounting events to those that can be expressed in money terms. This convention thus excludes the recording of many other economic factors that are being debated under the title of social responsibility accounting. For example, no value is attributed to key employees within the organisation. Monetary measurements are used because if all the items covered by an accounting statement are stated as an amount of money, then the cost of the items can be seen and their aggregate cost determined. There is thus a unity of meaning that makes financial statements readily understood and provide a common denominator for financial analysis.

10.2.3 The historical cost convention

The historical cost of an asset is the original amount paid for an asset when it was acquired. An advantage of this convention is that the historical cost is objective. We saw in Chapter 6 that non-current assets are stated at historical cost, less accumulated depreciation. If some other value was used, for example the amount the asset could be sold for, this would be subjective and as a result the financial statements may be less reliable for users.

10.2.4 The objectivity convention

Financial statements should not be influenced by the personal bias of the person preparing them. Thus, figures used in financial statements should be objective. Ideally, this should mean that any two accountants would produce the same figure, for example, for profit. In practice, there is always some judgement when preparing financial statements but when exercising that judgement the accountant should be neutral and not trying to produce, for example, a larger, or smaller, profit to benefit his/her own purposes. Financial statements which are objective should be reliable.

10.2.5 The dual aspect convention

This convention is the basis of double-entry bookkeeping and it means that every transaction entered into has a double effect on the position of the entity as recorded in the ledger accounts at the time of that transaction.

10.2.6 The realisation convention

This convention states that we recognise sales revenue as having been earned at the time when goods or services have been supplied and a sales invoice issued. Sales revenue is not realised when a customer places an order, as at that stage it is too early to say whether an eventual sale will be made. On the other hand, we should not wait until the cash is received from a customer before recognising that a sale has been made.

The other side of the realisation concept is to ask at what stage an asset, in this case a receivable, should be recognised. Thus we recognise a receivable when an invoice is raised; we do not recognise a receivable when an order is placed as it is too early to say that we have an 'asset'. On the other hand, if we only recognised revenue when cash was received, statements of financial position would not have receivables!

The words 'realised' and 'recognised' are important. Recognised means that an item is included in financial statements; items are recognised when they are realised.

Take particular care with goods sold on a 'sale-or-return' basis – the goods are not strictly 'sold' until they have been accepted by the buyer or the deadline for return has passed. If the full sales value of the goods has been included with sales and receivables (and the full cost taken out of inventories), the amounts that could still be returned should be taken out of sales/receivables and added back into inventories. The profit is then automatically included in the period in which it was actually earned.

10.2.7 The periodicity convention

It can be argued that the only correct measurement of an organisation's profitability is that which is made at the end of the organisation's life. However, there is a need to assess the financial position (i.e. statement of financial position) and performance (i.e. income statement) of an organisation during its life by producing periodic financial statements.

This assumes that transactions can be identified with a particular period, but in reality a number of other conventions (such as matching, realisation, prudence and accrual) are used to determine the treatment required.

The convention also enables comparisons to be made between one period and the other.

10.2.8 The accruals and matching conventions

There are two conventions combined here, but they interrelate. They arise from the periodicity convention and the need to identify transactions with particular accounting periods.

The accruals convention states that expenditure incurred in a particular accounting period should be accounted for in that period, irrespective of whether or not it has been invoiced or paid for. For example, if a business has engaged lawyers to do some legal work, the accrual may be made for that legal work even though the lawyers may not have yet submitted their invoice. Similarly, revenue that has been earned in that period should be accounted for in that period, irrespective of the date of invoice or the receipt of monies from the transaction. For example, if a business has some money in a deposit account at a bank, an accrual may be made for the interest due to be received even though the interest has not yet appeared on the bank statement. The convention applies equally to all transactions, whether involving revenue, expenses, assets or liabilities. If the transaction has occurred during the period, then it should be accounted for.

The matching convention is similar, but goes one step further, in that it attempts to match the revenue earned in a period with the expenses consumed *in earning that revenue*. It may happen that expenditure has been incurred in a period, but it has not been used to generate revenue during that same period. An example of this is goods purchased that remain unused at the end of the period. They have not been used to generate revenue in the period of purchase, so they are not included as part of the cost of goods sold in that period; on the assumption that they will be used to generate revenue in the future, they are carried forward and matched with the sales of the future. Thus the trading account has 'cost of goods sold' rather than 'purchases' as the expense item, and closing inventories are carried forward to be matched with the sales revenue of the next period.

This creates a problem in that the accruals convention states that the expense should be accounted for in that period, but the matching convention states that expense should be matched to revenue.

Generally, a prudent view is taken of expenses. If they have been incurred during the period, they are taken into that period's income statement, even though they *may* have been incurred to provide future revenue. It is only where they can be reasonably identified with future earning potential that they are carried forward to future periods, and so most expenses are charged to the income statement for the period in which they were incurred.

Similarly, a prudent view must also be taken of revenue. If monies have been received during a period in respect of revenue that has not yet been earned (e.g. the receipt of a deposit for a customer's order that has not yet been fulfilled), this must not be treated as revenue in that period, but carried forward until the order has been satisfied, and matched with the relevant expense incurred.

10.2.9 The materiality convention

Accounting statements are prepared for the benefit of various user groups. It is essential that the information provided is both significant and easily understood. The materiality convention ensures that the information provided is clear by omitting items that are not significant to the user in understanding the overall financial position of the organisation. Thus the materiality convention should make the financial statements *relevant* to users. The distinction between what is significant and what is not varies depending on the size of the organisation, and is a matter for judgement. Determining at what point an item becomes material depends partly on value, partly on the nature of the item concerned and partly on its effect on the results that will be reported.

As a general rule, items with a relatively small (5 per cent of net profit) monetary value are not significant unless they change a profit into a loss or vice versa or affect sensitive issues. The convention can be applied to the classification of items as 'revenue expenditure' rather than 'capital expenditure'. For example, the purchase of storage boxes for floppy disks is strictly capital expenditure as the boxes will be used over several years (and therefore they should be depreciated over their estimated useful life). However, their value is very small and therefore it is justifiable to treat them as revenue expenditure and included in the income statement in the period in which they were bought. Another example is the treatment of inventories of stationery at the end of a period – the matching convention dictates that the cost of unused inventory should be carried forward as an asset, but most organisations would find this cumbersome, and the effect on profit minimal, and therefore many would choose to make no adjustment for such inventories, unless their value is material.

Materiality can also be applied to 'aggregation'. Material items should be disclosed separately in the financial statements, but immaterial items may be aggregated together. For example, the charge for depreciation and the loss on sale of a non-current asset could be aggregated where both are immaterial.

Materiality can be applied to 'offsetting'. In general, assets and liabilities should not be offset; nor should revenue and expenses. However, where the amounts are immaterial, then offsetting may occur. For example, discounts received and discounts allowed should normally be shown separately, but if they are immaterial, they may be offset to give a net figure.

10.2.10   The stable monetary unit convention

Financial statements are prepared in monetary terms, using the dollar, yen and so on. It is assumed that the monetary value of a currency is stable from one period to the next; however, this is not the case as most economies experience inflation. No adjustment is made to financial statements to allow for inflation or deflation. This means that when comparing the profit of 1 year with the next, this is not a true comparison as part of any increase may be attributable to inflation.

10.2.11   The going concern convention

The going concern convention assumes that the business will continue in operation for the foreseeable future, which is taken to be at least 1 year. In previous chapters you have implicitly implemented this convention; for example, in calculating depreciation, you have assumed that there will be future years against which the cost of the non-current asset can be allocated. When calculating accruals and prepayments, you have assumed that there will be a next year.

This convention has particular importance for valuing assets in the statement of financial position. For example, if a business was not a going concern, then we would have to value non-current assets at their estimated selling price which might be less than cost, less accumulated depreciation. Similarly, we might have to reduce the value of inventories, if we anticipated that we would be forced to sell all the inventories in a very short period of time and would have to reduce the price to achieve this.

10.2.12   The consistency convention

The consistency convention is that the accounting treatment of like items should be consistently applied from one accounting period to the next. The usefulness of financial accounting lies to a considerable extent in the conclusions that may be drawn from the comparison of the financial statements of 1 year with those of a preceding year, or of one company with another. Much of the information thus derived would be useless if the choice of accounting methods were not applied consistently year by year. An example of an area where consistency is important is the method of valuing inventories.

The convention is also applied to the treatment of groups of similar items. For example, the same depreciation method should be used for similar types of non-current asset, and the same methods for valuing inventories should be used for similar types of inventories.

10.2.13   The prudence convention

When preparing financial statements there may be some uncertainty about some transactions. The prudence convention requires that caution should be applied when exercising judgement about these uncertainties. The convention of prudence ensures that a business should not lay claim to any profits before they have been earned with reasonable certainty. Also, it should anticipate losses that it expects to incur in future periods by immediately writing them off to the income statement. Whenever a subjective judgement must be included in the financial statements, the figure that gives the lower profit should be chosen. This prevents profits being overstated. Similarly, assets should not be overstated for statement of financial position purposes, but liabilities are generally recognised even where their likelihood is only possible, provided that their value can be estimated with sufficient reliability.

 ## Exercise 10.1

Explain briefly the meaning of the following conventions:

- going concern;
- consistency;
- accruals;
- prudence;
- duality;
- realisation;
- matching.

 ## Solution

- *Going concern*. The financial statements are prepared on the basis that the business is to continue for the foreseeable future and therefore, for example, non-current assets are stated at cost (less accumulated depreciation) as if they will continue to be used, and are not valued as if they are to be disposed of at their fair value.
- *Consistency*. The accounting treatment of like items is consistently applied from one period to the next. This enables comparisons between periods to be made.
- *Accruals*. Revenues and expenses are recognised (recorded) as they are earned or incurred (irrespective of whether or not they are paid for).
- *Prudence*. A business should not claim to have made profits or gains before they have been earned with reasonable certainty, but should anticipate fully any losses that are expected to occur. This prevents overstating of assets or profits.
- *Duality*. Every transaction has two effects, hence 'double-entry bookkeeping'.
- *Realisation*. Revenue and profits should not be anticipated but should be recognised in financial statements when they are realised in the form of cash, or other asset which can be converted into cash. Thus sales revenue is realised when it creates a receivable for which there is a legal claim if the customer does not pay.
- *Matching*. Revenues and expenses are 'matched' with the period in which they are earned or consumed; they are also matched with each other, in that the revenue from a transaction is matched with the expense incurred in producing that revenue in order to arrive at a figure for profit.

10.3 Accounting policies and estimation techniques

Accounting policies are the principles, conventions, rules etc. applied by a company when calculating the assets and liabilities, revenue and expenses, which will appear in the statement of financial position and income statement. The management should use those policies which it believes will be most useful to those who rely on the financial statements. These users will include, for example, shareholders and lenders, as discussed in Chapter 1. The management can assess which policies will be most useful by considering the characteristics of useful information, as discussed in Chapter 1. These include, for example, relevance and reliability.

The implementation of accounting policies requires certain items to be estimated. We have seen that the preparation of financial statements relies on judgement and that not all figures can be called 'accurate'. Accountants have developed a number of techniques to arrive at figures which have to be estimated. For example, we have seen that companies calculate an allowance for receivables, but this is only an estimate as to which trade receivables will not pay. This allowance may be calculated as a percentage of total receivables or as an allowance for specific customers. Either way, both of these are techniques to estimate bad debts. Another example is depreciation, where the straight-line method and the reducing-balance method are two techniques used to estimate the consumption of a non-current asset in a specific period.

10.4 The historical cost convention and its alternatives

Traditionally, financial statements have been prepared using the *historical cost convention* – and, to a large extent, still are.

Historical cost accounting. A system of accounting in which all values are based on the historical costs incurred.

This means that all of the assets, liabilities, expenses and revenue are recorded using the costs and prices ruling at the time of the transaction as the basis of any accounting entries. This method is objective as each value can be supported by the amount paid to the third party at the time of the transaction.

However, it is accepted that this convention has many shortcomings, and over the years many attempts have been made by accountants to develop alternative valuation methods. The main difficulty with the convention is that in times of changing price levels, it has the effect of overstating profits and understating asset values.

Consider the purchase of a machine for $5,000, which has an expected life of 5 years. Two years later a similar machine is bought for $6,000. Using the historical cost convention, the statement of financial position will show the total cost of these machines as $11,000. Indeed, this is the sum of money paid, but the value of the money used differs. On the basis that each machine will last 5 years we might calculate that the annual cost of using the first machine is $1,000, whereas for the second machine it is $1,200. But is this the real cost of using the machines? If they were to be replaced they would presumably cost at least $6,000 each. Using this value, the real cost of 1 year's use is:

$6,000/5 = $1,200 \times 2 = $2,400

The same principle also applies to inventories and any other items where there is a time period that elapses between acquiring the resource and matching the cost of that resource against the revenue it generates. It can be seen that the use of the historical cost convention thereby overstates profits and understates statement of financial position asset values. This reduces the usefulness of financial statements produced using this convention.

10.4.1 The theory of capital maintenance

If the historical cost convention is used to prepare financial statements, the resulting profit could be mistakenly regarded as satisfactory, especially if it equals or exceeds that of the previous year. But in inflationary times, the profit may only be sufficient to replace inventories, assets and pay for expenses, if the same level of activity is to be maintained. In that case, it is not really a 'profit' at all, as we think of profits as being an improvement. Indeed, the profit may not even be sufficient to maintain that level of activity, and – even worse – if some or all of the profits are paid out to the owners of the business, the level of activity may have to be reduced. In this case, the organisation has failed to maintain sufficient capital to support the level of activity.

Two methods have been used as the basis of solving this problem: *current purchasing power accounting* and *current cost accounting*.

10.4.2 Current purchasing power (CPP) accounting

This method of accounting considers the effects of changing price levels by reference to an index, for example movements in the retail price index (RPI) in the UK. It distinguishes between monetary and non-monetary items.

Retail price index

The RPI is a measure of inflation published each month. It is based on the prices of items bought by the average family. Consequently, it reflects the buying power of the currency unit to the domestic family/individual investor. It may bear little resemblance to the effects of inflation on the costs incurred by an organisation.

Monetary items

Examples of monetary items include cash and bank balances, receivables and payables. These are valued in a currency – such as dollar, yen or sterling – regardless of the changes in the price level. In a period of inflation, the holders of monetary assets suffer a loss in the real value of those assets because of a reduction in purchasing power over time. Holders of monetary liabilities make purchasing power gains.

Non-monetary assets

These are items that do not suffer a loss in value in a period of changing price levels. They include non-current assets, inventories and shareholders' equity (ordinary shares and reserves). This assumption presumes that when items are sold, the price charged will compensate for any changes in price level.

Holding gains and losses

The holding of monetary items will, in periods of inflation, give rise to holding gains or losses.

Example 10.A

Assume that inflation is 1 per cent per month.

The asset of a receivable balance in respect of a credit sale made today is valued at $1,000. In 2 months' time the receivable pays the account in full. Although $1,000 is received, with inflation of 1 per cent per month, the money needed to buy the same items as could be bought with $1,000 today is:

$$\$1,000 \times 1.01^2 = \$1,020$$

Since only $1,000 is received there is a holding loss of $20.

The customer, who had a liability of $1,000, has made a holding gain because the value of the money paid in 2 months' time is less than the value of $1,000 today. The calculation is as shown above, but for the customer there is a holding gain of $20.

The principle behind CPP accounting is that the financial statements should be adjusted to reflect the inflationary gain or loss on monetary items. The amount of this gain or loss is calculated by reference to an index which measures inflation, such as the RPI in the UK.

10.4.3 Current cost accounting

Current cost accounting (CCA) is a method of adjusting historical cost accounts for the effects of changing price levels by using indices specific to the organisation. For example, the property may be adjusted for an index related to property values, the equipment for an index for machinery and the inventories for an index relating to the items in inventory. Thus CCA attempts to measure the actual rate of inflation experienced by the business. This may be contrasted to CPP, which measures the rate of inflation experienced by the owners of the business.

10.4.4 Fair value

Non-current assets may also be valued at their fair value. The fair value may be defined as the value of an asset which would be agreed between a buyer and a seller of that asset. For example, if A is selling his car and B wishes to buy the car, A may initially ask for a high price and B may offer a low price. After a period of bargaining a price will be agreed at which the car changes hands, and this price is its 'fair value'. The advantage of valuing assets at fair value is that this provides relevant and up-to-date information to those using the financial statements; the disadvantage is that the information may not be reliable. Until an asset is actually sold, it is not possible to be precise about its fair value. It can be argued that valuing assets at fair value is contrary to the convention of prudence, which states that gains should not be anticipated.

10.4.5 Value to the business (or deprival value)

In several places in this learning system we have mentioned that there are a number of different ways in which we could value a non-current asset. It is possible to bring these different methods together into one single method called 'value to the business'. This method combines together replacement cost, fair value, less costs to sell, and net realisable value.

Replacement cost is the amount a company would have to pay today to purchase a new asset.

Fair value, less costs to sell (or net realisable value), is the amount an asset could be sold for, less costs of making the sale.

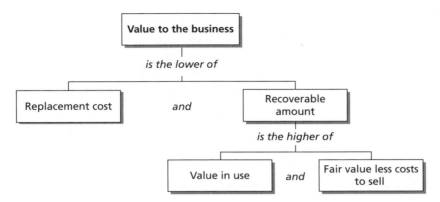

Figure 10.1 Value to the business

Value in use is the total future revenue that an asset will generate, after allowing for the fact that the revenue will be received in the future, rather than now. Thus future revenue will be affected by inflation, risk and the fact that money 'now' is more valuable than money in the 'future'. (For the simple reason that money 'now' can be invested to earn interest.)

These three factors mean that the future revenue must be 'discounted' (reduced) to find its present value.

'Value to the business' is a logical process by which an asset may be valued and follows some of the accounting conventions mentioned above.

It works as follows. An asset will generate revenue in one of two ways – through use or being sold. If the amount that could be earned from use was less than the amount from sale, then logically a company would sell the asset rather than use it. Thus the 'recoverable amount' from an asset is the higher of 'sale' or 'use'.

If an asset can earn more than its replacement cost, that is a profit can be made, then a company would buy such an asset, and at the end of its useful life, buy another. However, this profit should not be anticipated (prudence) and the asset should be valued at its replacement cost, being less than its recoverable amount.

However, if the recoverable amount were less than its replacement cost (in other words a loss will be made), then that loss should be recognised now (prudence) and the asset valued at the lower figure of 'recoverable' amount.

Figure 10.1 illustrates the possible choices when determining the value to the business of an asset. You should try making up your own numbers and entering them in Figure 10.1, and see how an asset should be valued. You should then work out why that is the best valuation.

For example, if RC is $10, VIU $6, and NRV $8, the asset would be valued at $8.

10.4.6   The valuation of intangible assets

An intangible asset is one that does not have a physical substance. Examples include:

- patents;
- trademarks;
- goodwill;
- research and development costs;
- intellectual capital (the value of employees' knowledge and skills).

In Chapter 6, Section 6.8, we looked at the accounting treatment of intangible assets. In this chapter we look at how the accounting conventions apply to intangible assets.

Intangible assets affect the value of a business and challenge our use of the historical cost convention. They are all items that cause accountants difficulty in their valuation, mainly because of the subjective nature of the value of such items. The general principle on which all intangibles are valued is whether or not they have the potential to earn profits in the future. In other words, do they have a value in use, and can it be quantified with a reasonable degree of accuracy?

We shall look at one of the intangibles above in order to appreciate the difficulties involved and the approach to be taken in their valuation.

The valuation of research and development costs

Some businesses spend money on research and development (R&D), and this gives difficulties for accountants. General R&D costs, which do not lead to a specific new product or method of production, are always written off to the income statement in the period in which the costs are incurred. However, there is an argument for regarding some development costs as capital expenditure if they comply with the following criteria:

- they are directed towards the development of a specific product or production method;
- the outcome of the research is known with reasonable certainty;
- the future revenue is likely to exceed the costs.

If these three criteria are met, the expenditure can be included in the statement of financial position, and is written off when the product or production method commences.

 ## Exercise 10.2

List and briefly describe as many examples as you can of different methods of valuing assets.

 ## Solution

- Original cost/historical cost – as evidenced on invoice.
- Carrying amount – cost less accumulated depreciation (i.e. original cost, less reduction due to proportion of asset used up).
- Fair value – professional or other valuation of asset, often used where asset value has increased, for example land and buildings, and where the fair value is the amount that could be obtained on the open market.
- Replacement cost – of replacing asset with its current equivalent.
- Current cost accounting – original cost adjusted by an industry-specific index, less accumulated depreciation.
- Current purchasing power accounting – original cost adjusted by a general index, less accumulated depreciation.
- Fair value less costs to sell (Net realisable value) – amount expected to be received from the sale of an asset, less costs of selling.

Exercise 10.3

Make brief notes on the shortcomings of the historical cost convention, and briefly describe two alternative methods of accounting that attempt to recognise changing price levels.

 Solution

Shortcomings of historical cost convention. Asset values are out of date, perhaps too low. This prevents comparison between businesses with newer assets and return on capital employed is distorted by inflation. No account is taken of gains that arise until they are realised, even though they may have occurred during previous periods. Profit is the increase in net assets during the period, but this figure cannot be fully determined using historical costs.

Current cost accounting applies industry- or asset-specific price indices to the costs of goods sold and assets consumed, to produce values that are based on the cost at the time of consumption. Because assets consumed are valued at a current value, profits are lower and are said to more accurately represent the increase (or decrease) in the capital of the organisation.

Current purchasing power accounting applies a general price index to the non-monetary items in the historical cost financial statements, thus showing the change in the general purchasing power of money. The value of the net assets is, therefore, restated according to the index applied; only if this results in an increase in net assets over the previous period is there said to be a 'real' profit for the period.

In a current value system of accounting, assets and liabilities are remeasured regularly so that changes in value are recorded as they occur; this results in the computation of a profit that reflects the organisation's ability to continue to operate at the same, or an improved, level of activity as in the past (or at a reduced level, if a loss occurs).

 Exercise 10.4

Explain briefly what is meant by the term *capital maintenance*.

 Solution

Capital maintenance is the concept that profit is earned only if the value of the organisation's net assets – or alternatively the organisation's operating capability, that is, its physical productive capacity – is greater at the end of the accounting period than it was at the beginning. The amount of profit earned is the amount of this increase.

One of the criticisms of historical cost financial statements is that they fail to comply with this concept. Under historical cost accounting (HCA), profit is measured as the increase in net assets valued in terms of a monetary unit – say, the dollar – which is not stable over time. The result is that HCA profits often do not represent true increases in the worth of a business, because apparent increases in asset values may be nothing more than the effect of inflation on the unit used to value them.

If financial statements are prepared under the historical cost convention, the profit reported may not be sufficient to support the organisation at the same level of activity in the future, especially if this profit is then paid out to the owner(s) of the organisation.

10.5 Regulations in accounting

There is little regulation regarding the preparation of financial statements for sole traders and partnerships, other than to satisfy the tax authorities of the profits made in each accounting period. However, with regard to the financial statements of limited companies, charities and so on, there are several types of regulation and guidance to assist the accountant in preparing such financial statements, and most of the principles they encompass can and should be equally applied to other organisations.

10.5.1 Company law

Most countries have legislation applying to companies and this is generally known as 'company law'. The amount of detail in company law will vary between countries but in general they cover broad issues rather than detailed aspects of accounting. Company law often states which companies are required to have their financial statements audited by a registered auditor.

10.5.2 The accountancy profession

Many countries have their own professional accountancy qualification. In the USA, for example, they are known as Certified Public Accountants (CPA). Some countries do not have their own professional accountancy qualification in which case trainee accountants take the qualification of another country. This will also apply if students in a country believe that the accountancy qualification in another country is more prestigious than their own domestic qualification. Thus some professional accountancy bodies which were originally just domestic have become international qualifications. Two examples in the UK are:

- The Chartered Institute of Management Accountants (CIMA),
- The Association of Chartered Certified Accountants (ACCA).

These bodies insist on their members being properly qualified, not only by passing examinations but also by obtaining appropriate practical experience, updating their skills and knowledge on a regular basis, and maintaining certain professional standards based on an ethical code.

10.5.3 International accounting standards

The Fundamentals of Financial Accounting syllabus states that no knowledge of any specific accounting treatment contained in the international financial reporting standards (IFRSs) is necessary. This Learning System has not, therefore, made mention of these

IFRSs, but nevertheless this text is based on IFRSs. The influence of IFRSs on the text has three main affects:

1. *Terminology.* This text uses the words, phrases, definitions and so on found in IFRSs.
2. *Presentation.* The presentation of the financial statements and particularly the statement of financial position and statement of cash flows follow the IFRS formats. The syllabus states that the formats in IAS 1 *Presentation of Financial Statements* (*Revised*) and IAS 7 *Statement of Cash Flows* are to be followed when preparing these financial statements.
3. *Technical.* The technical requirements of the IFRS have been followed, for example, in the discussion above in accounting for goodwill.

These IFRSs are very important and a brief description of how they are issued is given below.

There are four separate but related bodies which control the setting of IFRSs. They are organised as in the figure below.

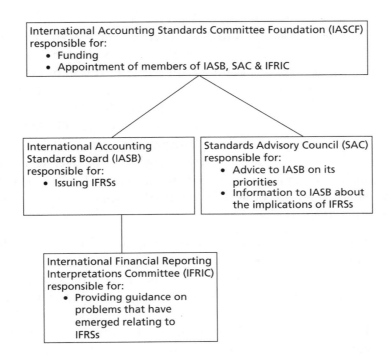

Members of these bodies are drawn from preparers of financial statements, (accountants) and users of financial statements (banks, analysts, stock exchange, government, etc.), all from different parts of the world.

The IASB sets IFRSs; a previous body, known as the International Accounting Standards Committee (IASC) set International Accounting Standards (IAS). When the IASB came into existence it adopted all of the IAS issued by the IASC. Thus we have in existence two sets of standards – IFRS and IAS, with the IAS being the older standards. In general, when reference is made to IFRS, it includes the IASs.

Many countries which previously set their own accounting standards still have their own standard-setting boards, for example the Financial Accounting Standards Board (FASB) in the USA, and the Accounting Standards Board (ASB) in the UK. However, these national boards are working with the IASB and are trying to reach convergence between their own national standards and the international standards.

Countries in the European Union (EU) – for example Germany, France, Italy and the UK – are generally required to use IFRSs when preparing the financial statements of companies listed (quoted) on a stock exchange. Once an IFRS has been developed by the IASB it is scrutinised by the EU to see whether it should be adopted for use by member states. It takes advice from two committees before adopting an IFRS – the Accounting Regulatory Committee and the European Financial Reporting Advisory Group (EFRAG). So far all IFRSs have been adopted, apart from certain sections of one particular standard.

Accountants are obliged to follow accounting standards and the enforcement of IFRSs is left to each individual country. In the UK, for example, the enforcement agencies are the Financial Services Authority (FSA) and the Financial Reporting Review Panel (FRRP).

10.5.4 The IASB Framework for the Preparation and Presentation of Financial Statements (the 'Framework')

Accounting is a social science not a natural science, like physics and chemistry. Whereas physics and chemistry have natural laws, accounting has to develop its own 'laws', which are the conventions listed above. It is important that the IFRSs produced by the IASB are consistent with the conventions and that the accounting standards are consistent with each other. In order to help ensure that this occurs the IASC produced a document which provides a framework within which all standards are set. This document underpins all accounting standards and provides the platform from which all future standards will be developed. This document is the 'Framework', which we have already mentioned in Chapter 1, and which has implicitly been the basis for many of the discussions in the preceding chapters. The Framework deals with the fundamental issues in financial reporting and a brief list of its contents is given below.

- The objective of financial statements – to provide useful information, such as statement of financial position and income statement to users.
- Underlying assumptions and qualitative characteristics – these are the conventions discussed above, for example accruals, going concern, materiality, prudence and recognition.
- The elements of financial statements – these are the five main components of an income statement and statement of financial position – revenue and expense, assets, capital and liabilities.
- The measurement of profit and capital maintenance – different methods of measuring profit, for example CPP and CCA, and the concept of capital maintenance, using different methods of asset valuation, for example value in use and replacement cost.

10.6 The role of the auditor

As we have seen, financial statements are prepared to provide information to a variety of different user groups. If the statements are to be useful they must be reliable and reasonably accurate. Accounting systems must therefore be designed to ensure that sufficient accuracy exists. In accounting terms we refer to financial statements as giving a fair presentation, or as being *true and fair*. It is the role of the auditor to ascertain that the financial statements are properly prepared in accordance with company law and accounting standards.

It is not, however, the responsibility of the auditor to actually prepare the financial statements – this is the responsibility of management (the directors in a limited company). In some cases, the auditors *are* engaged to prepare the financial statements, but this is in addition to their audit duties, and is still the responsibility of management. There is more about this in Section 10.7.

Some organisations are required by law to have their financial statements audited by an independent, qualified accountant. Others choose to have their financial statements audited on a voluntary basis, as the existence of an audit report may be beneficial to them.

10.6.1 Fair presentation or true and fair

Fair presentation or 'true and fair' means that financial statements prepared for external publication should fairly reflect the financial position of the organisation. They should be free of serious errors arising from negligence or deliberate manipulation. It may not be economically viable to test every single transaction, or to ensure 100 per cent accuracy, but fair presentation assumes that the financial statements do not contain any significant errors that would affect the actions of those reading them. This is based on the materiality convention discussed below. It is the duty of the registered auditor to test the financial statements for material misstatement and to report on whether they are presented fairly.

The materiality convention and the auditor

The purpose of an audit is to allow the auditor to form an opinion and to report accordingly on whether or not the financial statements fairly present the company.

In doing this the auditor will perform various tests based on the accounting records and other information gained from minutes of board meetings and discussions with the directors. In doing so, the auditor will not be able to check everything in the smallest detail. Instead, the implications of potential errors will be considered – if they would not affect the overall fair presentation of the reports they are not significant, that is, not material. If it were not for the materiality convention, then financial statements would always be required to be 100 per cent accurate, which would be very expensive and impractical, and the extra accuracy would be of limited extra benefit to the users of the financial statements.

There are two main types of tests that the auditor may choose to carry out. The first is known as *compliance testing*, which involves assessing the reliability of accounting systems, procedures and controls. If these appear to be working satisfactorily, the auditors can place a degree of reliance on them that means that they do not need to test those areas in detail. If there are areas of doubt, areas of high risk or items of a material nature, the auditors may choose to carry out more detailed testing, known as *substantive testing*.

 Exercise 10.5

Explain what is meant by the convention of materiality as used by accountants. Give examples of occasions where materiality might affect the treatment of an item in the financial statements of an organisation.

 Solution

Materiality is concerned with the importance of information to its users. Items that might affect the decisions made by a user should be clearly stated; items that are insignificant need not be highlighted. Small items of miscellaneous expense can be grouped together under general headings; larger items should be identified separately.

An example might be to treat sundry stationery items as expenses as soon as they are purchased, or to value the inventories of stationery remaining at the end of a period and include it as an asset on the statement of financial position. Another example might be to regard office staplers as expenses because of their low value, or as non-current assets to be depreciated because of their long useful life. A third example might be to disclose the sale of a section of the business, even though the proceeds were small – the amount might be insignificant but the effect on the future of the business might materially affect someone's opinion. The degree of materiality of items in the financial statements will affect the level of testing carried out by the auditor.

 Exercise 10.6

Explain what is meant by a fair presentation when applied to the audit of an organisation's financial statements.

 Solution

Fair presentation exists if the financial statements as presented enable the users and potential users to gain a picture of the affairs of the organisation that is sufficient to make proper judgements. It does not mean that the financial statements are completely accurate, but that any inaccuracies that exist would not affect the view of the financial statements. The audit does not guarantee to uncover every error or possible fraud, but does imply that the systems in use by the organisation would have a reasonable chance of preventing errors and fraud.

10.6.2 The role of the external auditor

The purpose of the external audit is to form an opinion on the financial statements. The role of the external auditor will vary depending on the size of the organisation and whether or not it has its own internal audit department. The work can be divided into two categories:

1. testing the reliability of the systems and procedures used (compliance testing);
2. testing specific transactions to ensure that they have been accounted for accurately (substantive testing).

On the basis of the above, together with their findings and tests carried out by internal audit (if appropriate), an opinion will be formed and expressed in an audit report.

Auditors do not check every entry in the ledger accounts. They design their audit programme primarily to test that there are proper control systems and procedures in place to accurately record the financial position of the organisation. Depending on their opinion of the systems and procedures in place, they will conduct additional, more detailed tests in some areas, such as tracing particular transactions through the system (*testing the audit trail*, as mentioned in Section 9.2.2). They will also perform tests on the control systems,

THE REGULATORY FRAMEWORK OF ACCOUNTING

such as reconciliations, the segregation of duties, authorisation procedures and documentation, and will check the existence of non-current assets.

They are also concerned to ensure that items are properly valued in accordance with accepted accounting practice, as discussed earlier in this chapter.

At the conclusion of the audit, an audit report is produced, summarising their findings.

The auditor and fraud

It is not the auditor's duty to detect fraud. Auditors should structure their audit tests in such a way that instances of fraud are likely to be brought to their attention, but the discovery of fraud has no more importance to them than the discovery of errors and omissions.

10.6.3 The role of the internal auditor

Many larger organisations have their own internal audit department. The work of internal audit falls into two categories:

- advising on accounting systems;
- carrying out tests on the accounting records and internal management reports.

10.6.4 The value-for-money audit

The audit of an organisation does not have to be strictly confined to the legal requirements. Audits can be carried out on a number of other areas, such as the efficiency of management, the design and implementation of computerised systems, and so on. One type of audit is the *value-for-money audit*, in which the organisation's expenditure is scrutinised to ensure its maximum effectiveness in earning profits. Expenditure could include that on non-current assets, current assets or expenses.

Such audits can be carried out by either internal or external auditors.

10.7 The role of management

In a sole trader's business it is entirely up to the sole trader to manage his or her business affairs as she or he wishes. If he or she does not make a good job of it, there is only himself or herself to suffer as a result, and only himself or herself to answer to.

In a limited company, however (and in other types of organisation, such as charities, clubs and societies), management are not necessarily the same people who provide its capital, nor will they be the prime beneficiaries of the organisation's continued success. In a limited company, it is the shareholders who provide the capital, and who expect that capital to be used properly and wisely, to produce profits, or to enable them to sell their shares successfully in the future. In a charity, club or society, the beneficiaries are those who enjoy the rewards of membership or other benefits derived from the organisation.

However, the shareholders/members/beneficiaries often are not involved in the running of the organisation; they appoint (or elect) others to manage things for them. In a company, those people are the directors; in a charity, club or society, they are the trustees or the members of the committee.

It is the responsibility of *management*, whoever they are, to ensure that the assets of the organisation are safeguarded. This might involve ensuring that

- all assets are recorded correctly, exist, and are properly maintained and insured;
- procedures are in place to prevent misappropriation or misuse of assets;
- the accounting system is efficient and effective;
- no expenditure is undertaken, or liability incurred, without proper procedures for its authorisation and control;
- the financial statements are prepared in accordance with current legislation and accounting standards.

The term often given to these responsibilities is 'the stewardship function'. Management acts as stewards on behalf of shareholders, members and other beneficiaries, and may be answerable if they fail in this duty. That is not to say that it is their responsibility to make as much profit as possible, or even that they are to blame if losses are made, but they must take appropriate steps to minimise the risks, within the confines of the business world.

10.8 Summary

In this chapter we have looked at:

- the main accounting conventions underlying the preparation of financial statements;
- the limitations of the historical cost convention and the methods suggested for remedying them;
- the regulatory framework, which includes company law and accounting standards;
- an outline of the purpose of internal and external audit;
- the stewardship role of management.

Revision Questions

❓ **Question 1** Multiple choice

1.1 If, at the end of the financial year, a company makes a charge against the profits for stationery consumed but not yet invoiced, this adjustment is in accordance with the convention of:

(A) materiality.
(B) accruals.
(C) consistency.
(D) objectivity.

1.2 You are the accountant of ABC Ltd and have extracted a trial balance at 31 October 20X4. The sum of the debit column of the trial balance exceeds the sum of the credit column by $829. A suspense account has been opened to record the difference. After preliminary investigations failed to locate any errors you have decided to prepare draft financial statements in accordance with the prudence convention.
The suspense account balance would be treated as:

(A) an expense in the income statement.
(B) additional revenue in the income statement.
(C) an asset in the statement of financial position.
(D) a liability in the statement of financial position.

1.3 A fair presentation is one that

(A) occurs when financial statements have been prepared in accordance with International Financial Reporting Standards.
(B) occurs when the financial statements have been audited.
(C) shows the financial statements of an organisation in an understandable format.
(D) shows the assets on the statement of financial position at their fair value.

1.4   The historical cost convention:

(A) fails to take account of changing price levels over time.
(B) records only past transactions.
(C) values all assets at their cost to the business, without any adjustment for depreciation.
(D) has been replaced in accounting records by a system of current cost accounting.

1.5   Your company sells goods on 29 December 20X3 on sale or return; the final date for return or payment in full is 10 January 20X4. The costs of manufacturing the product are all incurred and paid for in 20X3 except for an outstanding bill for carriage outwards that is still unpaid.

The associated revenues and expenses of the transaction should be dealt with in the income statement by:

(A) including all revenues and all expenses in 20X3.
(B) including all revenues and all expenses in 20X4.
(C) including expenses in 20X3 and revenues in 20X4.
(D) including the revenue and the carriage outwards in 20X4, and the other expenses in 20X3.

1.6   In times of rising prices, the historical cost convention has the effect of:

(A) valuing all assets at their cost to the business.
(B) recording goods sold at their cost price, even if they are worth less than that cost.
(C) understating profits and overstating statement of financial position asset values.
(D) overstating profits and understating statement of financial position asset values.

1.7   If the owner of a business takes goods from inventories for his or her own personal use, the accounting convention to be considered is:

(A) prudence.
(B) capitalisation.
(C) money measurement.
(D) separate entity.

1.8   Sales revenue should be recognised when goods and services have been supplied; costs are incurred when goods and services have been received.

The accounting convention that governs the above is:

(A) accruals.
(B) materiality.
(C) realisation.
(D) dual aspect.

1.9   The capital maintenance convention implies that

(A) the capital of a business should be kept intact by not paying out dividends.
(B) a business should invest its profits in the purchase of capital assets.
(C) non-current assets should be properly maintained.
(D) profit is earned only if the value of an organisation's net assets or its operating capability has increased during the accounting period.

1.10   In times of rising prices, the historical cost convention:

  (A) understates asset values and profits.
  (B) understates asset values and overstates profits.
  (C) overstates asset values and profits.
  (D) overstates asset values and understates profits.

1.11   The accounting convention that dictates that non-current assets should be valued at cost, less accumulated depreciation, rather than their enforced saleable value, is:

  (A) net realisable value.
  (B) prudence.
  (C) realisation.
  (D) going concern.

1.12   Net profit was calculated as being $10,200. It was later discovered that capital expenditure of $3,000 had been treated as revenue expenditure, and revenue receipts of $1,400 had been treated as capital receipts.
      The correct net profit should have been:
      $..........

1.13   Goodwill is most appropriately classed as:

  (A) a current asset.
  (B) an intangible asset.
  (C) a fictitious liability.
  (D) owner's capital.

1.14   A major aim of the internal auditors is to:

  (A) reduce the costs of the external auditors by carrying out some of their duties.
  (B) support the work of the external auditors.
  (C) prepare the financial statements.
  (D) report to shareholders on the accuracy of the financial statements.

1.15   Which one of the following is *not* a necessary part of the stewardship function?

  (A) To maximise profits.
  (B) To safeguard assets.
  (C) To ensure adequate controls exist to prevent or detect fraud.
  (D) To prepare the financial statements.

1.16   Who issues International Financial Reporting Standards:

  (A) The International Auditing and Assurance Standards Board (IAASB).
  (B) The Stock Exchange.
  (C) The International Accounting Standards Board (IASB).
  (D) The government.

1.17   Which of the following is *not* an accounting convention?

  (A) Prudence
  (B) Consistency
  (C) Depreciation
  (D) Accruals

1.18 When preparing financial statements in periods of inflation, directors:

(A) must reduce asset values.
(B) must increase asset values.
(C) must reduce dividends.
(D) need make no adjustments.

1.19 Which of the following statements is correct?

(A) External auditors report to the directors.
(B) External auditors are appointed by the directors.
(C) External auditors are required to give a report to shareholders.
(D) External auditors correct errors in financial statements.

1.20 What is an audit trail in a computerised accounting system?

(A) A list of all the transactions in a period.
(B) A list of all the transactions in a ledger account in a period.
(C) A list of all the items checked by the auditor.
(D) A list of all the nominal ledger codes.

1.21 The concept of capital maintenance is important for:

(A) the sources of finance.
(B) the measurement of profit.
(C) the relationship of debt to equity.
(D) the purchase of non-current assets.

1.22 Internal control includes 'detect' controls and 'prevent' controls. Which of the following is a detect control?

(A) Signing overtime claim forms.
(B) Matching purchase invoices with goods received notes.
(C) Preparing bank reconciliations.
(D) Matching sales invoices with delivery notes.

1.23 Which of the following statements is *not* correct?

(A) Internal auditors review value for money.
(B) Internal auditors should not liaise with external auditors.
(C) Internal audit is part of internal control.
(D) Internal audit should be independent of the activities it audits.

1.24 The fundamental objective of an external audit of a limited company is to:

(A) give advice to shareholders.
(B) detect fraud and errors.
(C) measure the performance and financial position of a company.
(D) provide an opinion on the financial statements.

1.25 Which *one* of the following statements most closely expresses the meaning of fair presentation?

(A) There is only one 'fair presentation' view of a company's financial statements.
(B) Fair presentation means there are no errors in the financial statements.
(C) Fair presentation means the financial statements are accurate.
(D) Fair presentation is largely determined by compliance with IFRSs.

1.26 A company includes in inventories goods received before the year end, but for which invoices are not received until after the year end. This is in accordance with:

(A) the historical cost convention.
(B) the accruals convention.
(C) the consistency convention.
(D) the materiality convention.

1.27 When there is inflation, the historical cost convention has the effect of:

(A) overstating profits and understating statement of financial position values.
(B) understating profits and overstating statement of financial position values.
(C) understating cash flow and overstating cash in the statement of financial position.
(D) overstating cash flow and understating cash in the statement of financial position.

1.28 Which of the following is *not* a reason for providing depreciation on tangible non-current assets.

(A) They have a limited useful life.
(B) They are part of the cost of generating the revenue for a period, and that cost should be matched with the revenue.
(C) Depreciation is an expense in running a business.
(D) It is a means of valuing an asset.

1.29 Which of the following is *not* correct?

(A) Depreciation reduces the net profit of an organisation.
(B) Providing depreciation generates cash.
(C) If depreciation is not charged, capital will not be maintained.
(D) By not charging depreciation, it might appear that profits have risen in line with inflation.

? Question 2

The external auditors of OBJ plc have identified several areas of weakness in the company's accounting procedures. One area of weakness is the classification of capital and revenue transactions. They feel that incorrect classification of material items could result in the failure of the financial statements to provide a fair presentation.

Requirements

Insert the missing word in these sentences:

(a) _____ expenditure is expenditure on items that are not intended to be sold but are intended to be retained in the business to enable additional profits to be made.

(b) _____ expenditure is expenditure on items that are either intended to be sold or are used up in a short space of time and have no lasting effect on the business.

(c) The auditors have also identified that the following transactions have been omitted from the accounts:

1. Plant purchased for $18,800 cash including $500 for delivery and $2,800 sales tax.
2. Motor vehicle purchased at the beginning of the accounting period for $16,355 cash, including $140 for annual vehicle licence tax and sales tax of $415. (*Note*: Assume that sales tax on motor vehicles cannot be reclaimed.)
3. Replacement engine for a commercial vehicle, costing $1,300 cash.
4. Sale of a non-current asset for $12,000 cash. This asset had cost $30,000 and it had been depreciated by $20,000.

OBJ plc's accountant has calculated the following figures at the year end of 30 April 20X7:

Net profit	$475,350
Non-current assets	$272,330

(i) Complete the table below to indicate the journal entries necessary to correct each of the above errors.

Item	Name of account	Debit ($)	Credit ($)
1.			
2.			
3.			
4.			

(ii) Insert the missing items into the table below in order to recalculate net profit and non-current assets after adjusting for the above transactions. Ignore any depreciation on the non-current assets purchased:

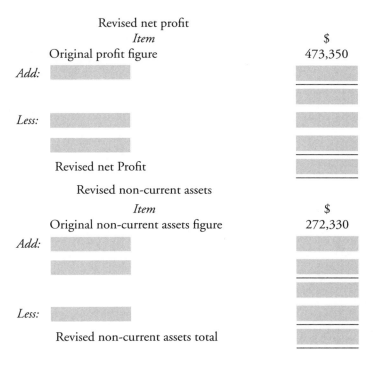

Revised net profit	
Item	$
Original profit figure	473,350
Add:	
Less:	
Revised net Profit	

Revised non-current assets	
Item	$
Original non-current assets figure	272,330
Add:	
Less:	
Revised non-current assets total	

? Question 3

(a) Which convention affects the treatment of sales on credit in an organisation's ledger accounts?

(b) Which convention justifies an allowance for receivables?

Solutions to Revision Questions

10

☑ Solution 1

1.1 Answer: (B)

The accruals convention implies that the profits must be charged with expenses consumed, irrespective of whether or not an invoice has been received.

1.2 Answer: (D)

The suspense account balance is a credit one; this represents either a revenue item or an expense. As it would be imprudent to assume the difference is due to an item of revenue, the only course open is to include the balance as a liability on the statement of financial position.

1.3 Answer: (A)

Part of an audit involves determining that the financial statements give a 'fair presentation', but it does not guarantee that this is the case; in addition, many organisations who do not have an audit performed still produce financial statements that show a fair presentation. Thus answer B is not wholly correct. Fair presentation does not necessarily mean that the financial statements are understandable or use fair values.

1.4 Answer: (A)

Transactions are normally included at their original cost to the business, but that does not preclude reductions in these figures for depreciation and other adjustments, therefore C is incorrect. The accounting professions have attempted to introduce systems of current cost accounting in the past, but these have not been successful.

1.5 Answer: (B)

Revenues must be matched with the expenses incurred in earning those revenues. Goods sold on sale or return are not officially sold until the date for returning them has passed. The costs should not be included as an expense until that same date.

The associated revenues and expenses are therefore dealt with in 20X4. The carriage outwards will be dealt with as it is incurred – which is also 20X4 in this case.

1.6 Answer: (D)

(A) is incorrect because assets can be revalued upwards or downwards from their original cost, and depreciated, even under the historical cost convention. (B) is incorrect as goods should be recorded at the lower of their cost or their net realisable value. (C) is incorrect because profits are calculated without adjustment for the increased cost of replacement inventories, and asset values would be lower than their current value.

1.7 Answer: (D)

The separate entity convention states that the transactions of the business and those of the owner should be kept separate. Therefore, any money, goods or services taken out of the business by the owner should be treated as private transactions.

1.8 Answer: (C)

1.9 Answer: (D)

1.10 Answer: (B)

1.11 Answer: (D)

1.12 Treating capital expenditure as revenue will have reduced profits; treating revenue receipts as capital will have reduced revenue. Thus the profit should have been higher by both of these items.

$$\$10,200 + \$3,000 + \$1,400 = \$14,600$$

1.13 Answer: (B)

Goodwill arises when more is paid for the assets of a business than their fair value. Thus, an additional asset is acquired which is intangible.

1.14 Answer: (B)

1.15 Answer: (A)

Stewardship is concerned with ensuring that there are procedures in place to safeguard assets, provide properly for liabilities, protect against misuse of assets and report adequately to the shareholders or stakeholders of the organisation.

1.16 Answer: (C)

1.17 Answer: (C)

1.18 Answer: (D)

1.19 Answer: (C)

1.20 Answer: (A)

1.21 Answer: (B)

1.22 Answer: (C)

1.23 Answer: (B)

1.24 Answer: (D)

1.25 Answer: (D)

1.26 Answer: (B)

1.27 Answer: (A)

1.28 Answer: (D)

1.29 Answer: (B)

 Solution 2

- Parts (a) and (b) require an explanation of the meanings of 'capital' and 'revenue' expenditure.
- Part (c)(i) requires journal entries for four transactions. Take care to take the sales tax on plant to the sales tax account and not to include it with the cost of plant. But in the case of the motor vehicles, sales tax should be included with the cost as it cannot be reclaimed. The annual vehicle licence tax is an expense and should not be included with the cost. For the disposed asset, the ledger entries can be made in various ways and your answer may allow any reasonable combination of entries that achieves the result of removing the asset cost and depreciation from the financial statements so that the profit or loss on disposal can be calculated.
- Part (c)(ii) requires a recalculation of net profit and non-current assets after the adjustments have been made. Take each adjustment in turn and determine whether or not it has any effect on either of these items.

(a) Capital expenditure is expenditure on items that are not intended to be sold but are intended to be retained in the business for some time to enable additional profits to be made.

(b) Revenue expenditure is expenditure on items that are either intended to be sold or are used up in a short space of time and have no lasting effect on the business.

(c) (i) Journal entries

Item	Name of account	Debit ($)	Credit ($)
1.	Plant at cost	16,000	
	Sales tax	2,800	
	Cash book		18,800
2.	Motor vehicles	16,215	
	Motor expenses	140	
	Cash		16,355
3.	Engine repairs	1,300	
	Cash		1,300
4.	Non-current assets		10,000 (carrying amount)
	Cash	12,000	
	Disposals	10,000	
	Disposals		12,000

THE REGULATORY FRAMEWORK OF ACCOUNTING

(ii) Revised net profit

	$
Original figure	475,350
Add: Profit on disposa	2,000
	477,350
Less:	
Motor expenses	(140)
Engine repairs	(1,300)
Revised net Profit	475,910

Revised non-current assets

	$
Original figure	272,330
Add:	
Plant at cost	16,000
Motor vehicles	16,215
	304,545
Less: disposed asset	(10,000)
Revised non-current-assets total	294,545

 Solution 3

(a) Realisation convention
(b) Prudence convention.

11

Incomplete Records; Income and Expenditure Statements

Incomplete Records; Income and Expenditure Statements

11

LEARNING OUTCOMES

When you have completed this chapter, you should be able to:

▶ prepare accounts from incomplete records;

▶ prepare income and expenditure accounts.

11.1 Introduction

So far, we have been looking at the preparation of financial statements from a ledger, with the results summarised in the trial balance. But not every business uses the full system of daybooks, ledger accounts and so on. Particularly in small businesses, there may not be management time or the financial expertise available. Even in larger businesses, it occasionally happens that accounting records are lost, damaged or destroyed. For all these reasons it may sometimes be necessary to prepare an income statement and statement of financial position from more limited information than we have been given in previous chapters. The same difficulties may apply to records maintained by non-profit-making bodies, such as clubs and societies, and many of the techniques covered in this chapter apply to both.

All the contents of this chapter should be considered important for the examination, as it provides a good test of your knowledge of bookkeeping, which is essential to pass the computer-based assessment. The ability to prepare financial statements from incomplete records may be regarded as more difficult than from complete records, which you have studied in the previous chapters.

11.2 Calculating 'missing figures'

If an organisation does not keep its records in double-entry form, with the production of a trial balance, the preparation of the income statement and statement of financial position may require some figures to be ascertained from other records and information. For example, a common situation is where the owner of a business has not kept records of his drawings from the business, but there are other figures available that would enable the drawings figure to be determined.

The accounting equation is usefully employed in this situation:

Assets = Liabilities + Capital

From this the value of capital can be calculated at any time. A change in the value of capital can be caused by only three things:

1. an introduction/withdrawal of capital;
2. net profit or loss for the period;
3. drawings.

Thus, if the opening and closing values of capital are known then, provided that the value of profit and of capital introductions/withdrawals are known, the value of drawings can be calculated.

In an organisation that does not keep full ledger accounts, there may be several figures that need to be determined with the aid of other figures that can be verified. There are several techniques to identify these missing figures.

11.2.1 Sales figures

It is common in organisations that do not keep full bookkeeping records to find that some figures regarding sales are unavailable. It might be that opening receivables lists have been mislaid, or cash sales have not been recorded, or discounts given to customers might have been overlooked. Drawing up the equivalent of a sales ledger control account will enable the missing figure to be determined. Of course, it will not be a 'proper' sales ledger control account, because there is unlikely to be a sales ledger, but the technique is the same.

The idea is to insert in the ledger accounts all known information, and then to derive the missing information as a balancing figure.

To take sales as an example:

- we probably know our opening figure for receivables – it is the figure that appeared in last year's statement of financial position;
- we probably know our closing receivables – they are the people who owe us money *now*;
- bank statements should indicate the amount received from customers in the form of cheques and other types of receipts (though we may have to look back through all the statements for the period in order to derive this information);
- we may have records of cash sales (e.g. till rolls) that will indicate the amounts received from cash customers;
- by entering all these known amounts into the sales total account we can derive a sales figure for the period as a balancing figure.

Note that, although we normally exclude cash sales from the sales ledger control account, it is permissible to include them in the 'sales total account' in order to get a complete total of sales, whether for cash or on credit.

Example 11.A

Jaswinder knows that his receivables at 1 January 20X1 were $27,000, and during the year he received $140,000 in cheques from customers, after allowing $2,000 in cash discounts for prompt payment. He wrote off a bad debt of $5,000 during the year, and his closing receivables at 31 December 20X1 amount to $24,500. Calculate the value of his sales for the year.

Solution

This can be done by drawing up a sales ledger control account, and inserting the known figures. The unknown figure for sales can then be determined as the figure required to balance the account.

Sales ledger control account

20X1		$	20X1		$
1 Jan.	Balance b/fwd	27,000	In year	Bank	140,000
In year	Sales		In year	Cash discounts allowed	2,000
			In year	Bad debts written off	5,000
			31 Dec.	Balance c/fwd	24,500
		171,500			171,500

The missing figure of sales is the figure required to make the control account balance, that is, $144,500. This technique can be used to identify any figure missing in respect of sales or receivables.

11.2.2 Purchases figures

These are calculated in the same way as sales figures.

11.2.3 Expenses figures

As with purchases, a ledger account is drawn up that is entered up with the known figures, and the missing figure is deduced as the figure required to make the account balance.

Example 11.B

Jaswinder paid an electricity bill during the year of $550. On 1 January, he knew that $120 was owing for electricity consumed in the previous year, and on 31 December he knew that $140 had been consumed in the current year, but not yet billed.

The ledger account for electricity would appear as follows:

			Electricity			
20XI		$	20XI			$
In year	Bank	550	1 Jan.	Balance b/fwd		120
31 Dec.	Balance c/fwd	140	31 Dec.	Income statement		?
		690				690

The missing income statement figure is $570.

11.2.4 Opening capital

It is also common for the opening capital figure to be missing. This can be determined by drawing up an opening statement of financial position and using the accounting equation to calculate the capital. You will remember the accounting equation:

$$\text{Assets} = \text{Liabilities} + \text{Capital}$$

If you can list the opening assets and liabilities, you can calculate the opening capital, or indeed any other opening figure that is missing.

11.2.5 Cash and bank summaries

It is common for incomplete records questions to commence with a summary of the cash and bank transactions. Such a summary is called a *receipts and payments account*. Very often, there is a missing figure in these – commonly the figure for owner's drawings. Preparing such a summary (which is in effect just a copy of the cash book) enables the missing figure to be determined.

Example 11.C

Since commencing business several years ago as a cloth dealer, Shareef has relied on annual receipts and payments accounts for assessing progress. These accounts have been prepared from his business bank account through which all business receipts and payments are passed.

Shareef's receipts and payments account for the year ended 31 March year 10 is as follow:

Receipts and payments account				
	$			$
Opening balance	1,680	Drawings		6,300
Sales receipts	42,310	Purchases payments		37,700
Proceeds of sale of grandfather clock	870	Motor van expenses		2,900
Loan from John Scott	5,000	Local business tax		570
Closing balance	1,510	Wages – John Jones		3,200
		Workshop rent		700
	51,370			51,370

Additional information

(a) The grandfather clock sold during the year ended 31 March year 10 was a legacy received by Shareef from the estate of his late father.

(b) The loan from John Scott was received on 1 January year 10. Interest is payable on the loan at the rate of 10 per cent per annum.

(c) In May year 10, Shareef received from his suppliers a special commission of 5 per cent of the cost of purchases during the year ended 31 March year 10.

(d) On 1 October year 9, Shareef engaged John Jones as a salesman. In addition to his wages, Jones receives a bonus of 2 per cent of the business's sales during the period of his employment; the bonus is payable on 1 April and 1 October in respect of the immediately preceding 6-month period.

Note: It can be assumed that sales have been at a uniform level throughout the year ended 31 March year 10.

(e) In addition to the items mentioned above, the assets and liabilities of Shareef were as follows:

	Year 9	Year 10
At 31 March	($)	($)
Motor van at cost	4,000	4,000
Inventories at cost	5,000	8,000
Trade receivables	4,600	12,290
Motor vehicle expenses prepaid	–	100
Workshop rent accrued due	–	200
Trade payables	2,900	2,200

(f) It can be assumed that the opening and closing balances in the above receipts and payments account require no adjustment for the purposes of Shareef's financial statements.

(g) As from 1 April year 9, it has been decided to calculate the depreciation on the motor van annually at the rate of 20 per cent of the cost. (It is assumed that the motor van will have no residual value.)

You are required to produce the income statement for the year ended 31 March year 10 and a statement of financial position at that date of Shareef.

Solution

The value of sales and purchases can be found by using total accounts:

Sales total account

	$		$
Balance b/d	4,600	Sales receipts	42,310
Sales	50,000	Balance c/d	12,290
	54,600		54,600

Purchases total account

	$			$
Purchases payments	37,700	Balance b/d		2,900
Balance c/d	2,200	Purchases		37,000
	39,900			39,900

It is then a fairly simple matter to complete the income statement.

Income statement of Shareef for the year ended 31 March year 10

	$	$
Sales		50,000
Opening inventories	5,000	
Purchases	37,000	
	42,000	
Closing inventories	(8,000)	
		(34,000)
Gross profit		16,000
Motor van expenses	2,800	
Workshop rent	900	
Local business tax	570	
Wages – John Jones	3,700	
Loan interest	125	
Depreciation	800	
	8,895	
Commission receivable	(1,850)	
		(7,045)
Net profit		8,955

The opening capital value can be calculated by applying the accounting equation to the values of assets and liabilities at 31 March year 9.

Assets	$
Motor van	4,000
Inventories	5,000
Trade receivables	4,600
Bank	1,680
	15,280
Liabilities	
Payables	2,900
Capital at 31 March year 9	12,380
	15,280

Statement of financial position of Shareef as at 31 March year 10

Assets	Cost $	Acc. Depreciation ($)	Carrying Amount ($)
Non-current assets			
Motor van	4,000	(800)	3,200
Current assets			
Inventories		8,000	
Receivables		12,290	
Prepayments		100	
Commission receivable		1,850	
			22,240
			25,440
Capital and liabilities			
Capital at the start of the year 10			12,380
Capital introduced			870
Net profit			8,955
			22,205
Less: drawings			(6,300)
Capital at the end of the year 10			15,905
Non-current liability			
Loan from John Scott			5,000
Current liabilities			
Trade payables		2,200	
Accrued rent		200	
Wage bonus		500	
Loan interest		125	
Bank overdraft		1,510	
			4,535
			25,440

The approach taken in this solution is typical of what is needed.

- Head up a sheet of paper for the income statement and another for the statement of financial position.
- Work line by line through the standard income statement format — sales, opening inventories, purchases and so on — entering the details given in the question. Workings may be needed for some of the figures, particularly sales and purchases. If so, do them on a separate sheet of paper and cross-reference as appropriate.
- Work through the statement of financial position in the same way, if necessary calculating as a working the opening balance of capital brought forward.

You should now attempt to put this into practice by attempting the following example.

Example 11.D

Angela is in business but does not keep full accounting records. For the year ended 31 December 20X5 she is able to provide you with the following information:

	At 1 January ($)	At 31 December ($)
Inventories	2,950	3,271
Receivables	325	501
Payables for purchases	736	1,014
Accrued wages payable	74	83

You are able to prepare the following summary of her cash and bank transactions for the year:

Cash	$	Bank	$
Opening balance	49	Opening balance	920
Receipts		Receipts	
Shop takings	5,360	Cheques from customers	1,733
Cheques cashed	260	Shop takings paid in	3,995
	5,669		6,648
Payments		Payments	
Purchases	(340)	Purchases	(2,950)
Wages	(102)	Wages	(371)
Other expenses	(226)	Other expenses	(770)
Drawings	(820)	Purchase of van	(1,250)
Paid into bank	(3,995)	Cash withdrawn	(260)
Closing balance	186	Closing balance	1,047

Angela believes that one customer owing $27 will definitely not pay. On the basis of past experience, she believes that about 4 per cent of the remaining receivables may not pay. The van is to be depreciated at the rate of 20 per cent per annum, straight line, and assuming no residual value.

You are required to prepare Angela's income statement and statement of financial position for 20X5.

Solution

Begin with the income statement, using total accounts to calculate sales and purchases.

Income statement of Angela for the year ended 31 December 20X5

	$	$
Sales (W1)		7,269
Opening inventories	2,950	
Purchases (W2)	(3,568)	
	6,518	
Less: closing inventories	(3,271)	
Cost of goods sold		(3,247)
Gross profit		4,022
Wages (W3)	482	
Other expenses (226 + 770)	996	
Bad debts	27	
Change in allowance for receivables (501 − 27) × 4%	19	
Depreciation (20% × 1,250)	250	
		(1,774)
Net profit for the year		2,248

Statement of financial position of Angela as at 31 December 20X5

Assets	Cost ($)	Acc. Depreciation ($)	Carrying Amount ($)
Non-current assets			
Van	1,250	(250)	1,000
Current assets			
Inventories		3,271	
Receivables less allowance (474 − 19)		455	
Bank		1,047	
Cash		186	
			4,959
			5,959

Capital and Liabilities		
Balance at 1 January 20X5 (W4)		3,434
Net profit for the year	2,248	
Less: drawings	(820)	
Retained profit for the year		1,428
		4,862
Current liabilities		
Payables	1,014	
Accrued wages	83	
		1,097
		5,959

Workings

1. Sales

Sales total account

	$		$
Balance b/f	325	Cash – shop takings	5,360
Sales (balancing figure)	7,269	Bank	1,733
		Bad debt	27
		Balance c/d (501 − 27)	474
	7,594		7,594

2. Purchases

Purchases total account

	$		$
Cash	340	Balance b/f	736
Bank	2,950	Purchases (balancing figure)	3,568
Balance c/d	1,014		
	4,304		4,304

3. Wages

Wages account

	$		$
Cash	102	Balance b/f	74
Bank	371	Income statement	482
Balance c/d	83		
	556		556

4. Capital as at 1 January 20X5

	$
Inventories	2,950
Receivables	325
Bank	920
Cash	49
	4,244
Less: liabilities (736 + 74)	(810)
	3,434

11.3   Financial statements of non-profit-making bodies

In this section we look at the financial statements of organisations such as clubs and societies, which are not primarily set up for the purpose of trading and making a profit (although they may engage in some trading activities, for example, running a bar for the use of members and visitors).

11.3.1   Accounting terminology for non-profit-making bodies

In Chapter 1, we learned that some organisations exist, not with the main intention of making profits in the long term, but with the objective of providing facilities to their members or others who may benefit from their activities. These organisations are often clubs and societies. They may have trading activities, and they will often engage in profitable activities that increase the net assets of the organisation. However, this increase in net assets is not attributed directly to the members, but is used to expand and improve the organisation, or to provide benefits for those whom the organisation exists to support.

Local government is another example of a non-profit-making organisation, but the financial statements of local government are outside the scope of your syllabus.

The financial statements prepared for these organisations are similar to those prepared for other trading organisations described earlier in this text, and they utilise the same accounting concepts and principles, but some of the terminology used is different. It is usual for the following to be prepared for these organisations.

Receipts and payments account. This is a summary of the organisation's cash and bank transactions for a period. It is common for these organisations to operate a single-entry accounting system and thus the receipts and payments account is the starting point for the preparation of other accounting statements.

Income and expenditure statement (or account). This is similar to the income statement of a trading organisation. It shows the income and expenditure of a particular period and follows the same accounting principles as described for trading organisations earlier in this text. The word 'income' is used rather than revenue. Also, instead of using the terms *profit* and *loss*, the difference between the income and expenditure of the period is referred to as *surplus* or *deficit*. The reason for this is that the organisation does not, in principle, exist in order to make a profit. Sometimes, however, the organisation has sections within itself or holds specific events with the deliberate intent of making profits that are used to subsidise the costs of the organisation's other activities: for example, it may have a bar selling drinks at a profit, or might hold a dinner dance for which tickets are sold. In these circumstances a separate 'trading account' is prepared for each such activity. The profit or loss arising is transferred to the income and expenditure account.

Statement of financial position

The statement of financial position of a non-trading organisation is similar to that of a sole trader, showing assets and liabilities at the statement of financial position date. However, the organisation does not have an owner. The equivalent of the owner's capital is referred to as the *accumulated fund*.

11.3.2 Accounting for membership fees and subscriptions

Another significant difference between these organisations and the trading organisation is that their income is mainly derived from their members in membership fees. Different organisations have different membership schemes but the most common are as follows.

Annual membership fees

This type of scheme requires members to pay a fee annually in order to retain membership. In accounting terms, this normally coincides with the date for preparing the annual financial statements, but care must be taken to adjust appropriately for subscriptions in advance (a liability) and for subscriptions in arrears (an asset). If a member has outstanding subscriptions it is unlikely that legal action will be taken to recover them (because of the legal costs involved and the difficulty of proving the debt), so it is common for them to be written off as a bad debt. However, each organisation will have its own policy.

Example 11.E

A club receives subscriptions during 20X8 of $17,400. At the start of 20X8, $100 was owing for fees in respect of 20X7, and $300 had been paid during the previous year in respect of 20X8 fees. At the end of 20X8, $150 was still owing for 20X8 fees, and $250 had been paid in advance for 20X9. The subscriptions account would appear as follows:

Subscriptions receivable

20X8		$	20X8		$
1 Jan.	In arrears	100	1 Jan.	In advance	300
				Received	17,400
31 Dec.	In advance	250	31 Dec.	In arrears	150
	Income and expenditure	17,500			
		17,850			17,850
20X9			20X9		
1 Jan.	In arrears	150	1 Jan.	In advance	250

Entrance fees

These are fees payable in addition to the annual subscription when a person first joins the organisation as a member (they may also be referred to as joining fees). For accounting purposes they are normally considered to relate to the number of years and credit is taken for them gradually in the income and expenditure statement. The time period used is a matter for the organisation to decide but, for example, if a period of 5 years were used and the entrance fee paid were $50, then $10 would be treated as revenue in each of the 5 year's; income and expenditure statements following the admission to membership.

The accounting treatment would be to create a liability in the statement of financial position on receipt of the $50 and then to transfer $10 from this account each year. This is shown below:

Entrance fees			
	$		$
Income and expenditure	10	Bank	50

Life membership fees

As its name suggests, this means that a member only makes one payment and for this receives membership for life. In accounting terms, this is treated similarly to the entrance fees described above: a statement of financial position liability is created on receipt of the fee, and a proportion of it is transferred to the income and expenditure statement over a period of time in accordance with the policy of the organisation.

Example 11.F

A club received the following life membership fees in each of its first 2 years:

	$
Year 1	1,500
Year 2	800

The club's policy is to take credit for life membership fees in equal amounts over 10 years. The entries in the ledger accounts would appear as follows:

	$		$
Income and expenditure	150	Bank	1,500
Balance c/d	1,350		
	1,500		1,500
Income and expenditure	230	Balance b/d	1,350
Balance c/d	1,920	Bank	800
	2,150		2,150

The amount transferred to income and expenditure in year 2 is made up of:

	$
10% of year 1 fees = 10% × $1,500	150
10% of year 2 fees = 10% × $800	80
	230

You should note that some organisations will offer their members a choice of these schemes, so that different techniques will be required for different membership schemes. In each case the policy of the organisation must be used to determine the accounting treatment required.

11.3.3 The financial statements of non-trading organisations

Example 11.G

The following receipts and payments account for the year ended 31 March year 11 for the Green Bank Sports Club has been prepared by the treasurer, Waseem.

Receipts and payments account

Receipts	$	Payments	$
Balances b/d		Painting of clubhouse	580
1 April year 10		Maintenance of grounds	1,310
Cash in hand	196	Bar steward's salary	5,800
Bank current account	5,250	Insurances	240
Members' subscriptions		General expenses	1,100
Ordinary	1,575	Bank investment account	1,500
Life	800	Secretary's honorarium	200
Annual dinner ticket sales	560	Annual dinner expenses	610
Bar takings	21,790	New furniture and fittings	1,870
		Bar purchases	13,100
		Rent of clubhouse	520
		Balances c/f,	
		31 March year 11	
		Bank current account	3,102
		Cash in hand	239
	30,171		30,171

The following additional information has been given:

i. Ordinary membership subscriptions received in advance at 31 March year 10 were $200. The subscriptions received during the year ended 31 March year 11 included $150 in advance for the following year.

ii. A life membership scheme was introduced on 1 April year 9. Under the scheme, life membership subscriptions are $100 and are apportioned to revenue over a 10-year period. Life membership subscriptions totalling $1,100 were received during the first year of the scheme.

iii. The club's bank investment account balance at 31 March year 10 was $2,676. During the year ended 31 March year 11 interest of $278 was credited to the account.

iv. All the furniture and fittings in the club's financial statements at 31 March year 10 were bought in January year 8 at a total cost of $8,000. It is the club's policy to calculate depreciation annually on non-current assets at 10 per cent of the cost of such assets held at the relevant year end. The furniture and fittings are not expected to have any residual value.

v. Other assets and liabilities of the club were:

At 31 March	Year 10 $	Year 11 $
Bar inventories	1,860	2,110
Insurances prepaid	70	40
Rent accrued due	130	140
Bar purchases payables	370	460

You are required:

(a) to draw up the bar trading and income statement for the year ended 31 March year 11;

(b) to draw up the club's income and expenditure statement for the year ended 31 March year 11 and a statement of financial position at that date;

(c) to outline the advantages and disadvantages of receipts and payments accounts for organisations such as the Green Bank Sports Club.

Solution

(d) Bar trading account of Green Bank Sports Club for the year ended 31 March year 11

	$	$
Bar takings		21,790
Opening inventories	1,860	
Purchases	13,190	
	15,050	
Closing inventories	(2,110)	
		(12,940)
Gross profit		8,850
Bar steward's salary		(5,800)
Net profit		3,050

(e) Income and expenditure statement of Green Bank Sports Club for the year ended 31 March year 11

	$	$
Income		
Ordinary subscriptions	1,625	
Life subscriptions	190	
Bank interest	278	
Bar profit	3,050	
		5,143
Expenditure		
Painting of clubhouse	580	
Maintenance of grounds	1,310	
Insurances	270	
General expenses	1,100	
Secretary's honorarium	200	
Loss on annual dinner	50	
Rent of clubhouse	530	
Depreciation of furniture and fittings	987	
		5,027
Surplus for the year		116

Statement of financial position of Green Bank Sports Club as at 31 March year 11

Assets	Cost ($)	Accumulated Depreciation ($)	Carrying Amount ($)
Non-current assets			
Furniture and fittings	9,870	(3,387)	6,483
Current assets			
Bar inventories		2,110	
Insurance prepaid		40	
Bank investment		4,454	
Bank current account		3,102	
Cash in hand		239	
			9,945
			16,428
Accumulated Fund and Liabilities			
Accumulated fund b/f			13,962
Surplus for the year			116
			14,078
Life membership fund			1,600
			15,678
Current liabilities			
Bar purchase payables		460	
Subscriptions in advance		150	
Rent accrual		140	
			750
			16,428

(f) The receipts and payments account provides a summary of the cash and bank transactions that have occurred during year 11.

Advantages

- It can easily be reconciled to bank statements and balances of cash in hand.
- It is easy to understand.

Disadvantages

- It does not recognise revenue and expenses as they arise, only as monies are received and paid. As such it does not conform to the accruals or matching conventions.
- It does not show the assets/liabilities of the club, and does not differentiate between capital and revenue expenditure.

Exercise 11.1

The Teesdon Tennis Club had the following assets and liabilities on 1 January 20X1:

	$
Land and buildings	45,000
Equipment	7,000
Cash in bank	1,360
Subscriptions in arrear	190
Subscriptions in advance for 20X1	70
Rent paid in advance	60

During the year ended 31 December 20X1 the club had the following receipts:

	$
Subscriptions for the year 20X1	9,000
Subscriptions from previous years	190
Subscriptions in advance for 20X2	70
Hire of courts	750
Loans from club members	5,000

and made the following payments:

	$
General expenses	5,400
Rent (for 12 months 1 April 20X1–31 March 20X2)	360
New furniture (cost $5,000 balance payable 20X2)	2,500
Repaid loan in part	1,500

You are required:

(a) to calculate the accumulated fund on 1 January 20X1;

(b) to prepare the subscriptions account;

(c) after allowing for depreciation of equipment by $2000, to prepare:

   (i) the receipts and payments account;

   (ii) the income and expenditure statement for the year ended 31 December 20X1 and a statement of financial position on that date.

Solution

(a) Accumulated fund on 1 January 20X1

$45,000 + $7,000 + $1,360 + $190 − $70 + $60 = $53,540

(b)

	Subscriptions		
20X1	$	20X1	$
Balance b/f	190	Balance b/f	70
Income and expenditure a/c	9,070	Bank	9,260
Balance c/f	70		
	9,330		9,330
		20X2	
		Balance b/f	70

(c) (i) Receipts and payments account for the year ended 31.12.20X1

20X1	$	20X1	$
Balance b/f	1,360	General expenses	5,400
Subscriptions	9,260	Rent	360
Hire of courts	750	Furniture	2,500
Loan from club members	5,000	Loan repayment	1,500
		Balance c/f	6,610
	16,370		16,370

(ii) Income and expenditure statement for the year ended 31.12.20X1

	$	$
Subscriptions	9,070	
Hire of courts	750	
		9,820
General expenses	5,400	
Rent	330	
		(5,730)
Surplus of income over expenditure		4,090

Statement of financial position as at 31.12.20X1

Assets	$	$
Non-current assets (carrying amount)		
Land and buildings		45,000
Equipment		12,000
		57,000
Current assets		
Rent paid in advance	90	
Cash at bank	6,610	
		6,700
		63,700
Accumulated fund and liabilities		
Accumulated fund balance b/f		53,540
Surplus for the year		4,090
		57,630
Long-term liability		
Loans from club members		3,500
Current liabilities		
Subscriptions paid in advance	70	
Payables for furniture	2,500	
		2,570
		63,700

11.4 Summary

In this chapter we have looked at the main techniques involved in preparing financial statements:

- from incomplete records;
- for non-profit-making organisations.

Apart from the use of some new terminology in the financial statements of non-profit-making organisations, this chapter builds on the knowledge and skills of previous chapters, in particular:

- the preparation of control accounts;
- the distinction between capital and revenue transactions;
- adjustments for accruals and prepayments;
- the accounting equation: Assets = Liabilities + Capital.

Revision Questions

Question 1 Multiple choice

1.1 In a not-for-profit organisation, the accumulated fund is:

   (A) long-term liabilities plus current liabilities plus current assets.
   (B) non-current assets less current liabilities less long-term liabilities.
   (C) the balance on the general reserves account.
   (D) non-current assets plus net current assets less long-term liabilities.

1.2 An income and expenditure statement (or account) is:

   (A) a summary of the cash and bank transactions for a period.
   (B) another name for a receipts and payments account.
   (C) similar to an income statement in reflecting revenue earned and expenses incurred during an period.
   (D) a statement of financial position as prepared for a non-profit-making organisation.

1.3 A club received subscriptions during 20X5 totalling $12,500. Of these, $800 related to 20X4 and $400 related to 20X6. There were subscriptions in arrears at the end of 20X5 of $250. The subscriptions to be included in the income and expenditure statement for 20X5 amount to:
   $..................

1.4 Life membership fees payable to a club are usually dealt with by:

   (A) crediting the total received to a life membership fees account and transferring a proportion each year to the income and expenditure statement.
   (B) crediting the total received to the income and expenditure statement in the year in which these fees are received.
   (C) debiting the total received to a life membership fees account and transferring a proportion each year to the income and expenditure statement.
   (D) debiting the total received to the income and expenditure statement in the year in which these fees are received.

1.5 A club's membership fees account shows a debit balance of $150 and a credit balance of $90 at 1 June 20X7. During the year ending 31 May 20X8, subscriptions received amounted to $4,750. Subscriptions overdue from the year ended 31 May 20X7, of $40, are to be written off. On 31 May 20X8, subscriptions paid in advance amount to $75.

The amount to be transferred to the income and expenditure statement for the year ending 31 May 20X8 is:

$..................

1.6 A receipts and payments account is similar to:

(A) an income and expenditure statement.
(B) an income statement.
(C) a trading account.
(D) a cash book summary.

1.7 The subscriptions receivable account of a club commenced the year with subscriptions in arrears of $50 and subscriptions in advance of $75. During the year, $12,450 was received in subscriptions, including all of the arrears and $120 for next year's subscriptions. The amount to be taken to the income and expenditure statement for the year is:

$..................

1.8 The difference between an income statement and an income and expenditure statement is that

(A) an income and expenditure account is an international term for an income statement.
(B) an income statement is prepared for a business and an income and expenditure statement is prepared for a non-profit-making organisation.
(C) an income statement is prepared on an accruals basis and an income and expenditure statement is prepared on a cash flow basis.
(D) an income statement is prepared for a manufacturing business and an income and expenditure statement is prepared for a non-manufacturing business.

Question 2

Potter has always kept his accounts in proper double-entry form, but they were all destroyed following a fire at his offices on 31 December 20X5. His accountants had the following statement of financial position as at 31 December 20X4:

Assets	$	$
Non-current assets (carrying amount)		
Land and buildings		80,000
Motor vehicles		8,000
Fixtures		7,500
		95,500
Current assets		
Inventories	18,800	
Receivables	16,200	
Bank	9,600	
		44,600
		140,100
Capital and liabilities		
Capital		97,200
Long-term liabilities		
10%loan		30,000
Current liabilities		
Trade payables	11,000	
Accrued expenses:		
Loan interest	1,500	
Local business tax	400	
		12,900
		140,100

You obtain the following additional information:

(i) Cheques received from receivables during the year were $78,900; sales amounted to $80,500 and cash discount was allowed to some receivables.

(ii) Purchases during the year were $45,250 and payables at 31 December 20X5 were $9,550.

(iii) Payments made by cheque during the year included wages $9,600, motor expenses $2,250, general expenses $2,550, loan interest $3,000, drawings $4,000 and local business tax for the 18 months to 31 March 20X6 $2,400.

(iv) A bill of $500 for motor expenses was awaited at 31 December 20X5.

(v) At 31 December 20X5, inventories were $16,000 and receivables $17,300.

(vi) Depreciation is to be charged on the carrying amount at 25 per cent on motor vehicles and at 20 per cent on fixtures.

Requirements

Prepare financial statements for 20X5 by inserting the missing figures in the workings, income statement and statement of financial position.

Workings

$

Purchases

Opening payables

Closing payables

Paid to payables

$

Sales

Opening receivables

Cheques received

Closing receivables

Cash discount

Local business tax

$

Bank summary

Opening balance

Receipts

$

Payments

Depreciation

$

Income statement of Potter for the year ended 31 December 20X5

	$	$
Sales		
Less: cost of sales		
Opening inventories		
Purchases		
Less: closing inventories		
Gross profit		
Less: expenses		
Discounts allowed		
Wages and salaries		
Local business tax		
Motor expenses		
General expenses		
Loan interest		
Depreciation		
Net profit for the year		

Statement of financial position of Potter as at 31 December 20X5

Assets   *Carrying Amount ($)*
Non-current assets

Current assets

Capital and liabilities

Long-term liabilities

Current liabilities

Question 3

The following is the receipts and payments account of the Long Lane Social Club for the year ended 31 December 20X5:

Receipts	$	Payments	$
Balance at 1 January	2,300	Bar licence fees	2,000
Bar takings	139,050	Cleaner's wages	4,340
Sales of refreshments	5,400	Refreshments purchased	2,890
Sales of dance tickets	1,880	Secretary's expenses	3,690
Sale of equipment	2,400	General expenses	2,090
Subscriptions	4,120	Payables for bar supplies	93,030
		Invested in bank deposit a/c	16,000
		Barperson's wages	9,500
		New equipment	8,000
		Rent	3,620
		Dance expenses	2,700
		Balance at 31 December	7,290
	155,150		155,150

Other assets and liabilities at 1 January and 31 December were as follows:

	1 Jan.	31 Dec.
	$	$
Premises at cost	105,000	105,000
Equipment at cost	5,400	?
Payables for bar supplies	2,270	1,960
Subscriptions in advance	480	350
Subscriptions in arrears	–	280
Inventories of bar supplies	9,500	8,350
Rent prepaid	1,000	1,100

You are also told that

(i) All the equipment owned at the start of the year was sold and replaced during the year. Depreciation of 10 per cent per annum is to be provided on the new equipment. It is assumed that the equipment will have no residual value.

(ii) The bank had credited $1,000 interest to the bank deposit account at 31 December 20X5.

Requirements
(a) Prepare a bar trading account for the year ended 31 December 20X5.
(b) Prepare an income and expenditure account for the year to 31 December 20X5.
(c) Prepare a statement of financial position at 31 December 20X5 by inserting the missing figures in the workings, income statement and statement of financial position.

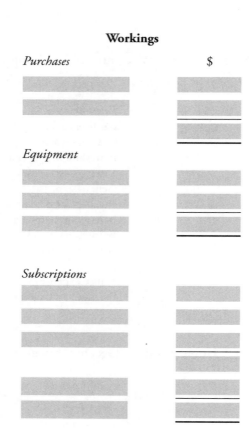

Workings

Purchases $

Equipment

Subscriptions

(a) Bar trading account of Long Lane Social Club for the year ended 31 December 20X5

	$	$
Sales		
Less: cost of sales		
Opening inventories		
Purchases		
Less: closing inventories		
Gross profit		
Less: expenses		
Barperson's wages		
Bar licence fees		
Net profit		

(b) Income and expenditure statement of Long Lane Social Club for the year ended 31 December 20X5

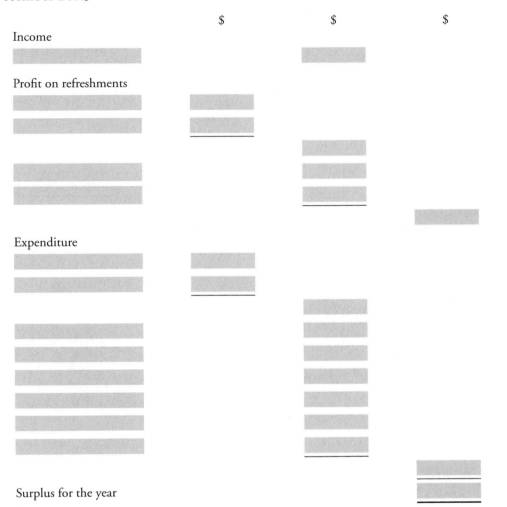

	$	$	$
Income			
		▭	
Profit on refreshments			
	▭		
	▭		
		▭	
		▭	
		▭	
			▭
Expenditure			
	▭		
	▭		
		▭	
		▭	
		▭	
		▭	
		▭	
		▭	
		▭	
			▭
Surplus for the year			▭

(c) Statement of financial position of Long Lane Social Club as at 31 December 20X5

Assets	*Cost* ($)	*Accumulated dep'n* ($)	*Carrying Amount* ($)
Non-current assets			
	▭	▭	▭
	▭	▭	▭
	▭	▭	
Current assets			
		▭	
		▭	
		▭	
		▭	
		▭	
		▭	

Accumulated fund and liabilities

Accumulated fund

Current liabilities

Statement of affairs of Long Lane Social Club as at 1 January 20X5

	$	$
Assets		

Less: liabilities

❓ Question 4

The HB tennis club was formed on 1 April 20X0 and has the following receipts and payments account for the 6 months ended 30 September 20X0:

Receipts	$	*Payments*	$
Subscriptions	12,600	Purchase of equipment	4,080
Tournament fees	465	Groundsperson's wages	4,520
Bank deposit interest	43	Rent	636
Sale of club ties	373	Heating and lighting	674
Life membership fees	4,200	Postage and stationery	41
		Court maintenance	1,000
		Tournament prizes	132
		Purchase of club ties	450
		Balance c/d	6,148
	17,681		17,681

Notes:

1. The annual subscription fee is $300. On 30 September, there were five members who had not paid their subscriptions, but this money was received on 4 October 20X0.
2. The equipment is expected to be used by the club for 5 years, after which time it will need to be replaced. Its estimated scrap value at that time is $50.
3. During the 6 months, the club purchased 100 ties printed with its own design. Forty of these ties remained unsold at 30 September 20X0.
4. The club has paid rent in advance on 30 September 20X0 of $68.
5. The club treasurer estimates that the following amounts should be accrued for expenses:

	$
Grounds person's wages	40
Postage and stationery	12
Heating and lighting	53

6. The life membership fees received relate to payments made by four families. The scheme allows families to pay $1,050, which entitles them to membership for life without further payment. It has been agreed that such receipts would be credited to income and expenditure in equal instalments over 10 years.

Requirements

(a) Calculate the following items to be included in the income and expenditure statement for the period, using the boxes provided.

   (i) Subscriptions

	$
Subscriptions received for the year	
Subscriptions accrued for the year	
Total subscriptions for the year	
Subscriptions for the 6 months	

INCOMPLETE RECORDS; INCOME AND EXPENDITURE STATEMENTS

(ii) Profit from the sale of club ties

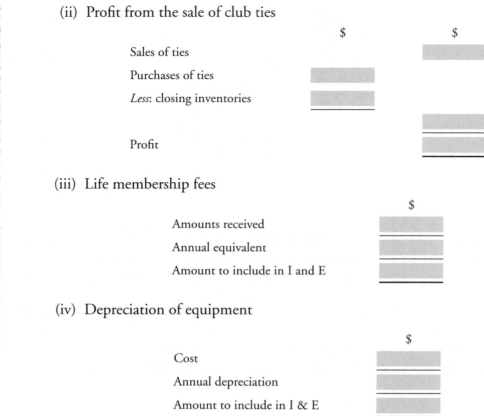

	$	$
Sales of ties		
Purchases of ties		
Less: closing inventories		
Profit		

(iii) Life membership fees

	$
Amounts received	
Annual equivalent	
Amount to include in I and E	

(iv) Depreciation of equipment

	$
Cost	
Annual depreciation	
Amount to include in I & E	

(b) Insert the missing items into the income and expenditure statement given below.
Income and expenditure statement of HB Tennis Club for the 6 months ended 30 September 20X0

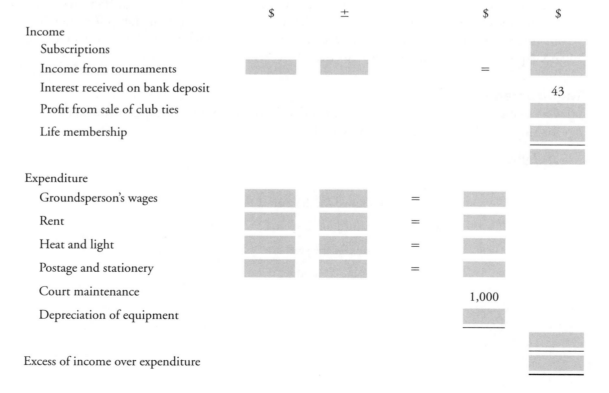

	$	±	$	$
Income				
Subscriptions				
Income from tournaments			=	
Interest received on bank deposit				43
Profit from sale of club ties				
Life membership				
Expenditure				
Groundsperson's wages			=	
Rent			=	
Heat and light			=	
Postage and stationery			=	
Court maintenance			1,000	
Depreciation of equipment				
Excess of income over expenditure				

Question 5

The Questing Theatre Club is an amateur dramatic club that rents premises in which it has established a theatre and bar for the use of its members. The club's treasurer has produced the following summary of the club's receipts and payments during the year ended 31 May 20X2:

Receipts and payments account for the year ended 31 May 20X2

Receipts	$	Payments	$
Cash and bank balances b/f	1,120	Secretarial expenses	550
Members' subscriptions	4,460	Rent of premises	1,990
Donations	500	Production expenses	18,800
Bar takings	25,900	Bar suppliers	14,700
Ticket sales	17,320	Bar expenses	4,180
Grants and subsidies	13,800	Fees of guest artists	900
		Stationery, printing & publicity	1,100
		Purchase of theatre equipment	15,100
		Other expenses	4,820
		Cash and bank balances c/f	960
	63,100		63,100

The treasurer has also been able to supply the following information:

	1 June 20X1	31 May 20X2
	$	$
Subscriptions in arrears	350	460
Subscriptions in advance	160	60
Owing to bar suppliers	1,300	1,650
Bar inventories	2,670	2,330
Production expenses owing	2,490	1,540
Stationery, printing and publicity prepaid	400	300
Valuation of bar equipment	14,500	11,500
Valuation of theatre equipment	35,000	46,000

The club's chairman is keen that the report given to members should show the profit or loss made by the bar and the surplus or deficit made on theatre productions. Only those items that can be directly allocated to the bar or the theatre productions are to be included.

Requirements

(a) Prepare the club's subscriptions account using the ledger account below:

Subscriptions

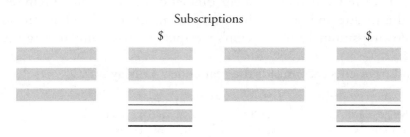

(b) Prepare the bar trading account by completing the boxes in the statements below:

  (i) Bar purchases

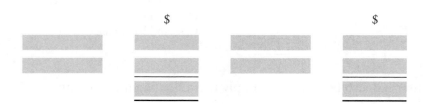

  (ii) Bar trading account for the year ended 31 May 20X2

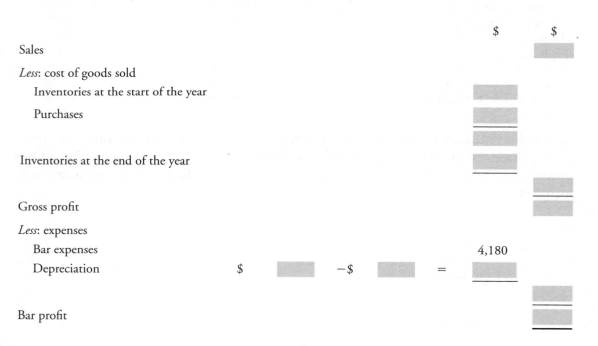

	$	$
Sales		
Less: cost of goods sold		
Inventories at the start of the year		
Purchases		
Inventories at the end of the year		
Gross profit		
Less: expenses		
Bar expenses	4,180	
Depreciation	$ ☐ −$ ☐ = ☐	
Bar profit		

(c) Prepare the productions trading account by inserting the missing items into the boxes in the statements below:

   (i) Productions expenses

$ $

   (ii) Depreciation of theatre equipment

$ $

   (iii) Productions trading account for the year ended 31 May 20X2

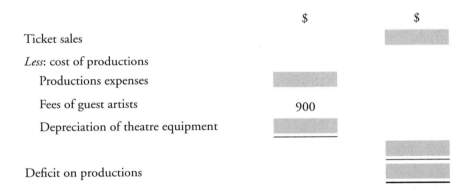

	$	$
Ticket sales		
Less: cost of productions		
Productions expenses		
Fees of guest artists	900	
Depreciation of theatre equipment		
Deficit on productions		

(d) Prepare the Questing Theatre Club's income and expenditure statement for the year ended 31 May 20X2 by inserting the missing items into the statements below.

   (i) Stationery, printing and publicity

$ $

(ii) Income and expenditure statement of Questing Theatre Club for the year ended 31 May 20X2

	$	$
Income		
Member subscriptions		▨
Donations		500
Surplus on bar		▨
Grants and subsidies		13,800
		▨
Expenditure		
Deficit on productions	▨	
Secretarial expenses	550	
Rent of premises	1,990	
Stationery, printing and publicity	▨	
Other expenses	4,820	
		▨
Surplus		▨

Solutions to Revision Questions

 Solution 1

1.1 Answer: (D)

Accumulated fund is equivalent to capital, so answer D is correct.

1.2 Answer: (C)

An income and expenditure statement (or account) is commonly prepared by a not-for-profit organisation as an alternative to an income statement. A summary of cash and bank transactions, and a receipts and payments account, are one and the same thing: they both include capital transactions, for example, payments for non-current assets, and neither takes account of accrued and prepaid income or expenses. Thus answers A and B are incorrect. A statement of financial position is a statement of assets, liabilities and capital or accumulated fund.

1.3 The calculation is:

	$
Subscriptions received in 20X5	12,500
Less: relating to 20X4	(800)
Less: relating to 20X6	(400)
	11,300
Add: subscriptions in arrears	250
	11,550

1.4 Answer: (A)

Life membership fee represents income in advance and this is credited to a life membership fees account. A proportion of income is transferred to the income and expenditure statement over the assumed life of the membership.

1.5

		Subscriptions account			
		$			$
1/6/X7	Balance b/f	150	1/6/X7	Balance b/f	90
31/5/X8	Balance c/f	75		Bank	4,750
31/5/X8	I & E*	4,655		Bad debts	40
		4,880			4,880

*Balancing figure

1.6 Answer: (D)

A receipts and payments account is a summary of the cash and bank transactions.

1.7

	$
Received in year	12,450
Arrears at the beginning	(50)
In advance at the beginning	75
In advance at the end	(120)
Total to income and expenditure	12,355

1.8 Answer: (B)

✓ Solution 2

- This is a straightforward incomplete records question, involving the calculation of several missing figures. The preparation of a 'workings' section, clearly labelled, is essential in providing these figures.
- This question also requires you to prepare a bank summary to determine the end-of-year bank balance.

Workings

	$
Purchases	45,250
Opening payables	11,000
	56,250
Closing payables	(9,550)
Paid to payables	46,700
Sales	80,500
Opening receivables	16,200
	96,700
Cheques received	(78,900)
	17,800
Closing receivables	(17,300)
Cash discount	500

Local business tax

	$
Paid	2,400
Accrued at start	(400)
	2,000
Prepaid at end	400
	2,400

Bank summary

	$	$
Opening balance		9,600
Receipts		
Receivables		78,900
		88,500
Payments		
Payables	46,700	
Wages	9,600	
Motor expenses	2,250	
General expenses	2,550	
Loan interest	3,000	
Drawings	4,000	
Local business tax	2,400	
		(70,500)
Closing bank balance		18,000

Depreciation

	$
Motor vehicles (25% × $8,000)	2,000
Fixtures (20% × $7,500)	1,500

Income statement of Potter for the year ended 31 December 20X5

	$	$
Sales		80,500
Less: cost of sales		
Opening inventories	18,800	
Purchases	45,250	
	64,050	
Less: closing inventories	(16,000)	
		(48,050)
Gross profit		32,450
Less: expenses		
Discounts allowed	500	
Wages and salaries	9,600	
Local business tax	1,600	
Motor expenses	2,750	
General expenses	2,550	
Loan interest	3,000	
Depreciation	3,500	
		(23,500)
Net profit for the year		8,950

Statement of financial position of Potter as at 31 December 20X5

Assets		Carrying Amount ($)
Non-current assets		
Land and buildings		80,000
Motor vehicles		6,000
Fixtures		6,000
		92,000
Current assets		
Inventories	16,000	
Receivables	17,300	
Prepayments	400	
Bank	18,000	
		51,700
		143,700
Capital and liabilities		
Capital at 1 January		97,200
Profit for the year		8,950
		106,150
Less: drawings		(4,000)
		102,150
Long-term liabilities		
Loan		30,000
Current liabilities		
Payables	9,550	
Accrued expenses		
Motor expenses	500	
Loan interest	1,500	
		11,550
		143,700

Solution 3

- Prepare workings for missing figures.
- Take care with subscriptions in advance and in arrears.
- An income and expenditure statement is drawn up using the same principles as an income statement. Revenue is earned during the period, irrespective of its receipt or non-receipt, and expenditure includes expenses incurred during the period, irrespective of payment.

Workings

Purchases	$
Paid to payables	93,030
Less: opening payables	(2,270)
	90,760
Equipment	
Carrying amount at 1 January	5,400
Proceeds of sale	(2,400)
Loss on disposal	3,000
Subscriptions	
Received during the year	4,120
In advance at the start of the year	480
In arrears at the end of the year	280
	4,880
Less: in advance at the end of the year	(350)
Income and expenditure statement	4,530

(a) Bar trading account of Lane Social Club for the year ended 31 December 20X5

	$	$
Sales		139,050
Less: cost of sales		
Opening inventories	9,500	
Purchases	92,720	
	102,220	
Less: closing inventories	(8,350)	
		(93,870)
Gross profit		45,180
Less: expenses		
Barperson's wages	9,500	
Bar licence fees	2,000	
		(11,500)
Net profit		33,680

(b) Income and expenditure statement of Long Lane Social Club for the year ended 31 December 20X5

	$	$	$
Income			
Bar profit		33,680	
Profit on refreshments			
Sales	5,400		
Purchases	(2,890)		
		2,510	
Subscriptions		4,530	
Interest receivable		1,000	
			41,720
Expenditure			
Loss on dance: ticket sales	1,880		
Expenses	2,700		
		820	
Cleaner's wages		4,340	
Secretary's expenses		3,690	
General expenses		2,090	
Rent		3,520	
Loss on sale of equipment		3,000	
Depreciation		800	
			(18,260)
Surplus for the year			23,460

(c) Statement of financial position of Long Lane Social Club as at 31 December 20X5

Assets	Cost ($)	Accumulated dep'n ($)		Carrying amount ($)
Non-current assets				
Premises	105,000	–		105,000
Equipment	8,000	(800)		7,200
	113,000	(800)		112,200
Current assets				
Bar inventories		8,350		
Subscriptions in arrears		280		
Rent prepaid		1,100		
Bank deposit		17,000		
Bank		7,290		
				34,020
				146,220
Accumulated fund and liabilities				
Accumulated fund				
Balance at 1 January 20X5 (see note i)				120,450
Surplus for the year				23,460
				143,910
Current liabilities				
Payables			1,960	
Subscriptions in advance			350	
				2,310
				146,220

Note:

(i) The opening accumulated fund can be taken as the balancing figure, as the question does not specifically ask for a separate calculation of this. However, if you wish to check the accuracy of the figure, then an opening statement of affairs can be produced.

Statement of affairs of Long Lane Social Club as at 1 January 20X5

	$	$
Assets		
Premises		105,000
Equipment		5,400
Bar inventories		9,500
Rent prepaid		1,000
Bank		2,300
		123,200
Less: liabilities		
Payables	2,270	
Subscriptions in advance	480	
		(2,750)
Accumulated fund on 1 January 20X5		120,450

✓ Solution 4

- Identify the capital and revenue receipts/payments.
- Adjust the receipts and payments for the effects the notes produce.
- Prepare the financial statements in good format.

(a) (i) Subscriptions

	$
Subscriptions received for the year	12,600
Subscriptions accrued for the year	1,500
Total subscriptions for the year	14,100
Subscriptions for the 6 months	7,050

(ii) Profit from the sale of club ties

	$	$
Sales of ties		373
Purchases of ties	450	
Less: closing inventories	(180)	
		(270)
Profit		103

(iii) Life membership fees

	$
Amounts received	4,200
Annual equivalent	420
Amount to include in I & E	210

(iv) Depreciation of equipment

	$
Cost	4,080
Annual depreciation	806
Amount to include in I & E	403

(b) Income and expenditure statement of HB Tennis Club for the 6 months ended 30 September 20X0

	$	$
Income		
Subscriptions		7,050
Income from tournaments (465 − 132)		333
Interest received on bank deposit		43
Profit from sale of club ties		103
Life membership (4 × $1,050/10 × 6/12)		210
		7,739
Expenditure		
Groundsperson's wages ($4,520 + $40)	4,560	
Rent ($636 − $68)	568	
Heat and light ($674 + $53)	727	
Postage and stationery ($41 + $12)	53	
Court maintenance	1,000	
Depreciation of equipment	403	
		(7,311)
Excess of income over expenditure		428

 ## Solution 5

- The bar trading account requires a calculation of bar purchases.
- A separate 'surplus on theatre productions' calculation is required.
- The theatre productions deficit includes depreciation of the theatre equipment (but not the cost of the equipment, as this is a capital item). The value of the theatre equipment has gone up during the year owing to the new purchases, but has then fallen to take account of depreciation.
- The income and expenditure statement follows the normal accounting rules involved in the preparation of income statements, that is, it should include the income earned and the expenses consumed during the period, with relevant adjustments for accruals and prepayments.
- Grants and subsidies are to be treated as revenue receipts on the assumption that they were received in respect of revenue expenditure.

(a) Subscriptions

	$		$
Subscriptions in arrears b/f	350	Subscriptions in advance b/f	160
Subscriptions in advance c/f	60	Receipts	4,460
Income and expenditure	4,670	Subscriptions in arrears c/f	460
	5,080		5,080

(b) (i) Bar purchases

	$		$
Payments to suppliers	14,700	Owing at 1.6.X1	1,300
Owing at 31.5.X2	1,650	Purchases	15,050
	16,350		16,350

(ii) Bar trading account for the year ended 31 May 20X2

	$	$
Sales		25,900
Less: cost of goods sold		
Inventories at the start of the year	2,670	
Purchases	15,050	
	17,720	
Inventories at the end of the year	(2,330)	
		(15,390)
Gross Profit		10,510
Less:		
Bar expenses	4,180	
Depreciation (14,500 − 11,500)	3,000	
		(7,180)
Bar profit		3,330

(c) (i) Productions expenses

	$		$
Payments	18,800	Owing at 1.6X1	2,490
Owing at 31.5.X2	1,540	Purchases	17,850
	20,340		20,340

(ii) Depreciation of theatre equipment

	$		$
Value at 1.6.X1	35,000	Value at 31.5.X2	46,000
Purchases	15,100	Depreciation	4,100
	50,100		50,100

(iii) Productions trading account for the year ended 31 May 20X2

	$	$
Ticket sales		17,320
Less: cost of productions		
Productions expenses	17,850	
Fees of guest artists	900	
Depreciation of theatre equipment	4,100	
		(22,850)
Deficit on productions		(5,530)

(d) (i) Stationery, publicity and printing

	$		$
Prepaid at 31.5.X1	400	Prepaid at 31.5.X2	300
Payments	1,100	Income and expenditure	1,200
	1,500		1,500

(ii) Income and expenditure statement Questing Theatre Club for the year ended 31 May 20X2

	$	$
Income		
Member subscriptions		4,670
Donations		500
Surplus on bar		3,330
Grants and subsidies*		13,800
		22,300
Expenditure		
Deficit on productions	5,530	
Secretarial expenses	550	
Rent of premises	1,990	
Stationery, printing and publicity	1,200	
Other expenses	4,820	
		(14,090)
Surplus		8,210

*Grants and subsides have been treated as revenue receipts.

12

The Manufacturing Account

The Manufacturing Account

12

12.1 Introduction

In our examples so far we have been dealing with businesses that purchase goods for onward sale to customers – in other words, with retail and wholesale businesses. We now turn our attention to manufacturing businesses.

In most respects the financial statements of a manufacturing business show no differences from what we have already learned. Its statement of financial position will be identical, though it is worth noting that the asset of inventories in a manufacturing company may be made up of four separate items: *bought-in-goods* (those bought in as finished goods and to be sold to customers), *finished goods* (those already manufactured and ready for sale to customers), *work in progress* (i.e. partly completed goods), and *raw materials* (purchased from suppliers and not yet used in production).

The income statement will be almost identical. The one exception is that instead of the cost of finished goods purchased in the year, the trading account will show the cost of finished goods manufactured in the year.

It is this final item that leads to the one major difference in the financial statements of a manufacturing business. Establishing the cost of finished goods manufactured in the year is not such a simple process as finding the total of finished goods purchased by a retailer. Indeed, it requires a whole new account – the *manufacturing account* – to arrive at this cost. The manufacturing account, in an identical way to the trading account, is a sub-section of the income statement. The name 'manufacturing account' does not appear within the income statement but it is nevertheless a very important part of the income statement.

12.2 Why is a manufacturing account needed?

Manufacturers may sell their finished product directly to the public, or may sell it to a wholesaler/retailer or to another trading organisation. The income statement is used to

413

bring together the revenue and expenditure of trading and operating the business, and this still applies to a manufacturing business. However, the calculation of the cost of goods sold by a retail or wholesale organisation is fairly straightforward, that is, opening inventories, plus purchases, less closing inventories. Calculating the costs of manufacturing products is often more complex than this, as the firm will incur not only the cost of materials but also labour costs and other expenses incurred in manufacturing. The manufacturing account is used to bring together the costs of manufacturing during the period.

12.2.1 Inventories in manufacturing organisations

The manufacturing process will involve three stages:

Stage 1. The acquisition of raw materials.
Stage 2. The modification or processing of those materials, with the addition of labour and other expenses.
Stage 3. The production of finished goods.

However, some raw materials purchased during a period will still be unmodified at the end of the period, while some will only be partly modified. In addition, there will be some finished goods produced during the period that remain unsold. The organisation might also buy in ready-made items for sale. Therefore, at the beginning and end of a period, there could be four types of inventories on the statement of financial position:

- raw materials;
- work in progress (partly finished goods);
- finished goods;
- bought-in goods.

It is important to remember that the trading account must still be used to show the sales revenue earned and the cost of goods sold, not the cost of goods manufactured. The trading account will therefore bring together opening inventories of finished goods, cost of completed goods manufactured during the period, less closing inventories of finished goods. The manufacturing account will contain all of the manufacturing costs, with adjustments for opening and closing inventories of raw materials and work in progress.

It is also important to appreciate that the manufacturing account is used solely to bring together *expenses* – it does not include any revenue from sales.

12.3 Costs to include in the manufacturing account

We have already mentioned that the cost of raw materials will be contained within the manufacturing account. The calculation of raw materials consumed in the manufacturing process is exactly the same as the calculations you have previously used in the trading account of retail and wholesale organisations, that is:

- opening inventories of raw materials;
- *plus* purchases of raw materials (including carriage inwards and less returns);
- *less* closing inventories of raw materials.

However, other manufacturing costs must also be considered.

The following terms are considered key to understanding the manufacturing account.

12.3.1   Other direct costs

A direct cost is one that can be identified with units of production; very often it is a cost that varies according to the level of production. You will learn more about this cost behaviour in your studies of *Fundamentals of Management Accounting*. Obviously, raw materials are direct costs in that they directly vary with the level of production.

Examples of other direct costs are:

- *Direct labour (also known as production labour)*. The wages and associated costs of those producing the goods;
- *Direct expenses*. Other costs that can be identified with units of production. These are more difficult to establish, as most expenses are more general in nature, but examples of direct expenses might be equipment hire for a special production run, power costs for a particular machine, and royalties payable on the production of certain products. You will not encounter direct expenses very often, however, and such expenses are likely to be highlighted if they are to be regarded as such.

12.3.2   Prime cost

The prime cost is the total of direct costs, that is, direct materials consumed, direct labour and direct expenses (if any). It should be clearly shown as a subtotal in the manufacturing account.

12.3.3   Indirect costs

These include all the other costs of manufacturing that are not part of prime cost. They are also referred to as *manufacturing overheads, production overheads* or *factory overheads*. Examples include:

- factory rent;
- factory heating, lighting and insurance;
- wages and salaries paid to factory supervisors and maintenance engineers (also known as *indirect factory labour*);
- depreciation of non-current assets used in manufacturing.

Note that only costs associated with manufacturing are included. Do not include costs associated with selling, distribution of goods sold or general administrative costs.

12.3.4   Factory cost of production

Factory cost of production is the total of prime cost and indirect costs consumed in the factory, and is another important subtotal to be shown in the manufacturing account.

12.3.5   Work in progress

The factory cost of production is the total of new costs introduced to the factory. However, there may already be some work in progress in the factory system at the start of the period. Some of this will be completed during the period, but there will probably still be some unfinished, and some new work in progress at the end of the period. We need to adjust the factory cost of production to add in the opening work in progress and deduct the closing work in progress. This is shown in the final section of the manufacturing account.

12.3.6 Factory cost of goods completed

This is the end result of the manufacturing account, and its balance is incorporated into the trading account.

12.4 Layout of manufacturing and trading accounts

As stated earlier, the trading account is the place to show the sales revenue earned and the cost of goods sold. In manufacturing organisations, however, the calculation of cost of goods sold will not include purchases and inventories of raw materials, but will instead include the factory cost of goods completed and opening and closing inventories of finished goods. The part of the income statement in the box is the manufacturing account; in effect the 'factory cost of goods completed' is a substitute for the 'purchases' which we have previously found in the trading account of a retailer.

Income statement (extract) for the year ended 31 December 20X1

	$	$	$	$
Sales				645,000
Less: cost of goods sold				
Opening inventories of finished goods			55,000	
Opening inventories of raw materials		12,000		
Purchases of raw materials		235,000		
				247,000
Closing inventories of raw materials		(14,000)		
Raw materials consumed		233,000		
Direct manufacturing wages		153,000		
Direct factory expenses		15,000		
Prime cost		401,000		
Production overhead				
Factory supervisors' wages	30,000			
Heating and lighting	16,000			
Factory rent	12,000			
		58,000		
Factory costs incurred		459,000		
Opening work in progress	26,000			
Closing work in progress	(21,000)			
		5,000		
Factory cost of goods completed			464,000	
			519,000	
Less: closing inventories of finished goods			(35,000)	
Cost of goods sold				(484,000)
Gross profit				161,000

12.5 Income statement for manufacturing organisations

These are exactly as for other organisations. The income statement will implicitly have two sub-sections – the manufacturing account and the trading account, and will contain sundry revenues and all other expenses incurred in running the business.

12.6 Statements of financial position for manufacturing organisations

These are also prepared as for other organisations, except that there is likely to be three or four types of inventories to be shown, that is:

- raw materials;
- work in progress;
- finished goods (manufactured goods);
- bought-in goods for resale.

12.7 The accounting system for manufacturing organisations

Ledger accounts will be prepared in the same way as for other organisations, except that there will be additional ledger accounts for items connected with manufacturing, such as direct factory labour, indirect factory labour, and inventories of work in progress and finished goods. Some items of expense, however, may not be separately established or invoiced. For example, premises insurance might consist of a single invoice covering all the buildings. In such cases, it is necessary to apportion the expenses between manufacturing and other elements (often described as 'factory' and 'office'). In computer-based assessment questions, you will be told what proportions to apply.

The manufacturing account, just as the trading account, and income statement as a whole, is part of the double-entry bookkeeping system. Hence it is called the manufacturing 'account' and is a ledger account which can be debited and credited. The items that appear in it will all have an equivalent opposite entry in either the nominal ledger or the trading account. For example, expenses such as direct factory labour will be debited to the direct factory labour ledger account during the year, and then, at the end of the year, the balance will be transferred to the manufacturing account (debit manufacturing account; credit direct factory labour).

The balance on the manufacturing account is transferred to the trading account at the end of the year (debit trading account; credit manufacturing account).

The key to questions in this area is to adopt a methodical approach. Remember that your aim in the manufacturing account is to arrive at the total cost of manufacturing the finished goods completed in the year. This can be regarded as comprising three elements:

- the costs directly attributable to the goods produced (such as the raw materials they contain, and the wages of personnel directly involved in manufacturing);

- the indirect factory costs (sometimes called factory overheads). These might include the costs of heating and lighting the factory, the rent on factory premises and the wages of factory supervisors;
- an adjustment for opening and closing work in progress, similar to the treatment of opening and closing inventories of finished goods in a trading account.

Example 12.A

G Club is a manufacturer of spare parts and the following balances were some of those appearing in his books at 31 December year 4.

	$
Capital	56,932
Inventories at 1 January year 4	
Raw materials	11,000
Work in progress	16,000
Finished goods	20,090
Inventories at 31 December year 4	
Raw materials	17,000
Work in progress	18,000
Finished goods	18,040
Wages	
Direct manufacturing	203,080
Factory supervisors	13,325
General office	10,200
Warehouse	19,300
Direct factory power	95,000
Heating and lighting	9,000
Purchase of raw materials	256,000
Carriage outwards	986
Plant and machinery	80,000
Premises	120,000
Returns inwards	420
Office equipment	15,000
Rent	6,000
Administrative expenses	1,800
Receivables	14,000
Payables	12,000
Cash in hand	3,662
Sales	800,290
Bank overdraft	25,641

For the year ended 31 December year 4, *you are required* to prepare:

(a) the income statement of G Club;
(b) the statement of financial position of G Club.

The costs of heating and lighting, and rent are to be apportioned as follows: factory 1/2, warehouse 1/3, offices 1/6.

Solution

(a) Income statement of G Club for the year ended 31 December year 4

	$	$	$	$
Sales				800,290
Less: returns inwards				(420)
				799,870
Opening inventories of finished goods			20,090	
Opening inventories of raw materials		11,000		
Purchases of raw materials		256,000		
		267,000		
Closing inventories of raw materials		(17,000)		
Raw materials consumed		250,000		
Direct manufacturing wages		203,080		
Direct factory power		95,000		
Prime cost		548,080		
Production overhead				
Factory supervisors' wages	13,325			
Heating and lighting	4,500			
Rent	3,000			
		20,825		
Factory costs incurred		568,905		
Opening work in progress	16,000			
Closing work in progress	(18,000)			
		(2,000)		
Factory cost of goods completed			566,905	
			586,995	
Closing inventories of finished goods			(18,040)	
Cost of sales				(568,955)
Gross profit				230,915
Warehouse costs				
Wages		19,300		
Heating and lighting		3,000		
Rates		2,000		
			24,300	
Office costs				
Wages		10,200		
Heating and lighting		1,500		
Rates		1,000		
Administration expenses		1,800		
			14,500	
Selling and distribution costs				
Carriage outwards			986	
				(39,786)
Net profit for the year				191,129

(b) Statement of financial position of G Club as at 31 December year 4

Assets	$	$	$
Non-current assets			
Premises			120,000
Plant and machinery			80,000
Office equipment			15,000
			215,000
Current assets			
Inventories			
Raw materials	17,000		
Work in progress	18,000		
Finished goods	18,040		
		53,040	
Receivables		14,000	
Cash in hand		3,662	
			70,702
			285,702
Capital and liabilities			
Capital			56,932
Add: net profit			191,129
			248,061
Current liabilities			
Payables		12,000	
Bank overdraft		25,641	
			37,641
			285,702

Exercise 12.1

What are the component parts of prime cost?

Solution

The component parts of prime cost are direct materials, direct labour and direct expenses (overheads).

12.8 Summary

In this chapter we have looked at the production of an income statement, incorporating manufacturing and trading accounts, and a statement of financial position for a manufacturing organisation. You should be able to identify the items that are to be included in the manufacturing account, in particular:

- the calculation of prime cost;
- factory cost of production;

- factory cost of goods completed;
- the adjustment for work in progress at the beginning and end of the period.

You should appreciate that the only difference in the trading account from that of a non-manufacturing organisation is the substitution of 'factory cost of goods completed' for 'purchases'.

Manufacturing accounts are quite straightforward if you take care with your workings, and adopt a methodical approach. Make sure that you clearly label workings, and cross-reference them to the financial statements: this is much clearer than attempting to squash them on to the face of the financial statements themselves, as some of them may involve several elements to their calculation. A suggested approach is as follows:

- *Step 1*. Read the question completely before starting. Note particularly if a statement of financial position is required or not.
- *Step 2*. Label the trial balance with the destination of the various items. If a statement of financial position is not required, you will not need all of the items on the statement of financial position (e.g. bank balances, receivables, payables).
- *Step 3*. Set out a page of workings before you start. Work through the notes to the financial statements, in the order given, and make the necessary adjustments:

    (A) adjust the trial balance figures for any accruals and prepayments, then split between manufacturing and the rest of the income statement.
    (B) calculate depreciation and split between manufacturing and the rest of the income statement;
    (C) calculate any other adjustments, for example, bad debts and allowance for receivables;
    (D) adjust for any other items, such as goods on sale or return, errors and corrections.

- *Step 4*.

    (A) Enter the sales, less any returns inwards in the trading account.
    (B) Enter opening inventories of finished goods in the trading account.
    (C) Commence your manufacturing account and enter all relevant figures, using your workings where necessary:
        - raw materials opening inventories, plus purchases, less closing inventories (remember to adjust for returns outwards and carriage inwards);
        - other direct costs, for example, wages, direct power, to give prime cost;
        - indirect factory costs (production overheads);
        - adjust for work in progress (add opening inventories, deduct closing inventories);
        - the final result is the factory cost of goods completed.

- *Step 5*. Complete the trading account:

    (A) less closing inventories of finished goods;
    (B) this gives cost of goods sold;
    (C) the difference between sales and cost of good sold is gross profit.

- *Step 6*. Prepare the remainder of the income statement, using your workings where necessary.
- *Step 7*. Prepare the statement of financial position (if required), remembering that you are likely to have several types of closing inventories to show.

Revision Questions

Question 1 Multiple choice

1.1 The following information relates to a company at its year end:

	$
Inventories at beginning of year	
Raw materials	10,000
Work in progress	2,000
Finished goods	34,000
Inventories at end of year	
Raw materials	11,000
Work in progress	4,000
Finished goods	30,000
Purchases of raw materials	50,000
Direct wages	40,000
Royalties on goods sold	3,000
Production overheads	60,000
Distribution costs	55,000
Administration expenses	70,000
Sales	300,000

The cost of goods manufactured during the year is: $................

1.2 If work in progress decreases during the period, then:

(A) prime cost will decrease.
(B) prime cost will increase.
(C) the factory cost of goods completed will decrease.
(D) the factory cost of goods completed will increase.

1.3 An increase in the figure for work in progress will:

(A) increase the prime cost.
(B) decrease the prime cost.
(C) increase the cost of goods sold.
(D) decrease the factory cost of goods completed.

423

1.4 Your firm has the following manufacturing figures:

	$
Prime cost	56,000
Factory overheads	4,500
Opening work in progress	6,200
Factory cost of goods completed	57,000

Closing work in progress is: $..............

1.5 The prime cost of goods manufactured is the total of:

(A) all factory costs before adjusting for work in progress.
(B) all factory costs of goods completed.
(C) all materials and labour.
(D) direct factory costs.

1.6 The following information relates to M Ltd:

At 30 September	20X1	20X0
	$'000	$'000
Inventories of raw materials	75	45
Work in progress inventories	60	70
Inventories of finished goods	100	90
For the year ended 30th September 20X1		
Purchases of raw materials	$ 150,000	
Manufacturing wages	$ 50,000	
Factory overheads	$40,000	

The prime cost of production in the manufacturing account for the year ended 30 September 20X1 is:
$..............

Question 2

M makes agricultural machinery, for sale to major suppliers in the industry. The following figures are extracted from his trial balance at the end of the most recent year.

	$'000
Sales	2,200
Purchases of parts	650
Carriage inwards	40
Carriage outwards	100
Returns inwards	80
Returns outwards	60
Manufacturing labour	200
Factory supervisory labour	75
Office salaries	108
Other costs	
Heating and lighting	165
Rent and insurance	122
Factory machinery at cost	1,000
Accumulated depreciation of factory machinery	400
Delivery vehicles at cost	300
Accumulated depreciation of vehicles	100
Office machinery at cost	120
Accumulated depreciation of office machinery	80
Opening inventories	
Raw materials	175
Work in progress	425
Finished goods	115

At the end of the year, the following information is also available:

(a)

	$'000
Closing inventories	
Raw materials	147
Work in progress	392
Finished goods	138

(b)

	$'000
Heat and light accrued	15
Rent prepaid	22

(c) Seventy-five per cent of heat, light, rent and insurance is considered to be applicable to the manufacturing processes.

(d) Depreciation is to be calculated as follows:
- factory machinery, 10 per cent, straight line;
- delivery vehicles, 20 per cent, reducing balance;
- office machinery, 25 per cent, reducing balance.

(e) Delivery vehicles are used entirely for the delivery of finished goods.

(f) Office machinery is used 25 per cent for the operation of factory information systems.

THE MANUFACTURING ACCOUNT

Requirements

Insert the missing items into the income statement below:

Income statement of M for the year ended . . .

	$'000	$'000	$'000	$'000
				▨
Sales				▨
Less: returns inwards				▨
Opening inventories of finished goods			▨	
Opening inventories of raw materials		▨		
Purchases	▨			
Carriage inwards	▨			
	▨			
Less: returns outwards	▨			
		▨		
		▨		
Less: closing inventories of raw materials		▨		
Direct materials		▨		
Direct labour		▨		
Prime cost		▨		
Factory indirect overheads				
Supervisory labour	▨			
Heat and light ┄┄% × $┄┄	▨			
Rent and insurance ┄┄% × $┄┄	▨			
Depreciation				
Factory machinery ┄┄% × $┄┄	▨			
		▨		
Factory cost of production		▨		
Opening work in progress	▨			
Less: closing work in progress	▨			
		▨		
Factory cost of goods completed			▨	
			▨	
Less: closing inventories of finished goods			▨	
Cost of sales				▨
Gross profit				▨
Expenses				
Carriage outwards			▨	
Office salaries			▨	
Heat and light ┄┄% × $┄┄			▨	
Rent and insurance ┄┄ × $┄┄			▨	
Depreciation				
Delivery vehicles ┄┄% × $┄┄			▨	
Office machinery ┄┄% × $┄┄			▨	
				▨
Net profit				▨

Solutions to Revision Questions 12

✓ Solution 1

1.1 Cost of goods manufactured is found as follows:

	$
Opening inventories of raw materials	10,000
Purchases of raw materials	50,000
Less: closing inventories of raw materials	(11,000)
	49,000
Direct wages	40,000
Prime cost	89,000
Production overheads	60,000
	149,000
Less: increase in work in progress	(2,000)
Cost of goods manufactured	147,000

1.2 Answer: (D)

A decrease in work in progress means fewer goods are partly complete, thus the value of completed goods will be higher.

1.3 Answer: (D)

(A) and (B) are incorrect as work in progress has no effect on prime cost. The change in work in progress has no effect on cost of goods sold, as this depends on inventories of finished goods, therefore (C) is incorrect. An increase in work in progress means that more production is in a partly finished state and therefore less hasbeen completed.

1.4

	$
Prime cost	56,000
Factory overheads	4,500
Opening WIP	6,200
Factory cost of goods completed	(57,000)
Therefore, closing WIP is	9,700

1.5 Answer: (D)

1.6 $170,000

Solution 2

- Categorise items before you start the income statement.
- Remember to make adjustments for accruals and prepayments, and the calculation of depreciation, before splitting items between manufacturing account, trading account and the remainder of the income statement.
- Some items in the question might not be required for your answer.

Income statement of M for the year ended . . .

	$'000	$'000	$'000	$'000
Sales				2,200
Less: returns inwards				(80)
				2,120
Opening inventories of finished goods			115	
Opening inventories of raw materials		175		
Purchases	650			
Carriage inwards	40			
	690			
Less: returns outwards	(60)			
		630		
		805		
Less: closing inventories of raw materials		(147)		
Direct materials		658		
Direct labour		200		
Prime cost		858		
Factory indirect overheads				
Supervisory labour	75			
Heat and light (75% × (165 + 15))	135			
Rent and insurance (75% × (122 − 22))	75			
Depreciation				
Factory machinery (10% × $1,000)	100			
		385		
Factory cost of production		1,243		
Opening work in progress	425			
Less: closing work in progress	(392)			
		33		
Factory cost of goods completed			1,276	
			1,391	
Less: closing inventories of finished goods			(138)	
Cost of sales				(1,253)
Gross profit				867
Expenses				
Carriage outwards			100	
Office salaries			108	
Heat and light (25% × (165 + 15))			45	
Rent and insurance (25% × (122 − 22))			25	
Depreciation				
Delivery vehicles (20% × $200)			40	
Office machinery (25% × (120 − 80))			10	
				(328)
Net profit				539

13

The Financial Statements
of Limited Companies and
the Statement of Cash Flows

The Financial Statements of Limited Companies and the Statement of Cash Flows

13

LEARNING OUTCOMES

When you have completed this chapter, you should be able to:

► prepare a statement of comprehensive income, statement of changes in equity and statement of financial position, from a trial balance, for limited companies;

► prepare a statement of cash flows.

13.1 Introduction

Many businesses are constituted in the form of limited companies. The nature of limited companies was mentioned very briefly in Chapter 1 and you should refer back to refresh your memory. In this chapter we look at some of the features of limited companies that have an impact on the content and presentation of their financial statements.

We also look at two further accounting statements that companies are required to include in their financial statements – the statement of changes in equity and the statement of cash flows.

13.2 Limited companies

As trading organisations grow in size, the limited financial resources of their owners often restrict the organisation's ability to grow any further. In order to avoid this difficulty many larger organisations use a company structure. A company is a separate legal entity that may sue and be sued. It may have many owners who may or may not be directly involved in the day-to-day running of the business. Each of these owners is known as a shareholder or member of the company; they buy shares in the company that when first issued form the company's capital. The liability of the members to the company is limited. This means that if a company's assets are insufficient to pay its liabilities the shareholders cannot be required to pay more than the amount paid, or agreed to be paid for their shares, and thus their personal assets are protected. This contrasts with the position of sole traders. In law, the business of a sole trader and the individual owning the business are the same person. Thus the business obligations must be met by its owner even if this means selling private assets or leads to the individual being declared bankrupt.

The financial statements of a company are normally filed annually at a public bureau, in a form prescribed by company law and international financial reporting standards (IFRSs) (this is not within your syllabus and is not included in this Learning System). However, the internal financial statements of companies are within your syllabus and use the same principles as have already been learned to prepare the financial statements of sole traders.

13.2.1 The financial statements of companies

The accounting statements of companies comprise:

1. a statement of comprehensive income, which may include a manufacturing account (if appropriate, depending on the organisation's activities dealt with in Chapter 12) and a trading account;
2. a statement of changes in equity;
3. a statement of financial position;
4. a statement of cash flows.

The statement of comprehensive income comprises an income statement, which you will already be familiar with from the previous chapters. It has an additional section which is discussed in more detail in Section 13.2.8 below.

The only statements different from those of a sole trader are the statement of changes in equity and the statement of cash flows. The statement of changes in equity shows the increase or decrease in equity in a company, where the equity is the name for 'capital' in a limited company. Thus in a limited company the accounting equation is assets = equity + liabilities.

In a sole trader's statement of financial position we show the change in capital as:

	$
Capital brought forward at the beginning of the year	X
Add: capital introduced (if any)	X
Add: profit for the year	X
Less: drawings for the year	(X)
Capital at the end of the year	X

This is effectively the same as the statement of changes in equity in a company, except that in company financial statements the statement of changes in equity is shown as a separate financial statement and only the final total is entered in the statement of financial position. Also, in company financial statements any capital introduced would be 'share' capital, and the money taken out by the owners is called 'dividends', not drawings. The statement of changes in equity is discussed in more detail in Section 13.2.9.

13.2.2 Presentation of company income statements

There are a few details in which the financial statements of a company will differ from those of a sole proprietor. In some cases this is because there are new items, for example dividends, and sometimes because a slightly different presentation is used to reflect the different nature of a limited company.

One such detail is that in the income statement of a sole proprietor the last line is 'net profit'. In the statement of comprehensive income of company accounts, it is normal to calculate a profit called 'operating profit' which is the profit before any interest received or paid.

An example is shown below:

Statement of comprehensive income of ABC Ltd for the year ended 20X8

	$'000
Sales	1000
Cost of sales	(640)
Gross profit	360
Expenses – (e.g. rent, power, telephone etc.)	(100)
Operating profit	260
Interest received	5
Interest paid	(20)
Profit before tax	245

Note that the line after interest paid is called 'profit before tax'.

13.2.3 Taxation in company financial statements

An additional item that appears in the financial statements of companies is that of taxation. In a sole trader's business, this is a personal charge, and so does not appear in the financial statements. But in the case of a limited company, a company is a separate legal entity and as such is liable to pay tax on its profits and so it does appear in the financial statements. At the end of each year an estimate is made by the company of the amount of its taxation liability and an accrual is made in its accounts by debiting the tax expense to the statement of comprehensive income and crediting a liability account 'income tax liability'. When the liability is finally agreed with the tax authorities there may be a difference compared with the estimate: the difference is compensated for when preparing the estimate for the following year's tax liability.

In this Learning System, the tax on company profits is referred to by the generic name 'income tax' though in different countries it may have another name, for example corporation tax in the UK.

The income tax will appear in the statement of comprehensive income, continuing the example above, as follows:

Profit before tax	245
Income tax	(80)
Profit for the period	165

Note that the final line is 'profit for the period'. The period of the statement of comprehensive income will appear at the top of the statement, in this case year ended 20X8.

13.2.4   Directors of limited companies

Limited companies are owned by the shareholders, but it is not common, especially in larger companies, for the shareholders to be involved in the day-to-day running of the company. Instead, the shareholders appoint directors to carry out those duties. Directors are merely employees of the company, and their duties are remunerated by salaries, fees, commission and so on, all of which are regarded in the same way as wages paid to any other employee, and appear in the statement of comprehensive income as an expense. Of course, in some companies, directors also own shares, but the two roles (as director and shareholder) are separate, and are recorded separately.

13.2.5   Sources of finance for a limited company

The statement of financial position of a company is similar to that of a sole trader, but there are usually a number of different sources of finance. Many companies raise their own loan finance in the form of debentures.

Debentures

Debenture. The written acknowledgement of a debt by a company and normally containing details as to payment of interest and the terms of repayment of principal.

A debenture may be secured on some or all of the assets of the company. This means that if the company fails to repay the loan, or cannot keep up with the interest payments, the debenture holders can seize the assets on which their loan is secured and sell them to recover their money.

In accounting terms, a debenture is the same as a loan; it may be a current or non-current liability depending on the date of repayment of the principal. The interest payments are compulsory, irrespective of the level of profits, and are a normal expense, accounted for on an accruals basis (i.e. the full amount of interest arising during the accounting period must be charged in the statement of comprehensive income, regardless of the date of payment of that interest).

Share capital

The owners' investment is in the form of shares. The most common forms of share are ordinary shares and preference shares.

Ordinary shares. Shares that entitle the holders to the remaining divisible profits (and, in a liquidation, the assets) after prior interests – for example, payables and prior-charge capital – have been satisfied.

Preference Shares. Shares carrying a fixed rate of dividend, the holders of which, subject to the conditions of issue, have a prior claim to any company profits available for distribution. Preference shareholders may also have a prior claim to the repayment of capital in the event of a winding up.

When presenting a company statement of financial position, each of these types of share capital should be shown as a separate source of finance.

When a company is formed, the legal documents state the authorised share capital of the company. This is analysed into a number of shares, each having a *nominal* value.

The *authorised share capital* is the amount of capital that may be issued without obtaining permission from the company's shareholders. The nominal value is also known as the *par value*.

Issues of shares by a company may be at nominal value or at a higher price. If they are issued at the higher price, the difference between this and the nominal value is known as the *share premium*.

When shares are issued, there are a number of stages before the share certificates are issued to their owners. Often, part of the issue price is payable on application for the shares, with further payments being requested later.

Example 13.A

Z Ltd plans to issue 100,000 ordinary shares of $1 nominal value at an issue price of $1.50 each. $0.75 per share is payable on application, $0.25 per share on confirmation that the shares have been issued and the balance of $0.50 per share on first call by Z Ltd in 3 months' time. This is for the share premium.

The double entry to record the receipt of the application monies is as follows:

	Debit ($)	Credit ($)
Bank	75,000	
Application a/c (Being cash received from applicants.)		75,000
Allotment a/c	25,000	
Application a/c	75,000	
Share capital		100,000

(Being the creation of share capital from successful applications and the recording of amounts due on allotment.)

When the allotment monies are received the entry is:

	Debit ($)	Credit ($)
Bank	25,000	
Allotment a/c		25,000

In 3 months' time, Z Ltd will request the final payment of $0.50 per share. This is known as a call for payment. In this example, this represents the share premium. The double entry would be:

	Debit ($)	Credit ($)
Bank	50,000	
Share premium		50,000

Share premiums are also a type of reserve. Reserves are explained in more detail below. When the statement of financial position is drawn up, the 'Equity' section will show:

	$
Ordinary shares of $1 each	100,000
Share premium	50,000

13.2.6 Dividends

The amount paid to the company's shareholders as a return for investing in the company is known as a dividend. Dividends are often paid in two instalments: one during the year is known as an *interim dividend*; the other, which is usually paid after the end of the financial year, is known as a *final dividend*. The total amount of the dividends is shown in the statement of changes in equity.

Particular attention has to be given to the final dividend at the end of the year. The normal procedure is for directors to *propose* a final dividend; this is then voted upon as a resolution at the annual general meeting which takes place after the year end. If the proposal is approved, then the directors *declare* that a dividend will be paid. The key point here is, at what time should we recognise the final dividend in company financial statements? The answer is, only when the dividend has been declared.

This means that in most circumstances the dividends which are *paid* in a year are the final dividends of the previous year and the interim dividend of the current year.

Example 13.B

A company has a year end of 31 December. On the 1 July 20X7, the directors declare an interim dividend of $10,000. On the 31 December 20X7, the directors propose a final dividend of $12,000. On the 1 March 20X8 at the annual general meeting the proposed final dividend for 20X7 is approved, and the directors declare that the dividend will be paid. On the 1 July 20X8, the directors declare an interim dividend of $11,000. On the 31 December 20X8, the directors propose a final dividend of $13,000. On the 1 March 20X9 at the annual general meeting the proposed final dividend for 20X8 is approved, and the directors declare that the dividend will be paid.

What will be the dividends appearing in the statement of changes in equity in the year ended 20X8?

Final dividend for 20X7	$12,000
Interim dividend for 20X8	$11,000
	$23,000

The $23,000 will appear in the trial balance for the year ended 31 December 20X8. The double entry will be debit 'dividends', credit 'bank'.

Directors do not have to pay the dividends in two instalments – interim and final – and in some companies there may only be one dividend payment at the end of the year. In this case, the dividend that will normally appear in the statement of changes in equity will be the dividend which was proposed in the previous year but declared and paid in the current year. For example, the financial statements for 20X4 will include the proposed dividend of 20X3.

It should be noted that the directors do not have to propose any dividends – the payment of dividends is entirely at their discretion. If the shareholders were not happy with this situation, they would remove these directors and replace them with directors who were prepared to propose a dividend.

There may be some occasions where the directors *declare* a final dividend before the end of the year, but do not pay the dividend until after the year end. This may occur where a meeting of the shareholders has been held before the year end to approve a proposed dividend. In this situation, the accruals convention will be applied, and the declared dividend will appear in the statement of changes in equity, and there will also be a 'dividend liability' in the current liabilities in the statement of financial position.

Example 13.C

A company has a year end of 31 March. In the year ended 31 March 20X2 no interim dividend was paid, but on the 29 March 20X2 the shareholders approved the payment of a proposed dividend of $15,000. The dividend was paid on 15 April 20X2.

What entries would appear in the financial statements for the year ended 31 March 20×2 in relation to dividends?

Statement of changes in equity	$15,000
Statement of financial position – current liabilities – dividend liability	$15,000

Dividends on ordinary shares

Ordinary shareholders are also known as *equity shareholders*. Their shares do not qualify for any special benefits, although they are often entitled to vote at general meetings. An ordinary shareholder is not entitled to any particular dividend payment, although if the directors decide to declare a dividend it can be as small or as large as they see fit. The ordinary shareholders are regarded as the 'main' shareholders in a company. The profits that are retained in the company belong to them, and would be repaid to them in the event that the company ceases to exist.

Do take care, when computing dividends, to read the question carefully. If the question states that the ordinary dividend is to be 10¢ per share, you need to calculate how many shares are in issue. For example, if the share capital in the statement of financial position is described as 'Ordinary shares of $0.5' and they are stated at $500,000, then there are 1 million ordinary shares. The dividend in this example would be 1 million ×10¢ = $100,000.

Dividends on preference shares

Preference shareholders are so known because they received preferential treatment in the payment of dividends, and in the repayment of capital in the event that the company ceases to exist. A preference share carries a fixed rate of dividend. The important point to remember is that if the ordinary shareholders are to receive a dividend, then the preference shareholders must receive theirs first.

There are many different types of preference shares and you will study these in more detail in later studies. For the purposes of this Learning System, it is assumed that all preference shares are 'irredeemable', which means that the preference shares have no fixed repayment date. In any questions containing preference shares, the dividends will have been paid and there will be no need to make any further adjustment.

13.2.7 Reserves

There are two types of reserves: *capital reserves* and *revenue reserves*. The difference between these is that capital reserves may not be distributed as dividends. Examples of capital reserves are share premium (see above) and revaluation reserves – created when a company revalues its assets (often land and buildings). Since the increase in value is based on a professional valuation and has not been realised by a sale, the increase in value (or profit) cannot be distributed to shareholders. For example, if a company had property in the statement of financial position at $200,000 and it was revalued to $275,000, the property would be increased to $275,000 in the statement of financial position and a revaluation reserve would be created for $75,000.

Revenue reserves are the accumulated and undistributed profits of a company. The most common is the balance remaining on the statement of changes in equity at the end of each year. This appears as a reserve called 'retained earnings' in the statement of financial position. However, the directors may decide to set aside a portion of the remaining profits into a separate reserve account, for either general or specific purposes. A specific reserve is used to identify the accumulation of profits for a specific future purpose. Despite the fact that several revenue reserve accounts may exist, they are all available to be used for the payment of dividends if required.

It is important to realise that the existence of reserves does not indicate a fund of cash. The creation of a reserve may well be simply a bookkeeping transaction, debiting retained profits reserve and crediting general reserve.

13.2.8 Statement of comprehensive income

We introduced the statement of comprehensive income very briefly in Section 13.2.1. We now return to this subject to discuss it in more detail. In previous chapters we have referred to the income statement when discussing the revenue and expenses in sole proprietors. In limited companies this is referred to as the statement of comprehensive income. The statement of comprehensive income has two sections – the 'income statement' section and the 'other comprehensive income' section. The income statement section is similar to that of sole proprietors, except for differences in terminology and taxation noted in Sections 13.2.2 and 13.2.3. respectively. The 'income statement' section includes all items from 'Sales' to 'Profit for the period'.

The section for 'other comprehensive income' can contain several items and you will learn about these later in your studies at more advanced levels. With regard to the assessment for Fundamentals of Financial Accounting, there is only one item you need to know, and that is the revaluation of property. If a company revalues a property, then the amount of the gain is included in 'other comprehensive income'. This gain is added to the profit for the period to give 'total comprehensive income for the period'. An illustration of this is given below.

Statement of comprehensive income of ABC Ltd
for the Year Ended 30 June 20X8

	$'000
Sales	1000
Cost of sales	(640)
Gross profit	360
Expenses (e.g. rent, power, telephone, etc.)	(100)
Operating profit	260
Interest received	5
Interest paid	(20)
Profit before tax	245
Income tax	(80)
Profit for the period	165
Other comprehensive income	
Gain on property revaluation net of tax	25
Total comprehensive income for the period	190

Although the first section has been referred to above as the 'income statement' section, this title does not appear in the statement.

A company may choose to present its statement of comprehensive income as two separate statements. In this case the two statements are called the 'income statement ' and the 'statement of comprehensive income'. The title 'income statement' does appear, and the statement of comprehensive income begins with the profit for the period.

The two statements would be presented as follows:

Statement of comprehensive income of ABC Ltd for the Year Ended 30 June 20×8

Income Statement

	$'000
Sales	1000
Cost of sales	(640)
Gross profit	360
Expenses (e.g. rent, power, telephone, etc.)	(100)
Operating profit	260
Interest received	5
Interest paid	(20)
Profit before tax	245
Income tax	(80)
Profit for the period	165

Statement of comprehensive income

	$'000
Profit for the period	165
Other comprehensive income	
Gain on property revaluation net of tax	25
Total comprehensive income for the period	190

As can be seen above, there is little difference in practice between the two presentations.

In this Learning System, it will normally be assumed that a single statement is prepared and this will be referred to as the 'statement of comprehensive income'. There will only rarely be an 'other comprehensive income' section, as this only applies when there is a revaluation of property.

A minor point is that the tax on the gain on the property revaluation should be disclosed. This can either be disclosed in the statement of comprehensive income or in a note. For example, using ABC Ltd above, this could be shown as:

Other comprehensive income	$'000	$'000
Gain on property revaluation before tax	30	
Less income tax	(5)	
Gain on property revaluation net of tax		25

Alternatively the tax may be shown as a note.

Other comprehensive income	
Gain on property revaluation net of tax *(Note 1)*	25

Note 1: income tax on gain on property revaluation $5,000

The tax will be included as an accrual under non-current liabilities in the statement of financial position.

The total comprehensive income for the year will be shown in the statement of changes in equity, analysed between profit for the period and the net gain on property revaluation. For purposes of the assessment, if the examiner refers to:

- an income statement, then just an income statement is required
- a statement of comprehensive income, then either:
  - a statement with two sections is required, as in the first illustration above
  - or, two statements are required, as in the second illustration above

In general, the examiner will make clear from the amount of information given and the nature of the question the exact format required to answer the question.

- 'other comprehensive income', then just this section of a comprehensive income statement is required.

13.2.9 Statement of changes in equity

We introduced the statement of changes in equity very briefly in Section 13.2.1 and now that we have discussed share capital, reserves and dividends in more detail, we can return to the statement of changes in equity. As the name implies, the statement shows the change in equity from the beginning of the year to the end of the year. Equity is the shareholders' capital in the company and comprises shares and reserves. These may be increased by, for example:

Share issues
Total comprehensive income.

These may be decreased by, for example:

Dividends.

There may be a transfer between reserves; this will not increase or decrease the reserves in total but will change the individual balances.

A full example of a statement of changes in equity is given below.

Statement of changes in equity of Hi Tech Ltd for the year ended 31 December 20X8

	Ordinary Shares $'000	Share Premium $'000	Revaluation Reserve $'000	General Reserve $'000	Retained Earnings $'000	Total $'000
Balance 1.1.X8	1,000	500	300	100	400	2,300
Profit for the year					600	600
Dividends					(200)	(200)
Shares issued	600	150				750
Transfer				75	(75)	
Revaluation property			80			80
Balance 31.12.X8	1,600	650	380	175	725	3,530

The statement of changes in equity shows the result of transactions between the owners of a limited company and its owners. This will typically be the retention of profit, the payment of dividends and the issue of shares.

The equity has changed from $2,300 to $3,530 in the year.

The equity would appear in the statement of financial position as follows:

Statement of financial position of Hi Tech Ltd as at 31 December 20X8

Equity	$'000
Ordinary shares	1,600
Share premium	650
Revaluation reserve	380
General reserve	175
Retained earnings	725
	3,530

In the Learning System, where there is no change in a component of equity, the statement of changes in equity will not be presented in full but only those columns which have changed.

These points are brought together in the following example.

Example 13.D

The trial balance of ABC Ltd at 30 September year 1 is set out below:

	Debit ($'000)	Credit ($'000)
Premises at cost	800	
Plant and equipment at cost	460	
Motor vehicles at cost	124	
Accumulated depreciation at 1.10 year 0:		
Premises		160
Plant and equipment		210
Motor vehicles		63
Inventories at 1.10 year 0		
Raw materials	41	
Work in progress	27	
Finished goods	76	
Sales of finished goods		2,702
Purchase of raw materials	837	
Carriage inwards	24	
Direct wages	658	
Heat, light and power	379	
Salaries	96	
Advertising	45	
Telephone, postage and stationery	23	
Trade receivables and payables	256	113
Employee income tax payable		57
Balance at bank	363	
Ordinary shares of $1 each		650
5% preference shares of $1 each		100
Share premium		250
Retained earnings		432
10% debentures (repayable year 20)		200
Bank deposit account	496	
Bank interest received		19
Ordinary dividend paid	31	
Preference dividend paid	5	
Rent	215	
	4,956	4,956

Notes:

1. The closing inventories at 30 September year 1 valued at cost were as follows:

	$
Raw materials	37,000
Work in progress	18,000
Finished goods	39,000

2. An analysis of the raw materials consumed during the year shows that $73,000 related to the use of indirect materials.

3. The following amounts had been prepaid on 30 September year 1:

	$
Rent	25,000
Telephone	2,000

4. The following amounts should be accrued for expenses at 30 September year 1:

	$
Direct wages	57,000
Salaries	14,000
Heat, light and power	61,000

5. An analysis of the salaries cost for the year is:

	$
Production	49,000
Selling and distribution	30,000
Administration	31,000

6. An allowance for receivables is to be created equal to 5 per cent of closing receivables after writing off a bad debt of $16,000. These expenses are to be treated as selling and distribution items.
7. During the year, a motor vehicle was sold for $13,000 when it had a carrying amount of $14,000. Its original cost was $24,000. The only entry made in respect of this transaction was to credit sales of finished goods and debit bank with the proceeds.
8. Depreciation is to be calculated on all non-current assets held on 30 September year 1, at the following rates:

Premises	5% p.a. on cost
Plant and equipment	20% p.a. reducing balance
Motor vehicles	20% p.a. on cost

It is assumed that none of the non-current assets has any expected residual value. The depreciation charge for the year is to be apportioned as follows:

	Production	Selling	Admin.
Premises	80%	10%	10%
Plant and equipment	70%	10%	20%
Motor vehicles	20%	60%	20%

9. Other expenses are to be apportioned as follows:

	Production	Selling	Admin.
Heat, light and power	80%	10%	10%
Telephone, postage and stationery	10%	60%	30%
Rent	70%	10%	20%

10. Income tax of $39,000 on the profit for the year is to be accrued.
11. It is proposed to transfer $100,000 into general reserves.
12. The premises were revalued to $850,000, and the tax on the gain is $10,000.

You are required:

(a) to prepare the statement of comprehensive income, incorporating the manufacturing and trading accounts for the year ended 30 September year 1;
(b) to prepare the statement of changes in equity for the year ended 30 September year 1;
(c) to prepare the company's statement of financial position at 30 September year.

Solution

(a) Statement of comprehensive income of ABC Ltd for the year ended 30 September year 1

	$'000		$'000
Sales (2,702–13)			2,689
Opening inventories of finished goods		76	
Opening inventories of raw materials	41		
Purchases of raw materials	837		
Carriage inwards	24		
	902		
Closing inventories of raw materials	(37)		
	865		
Indirect materials consumed	(73)		
Direct materials consumed	792		
Direct wages (658 + 57)	715		
Prime cost	1,507		
Production overhead			
Indirect materials consumed	73		
Heat, light and power ((379 + 61) × 80%)	352		
Telephone, postage, stationery ((23 − 2) × 10%)	2.1		
Salaries	49		
Rent ((215 − 25) × 70%)	133		
Depreciation			
Premises ((5% × 800) × 80%)	32		
Plant ((20% × 250) × 70%)	35		
Motor vehicle ((20% × 100) × 20%)*	4		
Loss on disposal of vehicle (1 × 20%)	0.2		
Factory cost incurred	2,187.3		
Opening work in progress	27		
Closing work in progress	(18)		
Factory cost of goods completed		2,196.3	
		2,272.3	
Closing inventories of finished goods		(39)	
			(2,233.3)
Gross Profit			455.7

	$'000	$'000
Gross profit		455.7

Selling and distribution

Heat, light and power (440 × 10%)	44	
Telephone, postage and stationery (21 × 60%)	12.6	
Advertising	45	
Salaries	30	
Rent (190 × 10%)	19	
Depreciation		
Premises (40 × 10%)	4	
Plant (50 × 10%)	5	
Motor vehicle (20 × 60%)	12	
Loss on disposal of vehicle (1 × 60%)	0.6	
Bad debt written off	16	
Change in allowance for receivables ((256 − 16) × 5%)	12	
		(200.2)

Administration

Heat, light and power (440 × 10%)	44	
Telephone, postage and stationery (21 × 30%)	6.3	
Salaries	31	
Rent (190 × 20%)	38	
Depreciation		
Premises (40 × 10%)	4	
Plant (50 × 20%)	10	
Motor vehicle (20 × 20%)	4	
Loss on disposal of vehicle (1 × 20%)	0.2	
		(137.5)
Operating profit		118.0
Interest received	19	
Interest paid (10% × $200)	(20)	
		(1)
Profit before taxation		117
Income tax		(39)

Profit for the period		78
Other comprehensive income		
Gain on property revaluation before tax	50	
Less income tax	(10)	
Gain on property revaluation net of tax		40
Total comprehensive income		118

(b) Statement of changes in equity of ABC Ltd for the year ended 30 September year 1

	Revaluation Reserve	General Reserve	Retained Earnings	Total
Balance at 1 October year 0			432	432
Comprehensive income for the period	40		78	118
Dividends – ordinary			(31)	(31)
Dividends – preference			(5)	(5)
Transfer to general reserve		100	(100)	0
Balance at 30 September year 1	40	100	374	514

(c) Statement of financial position of ABC Ltd as at 30 September year 1

Assets	Cost ($'000)	Acc. Depn ($'000)	Carrying Amount ($'000)
Non-current assets			
Premises	850	(200)	650
Plant and equipment	460	(260)	200
Motor vehicles	100	(73)	27
	1,410	(533)	877
Current assets			
Inventories			
Raw materials	37		
Work in progress	18		
Finished goods	39		
		94	
Receivables	240		
Less: allowance	(12)		
		228	
Prepayments		27	
Bank deposits		496	
Balance at bank		363	
			1,208
			2,085
Equity and liabilities			
Ordinary shares of $1 each			650
Preference shares of $1 each			100
Share premium			250
Revaluation reserve			40
General reserves			100
Retained earnings			374
			1,514
Non-current liabilities			
10% debentures		200	
Income tax on gain		10	210
Current liabilities			
Trade payables		113	
Employee income tax payable		57	
Accruals		132	
Debenture interest		20	
Income tax		39	
			361
			2,085

Note:

• On the assumption that the debentures have been in issue throughout the year, it is necessary to provide for a full year's interest, and to show a liability for that interest on the statement of financial position.

Exercise 13.1

Draw up an outline statement of comprehensive income, statement of changes in equity and statement of financial position to show the position of the following items:

1. gross profit,
2. profit before tax,
3. non-current assets,
4. current liabilities,
5. income tax,
6. interest paid transfers to reserves,
7. profit for the year,
8. intangible assets,
9. retained earnings at the start of the year,
10. retained earnings at the end of the year,
11. current assets,
12. non-current liabilities,
13. equity,
14. other comprehensive income.

 Solution

Statement of comprehensive income

Gross profit	X
Less: expenses	(X)
Operating profit	X
Interest paid	(X)
Profit before tax	X
Income tax	(X)
Profit for the period	X
Other comprehensive income	X
Total comprehensive income	X

Statement of changes in equity

	Reserve	Retained earnings	Total
Balance at the start of the period			
Retained earnings for the year			
Dividends			
Transfer to reserves			
Balance at the end of the period			

Statement of financial position

Non-current assets	X
Intangible assets	X
Current assets	X
	X
	X
Equity	X
Non-current liabilities	X
Current liabilities	X
	X

13.3   Statement of cash flows

In this section we shall illustrate the preparation of a statement of cash flows, which is often prepared for limited companies but may also be prepared for other types of organisation. It should be noted that a 'cash flow statement' has been renamed 'statement of cash flows' in accordance with IAS 1 (Revised) *Presentation of Financial Statements*.

13.3.1   What is a statement of cash flows?

A statement of cash flows recognises the importance of liquidity to a business by reporting the effect of the transactions of the business during the period on the bank, cash and similar liquid assets. At its simplest, it is a summary of receipts and payments during the period, but this method of presentation does not answer a common question asked by the readers of financial statements: 'Why does the profit made during the period not equate to an increase in cash and bank balances?' What is needed, therefore, is a statement that commences with the profit made during the period, and shows how that profit, and other transactions during the same period, have affected the flow of cash into and out of the company.

The syllabus states that the presentation for a statement of cash flows should be based on IAS 7 *Statement of Cash Flows* and that requirement is followed in this Learning System.

13.3.2   Why does the profit earned not equal the change in bank and cash balances?

There are three main reasons why this does not occur:

1. Profit is calculated on an accruals basis, which means that revenue is taken when it is earned, not when it is received, and expenses are deducted on the same basis to match with that revenue. Bank and cash balances change when monies are received and paid out. Thus the bank balance will be different from profit due to items such as the inventories balance, unpaid receivables and payables, accruals and prepayments, both at the start and at the end of the period. For example, an increase in inventories means more cash has flowed out; an increase in receivables means less cash has flowed in; an increase in payables means less cash has flowed out.
2. The calculation of profit includes some items that do not affect cash at all or affect it differently. For example, profit is after deducting depreciation, which involves no movement in cash. The profit or loss on disposal of a non-current asset will be taken into the profit calculation, but it is the *proceeds of sale* that affect cash. In addition, there may

be other accrued items in the statement of comprehensive income, for example taxation. Similarly, the change in allowance for receivables is a non-cash item. These do not affect cash at the same time as the accrual is made, for example, taxation may be paid after the year end, thus the amount of tax paid out during a period will be the bill for the previous year, not that for the current year.

3. Bank and cash balances are affected by some items that do not affect profit, such as the purchase of non-current assets (only depreciation affects profit), the raising of additional capital or the repayment of loans.

The statement of cash flows has three sections:

1. Cash flows from operating activities

   As the name implies, this is the cash flow from operating the business and mainly relates to the income statement. This is called 'cash generated from *operations*'. Cash from operating *activities* is then calculated after deducting:

   > Interest paid
   > Income tax paid

2. Cash flows from investing activities

   This has four main sections:

   > Purchase of non-fixed assets
   > Proceeds on sale of non-fixed assets
   > Interest received
   > Dividend received

3. Cash flows from financing activities

   This has four main sections:

   > Proceeds from issuing shares
   > Proceeds from loans
   > Repayment of loans
   > Payment of dividends

13.3.3 Cash flows from operating activities – cash generated from operations

The starting point for a statement of cash flows is the cash flow from operations. 'Operations' are the normal, everyday activity of the company that earn it profit, and that result in cash flow. For the purposes of a statement of cash flows, we begin with the operating profit in the statement of comprehensive income, and then proceed to convert this into cash flow.

The result will be as follows:

	$	$
Operating profit		X
Add:		
Depreciation charge for the period	X	
Loss on disposal of non-current assets	X	
Decreases in inventories levels	X	
Decreases in receivables	X	
Increases in payables	X	
		X
Or		
Less:		
Profit on disposal of non-current assets	X	
Increases in inventories levels	X	
Increases in receivables	X	
Decreases in payables	X	
		(X)
Cash generated from operations		X

Example 13.E

A company had the following items on its statements of financial position at the end of year 1 and year 2:

	Year 1 ($)	Year 2 ($)
Inventories	35,000	25,000
Receivables	24,000	28,000
Payables	31,000	33,000

In addition, the statement of comprehensive income for year 2 included the following items:

	$	$
Gross profit		90,000
Less:		
General expenses	17,000	
Depreciation on plant	10,000	
Loss on disposal of plant	4,000	
		(31,000)
Operating profit		59,000
Add: interest receivable		(13,000)
Less: interest payable		(3,000)
Profit before tax		69,000

Solution

Its cash generated from operations for year 2 would be as follows:

	$
Operating profit	59,000
Add:	
Depreciation	10,000
Loss on disposal of non-current assets	4,000
Decrease in inventories	10,000
Increase in payables	2,000
Less: increase in receivables	(4,000)
Cash generated from operations	81,000

13.3.4 Cash flows from operating activities – net cash from operating activities

We now need to calculate the cash from operating activities by deducting the following items from cash generated from operations:

(a) interest paid;

(b) tax paid;

Note that in both cases, it is the sum actually paid during the period that is included. In the case of tax, this will often be last year's tax liability.

13.3.5 Cash flows from investing activities

This section of the statement of cash flows shows the purchase of non-current fixed assets and the proceeds on their disposal. Whilst in practice all the relevant information would be known, in the computer-based assessment it is quite common for a question to give you only part of the information, and you have to calculate the missing information. An example of this is shown below relating to the purchase/sale of a non-current asset.

The interest and dividends received is straight forward and you can find these figures in the statement of comprehensive income.

13.3.6 Cash flows from financing activities

This section of the statement of cash flows shows the proceeds from issuing shares. A computer-based assessment question will often not tell you that shares have been issued; you have to work this out by looking to see if the ordinary or preference share capital has increased. Similarly, you will have to look at any debentures or loans to see if they have increased, in which there will be a cash flow in, or if they have decreased, in which case there will be a cash flow out.

The payment of dividends will be found in the statement of changes in equity. This figure will normally be the cash paid to shareholders in the year. However, you should check to see if there is an accrual for dividends under current liabilities in the statement of financial position.

If there is, this means that the directors have declared a dividend before the year end, but paid it after the year end. If this is the case, then you will have to work out what cash was actually paid to the shareholders for dividends. This is similar to the treatment of taxation and an example is given below.

Example 13.F

Continuing from Example 13.E, suppose that the dividends in the statement of changes in equity was $30,000 and that other items on the statements of financial position were as follows:

	Year 1 ($)	Year 2 ($)
Non-current assets*		
Plant at cost	100,000	120,000
Acc. depreciation	(20,000)	(22,000)
	80,000	98,000
Current assets		
Bank and cash	63,000	101,000
Share capital	100,000	120,000
Non-current liabilities		
Debenture	30,000	21,000
Current liabilities		
Taxation	12,000	16,000
Dividends	20,000	30,000

*Plant which had cost $15,000 and had a carrying amount of $7,000 was sold during the year.

Notice that the plant at cost has increased by $20,000 although we know that an asset with a cost of $15,000 has been sold. This means that an asset must have been purchased for $35,000. Similarly, notice that the depreciation given in the statement of comprehensive income was $10,000 – and yet the accumulated depreciation in the statement of financial position has increased by only $2,000. This is because the accumulated depreciation on the asset sold must have been $8,000. There must have been an asset sold during the year, and its cost and depreciation will have been taken out of the ledger accounts. Refer back to Chapter 6 to revise the ledger accounts for disposals of non-current assets. If the plant had a carrying amount of $7000 and it was sold at a loss of $4,000, then the proceeds must have been $3,000. Thus we have been able to work out the missing information of how much was received when the plant was sold. We can reconstruct the relevant non-current-asset accounts as follows:

Plant at cost

	$		$
Opening balance b/d	100,000	Disposal	15,000
Purchases (balancing figure)	35,000	Closing balance c/d	120,000
	135,000		135,000

Plant disposals

	$		$
Plant at cost	15,000	Plant depreciation	8,000
		Loss on disposal	4,000
		Proceeds of sale (balancing figure)	3,000
	15,000		15,000

We can now prepare the statement of cash flows for the year ended year 2 as follows:

	$	$
Cash flow from operating activities		
Cash generated from operations (from example 13.E above)		81,000
Less: interest paid		(3,000)
Less: tax paid (i.e. last year's)		(12,000)
Net cash from operating activities		66,000
Cash flows from investing activities		
Proceeds of sale of non-current assets	3,000	
Less: payments to acquire non-current assets	(35,000)	
Interest received	13,000	
Net cash used in investing activities		(19,000)
Cash flows from financing activities		
Equity dividends paid (i.e. last year's)	(20,000)	
Proceeds from issue of shares	20,000	
Less: repayment of debentures	(9,000)	
Net cash used in financing activities		(9,000)
Net increase in bank and cash		38,000
Bank and cash at the beginning of the period		63,000
Bank and cash at the end of the period		101,000

 ## Exercise 13.2

From the following information, construct a statement of cash flows:

	$
Operating profit for the year, after charging depreciation of $22,300	215,500
Purchase of non-current assets during the year	80,000
Repayment of non-current loan	45,000
Issue of shares at par	100,000
Changes in working capital during the year	
Increase in inventories	22,500
Decrease in receivables	18,000
Decrease in payables	14,500
Taxation paid	25,000
Dividends paid	5,000

Solution

Statement of cash flows

		$
Cash flows from operating activities		
Operating profit		215,500
Add:		
Depreciation		22,300
Decrease in receivables		18,000
Less:		
Increase in inventories		(22,500)
Decrease in payables		(14,500)
Cash generated from operations		218,800
Taxation paid		(25,000)
		193,800
Cash flows from investing activities		
Purchase of non-current assets		(80,000)
Cash flows from financing activities		
Issue of shares	100,000	
Loan repaid	(45,000)	
Dividends paid	(5,000)	
		50,000
Net increase in cash		163,800

Exercise 13.3

List as many examples as you can of cash flows in or out of a business that do not affect profit for the period.

 Solution

- Cash flows in – shares issued, loans received, proceeds of sale of non-current assets (as opposed to profit on disposal) and reduction in receivables' balances due to monies being received.
- Cash flows out – dividends paid, loans repaid, non-current assets purchased and reduction in payables' balances due to monies being paid out.

13.3.7 Statement of cash flows for sole traders

The preparation of a statement of cash flows is not restricted to limited companies. Indeed, the statement is a useful source of information for any kind of organisation.

For sole traders, dividends would be replaced by cash drawings, and share capital issued would be replaced by cash introduced by the owner. Taxation would not appear at all, being a private transaction. Otherwise, the preparation of the statement of cash flows would follow the same principles as for limited companies.

13.4 Summary

In this chapter we have looked at:

- the preparation of financial statements for limited companies;
- the preparation of a statement of changes in equity;
- the treatment of certain transactions in the financial statements of companies:
  - taxation,
  - other comprehensive income,
  - the revaluation of property,
  - dividends,
  - debentures,
  - reserves.
- the bookkeeping entries to record the issue of shares;
- the preparation of a cash flow statement;
- why profit does not equal cash flow.

Revision Questions

13

? **Question 1** Multiple choice

1.1 Revenue reserves are:

(A) accumulated and undistributed profits of a company.
(B) amounts that cannot be distributed as dividends.
(C) amounts set aside out of profits to replace revenue items.
(D) amounts set aside out of profits for a specific purpose.

1.2 A company has $100,000 of ordinary shares at a par value of 10¢ each and 100,000 5 per cent preference shares at a par value of 50¢ each. The directors decided to declare a dividend of 5¢ per ordinary share.

The total amount to be paid out in dividends amounts to:
$...............

1.3 The correct ledger entries needed to record the issue of 200,000 $1 shares at a premium of 30¢, and paid for by cheque, in full, would be:

	Debit $	Credit $
Share premium		
Share capital		
Bank		

1.4 A company has authorised share capital of one million ordinary shares of $1 each, of which 800,000 have been issued at a premium of 50¢ each, raising capital of $1,200,000. The directors are considering allocating $120,000 for dividend payments this year. This amounts to a dividend of:

$............... per share

1.5   Which one of the following would you expect to find in the statement of changes in equity in a limited company for the current year?

(A) Ordinary dividend proposed during the current year, but paid in the following year.
(B) Ordinary dividend declared during the current year, but paid in the following year.
(C) Directors' fees.
(D) Auditors' fees.

1.6   A business has made a profit of $8,000 but its bank balance has fallen by $5,000. This could be due to:

(A) depreciation of $3,000 and an increase in inventories of $10,000.
(B) depreciation of $6,000 and the repayment of a loan of $7,000.
(C) depreciation of $12,000 and the purchase of new non-current assets for $25,000.
(D) the disposal of a non-current asset for $13,000 less than its carrying amount.

1.7   A company has authorised capital of 50,000 5 per cent preference shares of $2 each and 500,000 ordinary shares with a par value of 20¢ each. All of the preference shares have been issued, and 400,000 ordinary shares have been issued at a premium of 30¢ each. Interim dividends of 5¢ per ordinary share plus half the preference dividend have been paid during the current year. A final dividend of 15¢ per ordinary share is declared and half the preference dividend. The total of dividends payable for the year is:

$...............

1.8   A business's bank balance increased by $750,000 during its last financial year. During the same period it issued shares of $1 million and repaid a debenture of $750,000. It purchased non-current assets for $200,000 and charged depreciation of $100,000. Working capital (other than the bank balance) increased by $575,000. Its profit for the year was:

$...............

1.9   The record of how the profit or loss of a company has been allocated to dividends and reserves is found in the:

(A) capital account.
(B) statement of comprehensive income.
(C) reserves account.
(D) statement of changes in equity.

1.10   Revenue reserves would decrease if a company:

(A) sets aside profits to pay future dividends.
(B) transfers amounts into 'general reserves'.
(C) issues shares at a premium.
(D) pays dividends.

1.11 A business can make a profit and yet have a reduction in its bank balance. Which one of the following might cause this to happen?

(A) The sale of non-current assets at a loss.
(B) The charging of depreciation in the statement of comprehensive income.
(C) The lengthening of the period of credit given to customers.
(D) The lengthening of the period of credit taken from suppliers.

1.12 Which one of the following does not form part of the equity capital of a limited company?

(A) Debentures.
(B) Share premium.
(C) Revaluation reserve.
(D) Ordinary share capital.

1.13 A particular source of finance has the following characteristics: a fixed return, a fixed repayment date, it is secured and the return is classified as an expense.

Identify the source of finance:

(A) Ordinary share.
(B) Bank overdraft.
(C) Debenture.
(D) Preference share.

1.14 Extracts from the financial statements of CFS Ltd are set out below.

Statement of comprehensive income CFS Ltd for the year ended 31 December 20X8

	$'000	$'000
Turnover		300
Cost of sales		(150)
Gross profit		150
Profit on sale of non-current asset		75
		225
Expenses	15	
Depreciation	30	
		(45)
Net profit		180

	Balances as at 31 December	
	20X7	20X8
	$'000	$'000
Inventories, receivables, current liabilities (net)	40	50

What figure would appear in the statement of cash flows of CFS Ltd for the year ended 31 December 20X8 in respect of cash generated from operations?

$...............

1.15 The movement on the plant and machinery account for X Ltd is shown below:

	$
Cost b/f	10,000
Additions	2,000
Disposals	(3,000)
Cost c/f	9,000
Acc. Depreciation b/f	2,000
Charge for the year	1,000
Disposals	(1,500)
Acc. Depreciation c/f	1,500
Carrying amount b/f	8,000
Carrying amount c/f	7,500

The profit on the sale of the machine was $500. What figures would appear in the statement of cash flows of X Ltd?

(A) Movement on plant account $500 and profit on disposal of $500.
(B) Movement on plant account $500 and proceeds on sale of plant $2,000.
(C) Purchase of plant $2,000 and profit on disposal of $500.
(D) Purchase of plant $2,000 and proceeds on sale of plant $2,000.

1.16 'Other comprehensive' income is found in the:

(A) Statement of financial position.
(B) Statement of cash flows.
(C) Statement of changes in equity.
(D) Income statement.
(E) The ledger accounts.
(F) None of these.

1.17 'The revaluation of a property is shown:

(A) Property in the statement of financial position, comprehensive income and revaluation reserves.
(B) Property in the statement of financial position, statement of changes in equity and revaluation reserves.
(C) Property in the statement of financial position, income statement and revaluation reserves.
(D) None, as companies are not allowed to revalue property.

1.18 'The tax on the gain on the revaluation of property is shown in the:

(A) Property account.
(B) Revaluation reserve.
(C) Statement of change in equity.
(D) Statement of comprehensive income.

1.19 'Which of the following statements is false with regard to limited companies?

(A) Limited companies are not allowed to report an income statement.
(B) Limited companies must report total comprehensive income.
(C) Limited companies must report 'other comprehensive income'.
(D) There are two alternative formats for presenting comprehensive income.

1.20 'An income statement includes the following line items:

(A) Sales to gross profit.
(B) Sales to operating profit.
(C) Sales to profit before tax.
(D) Sales to profit for the period.

? Question 2

Omit Ltd has the following statement of comprehensive income for the year ended 31 December 20X1 (draft):

	$
Sales	1,210,213
Cost of sales	(943,000)
Gross profit	267,213
Administrative salaries	(110,100)
Other expenses	(28,956)
Profit for the period	128,157

Omit Ltd has the following statement of financial position as at 31 December 20X1 (draft):

Assets	$	$	$
Non-current assets			596,294
Current assets			
Inventories	186,200		
Receivables	252,111		
Cash	87,800		
			526,111
			1,122,405
Equity and liabilities			
Share capital			100,000
Retained earnings			878,342
			978,342
Current liabilities			
Trade payables	120,290		
Employee income tax	13,205		
Social security tax	10,568		
			144,063
			1,122,405

Analytical review has revealed that the financial statements have shown a marked and unexpected improvement over last year's figures in certain key areas. You ascertain that the main reason for this is that the December payroll journal and cheques paid to the tax authorities have not been processed.

	Manufacturing staff	*Administration staff*
	$	$
Net pay	29,799	5,999
Employee income tax	10,800	2,286
Social security tax – employees	4,212	859
Social security tax – employers	4,683	956

Taxes deducted in 1 month are paid to the tax authority in the following month.

Requirements

(a) Insert the missing items into the journals given below.

Payment journal	*Debit ($)*	*Credit ($)*
Employee income tax payable		
Social security tax payable		
Cash		

Payroll journals

Manufacturing staff		
Cost of sales		
Cash		
Employee income tax payable		
Social security tax payable		
Administration staff		
Administrative salaries		
Cash		
Employee income tax payable		
Social security tax payable		

(b) Complete the following boxes in order to calculate the revised cash balance at 31 December 20X1.

	±	$
Cash balance per original statement of financial position		87,800
Revised cash balance		

(c) Insert the missing items into the financial statements below, to take account of the necessary adjustments in Part (a):

Statement of comprehensive income for the year ended 31 December 19X1 (draft)

	$	±	$		$
Sales					1,210,213
Cost of sales	(943,000	▨	)		▨
Gross profit					▨
Admin. salaries	(110,100	▨	)	=	▨
Other expenses					(28,956)
Profit for the period					▨

Statement of financial position as at 31 December 19X1 (draft)

Assets	$	$
Non-current assets		596,294
Current assets		
Inventories	186,200	
Receivables	252,111	
Cash	▨	
		▨
		▨

Equity and liabilities		
Share capital		100,000
Retained earnings		▨
Current liabilities		▨
Trade payables	120,290	
Employee income tax	▨	
Social security tax	▨	
		▨
		▨

Question 3

The following list of balances as at 30 April 20X2 has been extracted from the books of River Garages Ltd after the preparation of the draft financial statements for the year ended on that date.

		$	
Freehold land and buildings			
At cost		100,000	
Accumulated depreciation		20,000	
Plant and machinery			
At cost		58,000	
Accumulated depreciation		16,400	
Motor vehicles			
At cost		36,000	
Accumulated depreciation		8,500	
Inventories at cost		24,700	
Trade receivables		4,500	
Amounts prepaid		1,600	
Balance at bank		4,300	
Trade payables		7,900	
Ordinary shares of $1 each, fully paid		100,000	
Retained earnings			
At 1 May 20X1	7,600		
Year ended 30 April 20X2	<u>40,000</u>		
		47,600	
8% loan stock		30,000	
Suspense account		1,300	debit

Subsequently, the following discoveries have been made:

1. The company's inventories at 30 April 20X2 of $24,700 includes a motor car (J168 MRK) at $10,000. However, this vehicle was taken out of inventories on 1 February 20X2 for the use of the company's workshop manager.

   Note: It is company policy to provide for depreciation on motor vehicles at the rate of 25 per cent per annum on cost. Depreciation is to be time apportioned from the date of bringing the car into use as a non-current asset. Assume that there is no expected residual value.

2. A receipt of $1,000 from J Green, receivable, in February 20X2, was credited to sales as $1,400.

3. Interest on the 8 per cent loan stock is paid annually in arrears on 1 May. No provision for the loan interest has been made in the draft financial statements for the year ended 30 April 20X2.

4. No entry has been made in the company's books for a credit purchase of raw materials costing $2,000 on 14 April 20X2 from T Conway. However, a debit balance of $2,000 at 30 April 20X2 on T Conway's account in the company's books arises from a payment made to T Conway on that date.
5. The remaining balance of the suspense account arises from a prepayment at 30 April 20X2 for insurance, being omitted from the company's list of balances on that date.

Note: River Garages Limited does not maintain either a sales ledger total (or control account) or a purchases ledger total (or control account).

Requirements

(a) Insert the missing items into the journal given below, to correct items 1–4 above.

Item	Account name	Debit or credit?	$
1.			
2.			
3.			
4.			

(b) Insert the missing items into the following boxes in order to calculate the remaining balance on the suspense account, after correcting the four errors in the journal above.

	Debit or credit?	$
Suspense account balance arising per list of balances at 30 April 20X2		
Correction required re item number		
Remaining balance on suspense account		

(c) Insert the missing items into the journal given below, to correct item 5.

Item	Account name	Debit or credit?	$
5.			

(d) Complete the table below to recalculate the profit for the year ended 30 April 20X2, after adjusting for all the above items:

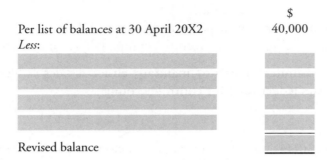

	$
Per list of balances at 30 April 20X2	40,000
Less:	
Revised balance	

(e) Insert the missing items into the revised statement of financial position at 30 April 20X2, given below, after taking account of the necessary adjustments

Statement of financial position as at 30 April 20X2

Assets	Cost ($)		Carrying amount ($)
Non-current assets			
Land and buildings	100,000	(20,000)	80,000
Plant and machinery	58,000	(16,400)	41,600
Motor vehicles			
Current assets			
Inventories			
Trade receivables			
Amounts prepaid			
Balance at bank			

Equity and liabilities

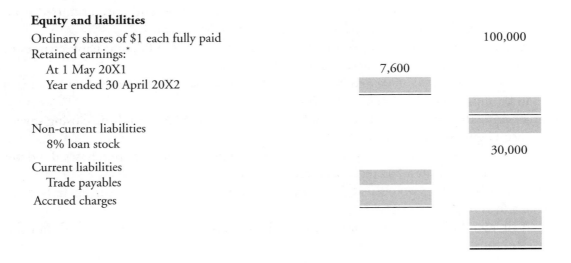

Ordinary shares of $1 each fully paid		100,000
Retained earnings:*		
At 1 May 20X1	7,600	
Year ended 30 April 20X2		
Non-current liabilities		
8% loan stock		30,000
Current liabilities		
Trade payables		
Accrued charges		

*Rather than show a statement of changes in equity, the movement has been shown in the statement of financial position.

? Question 4

The accountant of Fiddles plc has begun preparing financial statements, but the work is not yet complete. At this stage, the items included in the trial balance are as follows:

	$'000
Land	100
Buildings	120
Plant and machinery	170
Accumulated depreciation	120
Share capital	100
Retained earnings	200
Receivables	200
Payables	110
Inventories	190
Operating profit	80
Debentures (16%)	180
Allowance for receivables	3
Bank balance (asset)	12
Suspense	1

Notes (i)–(vii) are to be taken into account.

(i) The sales ledger control account figure, which is used in the trial balance, does not agree with the total of the sales ledger balances. A contra of $5,000 has been entered correctly in the individual ledger accounts but has been entered on the wrong side of both control accounts.

A batch total of sales of $12,345 has been entered in the double-entry system as $13,345, although individual ledger account entries for these sales were correct.

The balance of $4,000 on sales returns account has inadvertently been omitted from the trial balance, though correctly entered in the ledger records.

(ii) A standing order of receipt from a regular customer for $2,000, and bank charges of $1,000, have been completely omitted from the records.

(iii) A receivable for $1,000 is to be written off. The allowance for receivables balance is to be adjusted to 1 per cent of receivables.

(iv) The opening inventories figure had been overstated by $1,000 and the closing inventories figure understated by $2,000.

(v) Any remaining balance on suspense account should be treated as purchases if a debit balance and as sales if a credit balance.

(vi) The debentures were issued 3 months before the year end. No entries have been made as regards interest.

(vii) A dividend of 10 per cent of share capital was declared before the year end, but not paid until after the year end.

Requirements

(a) Insert the missing items in the journal entries to cover items in notes (i)–(v) above. You are not to open any new accounts and may use only those accounts included in the trial balance as given.

Journal

	Debit ($)	Credit ($)
(i)		
(ii)		
(iii)		
(iv)		
(v)		

(b) Insert the missing items in the financial statements.

Revised operating profit

$

(i)

(ii)

(iii)

(iv)

(v)

Revised operating profit

**Statement of comprehensive
income of Fiddles plc**

$

Operating profit

Statement of changes in equity of Fiddles plc

	Retained earnings
Balance at start	

Statement of financial position of Fiddles plc

Assets	$	$	$
Non-current assets			
Plant and machinery			
Current assets			
Bank			
Equity and liabilities			
Non-current liability			
Current liabilities			

? **Question 5**

The statement of financial position of OGN Ltd as at 31 December 20X4 was as follows:

Assets	$'000	$'000	$'000
Non-current assets			7,500
Current assets			
Inventories	2,000		
Receivables	5,000		
			7,000
			14,500
Equity and liabilities			
7,000 ordinary shares of $1 each			7,000
General reserves			1,500
Retained earnings			1,000
			9,500
Current liabilities			
Trade payables		4,000	
Bank overdraft		1,000	
			5,000
			14,500

During 20X5 a profit for the period of $1.5 million is made, after charging depreciation of $750,000. $1 million is transferred to general reserves. Closing inventories at 31 December 20X5 are $1.8 million and receivables are reduced by $1.5 million. Payables at 31 December 20X5 amount to $3 million.

During the year, two million additional ordinary shares are issued at a premium of 50c each, paid for immediately in cash. No dividends are declared for the year and no non-current assets are purchased.

Requirements

(a) Insert the missing items into the boxes below to calculate the bank balance at 31 December 20X5 by establishing the movement in cash during the period.

	$'000
Cash flow from operating activities	
Profit for the period	1,500
*Add/less:** depreciation	
*Add/less:** increase/decrease* in inventories	
*Add/less:** increase/decrease* in receivables	
*Add/less:** increase/decrease* in payables	

Cash flow from financing activities

Add/less: ▓▓▓▓▓▓▓▓▓▓▓▓▓▓▓▓▓▓▓▓ ▓▓▓▓▓▓

Increase/decrease* in cash and bank ▓▓▓▓▓▓

Add/less: opening bank balance (overdraft) (1,000)

Closing bank balance ▓▓▓▓▓▓

*Delete as appropriate.

(b) Insert the missing items into the statement of changes in equity for the year ended 31 December 20X5, provided below:

	Ordinary Shares $'000	Share Premium $'000	General Reserves $'000	Retained Earnings $'000	Total $'000
Balance at the start of the period	▓▓▓	▓▓▓	▓▓▓	▓▓▓	▓▓▓
▓▓▓	▓▓▓	▓▓▓	▓▓▓	▓▓▓	▓▓▓
▓▓▓	▓▓▓	▓▓▓	▓▓▓	▓▓▓	▓▓▓
▓▓▓	▓▓▓	▓▓▓	▓▓▓	▓▓▓	▓▓▓
Balance at the end of the period	▓▓▓	▓▓▓	▓▓▓	▓▓▓	▓▓▓

(c) Insert the missing items into the statement of financial position at 31 December 20X5, provided below.

Statement of financial position as at 31 December 20X5

Assets	$	$
Non-current assets		7,500
Less: accumulated depreciation		▓▓▓▓
		▓▓▓▓
Current assets		
Inventories	1,800	
Receivables	▓▓▓▓	
Bank	▓▓▓▓	
		▓▓▓▓
		▓▓▓▓
Equity and liabilities		
▓▓▓ ordinary shares of $1 each		▓▓▓▓
Share premium account		▓▓▓▓
General reserves		▓▓▓▓
Retained earnings		▓▓▓▓
		▓▓▓▓
Current liabilities Payables		3,000
		▓▓▓▓

(d) Complete the missing words in the following sentences

(i) _____ is that ascribed to shares when authorised, appears on the share certificate and used for _____ calculations.

(ii) _____ are long-terms loans with a _____ interest rate, payable irrespective of profits. They may be _____ in the future, and _____ on non-current assets.

(iii) Profits are transferred to _____ _____ to limit the profits available for payment of current/future dividends.

(iv) _____ are proposed by the directors, but are not payable until approved by _____ at the annual general meeting.

? Question 6

ABC Ltd prepares its financial statements to 31 October each year. Its trial balance at 31 October 20X3 was as follows:

	Debit ($'000)	Credit ($'000)
Premises – cost	600	
Manufacturing plant – cost	350	
Office equipment – cost	125	
Accumulated depreciation at 1 November 20X2		
Premises		195
Manufacturing plant		140
Office equipment		35
Inventories at 1 November 20X2		
Raw materials	27	
Work in progress	18	
Finished goods	255	
Sales of finished goods		2,350
Purchases of raw materials	826	
Returns inwards and outwards	38	18
Direct wages	575	
Heat, light and power	242	
Salaries	122	
Printing, postage and stationery	32	
Rent and insurances	114	
Loan interest paid	12	
Loan		250
Trade receivables and payables	287	75
Allowance for receivables		11
Sales tax account		26
Dividend paid	10	
Ordinary shares of $1 each		500
Share premium account		100
Retained earnings		442
Bank balance	509	
	4,142	4,142

The following additional information at 31 October 20X3 is available:

  (i) Closing inventories

Raw materials	$24,000
Work in progress	$19,000
Finished goods	$147,000

 (ii) Prepayments

Rent	$17,000
Insurance	$4,000

(iii) Accruals

Direct wages	$15,000
Salaries	$8,000

(iv) Salaries are to be apportioned as follows

Manufacturing	20%
Administration	80%

 (v) Bad debts to be written off amount to $47,000, including sales tax at 17.5 per cent. The company maintains a separate bad debts account. The debts have all been outstanding for more than 6 months.

Note: In the case of bad debts that have been outstanding for more than 6 months, the sales tax (which will already have been accounted for on the sale of the goods) can be reclaimed from the tax authorities.

 (vi) The allowance for receivables is to be amended to 2.5 per cent of receivables, after adjusting for bad debts written off.

(vii) Depreciation of non-current assets is to be provided as follows:

Premises	2 per cent on cost (not the revalued figure)
Plant	10 per cent on cost
Office equipment	20 per cent on reducing balance

Twenty-five per cent of premises depreciation is to be apportioned to the manufacturing account.

Note: It is to be assumed that there is no expected residual value.

(viii) The loan was taken out on 1 November 20 × 2, and the capital is to be repaid as follows:

1 January 20X4	$100,000
1 January 20X5	$100,000
1 January 20X6	$50,000

Interest is to be charged on the outstanding capital at 20 per cent per annum.

(ix) Other expenses are to be apportioned as follows:

Heat, light and power	1/2 manufacturing
	1/2 selling and administration
Rent and insurance	1/3 manufacturing
	2/3 administration

(x) One line of finished goods inventories, currently recorded at $8,000, has a net realisable value of $3,000.

(xi) A final dividend of 10¢ per share is to be proposed.

(xii) An accrual for income tax of $35,000 is to be made on the profits of the year.

(xiii) The premises are to be revalued to $700,000, and the potential tax liability is $30,000.

Requirements

(a) Insert the missing items into the manufacturing account for the year ended 31 October 20X3.

Manufacturing account of ABC Ltd for the year ended 31 December 20X3

	$'000	$'000	$'000
Direct materials			
Direct labour			
Prime cost			
Indirect factory costs			
Total factory cost			
Change in work in progress			
Factory cost of goods completed			1,616

(b) Insert the missing items into the statement of comprehensive income for the year ended 31 October 20X3.

Comprehensive income statement of ABC Ltd for the year ended 31 October 20X3

	$'000	$'000
Sales		
Less: cost of goods sold		
Factory cost of goods completed	1,616	
Gross profit		
Less: expenses		
Operating profit		
Profit before tax		
Income tax		
Profit for the period		
Other comprehensive income		
Gain on property revaluation before tax		
Income tax		
Gain on property revaluation after tax		
Total comprehensive income		

(c) Insert the missing items into the statement of changes in equity for the year ended 31 October 20X3.

	Revaluation Reserve	Retained Earnings	$'000
Balance at start of period			
Balance at end of period			

(d) Insert the missing items into the statement of financial position at 31 October 20X3.

Statement of financial position of ABC Ltd as at 31 October 20X3

Assets	Cost ($'000)	Acc. Dep'n ($'000)	Carrying Amount ($'000)
Non-current assets			
Current assets			
Equity and liabilities			
Non-current liability			
Current liabilities			

Question 7

FPC Ltd is a manufacturing company that sells its goods to wholesalers. Its trial balance at 31 March 20X6 was as follows:

	Debit ($)	Credit ($)
Issued share capital, $1 ordinary shares		750,000
10% debentures, repayable 2X15		200,000
Retained earnings at 1 April 20X5		98,000
Premises – at cost	900,000	
Premises – accumulated depreciation at 1 April 20X5		360,000
Plant – at cost	150,000	
Plant – accumulated depreciation at 1 April 20X5		75,000
Sales		2,960,000
Raw materials purchased	1,500,000	
Carriage outwards	10,000	
Carriage inwards	15,000	
Returns outwards		22,000
Returns inwards	14,000	
Receivables	220,000	
Payables		300,000
Bank balance	500,000	
Inventories at 1 April 20X5		
Raw materials	60,000	
Work in progress	30,000	
Finished goods	70,000	
Direct labour	600,000	
Discounts allowed	4,000	
Discounts received		2,500
Rent	120,000	
Insurance	100,000	
Factory supervisors' salaries	150,000	
Office wages and salaries	175,000	
Sales officers' commission	113,500	
Administration expenses	45,000	
Sales tax account		8,500
Allowance for receivables at 1 April 20X5		7,000
Bad debts written off	6,500	
	4,783,000	4,783,000

The following additional information at 31 March 20X6 is available:

(i) Closing inventories:

	$
Raw materials	80,000
Work in progress	42,500
Finished goods	100,000

(ii) Rent prepaid amounts to $10,000.
Insurance prepaid amounts to $20,000.
Twenty per cent of rent and insurance is to be regarded as factory cost.

(iii) Direct labour accrued amounts to $17,500.

(iv) Included in the above trial balance are finished goods sold on a sale or return basis, which must be accepted or rejected by 15 April 20X6. Their selling price is $35,000 and their cost price is $27,000. Sales tax is not applicable on these goods.

(v) The premises are to be depreciated at 2 per cent per annum, straight line. The plant is to be depreciated at 10 per cent per annum, straight line. Twenty-five per cent of premises depreciation is to be regarded as factory cost. Seventy-five per cent of plant depreciation is to be regarded as factory cost.

(vi) The allowance for receivables is to be amended to 5 per cent of receivables.

(vii) Sales officers' commission for the year is to be 5 per cent of net sales.

(viii) Administration expenses include stationery, which has been recorded at its total invoice value of $9,400, including sales tax at 17.5 per cent. The sales tax is reclaimable.

(ix) The debentures were issued on 1 October 20X5. Interest is due on 1 April and 1 October annually in arrears.

(x) Corporation tax of $22,000 is to be accrued for the year.

(xi) A dividend of 3c per share is proposed.

Requirements

(a) Insert the missing items into the statement of comprehensive income for the year ended 31 March 20X6.

	$	$	$	$
Sales				
Less returns				
Net sales				
Opening inventories of finished goods				
Opening inventories of raw material				
Less: closing inventories of raw material				
Direct material				
Direct labour				
Prime cost				
Factory indirect expenses				
Opening work in progress				
Less: closing work in progress				
Factory cost of goods completed				
Less: closing inventories of finished goods				
Cost of goods sold				
Gross profit				
Discount received				

	$	$
Less: expenses		
▨▨▨▨▨▨▨	▨▨	
▨▨▨▨▨▨▨	▨▨	
▨▨▨▨▨▨▨	▨▨	
▨▨▨▨▨▨▨	▨▨	
▨▨▨▨▨▨▨	▨▨	
▨▨▨▨▨▨▨	▨▨	
▨▨▨▨▨▨▨	▨▨	
▨▨▨▨▨▨▨	▨▨	
▨▨▨▨▨▨▨	▨▨	
▨▨▨▨▨▨▨	▨▨	
▨▨▨▨▨▨▨	▨▨	
		▨▨
Operating profit		▨▨
▨▨▨▨▨▨▨		▨▨
Profit before tax		▨▨
▨▨▨▨▨▨▨		▨▨
Profit for the period		▨▨

(b) Insert the missing items into the statement of changes in equity for the year ended 31 March 20X6.

	$'000
Balance at start of period	▨▨
▨▨▨▨▨▨▨	▨▨
Balance at end of period	▨▨

(c) For each of the following items that appear in the financial statements of FPC Ltd, state an accounting convention which affects its treatment:

(i) inventories of raw materials.
(ii) goods on sale or return.
(iii) allowance for receivables.

(i) ▨▨▨▨▨
(ii) ▨▨▨▨▨
(iii) ▨▨▨▨▨

? Question 8

Avtar Ltd had the following statement of financial position at 31 March 20X1 and 20X2:

Assets	20X1 ($'000)	20X2 ($'000)
Non-current assets at cost	1,000	1,300
Accumulated depreciation	(400)	(600)
	600	700
Current assets		
Inventories	800	1,400
Receivables	2,700	3,100
Bank	200	–
	4,300	5,200
Equity and liabilities		
Share capital	1,000	1,300
Share premium account	500	700
Retained earnings	1,200	1,240
	2,700	3,240
Current liabilities		
Payables	1,300	1,580
Declared ordinary dividend	300	260
Bank overdraft	–	120
	4,300	5,200

During the year to 31 March 20X2, non-current assets costing $50,000 were sold for $40,000 cash. Accumulated depreciation on these to 31 March 20X1 was $20,000.

Requirements

(a) Insert the missing figures into the ledger accounts below in order to calculate the additions to non-current assets, the profit or loss on sale of non-current assets, and the depreciation charge in the income statement for the year to 31 March 20X2.

Non-current assets at cost

	$'000		$'000
Balance b/f		Disposals a/c	
Additions		Balance c/f	

Non-current assets – accumulated depreciation

	$'000		$'000
Disposals a/c		Balance b/f	
Balance c/f		Charge for the year	

Non-current assets – disposals

	$'000		$'000
Non-current assets at cost		Non-current assets acc. depn.	
Profit on sale of non-current assets		Disposal proceeds	

(b) Insert the missing items into the statement of cash flows given below for the year ending 31 March 20X2.

	$'000	$'000	$'000
Cash flow from operating activities			
Increase in retained earnings		−	=
Add dividends declared			
Add depreciation charge for the year			
Deduct profit on sale of non-current assets			
Add/less* increase/decrease* in			
Add/less* increase/decrease* in			
Add/less* increase/decrease* in			
Cash flow from investing activities			
Cash flow from financing activities			
Increase/decrease* in bank			
Bank at beginning of period			
Bank at end of period			

*Delete as appropriate.

Question 9

Meltdown Ltd owns a property which it bought five years ago for $400,000. It has recently had the property valued by a firm of valuers at $460,000. The company's accountants have advised that the potential tax liability if the property were sold for its current value would be $18,000.

You are required to prepare the following extracts from the financial statements of Meltdown Ltd.

Meltdown Ltd – Statement of comprehensive income

Profit for the period	100
Other comprehensive income	
Revaluation of property before tax	
Tax on revaluation	_____
Total comprehensive income	_____

Meltdown Ltd – Statement of changes in equity

	Revaluation Reserve	Retained Earnings	Total

Meltdown – Statement of financial position

Non-current assets – Property	_____
Equity – Revaluation reserve	_____
Non – current liabilities income tax	_____

Solutions to Revision Questions

✔ Solution 1

1.1 Answer: (A)

Revenue reserves can be distributed as dividends, so (B) is incorrect. Revenue reserves are not set aside to replace revenue items; they could be set aside for a specific purpose but this is only one use of revenue reserves.

1.2 The share capital consists of:

	$
Preference shares, 100,000 at 50¢	50,000
Ordinary shares, 1,000,000 at 10¢	100,000

Thus the preference dividend amounts to 5 per cent of $50,000, that is $2,500, and the ordinary dividend amounts to 5¢ × 1 million shares = $50,000, giving a total dividend of $52,500.

1.3

	Debit	Credit
Share premium		60,000
Share capital		200,000
Bank	260,000	

1.4 Dividends are declared only on issued shares, and are based on the par value. A dividend of $120,000 on par value shares of $800,000 is 15¢ per share.

1.5 Answer: (B)

Dividends *proposed* are shown in the statement of changes in equity in the following year. The dividend should be approved at the annual general meeting and subsequently paid. Directors' and auditors' fees are normal business expenses and appear in the statement of comprehensive income.

1.6 Answer: (C)

	$
Profit	8,000
Add: depreciation	12,000
Net cash inflow	20,000
Purchase of non-current assets	(25,000)
Decrease	(5,000)

1.7

	$
Preference dividend for year (5% × $100,000)	5,000
Ordinary dividend for year (20¢ × 400,000 shares)	80,000
Total dividend	85,000

1.8

	$'000
Profit for the year	1,175
Add: depreciation	100
Less: increase in working capital	(575)
	700
Add: issue of shares	1,000
Less: repayment of debentures	(750)
Less: purchase of non-current assets	(200)
Increase in bank balance	750

1.9 Answer: (D)

With regards to (A), a company does not have a single capital account – its capital consists of several accounts.

1.10 Answer: (D)

(A) and (B) are both forms of revenue reserve. Issuing shares at a premium increases reserves, but they are capital reserves anyway.

1.11 Answer: (C)

Lengthening the period of credit given to customers reduces the amount of cash coming in. Lengthening the period of credit taken from suppliers has the opposite effect. The sale of non-current assets at whatever value results in cash coming in, while depreciation has no effect on cash at all.

1.12 Answer: (A)

All the others are part of the equity capital.

1.13 Answer: (C)

1.14

	$'000
Net profit	180
Add: depreciation	30
Less: profit on sale of non-current asset	(75)
Less: change in working capital	(10)
	125

1.15   Answer: (D)

1.16   (F) None of these. 'Other comprehensive' income is found in the comprehensive income statement; it is not found in the income statement, which shows all items from revenue down to profit for the period.

1.17   (A) Property in the statement of financial position, comprehensive income and revaluation reserves. The property is revalued, the gain is shown in 'other' comprehensive income and the gain is added to revaluation reserves in the statement of financial position.

1.18   (D) The tax on the gain on the revaluation of a property is shown in the statement of comprehensive income, within the 'other comprehensive income'. (Alternatively, it could be shown as a note to this statement.)

1.19   (A) Limited companies are allowed to report an income statement as a separate financial statement.

1.20   (D) Sales to profit for the period.

✓ Solution 2

- Part (a) involves payroll entries. Remember that employers' social security tax is not deducted from employees' wages but is an additional expense of the firm. The gross wages represent the amount to be charged in the statement of comprehensive income in addition to the employers' social security tax. The amount to be paid to the tax authorities will include both types of social security tax and the employers' income tax deducted. Any amounts still outstanding at the year end will be included with current liabilities on the statement of financial position.
- Part (b) requires you to prepare corrected financial statements. If you have dealt incorrectly with the items in Part (a) you may not be able to complete this section correctly.

(a)

Payment journal of Omit Ltd

		Debit ($)	Credit ($)
Dr	Employee income tax payable	13,205	
Dr	Social security tax payable	10,568	
Cr	Cash		23,773

Payroll journals

		Debit ($)	Credit ($)
Manufacturing staff			
Dr	Cost of sales (29,799 + 10,800 + 4,212 + 4,683)	49,494	
Cr	Cash		29,799
Cr	Employee income tax payable		10,800
Cr	Social security tax payable		8,895
Administration staff			
Dr	Administrative salaries	10,100	
	(5,999 + 2,286 + 859 + 956)		
Cr	Cash		5,999
Cr	Employee income tax payable		2,286
Cr	Social security tax payable (859 + 956)		1,815

(b)

	±	$
Cash balance per original statement of financial position		87,800
Revised cash balance	−	23,773
	−	29,799
	−	5,999
Revised cash balance		28,229

(c) **Statement of comprehensive income for the year ended 31 December 19X1 (draft)**

	$
Sales	1,210,213
Cost of sales (943,000 + 49,494)	(992,494)
Gross profit	217,719
Administrative salaries (110,100 + 10,100)	(120,200)
Other expenses	(28,956)
Profit for the period	68,563

Statement of financial position as at 31 December 19X1 (draft)

Assets	$	$
Non-current assets		596,294
Current assets		
Inventories	186,200	
Receivables	252,111	
Cash	28,229	
		466,540
		1,062,834

Equity and liabilities

Share capital		100,000
Retained earnings (878,342 − 49,494 − 10,100)		818,748
		918,748
Current liabilities		
Trade payables	120,290	
Employee income tax (10,800 + 2,286)	13,086	
Social security tax (8,895 + 1,815)	10,710	
		144,086
		1,062,834

☑ Solution 3

- This question involves consideration of a range of errors that have occurred prior to the preparation of financial statements as presented. Item 1 requires the motor car to be taken out of the inventories figure and to be included with non-current assets and depreciated as appropriate. Item 2 requires amendment of the sales figure and the suspense account. Item 4 arises because the purchase has been omitted from the books – the resulting debit balance on T Conway's account in the purchase ledger would highlight this omission.

(a) Item

			$	
1.	Motor vehicles	Debit	10,000	
	Inventories	Credit	10,000	
	Retained earnings	Debit	625*	* = (10,000 × 25% × 3/12)
	Accumulated depreciation	Credit	625	
2.	Retained earnings	Debit	1,400	
	Receivables	Credit	1,000	
	Suspense account	Credit	400	
3.	Retained earnings	Debit	2,400	
	Accrued interest	Credit	2,400	
4.	Retained earnings	Debit	2,000	
	Payables	Credit	2,000	

(b)

Suspense account balance at 30.04.X2	Debit	1,300
Correction required re item no. 2	Credit	(400)
Remaining balance on suspense account	Debit	900

(c)

Item	Account name	Debit or credit?	$
5.	Insurance prepaid*	Debit	900
	Suspense account	Credit	900

*No actual entry is needed in the insurance account, but the amount must be included with amounts prepaid on the statement of financial position.

(d)

Profit for the year ended 30 April 20X2

	$	$
Per list of balances at 30 April 20X2		40,000
Less:		
Motor car depreciation (25% × (25% × $10,000))	625	
Receipt wrongly credited to sales	1,400	
Loan interest accrued due	2,400	
Raw material purchase omitted	2,000	
		(6,425)
Revised balance		33,575

(e)

Statement of financial position as at 30 April 20X2

Assets	Cost ($)	Accumulated depreciation ($)	Carrying Amount ($)
Non-current assets			
Freehold land and buildings	100,000	(20,000)	80,000
Plant and machinery	58,000	(16,400)	41,600
Motor vehicles	46,000	(9,125)	36,875
	204,000	(45,525)	158,475
Current assets			
Inventories ($24,700 − $10,000)		14,700	
Trade receivables ($4,500 − $1,000 − $2,000)		1,500	
Amounts prepaid ($1,600 + $900)		2,500	
Balance at bank		4,300	
			23,000
			181,475
Equity and liabilities			
Ordinary shares of $1 each fully paid			100,000
Retained earnings*			
At 1 May 20X1		7,600	
Year ended 30 April 20X2		33,575	
			41,175
			141,175
Non-current liabilities			
8% loan stock			30,000
Current liabilities			
Trade payables		7,900	
Accrued charges		2,400	
			10,300
			181,475

*Rather than show a statement of changes in equity, the movement has been shown in the statement of financial position.

☑ Solution 4

- This is quite a complex question involving the correction of errors and adjustments to the figures contained in the ledger accounts, prior to the preparation of financial statements.
- The correction of the control account is particularly important as it is part of the trial balance.
- The adjustments to opening and closing inventories also require careful consideration: the error in opening inventories means that the retained earnings balance brought forward is overstated and the operating profit for the period is understated; the error in closing inventories means that the operating profit figure in the list of balances is understated and the inventories figure is understated.
- The debenture interest should be calculated as one-quarter of the annual figure, as they have been issued for only 3 months.

(a) Journal

		Debit ($)	*Credit ($)*
(i)	Payables	10,000	
	Receivables		10,000
	Operating profit (sales)	1,000	
	Receivables		1,000
	Operating profit (sales returns)	4,000	
	Suspense account		4,000
(ii)	Bank ($2,000 − $1,000)	1,000	
	Operating profit (bank charges)	1,000	
	Receivables		2,000
(iii)	Operating profit (bad debts w/off)	1,000	
	Receivables		1,000
	Allowance for receivables (Note 1)	1,140	
	Operating profit (reduction in allowance)		1,140
(iv)	Inventories	2,000	
	Operating profit (closing inventories)		2,000
	Retained earnings b/fwd	1,000	
	Operating profit		1,000
(v)	Suspense (balance) (Note 2)	3,000	
	Operating profit (sales)		3,000

Notes:

1. The allowance for receivables is to become 1 per cent of $186,000 = $1,860 (a reduction of $1,140).
2. The balance of the suspense account was $1,000 debit (found by adding up the balances given in the question); transaction (i) above credited the suspense account with $4,000, therefore the final balance was $3,000 credit – and as per the instruction in note (v), this is to be added to the sales account.

(a) Revised operating profit

	$
Original operating profit	80,000
(i) Receivables	(1,000)
Suspense	(4,000)
(ii) Bank	(1,000)
(iii) Receivables	(1,000)
Allowance for receivables	1,140
(iv) Inventories	2,000
Retained earnings b/fwd	1,000
(v) Suspense	3,000
Revised operating profit	80,140

Statement of comprehensive income of Fiddles plc

	$
Operating profit	80,140
Debenture interest	(7,200)
Profit for the period	72,940

Statement of changes in equity of Fiddles plc

	$
Balance at start of period (200,000 − 1,000)	199,000
Profit for the period	72,940
Dividend	(10,000)
Balance at end of period	261,940

Statement of financial position of Fiddles plc

Assets	$	$	$
Non-current assets			
Land			100,000
Buildings			120,000
Plant and machinery			
Cost		170,000	
Accumulated depreciation		120,000	
			50,000
			270,000
Current assets			
Inventories		192,000	
Receivables	186,000		
Less: allowance	1,860		
		184,140	
Bank		13,000	
			389,140
			659,140
Equity and liabilities			
Share capital			100,000
Retained earnings			261,940
			361,940
Non-current liabilities			
Debentures			180,000
Current liabilities			
Payables		100,000	
Debenture interest		7,200	
Dividends declared		10,000	
			117,200
			659,140

Solution 5

- This question involves the preparation of a statement of cash flows by analysing changes in the statement of financial position, together with the adjustment of profit for items that do not affect cash.
- Transfers to reserves must be added back before arriving at operating profit; this must then be adjusted by adding back depreciation for the year.

(a)

	$'000
Cash flow from operating activities	
Profit for the year ended 20X5	1,500
Add: depreciation	750
Add: decrease in inventories	200
Add: decrease in receivables	1,500
Less: decrease in payables	(1,000)
	2,950
Cash flow from financing activities	
Issue of shares	3,000
Increase in cash and bank	5,950
Opening bank balance	(1,000)
Closing bank balance	4,950

(b) **Statement of changes in equity of OGN Ltd for the year ended 31 December 20X5**

	Ordinary Shares $'000	Share Premium —	General Reserves $'000	Retained Earnings $'000	Total $'000
Balance at the start of the period	7,000		1,500	1,000	9,500
Retained earnings				1,500	1,500
Transfer to general reserve			1,000	(1,000)	—
Issue of ordinary shares	2,000	1,000			3,000
Balance at the end of the period	9,000	1,000	2,500	1,500	14,000

(c)

Statement of financial position of OGN Ltd as at 31 December 20X5

Assets	$'000	$'000
Non-current assets		7,500
Less: accumulated depreciation		(750)
		6,750
Current assets		
Inventories	1,800	
Receivables	3,500	
Bank	4,950	
		10,250
		17,000
Equity and liabilities		
9,000 ordinary shares of $1 each		9,000
Share premium account		1,000
General reserves		2,500
Retained earnings		1,500
		14,000
Current liabilities		
Trade payables		3,000
		17,000

(d)

(i) Par (or nominal) value is that ascribed to shares when authorised, appears on the share certificate and used for dividend calculations.

(ii) Debentures are long-terms loans with a fixed interest rate, payable irrespective of profits. They may be redeemable in the future, and secured on non-current assets.

(iii) Profits are transferred to general reserves to limit the profits available for payment of current/future dividends. They may be reversed in the future.

(iv) Dividends are proposed by the directors, but are not payable until approved by members at the annual general meeting.

☑ Solution 6

- Commence this question by preparing a workings section, adjusting for the various points given to you in the notes, with adjustments and apportionments clearly labelled.
- It might also help to label the figures in the trial balance according to their destination, that is, manufacturing account, statement of comprehensive income, statement of changes in equity, statement of financial position – and a note of items to be apportioned between different accounts.

(a)

Manufacturing account of ABC Ltd for the year ended 31 October 20X3

	$'000	$'000	$'000
Opening inventories of raw materials		27	
Purchases of raw materials	826		
Less: returns	(18)		
		808	
		835	
Less: closing inventories of raw materials		(24)	
Direct materials			811
Direct labour (575 + 15)			590
Prime cost			1,401
Indirect factory costs			
Heat, light and power (50% × $242)		121	
Salaries (20% × (122 + 8))		26	
Rent and insurance (1/3 × (114 − 21))		31	
Depreciation of plant (10% × $350)		35	
Depreciation of premises (25% × (2% × 600))		3	
			216
Total factory cost			1,617
Change in work in progress			
Opening inventories		18	
Less: closing inventories		(19)	
			(1)
Factory cost of goods transferred			1,616

(b) **Trading and statement of comprehensive income of ABC Ltd for the year ended 31 October 20X3**

	$'000	$'000
Sales		2,350
Less: returns		(38)
		2,312
Less: cost of goods sold		
Opening inventories of finished goods	255	
Factory cost of goods transferred	1,616	
	1,871	
Less: closing inventories of finished goods	(147)	
		(1,724)
Gross profit		588
Less: expenses		
Heat, light and power	121	
Salaries	104	
Printing, post and stationery	32	
Rent and insurance	62	
Change in allowance for receivables	(5)	
Bad debts written off	40	
Inventories written down	5	
Depreciation		
Premises	9	
Office equipment	18	
		(386)
Operating profit		202
Loan interest payable		(50)
Profit before tax		152
Income tax		(35)
Profit for the period		117
Other comprehensive income		
Gain on property revaluation before tax	100	
Income tax	(30)	
Gain on property revaluation after tax		70
Total comprehensive income		187

(c) **Statement of changes in equity of ABC Ltd for the year ended 31 October 20X3**

	Revaluation Reserve	Retained Earnings	$'000
Balance at start of period		442	442
Total comprehensive income	70	117	187
Dividends paid	—	(10)	(10)
Balance at end of period	70	549	619

(d)   **Statement of Financial position of ABC Ltd as at 31 October 20X3**

	Cost ($'000)	Acc. Dep'n ($'000)	Carrying amount ($'000)
Assets			
Non-current assets			
Premises	700	(207)	493
Plant	350	(175)	175
Office equipment	125	(53)	72
	1,175	(435)	740
Current assets			
Inventories			
Raw materials	24		
Work in progress	19		
Finished goods	142		
		185	
Receivables	240		
Less: allowance	(6)		
		234	
Prepayments		21	
Bank balance		509	
			949
			1,689
Equity and liabilities			
Ordinary share capital			500
Share premium account			100
Revaluation reserve			70
Retained earnings			549
			1,219
Non-current liability			
Loan repayable			150
Current liabilities			
Trade payables		(75)	
Accruals		(61)	
Sales tax liability		(19)	
Income Tax		(65)	
Loan repayable in 12 months		(100)	
			320
			1,689

Note that the dividend is ignored because it is only proposed.

 ## Solution 7

- This question involves a manufacturer, with all the usual adjustments and apportionments required.
- Prepare a workings section, with adjustments and apportionments clearly labelled.

(a)   **Statement of comprehensive income of FPC Ltd for year ended 31 March 20X6**

	$	$	$	$
Sales				2,925,000
Less: returns				(14,000)
Net sales				2,911,000
Opening inventories of finished goods			70,000	
Opening inventories of raw material		60,000		
Purchases	1,500,000			
Carriage inwards	15,000			
	1,515,000			
Less: returns outwards	(22,000)			
Net purchases		1,493,000		
		1,553,000		
Less: closing inventories of raw material		(80,000)		
Direct material		1,473,000		
Direct labour		617,500		
Prime cost		2,090,500		
Factory indirect expenses				
Rent and rates	22,000			
Insurance	16,000			
Factory supervisors' salaries	150,000			
Depreciation – premises	4,500			
Depreciation – plant	11,250			
		203,750		
		2,294,250		
Opening work in progress	30,000			
Less: closing work in progress	(42,500)			
		(12,500)		
Factory cost of goods completed			2,281,750	
			2,351,750	
Less: closing inventories of finished goods			(127,000)	
Cost of goods sold				(2,224,750)
Gross profit				686,250
Discount received				2,500
				688,750

	$	$
Less: expenses		
Carriage outwards	10,000	
Discount allowed	4,000	
Rent	88,000	
Insurance	64,000	
Office wages and salaries	175,000	
Sales officers' commission	145,000	
Administration expenses	43,600	
Allowance for receivables	2,250	
Bad debts written off	6,500	
Depreciation – premises	13,500	
	3,750	
Depreciation – plant and machinery		(556,150)
Operating profit		132,600
Debenture interest paid		(10,000)
Profit before tax		122,600
Income tax		(22,000)
Profit for the period		100,600

Workings

Rent	as per trial balance $120,000, less prepaid $10,000 = $110,000
	20% factory = $22,000; 80% administration = $88,000
Insurance	as per trial balance $100,000, less prepaid $20,000 = $80,000
	20% factory = $16,000; 80% administration = $64,000
Direct labour	as per trial balance $600,000, add accrued $17,500 = $617,500
Sales	as per trial balance $2,960,000, less sale or return $35,000 = $2,925,000
Receivables	as per trial balance $220,000, less sale or return $35,000 = $185,000
Depreciation	plant: 10% of $150,000 = $15,000
	75% factory = $11,250; 25% administration = $3,750
	premises: 2% of $900,000 = $18,000
	25% factory = $4,500; 75% administration = $13,500
Allowance for receivables	5% of $185,000 = $9,250, less previous balance $7,000 = $2,250
Sales officers' commission	5% of $2,911,000 = $145,550, less already paid $113,500 = $32,050 accrued
Administration expenses	as per trial balance $45,000, less incorrect sales tax $1,400 = $43,600

(b)   **Statement of changes in equity of FPC Ltd for year ended 31 March 20X6**

	$'000
Balance at start of period	98,000
Profit for the period	100,600
Balance at end of period	198,600

Note: The dividend is ignored because it is proposed.

(c) (i)   consistency convention
     (ii)   matching convention
     (iii) prudence convention

 ## Solution 8

(a)

Non-current assets at cost

	$'000		$'000
Balance b/f	1,000	Disposals a/c	50
Additions	350	Balance c/f	1,300
	1,350		1,350

Non-current asset – accumulated depreciation

	$'000		$'000
Disposals a/c	20	Balance b/f	400
Balance c/f	600	Charge for the year	220
	620		620

Non-current assets – disposals

	$'000		$'000
Non-current assets at cost	50	Non-current assets acc. depn.	20
Profit on sale of non-current assets	10	Disposal proceeds	40
	60		60

(b)

Statement of cash flows for the year ended 31 March 20X2

		$'000
Cash flow from operating activities		
Increase in retained earnings (1,240 − 1,200)		40
Add: dividends declared		260
Add: depreciation		220
Less: profit on sale of non-current assets		(10)
		510
Less: increase in inventories		(600)
Less: increase in receivables		(400)
Add: increase in payables		280
		(210)
Cash flow from investing activities		
Proceeds of sale of non-current assets	40	
Non-current assets purchased	(350)	
		(310)
Cash flow from financing activities		
Dividends declared	(300)	
Shares issued	500	
		200
Decrease in bank balance		(320)
Bank at beginning of period		200
Bank at end of period		(120)

☑ Solution 9

Meltdown Ltd–Statement of comprehensive income

Profit for the period		100
Other comprehensive income		
Revaluation of property before tax	60	
Tax on revaluation	(18)	
		42
Total comprehensive income		142

Meltdown Ltd–Statement of changes in equity

	Revaluation Reserve	Retained Earnings	Total
	42	100	142

Meltdown–Statement of financial position

Non-current assets Property	460
Equity–Revaluation reserve	42
Non-current liabilities Income tax	18

14

The Interpretation of Financial Statements

The Interpretation of Financial Statements

14

LEARNING OUTCOMES

When you have completed this chapter, you should be able to:

► calculate and interpret basic ratios.

14.1 Introduction

You have now reached one of the most important areas of study in this subject – the use and interpretation of accounting information. You now know how to prepare financial statements for various organisations, from a variety of different sources of data, but now we return to the content of Chapter 1 and the questions it posed: *What is accounting, who uses financial statements and for what purpose, and what makes financial statements useful?* The mechanics of the preparation of financial statements form only the start of the accounting process, the end result of which is to provide users with information to enable them to make decisions. The mere presentation of a set of financial statements does not necessarily achieve that objective, and this chapter looks at ways of making that information more meaningful.

Understanding the whole of this chapter should be regarded as essential for examination success.

14.2 What is meant by 'interpretation of financial statements'?

Financial statements provide a great deal of information. However, one difficulty with these statements is that they show only absolute figures for a particular period, and at the end of that period. To enable users to make informed decisions, the statements on their own do not always provide sufficient information, even though they have been prepared in accordance with international financial reporting standards.

Example 14.A

Suppose that Company A has a trading account that shows sales revenue of $100,000 and the profit for the year is $5,000. What does this tell you? It tells you that the sales revenue is $100,000 and the profit is $5,000. Is this good or bad? Is this to be expected? Is this comparable with other organisations? Can a user of the financial statements make decisions on the basis of this information?

The answer is no. That information on its own is not of use. Let us consider two other companies as well. Company B has sales revenue of $200,000 and profit form the year of $6,000. Company C has sales revenue of $300,000 and profit for the year of $4,500. Which of the three organisations is best? That depends on what the user is looking for.

If the user is looking for the organisation with the highest revenue, that is Company C. If (s)he is looking for the organisation with the highest profit, that is Company B. Which organisation is most successful, in terms of its profit? You might think it is Company B, with its higher profit. But Company B achieved that profit from sales of $200,000, whereas Company A had only half that level of sales yet achieved a profit of only $1,000 less than Company B.

We are now embarking on an important area of accounting, that of *comparison*. We are starting to compare profit with sales revenue, and we are comparing one firm with another. That is the key technique of the interpretation of financial statements – comparison of one with another.

Let us tabulate the information given above:

Company	Sales revenue	Profit
A	$100,000	$5,000
B	$200,000	$6,000
C	$300,000	$4,500

There are comparisons we can make here. Although Company B had the highest profit, it was only 3 per cent of its sales revenue. That is found by the following formula:

$$\frac{Profit}{Sales} \times 100$$

Company A achieved a profit of 5 per cent of sales, and Company C achieved a profit of only 1.5 per cent. So Company C looks poor.

But that is taking only 1 year as information. It would be useful to look at last year's results and see if any of the companies have improved their profits.

It might also be useful to compare the profit with other figures, apart from sales. Suppose that the capital employed in Company A is $50,000. A profit of $5,000 is a 10 per cent return on that capital. Suppose that Company C's capital employed is only $30,000. Its return on that capital is 15 per cent – so an investor might prefer to choose Company C, while a lender might prefer Company B.

The point is that different users are looking for different information, which a set of financial statements on its own does not necessarily provide. Comparing figures with other figures is a useful additional tool in providing information to support decision-making. These tools are known as the techniques of ratio analysis.

14.3 Calculating ratios

A ratio is simply a comparison of one figure with another. In the above examples, we calculated the *percentage* of profit compared with sales revenue for each year.

Using the formula above, for Company A the calculation is:

$$\frac{5,000}{100,000} \times 100 = 5\%$$

Calculating a percentage is only one method of presenting a ratio. The same figures could be presented as a fraction:

$$\frac{5,000}{100,000} = \frac{1}{20}$$

which means that profit was $\frac{1}{20}$ of sales revenue. The figures could also be shown as a simple comparison:

5,000 : 100,000 or 1 : 20

which means that each $1 of profit required $20 of sales revenue.

There are other types of ratios, which will be explained later in the chapter.

14.3.1 Using the ratios

Calculating the ratios is only one step in the analysis process. Once that is done, the results must be compared with other results. Comparison is commonly made between:

- previous accounting periods;
- other companies (perhaps in the same type of business);
- budgets and expectations;
- government statistics;
- other ratios.

14.4 Types of ratios

Ratios can be classified into various groupings, according to the type of information they convey. The main groupings are as follows:

- profitability (performance) ratios;
- liquidity (solvency) ratios;
- efficiency (use of assets) ratios;
- capital structure (gearing) ratios;
- security (investors) ratios.

The last group, security ratios, is not part of your syllabus for this subject. The above list is not exhaustive – a ratio can be compiled from any data if it can be usefully interpreted.

The following income statement and statement of financial position will be used to illustrate the calculation of accounting ratios and interpret them.

Income statement for the year ended 31 December year 8

	$	$
Sales		23,636
Opening inventories	1,225	
Purchases	8,999	
	10,224	
Closing inventories	(1,425)	
Cost of sales		(8,799)
Gross profit		14,837
Expenses		(5,737)
Operating profit		9,100
Interest payable on bank loan		(450)
Profit before tax		8,650
Income tax		(1,000)
Profit for the period		7,650

Statement of financial position as at 31 December year 8

Assets	$	$
Non-current assets		14,135
Current assets		
Inventories	1,425	
Receivables	542	
Bank	7,037	
Cash in hand	697	
		9,701
		23,836
Equity and liabilities		
Equity		18,250
Non-current liability		
Bank loan		4,500
Current liability		
Payables		1,086
		23,836

14.5 Profitability ratios

These are also known as *performance ratios*. They compare profit at different levels with other figures, and are often presented as percentages.

14.5.1 Gross profit margin

This ratio (also known as the *gross profit to sales revenue ratio*) is calculated by:

$$\frac{\text{Gross Profit}}{\text{Sales}} \times 100 = \frac{14{,}837}{23{,}636} \times 100 = 62.8\%$$

It is normally expressed as a percentage, but do try to understand the meaning of the percentage. The calculation shows that for every $1 of sales revenue, 62.8 ¢ were available to support the remaining expenses, the possible payment of dividends and the retention of profits for the future. While its value is useful for comparing the results of similar businesses, the trend of gross profit margins over time is a more appropriate use of the ratio.

Suppose the ratio in the previous year had been 64.3 per cent. How can we interpret the decline over the year?

There are several possibilities:

- sales revenue declined;
- sales revenue remained the same, but costs have increased;
- sales revenue increased, but costs increased by a greater proportion;
- it was necessary to keep sales prices steady, despite rising costs, in order to retain market share;
- suppliers increased their prices, or perhaps the firm lost the advantage of trade discounts;
- the sales mix changed: if several different products are being sold they will not all be equally profitable. It is possible that in the current year we sold a higher proportion of the less profitable products.

You can perhaps see that the above changes can be classified as either *volume changes* or *price changes*.

The gross profit margin could be a measure of the effectiveness of the sales team, pricing policies, purchasing methods and (in a manufacturing organisation) the production processes.

The decline will not be as a result of holding inventories, as this is adjusted for in the cost of sales calculation.

14.5.2 Gross profit mark-up

This ratio is an alternative measure of profitability. It is calculated by:

$$\frac{\text{Gross Profit}}{\text{Cost of sales}} \times 100 = \frac{14{,}837}{8{,}799} \times 100 = 168.6\%$$

It shows us that the selling price of the goods was equal to the cost of those goods, plus 168.6 per cent of the cost. In other words, for every $1 we spent on the cost of goods, we added $1.69 (approximately) to arrive at a selling price of $2.69.

Similar comments apply to this ratio as were applied to the gross profit margin.

14.5.3 Operating profit margin

This is calculated by:

$$\frac{\text{Operating profit}}{\text{Sales}} \times 100 = \frac{9{,}100}{23{,}636} \times 100 = 38.5\%$$

The value of this ratio lies in its comparison over time and with other organisations and the industry average. In this example the operating profit percentage was 38.5 per cent. In itself, this has no meaning – only by comparing it as stated is it possible to derive any benefit from the calculation. To interpret this percentage fully would involve an examination of its components. Given that operating profit is equal to gross profit less expenses, a change in this percentage could arise either from a change in gross profit or from a change in one or more of the expenses deducted from gross profit. Further analysis would be needed.

14.5.4 Return on capital ratios

People who invest their money in a business are interested in the return the business is earning on that capital. Expressing this return in the form of a ratio enables comparison with other possible investment opportunities.

This ratio is a key measure of return. It measures the amount of earnings generated per $1 of capital, and is usually stated as a percentage. The ratio can be calculated in several different ways, according to the information required of it, and depending on what is meant by the two terms 'capital employed' and 'return'. In this Learning System, two methods of calculating the return on capital are discussed – the return on total capital employed (ROCE) and the return on equity (ROE).

- *Capital employed* can consist of total capital employed (equity + non-current liabilities) or just equity. In using *total capital employed* we include long-term loans as well as equity, and this is used when calculating ROCE. When calculating ROE, just the equity is used. You should remember that equity is share capital plus all of the reserves. Furthermore, it is more correct to use the average of capital employed during the year, as the profit has been earned throughout the year. The capital at the start of the year will have been different, having been affected by share issues, loan issues or repayments, and the addition of profit for the year. However, in many computer-based assessments, the question may just require you to use the capital at the end of the year.
- *Return* is another way of describing profit. The profit figure to be taken will depend on which figure is taken for capital employed. If capital employed is taken as being total capital employed, then it is the operating profit figure that is required to be used as the 'return', as this is the profit available to finance the total investment in the business. If the capital employed is equity, then the return is the 'profit for the period', which is the last line in the income statement. In other words, it is the profit for the year, after interest and after tax.

The basic formula for return on capital ratios is:

$$\frac{\text{Profit}}{\text{Average total capital employed}} \times 100$$

The ROCE is:

$$\frac{\text{Operating Profit}}{\text{Average capital employed by shareholders and lenders}} \times 100$$

This expresses the profit that is available to all providers of long-term capital, as a percentage of that capital. Using the figures from the financial statements above, the calculation is:

$$\frac{9,100}{18,925} \times 100 = 48\%$$

Average total capital employed is arrived at by taking the average of:

	$
Closing total capital employed (18,250 + 4,500)	22,750
Opening total capital employed (22,750 − 7,650 retained profit)	15,100
	37,850 ÷2 = $18,925

Note that the profit figure used when calculating opening capital is 'retained' profit. This would normally be the profit after the payment of dividends and would be found in the statement of changes in equity. However, in this example there are no dividends paid and therefore the figure is taken from the income statement.

Overdrafts less cash balances, that is net overdrafts, are normally excluded from capital employed. This assumes that overdrafts are temporary and are not considered to be a source of permanent finance for the business.

The ROE is:

$$\frac{\text{Profit for the period}}{\text{Average equity}} \times 100$$

This expresses the profit that is available only to shareholders, as a percentage of their funds. The calculation is also known as return on net assets, as equity = assets − liabilities. (Which is a rearrangement of the accounting equation.)

Using the figures in the financial statements above, the calculation is:

$$\frac{7,650}{14,425} \times 100 = 53\%$$

Average equity is arrived at by taking the average of:

	$
Closing equity	18,250
Opening equity (18,250 − 7,650 profit)	10,600
	28,850 ÷2 = $14,425

If it is not possible to calculate the average capital employed, then use the closing capital figure, but bear in mind that it may not be representative of the capital employed through out the year.

14.6 Liquidity ratios

These are also known as *solvency ratios*, as they refer to the ability of the business to pay its payables in the short term.

There are two main liquidity ratios.

14.6.1 The current ratio

This is also known as the *working capital* ratio, as it is based on working capital or net current assets. It is a measure of the liquidity of a business that compares its current assets with those payables due to be paid within 1 year of the statement of financial position date (otherwise known as current liabilities). It is calculated as:

$$\frac{\text{Current assets}}{\text{Current liabilities}} = \frac{9,701}{1,086} = 8.9{:}1$$

Notice how the ratio is expressed, as a comparison of assets with liabilities. The ratio can also be stated as:

Current assets : current liabilities

The importance of this ratio is the information it gives about the liquidity of a business. Current liabilities all have to be settled in cash within a reasonably short space of time. Does the company have sufficient liquid resources to do this? Clearly, its cash and bank balances are liquid; receivables should convert into cash quite soon; and inventories will presumably soon be sold, again eventually generating cash. The calculation tells us that the company has $8.90 in current assets with which to pay every $1 of its current liabilities.

A high ratio, such as the one in our example, means that current assets are easily sufficient to cover current liabilities. A ratio of below one – meaning that current liabilities exceed current assets – could imply danger of insolvency. It used to be thought that a ratio of 2:1 was ideal, but this depends on the type of business and its reliance on credit transactions.

Although a high ratio gives comfort to payables, it may mean that the company is holding more in current assets than it requires in the short term. This is wasteful, as current assets rarely earn income – inventories need to be sold in order to produce profits, receivables will not pay more than the amount outstanding, and bank balances may earn only very small amounts of interest. Indeed, a company with a high level of inventories might indicate difficulty in selling them, while a high level of receivables might indicate poor credit control.

14.6.2 The quick ratio

This is also known as the *acid test ratio* and is calculated by:

$$\frac{\text{Current assets excluding inventories}}{\text{Current liabilities}} = \frac{8,276}{1,086} \times 100 = 7.6{:}1$$

or it can be expressed as:

Current assets excluding inventories : current liabilities

This is similar to the current ratio, but takes the more prudent view that inventories may take some time to convert into cash, and therefore the true liquidity position is measured by the relationship of receivables and cash only to current liabilities. The calculation tells us that the company has $7.60 in 'quick' assets with which to pay each $1 in its current liabilities. Again, a very high ratio is very comforting, but may be wasteful as mentioned above. Generally, a ratio of 1:1 is considered 'ideal' but many retail companies with very regular cash sales have very low ratios, due to their lack of receivables.

A low ratio might need further investigation before conclusions can be drawn, for example, if the current liabilities figure includes payables not due for payment until well into the next accounting period (e.g. income tax), the figure may be distorted.

14.7 Efficiency ratios

These are also referred to as *use of assets ratios*. They measure the efficiency of the management of assets, both non-current and current.

14.7.1 Asset turnover ratios

These ratios compare the assets with the sales revenue (turnover) that they have earned. The end result is often expressed in money value to represent the value of sales revenue for each $1 invested in those assets. The formula is:

$$\frac{\text{Sales revenue}}{\text{Assets}} = \$\ldots\ldots\ldots$$

The calculation can be performed on any combination of assets, from total net assets to individual groups of assets, such as plant and machinery.

Sales: total capital employed (capital turnover)
This is the sales revenue generated per $1 of average total capital employed.

$$\frac{\text{Sales revenue}}{\text{Average total capital employed}} = \frac{23,636}{18,925} = \$1,249$$

(See Section 14.5.4 for the calculation of average total capital employed).

The result tells us that we generated $1.249 in sales for every $1 invested in net assets.

Sales: non-current assets (non-current asset turnover)
This is the sales revenue generated per $1 of non-current assets.

$$\frac{\text{Sales revenue}}{\text{Non-current assets}} = \frac{23,636}{14,135} = £1.672$$

This tells us that for every $1 invested in non-current assets, sales revenue of $1.672 was earned. This figure is meaningless on its own – it is commonly compared with previous years' results, as comparison between firms is less useful.

14.7.2 Inventories days

Inventories may be analysed by calculating the ratio of inventories to cost of sales, and then multiplying by the number of days in a year to give inventories days.

The calculation is:

$$\frac{\text{Inventories}}{\text{Cost of Sales}} \times 365 = \text{inventories days}$$

$$\frac{1,425}{8,799} \times 365 = 59 \text{ days}$$

This figure gives the number of days that on average an item is in inventories before it is sold; this may alternatively be expressed as the number of days a firm could continue trading if the supply of goods ceased.

The calculation may also use average inventories:

$$\frac{1,325}{8,799} \times 365 = 55 \text{ days}$$

This tells us that in the past year, this was the average inventories days. By using the inventories at the end of the year, this tells us what the inventories days will be in the future, assuming cost of sales remains the same.

The number of inventories days is relevant to the context of the business; in a manufacturing company, it will approximate to the production cycle and in a cream cake shop to 1 day!

If inventories days are relatively high, this may indicate that inventories are too high and there is additional finance tied up in inventories which could perhaps be used more effectively elsewhere. If cash is paid out when the inventories are purchased, but the cash does not come back in until the inventories are sold to a customer, then this temporary negative cash flow will have to be financed by the company. Moreover, if the inventories are sold on credit terms and the customer does not pay for, say 1 month, then the delay in getting the cash back in is even longer.

If the inventories are too low, this may show an overzealous application of the 'just-in-time' concept and consequential risks of running out of inventories. It may also indicate a company meeting a cash flow crisis by running down inventories levels.

Inventories days needs to be compared to other companies and compared to previous years in the same company. Increasing inventories days may be investigated further by separately analysing raw materials (RM), work in progress (WIP) and finished goods (FG) to cost of goods sold. An increase in RM days may indicate mismanagement in the buying department; an increase in WIP may indicate production delays. If FG days increase, this may be a sign of decline in demand for the product and an increase in obsolete items.

The inventories ratio may also be expressed as the number of times an item turns over in a year – that is, how many times it is bought and sold during the year.

Inventories turnover is calculated as:

$$\frac{\text{Cost of sales}}{\text{Average inventories}} = \frac{8,799}{1,325} = 6.6 \text{ times}$$

You should note here that the word 'turnover' is being used to mean 'turn over' and is not referring to turnover, as in sales.

14.7.3 Receivables days

This is a measure of the average time taken by customers to settle their debts. It is calculated by:

$$\frac{\text{Receivables}}{\text{Sales}} \times 365 = \frac{542}{23,636} \times 365 = 8 \text{ days}$$

Where details are available, credit sales only should be considered.

'The sales figure will exclude sales tax but receivables will include sales tax, and so strictly speaking the figure is not comparing like-with-like. This sales tax on sales or receivables is not usually known and so this is inevitable. However, if the sales tax is known, then the figures should be adjusted so that both either include, or exclude, sales tax.

The result of this calculation should be compared with the number of days' credit normally allowed by the business to its customers. If it appears that customers are taking longer to pay than they should do, it may be necessary to take remedial action.

As with inventories days, a slowing down in the speed of collecting debts will have a detrimental effect on cash flow. On the other hand, it may be that the business has deliberately offered extended credit in order to increase demand.

14.7.4 Payable days

This is a measure of the average time taken to pay suppliers. Although it is not strictly a measure of asset efficiency on its own, it is part of the overall management of net current assets. It is calculated by:

$$\frac{\text{Payable}}{\text{Purchases}} \times 365 = \frac{1,086}{8,999} \times 365 = 44 \text{ days}$$

The purchases figure should exclude any cash purchases, if this information is available; where there is no purchases figure available the best alternative is to use cost of sales as the denominator. Similarly, payables should include only trade payables, not payables for expenses or non-current assets.

The purchases figure will exclude sales tax but payables will include sales tax, and so strictly speaking the figure is not comparing like-with-like. The sales tax on purchases or payables is not usually known and so this is inevitable. However, if the sales tax is known, then the figures should be adjusted so that both either include, or exclude, sale tax.

The result of this ratio can also be compared with the receivables days. A firm does not normally want to offer its customers more time to pay than it gets from its own suppliers, otherwise this could affect cash flow. Generally, the longer the payables payment period, the better, as the firm holds on to its cash for longer, but care must be taken not to upset suppliers by delaying payment, which could result in the loss of discounts and reliability.

It is important to recognise when using these ratios that it is the trend of ratios that is important, not the individual values. Payment periods are longer in some types of organisation than in others.

14.7.5 Total working capital ratio

This measures the total length of time for which working capital is tied up in inventories, receivables and payables, before becoming available for use. It is the total of the number of inventories days, receivables days, less payables days. From the preceding three sections, you can see that this is:

Number of days – inventories	59
Number of days – receivables	8
Less number of days – payables	(44)
Total working capital days	23

This tells us that it takes, on average, 23 days in which to sell the inventories, receive payment from receivables and pay the payables. The total of 23 days may not seem too lengthy for a manufacturing business, but it does indicate the level of working capital needed in order to finance the ordinary activities of the business, which may result in the need for an overdraft or other sources of finance.

14.8 Capital structure ratios

Different firms have different methods of financing their activities. Some rely mainly on the issue of share capital and the retention of profits; others rely heavily on loan finance; most have a combination of the two.

14.8.1 The gearing ratio (or leverage ratio)

Gearing is a measure of the relationship between the amount of finance provided by external parties (e.g. debentures) to the total capital employed. It is calculated by:

$$\frac{\text{Debt}}{\text{Total capital employed}} \times 100 = \frac{4{,}500}{22{,}750} \times 100 = 20\%$$

You should recall from the discussion above regarding the return on total capital employed (ROCE), that total capital employed is equity plus debt. This ratio has been calculated based on the capital employed at the date of the statement of financial position. An alternative would be to use the average capital employed and average loan capital during the year.

The more highly geared a business, the more profits that have to be earned to pay the interest cost of the borrowing. Consequently, the higher the gearing, the more risky is the owner's investment. Remember that dividends do not have to be paid out if the directors decide not to declare them, so there is reduced risk with low-geared companies, especially in times when profits are falling. On the other hand, a highly geared company might be more attractive to shareholders when profits are rising, because there are fewer of them to share out those profits.

An alternative method of calculating gearing is known as the *debt: equity ratio*. In this case, the loan capital is expressed as a percentage of equity capital.

In this example, it would be:

$$\frac{\text{Debt}}{\text{Equity}} = \frac{4{,}500}{18{,}250} \times 100 = 25\%$$

14.8.2 Interest cover

Connected to the gearing ratio is a measure of the number of times that the profit is able to 'cover' the fixed interest due on long-term loans. It provides lenders with an idea of the level of security for the payment. The formula is:

$$\frac{\text{Operating profit}}{\text{Interest payable}} = \frac{9{,}100}{450} = 20 \text{ times}$$

This shows lenders that their interest is covered 20 times by the current profits. This would normally be a fairly comfortable level, but of course, it is *future* profits that will determine the actual level of cover.

14.9 Ratio analysis for sole traders

All of the above ratios can be calculated for sole traders, as well as for limited companies.

 Exercise 14.1

Give the formulae for the following ratios:

(a) Return on capital employed (ROCE),
(b) Gross profit margin,
(c) Operating profit margin,
(d) Return on equity (ROE),
(e) Non-current assets turnover,
(f) Inventories days,
(g) Receivables days,
(h) Payables days,
(i) Current ratio,
(j) Quick ratio,
(k) Gearing ratio.

 Solution

Refer to the formulae above for the solutions.

14.10 Summary

This very important chapter is one worth spending time over. In a computer-bases assessment, not only will you be expected to calculate ratios, but you may need to be able to do any or all of the following:

- explain what the ratio attempts to show;
- discuss the results of your calculations;
- suggest possible reasons for good/poor results or differences from previous years, other companies or expectations.

Although ratios are a useful additional guide to decision-making, they are also very difficult to interpret fully without additional information.

Before calculating any ratios the nature of the business should be considered. The following list of questions is a useful starting point:

- What is the nature of its business?
- Does it need a lot of assets to operate?
- How has it obtained its funding (shareholders' capital, loan capital or internally generated profits)?
- Does it have a high or low operating profit margin on its business?
- Does it have high or low turnover in relation to the amount of capital that is tied up in the organisation? (High-margin companies will normally have slower rates of sales/turnover because they usually charge higher prices and/or operate in premium segments of a market.)
- Does the company appear to be financially unstable (i.e. does it have excessive debts in relation to its assets)?
- Do the level of inventories or any other asset, or number of employees appear to be too high or too low to support the organisation's level of activity/sales?
- Is there any information to tell whether the business is more or less efficient/profitable than other competitors in the same industry?

The answers to these questions and to others that are naturally associated with them are key to understanding how an organisation is currently performing and how it is likely to perform in the future. Trends in these indicators are of interest to internal managers and accountants, and also to external users. Examples of external users are:

- investors and potential investors use this type of information to decide whether to buy, sell or hold shares in a particular company;
- lenders and suppliers wish to know about the solvency of an enterprise and its ability to repay loans or debts incurred in relation to the supply of materials or services;
- governments charged with the responsibility for framing fiscal policy or industrial policy in different sectors of the economy will find much of interest in them. Many of the accounting figures are used to compile national statistics on industrial output, gross national product (GNP), wage levels and inflation trends.

External sources of comparative information will usually be industry averages compiled by government agencies or independent industry groups. These are readily available on the Internet.

Revision Questions

Question 1 Multiple choice

1.1 Given a selling price of $350 and a gross profit mark-up of 40 per cent, the cost price would be:

$...............

1.2 Sales are $110,000. Purchases are $80,000. Opening inventories are $12,000. Closing inventories are $10,000. Inventories days using average inventories are:

[   ] days

1.3 A business commenced with a bank balance of $3,250; it subsequently purchased goods on credit for $10,000; gross profit mark-up was 120 per cent; half the goods were sold for cash, less cash discount of 5 per cent; all takings were banked. The resulting operating profit was:

$...............

1.4 The rate of inventories turnover is six times where:

(A) sales are $120,000 and average inventories at selling price is $20,000.
(B) purchases are $240,000 and average inventories at cost is $40,000.
(C) cost of goods sold is $180,000 and average inventories at cost is $30,000.
(D) net purchases are $90,000 and closing inventories at cost is $15,000.

1.5 The formula for calculating inventories days is:

(A) cost of goods sold/inventories $\times$ 365.
(B) inventories/purchases $\times$ 365.
(C) cost of goods sold/inventories.
(D) inventories/cost of goods sold $\times$ 365.

1.6 A business operates on a gross profit margin of 33 $\frac{1}{3}$ per cent. Gross profit on a sale was $800, and expenses were $680. The operating profit margin is:

[   ] per cent.

1.7 A business has the following trading account for the year ending 31 May 20X8:

	$	$
Sales		45,000
Opening inventories	4,000	
Purchases	26,500	
	30,500	
Less: closing inventories	(6,000)	
		(24,500)
Gross profit		20,500

Its average inventories days for the year is:

☐ days

1.8 A company's gearing ratio would rise if:

(A) a decrease in long-term loans is less than a decrease in equity.
(B) a decrease in long-term loans is more than a decrease in equity.
(C) interest rates rose.
(D) dividends were paid.

1.9 A company has the following details extracted from its statement of financial position:

	$'000
Inventories	1,900
Receivables	1,000
Bank overdraft	100
Payables	1,000

Its liquidity position could be said to be:

(A) very well controlled, because its current assets far outweigh its current liabilities.
(B) poorly controlled, because its quick assets are less than its current liabilities.
(C) poorly controlled, because its current ratio is significantly higher than the industry norm of 1.8.
(D) poorly controlled, because it has a bank overdraft.

1.10 The gross profit mark-up is 40 per cent where:

(A) sales are $120,000 and gross profit is $48,000.
(B) sales are $120,000 and cost of sales is $72,000.
(C) sales are $100,800 and cost of sales is $72,000.
(D) sales are $100,800 and cost of sales is $60,480.

1.11 Revenue reserves would decrease if a company:

(A) sets aside profits to pay future dividends.
(B) transfers amounts into 'general reserves'.
(C) issues shares at a premium.
(D) pays dividends.

1.12 A company has the following current assets and liabilities at 31 October 20X8:

	$'000
Current assets	
Inventories	970
Receivables	380
Bank	40
	1,390
Current liabilities	
Payables	420

When measured against accepted 'norms', the company can be said to have:

(A) a high current ratio and an ideal acid test ratio.
(B) an ideal current ratio and a low acid test ratio.
(C) a high current ratio and a low acid test ratio.
(D) ideal current and acid test ratios.

1.13 Your company's income statement for the year ended 30 September 20X8 showed the following:

	$'000
Operating profit	1,200
Interest	(200)
Profit before tax	1,000
Income tax	(400)
Profit for the period	600

Its statement of financial position at 30 September 20X7 showed the following:

	$'000
Share capital	8,000
Retained earnings	1,200
	9,200
10% debenture	2,000
	11,200

Return on average capital employed (ROCE) for the year ended 30 September 20X8 is:

☐ per cent

1.14 A summary of the statement of financial position of M Ltd at 31 March 20X0 was as follows:

	$'000
Ordinary share capital	40
Share premium account	10
Retained earnings	10
	60
5% debentures	60
	120

If the operating profit for the year ended 31 March 20X0 was $15,000, what is the return on capital employed (ROCE)?

☐☐☐☐☐☐ per cent

1.15 The annual sales of a company are $235,000 including sales tax at 17.5 per cent. Half of the sales are on credit terms; half are cash sales. The receivables in the statement of financial position are $23,500.

What are the receivable days (to the nearest day)?

☐☐☐☐☐☐ days

1.16 The draft statement of financial position of B Ltd at 31 March 20X0 is set out below.

Assets	$	$
Non-current assets		450
Current assets		
Inventories	65	
Receivables	110	
Prepayments	30	
		205
		655
Equity and liabilities		
Ordinary share capital		400
Retained earnings		100
		500
Non-current liability		
Loan		75
Current liabilities		
Payables	30	
Bank overdraft	50	
		80
		655

What is the gearing of the company?

☐☐☐☐☐☐ per cent

? Question 2

The following information relates to PK, a sole trader.

During the year ended 30 June 20X6, he sold goods to the value of $240,000, which were all sold at a gross profit mark-up of 20 per cent. His administration costs during the year amounted to $32,000.

On 1 July 20X5 his opening inventories were $55,000 and at 30 June 20X6 the number of days' inventories on hand was 40. His receivables days was 30 days and his payables days were 50 days.

His current ratio was 2.2:1 and his non-current assets turnover ratio was 4:1. His return on capital employed was 10 per cent. There was a long-term loan with an outstanding balance of $3,438 at 30 June 20X6.

Requirements

Insert the missing items in the workings, PK's income statement and statement of financial position for the year ended 30 June 20X6.

Workings

Cost of sales	
Closing inventories	
Receivables	
Purchases	
	=
Payables	
Non-current assets	
Gross profit	
Profit for the period	
Capital employed	
Net current assets	
	=
Current assets	
	=
Bank balance	

Income statement of PK for the year ended 30 June 20X6

	$	$
Sales		
Less: cost of sales		
Opening inventories		
Purchases		
Less: closing inventories		
Gross profit		
Administration costs		
Profit for the period		

Statement of financial position of PK as at 30 June 20X6

Assets	$	$	$
Non-current assets			
Current assets			
Inventories			
Receivables			
Bank			
Capital and liabilities			
Opening capital			
Profit for the year			
Closing capital			
Non-current liability			
Long-term loan			
Current liabilities			
Payables			

Question 3

DEX Stores sells three different types of product. The business is made up of three different departments, each having its own manager, who is responsible for buying/selling a particular type of product. The owner determines the pricing policy of the entire operation and adds the following percentages to the cost of the goods to arrive at the selling prices:

Department A	40%
Department B	25%
Department C	100%

The takings during April 20X2 were:

Department A	$18,750
Department B	$11,750
Department C	$147,000

The opening inventories on 1 April 20X2, which the owner verified by a physical inventory count, were valued at cost:

Department A	$4,200
Department B	$7,800
Department C	$22,500

At the end of April, the owner decided to carry out a physical inventory count, but unfortunately could not do this until Sunday 3 May 20X2. The physical inventories held on that day, valued at cost, were:

Department A	$3,700
Department B	$8,100
Department C	$21,600

The following transactions occurred between the end of April and the physical inventories count:

	Department A ($)	Department B ($)	Department C ($)
Sales	420	250	1,500
Purchases	–	1,500	–
Returns inwards	–	–	300
Returns outwards	270	–	800

Purchases during April 20X2 amounted to:

Department A	$14,200
Department B	$8,400
Department C	$74,000

The owner has recently become concerned that the gross profit shown by the financial statements does not reconcile with these gross profit mark-ups and suspects that some of the inventories may be stolen.

THE INTERPRETATION OF FINANCIAL STATEMENTS

Requirements

(a) Insert the missing items into the following table in order to determine the value of inventories at 30 April 20X2.

	Department A ($)	Department B ($)	Department C ($)
Physical inventories at 3 May 20X2			
Add: sales at cost			
Less: purchases			
Less: returns inwards			
Add: returns outwards			
Theoretical inventories			

(b) Insert the missing items into the following table in order to determine the amount of inventories lost.

	Department A ($)	Department B ($)	Department C ($)
Opening inventories (1 April 20X2)			
Purchases in April 20X2			
Closing inventories (3 May 20X2)			
Cost of sales			
Add: mark-up			
Sales			
Actual takings			
Difference			

? Question 4

GH has the following statement of financial position at 30 April 20X5, with corresponding figures for the previous year:

	$	20X5 $	$	20X4 $
Assets				
Non-current assets		277,000		206,000
Current assets				
Inventories	46,000		42,000	
Receivables	37,500		36,000	
Cash and bank	12,500		54,000	
		96,000		132,000
		373,000		338,000
Capital and liabilities				
Capital at start		265,000		214,000
Capital introduced		20,000		–
Profit for the year		92,000		78,000
		377,000		292,000
Drawings		(30,000)		(27,000)
		347,000		265,000
Non-current liability				
Long-term liabilities		10,000		50,000
Current liabilities				
Payables		16,000		23,000
		373,000		338,000

The following information concerning the year to 30 April 20X5 is also available:

(i) Non-current assets were sold for $30,000. Their original cost had been $48,000 and depreciation of $12,000 had been charged in previous years.

(ii) Non-current assets costing $120,000 were purchased during the year.

Requirements

Insert the missing items in the workings and a statement of cash flows for the year to 30 April 20X5.

(a) Initial workings:

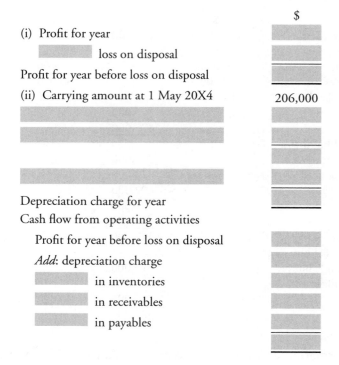

	$
(i) Profit for year	▢
▢ loss on disposal	▢
Profit for year before loss on disposal	▢
(ii) Carrying amount at 1 May 20X4	206,000
▢	▢
▢	▢
	▢
▢	▢
Depreciation charge for year	▢
Cash flow from operating activities	
Profit for year before loss on disposal	▢
Add: depreciation charge	▢
▢ in inventories	▢
▢ in receivables	▢
▢ in payables	▢
	▢

Statement of cash flows of GH for year ended 30 April 20X5

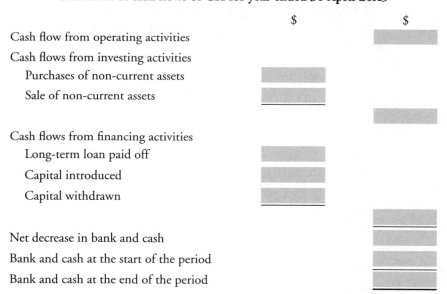

	$	$
Cash flow from operating activities		▢
Cash flows from investing activities		
Purchases of non-current assets	▢	
Sale of non-current assets	▢	
		▢
Cash flows from financing activities		
Long-term loan paid off	▢	
Capital introduced	▢	
Capital withdrawn	▢	
		▢
Net decrease in bank and cash		▢
Bank and cash at the start of the period		▢
Bank and cash at the end of the period		▢

? **Question 5**

The following trial balance has been extracted from the ledgers of JK Ltd at 31 March 20X3:

	$	$
Sales (all on credit)		647,400
Inventories (1 April 20X2)	15,400	
Trade receivables and payables	82,851	41,936
Purchases (all on credit)	321,874	
Carriage in	13,526	
Carriage out	32,460	
Electricity	6,994	
Local business tax	8,940	
Wages and salaries	138,292	
Postages and stationery	6,984	
Rent	14,600	
Sales tax control		16,382
Employees' income tax control		4,736
Motor vehicles		
At cost	49,400	
Cumulative depreciation		21,240
Bank deposit account	90,000	
Bank current account	77,240	
Ordinary shares of $1 each		50,000
Retained earnings		76,597
	858,291	858,291

The following notes are also relevant:

(i) Inventories at 31 March 20X3 $19,473.
(ii) Prepaid rent amounted to $2,800.
(iii) Accruals are estimated as follows:

Electricity	$946
Wages and salaries	$2,464

(iv) Depreciation on motor vehicles is to be calculated at 25 per cent per annum using the reducing-balance method.
(v) Accrued interest on the bank deposit account amounts to $7,200.
(vi) An accrual for income tax of $30,000 is to be made on the profits of the year.

Requirements
(a) Insert the missing items in: JK Ltd's income statement for the year ended 31 March 20X3.
(b) Insert the missing items in: JK Ltd's statement of financial position at 31 March 20X3.
(c) Calculate the:

Receivables days	☐ days
Payables days	☐ days
Inventories days (use average inventories)	☐ days

THE INTERPRETATION OF FINANCIAL STATEMENTS

(a)

Income statement of JK Ltd for the year ended 31 March 20X3

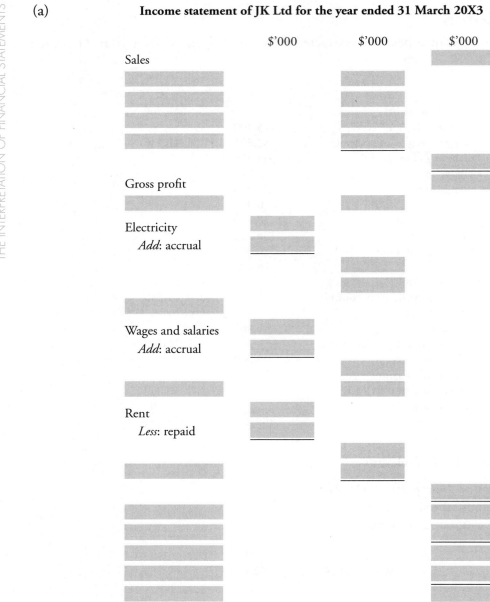

	$'000	$'000	$'000
Sales			
Gross profit			
Electricity			
Add: accrual			
Wages and salaries			
Add: accrual			
Rent			
Less: repaid			

(b)   **Statement of financial position of JK Ltd as at 31 March 20X3**

Assets	Cost ($'000)	Acc. Depreciation ($'000)	Carrying Amount ($'000)
Non-current assets			
Current assets			
Equity and liabilities			
Current liabilities			

? Question 6

The following figures have been extracted from the published financial statements of MBC plc, at 31 October 20X5:

	$m
Ordinary share capital	30
Share premium	3
Reserves	5
	38
6% debentures	10
	48

The profit for the period (after tax of $1 m) for the year to 31 October 20X5 was $4 m and dividends paid amounted to $0.5 m. The company is considering raising a further $10m in the next financial year to finance research and development.

THE INTERPRETATION OF FINANCIAL STATEMENTS

Requirements

(a) Insert the missing words, phrases or figures into the following:

(i) The gearing ratio formula is:

$$\frac{\$ \qquad}{\$ \qquad} \times 100 = \boxed{\qquad} \%$$

(ii) The gearing ratio for MBC plc is:

$$\frac{\$ \qquad}{\$ \qquad} \times 100 = \boxed{\qquad} \%$$

(iii) The return on total capital employed formula is:

$$\frac{\$ \qquad}{\$ \qquad} \times 100 = \boxed{\qquad} \%$$

(iv) The return on total capital employed for MBC plc is:

$$\frac{\$ \qquad}{\$ \qquad} \times 100 = \boxed{\qquad} \%$$

(b) If the company raises an additional $10m through the issue of shares:

(i) Calculate the gearing ratio for the next year:

$$\frac{\$ \qquad}{\$ \qquad} \times 100 = \boxed{\qquad} \%$$

(ii) Calculate the ROCE for the next year:

$$\frac{\$ \qquad}{\$ \qquad} \times 100 = \boxed{\qquad} \%$$

(c) If the company raises an additional $10m through the issue of 6 per cent debentures:

(i) Calculate the gearing ratio for the next year:

$$\frac{\$ \qquad}{\$ \qquad} \times 100 = \boxed{\qquad} \%$$

(ii) Calculate the ROCE for the next year:

$$\frac{\$ \qquad}{\$ \qquad} \times 100 = \boxed{\qquad} \%$$

(d) Insert the missing word in these sentences:

(i) _____ research is into new scientific or technological principles.

(ii) _____ research infers a more practical nature, but not necessarily leading to a practical application.

(iii) _____ expenditure is where there is a clearly defined outcome and which is expected to produce profits.

Question 7

DWS Ltd prepares its financial statements to 30 September each year. On 30 September 20X4 its trial balance was as follows:

	Debit ($)	Credit ($)
Plant and machinery		
Cost	125,000	
Acc. depreciation at 1 October 20X3		28,000
Office equipment:		
Cost	45,000	
Acc. depreciation at 1 October 20X3		15,000
Inventories at 1 October 20X3	31,000	
Purchases and sales	115,000	188,000
Returns inwards and outwards	8,000	6,000
Selling expenses	12,000	
Heat and light	8,000	
Wages and salaries	14,000	
Directors' fees	5,000	
Printing and stationery	6,000	
Telephone and fax	6,000	
Rent and insurance	4,000	
Trade receivables and payables	35,000	33,000
Allowance for receivables at 1 October 20X3		4,000
Bank	3,000	
Petty cash	1,000	
Dividend paid	2,000	
Ordinary shares of 50¢ each		100,000
Share premium account		8,000
General reserve		7,000
Retained earnings balance at 1 October 20X3		34,000
Suspense account	3,000	
	423,000	423,000

The following additional information at 30 September 20X4 is available:

(i) Closing inventories of goods for resale amount to $53,000.
(ii) Prepayments:

Telephone and fax rental	$1,000
Insurance	$1,000

(iii) Accruals:

Wages and salaries	$1,500
Directors' fees	2% of net turnover
Auditor's fees	$3,500

(iv) Bad debts to be written off amount to $3,000.

(v) Allowance for receivables is to be amended to 5 per cent of receivables, after adjusting for bad debts written off.

(vi) The following bookkeeping errors are discovered:

- The purchase of an item of inventory has been debited to the office equipment account, cost $1,200.
- The payment of $1,300 to a payable has been recorded by debiting the bank account and crediting the payable's account.

Any remaining balance on the suspense account is to be added to prepayments or accruals, as appropriate, on the statement of financial position.

(vii) The figure in the trial balance for the bank balance is the balance appearing in the cash book, prior to the reconciliation with the bank statement. Upon reconciliation, it is discovered that

- unpresented cheques amount to $3,000;
- bank charges not entered in the ledgers amount to $4,000.

(viii) Depreciation of non-current assets is to be calculated as follows:

Plant and machinery	10% on cost
Office equipment	33 ⅓ % on the reducing balance at the end of the year

(ix) A final dividend of 1.5¢ per share was declared before the year end, but not paid until after the year end.

(x) $10,000 is to be transferred to general reserves.

(xi) An accrual of $1,000 for income tax is to be made.

Requirements

(a) Insert the missing items in the income statement for the year ended 30 September 20X4.

Income statement of DWS Ltd for the year ended 30 September 20X4

	$	$
Sales		
Gross profit		
Operating profit		

(b) Insert the missing figures in the statement of changes in equity for the year ended 30 September 20X4.

	General Reserve $	Retained Earnings $	Total $
Balance at the start of the period			

(c) Insert the missing items in the statement of financial position at 30 September 20X4.

Statement of financial position of DWS Ltd as at 30 September 20X4

Assets	Cost ($)	Acc. Depreciation ($)	Carrying Amount ($)
Non-current assets			
Current assets			
Equity and liabilities			
Current liabilities			

(d) Calculate the current ratio and the quick ratio.

Current ratio

Ratio	▓▓▓▓	:	▓▓▓▓				
Figures	▓▓▓▓	:	▓▓▓▓	=	▓▓▓▓	:	▓▓▓▓

Quick ratio

Ratio	▓▓▓▓	:	▓▓▓▓				
Figures	▓▓▓▓	:	▓▓▓▓	=	▓▓▓▓	:	▓▓▓▓

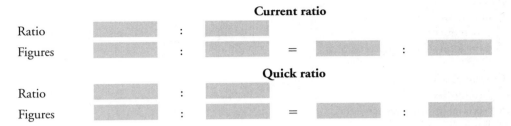

Question 8

You are considering the purchase of a small business, JK, and have managed to obtain a copy of its financial statements for the last complete accounting year to 30 September 20X3. These appear as follows:

Income statement for the year to 30 September 20X3

	$	$
Sale		385,200
Less: cost of goods sold		
Opening inventories	93,250	
Purchases	174,340	
Less closing inventories	(84,630)	
		(182,960)
Gross profit		202,240
Less: expenses		
Selling and delivery costs	83,500	
Administration costs	51,420	
Depreciation	36,760	
		(171,680)
Net profit		30,560

Statement of financial position as at 30 September 20X3

Assets	$	$
Non-current assets		
Assets at cost	235,070	
Less accumulated depreciation	(88,030)	
		147,040
Current assets		
Inventories	84,630	
Receivables and prepayments	36,825	
Bank and cash	9,120	
		130,575
		277,615
Capital and liabilities		
Capital at 1 October 20X2		197,075
Net profit for the year		30,560
Proprietor's drawings		(12,405)
		215,230
Current liabilities		
Payables and accruals		62,385
		277,615

Requirements

Calculate the following accounting ratios from the financial statements presented above:

(i) Net profit percentage

 × 100 = %

(ii) Return on capital employed

 × 100 = %

(iii) Current ratio

× 100 = %

(iv) Quick (acid test) ratio

 × 100 = %

Question 9

The draft financial statements for B Ltd are set out below.

Income statement of B Ltd for the year ended 30 September 20X7

	$'000
Turnover	600
Cost of sales	(410)
Gross profit	190
Profit on sale of non-current asset	10
	200
Operating expenses	(70)
Depreciation	(30)
Operating profit	100
Interest	(15)
Profit for the period	85

Note: Dividends of $50,000 were declared before the year end and paid after the year end.

Statement of financial position of B Ltd as at 30 September 20X6 and 20X7

	20X7 $'000	20X7 $'000	20X6 $'000	20X6 $'000
Assets				
Non-current assets (see note)		450		520
Current assets				
Inventories	65		50	
Receivables	80		30	
Bank and cash	30		15	
		175		95
		625		615
Equity and liabilities				
Share capital		400		400
Retained earnings		95		60
		495		460
Long-term liability				
Loan		20		100
Current liabilities				
Payables	60		20	
Dividends	50		35	
		110		55
		625		615

Note: B Ltd purchased non-current assets for $40,000 during the year ended 30 September 20X7.

Requirements

Insert the missing items into the cash-flow statement and workings below.

Cash-flow statement of B Ltd for the year ended 30 September 20X7

	$'000	$'000
Cash flow from operating activities		
Cash generated from operations – see workings		
Interest		
Cash flows from investing activities		
Cash flows from financing activities		
Net increase in bank and cash		

Workings

	$
Operating activities	
Operating profit	
Adjustment for non-cash flow items	
Adjustment for working capital	
Sale of non-current assets	

Solutions to Revision Questions

14

✓ Solution 1

1.1 Mark-up is gross profit as a percentage of cost of sales, so a mark-up of 40 per cent will result in a selling price of 140 per cent of cost of sales. Thus, if the selling price is $350, this represents 140 per cent of the cost of sales, therefore 100 per cent would be $350/140 \times 100 = \$250 = $ cost price.

  This can be confirmed by checking that 40 per cent of $250 gives a mark-up of $100, and hence a selling price of $350.

  A common mistake is candidates simply calculate 40 per cent of $350 to arrive at $140 as the mark-up (and hence $210 as the cost of sales); this is obviously incorrect as the mark-up is *not* 40 per cent of sales, but 40 per cent of cost of sales.

1.2 Inventories days is found by dividing cost of goods sold by average inventories and multiplying by 365. Average inventories is:

$$\left(\frac{12{,}000 + 10{,}000}{2}\right) = £11{,}000.$$

Cost of goods sold is found as follows:

	$
Opening inventories	12,000
Purchases	80,000
	92,000
Less: closing inventories	(10,000)
Cost of goods sold	82,000

Rate of inventories turnover is therefore:

$$\frac{\$11{,}000}{\$82{,}000} \times 365 = 49 \text{ days}$$

1.3   The answer can be found as follows:

	$
Cost of goods purchased	10,000
Cost of half the goods that have been sold	5,000
Gross profit mark-up on these goods = 5,000 × 120%	6,000
Therefore, selling price =	11,000
Cash discount given = 5% of $11,000	550
Therefore, operating profit = gross profit less discount	5,450

1.4   Answer: (C)

The rate of inventories turnover is found by dividing cost of goods sold by average inventories at cost. Only (C) gives the correct answer of 6 times.

1.5   Answer: (D)

You need only know the correct formula here.

1.6   Reconstruction of income statement:

	$	
Sales	2,400	(100%)
Cost of sales	(1,600)	(66%)
Gross profit	800	(33%)
Expenses	(680)	
Operating profit	120	(i.e. 5%)

1.7   Inventories days is:

$$\frac{\text{Average inventories}}{\text{Cost of goods sold}} \times 365 = \frac{[(4000 + 6000)/2]}{24,500} \times 365 = 74 \text{ days}$$

1.8   Answer: (A)

The gearing ratio is the proportion of long-term loans to shareholders' funds, thus it follows that if long-term loans decrease less than equity, the gearing ratio will rise.

1.9   Answer: (C)

The current ratio is current assets: current liabilities, that is 2,900:1,100 = 2.6:1. The quick ratio is current assets minus inventories: current liabilities, that is 1,000:1,100 = 0.9:1. The current ratio is high compared with the industry standard of 1.8:1, while the quick ratio is within acceptable limits of the 'norm' of 1:1. Without any evidence of the reason for the high inventories levels, its current ratio would appear to be higher than is required, and hence liquidity is poorly controlled.

1.10   Answer: (C)

	$
Sales were	100,800
Cost of sales was	(72,000)
Gross profit	28,800

Gross profit mark-up = Gross profit/Cost of sales × 100 = 28,800/72,000 × 100 = 40%

1.11   Answer: (D)

Transfers between revenue reserves, as mentioned in (A) and (B), have no effect on the overall total of revenue reserves; issuing shares at a premium increases capital reserves; the paying of dividends must be from revenue reserves, so these will decrease.

1.12   Answer: (A)

Current ratio	1,390:420 = 3.3:1	(i.e. high)
Acid test ratio	420:420 = 1:1	(i.e. ideal)

1.13   ROCE = Profit before interest and tax/Average capital employed × 100
Average capital employed = Opening capital + closing capital/2
Closing capital employed = Opening capital plus profit for the year
= 11,200 + 600 = $11,800
Average capital employed = 11,200 + 11,800/2 = $11,500
Thus ROCE = 1,200/11,500 × 100 = 10.43%

1.14   Operating profit/Capital employed = $15,000 = $120,000 × 100 = 12.5%

1.15   Receivables including sales tax/Credit sales including sales tax = $23,500/$117,500 × 365 days = 73 days

1.16   Gearing = Debt/Debt + equity = 75/75 + 500 = 13% (alternative answer debt/equity = 75/500 = 15%)

Solution 2

Workings

Cost of sales	Sales = 120% of cost of sales
	Cost of sales = $240,000 \times {}^{100}\!/_{120}$ = $200,000
Closing inventories	$200,000 × 40/365 = $21,918
Receivables	$240,000 × 30/365 = $19,726
Purchases	Opening inventories + purchases − closing inventories = cost of sales, therefore
	Purchases = cost of sales − opening inventories + closing inventories =
	$200,000 − $55,000 + $21,918 = $166,918
Payables	$166,918 × 50/365 = $22,865
Non-current assets	Sales/4 = $240,000/4 = $60,000
Gross profit	Sales − cost of sales = $240,000 − $200,000 = $40,000
Profit for the period	Gross profit − administration expenses =
	$40,000 − $32,000 = $8,000
Capital employed	Return on capital employed = 10%, therefore average capital employed = $8,000 × 10 = $80,000. If a profit of $8,000 has been made, then opening capital employed must be $4,000 lower than the average ($76,000), and closing capital employed must be $4,000 higher than the average ($84,000)
Net current assets	Capital employed − non-current assets + long-term loans = $84,000 − $60,000 + $3,438 = $27,438
Current assets	Inventories + receivables = $21,918 + $19,726 = $41,644
	The current ratio is 2.2:1, thus the bank balance cannot be overdrawn. Current assets must be Current liabilities × 2.2 = $22,865 × 2.2 = $50,303
Bank balance	Total current assets − (inventories + receivables) = $50,303 − $41,644 = $8,659

Income statement of PK for the year ended 30 June 20X6

	$	$
Sales		240,000
Less: cost of sales		
Opening inventories	55,000	
Purchases	166,918	
	221,918	
Less: closing inventories	(21,918)	
		(200,000)
Gross profit		40,000
Administration costs		(32,000)
Profit for the period		8,000

Statement of financial position of PK as at 30 June 20X6

Assets	$	$
Non-current assets		60,000
Current assets		
Inventories	21,918	
Receivables	19,726	
Bank	8,659	
		50,303
		110,303
Capital and liabilities		
Opening capital		76,000
Profit for the year		8,000
Closing capital		84,000
Non-current liability		
Long-term loan		3,438
Current liabilities		
Payables		22,865
		110,303

✅ Solution 3

(a)

	Department A ($)	Department B ($)	Department C ($)
Physical inventories at 3 May 20X2	3,700	8,100	21,600
Add: sales at cost	300	200	750
Less: purchases	–	(1,500)	–
Less: returns inwards	–	–	(150)
Add: returns outwards	270	–	800
Theoretical inventories	4,270	6,800	23,000

(b) **Calculation of theoretical sales value**

	Department A ($)	Department B ($)	Department C ($)
Opening inventories (1 April 20X2)	4,200	7,800	22,500
Purchases in April 20X2	14,200	8,400	74,000
	18,400	16,200	96,500
Closing inventories (from above)	(4,270)	(6,800)	(23,000)
Cost of sales	14,130	9,400	73,500
Add: mark-up	5,652	2,350	73,500
Sales	19,782	11,750	147,000
Actual takings	(18,750)	(11,750)	(147,000)
Difference	1,032	Nil	Nil

The owner's suspicions justify investigation in respect of Department A.

Solution 4

(a) Initial workings:

		$
(i)	Profit for year	92,000
	Add: loss on disposal	6,000
	Profit before loss on disposal	98,000
(ii)	Carrying amount at 1 May 20X4	206,000
	Less: disposal ($48,000 − $12,000)	(36,000)
	Add: additions	120,000
		290,000
	Carrying amount 30 April 20X5	(277,000)
	Depreciation charge for year	13,000
	Cash flow from operating activities	
	Profit before loss on disposal	98,000
	Add: depreciation charge for year	13,000
	Increase in inventories	(4,000)
	Increase in receivables	(1,500)
	Decrease in payables	(7,000)
		98,500

Cash-flow statement of GH for year ended 30 April 20X5

	$	$
Cash flow from operating activities		98,500
Cash flows from investing activities		
Purchases of non-current assets	(120,000)	
Sale of non-current assets	30,000	
		(90,000)
Cash flows from financing activities		
Long-term loan paid off	(40,000)	
Capital introduced	20,000	
Capital withdrawn	(30,000)	
		(50,000)
Net decrease in bank and cash		(41,500)
Bank and cash at the start of the period		54,000
Bank and cash at the end of the period		12,500

Solution 5

(a) Income statement of JK Ltd for the year ended 31 March 20X3

	$'000	$'000	$'000
Sales			647,400
Opening inventories		15,400	
Purchases		321,874	
Carriage inwards		13,256	
Closing inventories		(19,473)	
			(331,057)
Gross profit			316,343
Carriage outwards		32,460	
Electricity	6,994		
Add: accrual	946		
		7,940	
Local business tax		8,940	
Wages and salaries	138,292		
Add: accrual	2,464		
		140,756	
Postage and stationery		6,984	
Rent	14,600		
Less: prepaid	(2,800)		
		11,800	
Depreciation of vehicles		7,040	
			(215,920)
Operating profit			100,423
Interest receivable			7,200
Profit before tax			107,623
Income tax			(30,000)
Profit for the period			77,623

(b) Statement of financial position of JK Ltd as at 31 March 20X3

	Cost ($'000)	Acc. Depreciation ($'000)	Carrying Amount ($'000)
Assets			
Non-current assets			
Motor vehicles	49,400	(28,280)	21,120
Current assets			
Inventories	19,473		
Receivables	82,851		
Interest receivable	7,200		
Prepayment	2,800		
Bank deposit account	90,000		
Bank current account	77,240		
			279,564
			300,684
Equity and liabilities			
Ordinary shares of $1 each			50,000
Retained earnings			154,220
			204,220
Current liabilities			
Payables	41,936		
Accrual for expenses	3,410		
Income tax	30,000		
Sales tax	16,382		
Employees' income tax	4,736		
			96,464
			300,684

Workings

Retained earnings: $76,597 + $77,623 = $154,220

(c) Receivables days:

$$\frac{\text{Closing receivables} \times 365}{\text{Credit Sales}} = \frac{82,851 \times 365}{647,400} = 47 \text{ days}$$

Payable days:

$$\frac{\text{Closing payables} \times 365}{\text{Credit purchases}} = \frac{41,936 \times 365}{321,874} = 48 \text{ days}$$

Inventories days:

$$\frac{\text{Average inventories}}{\text{Cost of good sold}} = \frac{17,437 \times 365}{331,057} = 19 \text{ days}$$

Solution 6

(a) (i) Gearing ratio

$$\frac{\text{Debt}}{\text{Total capital employed}} \times 100$$

(ii) Gearing ratio for MBC plc

$$\frac{10}{48} \times 100 = 20.8\%$$

(iii) ROCE

$$\frac{\text{Operating profit}}{\text{Average total capital employed}} \times 100$$

(iv) ROCE for MBC plc

$$\frac{£4\,\text{m} + £0.6\,\text{m} + £1\,\text{m}}{(£48\,\text{m} + £44.5\,\text{m}) \div 2} \times 100 = 12.1\%$$

Note that the interest on the debenture is added back ($10m × 6% = $0.6 m), and that to calculate average capital, an adjustment is made for the retained profit of $3.5 m, which is the profit for the period, after the dividend.

(b) (i) $\dfrac{10}{58} \times 100 = 17.2\%$

(ii) $\dfrac{5.6}{53} \times 100 = 10.6\%$

(c) (i) $\dfrac{20}{58} \times 10 = 34.5\%$

(ii) $\dfrac{5.6}{53} \times 100 = 10.6\%$

(d) (i) Pure research is into new scientific or technological principles.
(ii) Applied research infers a more practical nature, but not necessarily leading to a practical application.
(iii) Development expenditure is where there is a clearly defined outcome and which is expected to produce profits.

THE INTERPRETATION OF FINANCIAL STATEMENTS

 Solution 7

(b) Income statement of DWS Ltd for the year ended 30 September 20X4

	$	$
Sales		188,000
Less: returns inwards		(8,000)
		180,000
Opening inventories	31,000	
Purchases (115,000 + 1,200)	116,200	
Returns outward	(6,000)	
Closing inventories	(53,000)	
Cost of goods sold		(88,200)
Gross profit		91,800
Selling expenses	12,000	
Heat and light	8,000	
Wages and salaries (14,000 + 1,500)	15,500	
Directors' fees (5,000 + 3,600)	8,600	
Printing and stationery	6,000	
Telephone and fax (6,000 − 1,000)	5,000	
Rent insurance (4,000 − 1,000)	3,000	
Auditor's fees	3,500	
Bad debts written off	3,000	
Change in allowance for receivables (see workings)	(2,400)	
Bank charges accrued	4,000	
Depreciation of plant and machinery	12,500	
Depreciation of office equipment	9,600	
		(88,300)
Operating profit		3,500
Income tax		(1,000)
Profit for the period		2,500

Statement of changes in equity of DWS Ltd for year ended 30 September 20X4

	General Reserve	*Retained Earnings*	*Total*
	$	$	$
Balance at the start of the period	7,000	34,000	41,000
Profit for the period		2,500	2,500
Dividends		(5,000)	(5,000)
Transfer to general reserve	10,000	(10,000)	
Balance at the end of the period	17,000	21,500	38,500

(b) Statement of financial position of DWS Ltd at 30 September 20X4

Assets	Cost ($)	Acc. Depreciation ($)	Carrying Amount ($)
Non-current assets			
Plant and machinery	125,000	(40,500)	84,500
Office equipment	43,800	(24,600)	19,200
	168,800	(65,100)	103,700
Current assets			
Inventories	53,000		
Receivables (32,000 − 1,600)	30,400		
Prepayments (3,000 + 2,000)	5,000		
Petty cash	1,000		
			89,400
			193,100
Equity and liabilities			
Ordinary shares of 50c each			100,000
Share premium account			8,000
General reserve account			17,000
(7,000 + 10,000)			
Retained earnings			21,500
			146,500
Current liabilities			
Payables (33,000 − 2,600)	30,400		
Accruals (1,500 + 3,600 + 3,500)	8,600		
Overdraft	3,600		
Income tax	1,000		
Declared final dividend	3,000		
			46,600
			193,100

(c)   Current ratio
        Current assets : Current liabilities
        89,400 : 46,600 = 1.92:1
      Quick ratio
        Current assets less inventories : Current liabilities
        (89,400 − 53,000) : 46,600 = 0.78:1

Workings
Re note (vi)

	$
Increase purchases by	1,200
Decrease office equipment by	1,200
Decrease bank by	2,600
Decrease payables by	2,600

This leaves the $3,000 suspense account balance 'untouched'. Therefore, increase prepayments by $3,000 as instructed.

Re notes (iv) and (v)

	$
Receivables in trial balance	35,000
Bad debt written off	(3,000)
	32,000

Five per cent of $32,000 is $1,600; therefore decrease allowance by $2,400.

Depreciation calculations
Plant and machinery: (10% of $125,000) = $12,500
Office equipment: (($45,000 − $1,200) −$15,000) × 33.33% = $9,600

 Solution 8

  (i) Net profit/sales × 100
      30,560/385,200 × 100 = 7.93%
 (ii) Either
      Net profit/average capital employed × 100
      30,560/[(197,075 + 215,230)/2] = 206,152.5 × 100 = 14.82%
      or
      Net profit/closing capital employed × 100
      30,560/215,230 × 100 = 14.20%
(iii) Current assets/current liabilities
      130,575/62,385 = 2.09
 (iv) Quick assets/current liabilities
      45,945/62,385 = 0.74

Solution 9

Cash-flow statement of B Ltd for the year ended 30 September 20X7

	$'000	$'000
Cash flow from operating activities		
Cash generated from operations – see workings		95
Interest		(15)
		80
Cash flows from investing activities		
Sale of non-current assets – see workings	90	
Purchase of non-current asset	(40)	
		50
Cash flows from financing activities		
Dividends paid	(35)	
Repayment of loan	(80)	
		(115)
Net increase in bank and cash		15
Opening bank and cash		15
Closing bank and cash		30

Workings

	$
Operating activities	
Operating profit	100
Adjustment for non-cash flow items	
Profit sale of non-current asset	(10)
Depreciation	30
	120
Adjustment for working capital	
Inventories	(15)
Receivables	50
Payables	40
	95
Sale of non-current assets	
Carrying amount $(520 + 40 - 30 - 450)$	80
Profit on sale	10
Proceeds on sale	90

Preparing for the
Computer-Based Assessments
(CBAs)

Preparing for the Computer-Based Assessments (CBAs)

This section is intended for use when you are ready to start revising for your CBA. It contains:

- a summary of useful revision techniques;
- details of the format of the CBA;
- a bank of revision questions and suggested solutions;
- two mock CBAs.

These should be attempted when you consider yourself to be ready for the CBA.

Revision technique

Planning

The first thing to say about revision is that it is an addition to your initial studies, not a substitute for them. In other words, do not coast along early in your course in the hope of catching up during the revision phase. On the contrary, you should be studying and revising concurrently from the outset. At the end of each week, and at the end of each month, get into the habit of summarising the material you have covered to refresh your memory of it.

As with your initial studies, planning is important to maximise the value of your revision work. You need to balance the demands for study, professional work, family life and other commitments. To make this work, you will need to think carefully about how to make best use of your time.

Begin as before by comparing the estimated hours you will need to devote to revision. Prepare a written schedule setting out the areas you intend to cover during particular weeks, and break that down further into topics for each day's revision. To help focus on the key areas try to establish:

- which areas you are weakest on, so that you can concentrate on the topics where effort is particularly needed;
- which areas are especially significant for the CBA – the topics that are tested frequently.

555

Do not forget the need for relaxation and for family commitments. Sustained intellectual effort is only possible for limited periods, and must be broken up at intervals by lighter activities. And do not continue your revision timetable right up to the moment when you enter the assessment room: you should aim to stop work a day or even two days before the exam. Beyond this point the most you should attempt is an occasional brief look at your notes to refresh your memory.

Getting down to work

By the time you begin your revision you should already have settled into a fixed work pattern: a regular time of day for doing the work, a particular location where you sit, particular equipment that you assemble before you begin and so on.

You should have notes summarising the main points of each topic you have covered. Begin each session by reading through the relevant notes and trying to commit the important points to memory.

Usually this will be just your starting point. Unless the area is one where you already feel very confident, you will need to track back from your notes to the relevant chapter(s) in the *Learning System*. This will refresh your memory on points not covered by your notes and fill in the detail that inevitably gets lost in the process of summarisation.

Tips for the final revision phase

As the CBA approaches, consider the following list of techniques and make use of those that work for you.

- Summarise your notes into more concise form, perhaps on index cards that you can carry with you for revision on the way into work.
- Go through your notes with a highlighter pen, marking key conventions and definitions.
- Summarise the main points in a key area by producing a wordlist, mind map or other mnemonic device.
- On areas that you find difficult, rework questions that you have already attempted and compare your answers in detail with those provided in the *Learning System*.
- Rework questions you attempted earlier in your studies.
- Try out the new CIMA e-success CD's produced by CIMA PUBLISHING for further practice.

Format of the Assessment

Structure of the assessment

The computer-based assessment is 2 hours and comprises 50 compulsary questions with one or more parts.

All questions should be attempted if time permits.

CIMA uses objective test questions in the computer-based assessment. The most common types are:

- Multiple choice, where you have to choose the correct answer from a list of four possible answers. This could either be numbers or text.
- Multiple choice with more choices and answers, for example, choosing two correct answers from a list of eight possible answers. This could either be numbers or text.
- Single numeric entry, where you give your numeric answer, for example, profit is $10,000.
- Multiple entry, where you give several numeric answers, for example, the charge for electricity is $2,000 and accrual is $200.
- True/false questions, where you state whether a statement is true or false, for example, external auditors report to the directors is FALSE.
- Matching pairs of text, for example, the convention 'prudence' would be matched with the statement 'inventories revalued at the lower of cost and net realisable value'.
- Other types could be matching text with graphs and labelling graphs/diagrams.

Weighting of subjects

The current weightings for the syllabus sections are:

- Conceptual and regulatory framework – 20%
- Accounting systems – 20%
- Control of ccounting systems – 15%
- Preparation of accounts – 45%

In broad terms, the entire syllabus will be covered in each assessment.

Revision Questions

The following table links the learning outcomes in the syllabus to the revision questions found within this section.

Learning Outcomes	Questions

(i) Conceptual and Regulatory Framework – 20%

Identify the various user groups which need accounting information and the qualitative characteristics of financial statements	1.12, 1.13
Explain the function of and differences between financial and management accounting systems	1.14
Identify the underlying assumptions, policies and changes in accounting estimates	2.4
Explain and distinguish between capital and revenue, cash and profit, income and expenditure, assets and liabilities	1.7, 2.6, 3.1, 3.2, 5.11
Distinguish between tangible and intangible assets	
Explain the historical cost convention	5.1
Identify the basic methods of valuing assets on current cost, fair value and value in use bases, and their impact on profit measures and statement of financial position values	1.4
Explain the influence of legislation (e.g. Companies Acts, EC directives) and accounting standards on the production of published accounting information for organizations	1.15

(ii) Accounting Systems – 20%

Explain the purpose of accounting records and their role in the accounting system	2.9
Prepare cash and bank accounts, and bank reconciliation statements	1.9, 1.10, 3.4, 22
Prepare petty cash statements under an imprest system	5.3
Prepare accounts for sales and purchases, including personal accounts and control accounts	1.8, 2.11, 2.14, 3.5, 3.10, 4.7, 4.11, 7, 15, 24, 33
Explain the necessity for financial accounting codes and construct a simple coding system	1.16
Prepare nominal ledger accounts, journal entries and a trial balance	1.1, 1.2, 2.1, 2.12, 3.7, 4.3, 4.10, 28, 34
Prepare accounts for indirect taxes	2.3
Prepare accounts for payroll	4.6

(iii) Control of Accounting Systems – 15%

Identify the requirements for external audit and the basic processes undertaken	3.6, 5.4

Explain the purpose and basic procedures of internal audit	1.6
Explain the meaning of fair presentation	1.17
Explain the need for financial controls	1.11
Explain the purpose of audit checks and audit trails	8
Explain the nature of errors, and be able to make accounting entries for them	1.3, 2.2, 2.15, 3.8, 4.4, 4.9, 6, 9, 32
Explain the nature of fraud and basic methods of fraud prevention	18

(iv) Preparation of Accounts for Single Entities – 45%

Prepare accounts using accruals and prepayments	2.5, 3.9
Explain the difference between bad debts and allowances for receivables	5.13
Prepare accounts for bad debts and allowances for receivables	
Calculate depreciation	2.7, 3.11, 4.5, 5.12
Prepare accounts using each method of depreciation and for impairment values	
Prepare a non-current asset register	3.3, 5.2
Prepare accounts for inventories	2.8, 3.13, 5.10, 11.29
Prepare income statements, statements of changes in equity and statements of financial position from trial balance	1.5, 3.14, 4.1, 5.5, 5.15, 12, 13, 17, 20, 23, 25, 27, 30, 31
Prepare manufacturing accounts	2.10, 3.12, 4.12, 5.9
Prepare income and expenditure accounts	4.2, 5.6, 5.7, 26
Prepare accounts from incomplete records	5.8, 14
Interpret basic ratios	2.13, 3.15, 4.13, 4.14, 4.15, 5.14, 10, 19
Prepare statements of cash flows	4.8, 16, 21

Question 1

1.1 A company received an invoice from ABC Ltd for 40 units at $10 each, less 25 per cent trade discount, these being items purchased on credit and for resale. It paid this invoice minus a cash discount of 2 per cent. Which of the following journal entries correctly records the effect of the whole transaction in the company's books?

(A)

	Debit	Credit
ABC Ltd	300	
Purchases		300
Cash	292	
Discount allowed	8	
ABC Ltd		300

(B)

	Debit	Credit
Purchases	300	
ABC Ltd		300
ABC Ltd	300	
Discount allowed		8
Cash		292

(C)

	Debit	Credit
Purchases	300	
ABC Ltd		300
ABC Ltd	300	
Discount allowed		6
Cash		294

(D)

	Debit	Credit
ABC Ltd	400	
Purchases		400
Cash	294	
Discount allowed	106	
ABC Ltd		400

1.2 For which one of the following accounting uses is a spreadsheet least suitable?

(A) Preparing budgets and forecasts.
(B) Recording the dual aspect of accounting transactions.
(C) The preparation of financial statements from a trial balance.
(D) Entering sales invoices in a sales daybook.

1.3 The suspense account shows a debit balance of $100. This could be due to:

(A) entering $50 received from A Turner on the debit side of A Turner's account.
(B) entering $50 received from A Turner on the credit side of A Turner's account.
(C) undercasting the sales daybook by $100.
(D) undercasting the purchases daybook by $100.

1.4 The purchase of a business for more than the aggregate of the fair value of its separable identifiable assets results in the creation of a:

(A) share premium account.
(B) reserve account.
(C) suspense account.
(D) goodwill account.

1.5 A business has opening inventories of $12,000 and closing inventories of $18,000. Purchase returns were $5,000. The cost of goods sold was $111,000.

Purchases were:

$.........

1.6 The responsibility for ensuring that all accounting transactions are properly recorded and summarised in the financial statements lies with:

(A) the external auditors.
(B) the internal auditors.
(C) the shareholders.
(D) the directors.

1.7 A business incurs expenditure on the following research and development activities:

- $120,000 on pure research.
- $200,000 on applied research.
- $350,000 on product development.

The amount that could be capitalised is:

$.........

1.8 Your purchase ledger control account has a balance at 1 October 20X8 of $34,500 credit. During October, credit purchases were $78,400, cash purchases were $2,400, and payments made to suppliers, excluding cash purchases and after deducting cash discounts of $1,200, were $68,900. Purchase returns were $4,700.

The closing balance was:

$.........

1.9 Your firm's bank statement at 31 October 20X8 shows a balance of $13,400. You subsequently discover that the bank has dishonoured a customer's cheque for $300 and has charged bank charges of $50, neither of which is recorded in your cash book. There are unpresented cheques totalling $1,400. You further discover that an automatic receipt from a customer of $195 has been recorded as a credit in your cash book.

Your cash book balance, prior to correcting the errors and omissions, was:

$.........

1.10 Your firm's cash book shows a credit bank balance of $1,240 at 30 April 20X9. Upon comparison with the bank statement, you determine that there are unpresented cheques totalling $450, and a receipt of $140 that has not yet been passed through the bank account. The bank statement shows bank charges of $75 that have not been entered in the cash book.

The balance on the bank statement is:

$.........

1.11 Ensuring that the assets of a company are properly safeguarded and utilised efficiently and effectively is part of:

(A) the stewardship function exercised by the directors.
(B) the external auditor's responsibility.
(C) the function of the financial accountant.
(D) the internal auditor's responsibility.

1.12 Match the following users with their information requirements:

User	Requirements
1. The public	A. The ability of the company to continue, and to pay pensions in the future
2. The government	B. The use of information for taking operational decisions in running the company
3. Employees	C. The polices of a company and how those policies affect the community, for example, health and safety
4. Internal users	D. The performance and financial position of a company and its ability to pay dividends
5. Shareholders	E. The ability of a company to pay taxes, and to administer other taxes, for example, sales tax

1.13 A new student at a college asked the caretaker when and where the accounting exam would take place. The caretaker replied that he thought the economics exam was on a Monday in C/42.

State four characteristics of useful information which are breached by the caretaker's reply.

1. _____
2. _____
3. _____
4. _____

1.14 Management accounts differ from published financial statements because they:

(A) are forecasts of future income and expenditure.
(B) contain more detailed information.
(C) they are never shown to the external auditors.
(D) not prepared from the bookkeeping system.

Which of the above statements is TRUE?

1.15 The management accounts within a limited company are determined by:

(A) company law.
(B) company law and international financial reporting standards.
(C) the shareholders.
(D) the directors.

1.16 Which one of the following attributes is the most important for any code to possess in order to be of use in an accounting system?

(A) easy to change the code number.
(B) each code is a unique number.
(C) a combination of letters and digits to ensure input accuracy.
(D) linked to assets, liabilities, revenue, expenditure and capital.

1.17 A fair presentation (or 'true and fair view') occurs when:

    (A) the financial statements are correct.
    (B) the financial statements have been approved by the auditors.
    (C) the financial statements have been approved by the shareholders.
    (D) the financial statements have been prepared in accordance with international financial reporting standards.

(Total marks = 34)

Question 2

2.1 A credit balance on a ledger account indicates:

    (A) an asset or an expense.
    (B) a liability or an expense.
    (C) an amount owing to the organisation.
    (D) a liability or a revenue.

2.2 An error of principle would occur if:

    (A) plant and machinery purchased was credited to a non-current asset account.
    (B) plant and machinery purchased was debited to the purchases account.
    (C) plant and machinery purchased was debited to the equipment account.
    (D) plant and machinery purchased was debited to the correct account but with the wrong amount.

2.3 If sales (including sales tax) amounted to $27,612.50, and purchases (excluding sales tax) amounted to $18,000, the balance on the sales tax account, assuming all items are subject to sales tax at 17.5 per cent, would be:

Dr/Cr $

………………

2.4 The accounting convention that, in times of rising prices, tends to understate asset values and overstate profits, is the:

    (A) going concern
    (B) prudence
    (C) realisation
    (D) historical cost

2.5 An organisation's year end is 30 September. On 1 January 20X6 the organisation took out a loan of $100,000 with annual interest of 12 per cent. The interest is payable in equal instalments on the first day of April, July, October and January in arrears.

How much should be charged to the income statement for the year ended 30 September 20X6, and how much should be accrued on the statement of financial position?

Income statement	Statement of financial position
$	$

2.6 Recording the purchase of computer stationery by debiting the computer equipment account would result in:

(A) an overstatement of profit and an overstatement of non-current assets.
(B) an understatement of profit and an overstatement of non-current assets.
(C) an overstatement of profit and an understatement of non-current assets.
(D) an understatement of profit and an understatement of non-current assets.

2.7 Depreciation is best described as:

(A) a means of spreading the payment for non-current assets over a period of years.
(B) a decline in the market value of the assets.
(C) a means of spreading the net cost of non-current assets over their estimated useful life.
(D) a means of estimating the amount of money needed to replace the assets.

2.8 An organisation's inventories at 1 July was 15 units @ $3.00 each. The following movements occur:

3 Jul. 20X6	5 units sold at $3.30 each
8 Jul. 20X6	10 units bought at $3.50 each
12 Jul. 20X6	8 units sold at $4.00 each

Closing inventories at 31 July, using the FIFO cost formula would be:

$.........

2.9 Which *one* of the following is a book of prime entry *and* part of the double-entry system?

(A) The journal.
(B) The petty cash book.
(C) The sales daybook.
(D) The purchase ledger.

2.10 A manufacturer has the following figures for the year ended 30 September 20X6:

	$
Direct materials	8,000
Factory overheads	12,000
Direct labour	10,000
Increase in work in progress	4,000

Prime cost is:

$.........

2.11 A sales ledger control account had a closing balance of $8,500. It contained a contra to the purchase ledger of $400, but this had been entered on the wrong side of the control account.

The correct balance on the control account should be:

Dr $.........

2.12 Working capital will reduce by $500 if:

(A) goods costing $3,000 are sold for $3,500 on credit.
(B) goods costing $3,000 are sold for $3,500 cash.
(C) non-current assets costing $500 are purchased on credit.
(D) non-current assets with a carrying amount of $750 are sold for $250 cash.

2.13 From the following information regarding the year to 31 August 20X6, what are the payables days ?

	$
Sales	43,000
Cost of sales	32,500
Opening inventories	6,000
Closing inventories	3,800
Payables at 31 August 20X6	4,750

.... days

2.14 A trader who is not registered for sales tax purposes buys goods on credit. These goods have a list price of $2,000 and the trader is given a trade discount of 20 per cent. The goods carry sales tax at 17.5 per cent.

The correct ledger entries to record this purchase are to debit the purchases account and to credit the supplier's account with:

$.........

2.15 A suspense account was opened when a trial balance failed to agree. The following errors were later discovered:

- A gas bill of $420 had been recorded in the gas account as $240.
- Discount of $50 given to a customer had been credited to discounts received.
- Interest received of $70 had been entered in the bank account only.

The original balance on the suspense account was:

Dr/Cr $

....

(Total marks = 30)

? Question 3

3.1 Your company auditor insists that it is necessary to record items of plant separately and to depreciate them over several years, but that items of office equipment, such as hand-held stapling machines, can be grouped together and written off against profits immediately.

The main reason for this difference in treatment between the two items is because:

(A) treatments of the two items must be consistent with treatment in previous years.
(B) items of plant last for several years, whereas hand-held stapling machines last only for months.
(C) hand-held stapling machines are not regarded as material items.
(D) items of plant are revalued from time to time, whereas hand-held stapling machines are recorded at historical cost.

3.2 Which of the following best explains what is meant by 'capital expenditure'?

Capital expenditure is expenditure:

(A) on non-current assets, including repairs and maintenance.
(B) on expensive assets.
(C) relating to the issue of share capital.
(D) relating to the acquisition or improvement of non-current assets.

3.3 On 1 July 20X7, your non-current asset register showed a carrying amount of $47,500. The ledger accounts showed non-current assets at cost of $60,000 and accumulated depreciation of $15,000. It was discovered that the disposal of an asset for $4,000, giving rise to a loss on disposal of $1,500 had not been recorded in the non-current asset register.

After correcting this omission, the non-current asset register would show a balance that was:

(A) $3,000 lower than the ledger accounts.
(B) $1,500 lower than the ledger accounts.
(C) equal to the ledger accounts.
(D) $1,000 higher than the ledger accounts.

3.4 The bank statement at 31 October 20X7 showed an overdraft of $800. On reconciling the bank statement, it was discovered that a cheque drawn for $80 had not been presented for payment, and that a cheque for $130 from a customer had been dishonoured on 30 October 20X7, but that this had not been notified to you by the bank.

The correct bank balance to be shown in the statement of financial position at 31 October 20X7 is:

Overdrawn $.........

3.5 A credit entry of $450 on X's account in the books of Y could have arisen by:

(A) X buying goods on credit from Y.
(B) Y paying X $450.
(C) Y returning goods to X.
(D) X returning goods to Y.

3.6 The main purpose of an audit is to:

(A) detect errors and fraud.
(B) ensure that the financial statements are accurate.
(C) determine that the financial statements show a fair presentation (or true and fair view) of the financial state of the organisation.
(D) ensure that all transactions have been recorded in the books of accounts.

3.7 A computerised spreadsheet package is *most* suitable for:

(A) recording the dual effect of accounting transactions.
(B) maintaining an audit trail of transactions.
(C) performing bank reconciliations.
(D) preparing a cash budget.

3.8 Where a transaction is entered into the correct ledger accounts, but the wrong amount is used, the error is known as an error of:

(A) omission.
(B) original entry.
(C) commission.
(D) principle.

3.9 On 1 September, the motor expenses account showed 4 months' insurance prepaid of $80 and petrol accrued of $95. During September, the outstanding petrol bill is paid, plus further bills of $245. On 30 September there is a further outstanding bill of $120.

The amount to be shown in the income statement for motor expenses for September is:

$.........

3.10 Your organisation sold goods to PQ Ltd for $800 less trade discount of 20 per cent and cash discount of 5 per cent for payment within 14 days. The invoice was settled by cheque 5 days later. The entries required to record *both* of these transactions are:

		Debit ($)	Credit ($)
A	PQ Ltd	640	
	Sales		640
	Bank	608	
	Discount allowed	32	
	PQ Ltd		640
B	PQ Ltd	640	
	Sales		640
	Bank	600	
	Discount allowed	40	
	PQ Ltd		640
C	PQ Ltd	640	
	Sales		640
	Bank	608	
	Discount received	32	
	PQ Ltd		640
D	PQ Ltd	800	
	Sales		800
	Bank	608	
	Discount allowed	182	
	PQ Ltd		800

3.11 A non-current asset was purchased at the beginning of year 1 for $2,400 and depreciated by 20 per cent per annum by the reducing-balance method. At the beginning of year 4 it was sold for $1,200. The result of this was:

Income statement		$	

3.12 You are given the following information for the year ended 31 October 20X7:

	$
Purchases of raw materials	112,000
Returns inwards	8,000
Decrease in inventories of raw materials	8,000
Direct wages	42,000
Carriage outwards	4,000
Carriage inwards	3,000
Production overheads	27,000
Increase in work in progress	10,000

The value of factory cost of goods completed is:

$.........

3.13 Your organisation uses the weighted average cost formula for inventories. During August 20X7, the following inventories details were recorded:

Opening balance	30 units valued at $2 each
5 August	purchase of 50 units at $2.40 each
10 August	issue of 40 units
18 August	purchase of 60 units at $2.50 each
23 August	issue of 25 units

The cost of the balance at 31 August 20X7 was:

$.........

3.14 During September, your organisation had sales of $148,000, which made a gross profit of $40,000. Purchases amounted to $100,000 and opening inventories were $34,000.

The cost of closing inventories was:

$.........

3.15 During the year ended 31 October 20X7, your organisation made a gross profit of $60,000, which represented a mark-up of 50 per cent. Opening inventories were $12,000 and closing inventories were $18,000.

The rate of inventories turnover was:

.........time

(Total marks = 30)

Question 4

4.1 It is important to produce a trial balance prior to preparing the financial statements because:

(A) it confirms the accuracy of the ledger accounts.
(B) it provides all the figures necessary to prepare the financial statements.
(C) it shows that the ledger accounts contain debit and credit entries of an equal value.
(D) it enables the accountant to calculate any adjustments required.

4.2 The accumulated fund represents:

(A) the total of the shareholders' investment in a company.
(B) the carrying amount of net assets in a not-for-profit organisation.
(C) the excess of income over expenditure in a not-for-profit organisation.
(D) the bank balances of an organisation.

4.3 A computerised accounts package would be *most* useful in maintaining:

(A) the ledger accounts.
(B) the books of prime entry.
(C) a register of non-current assets.
(D) the inventories records.

4.4 An error of original entry would occur if the purchase of goods for resale was:

(A) debited and credited to the correct accounts using the incorrect amount in both cases.
(B) credited to the purchases account and debited to the supplier's account.
(C) debited to a non-current asset account.
(D) entered correctly in the purchases account, but entered in the supplier's account using the wrong amount.

4.5 The reducing-balance method of depreciating non-current assets is more appropriate than the straight-line method when:

(A) there is no expected residual value for the asset.
(B) the expected life of the asset is not capable of being estimated.
(C) the asset is expected to be replaced in a short period of time.
(D) the asset is consumed less in later years than in the early years of use.

4.6 Your organisation paid $240,500 in net wages to its employees during the year. Employees' tax and social security tax amounted to $64,000 and employer's social security tax was $22,000. Employees had contributed $12,500 to a pension scheme.

The amount to be charged against profits for the year, in respect of wages, is:

$.........

4.7 Your organisation has received a statement of account from one of its suppliers, showing an outstanding balance due to them of $1,350. On comparison with your ledger account, the following is determined:

- your ledger account shows a credit balance of $260;
- the supplier has disallowed cash discount of $80 due to late payment of an invoice;
- the supplier has not yet allowed for goods returned at the end of the period of $270;
- cash in transit of $830 has not been received by the supplier.

Following consideration of these items, the unreconciled difference between the two records is:

$.........

4.8 A statement of cash flows can *best* be described as:

(A) a statement showing the effects of profit on cash resources.
(B) a statement of cash inflows and outflows from operating activities.
(C) a statement showing the movement in working capital.
(D) a statement showing the inflows and outflows of cash.

4.9 Your organisation's trial balance at 31 October 20X9 is out of agreement, with the debit side totalling $500 less than the credit side. During November, the following errors are discovered:

- the sales journal for October had been undercast by $150;
- rent received of $240 had been credited to the rent payable account;
- the allowance for receivables, which decreased by $420, had been recorded in the allowance for receivables account as an increase.

Following the correction of these errors, the balance on the suspense account would be:

Dr/Cr $

....

4.10 On 1 November 20X9, your organisation purchased, on credit from XYZ Ltd, office equipment with a catalogue price of $1,000, less trade discount of 20 per cent and cash discount of 5 per cent, if paid for within 14 days. The correct journal entry to record the purchase on 1 November (ignoring sales tax) is:

		Debit ($)	Credit ($)
A	Office equipment	1,000	
	XYZ Ltd		750
	Discount received		250
B	Office equipment	1,000	
	XYZ Ltd		760
	Discount received		240
C	Office equipment	800	
	XYZ Ltd		800
D	Office equipment	800	
	XYZ Ltd		760
	Discount received		40

4.11 The following sales ledger control account contains some inaccurate entries:

Sales ledger control account

	$		$
Opening receivables	14,500	Credit sales	53,500
Discounts allowed	350	Returns	1,400
Receipts from receivables	51,200	Contra to purchase ledger	500

The correct closing receivables figure should be:

$.........

4.12 The following information relates to a business at its year end:

	$'000
Sales	600
Inventories at beginning of year	
Raw materials	20
Work in progress	4
Finished goods	68
Inventories at end of year	
Raw materials	22
Work in progress	8
Finished goods	60
Purchases of raw materials	100
Returns inwards	10
Returns outwards	15
Carriage inwards	8
Carriage outwards	12
Direct labour	80

The prime cost of goods manufactured during the year is:

$.........

4.13 An increase in the gross profit margin of a business is most likely to be due to which *one* of the following combinations:

	Selling price per unit	*Quantity sold*	*Cost per unit*
A	increased	no change	increased
B	no change	increased	no change
C	no change	no change	decreased
D	decreased	increased	increased

4.14 A business has the following capital and long-term liabilities:

	31.10.X8 ($m)	*31.10.X9 ($m)*
12% debentures	20	40
Issued share capital	15	30
Share premium	3	18
Retained earnings	22	12

On 31 October 20X9, its gearing ratio, compared with that on 31 October 20X8, has:

(A) risen, resulting in greater risk for shareholders.
(B) risen, resulting in greater security for shareholders.
(C) fallen, resulting in greater security for shareholders.
(D) remained the same.

4.15 A business has the following trading accounts:

	$'000	Year ended 31 October 20X8 $'000	$'000	Year ended 31 October 20X9 $'000
Sales		2,000		2,650
Less: cost of sales				
Opening inventories	75		85	
Purchases	1,260		1,330	
	1,335		1,415	
Less: closing inventories	(85)		(115)	
		(1,250)		(1,300)
Gross profit		750		1,350

During the year ended 31 October 20X9, inventories days, compared with that for the year ended 31 October 20X8, have:

(A) increased, with a possible beneficial effect on liquidity.
(B) increased, with a possible detrimental effect on liquidity.
(C) decreased, with a possible detrimental effect on liquidity.
(D) decreased, with a possible beneficial effect on liquidity.

(Total marks = 30)

❓ Question 5

5.1 In times of rising prices, the historical cost convention results in:

(A) inventories being valued at cost price if this is higher than their net realisable value.
(B) non-current assets being valued at their original cost, with no adjustment for depreciation.
(C) profits being overstated and statement of financial position values being understated.
(D) profits being understated and statement of financial position values being overstated.

5.2 An organisation's non-current asset register showed a carrying amount of $271,200. The non-current asset account in the nominal ledger showed a carrying amount of $251,200. The difference could be due to not having removed from the non-current asset register a disposed asset that had:

(A) disposal proceeds of $30,000 and a profit on disposal of $10,000.
(B) disposal proceeds of $30,000 and a carrying amount of $10,000.
(C) disposal proceeds of $30,000 and a loss on disposal of $10,000.
(D) disposal proceeds of $10,000 and a carrying amount of $10,000.

5.3 An organisation restores its petty cash balance to $250 at the end of each month. During October, the total expenditure column in the petty cash book was calculated as being $210, and hence the imprest was restored by this amount. The analysis columns, which had been posted to the nominal ledger, totalled only $200. This error would result in:

(A) the trial balance being $10 higher on the debit side.
(B) the trial balance being $10 higher on the credit side.
(C) no imbalance in the trial balance.
(D) the petty cash balance being $10 lower than it should be.

5.4 The *stewardship function* is carried out by:

(A) the internal auditors.
(B) the external auditors.
(C) the treasurer of a not-for-profit organisation.
(D) the management of an organisation.

5.5 An increase in inventories of $500, a decrease in the bank balance of $800 and an increase in payables of $2,400, will result in:

(A) an increase in working capital of $2,700.
(B) a decrease in working capital of $2,700.
(C) an increase in working capital of $2,100.
(D) a decrease in working capital of $2,100.

5.6 On 1 November 20X8, a club's membership subscriptions account showed a debit balance of $200 and a credit balance of $90. During the year ended 31 October 20X9, subscriptions received amounted to $4,800. On 31 October 20X9, subscriptions paid in advance amounted to $85, and subscriptions in arrears, and expected to be collected, amounted to $50.

The amount to be transferred to the income and expenditure statement in respect of subscriptions for the year ended 31 October 20X9 is:

$.........

5.7 The *accumulated fund* represents:

(A) the bank balances of an organisation.
(B) the carrying amount net assets in a not-for-profit organisation.
(C) the excess of receipts over payments in a not-for-profit organisation.
(D) the total of shareholders' funds.

5.8 A sole trader's income statement for the year ended 31 October 20X9 was drawn up as follows:

	$	$
Gross profit		87,000
Less: expenses		
Own wages	18,000	
Assistant's wages	8,000	
General expenses	16,000	
		(42,000)
Net profit		45,000

All wages were paid by cheque from the business bank account. During the year, the sole trader had paid his private telephone bills of $800 from the business bank account, and recorded these as 'drawings'. He had also paid $2,700 from his private funds for petrol (of which one-third was for private use), but had made no entries in his accounts for these payments.

His capital at 1 November 20X8 was $28,000. His capital at 31 October 20X9 is:

$.........

5.9   The following information is given for the year ended 31 October 20X0:

	$
Purchases of raw materials	56,000
Returns inwards	4,000
Increase in inventories of raw materials	1,700
Direct wages	21,000
Carriage inwards	2,500
Production overheads	14,000
Decrease in work in progress	5,000

The value of factory cost of goods completed is:

$.........

5.10   Your organisation uses the weighted average cost formula for inventories. During September 20X0, the following inventory details were recorded:

Opening balance	60 units valued at $4 each
6 September	Purchase of 100 units at $4.80 each
9 September	Sale of 80 units
12 September	Purchase of 120 units at $5 each
23 September	Sale of 50 units

The value of the inventory on 30 September 20X0 was:

$.........

5.11   Goodwill is most appropriately classed as:

(A) a fictitious asset.
(B) a semi-non-current asset.
(C) a tangible asset.
(D) an intangible asset.

5.12   The reducing-balance method of depreciating non-current assets is more appropriate than the straight-line method when:

(A) the expected life of the asset is short.
(B) the asset is expected to decrease in value by a fixed percentage of cost each year.
(C) the expected life of the asset cannot be estimated accurately.
(D) the asset is expected to be consumed less in later years than in the early years of its life.

5.13 An increase in the allowance for receivables would result in:

(A) a decrease in working capital.
(B) an increase in working capital.
(C) an increase in liabilities.
(D) an increase in net profit.

5.14 The gross profit mark-up is 60 per cent where sales are $240,000 and:

(A) cost of sales is $96,000.
(B) gross profit is $144,000.
(C) gross profit is $150,000.
(D) cost of sales is $150,000.

5.15 Revenue reserves would increase if a company:

(A) issues shares at a premium.
(B) makes a transfer from retained earnings to general reserves.
(C) retains profits.
(D) increases its current bank balances.

(Total marks = 30)

Question 6

The trial balance of OBX plc for the year ended 30 April 20X6 showed the following totals:

Debit $723,626   Credit $721,405

The totals included the sales ledger control account balance of $104,637.

A suspense account was opened for the difference. The profit for the year ended 30 April 20X6 was then calculated as being $227,642 and the suspense account balance was dealt with by including it on the statement of financial position as appropriate.

Later investigation revealed the following:

1. An invoice of $46 for stationery had been entered in the stationery account as $64, but was correctly entered in the payable's account.
2. One of the pages of the sales daybook had been incorrectly totalled as $2,463 instead of $2,643, and a credit sale of $325 had been omitted from another page.
3. Discounts allowed of $950 had been omitted from the sales ledger control account.
4. Bank interest received of $220 had been correctly entered in the revenue account but had not been entered in the cash book.
5. A contra entry between the sales and purchase ledgers of $426 had been debited to the sales ledger control account and credited to the purchase ledger control account.
6. During the year, a non-current asset costing $3,000 was sold for $750. Its carrying amount at the date of disposal was $920. The proceeds were entered in the cash book, but no other entries regarding the disposal were made.

Requirements

(a) Insert the missing items into the suspense account given below to record the correction of the above errors, carrying down any unresolved balance.

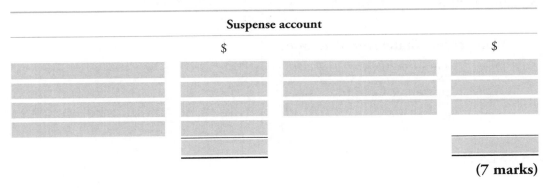

Suspense account

(7 marks)

(b) Insert the missing items into the sales ledger control account given below in order to calculate the corrected balance after the adjustment for the errors now discovered.

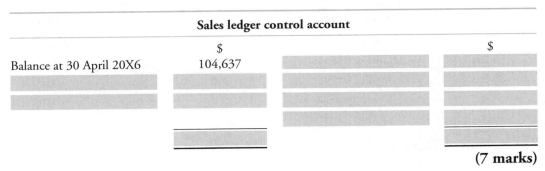

Sales ledger control account

	$		$
Balance at 30 April 20X6	104,637		

(7 marks)

(c) Insert the missing items below in order to calculate the revised net profit after the correction of the errors.

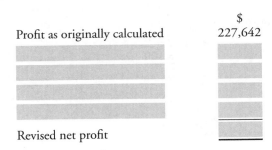

	$
Profit as originally calculated	227,642
Revised net profit	

(6 marks)
(Total marks = 20)

Question 7

M Kingston & Co. Ltd received the following statement of account from Wang & Son on 31 January 20X6:

Wang & Son Statement of account

Date: 31 January 20X6

To: M Kingston & Co. Ltd

High Lane

KE3 2DE

Date	Reference	Debits	Credits	Balance
20X6		$	$	$
1 Jan.	Balance b/f			3,000 Dr
13 Jan.	(a) Invoice 01256	1,000		4,000 Dr
15 Jan.	(b) Cash received		2,800	
	(c) Invoice 01287	3,600		4,800 Dr
16 Jan.	(d) Credit Note 0062	50		4,750 Dr
20 Jan.	(e) Invoice 01364	500		5,250 Dr
28 Jan.	(f) Invoice 01395	800		6,050 Dr
30 Jan.	(g) Credit Note 0070		100	5,950 Dr

The account of Wang & Son in the ledger of M Kingston & Co. Ltd is as follows:

Wang & Son

20X6			$	20X6			$
13 Jan.	(h)	Cash	2,800	1 Jan.	Balance b/f		3,000
	(i)	Discount	200	15 Jan.	Invoice 01256		1,000
18 Jan.	(j)	Credit Note 0062	150	17 Jan.	Invoice 01287		3,600
30 Jan.	(k)	Cash	1,400	22 Jan.	Invoice 01364		500
31 Jan.	(l)	Debit Note 65	300				
		Balance c/d	3,250				
			8,100				8,100

Requirements

(a) Insert the missing items below in order to reconcile the two balances.

	$
Balance per supplier's statement	5,950
Adjustments:	
Add/less:	
Add/less:	
Corrected balance	
Balance per ledger	3,250
Add/less:	
Add/less:	
Add/less:	
Add/less:	
Correct balance	

*Delete as appropriate.

(8 marks)

(b) Match the following descriptions to the letters (a) to (l).

(i) This is an invoice from Wang to Kingston. It will have been entered in Wang's records as soon as it was issued, but has not yet been received by Kingston. Letter _____

(ii) This is a credit note issued by Wang and entered in its records at once; it has not yet been received by Kingston. Letter _____

(iii) This is cash discount that has been deducted by Kingston upon payment of the outstanding balance at the beginning of January, ignored or disallowed by Wang. Letter_____

(iv) This is cash paid by Kingston at the end of the month, and entered in its ledger account at once; it has not yet been received by Wang. Letter _____

(v) This is a debit note issued by Kingston perhaps due to goods returned; credit note not yet received by Wang. Letter _____

(10 marks)

(c) The correct figure to be shown in the statement of financial position of M Kingston & Co. Ltd is $ _____ and is a current **asset/liability** (delete as appropriate).

(2 marks)
(Total marks = 20)

? Question 8

In connection with controls over accounting documents and records that would help to prevent errors or fraud in the operation of the computerised ledger, complete the missing words in these sentences:

(i) invoices relate to a properly authorised _____;

(ii) numbered _____ should be raised, for example by storekeeper, to ensure that goods have been inspected and taken into stores;

(iii) adequate _____ of duties exists;

(iv) purchase ledger records should be checked against _____ statements.

(8 marks)

? Question 9

At the year end of TD, an imbalance in the trial balance was revealed that resulted in the creation of a suspense account with a credit balance of $1,040.

Investigations revealed the following errors:

(i) A sale of goods on credit for $1,000 had been omitted from the sales account.

(ii) Delivery and installation costs of $240 on a new item of plant had been recorded as a revenue expense.

(iii) Cash discount of $150 on paying a supplier, JW, had been taken, even though the payment was made outside the time limit.

(iv) Inventories of stationery at the end of the period of $240 had been ignored.

(v) A purchase of raw materials of $350 had been recorded in the purchases account as $850.

(vi) The purchase returns daybook included a sales credit note for $230 that had been entered correctly in the account of the receivable concerned, but included with purchase returns in the nominal ledger.

Requirements

(a) Insert the missing items into the table below to show the journal entries required to correct each of the above errors.

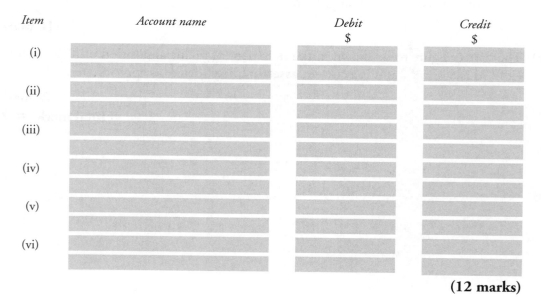

Item	Account name	Debit $	Credit $
(i)			
(ii)			
(iii)			
(iv)			
(v)			
(vi)			

(12 marks)

(b) Insert the missing items into the suspense account given below to show the corrections to be made.

Suspense account

	$	$	

(3 marks)

(c) Prior to the discovery of the errors, TD's gross profit for the year was calculated at $35,750 and the net profit for the year at $18,500.

Insert the missing items below in order to calculate the revised gross and net profit figures after the correction of the errors.

	$
Gross profit – original	35,750
*Add/less**:	
*Add/less**:	
*Add/less**:	
Revised gross profit	
Net profit – original	18,500
*Add/less**:	
*Add/less**:	
*Add/less**:	
*Add/less**:	
Revised net profit	

(5 marks)
(Total marks = 20)

? Question 10

ARH plc has the following results for the last 2 years of trading:

Income statement of ARH plc

For the year ended	31.12.X4	31.12.9X5
	$'000	$'000
Sales	14,400	17,000
Less: cost of sales	(11,800)	(12,600)
Gross profit	2,600	4,400
Less: expenses	(1,200)	(2,000)
Operating profit	1,400	2,400

Statement of changes in equity of ARH plc

For the year ended	31.12.X4	31.12.X5
Retained earnings start of period	320	1,200
Total comprehensive income for the period	1,400	2,400
Dividends paid	(520)	(780)
Retained earnings end of period	1,200	2,820

Statement of financial position of ARH plc

	At 31 December 20X4		At 31 December 20X5	
Assets	$'000	$'000	$'000	$'000
Non-current assets		2,500		4,000
Current assets				
Inventories	1,300		2,000	
Receivables	2,000		1,600	
Bank balances	2,400		820	
		5,700		4,420
		8,200		8,420
Equity and liabilities				
2.4 million ordinary shares of $1 each		2,400		2,400
Revaluation reserves		500		500
Retained earnings		1,200		2,820
		4,100		5,720
Non-current liabilities				
10% debentures		2,600		–
Current liabilities				
Payables		1,500		2,700
		8,200		8,420

Requirements

Calculate for 20X4 and 20X5 the:

(i) gross profit margin,
(ii) operating profit margin,
(iii) return on capital employed (ROCE), using average capital.

(6 marks)

 ## Question 11

(a) You are given the following details regarding inventory movements during April 20X6:

1 Apr.	100 units on hand, cost $10 each
8 Apr.	Inventory sold for $360, with a mark-up of 50%
18 Apr.	38 units purchased for $480 less trade discount of 5%
20 Apr.	50 units sold
23 Apr.	35 units sold
28 Apr.	20 units purchased for $260

You are required to insert the missing items into the inventory record cards given below, using the first in, first out (FIFO), last in, first out (LIFO) and average cost (AVCO) cost formulas, in order to determine the quantity and cost of closing inventory at 30 April 20X6.

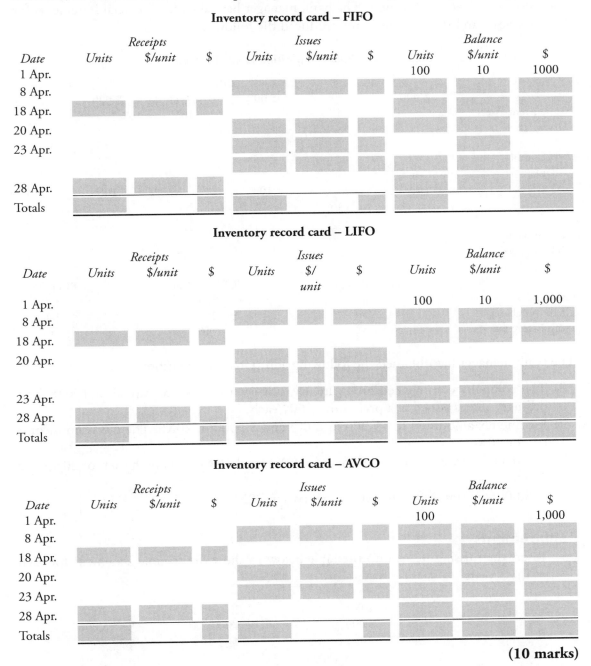

Inventory record card – FIFO

Inventory record card – LIFO

Inventory record card – AVCO

(10 marks)

(b)   If the physical inventory count carried out at 30 April revealed a closing inventory quantity of 50 units, which of the following could be possible reasons for the discrepancy.

   (i)   Recording of an issue at too high a level
  (ii)   Recording of a receipt at too high a level
 (iii)   Recording of a receipt at too low a level
 (iv)   Recording of an issue at too low a level.

(2 marks)
(Total marks = 12)

Question 12

The directors of R Ltd are hoping to negotiate an overdraft to provide working capital for a proposed expansion of business. The bank manager has called for financial statements for the last 3 years and the directors have produced the following extracts:

Statements of financial position as at 31 December

	20X4		20X5		20X6	
	$'000	$'000	$'000	$'000	$'000	$'000
Non-current assets		147		163		153
Current assets						
Inventories	27		40		46	
Receivables	40		45		52	
Bank	6		15		8	
	73		100		106	
		146		200		212
		293		363		365
Current liabilities						
(including tax)		33		45		43

	20X4 ($'000)	20X5 ($'000)	20X6 ($'000)
Credit sales	360	375	390
Credit purchases	230	250	280
Profit before tax	32	46	14

The bank manager has obtained the following additional information:

(i) The company commenced on 1 January 20X4 with an issued capital of 100,000 $1 ordinary shares issued at a premium of 60¢ each.

(ii) Income tax amounted to $5,000 in 20X5 and $6,000 in 20X6. There was no income tax for 20X4.

(iii) Dividends paid were of 5¢ per share in 20X4, and 10¢ per share in each of 20X5 and 20X6.

(iv) $18,000 was transferred to general reserves in 20X5.

Requirements

(a) Insert the missing items into the table below to show the income statement for each of the 3 years.

	20X4 $'000	20X5 $'000	20X6 $'000

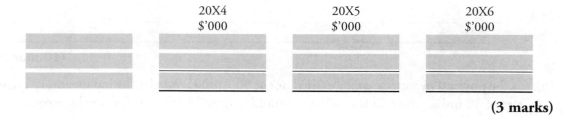

(3 marks)

(b) Insert the missing items into the table below to show the statement of changes in equity for each of the 3 years.

	20X4 $'000		20X5 $'000		20X6 $'000	
	Gen. res	Retained earnings	Gen. Res	Retained earnings	Gen. Res	Retained earnings
Balance at start of period						

(3 marks)

(c) Insert the missing items into the table below to show the capital section of the statement of financial position for each of the 3 years.

Description	20X4 ($'000)	20X5 ($'000)	20X6 ($'000)
Totals			

(4 marks)

(d) (i) The formula for receivables days is:

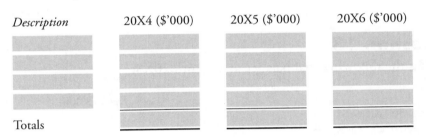

(ii) The receivables days in each of the 3 years is:

For 20X4:   days
For 20X5:   days
For 20X6:   days

(iii) The formula for payables days is:

(iv) The payables days in each of the 3 years is (*Note*: remember to exclude taxation from payables):

For 20X4:		days
For 20X5:		days
For 20X6:		days

(6 marks)

(e) Deleting text as appropriate, complete the following paragraph, which discusses how the above changes in receivables and payables days might affect the proposed overdraft.

The company appears to be *increasing/decreasing* the length of credit given to customers, which *slows down/speeds up* the receipt of cash. At the same time it is *increasing/decreasing* the length of credit from suppliers, which *slows down/speeds up* the payment of cash. These two actions combined will cause the amount of cash available to *increase/decrease*. If these payment periods could be brought more into line with each other, the amount of overdraft required will be *higher/lower*.

(6 marks)
(Total marks = 22)

Question 13

APW Ltd has the following trial balance at 30 April 20X8:

	Debit ($'000)	Credit ($'000)
Ordinary shares, 50¢ each		1,500
Irredeemable preference shares, 7%		400
Share premium account		200
Retained earnings at 1 May 20X7		580
8% debentures		500
Buildings – at valuation	3,500	
Buildings – accumulated depreciation at 1 May 20X7		1,300
Factory plant – cost	1,200	
Factory plant – accumulated depreciation at 1 May 20X7		200
Office equipment – cost	250	
Office equipment – accumulated depreciation at 1 May 20X7		50
Delivery vehicles – cost	600	
Delivery vehicles – accumulated depreciation at 1 May 20X7		360
Inventories at 1 May 20X7		
Raw materials	234	
Work in progress	182	
Finished goods	98	
Receivables and payables	136	124
Sales tax account		74
Employees' income tax and social security tax payable		62
Bank		248
Sales		2,660
Purchases of raw materials	785	
Carriage outwards	20	
Carriage inwards	40	
Returns	104	65
Direct labour	372	
Indirect factory labour	118	
Office salaries	130	

Indirect factory overheads	63	
Heat, light and power	120	
Rent and insurance	130	
Administration expenses	55	
Debenture interest	20	
Dividends paid – preference	28	
Dividends paid – ordinary	140	
Bank interest received		12
Bank charges	10	
	8,335	8,335

You are given the following information at 30 April 20X8:

(i) Inventories are as follows:

Raw materials	$256,000
Work in progress	$118,000
Finished goods	$123,000

You ascertain that finished goods consist of three products:

Product	Cost included in above valuation ($)	Net realisable value ($)
Alpha	71,000	75,000
Beta	31,000	23,000
Delta	21,000	23,000

(ii) Depreciation is to be calculated as follows:

Buildings	5% on valuation (of which 40% is to be apportioned to the factory)
Factory plant	10% on cost
Office equipment	20% on the reducing balance
Delivery vehicles	20% on cost

(iii) Wages and salaries costs accrued are:

	Direct labour ($)	Indirect factory labour ($)	Office salaries ($)
Gross wages	34,000	14,000	25,000
Employees' income Tax and social security deducted	6,700	2,800	3,900
Employer's social security tax	3,000	1,000	2,000

(iv) Income tax of $80,000 for the year is to be accrued.
(v) Heat, light and power accrued amounts to $15,000. Forty per cent of heat, light and power is to be apportioned to the factory.
(vi) Rent and insurance prepaid amounts to $10,000. Thirty per cent of rent and insurance is to be apportioned to the factory.
(vii) The debentures were issued in 20X4, and are due for repayment in 20Y4.

Requirements

(a)   Insert the missing items in the income statement for the year ended 30 April 20X8.

Income statement of APW Ltd for the year ended 30 April 20X8

	$'000	$'000	$'000	$'000
Sales				
Opening inventories of finished goods				
Opening inventories of raw material				
Prime cost				
Cost of production transferred to finished goods inventories				
Gross profit				

Operating profit

Profit before tax

(10 marks)

(b) Insert the missing items in the statement of changes in equity for the year ended 30 April 20X8.

Statement of changes in equity of APW Ltd for the year ended 30 April 20X8

Retained Earnings

Balance at start of period

(13 marks)

(c) Which are the two principal accounting conventions that affect the valuation of inventories.

(i) _____

(ii) _____

(7 marks)

(Total marks = 30)

Question 14

The computerised accounting system used by FLS Ltd developed a program error during the production of the trial balance at 30 September 20X8. The accountant presented you with the following balances and supporting information:

Authorised share capital comprised 10 million ordinary shares with a par value of 50¢ each, of which 6 million had been issued at a premium of 5¢ per share, and 1 million 5 per cent irredeemable preference shares issued at par, at $1 each.

The statement of finacial position at 30 September 20X7 included the following balances:

	$'000
Retained earnings	600
Revaluation reserve	1,250
Inventories	1,250
Land at valuation	5,800
Buildings at cost	3,800
Plant at cost	2,800
Accumulated depreciation on buildings	800
Accumulated depreciation on plant	600
Goodwill	2,000
Long-term loan	8,000
Administration costs prepaid	100
Ordinary dividends owing	300
Receivables	1,850
Allowance for receivables	80
Payables	1,050
Bank overdraft	520
Income tax owing	100

During the year to 30 September 20X8, the following transactions had been recorded:

	$'000
Sales	14,000
Purchases	7,400
Returns outwards	75
Selling and distribution costs paid	2,750
Administration costs paid	2,400
Bad debts written off	200
Preference dividend paid	50
Ordinary interim dividend paid	150
Final dividend from previous year paid	300
Half-year's loan interest paid	400
Income tax paid	100
Receipts from receivables	13,300
Payments to payables	7,525

At 30 September 20X8, the following additional figures were extracted:

	$'000
Trade receivables	2,350
Trade payables	850
Inventories	1,450

Requirements

(a)   Insert the missing items in the bank account for the year ended 30 September 20X8.

Bank account of FLS Ltd for the year ended 30 September 20X8

	$'000		$'000
		Balance b/fwd	
Balance c/fwd			

(3 marks)

(b)   Insert the missing items in a trial balance at 30 September 20X8.

Trial balance of FLS as at 30 September 20X8

	Debit ($'000)	Credit ($'000)
Retained earnings		
Revaluation reserve		
Inventories at 30 September 20X7		
Land at valuation		
Buildings at cost		
Plant at cost		
Accumulated depreciation on buildings at 30 September 20X7		
Accumulated depreciation on plant at 30 September 20X7		
Goodwill		
Long-term loan		
Allowance for receivables at 30 September 20X7		
Sales		
Purchases		
Returns outwards		
Selling and distribution costs		
Administration costs		
Bad debts written off		
Dividends paid – preference		
Dividends paid – ordinary		
Loan interest (half year)		
Receivables		
Payables		
Bank account		
Share capital – ordinary		
Share premium account		
Share capital – preference		

(10 marks)

(c)   Insert the missing items in an income statement, and statement of changes in equity, for the year ended 30 September 20X8, to include the following adjustments:

- the sales figure above includes $100,000 cash received with an order on 28 September 20X8; the goods were not despatched until 14 October 20X8;
- selling and distribution costs prepaid were $50,000 and administration costs accrued were $25,000;
- the allowance for receivables figure is to be amended to 2 per cent of trade receivables;

- calculation for depreciation is to be 2 per cent on cost for buildings, and 5 per cent on the reducing balance for plant;
- an accrual of $140,000 is to be made for income tax on the year's profits;
- a final dividend of 10c per ordinary share was declared before the year end and paid after the year end.

Income statement of FLS Ltd for year ended 30 September 20X8

	$'000	$'000	$'000

Gross profit

Operating profit

Loan interest

Profit before tax

Profit for the period

Statement of changes in equity of FLS Ltd for year ended 30 September 20X8

Retained earnings

Balance at start of period

(10 marks)

(d) Calculate the gearing ratio at 30 September 20X8.

Analysis of total capital employed

(7 marks)
(Total 30 marks)

$$\text{Gearing ratio} = \frac{}{} \times 100 = \%$$

? Question 15

You are responsible for maintaining the journals and ledger accounts for your organisation. Sales are currently all for cash, but the managers plan to offer credit to customers in the future, in order to increase business activity.

At 1 October 20X8, there are the following balances on payables accounts:

Ibrahim	$1,250
J Hall	$150

During the month of October 20X8, you compile the following journals:

Purchases daybook

Date 20X8	Name	Net ($)	Sales tax ($)	Gross ($)
4 Oct.	Ibrahim	6,000	1,050	7,050
11 Oct.	J Bolton	30,000	5,250	35,250
13 Oct.	Z Rhawandala	5,000	875	5,875
15 Oct.	Ibrahim	12,000	2,100	14,100
31 Oct.	Totals	53,000	9,275	62,275

Returns outwards daybook

Date 20X8	Name	Net ($)	Sales tax ($)	Gross ($)
3 Oct.	J Bolton	2,000	350	2,350
28 Oct.	Ibrahim	600	105	705
31 Oct.	Totals	2,600	455	3,055

Petty cash book

Date	Debit ($)	Details	Total ($)	Postage ($)	Travel ($)	Pur. Ledger ($)
1 Oct.	600	Balance b/f				
6 Oct.		Parcel post	65	65		
10 Oct.		Bus fares	20		20	
12 Oct.		G Hall (train ticket)	125		125	
14 Oct.		Parcel post	24	24		
16 Oct.		Travel reimbursed	85		85	
18 Oct.		Parcel post	27	27		
21 Oct.		J Hall	150			150
			496	116	230	150
31 Oct.	496	Bank				
		Balance c/f	600			
	1,096		1,096			

You have extracted the following details from the cash book for October:

- Cash sales in the month were $61,100, including sales tax at 17.5 per cent.
- Paid to Ibrahim on 4 October, his opening balance less cash discount of 2 per cent.

Requirements

(a) Insert the missing items into the following ledger accounts.

Note: in the 'Transactions' columns only *one* of the debit or credit columns is to be completed for each transaction. All other boxes must be completed.

Date	Description	Transactions Debit ($)	Credit ($)	Balance ($)	Debit or credit?
		Ibrahim			
1 Oct.	Balance b/f			1,250	Cr
		J Hall			
1 Oct.	Balance b/f			150	Cr
		J Bolton			

Z Rhawandala

Sales Tax

Sales

Purchases

Returns outwards

Post

Discounts received

Travel

(11 marks)

(b) You later realise that the purchase from Z Rhawandala is for office equipment. Insert the missing words in these sentences

    (i) Office equipment should have been debited to a _____.

    (ii) The profit will have been _____ by $5,000 less any depreciation charge.

(3 marks)
(Total marks = 14)

Question 16

AMS Ltd made a gross profit of $239,000 in the year to 31 August 20X8. Expenses amounted to $159,000, which included interest of $30,000 payable on a long-term loan, depreciation on plant of $50,000, and depreciation on premises of $25,000. Income tax in the income statement was $10,000 and dividends declared before the year-end, but paid after the year-end, were $45,000.

The statements of financial position of AMS Ltd at 31 August 20X8 and 20X7 were as follows:

	20X8	20X8	20X7	20X7
Assets	$'000	$'000	$'000	$'000
Non-current assets				
Premises		1,200		1,170
Plant and machinery		800		700
		2,000		1,870
Current assets				
Inventories	450		550	
Receivables	700		680	
Bank and cash	300		–	
		1,450		1,230
		3,450		3,100
Equity and liabilities				
Ordinary shares of $1 each		1,800		1,300
Share premium		400		300
Retained earnings		392		367
		2,592		1,967
Long-term liabilities				
Loan		200		400
Current liabilities				
Payables	600		670	
Taxation	10		12	
Dividends	45		11	
Bank overdraft			40	
		658		733
		3,450		3,100

During the year ended 31 August 20X8, plant that had cost $85,000 was sold at a loss of $10,000. The sale proceeds were $50,000. The loss was deducted in the income statement.

Requirements

(a) Insert the missing items into the cash-flow statement, and supporting workings, given below.

Calculation of operating profit

Cash generated from operations

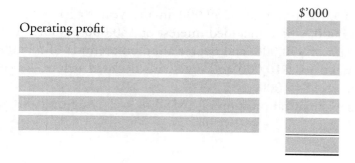

Operating profit

$'000

Purchase cost of non-current assets

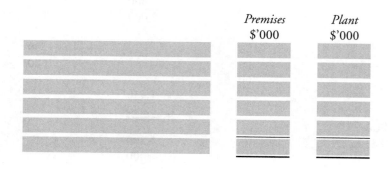

Premises $'000   *Plant* $'000

Cash-flow statement of AMS Ltd for the year ended 31 August 20X8

$'000 $'000

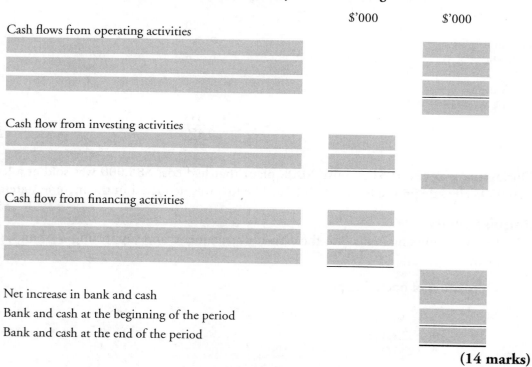

Cash flows from operating activities

Cash flow from investing activities

Cash flow from financing activities

Net increase in bank and cash
Bank and cash at the beginning of the period
Bank and cash at the end of the period

(14 marks)

(b) In connection with a statement of cash flows complete the missing words in the following sentences.

(i) A statement of cash flows shows _____ and _____ of cash during the period. It reconciles opening and closing _____ balances.

(ii) The income statement includes _____ items and excludes cash involved in _____ transactions.

(3 marks)
(Total marks = 17)

Question 17

BAK plc has the following trial balance at 30 April 20X9:

	Debit ($'000)	Credit ($'000)
Ordinary shares, 50¢		3,200
5% preference shares, $1		800
Share premium		640
General reserves		700
Retained earnings 1 May 20X8		420
Motor vehicles – cost	6,000	
Motor vehicles – acc. depreciation at 1 May 20X8		1,000
Office equipment – cost	1,200	
Office equipment – acc. depreciation at 1 May 20X8		360
Goodwill	1,000	
Research and development expenditure	846	
Inventories at 1 May 20X8	1,420	
Receivables	3,100	
Payables		1,770
Allowance for receivables at 1 May 20X8		102
Bank balance	2,476	
Ordinary dividends paid	80	
Preference dividends paid	40	
Purchases	7,390	
Sales		19,620
Returns inwards	320	
Carriage inwards	240	
Distribution costs	2,860	
Administration costs	970	
Salaries and wages	1,310	
Printing, stationery and advertising	900	
Premises costs	310	
Loan		2,000
Loan interest	100	
Loss on disposal of non-current assets	50	
	30,612	30,612

You are given the following information at 30 April 20X9:

(i) Closing inventories were $1,280,000.
(ii) Allowance for receivables is to be amended to 2 per cent of receivables.
(iii) Sales representatives are to receive a bonus of 2 per cent of net sales.
(iv) Auditors' fees accrued amount to $115,000.
(v) Printing, stationery and advertising costs include the purchase of inventories of advertising literature that cost $200,000. Twenty-five per cent of this is unusable, but the remainder is to be distributed during May 20X9.
(vi) Premises costs includes insurance prepaid of $80,000.

(vii) Research and development expenditure includes $396,000, which the directors feel should be carried forward in the statement of financial position; the remainder is to be written off against profits during the year.

(viii) The loan carries interest at 10 per cent per annum. The capital sum is due for repayment in two equal instalments, on 31 December 20X9 and on 31 December 20Y0.

(ix) Depreciation is to be charged as follows:
- on motor vehicles, at 20 per cent on cost;
- on office equipment, at 10 per cent on cost.

(x) An accrual is to be made for income tax of $900,000.

(xi) $1,000,000 is to be transferred to general reserves.

Requirements

(a) Insert the missing items into the following income statement.

Income statement of BAK plc for the year ended 30 April 20X9

	$'000	$'000	$'000
Sales			
Returns inwards			
Cost of sales			
Opening inventories			
Purchases			
Carriage inwards			
Closing inventories			
Gross profit			
Research and development expenses			
Distribution costs			
Administration costs			
Salaries and wages			
Printing, stationery and adverts			
Premises costs			
Loss on disposal of non-current assets			
Reduction in allowance for receivables			
Bonuses owing			
Depreciation of vehicles			
Depreciation of office equipment			
Auditors' fees			
Operating profit			
Loan interest			
Profit before tax			
Income tax			
Profit for the period			

(8 marks)

(b) Insert the missing items into the following statement of changes in equity.

Statement of changes in equity of BAK plc for the year ended 30 April 20X9

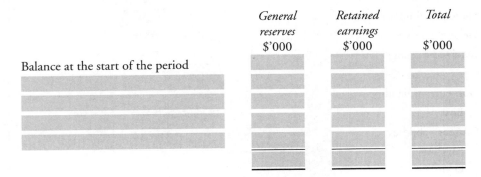

	General reserves $'000	Retained earnings $'000	Total $'000
Balance at the start of the period			

(4 marks)

(c) Insert the missing items into the following statement of financial position.

Statement of financial position of BAK as at 30 April 20X9

Assets	Cost $'000	Depreciation $'000	Carrying amount $'000
Non-current assets			
Tangibles			
Office equipment			
Vehicles			
Intangibles			
Goodwill			
Development expenditure			
Current assets			
Inventories of goods			
Inventories of advertising material			
Receivables			
Prepayments			
Bank			

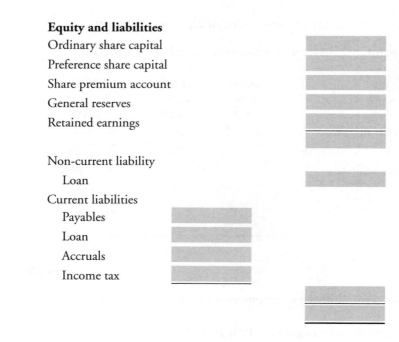

Equity and liabilities

Ordinary share capital

Preference share capital

Share premium account

General reserves

Retained earnings

Non-current liability

   Loan

Current liabilities

   Payables

   Loan

   Accruals

   Income tax

(10 marks)
(Total marks = 22)

Question 18

The computerised sales and purchase ledger shows the following totals at 30 April 20X9:

	$
Receivables outstanding	204,580
Credit balances on receivables accounts	12,460
Payables outstanding	134,290

At 1 April 20X9, the sales ledger control account showed a balance of $184,650, and the purchase ledger control account showed a balance of $142,320.

   At the end of April the following totals are extracted from the subsidiary books for April:

	$
Sales daybook (including cash sales of $3,450)	333,895
Purchases daybook	183,800
Returns outwards daybook	27,490
Returns inwards daybook	13,240
Refunds paid to receivables	8,255
Receipts from receivables, after deducting $2,115 cash discount	320,045
Dishonoured cheques from receivables	8,395
Bad debts written off	3,450
Payments to payables, after deducting $1,430 cash discount	196,360

It is also discovered that

(i) the purchase daybook figure is net of sales tax at 17.5 per cent; the other figures all include sales tax.

(ii) a receivable's balance of $2,420 has been offset against her balance of $3,650 in the purchase ledger.

(iii) allowance is to be made for receivables of 2.5 per cent of the net closing balance at 30 April 20X9.

(iv) a receivable has queried an invoice sent to him during the month for $1,400 plus sales tax at 17.5 per cent. It is found to be a duplicate of a previous invoice. It has been posted to his account in the sales ledger, but has not been included in the sales daybook.

(v) a supplier's account in the purchase ledger, with a debit balance of $800, has been included on the list of payables as a credit balance.

Requirements

(a) Insert the missing items into the following sales and purchase ledger control accounts for April 20X9.

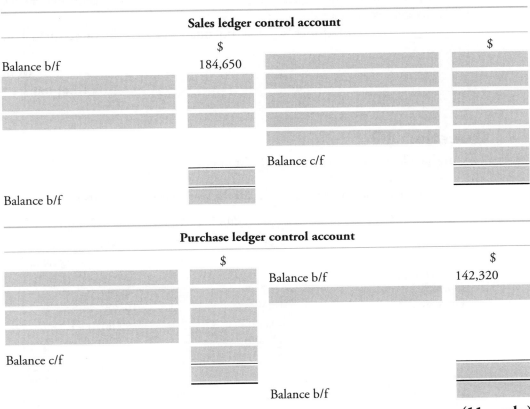

Sales ledger control account

	$		$
Balance b/f	184,650		
		Balance c/f	
Balance b/f			

Purchase ledger control account

	$		$
		Balance b/f	142,320
Balance c/f			
		Balance b/f	

(11 marks)

(b) Insert the missing items below, to identify the ledger that is out of balance with its control account.

Receivables	$	Payables	$
Control account total		Control account total	
Ledger account total	192,120	Ledger account total	134,290
Adjustment:		Adjustment:	
Revised ledger account total		Revised ledger account total	

The ledger that is out of balance with its control account is the _____ ledger.

(3 marks)

(c) In connection with controls within the accounting system that can reduce the risk of error and fraud, complete the missing words in these sentences.

(i) independent preparation of a _____ reconciliation statement on a regular basis;

(ii) regular preparation of a _____ _____ to confirm arithmetical accuracy of the ledger accounts;

(iii) _____ of duties so that no one person is involved in a complete process.

(6 marks)
(Total marks = 20)

Question 19

AJ Ltd has produced the following financial statements:

Trading and income statements for the year ended 31 December

	20X7 $'000	20X7 $'000	20X8 $'000	20X8 $'000
Sales		25,000		28,000
Cost of sales				
Opening inventories	2,200		2,300	
Purchases	18,400		16,200	
	20,600		(18,500)	
Less: Closing inventories	(2,300)		(2,800)	
		(18,300)		(15,700)
Gross profit		6,700		12,300
Less: Expenses		(4,200)		(6,200)
Operating profit		2,500		6,100
Income tax		(500)		(1,000)
Profit for the period		2,000		5,100
Retained earnings balance b/f		5,000		7,000
Retained earnings balance c/f		7,000		12,100

Statements of financial position as at 31 December

	20X7		20X8	
	$'000	$'000	$'000	$'000
Assets				
Non-current assets		18,000		23,000
Current assets				
Inventories	2,300		4,800	
Receivables	2,500		3,200	
Bank and cash	1,300		–	
		6,100		8,000
		24,100		31,000
Equity and liabilities				
Ordinary shares of $1 each		13,200		14,200
Retained earnings		7,000		12,100
		20,200		26,300
Current liabilities				
Payables	3,900		3,600	
Bank overdraft	–		1,100	
		3,900		4,700
		24,100		31,000

Requirements

(i) State the formulae for and calculate *three* profitability ratios for each of the 2 years.

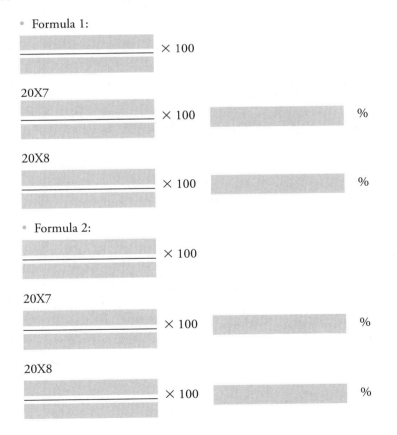

- Formula 1:

$$\frac{\rule{3cm}{0.4cm}}{\rule{3cm}{0.4cm}} \times 100$$

20X7

$$\frac{\rule{3cm}{0.4cm}}{\rule{3cm}{0.4cm}} \times 100 \qquad \rule{3cm}{0.4cm} \%$$

20X8

$$\frac{\rule{3cm}{0.4cm}}{\rule{3cm}{0.4cm}} \times 100 \qquad \rule{3cm}{0.4cm} \%$$

- Formula 2:

$$\frac{\rule{3cm}{0.4cm}}{\rule{3cm}{0.4cm}} \times 100$$

20X7

$$\frac{\rule{3cm}{0.4cm}}{\rule{3cm}{0.4cm}} \times 100 \qquad \rule{3cm}{0.4cm} \%$$

20X8

$$\frac{\rule{3cm}{0.4cm}}{\rule{3cm}{0.4cm}} \times 100 \qquad \rule{3cm}{0.4cm} \%$$

- Formula 3:

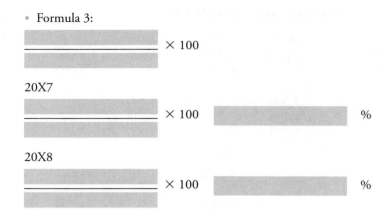

20X7

20X8

(ii) State the formulae for and calculate *two* liquidity and *two* efficiency ratios for each of the 2 years.

Liquidity ratios

- Formula 1:

20X7

20X8

- Formula 2:

20X7

20X8

(iii) Efficiency ratios

- Formula 1:

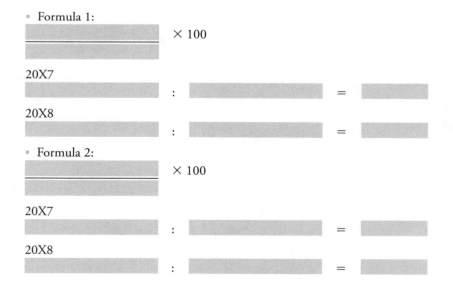

20X7

20X8

- Formula 2:

20X7

20X8

(21 marks)

Question 20

On 31 December 20X5 the accounting records of JB were partly destroyed by fire. Her accountant has provided the following list of assets, liabilities and capital at 31 December 20X4:

	$
Plant and machinery	128,000
Office equipment	45,000
Inventories	30,500
Receivables and prepayments	35,000
Payables and accruals	17,600
Bank overdraft	8,850
Loan (interest 10% per annum)	95,000
Capital	117,050

A summary of her receipts and payments during 20X5 can be extracted from the bank statements as follows:

	$
Receipts	
Capital paid in	22,000
Received from receivables	427,500
Payments	
Cash withdrawn	22,450
Loan repayments	20,000
Paid to payables	175,600
Rent paid	22,000
Wages	90,000
General expenses paid	12,500

The following additional information is obtained:

(i)   On 31 December 20X4, the receivables figure included $2,500 for rent paid in advance, and the payables figure included $4,300 for wages accrued for the last week of 20X4.

(ii) The plant and machinery had been purchased for $200,000 in 20X3 and was being depreciated at 20 per cent per annum on the reducing-balance basis.
The office equipment was bought during 20X4 and was being depreciated over 10 years on the straight-line basis, with a full year's depreciation in the year of purchase.

(iii) During 20X5, JB transferred a private motor vehicle worth $5,000 to her business.
It is to be depreciated over 4 years on the straight-line basis, with a full year's depreciation in the year of acquisition.

(iv) Of the cash withdrawn from the bank during 20X5, $6,750 was for wages, $4,200 was for cash payments to suppliers, $2,600 was for printing of advertising leaflets (of which half are still to be distributed), and the remainder was taken by JB for her own use.

(v)   The bank balance 31 December 20X5, according to the bank statement, after adjusting for unpresented cheques, was $106,700. Any difference is assumed to be cash sales banked, after deducting $30 per week wages paid to JB's daughter, who assists in the office.

(vi) The loan repayments from the bank account include $9,500 interest.

(vii) Other balances at 31 December 20X5 are

	$
Inventories	27,850
Rent paid in advance	2,700
Wages owing	5,250
Payables for supplies	12,200
Receivables	22,300

(viii) It is subsequently discovered that a receivable owing $16,000 has gone into liquidation, and a dividend of 20¢ in the $ is expected.

Requirements

(a) Insert the missing items into the income statement for JB for the year ended 31 December 20X5, given below.

You will need to calculate several figures for inclusion in the income statement before you commence. In a computer-based assessment, this question would probably be examined in smaller sections.

Income statement of JB for the year ended 31 December 20X5

	$	$	$
Credit sales			▨
Cash sales			▨
Less: cost of sales			▨
Opening inventories		30,500	
Credit purchases	▨		
Cash purchases	▨		
		▨	
		▨	
Closing inventories		(27,850)	
Gross profit			▨
Less: expenses			▨
Wages		▨	
Advertising expenses		▨	
Loan interest		9,500	
Rent		▨	
General expenses		12,500	
Bad debts written off		▨	
Depreciation			
Plant and machinery		▨	
Vehicle		▨	
Office equipment		▨	
			▨
Net profit			▨

(15 marks)

(b) Insert the missing figures into the statement of financial position for JB for 31 December 20X5, given below.

Statement of financial position of JB as at 31 December 20X5

Assets		*Carrying amount* ($)
Non-current assets		
Plant and machinery		
Office equipment		
Vehicle		
Current assets		
Inventories	27,850	
Receivables		
Prepayments		
Bank		
Capital and liabilities		
Capital at 1 January 20X5		
Add: capital introduced		
Add: profit		
Less: drawings		
Non-current liabilities		
Long-term loan		
Current liabilities		
Payables		
Accruals		

(10 marks)
(Total marks = 25)

? Question 21

You are presented with the following information relating to SH Ltd:

Income statement for the year ended 30 June 20X6

	$'000
Gross profit	980
Trading expenses	(475)
Depreciation	(255)
Operating profit	250
Retained earnings start of year	1,400
Operating profit for the year	250
Dividends declared before the year end and paid after the year end.	(80)
Retained earnings at the end of the year	1,570

Statement of financial position as at 30 June

Assets	20X5 ($'000)	20X6 ($'000)
Non-current assets at cost	3,000	3,500
Less: Accumulated depreciation	(2,100)	(2,300)
Carrying amount	900	1,200
Current assets		
Inventories	825	1,175
Receivables	5,200	5,065
Bank and cash	2,350	2,160
	8,375	8,400
	9,275	9,600
Equity and liabilities		
Ordinary shares of $1 each	2,800	3,200
Share premium	–	400
Retained earnings	1,400	1,570
	4,200	5,170
Current liabilities		
Payables	5,000	4,350
Dividends	75	80
	5,075	4,430
	9,275	9,600

During the year ended 30 June 20X6, non-current assets that had cost $230,000 were sold for $145,000. The loss on this disposal had been included in the trading expenses in the income statement.

Requirements

(a) Insert the missing items below in order to calculate the loss on disposal of non-current assets.

	$'000
Accumulated depreciation at 30 June 20X5/20X6*	
Add/less*: charge for the year	255
Accumulated depreciation at 30 June 20X5/20X6*	
Accumulated depreciation relating to disposal	
Proceeds	145
Carrying amount	
Loss on disposal	

(3 marks)

(b) Insert the missing items below to calculate the cash flow generated from operations during the year ended 30 June 20X6.

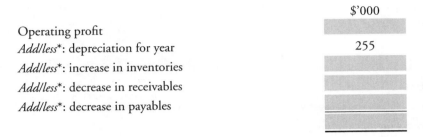

$'000

Operating profit

Add/less*: depreciation for year   255

Add/less*: increase in inventories

Add/less*: decrease in receivables

Add/less*: decrease in payables

*Delete as appropriate.

(4 marks)

(c) Insert the missing items below to produce the cash-flow statement for the year ended 30 June 20X6.

Note: show figures to be deducted in brackets.

Statement of cash flows of SH Ltd for year ended 30 June 20X6

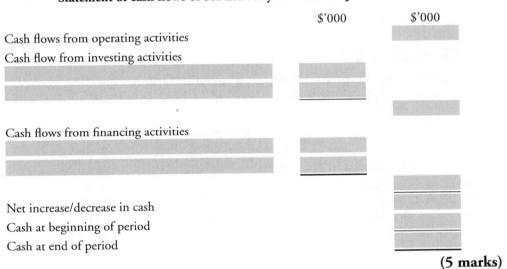

	$'000	$'000
Cash flows from operating activities		
Cash flow from investing activities		
Cash flows from financing activities		
Net increase/decrease in cash		
Cash at beginning of period		
Cash at end of period		

(5 marks)

(d) Calculate the current ratio and the liquid (or quick) ratio for *each* of the 2 years

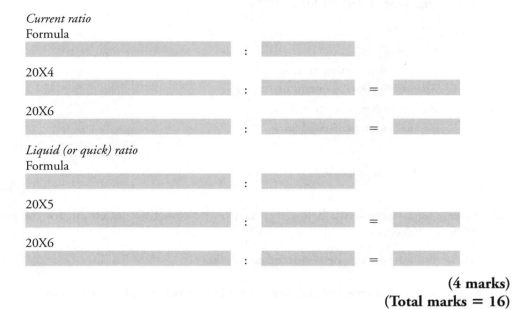

Current ratio
Formula

20X4

20X6

Liquid (or quick) ratio
Formula

20X5

20X6

(4 marks)
(Total marks = 16)

? Question 22

From the following information, prepare a statement reconciling the present bank balance as shown in the cash book with that shown on the bank statement at 16 November 20X6:

Cash book

Date		$	Date		$
10 Nov.	Balance b/fwd	5,327	11 Nov.	Purchase ledger	1,406
12 Nov.	Sales ledger	2,804	12 Nov.	Employees' income tax	603
13 Nov.	Cash sales	543	14 Nov.	Sales tax	435
15 Nov.	Sales ledger	1,480	16 Nov.	Cheques cashed	1,342
				Balance c/fwd	6,368
		10,154			10,154

Bank statement

Date		Debit ($)	Credit ($)	Balance ($)
10 Nov.	Balance			6,049
11 Nov.	Cheque 101204	420		5,629
12 Nov.	Cheque 101206	1,406		4,223
13 Nov.	Cheque 101205	302		
	Rent DD	844		3,077
14 Nov.	Paid in – cheques		2,804	
	Paid in – cash		543	6,424
15 Nov.	Credit transfer		685	
	Bank charges	130		
	Dishonoured cheque	425		
	Cheque 101207	603		5,951
16 Nov.	Cheque 101209	1,342		4,609

Insert the missing items in the schedules below.

Updating the cash book for items found on the bank statement not entered in books of MTR:

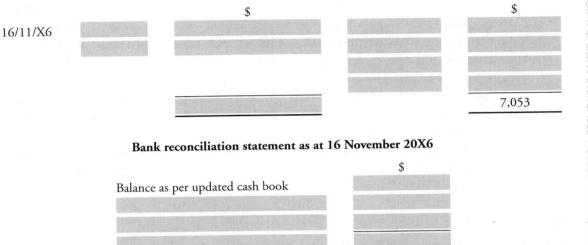

16/11/X6

7,053

Bank reconciliation statement as at 16 November 20X6

Balance as per updated cash book

(8 marks)

? Question 23

TYR Ltd produced the following trial balance at 31 October 20X7:

	Debit ($'000)	Credit ($'000)
Share capital – $1 ordinary shares		1,000
Reserves		425
12% debentures, repayable 2010		250
Land at valuation	495	
Premises at cost	350	
Acc. depreciation to 1 November 20X6		20
Plant and machinery at cost	220	
Acc. depreciation to 1 November 20X6		30
Patents and trademarks	200	
Inventories at 1 November 20X6	210	
Receivables	875	
Cash in hand	12	
Payables		318
Bank		85
Administration expenses	264	
Selling and distribution expenses	292	
Dividends paid	20	
Debenture interest	15	
Sales		2,569
Purchases	1,745	
Carriage inwards	15	
Carriage outwards	18	
Returns outward		34
	4,731	4,731

The following additional information at 31 October 20X7 is available:

(i) A physical inventories count reveals inventories at cost of $194,000.

(ii) Prepaid administration expenses amount to $12,000 and prepaid selling and delivery expenses amount to $28,000. Accrued administration expenses amount to $17,000.

(iii) During October 20X7 goods were sold on a 'sale or return' basis, with the final date for return being 25 November 20X7. The sale has been recorded as normal in the sales daybook and receivables' account, and the inventories have been excluded from the inventories count. The goods cost $7,000 and had a selling price of $12,000.

(iv) The land is to be revalued at $550,000. The tax on the gain is estimated at $15,000.

(v) The reserves account consists of share premium of $100,000 and revaluation reserve of $135,000, with the balance representing retained earnings.

(vi) The premises are to be depreciated at 4 per cent per annum straight line. The plant and machinery is to be depreciated at 10 per cent per annum straight line.

(vii) Income tax of $40,000 is to be accrued for the year.

Requirements

(a) Insert the missing items in the income statement for the year ended 31 October 20X7.

Income statement of TYR Ltd for the year ended 31 October 20X7

	$'000	$'000	$'000
Sales			
Cost of sales			
Gross profit			
Operating profit			
Profit for the period			
Other comprehensive income			
Gain on property revaluation before tax			
Income tax			
Gain on prperty revaluation after tax			
Total comprehensive income			

(7 marks)

(b) Insert the missing items in the statement of changes in equity for the year ended 31 October 20X7.

Statement of changes in equity of TYR Ltd for the year ended 31 October 20X7

	Share Capital $'000	Share Premium $'000	Revaluation Reserve $'000	Retained Earnings $'000	Total $'000
Balance at the start of the period					
Balance at the end of the period					

(3 marks)

(c) Insert the missing items in the statement of financial position at 31 October 20X7.

Statement of financial position of TYR Ltd as at 31 October 20X7

Assets	Cost or valuation $'000	Acc. Dep'n $'000	Carrying Amount $'000
Tangible non-current assets			
Intangible non-current assets			
Current assets			

Equity and liabilities

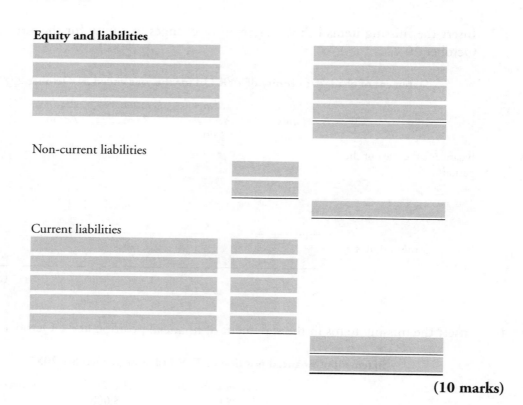

Non-current liabilities

Current liabilities

(10 marks)

(c)   Calculate the following ratios for the current year.

(i)   Gross profit mark-up

Formula

$\times$ 100 = $\times$ 100 =

(ii)   Operating profit margin

Formula

$\times$ 100 = $\times$ 100 =

(iii)   Current ratio:

Formula

: = : = :

(iv)   Acid test ratio

Formula

: = : = :

(10 marks)
(Total marks = 30)

? **Question 24**

At the beginning of September 20X7, GL had the following balances on the accounts of three of his receivables:

	$
A Barton	400
C Sikorski	1,200
F Gray	340

During September, the following sales and returns took place for the above receivables:

Sales

On 3 September to A Barton	goods $200 less trade discount of 20%, plus sales tax at 17.5%
On 8 September to C Sikorski	goods $800, plus sales tax at 17.5%
On 12 September to C Sikorski	goods $360 plus sales tax at 17.5%

Sales returns

On 5 September from A Barton	25% of the goods sold to him on 3 September
On 18 September from C Sikorski	15% of the goods sold to him on 8 September

The balance at the bank was $347 overdrawn on 1 September 20X7.
   The following bank transactions took place during September 20X7:

4 Sep.	A Barton paid the amount outstanding at 1 September, less 5% cash discount.
8 Sep.	C Sikorski paid the amount outstanding at 1 September, less 2.5% cash discount.
10 Sep.	Paid J Swinburn, a payable, for an invoice of $1,200, less 5% cash discount.
15 Sep.	Paid sales tax of $832 to tax authority, re the quarter ended 31 August 20X7.
17 Sep.	Paid P Taylor, a payable, $400 less 5% cash discount.
20 Sep.	including $150 annual vehicle licence tax and sales tax at 17.5%.
22 Sep.	C Sikorski paid the invoice of 8 September, less the credit note of 18 September. There was no cash discount allowed on this payment.
25 Sep.	Received a cheque from F Gray for 50% of his debt; the remainder is to be written off as a bad debt.
30 Sep.	Paid wages to employees, made up as follows:

Gross wages	$2,500
Employees' social security tax	$200
Employer's social security tax	$200
Employees' income tax	$300

30 Sep.	Banked receipts from receivables	$10,500
	Paid cheques to payables	$11,200

GL has a computerised sales ledger system, which produced the following aged receivables' printout at 30 September 20X7:

Current month	$12,000
30 to 60 days	$7,500
60 to 90 days	$3,600
over 90 days	$1,100

The balance on the allowance for receivables account at 1 September 20X7 was $450 credit. No further allowance for receivables has been made since that date. You are given the following additional information:

(i) The 'current month' total includes $60 for discounts allowed to receivables not recorded in the sales ledger.

(ii) The '30 to 60 days' total includes a balance of $200 to be taken as a contra entry in the purchase ledger.

(iii) The 'over 90 days' total includes a debt of $240 to be written off as bad.

(iv) The company decides to amend the allowance for receivables to the following amounts:

Over 90 days	20%
60 to 90 days	10%
30 to 60 days	5%
Current month	Nil

Requirements

(a) Insert the missing items in the cash book for September 20X7.

Cash book

Date	Details	Disc	$	Date	Details	Disc	$

(7 marks)

(b) Insert the xmissing items in the ledger accounts (in date order) for A Barton, C Sikorski and F Gray.

A Barton

Date		$	Date		$
		141			

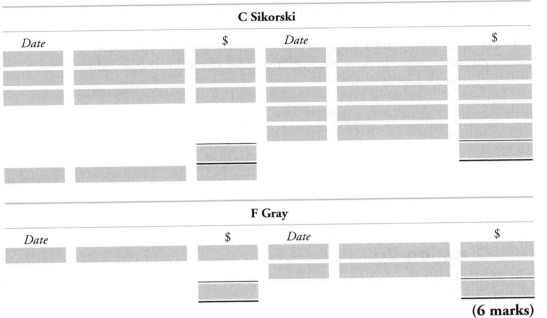

C Sikorski

Date		$	Date		$

F Gray

Date		$	Date		$

(6 marks)

(c) Insert the missing items in the change in the allowance for receivables.

Calculation of the allowance for receivables on 30 September 20X7

	Total receivables as per schedule $	Adjustments $	Revised Balances $		Allowance $
Current				at 0%	
30–60 days				at 5%	
60–90 days				at 10%	
90+ days				at 20%	
Revised cumulative allowance					

The allowance for receivables account will need to be increased by

(4 marks)

(d) Which is the principal accounting convention that governs the allowance for receivables?

(3 marks)

(Total marks =20)

? Question 25

You are required to state, for *each* of the transactions below whether there will be an **increase**, a **decrease**, or **no change** to each of: *non-current assets, working capital* and *profit*.

(i) dividends which were accrued in the statement of financial position for the year just ended have been paid by cheque in the current year;

(ii) non-current assets have been disposed of on credit, for more than their carrying amount;

(iii) a long-term bank loan has been repaid by increasing the overdraft;

(iv) goods sold on credit have been returned and the original sales value has been credited to the receivables' account.

	Non-current assets	Working capital	Profit
(i)	_____	_____	_____
(ii)	_____	_____	_____
(iii)	_____	_____	_____
(iv)	_____	_____	_____

(8 marks)

Question 26

The Monarch Sports Club has the following summary of its cash book for the year ended 30 June 20X7:

	$	$
Opening bank balance		12,500
Receipts		
Subscriptions	18,000	
Life membership fees	3,000	
Competition receipts	7,500	
Entrance fees	2,500	
Equipment sold	1,000	
		32,000
		44,500
Payments		
Transport to matches	3,700	
Competition prizes	4,300	
Coaching fees	2,100	
Repairs to equipment	800	
Purchase of new equipment	4,000	
Purchase of sports pavilion	35,000	
		(49,900)
Closing balance (overdrawn)		5,400

The following information is available regarding the position at the beginning and end of the accounting year:

	1 July 20X6	30 June 20X7
	$	$
Subscriptions in advance	1,100	900
Subscriptions in arrears	200	300
Coaching fees outstanding	150	450

Of the subscriptions outstanding at the beginning of the year, only half were eventually received.

The equipment sold during the year had a carrying amount of $1,200 at 1 July 20X6. Equipment is to be depreciated at 20 per cent per annum straight line. Life membership fees are taken to cover 10 years.

The treasurer insists that no depreciation needs to be charged to the sports pavilion, as buildings do not decrease in value. He says that the last club of which he was treasurer did charge depreciation on its buildings but that when the club came to replace them, there was still insufficient money in the bank to pay for the new building.

Requirements

(a) Insert the missing words in the following sentences

A _____ and _____ account is a summary of the cash and bank transactions for the relevant period; in essence, it is a summarised cash book.

An _____ and _____ statement is essentially the same as an income statement. It takes into account prepayments and accruals and distinguishes between capital and revenue items.

(4 marks)

(b) Insert the missing items in the income and expenditure statement for the Monarch Sports Club for the year ended 30 June 20X7.

Income and expenditure statement of Monarch Sports Club for the year ended 30 June 20X7.

	$	$
Income		
Annual subscriptions		
Receipts in year		
Add: Subs in advance at		
Less: Subs in arrears at		
Less: Subs in advance at		
Add: Subs in arrears at		
Expenses		
Surplus for year		

(8 marks)
(Total marks = 12)

Question 27

Robert Costello is a sole trader. His business mainly involves the sale of computer systems to small businesses and home users, including hardware and pre-loaded software. He also sells individual items of equipment from his shop. At 30 September 20X9, he extracts the following trial balance from his accounting records:

	Debit $	Credit $
Capital at 1 October 20X8		26,600
Loan from bank		40,000
Loan repayments made	12,600	
Inventories at 1 October 20X8	42,500	
Sales of computer systems		305,000
Other sales		5,500
Purchases	180,300	
General office expenses	8,800	
Car insurance	400	
Shop rental	24,000	
Local business tax	3,500	
Heating and lighting	2,400	
Wages	18,500	
Fixtures and fittings – cost	10,000	
Fixtures and fittings – acc. depreciation 1 October 20X8		3,600
Motor vehicle – cost	21,000	
Motor vehicle – acc. depreciation 1 October 20X8		5,000
Receivables	62,900	
Payables		15,200
Sales tax		4,500
Bank balance	18,500	
	405,400	405,400

You are given the following information at 30 September 20X9:

(i) Closing inventories of hardware and software were $45,200.

(ii) The figure in the accounts for shop rental includes $6,000 for the period from 1 October 20X9 to 31 December 20X9.

(iii) Local business tax for the year ending 31 March 20Y0 has been paid in full, amounting to $2,400.

(iv) Heating and lighting to be accrued is $350.

(v) The wages total recorded in the books consists of $15,000 that Robert paid to himself, and $3,500 paid to his father for assistance with bookkeeping.

(vi) During the year, sales of sundry items amounting to $5,640 (including sales tax at 17.5 per cent) were made for cash, and have not been recorded in the books. The cash was used to pay for stationery ($470 including sales tax), shop assistant's wages ($3,760) and petrol ($1,410 including sales tax).

(vii) During the year, a motor vehicle that had cost $8,000, and on which the accumulated depreciation was $5,000, was given in part exchange for a new vehicle costing $15,000. The part-exchange valuation was $2,000. The ledger accounts in the above trial balance contain the cost and accumulative depreciation of the disposed vehicle, and the balance paid by cheque for the new vehicle.

(viii) Fixtures and fittings are to be depreciated at the rate of 20 per cent per annum on the reducing-balance basis; motor vehicles are to be depreciated at the rate of 20 per cent per annum, straight line, with a full year's depreciation provided in the year of acquisition.

(ix) One of Robert's business customers is in financial difficulties, and is unable to pay the whole of his debt of $6,000. He offered to pay in six equal instalments, starting August 20X9, but so far has made no payment. Robert feels that he is likely to get half the money back. Other receivables are also showing signs of difficulties, and he thinks it might be prudent to make an allowance of 5 per cent for receivables.

(x) The bank loan was taken out on 1 January 20X9. The loan is being repaid in 40 monthly instalments of $1,400, including flat-rate interest of 12 per cent per annum on the amount borrowed.

Requirements

(a) Insert the missing items in Robert's income statement for the year 30 September 20X9.

Income statement of Robert Costello for the year ended 30 September 20X9

	$	$
Gross profit		
Net profit		

(12 marks)

(b)   Insert the missing items in Robert's statement of financial position 30 September 20X9

Balance sheet of Robert Costello as at 30 September 20X9

Assets	Cost	Acc. Dep'n	Carrying Amount
Non-current assets	$	$	$
Current assets			
Capital and liabilities			
Non-current liabilities			
Current liabilities			

(12 marks)
(Total marks = 24)

Question 28

Tanwir commenced in business on 1 October 20X9, with capital in the bank of $20,000. During his first month of trading, his transactions were as follows:

2 Oct.	Purchased inventories for $3,500 on credit from A Jones
3 Oct.	Paid $1,200 rental of premises, by cheque
5 Oct.	Paid $5,000 for office equipment, by cheque
10 Oct.	Sold goods costing $1,000, for $1,750, on credit to P Assad
15 Oct.	Returned inventories costing $500 to A Jones
18 Oct.	Purchased inventories for $2,400 on credit from A Jones
25 Oct.	Paid A Jones for the net purchases of 2 Oct., by cheque
28 Oct.	P Assad paid $500 on account, by cheque

Requirements

(a) Insert the missing items in the ledger accounts for the above transactions.

Capital

	$				$

Bank

	$				$

Purchases

	$		$

A Jones

	$				$

Rent payable

	$		$

Office equipment

	$		$

Sales

	$				$

P Assad

	$				$

Returns outwards

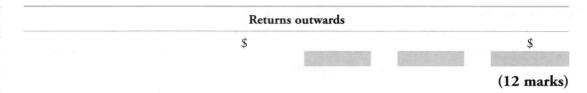

$ $

(12 marks)

(b) During his first year of trading, Tanwir brings his private car, valued at $6,000, into the business. The business made a net profit of $17,500 for the year, after deducting $650 for petrol that was paid out of his private funds. He has drawn $5,000 out of the business bank account for himself, as well as paying his home telephone bill of $450 from business funds.

Insert the missing items in the calculation of Tanwir's capital at the end of the first year of trading.

Calculation of Tanwir's closing capital

Closing capital

(5 marks)

(c) State the accounting convention that has governed the treatment of the items which make up Tanwir's capital at the end of the year.

 convention

(3 marks)
(Total marks = 20)

? Question 29

Jay Ltd values inventories on the first in, first out (FIFO) cost formula. During October 20X9, there are the following details regarding inventory of Product A:

1 Oct.	Balance in inventory	120 items valued at $8 each
3 Oct.	Purchases	180 items at $9 each
4 Oct.	Sales	150 items at $12 each
8 Oct.	Sales	80 items at $15 each
12 Oct.	Returns to the supplier	30 items purchased on 3 Oct.
18 Oct.	Purchases	300 items at $10 each
22 Oct.	Sales	100 items at $15 each
28 Oct.	Returns from customers	20 items sold on 22 Oct.

Requirements

(a) Insert the missing items in the stores ledger card for Product A for October 20X9 using the FIFO cost formula.

Note: Goods returned inwards are valued at the latest issue price.

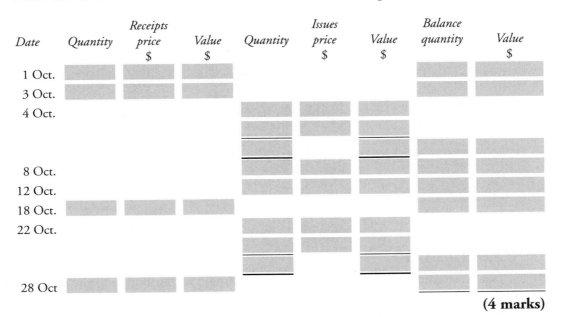

(4 marks)

(b) Insert the missing items in the stores ledger card for Product A for October using the AVCO (weighted average cost) cost formula.

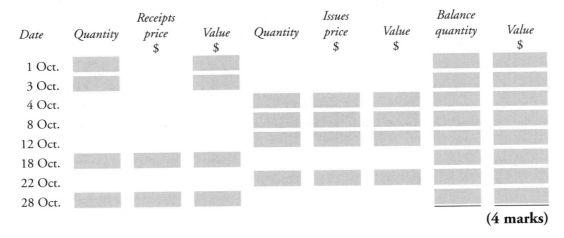

(4 marks)

(c) Calculate the gross profit for October using *both* methods of inventory valuation by inserting the missing items in the schedule below.

Trading accounts of Jay Ltd

	FIFO	AVCO
	$	$
Opening inventory		
Purchases		
Closing inventory		
Cost of sales		
Sales		
Gross profit		

(4 marks)
(Total marks = 12)

? Question 30

MMM Ltd is a recently formed company, which provides training and educational services. The company was formed with an authorised share capital of 1,000,000 $1 shares. The three shareholders, who are also directors, each purchased 120,000 shares at $1.40 per share. It is expected that the business will grow rapidly during the first 2 years, and that funds for that expansion will be sought by issuing shares to family members and obtaining bank finance.

During the first year of trading, a profit before tax of $48,800 was made, after deducting salaries to the three directors of $60,000 in total. Income tax of $6,500 was accrued for the year. As well as the salaries, the three directors paid dividends for themselves at 5¢ per share. They also decided to transfer $5,000 into general reserves.

During the second year of trading, profit before tax was $55,000. Family members purchased a further 30,000 shares at $1.50 per share, at the start of the year. Salaries were as in the first year. Dividends of 13¢ per share were paid. Income tax of $8,000 was accrued for the year, and a further $5,000 transferred into general reserves.

Requirement

Insert the missing items in the statement of changes in equity for each of years 1 and 2.

Statement of changes in equity of MMM Ltd

	Year 1				Year 2			
	Share capital $	Share premium $	General reserve $	Retained earnings $	Share capital $	Share premium $	General reserve $	Retained earnings $
Balance at start of period	–	–	–	–				
Balance at end of period								

(9 marks)

? Question 31

EMP plc is a retail organisation, with the following trial balance at 31 October 20X1:

	Debit $m	Credit $m
Ordinary shares of 50¢ each		200
Share premium account		16
General reserves		14
Retained earnings at 1 November 20X0		62
Plant and machinery		
Cost	250	
Acc. depreciation at 1 November 20X0		56
Office equipment		
Cost	90	
Acc. depreciation at 1 November 20X0		30
Inventories at 1 November 20X0	62	
Receivables and payables	84	80
Allowance for receivables at 1 November 20X0		8
Bank balance	8	
Purchases and sales	230	376
Returns inwards and outwards	16	12
Administrative expenses		
Wages and salaries	28	
Directors' fees	10	
Telephone costs	12	
Rent and insurances	8	
Heat and light	16	
Printing and stationery	12	
Distribution expenses	24	
Dividend paid	4	
	854	854

The following additional information at 31 October 20X1 is available:

(i)   Closing inventories of goods for resale are valued at $106 m.
(ii) Distribution expenses include $1 m carriage inwards and $3 m carriage outwards.
(iii) Prepayments

	$m
Telephone rental	1
Insurance	2

(iv) Accruals

	$m
Wages and salaries	3
Telephone call charges	4
Directors' fees	2
Auditors' fees	1

(v)   The figure in the trial balance for the bank balance is the balance appearing in the cash book prior to preparing a bank reconciliation. On receipt of the bank statement, it is discovered that
  - unpresented cheques amount to $3 m;
  - bank charges not recorded in the cash book amount to $2 m;
  - a cheque for $1 m from a customer has been dishonoured and not recorded in the ledgers.

(vi) Bad debts to be written off amount to $5 m (including the dishonoured cheque referred to in note (v) above), and the allowance for receivables is to be amended to 2.5 per cent of receivables.

(vii) Depreciation on non-current assets is to be provided as follows:
  - plant and machinery, 10 per cent on cost;
  - office equipment, 33 1/3 per cent on the reducing balance.

(viii) An accrual of $2 m is to be made for income tax.
(ix) $20m is to be transferred to general reserves.

Requirements

(a) Insert the missing items in the income statement for the year ended 31 October 20X1

Income statement of EMP plc for the year ended 31 October 20X1

	$m	$m	$m
Sales			
Cost of sales			
Gross profit			
Operating profit			

(9 marks)

(b) Insert the missing items in the statement of changes in equity for the year ended 31 October 20X1

Statement of changes in equity of EMP plc for the year ended 31 October 20X1

	General reserves $m	Retained earnings $m	Total $m
Balance at the start of the period			
Balance at the end of the period			

(3 marks)

(c) Insert the missing items in the statement of financial position at 31 October 20X1.

Statement of financial position of EMP plc at 31 October 20X1

	$m	Cost $m	Acc. Depreciation $m	Carrying Amount $m
Assets				
Non-current assets				
Current assets				
Equity and liabilities				
Current liabilities				

(8 marks)

(d) State the formulae for and calculate the following ratios by inserting the missing items.

(i) *Acid test or quick ratio*

(ii) *Inventories days*

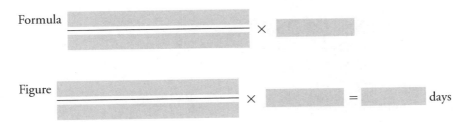

(4 marks)
(Total marks = 24)

? Question 32

Your organisation's year end is 31 October. Prior to producing the trial balance at 31 October 20X0, your supervisor has passed you the following list of errors and omissions

(i) Purchase of raw materials on credit from J Brown had been completely omitted. The list price was $9,000, less trade discount of 331/3 per cent, with cash discount of 2 per cent offered for payment before 31 October 20X0. The invoice is still outstanding at the end of the month.

(ii) Office equipment valued at $4,000 was received in part payment of a debt of $4,500 from Zhang. The balance of Zhang's debt is to be written off. No entries have been made for either of these transactions. No depreciation is to be charged on the office equipment.

(iii) Administration expenses paid, of $5,300, had been credited to administration expenses and debited to the bank account.

(iv) Office equipment had been disposed of during the year. The cost ($4,200) and accumulated depreciation ($3,320) had been correctly transferred to the disposals account, but no other entries had been made. The disposal proceeds of $720 have not yet been received.

(v) Staff wages accrued of $3,000 gross had been omitted. Employees' income tax was $450, employees' social security tax contributions were $120 and employer's social security tax contributions were $130. All payments will be made after 31 October 20X0.

Requirements

(a) Insert the missing items in the journal entries to correct the above errors and omissions.

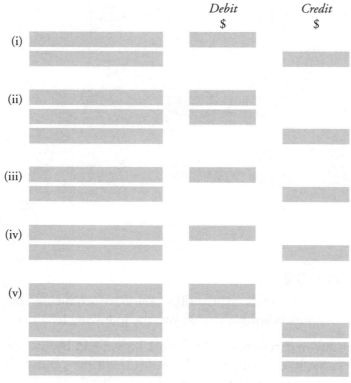

Journal entries

		Debit $	Credit $
(i)			

(7 marks)

(b) If the above errors had not been corrected, the net profit for the year ended 31 October 20X0 would have been $37,500. Recalculate the net profit after taking into account the above corrections, by inserting the missing figures in the schedule below.

Recalculated net profit

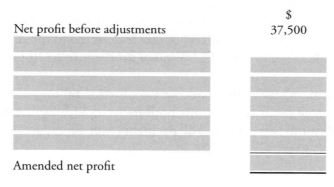

	$
Net profit before adjustments	37,500
Amended net profit	

(4 marks)

(c) A replacement engine had been purchased for a machine during the year. The whole cost of $25,000 had been charged to the 'machinery cost account', and depreciation of 10 per cent on the full amount had been charged. You are now informed that only $10,000 of the cost was deemed to be in respect of an improvement in the productive capacity of the machine.

You are required to:

(i) complete the missing words in the following sentences:_____ expenditure is the acquisition, production or enhancement of _____ assets. _____ expenditure includes the purchase of goods for resale, and expenditure on goods and services to be _____ during the reporting period.

(6 marks)

(ii) calculate the effect that the incorrect treatment of this expenditure will have had on the profit for the year, by inserting the missing figures in the schedule below.

Effect of incorrect treatment

(3 marks)
(Total marks = 20)

? Question 33

You are given the following information relating to PB's business for the month of October 20X0:

	$
Owing by customers at 1 October 20X0	95,760
Owing to customers at 1 October 20X0	3,400
Owing to customers at 31 October 20X0	5,750
Sales during the month	
Cash sales (including sales tax at 17.5%)	9,400
Credit sales (including sales tax at 17.5%)	757,875
Receipts from customers (including cash sales)	739,000
Discounts allowed to credit customers	2,450
Refunds made to credit customers	4,385
Returns inwards (excluding sales tax at 17.5%), all on credit	25,800
Bad debts written off	2,875
Dishonoured cheques from credit customers	15,215

The allowance for receivables is 2 per cent of net balance at 31 October 20X0.

In addition, PB was notified on 30 October 20X0 that she would be receiving a dividend of 20¢ in the pound from a previously written-off bad debt of $6,000. The amount was received in November 20X0.

She also has a customer owing $5,400, who is also a supplier of hers. The balance in the purchase ledger is $8,200, and she agreed to offset the balances.

You are required to prepare a sales ledger control account for PB for the month of October 20X0, using the information above, by inserting the missing items below.

Sales ledger control account

	$		$
Balance b/f		Balance b/f	
Balance c/f		Balance c/f	

(7 marks)

? **Question 34**

Your organisation maintains a single ledger account for rent, local business tax and insurance.

On 1 November 20X0, the following balances were to be brought forward on the account:

	$
Rent accrued for October 20X0	700
Local business tax prepaid to 31 March 20X1	550
Insurance prepaid to 31 December 20X0	400

During the next year, the following payments were made:

- *Rent.* $2,100 per quarter, payable on 1 November, 1 February, 1 May and 1 August. The May payment was made with the August payment.
- *Local business tax.* $1,200, for the year ending 31 March 20X2, paid on 8 April 20X1.
- *Insurance.* $3,000, for the year ending 31 December 20X1, paid on 28 December 20X0. In addition, a refund of insurance for the year ended 31 December 20X0, of $80, was received on 3 January 20X1.

Requirements

(a) Insert the missing items in the ledger account for rent, local business tax and insurance for the year ended 31 October 20X1, showing clearly the amount to be transferred to the income statement for the year, and the amounts accrued and/or prepaid at the end of the year.

Rent, local business tax and insurance

Date	Account	$	Date	Account	$

(8 marks)

(b) Insert the missing words in these sentences relating to the conventions of prudence and accruals.

The _____ *convention* stipulates that _____ and _____ should not be anticipated. However, _____, _____ and _____ should be provided for as soon as it is known that an _____ has been incurred that relates to the accounting period, or the possibility of a _____ or _____ exists.

The _____ (or _____) *convention* stipulates that _____ and _____ are matched with each other in accordance with the period to which they relate, regardless of the period in which the _____ or _____ occurs.

(5 marks)

(c) Your organisation made a net profit of $47,500 for the year ended 31 October 20X1. This was after charging depreciation of $8,200 and a loss on disposal of non-current assets of $1,200. The proceeds of sale of the non-current asset were $5,400.

During the year, the carrying amount of non-current assets rose by $18,000; receivables increased by $2,500; inventories decreased by $5,200 and payables increased by $1,800. The proprietor withdrew $7,000 of the profits for his own use, and paid off a long-term loan of $8,000.

Insert the missing items in the schedule for the change in the bank balance as a result of the above transactions.

Change in bank balance

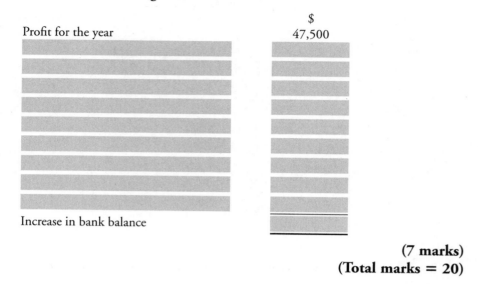

Profit for the year

$
47,500

Increase in bank balance

(7 marks)
(Total marks = 20)

Solutions to Revision Questions

✓ Solution 1

1.1 Answer: (C)

There are several ways a candidate could identify the correct answer here, including the process of elimination. Answers (A) and (D) cannot be right as they both include a debit to the cash account, and as the company is making a payment a credit to the cash account is required. The difference between answers (B) and (C) is the amount of cash discount given. This should be calculated as 2 per cent of the net goods value, that is, the value after deducting the trade discount. The net goods value is $400 less $100 trade discount = $300, therefore the cash discount is $6 and answer (C) is correct.

Taking the question in order of action, the initial purchase should be recorded ignoring the cash discount, as it is not known at the time of purchase whether payment will be made in time to become entitled to the cash discount. Trade discount is always deducted at once, and thus the initial entries are Debit purchases, Credit ABC Ltd with $300. On payment, ABC Ltd is debited with $300, the amount paid out (and credited to the bank) is $300 – $6 cash discount, and the discount is credited to Discount received (being an item of revenue).

1.2 Answer: (B)

A spreadsheet is ideal for preparing budgets and forecasts, using a columnar format with the accounting periods across the top and the items of revenue/expense and so on, down the columns. It is also ideal for use as a daybook, again with a columnar format with the invoice numbers and, listed vertically and the columns headed 'Gross', 'sales tax' and 'Net' (perhaps with further analysis columns). An extended trial balance could also be prepared using a spreadsheet, with the accounts listed vertically and the columns used for the trial balance figures, adjustments, income statement items and, finally, statement of financial position items. Double-entry records would require several spreadsheets, one for each account, and recording the dual aspect would mean locating the two relevant spreadsheets and the appropriate cells, making this application much more difficult.

1.3 Answer: (D)

The suspense account is debited or credited as a result of an imbalance in the trial balance. A debit balance would arise if the credit side of the trial balance were greater than the debit side. Option (A) would result in the debit side being greater than the credit side. Option (B) is a correct entry. Option (C) would make the credit side less than the debit side.

1.4 Answer: (D)

Share premium arises where shares are issued for more than their par value. Reserves are created from profits retained in the business or from the upward revaluation of non-current assets. The suspense account is created when there is an imbalance in the ledger accounts. Goodwill arises when the value of the assets purchased is less than the purchase price.

1.5 Reconstruction of cost of goods sold to establish the purchases figure:

	$	$
Opening inventories		12,000
Add: Purchases	122,000*	
Less: Returns	(5,000)	
		117,000
Closing inventories		(18,000)
Cost of goods sold		111,000
*Found by difference.		

1.6 Answer: (D)

1.7 Answer: $350,000

1.8

	$
Opening balance	34,500
Credit purchases	78,400
Discounts	(1,200)
Payments	(68,900)
Purchase returns	(4,700)
	38,100

1.9

	$	
Statement balance	13,400	
Add: dishonoured cheque	300	
Add: bank charges	50	
Less: Unpresented cheques	(1,400)	
Adjustment re error	(390)	(i.e. twice 195)
	11,960	

1.10

	$
Cash book balance	(1,240)
Unpresented cheques	450
Receipt not yet processed	(140)
Bank charges	(75)
As per statement	(1,005)

1.11   Answer: (A)

1.12   Answers: 1C, 2E, 3A, 4B, 5D

1.13   Reliable – the caretaker is not likely to know; the office staff should know.
Relevance – the economics exam is not likely to be relevant.
Complete – the student needs to know the precise date.
Understandable – C/42 is probably not understandable to the new student – this might be Block C, Room 42, or room C, block 42.

1.14   Answer: (B)

1.15   Answer: (D)

1.16   Answer: (B)

1.17   Answer: (D)

☑ Solution 2

2.1   Answer: (D)

2.2   Answer: (B)

2.3   Credit $962.50

2.4   Answer: (D)

2.5   Income statement $9000; Statement of financial position $3,000

2.6   Answer: (A)

2.7   Answer: (C)

2.8 $41.00

2.9   Answer: (B)

2.10 $18,000

2.11   Debit $7,700

2.12   Answer: (C)

2.13   57 days

2.14 $1,880

2.15   Debit $210

☑ Solution 3

3.1   Answer: (C)

3.2   Answer: (D)

3.3   Answer: (A)

3.4 Overdrawn $880

3.5 Answer: (D)

3.6 Answer: (C)

3.7 Answer: (D)

3.8 Answer: (B)

3.9 $385

3.10 Answer: (A)

3.11 Loss $28.80

3.12 $182,000

3.13 $180.00

3.14 $26,000

3.15 8 times

 Solution 4

4.1 Answer: (C)

4.2 Answer: (B)

4.3 Answer: (A)

4.4 Answer: (A)

4.5 Answer: (D)

4.6 $339,000

4.7 $90

4.8 Answer: (D)

4.9 Credit $190

4.10 Answer: (C)

4.11 $14,550

4.12 $171,000

4.13 Answer: (C)

4.14 Answer: (A)

4.15 Answer: (B)

Solution 5

5.1   Answer: (C)

5.2   Answer: (A)

	$
Disposal proceeds	30,000
Less: profit	(10,000)
Carrying amount	20,000

$$\$271,200 - \$20,000 = \$251,200$$

5.3   Answer: (B)

5.4   Answer: (D)

5.5   Answer: (B)

	$
Increase in inventories	500
Decrease in bank	(800)
Increase in payables	(2,400)
Decrease in working capital	(2,700)

5.6

Subscription account

	Dr $		Cr $
Balance b/f	200	Balance b/f	90
Paid in advance c/f	85	Receipts	4,800
Income and expenditure statement	4,655	Outstanding c/f	50
	4,940		4,940

5.7   Answer: (B)

5.8

	$	$
Opening capital		28,000
Capital introduced (petrol)		1,800
Add: profit		
Per IS	45,000	
Add back own wages	18,000	
Less: petrol	(1,800)	
		61,200
		91,000
Less: drawings		
Wages	18,000	
Telephone	800	
		(18,800)
Closing capital		72,200

5.9

	$
Purchase of raw material	56,000
Carriage inwards	2,500
Increase in inventories	(1,700)
Cost of material consumed	56,800
Direct wages	21,000
Prime cost	77,800
Production overhead	14,000
Decrease in work in progress	5,000
Production cost	96,800

5.10

	Qty	Price $	Total $
Opening inventories	60	4.00	240
Purchases	100	4.80	480
Balance	160	4.50	720
Sales	80	4.50	360
Balance	80	4.50	360
Purchases	120	5.00	600
Balance	200	4.80	960
Sales	50	4.80	240
Balance	150	4.80	720

5.11 Answer: (D)

5.12 Answer: (D)

5.13 Answer: (A)

5.14 Answer: (D)

$$60\% \text{ of } \$150,000 = \$90,000$$
$$\$150,000 + \$90,000 = \$240,000$$

5.15 Answer: (C)

Solution 6

(a)

Suspense account

	$		$
Stationery error	18	Trial balance difference	2,221
Discount allowed omitted	950	Sales daybook error	180
Proceeds of sale of non-current asset		Bank interest omitted	220
not entered in disposal account	750		
Balance carried down	903		
	2,621		2,621

(b)

Sales ledger control account

	$		$
Balance at 30 April 20X6	104,637	Discount allowed	950
Error in sales daybook	180	Contra to purchase ledger	426
Credit sale omitted	325	Contra to purchase ledger	426
		Balance carried down	103,340
	105,142		105,142

(c)

	$
Profit as originally calculated	227,642
Add: stationery error	18
Add: error in sales daybook total	180
Add: credit sale omitted	325
Less: loss on sale of non-current asset	(170)
Revised net profit	227,995

 Solution 7

This question involves the comparison of the statement received from a supplier with the ledger account maintained in the firm's purchase ledger. Remember that debits on one should appear as credits on the other. The technique is similar to that of bank reconciliations but there are added complications in the form of discounts assumed to be taken by the firm but not allowed by the supplier, and debit notes issued by the firm that have not yet been raised as credit notes by the supplier. The items to appear on the reconciliation will include items from both the statement and the ledger account; both are likely to be incorrect, and therefore the simplest way of reconciling the two is to prepare a calculation of the corrected balance for each and ensure that they agree.

(a)

	$
Balance per supplier's statement	5,950
Less: cash in transit	(1,400)
Less: Debit Note 65	(300)
Corrected balance	4,250
Balance per ledger	3,250
Add: discount disallowed	200
Amend Credit Note 0062	100
Invoice 01395 not yet received	800
Less: Credit Note 0070 not yet received	(100)
Correct balance	4,250

(b) (i) This is an invoice from Wang to Kingston. It will have been entered in Wang's records as soon as it was issued, but has not yet been received by Kingston. (f)

   (ii) This is a credit note issued by Wang and entered in its records at once; it has not yet been received by Kingston. (g)

   (iii) This is cash discount that has been deducted by Kingston upon payment of the outstanding balance at the beginning of January, ignored or disallowed by Wang. (i)

   (iv) This is cash paid by Kingston at the end of the month, and entered in its ledger account at once; it has not yet been received by Wang. (k)

   (v) This is a debit note issued by Kingston perhaps due to goods returned; credit note not yet received by Wang. (l)

(c) $4,250 current liability.

✅ Solution 8

   (i) invoices relate to a properly authorised order;
   (ii) numbered goods received notes (GRN) should be raised, for example by storekeeper, to ensure that goods have been inspected and taken into stores;
   (iii) adequate segregation of duties exists;
   (iv) purchase ledger records should be checked against suppliers' statements.

Solution 9

(a) TD: journal entries

		Debit $	Credit $
(i)	Suspense account	1,000	
	Sales		1,000
(ii)	Plant at cost	240	
	Delivery costs		240
(iii)	Discounts received	150	
	JW		150
(iv)	Stationery inventories (balance)	240	
	Stationery account		240
(v)	Suspense account	500	
	Purchases		500
(vi)	Returns outwards	230	
	Returns inwards	230	
	Suspense		460

(b)

Suspense account

		$			$
(i)	Sales	1,000		Balance per trial balance	1,040
(v)	Purchases	500	(vi)	Returns in and out	460
		1,500			1,500

(c) Revised gross and net profit figures

	$
Gross profit – original	35,750
Add: (i)	1,000
Add: (v)	500
Less: (vi)	(460)
Revised gross profit	36,790
Net profit – original	18,500
Add: increase in gross profit	1,040
Add: (ii)	240
Less: (iii)	(150)
Add: (iv)	240
Revised net profit	19,870

Solution 10

Ratios

		20X4	20X5
(i)	*Gross profit margin*		
	$\dfrac{\text{Gross profit}}{\text{Sales}} \times 100$	$\dfrac{2,600}{14,400} \times 100 = 18.1\%$	$\dfrac{4,400}{17,000} \times 100 = 25.9\%$
(ii)	*Operating profit margin*		
	$\dfrac{\text{Operating profit}}{\text{Sales}} \times 100$	$\dfrac{1,400}{14,400} \times 100 = 9.7\%$	$\dfrac{2,400}{17,000} \times 100 = 14.1\%$
(iii)	*Return on capital employed*		
	$\dfrac{\text{Operating profit}}{\text{Average total capital}} \times 100$	$\dfrac{1,400}{6,260} \times 100 = 22.4\%$	$\dfrac{2,400}{6,210} \times 100 = 38.6\%$

 Solution 11

(a) Inventory record card – FIFO

		Receipts			Issues				Balance	
Date	Units	$/unit	$	Units	$/unit	$	Units	$/unit	$
1 Apr.							100	10	1,000
8 Apr.				24	10	240	76	10	760
18 Apr.	38	12	456				38	12	456
20 Apr.				50	10	500	26	10	260
							38	12	456
23 Apr.				26	10	260			
				9	12	108	29	12	348
28 Apr.	20	13	260				20	13	260
Totals	58		716	109		1,108	49		608

Inventory record card – LIFO

		Receipts			Issues				Balance	
Date	Units	$/unit	$	Units	$/unit	$	Units	$/unit	$
1 Apr.							100	10	1,000
8 Apr.				24	10	240	76	10	760
18 Apr.	38	12	456				38	12	456
20 Apr.				38	12	456			
				12	10	120	64	10	640
23 Apr.				35	10	350	29	10	290
28 Apr.	20	13	260				20	13	260
Totals	58		716	109		1,166	49		550

Inventory record card – AVCO

Date	Units	Receipts $/unit	$	Units	Issues $/units	$	Unit	Balance $/unit	$
1 Apr.							100	10	1,000
8 Apr.				24	10	240	76	10	760
18 Apr.	38	12	456				114	10.67	1,216
20 Apr.				50	10	533	64	10.67	683
23 Apr.				35	10	373	29	10.67	310
28 Apr.	20	13	260				49	11.63	570
Totals	58		716	109		1,146	49		570

(b) (i) recording of an issue at too high a level.
    (ii) recording of a receipt at too low a level.

✓ Solution 12

(a)   **Income statements of R Ltd for years ended 31 December**

	20X4 $'000	20X5 $'000	20X6 $'000
Profit before tax	32	46	14
Income tax	–	(5)	(6)
Profit for the period	32	41	8

(b)   **Statement of changes in equity of R Ltd for years ended 31 December**

	20X4 $'000 Gen. Res	Retained Earnings	20X5 $'000 Gen. Res	Retained Earnings	20X6 $'000 Gen. Res	Retained Earnings
Balance at start of period	–	–	–	27	18	40
Total comprehensive income for the period	32			41		8
Dividends		(5)		(10)		(10)
Transfer to general reserve			18	(18)		
Balance at end of period	–	27	18	40	18	38

(c) Capital sections of statements of financial position of R Ltd as at years ended 31 December

	20X4 $'000	20X5 $'000	20X6 $'000
Share capital	100	100	100
Share premium account	60	60	60
General reserve account	–	18	18
Retained earnings	27	40	38
	187	218	216

(d) Receivables days

   (i) Receivables days $= \dfrac{\text{Closing receivables}}{\text{Credit sales}} \times 365$

   (ii) For 20X4 : $\dfrac{40}{360} \times 365 = 41$ days

      For 20X5 : $\dfrac{45}{375} \times 365 = 44$ days

      For 20X6 : $\dfrac{52}{390} \times 365 = 49$ days

Payables' days

   (iii) Payables days $= \dfrac{\text{Closing creditors}}{\text{Credit purchases}} \times 365$

   (iv) For 20X4 $\dfrac{33 \times 365}{230} = 52$ days

      For 20X5 $\dfrac{45 - 5 \times 365}{250} = 58$ days

      For 20X6 $\dfrac{43 - 6 \times 365}{280} = 48$ days

(e) The company appears to be *increasing* the length of credit given to customers, which *slows down* the receipt of cash. At the same time it is *decreasing* the length of credit from suppliers, which *speeds up* the payment of cash. These two actions combined will cause the amount of cash available to *decrease*. If these payment periods could be brought more into line with each other, the amount of overdraft required will be *lower*.

✅ Solution 13

(a) **Income statement of APW Ltd for the year ended 30 April 20X8**

	$'000	$'000	$'000	$'000
Sales				2,660
Returns inwards				(104)
				2,556
Opening inventories of finished goods			98	
Opening inventories of raw material		234		
Purchases of raw material	785			
Carriage inwards	40			
Returns outwards	(65)			
		760		
		994		
Closing inventories of raw material		(256)		
Cost of raw material consumed		738		
Direct wages (372 + 37)		409		
Prime cost		1,147		
Indirect factory labour (118 + 15)	133			
Indirect factory overheads	63			
Heat, light and power 40% (120 + 15)	54			
Rent and insurance 30% (130 − 10)	36			
Depreciation of factory plant (10% × 1,200)	120			
Depreciation of buildings 40% (3,500 × 5%)	70			
		476		
		1,623		
Add: Opening work in progress	182			
Less: Closing work in progress	(118)			
		64		
Cost of production			1,687	
			1,785	
Closing inventories of finished goods (123 − 8)			(115)	
				(1,670)
				886
Gross profit				
Carriage outwards	20			
Administration expenses	55			
Bank charges	10			
Office salaries (130 + 27)	157			
Heat, light and power (60% × 135)	81			
Rent and insurance (70% × 120)	84			
Depreciation of buildings (60% (5% × 3,500))	105			
Depreciation of office equipment (20% × 200)	40			
Depreciation of delivery vehicles (20% × 600)	120			
			672	
			214	
Operating profit				
Interest received	12			
Debenture interest (20 + 20)	(40)			
			(28)	
			186	
Profit before tax				
Income tax			(80)	
Profit for the period			106	

(b) **Statement of changes in equity of APW Ltd for the year ended 30 April 20X8**

	Retained earnings ($'000)
Balance at start of period	580
Total comprehensive income for the period	106
Ordinary dividends	(140)
Preference dividends	(28)
Balance at end of period	518

(c) The two principal accounting conventions that affect the valuation of inventories are the prudence and the matching (or accruals) conventions. As regards the prudence convention, it is generally accepted that inventories should be valued at the lower of cost or realisable value. Thus, one of the products (Beta) in the inventories list has been valued at less than original cost. Therefore, APW Ltd is expected under the prudence convention to recognise the loss, via an inventories write-down, that is, anticipate losses, but not take profits until they are reasonably certain.

In accordance with the matching convention, the cost of inventories sold in the accounting period is matched against the revenue generated from the sale of such inventories. Any inventories unsold in the period are carried forward as a current asset into the next period. In fact, the convention also applies to the valuation of such inventories, that is, it is to be valued at the cost of getting the inventories into a saleable condition, which in the case of a manufacturing company such as APW Ltd will include both variable and fixed production costs. While the above two conventions are the main ones involved, the consistency convention would also apply. The inventories cost formula used by APW Ltd should be applied consistently from one period to another. In most cases, such a company would use the FIFO cost formula.

Solution 14

(a)

Bank account of FLS Ltd for the year ended 30 September 20X8

	$'000		$'000
Receipts	13,300	Balance b/fwd	520
Balance c/fwd	895	Payments	7,525
		Selling and distribution costs	2,750
		Administration costs	2,400
		Preference dividend	50
		Ordinary dividend	150
		Last year's ordinary dividend	300
		Loan interest	400
		Income tax	100
	14,195		14,195

(b)

Trial balance FLS Ltd as at 30 September 20X8

	$'000 Debit	$'000 Credit
Retained earnings		600
Revaluation reserve		1,250
Inventories at 30 September 20X7	1,250	
Land at valuation	5,800	
Buildings at cost	3,800	
Plant at cost	2,800	
Accumulated depreciation on buildings at 30 September 20X7		800
Accumulated depreciation on plant at 30 September 20X7		600
Goodwill	2,000	
Long-term loan		8,000
Allowance for receivables at 30 September 20X7		80
Sales		14,000
Purchases	7,400	
Returns outwards		75
Selling and distribution costs	2,750	
Administration costs (2,400 + 100)	2,500	
Bad debts written off	200	
Dividends – preference	50	
Dividends – ordinary	150	
Loan interest (half year)	400	
Receivables	2,350	
Payables		850
Bank account		895
Share capital – ordinary		3,000
Share premium account		300
Share capital – preference		1,000
	31,450	31,450

(c)

Income statement of FLS Ltd for the year ended 30 September 20X8

	$'000	$'000	$'000
Sales (14, 000 − 100)			13,900
Opening inventories		1,250	
Purchases	7,400		
Returns outwards	(75)		
		7,325	
		8,575	
Closing inventories		(1,450)	
Cost of goods sold			(7,125)
Gross profit			6,775
Selling and distribution costs (2,750 − 50)		2,700	
Administration costs (2,500 + 25)		2,525	
Bad debts written off		200	
Change in allowance for receivables (80 − 47)		(33)	
Depreciation of buildings (2% of 3,800)		76	
Depreciation of plant 5% (2,800 − 600)		110	
			(5,578)
Operating profit			1197
Loan interest (400 + 400)			(800)
Profit before tax			397
Income tax			(140)
Profit for the period			257

Statement of changes in equity of FLS Ltd for the year ended 30 September 20X8

Retained earnings	
Balance at start of period	600
Total comprehensive income	257
for the period	
Preference dividends	(50)
Ordinary dividends (150 + 600)	(750)
Balance at end of period	57

(d) Analysis of total capital employed

	$
Ordinary share capital	3,000
Share premium	300
Preference share capital	1,000
Revaluation reserve	1,250
Retained earnings	57
Shareholders' funds	5,607
Long-term loan	8,000
Total capital employed	13,607

$$\text{Gearing ration} = \frac{\text{Loan capital}}{\text{Total capital}} \times 100 = \frac{8,000}{13,607} \times 100 = 59\%$$

Solution 15

(a) Ledger accounts

Transactions

Date	Description	Debit $	Credit $	Balance $
Ibrahim				
1 Oct.	Balance b/f			1,250 cr
4 Oct.	Purchase daybook		7,050	8,300 cr
4 Oct.	Cash book	1,225		7,075 cr
4 Oct.	Discount received	25		7,050 cr
15 Oct.	Purchase daybook		14,100	21,150 cr
28 Oct.	Returns out book	705		20445 cr
J Hall				
1 Oct.	Balance b/f			150 cr
21 Oct.	Petty cash book	150		NIL
J Bolton				
3 Oct.	Returns out book	2,350		2,350 dr
11 Oct.	Purchase daybook		35,250	32,900 cr
Z Rhawandala				
13 Oct.	Purchase daybook		5,875	5,875 cr
Sales tax				
31 Oct.	Purchase daybook	9,275		9,275 dr
31 Oct.	Returns out book		455	8,820 dr
31 Oct.	Cash sales		9,100	280 cr
Sales				
31 Oct.	Cash sales		52,000	52,000 cr
Purchases				
31 Oct.	Purchase daybook	53,000		53,000 dr
Returns outwards				
31 Oct.	Returns out book		2,600	2,600 cr
Postage				
31 Oct.	Petty cash book	116		116 dr
Discount received				
4 Oct.	Ibrahim		25	25 cr
Travel				
31 Oct.	Petty cash book	230		230 dr

(b) (i) Office equipment should have been debited to a non-current asset account.

(ii) The profit will have been understated by $5,000 less any depreciation charge.

✓ Solution 16

(a) Calculation of operating profit

	$'000
Gross profit	239
Expenses	(159)
Profit for the period	80
Add back interest	30
Therefore, operating profit	110

Cash generated from operations

	$'000
Operating profit	110
Add back depreciation (50 + 25)	75
Add back loss on disposal	10
Decrease in inventories	100
Increase in receivables	(20)
Decrease in payables	(67)
	208

Purchase cost of non-current assets

	Premises $'000	*Plant* $'000	
Carrying amount at 31 December 20X8	1,200	800	
Carrying amount at 31 December 20X7	(1,170)	(700)	
Depreciation charge	25	50	
Disposal – cost	–	85	
Disposal – acc. depn	–	(25)	
Purchases	55	210	(total $265,000)

Cash-flow statement of AMS Ltd for the year ended 31 August 20X8

	$'000	$'000
Cash flows from operating activities		
Cash generated from operations		208
Interest		(30)
Income tax		(12)
		166
Cash flow from investing activities		
Payments to acquire tangible non-current assets	(265)	
Receipts from sale of tangible non-current assets	50	
		(215)
Cash flow from financing activities		
Equity dividends paid	(11)	
Issue of ordinary shares (500 + 100)	600	
Repayment of long-term loans	(200)	
		389
Net increase in bank and cash		340
Bank and cash at the beginning of the period		(40)
Bank and cash at the end of the period		300

(b) (i) A statement of cash flows shows inflows and outflows of cash during the period. It reconciles opening and closing cash balances.

(ii) The income statement includes non-cash items, and excludes cash involved in capital transactions.

Solution 17

(a) **Income statement of BAK plc for the year ended 30 April 20X9**

	$'000	$'000	$'000
Sales			19,620
Returns inwards			(320)
			19,320
Cost of sales			
Opening inventories		1,420	
Purchases	7,390		
Carriage inwards	240		
		7,630	
		9,050	
Closing inventories		(1,280)	
Cost of goods sold			(7,770)
Gross profit			(11,530)
Research and development expenses (846 − 396)	450		
Distribution costs	2,860		
Administration costs	970		
Salaries and wages	1,310		
Printing, stationery and adverts (900 − 150)	750		
Premises costs (310 − 80)	230		
Loss on disposal of non-current assets	50		
Reduction in allowance for receivables (102 − 62)	(40)		
Bonuses owing (2% of 19,300)	386		
Depreciation of vehicles (20% of 6,000)	1,200		
Depreciation of office equipment (10% of 1,200)	120		
Auditors' fees (accrual)	115		
			(8,401)
Operating profit			3,129
Loan interest (100 + 100)			(200)
Profit before tax			2,929
Income tax			(900)
Profit for the period			2,029

(b) **Statement of changes in equity of BAK plc for the year ended 30 April 20X9**

	General reserves $'000	Retained earnings $'000	Total $'000
Balance at the start of the period	700	420	1,120
Total comprehensive income for the period		2,029	2,029
Ordinary dividends		(80)	(80)
Preference dividends		(40)	(40)
Transfer to general reserve	1,000	(1,000)	
Balance at the end of the period	1,700	1,329	3,029

(c)

Statement of financial position of BAK plc at 30 April 20X9

	Cost $'000	Depreciation $'000	Carrying amount $'000
Assets			
Non-current assets			
Tangibles			
Office equipment	1,200	(480)	720
Vehicles	6,000	(2,200)	3,800
	7,200	(2,680)	4,520
Intangibles			
Goodwill		1,000	
Development expenditure		396	
			1,396
			5,916
Current assets			
Inventories of goods	1,280		
Inventories of advertising material	150		
Receivables (3,100 − 62)	3,038		
Prepayments	80		
Bank	2,476		
			7,024
			12,940
Equity and liabilities			
Ordinary share capital			3,200
Preference share capital			800
Share premium account			640
General reserves (700 + 1,000)			1,700
Retained earnings			1,329
			7,669
Non-current liability			
Loan			1,000
Current liabilities			
Payables	1,770		
Loan	1,000		
Accruals (115 + 100 + 386)	601		
Income tax	900		
			4,271
			12,940

Solution 18

(a)

Sales ledger control account

	$		$
Balance b/f	184,650	Returns inwards	13,240
Credit sales	330,445	Received from receivables	320,045
Refunds to receivables	8,255	Discounts allowed	2,115
Dishonoured cheques	8,395	Bad debts written off	3,450
		Contras	2,420
		Balance c/f	190,475
	531,745		531,745
Balance b/f	190,475		

Purchase ledger control account

	$		$
Returns outwards	27,490	Balance b/f	142,320
Payments to payables	196,360	Credit purchases	215,965
Discounts received	1,430		
Contras	2,420		
Balance c/f	130,585		
	358,285		358,285
		Balance b/f	130,585

(b)   Reconciliation

	Receivables		*Payables*
	$		$
Control account totals	190,475		130,585
Ledger account totals	192,120		134,290
Adjustment re note (iv)	(1,645)	Adjustment re note (v)	(1,600)
	190,475		132,690

From this we can see that there would appear to be an error within the purchase ledger or its control account, as they do not agree.

(c)   Other internal controls that could be used are:
   (i) independent preparation of a bank reconciliation statement on a regular basis;
   (ii) regular preparation of a trial balance to confirm arithmetical accuracy of the ledger accounts;
   (iii) segregation of duties so that no one person is involved in a complete process.

Solution 19

(i) Profit ratios

	20X7	20X8
$\dfrac{\text{Gross profit}}{\text{Sales}} \times 100$	$\dfrac{6{,}700}{25{,}000} \times 100 = 26.8\%$	$\dfrac{12{,}300}{28{,}000} \times 100 = 43.9\%$
$\dfrac{\text{Gross profit}}{\text{Cost of sales}} \times 100$	$\dfrac{6{,}700}{18{,}300} \times 100 = 36.6\%$	$\dfrac{12{,}300}{15{,}700} \times 100 = 78.3\%$
$\dfrac{\text{Operating profit}}{\text{Sales}} \times 100$	$\dfrac{2{,}500}{25{,}000} \times 100 = 10\%$	$\dfrac{6{,}100}{28{,}000} \times 100 = 21.8\%$
$\dfrac{\text{Operating profit}}{\text{Average capital}} \times 100$	$\dfrac{2{,}500}{19{,}200} \times 100 = 13\%$	$\dfrac{6{,}100}{23{,}250} \times 100 = 26.2\%$

(ii) Liquidity ratios

Current assets:current liabilities 6,100:3,900 = 1.6:1 8,000:4,700 = 1.7:1
Current assets less inventories:current 3,800:3,900 = 0:97:13,200:4,700 = 0.68:1
liabilities

(iii) Efficiency ratios

Inventories days

$\dfrac{\text{Average Inventories}}{\text{Cost of sales}} \times 365$	$\dfrac{2{,}250}{18{,}300} \times 365 = 45 \text{ days}$	$\dfrac{2{,}550}{15{,}700} \times 365 = 59 \text{ days}$

Receivables days

$\dfrac{\text{Receivables}}{\text{Sales}} \times 365$	$\dfrac{2{,}500}{25{,}000} \times 365 = 37 \text{ days}$	$\dfrac{3{,}200}{28{,}000} \times 365 = 42 \text{ days}$

Payables days

$\dfrac{\text{Payables}}{\text{Purchases}} \times 365$	$\dfrac{3{,}900}{18{,}400} \times 365 = 77 \text{ days}$	$\dfrac{3{,}600}{16{,}200} \times 365 = 81 \text{ days}$
$\dfrac{\text{Expenses}}{\text{Sales}} \times 100$	$\dfrac{4{,}200}{25{,}000} \times 100 = 16.8\%$	$\dfrac{6{,}200}{28{,}000} \times 100 = 22.1\%$

Solution 20

Workings

1.

Reconstruction of JB cash book				
		$		$
Capital introduced		22,000	Balance b/f	8,850
Receipts from receivables		427,500	Cash withdrawn: Wages	6,750
		449,500	Purchases	4,200
			Advertising	2,600
			Drawings	8,900
Therefore, balancing figure			Loan repayments	20,000
Cash sales	10,160		Payments to payables	175,600
Less: wages	(1,560)	8,600	Rent	22,000
			Wages	90,000
			General expenses	12,500
			Balance c/d	106,700
		458,100		458,100

2. Calculation of credit sales

	$	
Receipts	427,500	
Less: opening receivables	(32,500)	(35,000 − 2,500)
Add: closing receivables	22,300	
	417,300	

3. Calculation of credit purchases

	$	
Payments	175,600	
Less: opening payables	(13,300)	(17,600 − 4,300)
Add: closing payables	12,200	
	174,500	

4. Calculation of closing receivables

	$
Receivables	22,300
Less: bad debt 80% of $16,000	(12,800)
	9,500

5. Office equipment

Original cost $45,000/9 \times 10 = 50,000$

Therefore, depreciation $= \$5,000$ p.a.

(a)   **Income statement of JB for the year ended 31 December 20X5**

	$	$	$
Credit sales (W2)			417,300
Cash sales			10,160
			427,460
Opening inventories		30,500	
Credit purchases (W3)	174,500		
Cash purchases	4,200		
		178,700	
		209,200	
Closing inventories		(27,850)	
			(181,350)
Gross profit			246,110
Wages (6,750 + 90,000 + 1,560 − 4,300 + 5,250)		99,260	
Advertising expenses ($2,600/2)		1,300	
Loan interest		9,500	
Rent (22,000 + 2,500 − 2,700)		21,800	
General expenses		12,500	
Bad debt written off (W4)		12,800	
Depreciation			
Plant and Machinery (20% × 128,000)		25,600	
Vehicle (25% × 5,000)		1,250	
Office equipment (W5)		5,000	
			(189,010)
			57,100

(b)   **Statement of financial statement of JB as at 31 December 20X5**

Assets	$	$	$
Non-current assets			
Plant and machinery			102,400
Office equipment			40,000
Vehicle			3,750
			146,150
Current assets			
Inventories	27,850		
Receivables (W4)	9,500		
Prepayments (2,700 + 1,300)	4,000		
Bank (W1)	106,700		
			148,050
			294,200
Capital and liabilities			
Capital at 1 January 20X5			117,050
Add: capital introduced			27,000
Add: profit			57,100
Less: drawings			(8,900)
			192,250
Non-current liability			
Long-term loan			84,500
Current liabilities			
Payables	12,200		
Accruals	5,250		
			17,450
			294,200

Solution 21

(a)   Calculation of loss on disposal

	$'000
Accumulated depreciation at 30 June 20X6	2,300
Less: Charge for the year	(255)
	2,045
Accumulated depreciation at 30 June 20X5	(2,100)
Therefore, accumulated depreciation relating to disposal	(55)
Proceeds	145
Carrying amount (230 − 55)	(175)
Therefore, loss on disposal	(30)

(b)   Calculation of cash generated from operations

	$'000
Operating profit (250 + 30)	280
Add: Depreciation for year	255
Increase in inventories	(350)
Decrease in receivables	135
Decrease in payables	(650)
	(330)

(c)   **Statement of cash flows of SH Ltd for year ended 30 June 20X6**

	$'000	$'000
Cash flows from operating activities		(330)
Cash flow from investing activities		
Purchase of non-current assets ((3,000 − 230) − 3,500)	(730)	
Sale of non-current assets	145	
		(585)
Cash flows from financing activities		
Proceeds from share issue	800	
Dividends paid	(75)	
		725
Net decrease in cash		(190)
Cash at beginning of period		2,350
Cash at end of period		2,160

(d)   Calculation of ratios

	20X5		20X6	
Current ratio				
CA : CL	8,375 : 5,075	1.65 : 1	8,400 : 4,430	1.90 : 1
Liquid or quick ratio				
CA less inventories : CL	7,550 : 5,075	1.49 : 1	7,225 : 4,430	1.63 : 1

Solution 22

Updating the cash book for items found on the bank statement not entered in books of MTR:

		$		$
16/11/X6	Balance b/fwd	6,368	Rent	844
	Receipt (credit transfer)	685	Bank charges	130
			Receivable a/c (dishon. cheque)	425
			Amended balance	5,654
		7,053		7,053

Bank reconciliation at 16 November 20X6

	$
Balance as per updated cash book	5,654
Add: Unpresented cheque	435
Less: Deposit not yet entered by bank	(1,480)
Balance as per bank statement	4,609

 Solution 23

(a)   **Income statement of TYR Ltd for the year ended 31 October 20X7**

	$'000	$'000	$'000
Sales (2,569 − 12)			2,557
Cost of sales			
Opening inventories		210	
Purchases	1,745		
Returns outward	(34)		
Carriage inwards	15		
		1,726	
		1,936	
Closing inventories (194 + 7)		(201)	
			(1,735)
Gross profit			822
Administration expenses (264 − 12 + 17)		269	
Selling and distribution expenses (292 − 28)		264	
Carriage outwards		18	
Depreciation			
Premises (4% of 350)		14	
Plant & equipment (10% of 220)		22	
			(587)
Operating profit			235
Debenture interest (15 + 15)			(30)
Profit before tax			205
Income tax			(40)
Profit for the period			165
Other comprehensive income		55	
Gain on property revaluation before tax		(15)	
Income tax			
Gain on property revaluation after tax			40
Total comprehensive income			205

(b)

Statement of changes in equity of TYR Ltd for the year ended 31 October 20X7

	Share capital $'000	Share premium $'000	Revaluation reserve $'000	Retained earnings $'000	Total $'000
Balance at the start of the period	1,000	100	135	190	1,425
Total comprehensive income for the period			40	165	205
Dividends paid				(20)	(20)
Balance at the end of the period	1,000	100	175	335	1,610

(c)

Statement of financial position of TYR Ltd as at 31 October 20X7

	Cost or valuation $'000	Acc. Dep'n $'000	Carrying amount $'000
Assets			
Tangible non-current assets			
Land	550	–	550
Premises	350	(34)	316
Plant and equipment	220	(52)	168
	1,120	(86)	1,034
Intangible non-current assets			
Patents and trademarks	200	–	200
	1,320	(86)	1,234
Current assets			
Inventories (194 + 7)	201		
Receivables (875 − 12)	863		
Prepayments (12 + 28)	40		
Cash	12		
			1,116
			2,350
Equity and liabilities			
Share capital			1,000
Share premium			100
Revaluation reserve account (135 + 40)			175
Retained earnings			335
			1,610
Non-current liabilities			
12% Debentures (2010)	250		
Income tax on gain property revaluation	15		
Current liabilities			265
Payables	318		
Bank	85		
Accrued expenses (17 + 15)	32		
Income tax	40		475
			2,350

(d) (i) Gross profit mark-up

$$\frac{\text{Gross profit}}{\text{Cost of sales}} \times 100 = \frac{822}{1,735} \times 100 = 47.4\%$$

This is lower than in the previous year. It may be due to increased price competition in the marketplace; a deliberate policy of offering tighter margins to improve volume of sales; or that the company has been less efficient in purchasing.

(ii) Operating profit margin

$$\frac{\text{Operating profit}}{\text{Sales}} \times 100 = \frac{205}{2,557} \times 100 = 8\%$$

This is much better than last year and would suggest that the company is deriving the benefits of economies of scale. Quite clearly, costs have risen at a lower rate than that of the revenue.

(iii) Current ratio

Current assest: current liabilities $= 1,116 : 560 = 2 : 1$

This is lower than last year's ratio and perhaps is a sign of increased efficiency in terms of managing the cash flow cycle. The calculations of the relevant efficiency ratios would give us more information on which to draw conclusions.

(iv) Acid test ratio

Current assents minus inventories: current liabilities
$= (1,116 - 201) : 560 = 1.63 : 1$

This is lower than last year, but may be considered to be unnecessarily high. The company appears to have a high proportion of receivables in relation to the turnover. As stated above, the calculation of the receivables days would assist in this evaluation.

 Solution 24

(a)

Cash book

Date	Details	Disc	$	Date	Details	Disc	$
4/9/X7	A Barton	20	380	1/9/X7	Balance b/f		347
8/9/X7	C Sikorski	30	1,170	10/9/X7	J Swinbum	60	1,140
22/9/X7	C Sikorski		799	15/9/X7	Sales tax		832
25/9/X7	F Gray		170	17/9/X7	P Taylor	20	380
30/9/X7	Receivables		10,500	20/9/X7	Motor vehicle a/c		9,400
30/9/X7	Balance c/f		12,430	20/9/X7	Motor expenses		150
				30/9/X7	Wages		2,000
				30/9/X7	Payables		11,200
		50	25,449			80	25,449
				1/10/X7	Balance b/f		12,430

(b)

A Barton

Date		$	Date		$
1/9/X7	Balance b/f	400	4/9/X7	Bank	380
3/9/X7	Sales	188	4/9/X7	Discount allowed	20
			5/9/X7	Returns inward	47
			30/9/X7	Balance c/f	141
		588			588
1/10/X7	Balance b/f	141			

C Sikorski

Date		$	Date		$
1/9/X7	Balance b/f	1,200	8/9/X7	Bank	1,170
8/9/X7	Sales	940	8/9/X7	Discount allowed	30
12/9/X7	Sales	423	18/9/X7	Returns inward	141
			22/9/X7	Bank	799
			30/9/X7	Balance c/f	423
		2,563			2,563
1/10/X7	Balance b/f	423			

F Gray

Date		$	Date		$
1/9/X7	Balance b/f	340	25/9/X7	Bank	170
			25/9/X7	Bad debts a/c	170
		340			340

(c) **Calculation of the allowance for receivables on 30 September 19X7**

	Total receivables as per schedule $	Adjustments $	Revised balances $	Allowance $
Current	12,000	(60)	11,940 at 0%	Nil
30–60 days	7,500	(200)	7,300 at 5%	365
60–90 days	3,600	–	3,600 at 10%	360
90+ days	1,100	(240)	860 at 20%	172
Revised cumulative allowance				897

Therefore, the allowance for receivables account will need to be increased by (credited with) $447 (897 − 450).

(d)   The principal accounting convention involved is the prudence convention.

Solution 25

	Non-current assets	Working capital	Profit
(i)	No change	No change	No change
(ii)	Decrease	Increase	Increase
(iii)	No change	Decrease	No change
(iv)	No change	Decrease	Decrease

 Solution 26

(a) A receipts and payments account is a summary of the cash and bank transactions for the relevant period; in essence, it is a summarised cash book.

An income and expenditure statement is essentially the same as an income statement. It takes into account prepayments and accruals and distinguishes between capital and revenue items.

(b) **Income and expenditure statement of Monarch Sports Club for the year ended 30 June 20X7**

	$	$
Income		
Annual subscriptions		
Receipts in year	18,000	
Add: Subs in advance at 1/7/X6	1,100	
Less: Subs in arrears at 1/7/X6	(100)	
Less: Subs in advance at 30/6/X7	(900)	
Add: Subs in arrears at 30/6/X7	300	
		18,400
Life membership (10% of 3,000)		300
Surplus on competitions (7,500 − 4,300)		3,200
Entrance fees		2,500
		24,400
Expenses		
Bad debts written off (subs from previous year)	100	
Transport to matches	3,700	
Coaching fees (2,100 − 150 + 450)	2,400	
Repairs to equipment	800	
Loss on disposal of equipment (1,200 − 1,000)	200	
Depreciation of new equipment (20% of 4,000)	800	
		(8,000)
Surplus for year		16,400

Solution 27

(a)

Income statement of Robert Costello for the year ended 30 September 20X9

	$	$
Sales (305,000 + 5,500 + 4,800)		315,300
Opening inventories	42,500	
Purchases	180,300	
	222,800	
Closing inventories	(45,200)	
Cost of sales		(177,600)
Gross profit		137,700
Loan interest	3,600	
Rental of shop (24,000 − 6,000)	18,000	
Local business tax (3,500 − 1,200)	2,300	
General office expenses	8,800	
Heating and lighting (2,400 + 350)	2,750	
Car insurance	400	
Wages (18,500 − 15,000 + 3,760)	7,260	
Depreciation of fixtures and fittings	1,280	
Depreciation of motor vehicle	3,000	
Loss on disposal	1,000	
Stationery	400	
Petrol	1,200	
Bad debts & allowance for receivables (3,000 + 2,845)	5,845	
		(55,835)
Net profit		81,865

(b)

Statement of financial position of Robert Costello as at 30 September 20X9

Assets	Cost	Acc. Dep'n	Carrying Amount
Non-current assets	$	$	$
Fixtures and fittings	10,000	(4,880)	5,120
Motor vehicle	15,000	(3,000)	12,000
	25,000	(7,880)	17,120
Current assets			
Inventories	45,200		
Receivables (62,900 − 5,845)	57,055		
Prepayments (6,000 + 1,200)	7,200		
Bank	18,500		
			127,955
			145,075

Capital and liabilities			
Balance on 1 October 20X8			26,600
Profit for year			81,865
Drawings			(15,000)
			93,465
Non-current liabilities			
Bank loan (40,000 − 9,000 − 12,000)			19,000
Current liabilities			
Payables	15,200		
Accrued expenses	350		
Sales tax (4,500 + 840 − 70 − 210)	5,060		
Bank loan	12,000		
			32,610
			145,075

Workings

(i) Closing inventories of $45,200 appears in the income statement as part of the cost of goods sold calculation and in the statement of financial position under current assets.

(ii) Deduct $6,000 from shop rental and include as a prepayment.

(iii) Half the $2,400 represents a prepayment.

(iv) Add $350 to heating and lighting and include as an accrual.

(v) Deduct $15,000 from wages and treat as drawings.

(vi) Increase sales by $4,800
Increase sales tax a/c by $840
Increase stationery by $400
Reduce sales tax a/c by $70
Increase wages by $3,760
Increase petrol by $1,200
Reduce sales tax a/c by $210.

(vii) Motor vehicle at cost will now be (21,000 − 8,000 + 2,000), that is $15,000.
The trial balance depreciation figure is to be eliminated.
There is a loss on disposal of $3,000 − $2,000, that is $1,000.

(viii) The depreciation charge re fixtures and fittings is 20% ($10,000 − $3,600) = $1,280.
The depreciation charge re the new motor vehicle is 20% of $15,000 = $3,000.

(ix) Write off $3,000 as a bad debt plus an allowance for receivables 5% (62,900 − 6,000) = $2,845.

(x) The $12,600 is $9,000 capital repayment, and $3,600 interest paid. Also, next year's capital repayments of $12,000 are to be treated as a current liability.

Solution 28

(a)

Capital

		$			$
			1/10/9X9	Bank	20,000

Bank

		$			$
1/10/X9	Capital	20,000	3/10/X9	Rent payable	1,200
28/10/X9	P Assad	500	5/10/X9	Office equipment	5,000
			25/10/X9	A Jones	3,000

Purchases

		$			$
2/10/X9	A Jones	3,500			
18/10/X9	A Jones	2,400			

A Jones

		$			$
15/10/X9	Returns outwards	500	2/10/X9	Purchases	3,500
25/10/X9	Bank	3,000	18/10/X9	Purchases	2,400
31/10/X9	Balance c/d	2,400			
		5,900			5,900
			1/11/X9	Balance b/d	2,400

Rent payable

		$			$
3/10/X9	Bank	1,200			

Office equipment

		$			$
5/10/X9	Bank	5,000			

Sales

		$			$
			10/10/X9	P Assad	1,750

P Assad

		$			$
10/10/X9	Sales	1,750	28/10/X9	Bank	500
			31/10/X9	Balance c/d	1,250
		1,750			1,750

Returns outwards

		$			$
			15/10/X9	A Jones	500

(b)   Calculation of Tanwir's closing capital

	$
Initial bank deposit	20,000
Vehicle introduced	6,000
Petrol payments	650
Profit for the year	17,500
Drawings	
Cash	(5,000)
Private telephone expenses	(450)
	38,700

(c)   The accounting convention involved is the business entity convention.

 Solution 29

(a)   FIFO cost formula

Date	Quantity	Receipts price $	Value $	Quantity	Issues price $	Value $	Balance quantity	Value $
1 Oct.	120	8	960				120	960
3 Oct.	180	9	1,620				300	2,580
4 Oct.				120	8	960		
				30	9	270		
				150		1,230	150	1,350
8 Oct.				80	9	720	70	630
12 Oct.				30	9	270	40	360
18 Oct.	300	10	3,000				340	3,360
22 Oct.				40	9	360		
				60	10	600		
				100		960	240	2,400
28 Oct.	20	10	200				260	2,600

(b)   AVCO cost formula

Date	Quantity	Repeipts price $	Value $	Quantity	Issues price $	Value $	Balance quanity	Value $
1 Oct.	120	8	960				120	960
3 Oct.	180	9	1,620				300	2,580
4 Oct.				150	8.6	1,290	150	1,290
8 Oct.				80	8.6	688	70	602
12 Oct.				30	9.0	270	40	332
18 Oct.	300	10	3,000				340	3,332
22 Oct.				100	9.8	980	240	2,352
28 Oct.	20	9.8	196				260	2,548

(c)   Trading accounts of Jay Ltd

	FIFO	AVCO
	$	$
Opening inventory	960	960
Purchases (1,620 + 3,000 − 270)	4,350	4,350
	5,310	5,310
Closing inventory	(2,600)	(2,548)
Cost of sales	2,710	2,762
Sales (1,800 + 1,200 + 1,500 – 300)	(4,200)	(4,200)
Gross profit	1,490	1,438

✅ Solution 30

Statement of changes in equity of MMM Ltd

Year 1

	Share capital	Share premium	General reserve $	Retained earnings $
Balance at the start of the period	–	–	–	–
Shares issued	360,000	144,000	–	–
Total comprehensive income for the period (48,800 − 6,500) (55,000 − 8,000)				42,300
Dividends				(18,000)
Transfer to reserves			5,000	(5,000)
Balance at the end of the period	360,000	144,000	5,000	19,300

Year 2

	Share capital $	Share premium	General reserve $	Retained earnings $
Balance at the start of the period	360,000	144,000	5,000	19,300
Shares issued	30,000	15,000		
Total comprehensive income for the period (48,800–6,500) (55,000–8,000)				47,000
Dividends				(31,200)
Transfer to reserves			5,000	(5,000)
Balance at the end of the period	390,000	159,000	10,000	30,100

Solution 31

(a)

Income statement of EMP plc for the year ended 31 October 20X1

	$m	$m	$m
Sales			376
Less: returns inwards			(16)
			360
Cost of sales			
Opening inventories		62	
Purchases	230		
Carriage inwards	1		
Returns outwards	(12)		
		219	
		281	
Closing inventories		(106)	
			(175)
Gross profit			185
Administrative expenses			
Wages and salaries (28 + 3)		31	
Directors' fees (10 + 2)		12	
Telephone costs (12 + 4 − 1)		15	
Rent and insurance (8 − 2)		6	
Heat and light		16	
Printing and stationery		12	
Audit fee		1	
Bank charges		2	
Distribution expenses (24 − 1)		23	
Bad debts written off		5	
Change in allowance for receivables (decrease)*		(6)	
Depreciation			
Plant (10% of 250)		25	
Office equipment 33.3% (90 − 30)		20	
			(162)
Operating profit			23
Income tax			(2)
Profit for the period			21

*Calculation of the decrease in allowance for receivables:

	$m
2.5% of (84 + 1 − 5) =	2
Brought forward figure	(8)
Therefore, a decrease of	(6)

(b)

Statement of changes in equity of EMP plc for the year ended 31 October 20X1

	General reserves $m	Retained earnings $m	Total $m
Balance at the start of the period	14	62	76
Total comprehensive income for the period		21	21
Dividends		(4)	(4)
Transfer to general reserves	20	(20)	
Balance at the end of the period	34	59	93

(c)

Statement of financial position of EMP plc as at 31 October 20X1

Assets	Cost $m	Acc. Depreciation $m	Carrying Amount $m
Non-current assets			
Plant and machinery	250	(81)	169
Office equipment	90	(50)	40
	340	(131)	209
Current assets			
Inventories		106	
Receivables		80	
Less: allowance		(2)	
		78	
Prepayments		3	
Bank		5	
			192
			401
Equity and liabilities			
Share capital			200
Share premium			16
General reserves (14 + 20)		34	
Retained earnings		59	
			93
			309
Current liabilities			
Trade payables		80	
Accruals		10	
Income tax		2	
			92
			401

(d) (i) *Acid test or quick ratio*

Current assets minus inventories : current liabilities $(192 - 106) : 98 = 0.88 : 1$

(ii) *Inventories days*

$$\frac{\text{Average inventories}}{\text{Cost of sales}} \times 365 = \text{inventories days}$$

$$\frac{(62 + 106)/2}{175} \times 365 = 175 \text{ days}$$

Solution 32

(a) Journal entries

		Debit $	Credit $
(i)	Purchases	6,000	
	J Brown (payable)		6,000
(ii)	Office equipment	4,000	
	Bad debts	500	
	Zhang (receivable)		4,500
(iii)	Administration expenses	10,600	
	Bank		10,600
(iv)	Receivables	720	
	Disposal account		720
(v)	Wages account	3,000	
	Wages account (employer's social security tax)	130	
	Employees' income tax payable		450
	Social security tax payable		250
	Wages payable		2,430

(b) Recalculated net profit

	$
Net profit before adjustments	37,500
Less:	
Purchases	(6,000)
Bad debts	(500)
Administration expenses	(10,600)
Loss on disposal	(160)
Wages accrual	(3,130)
Amended net profit	17,110

(c) (i) Capital expenditure is the acquisition, production or enhancement of non-current assets. Revenue expenditure includes the purchase of goods for resale, and expenditure on goods and services to be consumed during the reporting period.

(ii)

Effect of incorrect treatment

	$
Amount now deemed to be revenue expenditure	15,000
Adjustment to depreciation charge*	(1,500)
	13,500

that is, the profit will be $13,500 less than the original amount.

	$
*Original depreciation charge 10% of 25,000	2,500
Revised amount 10% of 10,000	(1,000)
	1,500

Solution 33

Sales ledger control account

	$		$
Balance b/f	95,760	Balance b/f	3,400
Credit sales	757,875	Receipts	729,600
Refunds	4,385	Discounts allowed	2,450
Dishonoured cheques	15,215	Returns inwards	30,315
Bad debt written back	1,200	Bad debts written off	2,875
		Contra	5,400
Balance c/f	5,750	Balance c/f	106,145
	880,185		880,185

 Solution 34

(a)

Rent, local business tax and insurance

Date	Account	$	Date	Account	$
1/11	Local business tax prepaid b/f	550	1/11	Rent accrued b/f	700
			3/1	Bank – insurance	80
1/11	Insurance prepaid b/f	400	31/10	Local business tax	500
1/11	Bank – rent	2,100		prepaid c/f*	
28/12	Bank – insurance	3,000		Insurance prepaid c/f*	500
1/2	Bank – rent	2,100		Income statement	12,470
8/4	Bank – local business tax	1,200			
1/8	Bank – rent	4,200			
31/10	Rent accrued c/f	700			
		14,250			14,250

Calculations:

$$\text{Rates prepaid} = 1,200/12 \times 5 = \$500$$
$$\text{Insurance prepaid} = 3,000/12 \times 2 = \$500$$

(b) The *prudence convention* stipulates that revenue and profits should not be anticipated. However, expenses, liabilities and losses should be provided for as soon as it is known that an expense has been incurred that relates to the accounting period, or the possibility of a liability or loss exists.

The *accruals (or matching) convention* stipulates that costs and revenues are matched with each other in accordance with the period to which they relate, regardless of the period in which the receipt or payment occurs.

(c) Change in bank balance

	$
Profit for the year	47,500
Add: depreciation charge	8,200
Add: loss on disposal	1,200
Less: purchase of non-current assets*	(32,800)
Sale of non-current assets	5,400
Increase in receivables	(2,500)
Decrease in inventories	5,200
Increase in payables	1,800
Less: drawings	(7,000)
Long-term loan paid off	(8,000)
Increase in bank balance	19,000
*Increase in non-current assets	18,000
Add: depreciation	8,200
Add: carrying amount of disposed assets	6,600
Therefore, purchases must be	32,800

Mock Assessment 1

Mock Assessment 1

Certificate in Business Accounting

Fundamentals of Financial Accounting

Illustrative Computer-based Assessment

Instructions: attempt all 50 questions

Time allowed: 2 hours

Do not look at or attempt this illustrative computer-based assessment until you have fully completed your revision and are about to sit your computer-based assessment.

Illustrative computer-based assessment 1: Questions

Question 1

The fundamental objective of an external audit of a limited company is to:

(A) give advice to shareholders.
(B) detect fraud and errors.
(C) measure the performance and financial position of a company.
(D) provide an opinion on the financial statements.

Question 2

A receives goods from B on credit terms and A subsequently pays by cheque. A then discovers that the goods are faulty and cancels the cheque before it is cashed by B.
  How should A record the cancellation of the cheque in his books?

(A) Debit payables, credit returns outwards.
(B) Credit bank, debit payables.
(C) Debit bank, credit payables.
(D) Credit payables, debit returns outwards.

Question 3

The profit of a business may be calculated by using which of the following formulae?

(A) Opening capital − drawings + capital introduced − closing capital.
(B) Closing capital + drawings − capital introduced − opening capital.
(C) Opening capital + drawings − capital introduced − closing capital.
(D) Closing capital − drawings + capital introduced − opening capital.

Question 4

The turnover in a company was $3 million and its receivables were 5 per cent of turnover. The company wishes to have an allowance for receivables of 4 per cent of receivables, which would make the provision 33% higher than the current provision. What figure would appear in the income statement?

Debit/Credit	$

 **Question 5**

Which of the following should be accounted for as capital expenditure?

(A) the cost of painting a building.
(B) the replacement of windows in a building.
(C) the purchase of a car by a garage for resale.
(D) legal fees on the purchase of a building.

Question 6

A business purchases a machine on credit terms for $18,000 plus sales tax at 15 per cent. The business is registered for sales tax. How should this transaction be recorded in the books?

		DR $	CR $
A	Machinery	18,000	
B	Payables		18,000
C	Machinery	20,700	
D	Payables		20,700
E	Sales tax	2,700	
F	Sales tax		2,700

Question 7

Which of the following statements most closely expresses the meaning of 'a fair presentation'?

(A) There is only one fair presentation of a company's financial statements.
(B) Fair presentation is determined by compliance with European Union directives.
(C) Fair presentation is determined by compliance with company law.
(D) Fair presentation is largely determined by reference to international financial reporting standards.

Question 8

On 1st May 20X0, A Ltd pays a rent bill of $2,400 for the period to 30th April 20X1. What is the charge to the income statement and the entry in the statement of financial position for the year ended 30th November 20X0?

Income Statement	Accrual or Prepayment	Statement of financial position
$		$

Question 9

S Ltd exchanged inventories for a delivery vehicle with T Ltd. The inventories had cost S Ltd $12,000 and the normal selling price was $14,000; the delivery vehicle had cost T Ltd $11,000 and the normal selling price was $15,000.

How should S Ltd value the vehicle in its statement of financial position?

$...............

 Question 10

Z's bank statement shows a balance of $1,650 overdrawn. The bank statement includes bank charges of $100 which have not been entered in the cash book. There are unpresented cheques totalling $950 and deposits not yet credited of $1,200. The bank statement incorrectly shows a direct debit payment of $320 which belongs to another customer.

The figure in the statement of financial position should be:

Overdrawn $...............

 Question 11

There is $200 in the till at the year end at F Ltd but the accountant suspects that some cash has been stolen. At the beginning of the year there was $100 in the till and receivables were $2000. Total sales in the year were $230,000. Receivables at the end of the year were $3,000. Cheques banked from credit sales were $160,000 and cash sales of $50,000 have been banked.

How much cash was stolen during the year?

$..................

 Question 12

A car was purchased for $10,000 on 1st April 20X0 and has been depreciated at 20 per cent per annum on straight-line basis. The company policy is to charge depreciation, once a year at the end of the year, on the cost of an asset in use at the year end. Assume there is no residual value. The car was traded in for a replacement vehicle on 1st August 20X3 for an agreed figure of $4,900. What was the profit or loss on the disposal of the vehicle for the year ended 31st December 20X3?

Profit or Loss	$

? Question 13

A company includes in inventories goods received before the year end but for which invoices are not received until after the year end. Which convention is this in accordance with?

(A) Historical cost.
(B) Accruals.
(C) Consistency.
(D) Materiality.

? Question 14

I Ltd operates the imprest system for petty cash. On 1st July there was a float of $250. During July the petty cashier received $50 from staff for using the photocopier and a cheque for $100 was cashed for an employee. In July, cheques were drawn for $600 for petty cash. It was decided to increase the cash float to $180 from 1st August. How much cash was paid out by the petty cashier in July?

$.................

? Question 15

Which of the following sentences does *not* explain the distinction between financial statements and management accounts?

(A) Financial statements are primarily for external users and management accounts are primarily for internal users.
(B) Financial statements are normally produced annually and management accounts are normally produced monthly.
(C) Financial statements are more accurate than management accounts.
(D) Financial statements are audited by an external audit and management accounts do not normally have an external audit.

? Question 16

When there is inflation, the historical cost convention has the effect of:

(A) overstating profits and understating statement of financial position values.
(B) understating profits and overstating statement of financial position values.
(C) understating cash flow and overstating cash in the statement of financial position.
(D) overstating cash flow and understating cash in the statement of financial position.

Question 17

When reconciling the payables ledger control account with the list of payables ledger balances of M, the following errors were found: the purchase daybook had been overstated by $600 and the personal ledger of a supplier had been understated by $200.

What adjustment must be made to correct these errors?

Control Account		**List of Payable Balances**	
Debit or Credit	$	*Increase or Decrease*	$

 # Question 18

B is a builder with a staff of ten employees. In April 20X0, he paid the following amounts:

Net salaries after employees' income tax and social security tax	$16,000
Employees' income tax and employees' social security tax for March 20X0	$7,000
Employer's social security tax for March 20X0	$3,000

He owes $8,000 for April's employees' income tax and employees' social security tax and $3,500 for April's employer's social security tax. What is the correct expense to be included in April's income statement?

$...................

 # Question 19

The following information relates to M Ltd:

	At 30th September	
	20X1	20X0
	$'000	$'000
Inventories of raw materials	70	50
Work in progress	60	70
Inventories of finished goods	100	90
For the year ended 30th September 20X1		
Purchases of raw materials	$165,000	
Manufacturing wages	$30,000	
Factory overheads	$40,000	

The prime cost of production in the manufacturing account for the year ended 30th September 20X1 is:

$ ....

Question 20

Are the following statements TRUE or FALSE?

(A) When valuing inventories at cost, inward transport costs should be included.

TRUE/FALSE ....

(B) When valuing inventories at cost, production overheads should be included.

TRUE/FALSE ....

 ## Question 21

On 30 June 20X0 an electricity ledger account had an accrual of $400 and a credit balance was brought down on 1 July 20X0. During the financial year electricity invoices totalling $5,000 were paid, including an invoice for $900 for the quarter ended 31 May 20X1.

What is the income statement charge for electricity payable for the year ended 30 June 20X1?

$...................

 ## Question 22

The allowance for receivables in the ledger of B Ltd at 31 October 20X0 was $11,000. During the year ended 31 October 20X1 bad debts of $7,000 were written off. Receivable balances at 31 October 20X1 were $140,000 and the company policy is to have an allowance for receivables of 5 per cent.

What is the charge for bad debts and change in the allowance for receivables in the income statement for the year ended 31 October 20X1?

$..................

Question 23

The following is an extract from the statement of financial position of IAS plc for the years ended 31 July 20X0 and 20X11.

	20X1	20X0
	$'000	$'000
Inventories	40	90
Receivables	55	10
Payables	45	30
Accruals	15	20

What figure would appear in the statement of cash flows of IAS plc for the year ended 31 July 20X0 as part of the cash generated from operations?

Question 24

The inventories at SOR Ltd were valued at $14,000 and excludes goods supplied to a customer on a sale or return basis. The customer still has 30 days within which to return the inventories. The goods on sale or return were purchased by SOR Ltd for $4,000 and were invoiced at a mark-up of 25 per cent.

The value of inventories at SOR Ltd should be:

$..................

 Question 25

A trial balance does not balance. Which of the following errors may be the cause of this failure to balance?

(A) The purchase of a machine had been debited to the machine repairs account.
(B) A cheque from a customer had been credited to the purchase ledger account of the customer.
(C) Goods returned inwards had been debited to the sales ledger account of the customer.
(D) The depreciation charge on machinery had been credited to the cost of machinery account.

 Question 26

S is employed by T Ltd. His pay details for January and February are as follows:

January:	Gross Salary $2,200;	Tax $500;	Social security $100;	Net pay $1,600.
February:	Gross Salary $2,500;	Tax $550;	Social security $110;	Net pay $1,840.

Tax and social security are payable to the government one month after they are deducted from employees' salaries.

How much cash did T Ltd pay out in February in connection with S's wages?

$..................

 Question 27

When a company produces a statement of comprehensive income, which of the following items is included in 'other comprehensive income'?

(A) Profit on sale of a non-current asset.
(B) Interest received.
(C) Government grant.
(D) Net gain on property revaluation.

? Question 28

N plc purchased a machine for $18,000. The transportation costs were $1,700 and installation costs were $500. The machine broke down at the end of the first month in use and cost $400 to repair. N plc depreciates machinery at 10% per annum on cost, assuming no residual value.

What is the carrying amount of the machine after one year, to the nearest dollar?

$...................

? Question 29

Which of the following might explain the debit balance on a purchase ledger account?

(A) The company took a cash discount to which they were not entitled and paid less than the amount due.
(B) The company mistakenly paid too much.
(C) The bookkeeper failed to enter a contra with the sales ledger.
(D) The bookkeeper failed to post a cheque paid to the account.

? Question 30

In a period of inflation, which of the following methods of charging inventory issues to production will give the lowest profit figure?

(A) Average cost
(B) LIFO
(C) FIFO
(D) Replacement cost

? Question 31

Which of the following provides the best explanation of the objective of an internal audit?

(A) The objective is to assist the directors of a company in the effective discharge of their financial responsibilities towards the members.
(B) The objective is to provide support to the external auditor.
(C) The objective is to detect fraud and error.
(D) The objective is to audit the financial statements.

Question 32

The following information at 5 January 20X2 relates to a club which has a year end of 31 December 20X1.

	$
Subscriptions for 20X0 unpaid at January 20X1	400
Subscriptions for 20X0 paid during the year ended 31 December 20X1	550
Subscriptions for 20X1 paid during the year ended 31 December 20X1	7,000
Subscriptions for 20X2 paid during the year ended 31 December 20X1	2,000
Subscriptions for 20X1 unpaid at 31 December 20X1	850

It is the club's policy to write off overdue subscriptions after 1 year.

What amount should be credited to the income and expenditure statement for the year ended 31 December 20X1?

$..................

 Question 33

Extracts from the financial statements of ASB Ltd are set out below.

Income statement for the year ended 31 December 20X1

		$'000
Turnover		400
Cost of sales		(175)
Gross profit		225
Profit on sale of non-current asset		80
		305
Expenses	35	
Depreciation	40	
Operating profit		(75)
		230

	31st December 20X0	31st December 20X1
	$'000	$'000
Inventories, receivables, current liabilities	50	65

What figure would appear in the statement of cash flows of ASB Ltd for the year ended 31 December 20X1 for cash generated from operations?

Question 34

The correct ledger entries to record the issue of 200,000 $1 Ordinary Shares at a premium of 20% and paid by cheque is:

		DR $	CR $
A	Bank	240,000	
B	Share capital		200,000
C	Share premium		40,000
D	Share premium		240,000
E	Share capital		240,000
F	Bank	200,000	
G	Share capital		160,000

Question 35

M plc's trial balance did not balance at 31 May 20X1. The following errors were discovered: insurance of $700 prepaid at 31 May 20X0 had not been brought down as an opening balance on the insurance account; wages of $6,000 had been incorrectly debited to the purchases account; the bookkeeper had failed to accrue for the telephone invoice owing at 31 May 20X1 of $400.

What was the difference on the trial balance?

$..................

Question 36

S is a builder who has numerous small items of equipment. He calculates his depreciation using the revaluation method. At the beginning of his financial year he valued his equipment at $11,475; he bought equipment costing $4,360 and he sold equipment for $3,257. At the end of his financial year he valued his equipment at $9,000.

What is his depreciation charge on equipment for the year?

$..................

Question 37

The operating profit margin in a company is 9% and the turnover to total capital employed ratio is 3.

What is the return on capital employed?

%

Question 38

The accounts for SPA plc are set out below.

Income statement of SPA plc for the year ended 30 November 20X2

	$'000	$'000
Turnover		6,000
Opening inventories	200	
Purchases	3,100	
Closing inventories	(400)	
Cost of sales		(2,900)
Gross profit		3,100
Operating expenses		(400)
Operating profit		2,700
Interest		(200)
Profit for the period		2,500

Statement of financial position of SPA plc as at 30 November 20X2

Assets	$'000	$'000
Non-current assets		3,500
Current assets		
Inventories	300	
Receivables	900	
Bank	50	
		1,250
		4,750
Equity and liabilities		
Share capital		2,200
Retained earnings		2,100
		4,300
Current liabilities		
Trade payables		450
		4,750

The return on capital employed in SPA is:

%

 # Question 39

The sales: total capital employed ratio in SPA using the total capital employed at the year end is:

:1

 # Question 40

The quick ratio in SPA is:

:1

Question 41

A credit balance of $800 brought down on X Limited's account in the books of Y Limited means that

(A) X Limited owes Y Limited $800.
(B) Y Limited owes X Limited $800.
(C) Y Limited has paid X Limited $800.
(D) Y Limited has overpaid X by $800.

 Question 42

Match the following user groups with their responsibilities.

A	The government	1	Appointing directors
B	The shareholders	2	Ensuring that all accounting transactions are properly recorded and summarized in the accounts
C	The internal auditors	3	Collecting statistical information useful in managing the economy
D	The directors	4	Reporting to the directors on internal systems

 Question 43

The following information relates to a company at its year end:

	$
Inventories at the beginning of the year	
Raw materials	22,000
Work in progress	4,000
Finished goods	63,000
Inventories at the end of the year	
Raw materials	25,000
Work in progress	1,000
Finished goods	72,000
Purchases of raw materials	220,000
Direct wages	300,000
Royalties on goods sold	45,000
Production overheads	360,000
Distribution costs	70,000
Administration expenses	290,000
Sales	1,400,000

The cost of goods manufactured during the year is:
$...............

Question 44

Your sales ledger control account has a balance at 1 November 20X1 of $30,000 debit. During November, credit sales were $67,000, cash sales were $15,000 and receipts from customers, excluding cash receipts, and after deducting cash discounts of $1,400 were $60,000. Sales returns were $4,000.

The closing balance on the sales ledger control account was:

$...............

 ## Question 45

In a not-for-profit organisation, the accumulated fund is:

(A) non-current assets plus net current assets less non-current liabilities.
(B) the balance on the general reserve.
(C) non-current assets plus working capital.
(D) non-current liabilities plus current liabilities minus current assets.

Question 46

Your company's bank statement at 31 July 20X1 shows a favourable balance of $10,300. You subsequently discover that the bank has dishonoured a customer's cheque for $500 and has charged bank charges of $150, neither of which is recorded in your cash book. There are unpresented cheques totalling $1,700. You further discover that a receipt from a customer of $400 has been recorded as a credit in your cash book.

Your cash book balance, prior to correcting the errors and omissions, was:

$...............

Question 47

Inventory is valued using FIFO. Opening inventory was 12 units at $4 each. Purchases were 60 units at $5 each, then issues of 18 units were made, followed by issues of 23 units.

Closing inventory is valued at:

$...............

 ## Question 48

A book of prime entry is one in which:

(A) transactions are entered prior to being recorded in ledger accounts.
(B) ledger accounts are maintained.
(C) the rules of double-entry bookkeeping do not apply.
(D) memorandum accounts are kept.

Question 49

Sales are $310,000, purchases are $165,000, opening inventories are $21,000, closing inventories are $18,000.

Inventories days are:

$ ....

 Question 50

Which two of the following statements are true?

(A) Sales less factory cost of goods completed equals gross profit.
(B) Prime cost is recorded in the trading account.
(C) Factory cost of goods completed is recorded in the trading account.
(D) Closing work in progress is not included in the statement of financial position.
(E) Royalty payments on goods manufactured are included in prime cost.
(F) Trade discounts on the purchase of raw matrerials are included in prime cost.

Illustrative computer-based assessment 1: Solutions

 ## Solution 1

Answer: (D)

 ## Solution 2

Answer: (C)

 ## Solution 3

Answer: (B)

 ## Solution 4

Turnover $3 million × 5% gives receivables of = $150,000
Allowance for receivables is 4% × $150,000 = $6,000
Existing allowance is $6,000 × 3/4 = $4,500
Change in allowance to income statement = debit $1,500

 ## Solution 5

Answer: (D)

 ## Solution 6

Answer: (A), (D), (E)

 ## Solution 7

Answer: (D)

 ## Solution 8

$2,400 for one year is $200 per month
Charge to income statement   7 × $200 = $1,400
Prepaid in statement of financial position   5 × $200 = $1,000

 ## Solution 9

$14,000

Solution 10

		$
Bank statement balance	overdrawn	(1,650)
Unpresented cheques		(950)
Outstanding deposits		1,200
Bank error		320
Cash book – credit balance		(1,080)

 Solution 11

Sales ledger control

Opening receivables	2,000	Cheques banked credit sales	160,000
Credit sales	161,000		
(balancing figure)		Closing receivables	3,000
	163,000		163,000

Cash account

Opening balance	100	Cash banked	50,000
Cash sales	69,000	Cash missing	18,900
($230,000 − $161,000)		Closing balance	200
	69,100		69,000

Cash missing is $18,900.

 Solution 12

1st April 20X0 Cost		10,000
Depreciation charge at 20%		
20X0	2,000	
20X1	2,000	
20X2	2,000	
		6,000
Carrying amount 1 August 20X3		4,000
Proceeds 1 August 20X3		4,900
Profit		900

 Solution 13

Answer: (B)

Solution 14

Cash Account

1st July bal b/d	250	Cash cheque	100
Photocopying	50	Cash paid out	620
Cash from bank	600	(balancing figure) 31st July bal c/d	180
	900		900

Cash paid out $620.

 ## Solution 15

Answer: (C)

 ## Solution 16

Answer: (A)

 ## Solution 17

Control Account		List of Payable Balances	
Debit or Credit	$	*Increase or Decrease*	$
Debit	600	Increase	200

 ## Solution 18

	$
Net salaries for April	16,000
Employees' social security and tax for April	8,000
Employer's social security	3,500
	27,500

 ## Solution 19

	$
Prime cost is direct materials and direct labour	
Opening inventories of raw materials	50,000
Purchases	165,000
Closing inventories of raw materials	(70,000)
Raw materials consumed	145,000
Manufacturing wages	30,000
	175,000

Solution 20

Include Inward Transport Costs	Include Production Overheads
Yes or No	Yes or No
Yes	Yes

 Solution 21

Electricity Account

		$			$
31 May 20X1	Invoices	5,000	1 Jul. 20X0	bal b/d	400
31 May 20X1	Accrual – $900 × 1/3	300	31 May 20X1	IS	4,900
		5,300			5,300

Answer is $4,900

 Solution 22

	$
Receivables ($140,000 × 5%)	7,000
Allowance for receivables at 31 October 20X0	(11,000)
Change in allowance	(4,000)
Bad debts written off	7,000
Income statement	3,000

 Solution 23

	$'000
Inventories	50
Receivables	(45)
Payables	15
Accruals	(5)
Cash generated from operations	15

 Solution 24

	$
Inventories at valuation	14,000
Goods on sale or return at cost	4,000
Inventories valuation	18,000

 Solution 25

Answer: (C)

Solution 26

	$
Net pay February	1,840
Tax January	500
Social security January	100
	2,440

 # Solution 27

(D) Net gain on property revaluation.
Items (A), (B) and (C) would be recorded in the 'income statement' part of a statement of comprehensive income.

 # Solution 28

	$
Cost of machine	18,000
Transportation	1,700
Installation	500
	20,200
Depreciation at 10%	(2,020)
Carrying amount	18,180

 # Solution 29

Answer: (B)

Solution 30

Answer: (D)

Solution 31

Answer: (A)

Solution 32

	$
Subscriptions paid for 20X0	7,000
Subscriptions owing for 20X0	850
	7,850

Solution 33

Operating profit	230
Add: depreciation	40
Less: profit on sale	(80)
	190
Increase working capital	(15)
Cash generated from operations	175

Solution 34

Answer: (A), (B), (C)

 ## Solution 35

Insurance balance omitted	$700
Wages mis-posted – not affect trial balance	Nil
Accrual omitted – not affect trial balance	Nil

Answer is $700

 ## Solution 36

	$
Valuation at the beginning of the year	11,475
Purchases	4,360
Disposals	(3,257)
	12,578
Valuation at end of year	(9,000)
Depreciation	3,578

 ## Solution 37

Operating profit margin % × turnover : total capital employed = ROCE

9% × 3 = 27%

 ## Solution 38

$$\frac{\text{Operating profit}}{\text{Total capital employed}} = \frac{£2,700,000}{£4,300,000} \times 100 = 63\%$$

 ## Solution 39

$$\frac{\text{Turnover}}{\text{Total capital employed}} = \frac{£6,000,000}{£4,300,000} = 1.39 : 1$$

 ## Solution 40

$$\frac{\text{Receivables} + \text{Bank}}{\text{Current liabilities}} = \frac{£900,000 + £50,000}{£450,000} = 2.11 : 1$$

 ## Solution 41

Answer: (B)

Solution 42

Answer: (A3) (B1) (C4) (D2)

 ## Solution 43

	$'000
Inventories at beginning of year – raw materials	22,000
Purchases	220,000
Inventories at end of year – raw materials	(25,000)
Direct wages	300,000
Production overheads	360,000
Inventories at beginning of year – work in progress	4,000
Inventories at end of year – work in progress	(1,000)
	880,000

 ## Solution 44

Sales ledger control account

		$			$
1 Nov. 20X1	Balance b/d	30,000		Bank	60,000
	Credit sales	67,000		Cash discounts	1,400
				Sales returns	4,000
			31 Nov. 20X1	Bal c/d	31,600
		97,000			97,000

 ## Solution 45

Answer: (A)

Solution 46

Bank reconciliation	$
Balance at bank 31 July 20X1	10,300
Unpresented cheques	(1,700)
	8,600
Opening balance in cash book – balancing figure	8,450
Dishonoured cheque	(500)
Bank charges	(150)
Error ($600 × 2)	800
	8,600

 ## Solution 47

	units	unit $	Total $
Opening inventories	12	4	48
Purchases	60	5	300
Issue	(12)	4	(48)
Issue	(6)	5	(30)
Issue	(23)	5	(115)
Closing inventories	31	5	155

Solution 48

Answer: (A)

 Solution 49

Average inventories is opening inventories $21,000 + closing inventories $18,000 = $39,000/2 = $19,500

Cost of goods sold is opening inventories $21,000 + purchases $165,000 − closing inventories $18,000 = $168,000

Inventories days is ($19,500 × 365)/$168,000 = 42 days

 Solution 50

Answer: (C), (E)

Mock Assessment 2

Mock Assessment 2

Certificate in Business Accounting

Fundamentals of Financial Accounting

Illustrative Computer-based Assessment

Instructions: attempt all 50 questions

Time allowed: 2 hours

Do not look at or attempt this illustrative computer-based assessment until you have fully completed your revision and are about to sit your computer-based assessment.

Illustrative computer-based assessment 2: Questions

Question 1

A business is normally said to have earned revenue when:

(A) an order has been placed.
(B) a customer is legally obliged to pay for goods delivered.
(C) cash has been received.
(D) goods have been manufactured and placed in inventories.

Which convention does this comply with? Convention...........

Question 2

The following information relates to NI Ltd at 30 June 20X6.

	$
Balance per cashbook – credit balance	5,200
Unpresented cheques	1,100
Bank charges not entered in the cash book	400
Receipts not yet credited by the bank	1,700
Dishonoured cheques not yet entered in the cash book	600

The balance shown on the bank statement at 30 June 20X6 was:
$ ....

Question 3

The following information relates to NBV Ltd for the year ended 31 July 20X5.

	$'000
Prime cost	370
Carriage outwards	90
Depreciation delivery vehicles	50
Factory indirect overheads	560
Increase in WIP	65
Decrease in inventories of finished goods	40

The factory cost of goods completed for the year ended 31 July 20X5 is:
$ ....

Question 4

An external auditor carried out the following tests:

(A) review of internal control.
(B) review of systems.
(C) vouching a purchase invoice.
(D) inspecting a non-current asset.

Which of the above are compliance tests?

Question 5

The following information relates to CT plc.

Machinery	$'000
Cost at 1 January 20X4	90
Additions	30
Disposal	(20)
Cost at 31 December 20X4	100
Accumulated depreciation at 1 January 20X4	20
Depreciation charge	5
Disposal	(3)
Accumulated depreciation at 31 December 20X4	22

The profit on disposal of a machine was $3,000.

The cash flow from investing activities of CT plc for the year ended 31 December 20X4 would include:

$.................   inflow/outflow.................

 Question 6

The accountant at SL Ltd is preparing quarterly financial statements on the 31 July 20X3 for the quarter ended 31 July 20X3. The last quarterly gas bill, payable in arrears, received by SL Ltd was dated 31 May 20X3 and amounted to $2,800. The accountant, when preparing the quarterly financial statements for the quarter ended 30 April had expected the May gas bill to be $2,100. The accountant expects the gas bill for the quarter ended 31 August 20X3 to be $3,900. Gas bills are paid on the day they are received. All under/over estimates on accruals are charged within the period.

The charge to the income statement for gas in the quarter to 31 July 20X3 should be:

$.................

Question 7

IT plc has a policy that all items of equipment which cost less than $1,000 are charged to an expense account rather than a non-current asset account. This is an example of the convention of:

(A) money measurement.
(B) prudence.
(C) going concern.
(D) materiality.

Question 8

Internal auditors report to the:

(A) government.
(B) external auditors.
(C) shareholders.
(D) management.

Question 9

KP Ltd is preparing financial statements for the year ended 30 June 20X3. Rent is payable quarterly in advance on 1 February, 1 May, 1 August and 1 November. The annual charge for rent was $3,600 and $4,800 for the year ended 31 January 20X3 and 20X4, respectively. The financial statements should show:

Rent expense = $.................   Accrual = $.................   Prepayment = $.................

 Question 10

DOB Ltd purchased a machine costing $20,000 on 1 August 20X2. The company estimated that the asset had a useful life of 4 years and an expected residual value of $2,000. The company uses the straight-line method of depreciation. The company's financial year end is 30 November. It is the company's policy to charge a full year's depreciation in the year of purchase and none in the year of disposal. On 1 November 20X5 the asset was sold for $5,500. The profit or loss on disposal in the year ended 30 November 20X5 was:

$...................   Profit/loss...................

 Question 11

The following information is an extract from the financial statements of FWD plc for the years ended 31 August 20X2 and 20X3.

	20X3 $'000	20X2 $'000
Inventories	22	16
Receivables	18	20
Bank	14	12
	54	48
Payables	(14)	(18)
	40	30

The statement of cash flows of FWD plc for the year ended 31 August 20X3 should include in the cash flow from operations:

$.................   inflow/outflow.................

 Question 12

Which of the following entries would not affect the totals in the trial balance agreeing?

(A) An invoice for $250 for rent has been omitted from the ledgers.
(B) A cash sale has been recorded as debit cash sales, credit cash.
(C) An invoice for vehicle expenses has been charged to the vehicle non-current asset account.
(D) A payment received from a supplier has been posted to the personal account twice.

? Question 13

Which of the following are not intangible non-current assets?

(A) Goodwill
(B) Trademark
(C) Investment
(D) Patent
(E) Brand
(F) Leasehold property

? Question 14

ASB Ltd bought computer equipment on the 1 January 20X1 for $32,000 and estimated that it would have a useful life of 5 years and would have a residual value of $4,000. ASB Ltd uses the straight-line method of depreciation. On the 31 December 20X2 it now considers that the remaining life is only 2 years and that the residual value will be nil.

The depreciation charge for the year ended 31 December 20X3 and 20X4 should be:

$....................

? Question 15

A company has a quick (acid) test ratio of 2:1. Current assets include inventories of $12,000 and trade receivables of $4,000. Trade payables are $8,000.

The bank balance is:

$.................. Debit/credit balance...................

? Question 16

Which one of the following does *not* help in the prevention of fraud and errors?

(A) Reconciliations
(B) Suspense accounts
(C) Organisation of staff
(D) Authorisation procedures

? Question 17

The FRC cycling club started in January 20X2 and the following fees were received in the years ended 31 December 20X2 and 20X3.

	20X2 $	20X3 $
Joining fees	11,000	13,000
Annual fees	8,000	10,000
Life membership fees	7,000	5,000
	26,000	28,000

Joining fees are recognised over a period of 4 years and life membership fees are recognised over 10 years.

The total amount of fees in the income and expenditure statement for the year ended 31 December 20X3 should be:

$ ....

? Question 18

IAS plc declared a final dividend of 5% for the year ended 28 February 20X3. The nominal value of the shares is 25¢. X bought 800 shares at a price of $5 in December 20X2 and the shares were valued at a price of $8 on 28 February 20X3.

X will receive a final dividend of:

$ ....

? Question 19

The internal financial statements of GH Ltd value inventories at replacement cost. The warehouse manager has produced the following schedule for the values of the three items (X1, X2 and X3) in inventories at the year end.

	First in/first out $'000	Net realizable value $'000	Replacement cost $'000
X1	15	25	35
X2	10	6	3
X3	14	16	15
	39	47	53

At what value should the inventories be stated in the statutory financial statements?

$ ....

? Question 20

The job descriptions of staff in the credit control department are normally segregated because:

(A) work is completed more efficiently.
(B) lower salaries can be paid.
(C) it motivates staff to perform better.
(D) it facilitates internal control.

? Question 21

The management accounts within a limited company are determined by:

(A) the directors.
(B) the shareholders.
(C) company law and accounting standards.
(D) company law.

Question 22

When the historical cost convention is applied, the capital of an entity is measured in terms of:

(A) money.
(B) money, adjusted for inflation.
(C) fair value.
(D) operating capability.

Question 23

If work in progress increases during an accounting period, then:

(A) prime cost will increase.
(B) prime cost will decrease.
(C) the factory cost of goods completed will increase.
(D) the factory cost of goods completed will decrease.

Question 24

The following information was extracted from the pay slip of JS, who received her net salary in cash, for the month ended 31 January 20X5.

	$
Gross salary of	5,000
Tax deducted	500
Employer's social security tax	400
Employee's social security tax	350
Employer's contribution to pension fund	190
Employee's contribution to pension fund	210
Voluntary deduction for payment to charity	30

Tax, social security tax, pension fund contributions and payments to charity are all payable in February 20X5.

The charge to the income statement, the balance on the payroll control account and the net pay for JS's salary for January was:

Charge to income statement	Balance on payroll control A/c	Net pay
$..................	$..................	$..................

 Question 25

In January 20X4, JR began trading as a car valeting service. He introduced small items of equipment with an estimated cost of $3,600. During the year ended December 20X4, he purchased new items of equipment for $1,700 and sold some items for $300. On 31 December, JR estimated the cost of his small items of equipment at $3,900.

Using the revaluation method, the depreciation charge for the year ended 31 December 20X4 was:

$ ....

MOCK ASSESSMENT 2

 Question 26

After the income statement for EH Ltd had been prepared, it was found that accrued expenses of $1,500 had been omitted and that closing inventories had been overvalued by $500.

The effect of these errors is an:

overstatement/understatement of profit .... $..................

 Question 27

A sales ledger control account at 1 June had an opening balance of $20,000. During June, sales were $180,000, being credit sales of $170,000 and cash sales of $10,000. Total receipts from cash and credit customers was $165,000. During the month, it was recognised that $3,000 of receivables were bad and that a further $5,000 may not be paid. During the month, there was a contra of $2,000 between the sales and purchase control accounts and customers returned goods at a value of $6,000.

The balance on the sales ledger control account at 30 June was:

$ ....

 Question 28

Which of the following would you expect to see in a statement of changes in equity?

	Yes	No
Dividends		
Total comprehensive income for the year		
Directors' salaries		
Revaluation of property		
Taxation		

 Question 29

CAD Ltd uses the weighted average cost formula for valuing inventories. On 1 April there were 80 units in inventory valued at $17 each. On 6 April, 30 units were purchased for $19 each; and on 20 April, 45 units were purchased for $20 each. On 25 April, 100 units were sold for $3,000. The value of the closing inventories at 30 April was:

$ ....

 Question 30

The following information related to M plc for the year ended 31 July 20X9:

	$
Prime cost	164,000
Factory overheads	227,000
Opening work in progress at 1 August 20X8	82,000
Factory cost of goods completed	342,000

The closing work in progress at 31 July 20X9 was:

$ ....

Question 31

VIP Ltd is registered for sales tax and received an invoice from a legal firm for $6,000 plus sales tax. The rate of sales tax on the services was 17.5%. The correct journal entries are:

Account	Dr	Cr
	$	$

Question 32

E Ltd received an invoice for the purchase of non-current asset equipment which was credited to the correct supplier's ledger account but debited to the equipment repairs account instead of the equipment account. The effect of not correcting this error on the financial statements would be:

(A) profit would be overstated and non-current assets would be understated.
(B) profit would be overstated and non-current assets would be overstated.
(C) profit would be understated and capital would be overstated.
(D) profit would be understated and non-current assets would be understated.

Question 33

The accountant at URP Ltd is preparing the annual financial statements. The company is in dispute with one of its suppliers which is currently the subject of a court case for a claim against the company for $300,000. URP Ltd has also made a claim against its insurance company for $200,000 and is waiting to hear if the insurance company will pay up.

The accountant has decided to accrue for the legal claim for $300,000 but to ignore the insurance claim of $200,000.

The accounting convention which underlies these decisions is:

.... convention

Question 34

The return on capital employed for ETC plc is 22% and the net asset turnover ratio is 4 times.

The operating profit margin is:

.... %

Question 35

Which of the following would *not* help detect errors in a computerised accounting system?

(A) Control accounts.
(B) Passwords.
(C) Batch processing.
(D) Coding systems.

Question 36

The total cost of salaries charged to a limited company's income statement is:

(A) cash paid to employees.
(B) net pay earned by employees.
(C) gross pay earned by employees.
(D) gross pay earned by employees plus employer's social security tax contributions.

 Question 37

The trading account for SUV Ltd for the year ended 31 July 20X8 was:

Trading Account for the year ended 31 July 20X8

		$'000
Sales		300
Opening inventories	25	
Purchases	125	
Closing inventories	(30)	
Cost of good sold		120
Gross profit		180

The trade payables at 31 July 20X8 was $28,000.
   The trade payables days at 31 July 20X8 was:
.... days

Question 38

The following is the aged receivables analysis for Z Ltd at 30 April 20X3.

Age of debt	Less than 1 month	1–2 months	2–3 months	Over 3 months
Amount ($)	18,000	30,000	14,000	12,000

The company makes an allowance for receivables as follows:

Allowance	0%	1%	8%	15%

The allowance for receivables at 1 May 20X2 brought forward was $6,000.
   The entry for the allowance for receivables in the income statement for the year ended 30 April 20X3 and the net receivables figure in the statement of financial position at that date should be:

Income statement	Statement of financial position
$.................. debit/credit..................	$..................

Question 39

The following information relates to companies X plc and Y plc, who are competitors selling carpets.

	X plc	Y plc
Gross profit percentage	25%	20%

Which of the following are possibly true based on the information provided?

(A) X plc has a higher selling price.
(B) X has lower purchasing costs.
(C) Y plc has lower closing inventories.
(D) Y plc has more closing inventories.

Question 40

Which of the following are accounting conventions and which are qualitative characteristics of financial statements?

	Accounting convention	Qualitative characteristic
Timely		
Material		
Relevant		
Objective		
Complete		

Question 41

On 1 October 20X6, LED Ltd owed a supplier $1,300. During the month of October, LED Ltd:

- purchased goods for $1,800 and the supplier offered a 4% discount for payment within the month.
- LED Ltd returned goods valued at $170 which had been purchased in September 20X6.
- sent a cheque to the supplier for payment of the goods delivered in October.

The balance on the supplier's account at the end of October 20X6 is:
$.................

Question 42

The main advantage of using a sales ledger control account is that:

(A) it ensures that the trial balance will always balance.
(B) it helps with credit control.
(C) it helps in detecting errors.
(D) double-entry bookkeeping is not necessary.

Question 43

The following information relates to B Ltd for the year ended 31 August 20X7.

	$
Retained profit for the year	25,000
Net cash inflow from operating activities	23,000
Dividend paid	2,000
Profit on sale of non-current assets	500
Proceeds on sale of non-current assets	6,000
Taxation paid	1,000
Interest paid	3,500
Payments for non-current assets	7,000
Issue of debentures	4,000

The statement of cash flows will show:

decrease/increase .... in cash of $ ....

Question 44

The property in Credit Crunch Ltd has been revalued from $300,000 to $400,000, and the tax on the gain is $25,000.

Complete the following items to enter the above information.

Amount included in total comprehensive income	$
Amount included in statement of changes in equity	$
Property in statement of financial position	$
Revaluation reserve	$
Non-current liabilities	$

Question 45

DRP Ltd operates an imprest system for petty cash. On 1 May the float was $325. It was decided that this should be increased to $400 at the end of May.

During May, the cashier paid $15 for gardening, $120 for stamps and $175 for repairs. The cashier received $40 from staff for the private use of the telephone and $70 for a cash sale. The amount to be drawn from the bank account for petty cash at the end of May is:

$..................

Question 46

An audit trail in a computerised accounting system is:

(A) a history of all transactions on a ledger account.
(B) information regarding all transactions in a period.
(C) a list of all transactions automatically posted from day books to ledgers.
(D) a list of all transactions checked by the internal auditor.

Question 47

The following are extracts from the financial statements of RSVP plc for the year ended 31 March 20X8.

	$'000
Issued ordinary shares of $1	450
Share premium account	75
Income statement reserve	40
Debenture	50
Profit before interest for the year ended 31 March 20X8	85

The return on total capital employed is:

.... %

 ## Question 48

There was a fire at the premises of NGO Ltd during the year ended 30 November 20X9 and the accounting records were partly destroyed. The accountant is trying to prepare the financial statements from these incomplete records. She discovers that the electricity account was overpaid by $400 on the 1 December 20X8 and that there was $300 owing on 30 November 20X9. During the year, electricity payments totalled $3,000.

The charge to the income statement for electricity for the year ended 30 November 20X9 is:

$ ....

Question 49

In order to confirm that financial statements show a true and fair view (fair presentation), the external auditor should ensure that the financial statements comply with:

(A) internal procedures as specified by the directors.
(B) the stock exchange listed company regulations.
(C) the accounting conventions.
(D) international financial reporting standards.

Question 50

CO Ltd purchased equipment for $60,000 on 1 July 20X5 with an estimated residual value of $4,000. The company's accounting year end is 31 December. It is CO Ltd's policy to charge a full year's depreciation in the year of purchase. CO Ltd depreciates its equipment on the reducing balance basis at 25% per annum.

The carrying amount of the equipment at 31 December 20X8 should be:

$..................

Illustrative computer-based assessment 2: Solutions

 ## Solution 1

Answer: (B) Convention: Realisation

 ## Solution 2

	Cash book $	Bank statement $
Balance per cash book/bank statement	(5,200)	(6,800)
Unpresented cheques		(1,100)
Bank charges	(400)	
Receipts not credited by bank		1,700
Dishonoured cheques	(600)	
	(6,200)	(6,200)

Answer: $6,800

 ## Solution 3

	$'000
Prime cost	370
Factory indirect overheads	560
Increase in WIP	(65)
Factory cost of goods completed	865

 ## Solution 4

Answer: (A), (B)

Solution 5

		$'000
Additions		(30)
Asset disposal – cost	20	
– depreciation	(3)	
– carrying amount	17	
Profit on disposal	3	
Proceeds on disposal		20
Cash outflow		(10)

Solution 6

		Dr $	Cr $
Gas account			
20X3			
May 1	Bal b/f ($2,100 × 2/3)		1,400
May 31	Bank	2,800	
Jul. 31	Accrual ($3,900 × 2/3)	2,600	
Jul. 31	Income statement		4,000
		5,400	5,400

 Solution 7

Answer: (D)

 Solution 8

Answer: (D)

 Solution 9

		Dr $	Cr $
Rent account			
1 Jul. 20X2	Bal b/f ($900 × 1/3)	300	
1 Aug. 20X2	Bank	900	
1 Nov. 20X2	Bank	900	
1 Feb. 20X3	Bank	1200	
1 May 20X3	Bank	1200	
30 Jun. 20X3	Income statement		4,100
30 Jun. 20X3	Bal c/d ($1200 × 1/3)		400
		4,500	4,500

Rent expense = $4,100   Accrual = $nil   Prepayment = $400

Solution 10

	$
Cost machine	20,000
Expected residual value	(2,000)
	18,000
Annual depreciation charge	
$18,000/4	4,500
Cost machine	20,000
Depreciation charge 3 years ($4500 × 3)	(13,500)
Carrying amount	6,500
Proceeds	(5,500)
Loss on disposal	1,000

 # Solution 11

	$'000
Inventories	(6,000)
Receivables	2,000
Payables	(4,000)
Cash outflow	(8,000)

 # Solution 12

Answer: (A), (B), (C)

 # Solution 13

Answer: (C), (F)

Solution 14

	$
Cost machine	32,000
Expected residual value	(4,000)
	28,000
Annual depreciation charge	
$28,000/5	5,600
Cost machine	32,000
Depreciation charge 2 years ($5600 × 2)	(11,200)
Carrying amount	20,800
Depreciation charge 20 × 3 & 20 × 4	
($20,800/2)	10,400

Solution 15

	$
Receivables	4,000
Bank	12,000
	16,000
Payables	8,000
Quick (acid) test	2:1

 # Solution 16

Answer: (B)

 # Solution 17

Fees – year ended 31 December 20X3

	$
Annual fees	10,000
Joining fees $(11000 + $13000)/4	6,000
Life membership fees $(7000 + $5000)/10	1,200
	17,200

 # Solution 18

800 shares at 25¢	$200
Dividends 5%	$10

 # Solution 19

	$'000
X1	15
X2	6
X3	14
	35

 # Solution 20

Answer: (D)

 # Solution 21

Answer: (A)

 # Solution 22

Answer: (A)

Solution 23

Answer: (D)

 Solution 24

	Income statement	Payroll control	Net pay
Gross salary	5,000		5,000
Tax deducted		(500)	(500)
Employer's social security tax	400	400	
Employee's social security tax		350	(350)
Employer's contribution to pension fund	190	190	
Employee's contribution to pension fund		210	(210)
Voluntary deduction for payment to charity		30	(30)
Net pay			
	5,590	1,680	3,910

 Solution 25

	$
Estimated cost equipment introduced	3600
Additional equipment	1700
Equipment sold	(300)
	5, 000
Estimated cost equipment December 20X4	(3,900)
Depreciation charge – year ended 31 December 20X4	1,100

 Solution 26

Overstatement $2,000

 Solution 27

Debit		Credit	
	$		$
Opening balance	20,000	Bank	155,000
Sales	170,000	Bad debts	3,000
		Contra	2,000
		Returns	6,000
		Closing balance	24,000
	190,000		190,000

Solution 28

	Yes	No
Dividends	✓	
Total comprehensive income for the year	✓	
Directors' salaries		✓
Revaluation of property	✓	
Taxation		✓

Solution 29

Date	Units	Average Price ($)	Total ($)
1 Apr.	80	17	1360
6 Apr.	30	19	570
	110	17.55	1930
20 Apr.	45	20	900
	155	18.26	2830
25 Apr.	(100)	18.26	(1826)
30 Apr.	55	18.26	1004

Solution 30

		$'000
Prime cost		164
Factory overheads		227
		391
Opening work in progress	82	
Closing work in progress	(131)	(49)
Factory cost of goods completed		342

Solution 31

Account	Dr ($)	Cr ($)
Legal fees	6000	
VAT	1050	
Trade payable		7050

Solution 32

Answer: (D)

Solution 33

Prudence convention

Solution 34

	ROCE		Operating profit margin		Net asset turnover
	22%	=	5.5%	×	4

 Solution 35

Answer: (B)

 Solution 36

Answer: (D)

 Solution 37

$28,000 × 365/$125,000 = 82 days

 Solution 38

Statement of financial position	Receivables $	%	Allowance for receivables $
<1 month	18,000	0%	0
1–2 months	30,000	1%	300
2–3 months	14,000	10%	1,400
>3 months	12,000	30%	3,600
			5,300

Allowance $	Allowance $	IS A/c $
1 May 20X2	30 April 20X3	
6,000	5,300	700 Credit
Income statement $700 credit		Statement of financial position $5,300

 Solution 39

Answer: (A), (B)

 Solution 40

	Accounting convention	Qualitative characteristic
Timely		✓
Material	✓	
Relevant		✓
Objective	✓	
Complete		✓

Solution 41

		$
1 Oct. 20X6	Opening balance	1,300
	Invoice	1,800
	Cheque	(1,728)
	Discount	(72)
	Goods returned	(170)
31 Oct. 20X6	Closing balance	1,130

 Solution 42

Answer: (C)

 Solution 43

	$
Net cash inflow from operating activities	23,000
Dividend paid	(2,000)
Proceeds on sale of non-current assets	6,000
Taxation paid	(1,000)
Interest paid	(3,500)
Payments for non-current assets	(7,000)
Issue of debentures	4,000
Increase	19,500

 Solution 44

Complete the following items to enter the above information.

Amount included in total comprehensive income	$75,000
Amount included in statement of changes in equity	$75,000
Property in statement of financial position	$400,000
Revaluation reserve	$75,000
Non-current liabilities	$25,000

Solution 45

1 May	Balance	325
	Gardening	(15)
	Stamps	(120)
	Repairs	(175)
	Telephone	40
	Sales	70
		125
	Drawn from bank	275
31 May	Balance	400

Solution 46

Answer: (B)

Solution 47

$$\frac{\text{Profit before interest}}{\text{Capital}} \qquad \frac{\$85,000}{\$615,000} = 13.8\%$$

Solution 48

	Electricity Account		
Dr	$	*Cr*	$
1 Dec 20X8 Bal b/f	400		
Bank	3,000		
		31 December 20X9 IS	3,700
31 December 20X9 Bal c/d	300		
	3,700		3,700

Solution 49

Answer: (D)

Solution 50

$60,000 × 75% × 75% × 75% × 75% = $18,984

Index

Index